A History
of
the
Modern
World

Contemporary Europe

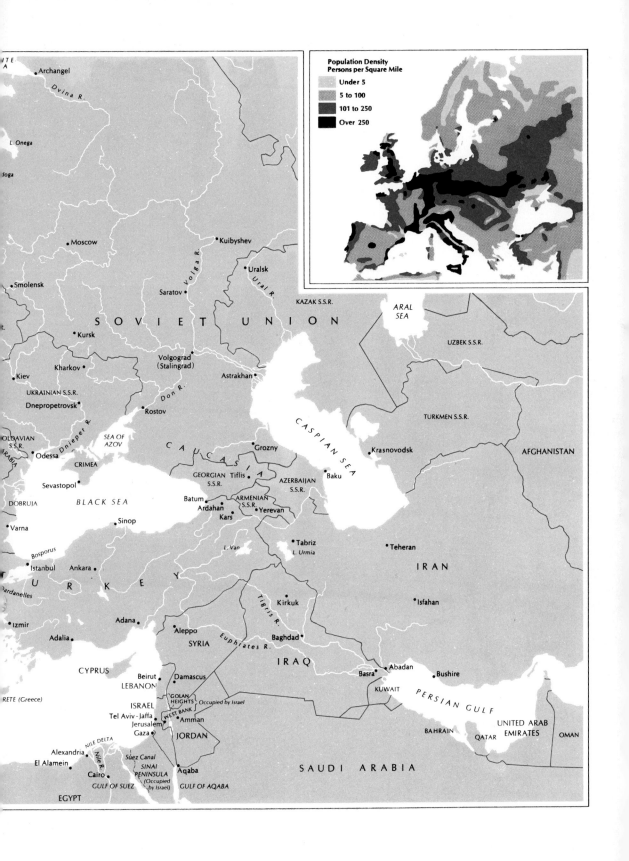

Population Density
Persons per Square Mile

Under 5
5 to 100
101 to 250
Over 250

Archangel

Dvina R.

L. Onega

oga

Moscow

Kuibyshev

Uralsk

Volga R.

Ural R.

Smolensk

Saratov

KAZAK S.S.R.

ARAL
SEA

Kursk

UZBEK S.S.R.

S O V I E T   U N I O N

Volgograd
(Stalingrad)

Astrakhan

Kiev

Kharkov

Don R.

Dnepropetrovsk

Rostov

TURKMEN S.S.R.

OLDAVIAN
S.S.R.

ABIA

Odessa

CRIMEA

Dnieper R.

SEA OF
AZOV

C A U C A S I A

Grozny

CASPIAN SEA

Krasnovodsk

AFGHANISTAN

Sevastopol

GEORGIAN
S.S.R.

Tiflis

AZERBAIJAN
S.S.R.

Baku

DOBRUJA

BLACK SEA

Batum

Ardahan

ARMENIAN
S.S.R.

Kars

Yerevan

Varna

Sinop

L. Van

Tabriz

L. Urmia

Teheran

I R A N

Bosporus

Istanbul

Ankara

T   U   R   K   E   Y

Isfahan

Dardanelles

Kirkuk

Tigris R.

Izmir

Adana

Aleppo

Euphrates R.

Baghdad

Adalia

SYRIA

I R A Q

Abadan

CYPRUS

Beirut

Damascus

Basra

Bushire

LEBANON

KUWAIT

P E R S I A N   G U L F

CRETE (Greece)

ISRAEL

GOLAN
HEIGHTS

Occupied by Israel

UNITED ARAB
EMIRATES

OMAN

Tel Aviv-Jaffa

WEST BANK

Amman

BAHRAIN

QATAR

Jerusalem

Gaza

JORDAN

Alexandria

NILE DELTA

Suez Canal

*SINAI
PENINSULA
(Occupied
by Israel)*

S A U D I   A R A B I A

El Alamein

Nile R.

Cairo

GULF OF SUEZ

Aqaba

GULF OF AQABA

EGYPT

fifth edition

A History
of
the
Modern
World
Since 1815

R. R. PALMER
JOEL COLTON

Alfred A. Knopf
New York

THIS IS A BORZOI BOOK PUBLISHED BY ALFRED A. KNOPF, INC.

Copyright 1950, © 1956, 1965, 1971, 1978   by Alfred A. Knopf, Inc.

All rights reserved under International and Pan-American Copyright Conventions. No part of this book may be reproduced in any form or by any means, electronic or mechanical, including photocopying, without permission in writing from the publisher. All inquiries should be addressed to Alfred A. Knopf, Inc., 201 East 50th Street, New York, N.Y. 10022. Published in the United States by Alfred A. Knopf, Inc., New York, and simultaneously in Canada by Random House of Canada Limited, Toronto. Distributed by Random House, Inc., New York.

Library of Congress Cataloging in Publication Data
Palmer, Robert Roswell, 1909–
  A history of the modern world.

  Bibliography: p.
  Includes index.
  1. History, Modern. I. Colton, Joel G., 1918–
joint author. II. Title.
[D209.P26   1977b]   909.08   77–9412
ISBN 0–394–32040–9 (v. 1) pbk.
ISBN 0–394–32041–7 (v. 2) pbk.

Published July 24, 1950. Reprinted seven times.

Second edition, revised, reset, and printed from new plates, with new maps, 1956. Reprinted fourteen times.

Third edition, revised, with new maps, 1965. Reprinted five times.

Fourth edition, revised, reset, and printed from new plates, with new maps and illustrations, 1971. Reprinted five times.

Fifth edition, revised, reset, and printed from new plates, with new maps and illustrations, 1978.

Fifth Edition
98765432

ACKNOWLEDGMENT IS HEREBY MADE FOR PERMISSION TO QUOTE FROM THE FOLLOWING WORKS:

World Population, by A. N. Carr-Saunders. Clarendon Press, Oxford (1936).

British Economic Growth, 1688–1959: Trends and Structure, by Phyllis Deane and W. A. Cole. Reprinted by permission of Cambridge University Press.

"The White Man's Burden" from The Five Nations by Rudyard Kipling. Reprinted by permission of The National Trust and Doubleday & Company, Inc.

European Historical Statistics 1750–1970, by B. R. Mitchell, pp. 316 and 396. Copyright ©1975 by Columbia University Press.

Manufactured in the United States of America

Preface

[Publisher's Note: In order to provide an alternative to the hardcover edition, *A History of the Modern World* is being made available in a two-volume paperbound edition. Volume 1, *To 1815*, includes chapters I–X; volume 2, *Since 1815*, chapters XI–XXI. The page numbering in these chapters remains the same as in the hardcover text, and footnotes refer to pages in both volumes.]

It is a pleasure to offer a fifth edition of a work that has been so well received in the past. The format is new and additional material has been included, but essentially *A History of the Modern World* retains its earlier character in content and coverage. Both authors, however, have worked over it carefully in the hope of making it more useful and attractive. We have condensed the language in many places and have made verbal alterations throughout. As a result, while a number of passages have been amplified, and the treatment of the years since the Second World War has been recast and enlarged for contemporary developments, the length of the book remains about as it was in the fourth edition.

Some additional maps, graphs, and illustrations have been incorporated. There is also a new Appendix, showing the populations of various countries and cities since the later Middle Ages. We have reviewed and in some cases expanded the captions for maps, charts, diagrams, and pictures, to make such visual materials more effective and more relevant to the text. The large bibliography, which has always been a special feature of the book, has been updated and now contains several thousand titles. In general, we have done what we could to make so long and complex a volume more manageable and digestible. The whole structure of chapters, sections and subsections, the frequent cross-references, the chronological tables, and the detailed index are intended for this purpose. A student's Study Guide also is available for those who may wish to use it.

Since its first edition the book has been designed to set forth the modern history of Europe and European civilization as a unit, and in its later chapters it attempts to tell the story of an integrated, or at least interconnected, world. Emphasis falls on situations and movements of international scope, or on what Europeans and their descendants have done and faced in common. National histories are therefore somewhat subordinated, and in each national history the points of contact with a larger civilization are treated most fully. Historic regional differences within Europe, as between eastern and western Europe, are brought out, and the history of the Americas is woven into the story at various points, as are developments of the last century in Asia and Africa. A good deal of institutional history is included. Considerable space is given to the history of ideas, not only in special sections devoted to ideas, but throughout the book in close connection with the account of institutions and events. Social and economic development bulks rather large, as does the impact of wars and revolutions. Since our own age is one in which much depends on political decision, we think of this volume as political history in the broadest sense, in that matters of many kinds, such as religion, economics, social welfare, and international relations, have presented themselves as public questions requiring public action by responsible citizens or official persons. It seems to us that many subjects of current research interest, such as women's history, family history, the history of the laboring classes, the history of minorities, or quantitative studies, are best understood when seen within a wider framework such as this book attempts to provide.

We are again glad to thank all those who have helped with the book over the years, and in particular the half-dozen persons who have acted as consultants for this fifth edition. We are indebted to David Follmer and James Kump of Alfred A. Knopf, Inc., the former for his initiative in bringing this new edition into being, the latter for his careful work as manuscript editor. Since they have left the important decisions to us, and all the actual writing is ours, we assume all responsibility for errors, imperfections, questionable judgments, and other possible shortcomings. Esther Palmer and Shirley Colton have contributed in innumerable ways to the newest edition of this history, which can stand as some kind of continuing monument to marriage, friendship, and intellectual collaboration.

R. R. PALMER
JOEL COLTON

Contents

Prologue:
A Revolutionary
Half-Century

The French Revolution
The Napoleonic Empire
The Peace Settlement of 1814–1815

T he reader will see, if only by looking at the page numbers, that this book is the second half of a larger work. It begins quite abruptly with Europe in the year 1815. It may be asked why a modern history should begin with 1815, and why an account of the modern world seems to be mainly about Europe.

There is no spectacular date to signify the opening of modern times. Yet it is necessary to begin somewhere, and the year 1815 is convenient, because it was in that year that Napoleon Bonaparte was finally defeated at Waterloo, and his attempt at building a European empire was ended. A long period of revolutionary turmoil came to a close in 1815. It had lasted for almost half a century if we count from the American Revolution, which had broken up the old British Empire, temporarily weakened France, and established the United States of America. The new American republic aroused great interest in Europe, for it gave a new meaning and a new force to ideas of constitutional government and of political rights and civil liberties. These ideas were magnified and geographically extended by the French Revolution of 1789. For twenty years, from 1794 to 1814, a renovated France dominated the European continent. The early stages of movements for Latin American independence also began. Looking either to Europe or the Americas, anyone forty years old in 1815 had personal memories of staggering events.

What such a person could not know was, of course, the future, which, as it turned out, was to be a time of extraordinary change. The century from 1815 to 1914, or from the collapse of Napoleon's empire to the First World War, was precisely the period when the modernization of Europe proceeded most rapidly. These hundred years saw the increasing use of power machinery in the Industrial Revolution, the revolution in transportation by the railroad and steamship, the rise of almost instant communications with the telegraph and ocean cables, the development of world markets, modern science, and huge manufacturing and commercial cities. Social classes were restructured; where formerly the difference between aristocrat and plebeian had been important, the big difference now was between those who possessed capital and those who depended wholly on their own labor. Politically, the century after 1815 was a time when national consciousness was acutely heightened and various societies were consolidated into national states. Democracy made advances and socialism appeared. The idea of revolution, derived in its modern form from the French Revolution, aroused hopeful expectations in some, and pessimistic fears in others. Meanwhile a vast emigration from Europe built up communities of European type overseas, notably in the United States, whose population rose between 1820 and 1910 from about nine to ninety million. The population of Europe itself more than doubled in these same years, exceeding 400 million at the close of the nineteenth century.

Europe thus created a combination of political and economic power such as had never yet been seen in the world's history. Able now to reach other parts of the earth more speedily and effectively than ever before, Europeans had an overwhelming impact on the ancient cultures of Asia, Africa, and America. The European ascendancy reached its height about the year 1900, with the penetration of China, the transformation of Japan, and the reduction of most of the rest of Asia and of Africa to the status of colonies within a half dozen empires. In the twentieth century the position of Europe has relatively declined, partly because of conflicts within Europe itself, but mainly because the apparatus which had made Europe so dominant can now be found in other parts of the world. Some, like the United States, are essentially offshoots of Europe. Others have neither had nor wanted connections with Europe until recent times. But all peoples in the twentieth century are caught up in a process of modernization or "development," which usually turns out to mean acquiring some of the technical, scientific, and organizational skills first exhibited by Europeans.

The "modern" world consists in a kind of uniform civilization that overlies many traditional cultures. Each region has its own familiar and deeper level of life, Europe and the United States as well as India or Bolivia, but above them all is the interconnected world of science, fast transportation, radio and television, industry and machines, trade and finance, loans and debts, investments and bank accounts. In most countries, as they become modern, there have been pressures for increased democracy, and all modern governments, democratic or not, must seek to arouse the energies and support of their populations. In a modern society old customs loosen, and ancestral religions are questioned. There is a demand for individual liberation, and an expectation of a higher standard of living. Everywhere there is a drive for more equality—between sexes and among races, between high and low incomes, between adherents of different religions, or between different parts of the same country. Movements for social change may be slow and gradual, or revolutionary and catastrophic, but movement of some kind is universal.

Such are a few of the indexes of modernity. Since they appeared first in the history of Europe, or of the European world in the extended sense in which the United States is included, the present book deals mainly with Europe, but gives increasing attention, in the later chapters, to the earth as a whole.

But before beginning at the date 1815, we must look briefly at what went before, and especially at the French Revolution of 1789, in which many of these indexes of modernity were prefigured.

THE FRENCH REVOLUTION

Unlike the Russian or Chinese revolutions of the twentieth century, the French Revolution ended in a compromise. In 1815 the forces of both the old order and the new era remained very much alive, and the conflict between them continued for generations. In France the Bourbon monarchy was restored in 1814–1815 (having been abolished in 1792), and the European powers that defeated Napoleon were all conservative in that they all opposed revolutionary activity. But the French Revolution had momentous and permanent effects. It had by no means failed, or only its most radical aims were unfulfilled, for it thoroughly transformed the institutions that preceded it, or what was now called the Old Regime. It had shaken Europe, the United States, Canada, Latin America, and the Ottoman Empire, which then spread over the Middle East. It impinged on all of them by the force of its ideals and the sheer weight of its power.

France, at the time of its Revolution, was the leading center of the arts and sciences of Europe. French was the most widely used international language. With 25 million inhabitants in 1789, France had three times as many people as England, and far more than Italy or Spain.[1] There were about as many Germans as Frenchmen, but the Germans could never act together since they lived in a multitude of states within the old and ineffectual Holy Roman Empire. Even Russia, before annexing parts of Poland in the 1790s, was probably no more populous than France. It is hence not surprising that France, revolutionized in the 1790s and then reorganized by Napoleon, exercised an enormous influence that is now hard to imagine.

The Old Regime and the Enlightenment

With the Revolution, the society and government that had existed before it came to be called the Old Regime. The phrase calls up a picture of absolute monarchs and obsequious courtiers, haughty nobles and timid middle classes, luxurious rich and suffering poor, influential archbishops and officious priests, all thrown together in a system of legal privilege and formal rank, with a feudal or seigneurial system of landed property, and a government whose authority rested on tradition, or on dynastic inheritance, or on the teachings of religion. All these things existed in France before 1789, though a closer examination would soon lead to serious qualifications. Louis XVI was indeed an absolute king, legally speaking, in that no one could rightfully oppose his express will or remove him from office. Whether France had any constitution was a debated question; if so, it could be found in no written document, but consisted in a hazy compound of varying customs and disputed rights. The king governed through a bureaucracy

[1] See Appendix III for populations of various countries.

of civil servants, who were in fact becoming more professional and more competent in the years before the Revolution. His freedom of action was limited by these bureaucrats, by the legal privileges of the nobility and the church, special arrangements with the great provinces, high courts of law called *parlements,* and the fact that many officials were irremovable because they had property rights in their own offices, which they had purchased or inherited. The Old Regime was thus in a perpetual state of stalemate and confusion. Repeatedly, before 1789, the king was persuaded to support reforms, only to be blocked by these privileged bodies.

The Revolution came from a breakdown of the government, and from mass insurrection following on food shortages which caused desperation among the poor, but when it came it drew on most of the advanced ideas in Europe, or on the thinking of what is called the Enlightenment. The eighteenth century saw a great increase in the number of writers appealing to a general audience, a proliferation of books, periodicals, pamphlets, and reading clubs, and hence the early stages in the formation of a public opinion. Scientific and geographical discoveries produced a new mood. Perhaps the main idea of the Enlightenment was that new forms of knowledge were now available, by which life on earth and in human society could be improved. There was an expectation of "progress"—a new word at the time—a belief that world history, however distressing, yet moved in a desirable direction, and that meanwhile most existing institutions could be deliberately changed for the better by the use of intelligence or "reason." The past was discredited, and the mere fact that a thing was done in a certain way was no argument in its favor. More specifically, the Enlightenment was skeptical of the mysteries of religion, opposed to the authority of the church, and critical of arbitrary and secretive government, which is called despotism. It was shocked by religious intolerance and judicial torture. Chaotic diversity in the laws, unfair taxation, conflicts of jurisdiction, and self-perpetuating local authorities all seemed unreasonable. Many privileges of the nobility now seemed absurd, and it was said in France, as in America, that people should obtain desirable positions on the basis of talent, not social status. Liberty, equality, the rights of the "citizen" and of the "nation" under a "constitution" were constantly talked about in France for twenty years before 1789. Yet no one foresaw or expected the Revolution, and there was no revolutionary party before the event—again in contrast to the Russian, Chinese, and other later revolutions. Nor was the Enlightenment democratic in a later equalitarian sense. It was mostly an affair of educated persons in the middle and upper classes, including many in the government itself. The collapse of government and popular rebellion gave such persons the opportunity to take action.

What happened was that the French government faced bankruptcy in the 1780s. The trouble arose from both mounting expenses and deficiency of income. Expenses had risen because of French intervention in the American Revolution, for which there was much enthusiasm in France, although the government aided the American insurgents for pragmatic reasons, to check the growing power of England. Government revenues were limited by the fact that much of the wealth of the country was tax-exempt. Legally the French people were divided into three "orders"—Clergy, Nobility, and Third Estate—and freedom from certain kinds of taxation was one of the privileges of the "privileged classes," the Clergy and the Nobility. Since members of these two orders owned a good deal of property, the government was unable to tap the full wealth of the country. Some of the clergy and the nobility were willing to pay more taxes, but only in return for concessions to the church and to the aristocracy that Louis XVI and his ministers were unwilling to grant.

The Revolution of 1789

Louis XVI was obliged to call an election, which, in the absence of other precedents, followed the pattern of the long obsolete Estates General. That is, each Frenchman voted as a member of one of the three "orders." There were less than 100,000 clergy, and no more than 400,000 nobles, in the population of 25,000,000. Yet each order chose its own deputies, who met in three equal houses in May of 1789. A majority in the noble house refused to surrender their corporate identity, while the house of the clergy was internally divided. The Third Estate, in which most of the deputies were lawyers and lesser government officers, with a few merchants and medical doctors, insisted that the three houses should merge into one—making three "orders" into a "nation." It declared itself to be a National Assembly, which it invited members of the other two houses to join. It also claimed the right and duty of writing a constitution. The assembly thus issued a challenge to the king, amounting to an arrogation of sovereign power. The insistence on producing a written constitution, to be accompanied by a declaration of rights, though it flowed from many currents in eighteenth-century thought, was a consequence also of the French enthusiasm for what had been done in the American Revolution. Louis XVI took an ambiguous position; he favored important changes, but supported the noble demand for separate representation, and began to concentrate troops near Paris, with the thought of dissolving the new self-styled National Assembly by force.

The Assembly was saved by the urban rioting and peasant insurrection that broke out in all parts of the country. The summer of 1789 was a time of economic as well as political crisis. Bread prices soared, food was scarce, there was hunger as well as the fear of actual starvation. The king's calling of the Estates General had aroused expectations of relief. As economic distress grew worse, and in the sudden politicizing of opinion, the popular misery was blamed on the stubbornness of the nobility and "aristocrats." Peasants attacked the châteaux of their manor lords, and forced the suspension of payments due on lands which they themselves already owned under "feudal" arrangements. Violence occurred in many provincial towns, where middle-class leaders, taking over from the older authorities, attempted to pacify mobs, provide food supplies, and preserve order. Disturbances in Paris led to an assault on the Bastille, which surrendered to insurrectionists on July 14. Neither the king nor the National Assembly dared to call on the army, for fear that the soldiers might fraternize with the rioters. The king reluctantly recognized the Assembly, which thus faced the task of satisfying the country. Widespread popular revolution had saved the Assembly from extinction, but it expressed the grievances of poor and uneducated men and women with which the Assembly was hardly prepared to deal, and it produced a kind of anarchy throughout the country, as manorial lords and big landowners were intimidated, town councils were ousted, and royal officials abandoned their posts. In these unfavorable circumstances the Assembly proceeded to write a constitution and to reorganize France.

The Constituent Assembly, as it was now called, took two years to complete its constitution. Involved also in legislative and administrative business, operating in a glare of publicity, egged on by militant and vocal activists, and obstructed by counterrevolutionaries who wished to terminate its proceedings, the Assembly worked under very different conditions from those in which the American state constitutions and the federal constitution of the United States had been devised. It did far more than construct a new mechanism of government. It in fact mapped out the outlines of what in later times would sometimes be called bourgeois society, and in any case of the liberal modern state.

It began with promises of a new era. In a memorable session, the night of August 4, 1789, the Assembly decreed the "abolition of feudalism." That is, the peasants were freed of all personal servitudes and of the payments made to lords under the seigneurial system, so that peasants who held land under such "feudal" tenures emerged as small property owners of more modern kind. Tax exemptions, church tithes, and provincial privileges were likewise abolished. A few weeks later the Assembly issued, as a preamble to the coming constitution, its famous Declaration of the Rights of Man and the Citizen. This held that "men are born and remain free and equal in rights," that these rights were "liberty, property, security and resistance to oppression," that sovereign power rested ultimately in the nation, that all public authorities were accountable to the nation, that taxation could only be by public consent, and that citizens must enjoy freedom from arrest and freedom of the press, religion, etc., within certain limits to be set by the law. The Declaration was soon translated into all European languages, and stood as a primary symbol of the Revolution.[2]

The Assembly made Louis XVI into a constitutional monarch, providing a legislature for which about half the adult males were to have an indirect vote. It changed the entire machinery of taxation, public expenditure, fiscal accounting, law courts, and local government. It abolished nobility, and ended the system by which public offices could be bought, sold, and inherited. It did away with trade guilds, internal tariffs, and other barriers to economic freedom within a national market, and began the discussions which resulted in the metric system and decimal currency. Protestants, Catholics, and the non-religious received the same rights. On the principle that citizenship could not depend on race or religion, the Assembly began the process of equalization of rights for Jews and for

---

[2] The Rights of Man, reinforced by Thomas Paine's book by that title in 1791, became the watchword of the eighteenth-century revolutions. Almost immediately, Mary Wollstonecraft supplemented it by her *Vindication of the Rights of Woman* (1792), thus opening up a long argument on the application of the word "man." In English as in French there is only one word for the two meanings. "Man" may mean either any member of the human race, male or female, child or adult (as in German *Mensch* and Latin *homo*), or simply an adult male (as in German *Mann*, Latin *vir*). The former usage will occur from time to time in the present book, and in these contexts the pronouns "he," "him" and "his" are of indeterminate gender. In the French Declaration of the Rights of Man the reference is to the human race in general, but it is true that throughout the French Revolution, and in all countries until much later, certain specific rights were restricted to the males, notably in voting, eligibility to office, education, family law, and some aspects of property law.

free blacks. (Slavery itself was abolished in the French colonies in the more radical days of 1794, to be reinstituted under Napoleon.) It took the initial steps in legal codification (to be completed under Napoleon), so that the whole country might have uniform laws instead of the numerous separate regions of historically developed law under the Old Regime. The old provinces such as Brittany and Languedoc disappeared as legal entities. In their place the Assembly divided the country into eighty-three departments, all structurally alike. The idea was to assure equality of taxation, administration, judicial facilities, and public services throughout the national territory. A pattern of standardization and centralization was thus created (and confirmed by Napoleon) for which France has been famous ever since.

Late in 1789 the Assembly also confiscated or nationalized all the property of the Catholic church, not only the actual church buildings but also the income-producing properties by which the church and many schools and welfare institutions were endowed. In the following years the revolutionary authorities likewise confiscated the property of émigrés, those who left the country because of hostility to the Revolution. All governments during the French Revolution had a high respect for private property; it was simply argued that the property of the church was not private, having been given by pious donors for public purposes over the centuries; and as for the confiscation of émigré property, it was no different in principle from the confiscation of Loyalist estates during the American Revolution. The nationalized properties represented a substantial proportion of all the rural and urban real estate in France. There was no intention for it to remain in the hands of the state. The purpose was to resell it and to use the proceeds to pay off the royal debt which had precipitated the Revolution, to pay compensation for various abolished rights, to finance the government in the collapse of tax collections, and after 1792 to finance the war. Paper money was issued against the nationalized land. With this paper money the government paid its bills, the paper entered into general circulation, and anyone holding the paper could use it, at face value, to acquire a piece of the new "national domain."

An enormous transfer of property ensued. Anyone who had money, or could obtain credit, might acquire a parcel of land, rural or urban. The whole process was facilitated by inflation, in which the paper money had more value for purchase of land than for buying other commodities. Middle-class persons mainly benefited, but some urban workers were able to buy the homes or shops that they had previously rented, many peasants were able to add to their holdings, and there were even cases of aristocrats who, if they could keep out of trouble, managed to expand their estates. In thus enlarging the number of owners of property, and of a property now freed from the church tithe and feudal restraints, the French Revolution was indeed the bourgeois revolution that Marxists and others have seen in it. But it never became a social revolution in the later sense, being rather a political revolution with great social consequences.

The new constitution, completed in 1791, lasted less than a year. The other measures taken by the Constituent Assembly proved more durable; most of them remained in effect in 1815, entering into the compromise in which the Revolution ended. The more purely constitutional features of the Assembly's work—the powers of the king, the composition of the legislature, the provisions for elections —collapsed in August 1792.

The Radical Phase and After

It is true, as is often said, that the most permanent achievements of the Revolution were already evident (or at least enacted) by 1791. The ensuing radical phase of the Revolution was less successful in its objectives, but it was no mere wild aberration. It was this phase that "saved" the Revolution, that is, prevented the reversal of what was done from 1789 to 1791. It also inspired later generations of revolutionaries who looked back on the "sun of '93," and produced a lasting fear of revolutionary agitation among comfortably situated people, including those who had benefited from the Revolution of '89.

From the beginning, the Revolution generated both radical and reactionary currents. Those most determined to press on with the Revolution, and to silence its enemies, became known as Jacobins. Among its enemies were (secretly) the king himself, various disgruntled nobles and their sympathizers, some of the clergy, ordinary persons alarmed by violence, the émigrés led by Louis XVI's two brothers, and as time passed the foreign powers. The two extremes reinforced each other. The rise of Jacobinism made some moderates despair of the Revolution, while the threat of counterrevolution turned others temporarily into Jacobins. The Assembly ran into a confrontation with the Catholic church. Having deprived the church of its property, and yet believing that religion was good for society, the Assembly subjected the church like everything else to a national reorganization, and undertook to pay salaries to its clergy. The pope and almost all the French bishops disapproved; the bulk of the clergy and the laity were divided. Revolution thus passed into religious schism. Partly for this reason, Louis XVI in June 1791 tried to escape from Paris, so as to put himself at the head of the counterrevolutionary forces. Arrested at Varennes, he was compelled to return. A few radicals murmured that France should now be a republic. Moderates preferred to hold on to a constitutional monarchy even with an unwilling and disloyal king. Their position became difficult with the approach of war, in which Louis XVI was rightly suspected of sympathizing with the foreign powers.

Royalty and aristocracy at the time were in their way international institutions. Kings and nobles had more contacts with each other than with their own peoples, and the "nation" was a revolutionary idea. The pleas of the émigrés were listened to in foreign courts. The French queen, Marie Antoinette, was the sister of the ruler of Austria. With the French king and queen virtually prisoners in their own country, the pressure rose for intervention to protect them. In France a few firebrands preached a kind of world revolution against all kings, although Robespierre and a few other Jacobins opposed it. War between France and Austria began in April 1792.

There were then (and throughout the nineteenth century) five principal states or "great powers" in Europe. France was one of them, as was Great Britain with its colonial empire. Austria, or rather the Austrian monarchy, was another; it included Austria itself, Hungary and Bohemia-Moravia (now Czechoslovakia), and had possessions in north Italy and in what is now Belgium. The kingdom of Prussia, with its capital at Berlin, extended along part of the Baltic coast, and controlled a few detached duchies in western Germany. The fifth great power was the Russian Empire, which reached from the Baltic Sea to the Pacific Ocean. In 1792 Poland was invaded by Russia and Prussia, and by 1795 it disappeared from the map. It remained to be seen what an invasion of France might mean. By 1793 France was at war not only with Austria but with Prussia and Great Britain as well, and also with the Dutch Netherlands, Spain, and the Italian Kingdom of Sardinia, which adjoined the southeastern corner of France. Since Belgium belonged to Austria, France was now virtually encircled by a league of conservative states intervening against its Revolution.

At first, in the summer of 1792, the French army was in a state of collapse. An Austro-Prussian force, on the point of invasion, issued a manifesto to the city of Paris, threatening it with fearful retribution unless Louis XVI was properly obeyed. Paris responded with a tremendous insurrection on August 10, 1792, in which Louis XVI was deposed, the new constitution scrapped, and a call issued for a newly elected National Convention. One of the first acts of the Convention was to proclaim the French Republic.

For more than a year the Convention, elected from all over the country, was hard pressed by the advanced revolutionary activists of Paris, the "sans-culottes," who had been brought to power by the insurrection of August 10. Members of the Convention were generally of the educated and substantial middle class. The sans-culottes, though a few erratic intellectuals acted as their spokesmen, were generally from the solid working-class world of artisans and shopkeepers. They were not the destitute, the riffraff, or the vagrant and criminal types that they were said to be by their enemies. Given their broad social origins, the two years after August 1792 have been called the "democratic" phase of the French Revolution. One result was to associate, in later times in France and Europe, the idea of democracy with the idea of revolutionary violence and excitement, and so to impede the gradual growth of politically democratic institutions. In any case, this crisis of the Revolution was not democratic in any liberal sense, but a time of revolutionary dictatorship and the Reign of Terror.

The Convention, composed of about 780 members, unanimously found Louis XVI guilty of collusion with the foreign powers, or treason, and a majority voted for his execution in January 1793. The death of the king committed the revolutionaries more firmly than ever to their course. Successful counterrevolution would destroy them; the grisly fate of the regicides who had put to death Charles I of England in 1649 was well remembered. And counterrevolution seemed all too probable in the spring of 1793. The leading French general defected to the Austrians, who began to cross the northern frontier. The British fleet occupied Toulon. In western France and in the great provincial cities there were revolts against Paris. The paper money lost value, prices rose, food was scarce, and the sans-culottes clamored for bread. They denounced big merchants, rich people, aristocrats, moderates, foreigners, and conspirators. They forced the Convention to expel some of its members, the Girondins, so that power passed to a more fierce and energetic group, the Mountain. The Convention set up a Committee of Public Safety which governed for about a year. Its best-known member was Maximilien Robespierre, though he was never a personal dictator, nor was there any leadership cult of the kind that twentieth-century revolutions were to make familiar.

The Revolution reached its climax in the latter half of 1793. A democratic constitution with universal male suffrage was proclaimed, but was suspended for the duration of the war. Price controls and requisitions of food pacified the sans-culottes, and enabled the government to provide for the army. The controls gave offense to the agricultural population, which, however, was relieved at this time of the last vestiges of the old seigneurial payments. Overwhelming numbers remained faithful to the Revolution, so that an army was raised of almost a million men; it was the largest ever seen in Europe, and the first national or citizen army; and it began to win victories against the hired professionals of Prussia and Austria. There were violent antireligious outbursts, churches were pillaged, and a republican calendar replaced the Christian era. Marriage became a civil contract, with divorce allowed. There were long discussions of universal primary education, but little was accomplished. Universities were abolished, to be replaced by special schools of more modern type; the famous engineering school, the Polytechnique, dates from this time. Eminent scientists worked for the government, to assist in producing cannon, muskets, gunpowder, and even military balloons.

Accompanying all this was the Terror, officially proclaimed in September 1793. The Terror, in the strict sense, lasted about a year, until the military emergency was over. Justified as necessary to strengthen the government in time of war, or as a means of promoting a democratic revolution, the Terror also unleashed irrational frenzies of suspicion, private vengefulness, and class hatred. Since the foreign war was compounded by civil war, the repression fell especially heavily on parts of France that were in rebellion against the revolutionary government, and in these areas far more peasants and workers than nobles and aristocrats became its victims. A Law of Suspects threatened not only enemies of the Revolution but even those who showed insufficient enthusiasm for it. Moderation became a fault. Revolutionary courts, open to the public and hence swayed by extremists, acquitted a few but sentenced about 17,000 persons to death. The guillotine, introduced in 1790 as a more humane means of capital punishment, became the usual method of execution. All told, about 40,000 men and women perished in the Terror, including those who died in the prisons, or were summarily dispatched when taken in the field with arms in their hands as rebels. Several hundred thousand were interned in large buildings such as schools, abbeys, and warehouses, but the Terror did not last long enough to develop anything like concentration camps.

Gradually the government, that is, the Committee of Public Safety, got control of the spontaneous lower-class activity of the sans-culottes. Revolutionary initiative became located in the government itself. Robespierre announced the theory of revolutionary dictatorship, intended to be a temporary regime leading to a democratic and constitutional order. He even tried to introduce a new state religion, the cult of the Supreme Being. He was ridiculed for his pains. The Terror mounted in Paris while it subsided elsewhere. The revolutionary leadership fell apart; its members became afraid of each other; and Robespierre was outlawed and put to death by the Convention in July 1794—Thermidor of the Year Two of the Republic.

A few weeks before Thermidor the French army won a great victory in Belgium. Thus began a series of military successes that were to last for twenty years, and would refashion Europe. In France the revolutionary dictatorship was dismantled. The democratic dream evaporated. A new regime, the Directory, under the constitution of 1795, tried to hold the Republic on a middle ground between equalitarian revolution and aristocratic-clerical-royalist reaction. It failed, and gave way to the Consulate, with Napoleon Bonaparte as First Consul. Bonaparte was a sensational young officer in the republican army, who had been promoted to general in 1793, at the height of the Terror, at the age of twenty-four.

As First Consul, from 1799 to 1804, Bonaparte imposed on France his own version of a compromise with the Revolution—to prevent the return both of the Bourbon monarchy and of the extreme or "democratic" revolutionaries, while preserving the main goals of the Constituent Assembly of 1789–1791. He reduced representative institutions to a pretense, censored the press, and stopped all public discussion of politics. He put down the lingering rebellion in western France, and imprisoned, or in a few cases executed, those caught in either republican or royalist conspiracies. To disarm the counterrevolution, as he said, or to desanctify it, he made an agreement with the pope, the "concordat," by which the church surrendered its claims to its former property, so that the new owners were reassured. Émigré bishops returned to France, and Catholic worship was protected by the government against the antireligious harassments of the preceding years. Non-Catholics continued to enjoy the equal rights obtained during the Revolution. New law codes—the civil code (Code Napoleon) and commercial and penal codes—combined the Revolutionary legislation with the jurisprudence of the Old Regime. By efficient management, many reforms projected at the beginning of the Revolution were made to work in practice. Most of the émigrés came back to France and tried to find a place for themselves in the new order. Bonaparte purposely chose as his subordinates both men who had taken part in the Revolution and those who had opposed it. He said that he offered a career open to talents, by which he meant not so much that poor boys should be encouraged to rise, as that even those of high birth must qualify by strict education, practical training, personal ability, and severe competition. Past politics and ancestral rank were supposed to be forgotten. A new elite composed of both bourgeois and aristocrats began to emerge, of the kind that would conduct French affairs throughout the nineteenth century.

Revolutionary and Conservative Forces in Europe

Although it was only in France that a real revolution occurred, complete with massive popular revolt, there were revolutionary currents in other countries, some of them antedating the French Revolution. Old Regime conditions existed even where there were no monarchies. In the republics of Venice and Genoa, as in Switzerland, the Dutch provinces, and the German free cities, there were hereditary patriciates, closed oligarchies, and self-selected ruling groups, as well as unequal taxation, local privileges, exclusive guilds, and confused legal jurisdictions. There were a hundred different tariff zones in Switzerland alone. Protestant as well as Catholic countries had their state churches, and persons outside such churches, though tolerated, had only limited rights. In differing degree, all European countries had been affected by the Enlightenment and by the American Revolution. There was dissatisfaction everywhere; the Dutch staged a revolution against the house of Orange in the 1780s, and the Belgian "democrats," as they explicitly called themselves, rebelled in 1789 against both their Austrian overlords and their own Belgian upper classes.

When war broke out in 1792 there was therefore much sympathy for the French, especially among the middle classes all over Europe. The message of liberty, equality, and fraternity was warmly received. When the French armies began to win victories, and so to move into enemy territory, they found supporters among the Belgians, Dutch, Italians, and Rhineland Germans. Such people generally wanted, not to be dominated by the French, but to use the French for their own purposes against their own Old Regimes. Eventually there was much disillusionment on both sides. Meanwhile, in 1794, the French simply annexed the Austrian Netherlands and bishopric of Liège—what in later times would become the kingdom of Belgium. In the next five years they absorbed the tiny German states west of the Rhine into the French Republic. Combining with the Dutch revolutionaries they set up a Batavian Republic in 1795, and by similar methods, as by-products of the war against Austria, and in conjunction with native supporters, the French established new republics in Italy and Switzerland. Each of these satellite republics had its constitution, declaration of rights, elected legislature, principles of civil equality, and new financial, judicial, and administrative arrangements modeled on the French.

Opposition to the Revolution was similarly international. There were Dutch and Swiss émigrés as well as French, all hoping to return to their former positions in their own countries and all urging the British and Austrians to pursue the war against France with vigor. At the head of the French émigrés was Louis XVI's next oldest brother, who took the title of Louis XVIII in 1795 (the boy "Louis XVII" having died in prison); but not even the conservative European governments recognized him until 1814, and he wandered about Europe for years, residing eventually in Russia, while the other Bourbon brother, the future King Charles X, lived for twenty years in England and Scotland. They engaged in conspiracies that became more futile as the years passed, since most of the French émigrés made their peace with Napoleon after 1800. Spokesmen for the established churches, whether Roman Catholic, Anglican, or Dutch Reformed, generally disliked the Revolution, but even the pope recognized the French Republic when he signed the concordat with Bonaparte. Prussia turned neutral after 1795, and Spain (though a Bourbon monarchy) even allied itself with regicide France, being more afraid of England. Great Britain, although it had entered the war reluctantly, became the main pillar of conservatism. Its wealth, its landed aristocracy, and its unwritten constitution were admired by partisans of the Old Regime in other countries. The British government, repressing democratic agitation in England and Scotland, carried on the war with its navy and with financial grants to its Continental allies. The counterrevolution won significant victories, as when the British put down the Irish rebellion, abolished the Irish parliament, and joined Ireland with the United Kingdom in 1801, and when Russia, Prussia, and Austria crushed the Polish uprising and divided Poland among themselves in 1795. For a time it seemed that they might at last overwhelm the French Revolution itself, for in 1799 the Austrians drove the French out of Italy, and a Russian army, aiming for France, operated as far west as Switzerland and Holland. The French were again able to defeat them. It was out of this crisis that General Bonaparte emerged as First Consul.

Bonaparte not only reached an apparent reconciliation with the pope, and not only invited back to France those émigrés who would accept him; he also, by his military victories, persuaded the Austrians and the British to make peace. For about a year in 1802 there was no war in Europe. Bonaparte's popularity in France was due to his role as a peacemaker. If only he had stayed out of war, his Consulate might have proved to be a more lasting solution to the problems raised by the Revolution. Such, however, was not to be the case.

THE NAPOLEONIC EMPIRE

In 1804 the French Republic was declared to be an Empire, and Bonaparte took the title of Napoleon I, Emperor of the French. Napoleon's personal ambitions were not yet satisfied, but the blame for renewal of hostilities was not altogether one-sided. The other powers were rightly afraid of him, but their own aims were not merely defensive, for they too had their ambitions, the British to obtain colonial and naval supremacy and to keep a balance of power on the Continent; the Russians, Austrians, and Prussians to make territorial acquisitions, and to prevent the resurgence of an independent Poland. For ten years it was Napoleon who prevailed. At its height, in 1810, his "French Empire" included not only France, as enlarged in the 1790s by the incorporation of Belgium and the German left bank of the Rhine, but two long tentacles along the seacoast, annexed as a countermeasure against British maritime influences: one to the north, comprising the Dutch Netherlands and the German North Sea shore; the other to the south, along the Italian coast as far as Rome. His "Grand Empire" included the French Empire proper, and also Spain, a Kingdom of Italy comprising most of north Italy and a Kingdom of Naples in the southern half of the peninsula, along with Switzerland, most of Germany, the nucleus of Poland set up as the Grand Duchy of Warsaw, and much of Croatia and Slovenia under the name of the Illyrian Provinces. At this time, in consequence of repeated Napoleonic victories, Russia, Austria, and Prussia were all technically allied with Napoleon. The Austrians even gave him a daughter of the house of Habsburg as his second wife; she became the mother of his only child. It was only the British, beyond his reach in their island, who consistently refused to recognize or deal with Napoleon in any way.

The powers that defeated Napoleon in 1814–1815 saw in him a symbol of the Revolution. They even called him a Jacobin. He was no revolutionary, but he had a revolutionary impact on Europe. He was a romantic egomaniac in his temperament, and a follower of the classical Enlightenment in his program. He favored almost everything that the Enlightenment had preached, from the subordination of the church to the reform of taxation and the assimilation of Jews. It was as an innovator, organizer, rationalizer, and modernizer that he presented himself to Europe. To the German philosopher Hegel he seemed to be the "World Spirit on horseback," or in other words he represented the progressive forces of Europe in a position of power.

Spread of the Revolution

Under Napoleon some of the changes introduced in France by the Revolution spread to much of the Continent. England remained fixed in its own ways, made even more conservative, and more satisfied in being different from the Continent, by its long struggle against the French Emperor. The new creations in Spain, Poland, and Croatia-Slovenia were too distant, or too unsettled, for the Napoleonic impact to be much felt. It was in Italy and Germany that native reformers for several years were most willing to work with Napoleon.

One change was simply the enlargement of territorial units, that is, of the area within which a person could go without passing a frontier, changing his money, finding different laws, dealing with unfamiliar officials, or meeting barriers to his trade or professional practice. The units were not yet national. But in north Italy a medley of city-states and duchies was merged into the Kingdom of Italy. In Germany the old Holy Roman Empire, consisting of some three hundred "states," was reorganized into a mere twenty. Most of the free cities disappeared, as did all the church states, where bishops or abbots had been the rulers. Thus Bavaria absorbed the free city of Nuremberg and the bishopric of Bamberg. Various princelings hitherto regarded as sovereign, but who in some cases had no more territory than an English landlord, were likewise "mediatized," becoming subjects of the king of Bavaria, Württemberg, or others, as the case might be. The German rulers who thus expanded their territories were among Napoleon's most ardent supporters. Those of Bavaria, Württemberg, and Saxony, hitherto only electoral princes, were promoted by Napoleon to the rank of "king."

Into these enlarged units the Napoleonic legal codes and administrative apparatus were introduced. Civil equality was a principle of the Code Napoleon; all citizens of the territory, whether noble or non-noble, were to be treated alike by the state in its judicial and financial operations. Expressing the new law of persons and property, the Code also undermined "feudalism." Seigneurial courts were replaced by local courts maintained by the state and subordinated to appellate and high courts ranged above them. Personal services of peasants to lords were abolished, and payments due to seigneurs were abolished or commuted. Large and small property owners remained, as well as those who owned none at all, but there was no longer one form of property for nobles and an inferior form for others. Property owners paid taxes in proportion to the amount of property that they owned, without regard to social status, and tax collection became more professional and efficient. Church courts were abolished, and persons of all religions received the same civil rights. A new system of local government replaced the quaint peculiarities of old-fashioned towns. Roads were improved, and uniform weights and measures were introduced. Each Napoleonic state also maintained its own army, under the Emperor's supreme command. Napoleon saw in his Grand Army another means of unifying Europe, and in fact, when he invaded Russia in 1812, only a third of his 600,000 soldiers were actually French.

Cosmopolitans for a while were well disposed toward Napoleon. Goethe, a humane man but no democrat, once called him "the expression of all that was reasonable, legitimate, and European in the revolutionary movement." His most irreconcilable enemies were the enemies of the French Revolution. But even in France his supporters gradually turned against him, disillusioned by his repeated wars, his repression of open discussion, and his increasing proclivity to ape the royalty of Europe. In other parts of the Grand Empire there began to be nationalist opposition, most especially in Spain, but also in Italy, the Netherlands, and Germany. In 1789 the "nation" had been a revolutionary conception, with liberal implications, directed against absolute rulers and hereditary privileged classes; the nation was a community of equal citizens capable of determining their own fate. Another kind of national feeling now began to develop, in which national identity meant a sense of difference from other nations, i.e., foreigners. The implications of this kind of nationalism were more conservative, for it stressed historic differences in culture, language, folkways, law, and local customs which the Napoleonic system attempted to override. In this view each nation had a spirit of its own, which the Germans called the *Volksgeist*, and which had to be protected against distortion or corruption by outsiders. One kind of national idea was primarily civic, the other primarily ethnic, and both kinds were to remain important, long after Napoleon's time, for Europe and for the world.

On a practical level, among the European powers, the most persistent adversary of Napoleon was Great Britain. Napoleon seriously planned an invasion of England in 1803, but gave it up. His ships attacked the British fleet, but were worsted at the naval battle of Trafalgar. The British responded by forming coalitions with Austria, Prussia, and Russia, whose armies they helped to finance, and which Napoleon defeated in the battles of Austerlitz, Jena, Friedland, and Wagram, all in central Europe, and all now commemorated in Paris as the names of two streets, a bridge, and a railway station. The contest between Britain and France settled into a trade war, in which each tried to undermine the other's economy by reducing its exports.

There was no military solution until Napoleon, to prevent Russia from trading with Britain, launched an invasion of Russia in 1812. He reached Moscow in September, only to find the city in flames, probably set by the Russians themselves in order to freeze him out of the country. He and his army were obliged to make a hasty and miserable retreat in the dead of winter. In the next year, with Prussia and Austria turning against him, a new alliance defeated him in Germany. The allies pressed on, entered Paris, and obliged him to abdicate. They exiled him to Elba on the Italian coast, in 1814, but he escaped from Elba, rallied surprising support in France, took again to the field, and was defeated again by a British and Prussian army at Waterloo, in Belgium. He was sent this time to the tiny island of St. Helena in the South Atlantic, where he died in 1821.

THE PEACE SETTLEMENT OF 1814–1815

The victorious allies believed that they had at last brought an end to the French Revolution and all its works. Yet there was no agreement on what should follow. The allied statesmen had no love for the Bourbon monarchy. In France, after more than twenty years, the Bourbons had been forgotten or remembered with distaste, except by handfuls of royalist true believers. Nevertheless, in the absence of any other acceptable solution, the Bourbon throne was "restored" and Louis XVIII recognized as king. Now a man of sixty, who had spent half his adult life in exile, he was at last prepared to compromise with the Revolution. He issued a constitutional charter, insisting that he did so by his own royal grace and authority, and refusing to accept the principle of national sovereignty; but the charter incorporated most of the great changes which since 1789 had entered into the fabric of French law and society. It also provided for a degree of freedom of speech, political life, and parliamentary government that had been unknown under Napoleon, though politics and voting were confined to a small number of large landowners. As for the allies, they also accepted a Bourbon restoration as most likely to have a stabilizing effect in Europe, since a Bourbon monarchy would be under no pressure to regain the conquests of the Republic and the Empire. It was with Louis XVIII that the allies signed a treaty of peace, by which France was returned to its boundaries of 1791.

To deal with other questions the powers agreed to hold an international congress at Vienna. The recession of the French flood left the future of much of Europe—Belgium, Holland, Germany, Poland, Italy, Spain—fluid and uncertain. There were many other debatable questions. Russia had ambitions against Turkey, and in 1809 had annexed Finland, which it held as an autonomous grand duchy only loosely connected with the tsarist empire. The Spanish empire in America had begun to disintegrate during the Napoleonic occupation of Spain. The British were in possession of all the French and Dutch overseas colonies, and of various islands off the coast of Europe.

Both Russia and Great Britain, before consenting to a general conference, specified certain matters that they would decide for themselves as not susceptible to international consideration. The Russians refused to discuss Turkey and the Balkans. They also kept Finland, as well as certain recent conquests in the Caucasus almost unknown to Europe. The British barred all colonial and overseas questions. They simply announced to Europe which of their colonial and insular conquests they would keep and which they would return.

In Europe, the British remained in possession of Malta, the Ionian Islands, and Heligoland. In America, they kept St. Lucia, Trinidad, and Tobago in the West Indies and reasserted their claims to the Pacific Northwest, or Oregon country, to which claims were also made by Russia, Spain, and the United States. Of former French possessions, the British kept the island of Mauritius in the Indian Ocean. Of former Dutch territories, they kept the Cape of Good Hope and Ceylon, but returned the Netherlands Indies. During the Revolutionary and Napoleonic wars in Europe the British had also made extensive conquests in India, bringing much of the upper Ganges valley under their rule. The British emerged, in 1814, as the controlling power in both India and the Indian Ocean. Indeed, of all the colonial empires founded by Europeans in the sixteenth and seventeenth centuries, and whose rivalry had been a recurring cause of war in the eighteenth, only the British now remained as a growing and dynamic system. Only the British in 1814 had a significant navy. With Napoleon defeated, with the Industrial Revolution bringing power machinery to their manufactures, and with no rival left in the contest for overseas dominion, the British embarked on their century of world leadership, which may be said to have lasted from 1814 to 1914.

The Congress of Vienna

The Congress of Vienna assembled in September 1814. Never had such a brilliant gathering been seen. All the states of Europe sent representatives; and many defunct states, such as the formerly sovereign princes and ecclesiastics of the late Holy Roman Empire, sent lobbyists to urge their restoration. But procedure was

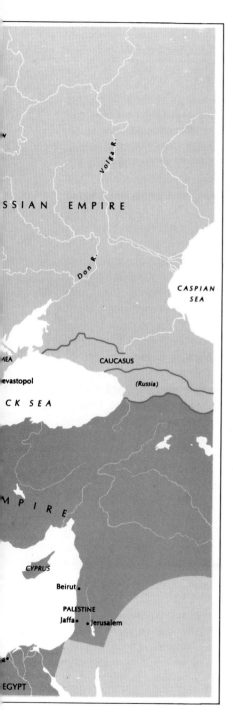

EUROPE, 1815

Boundaries are those set by the Congress of Vienna in 1815. In general, a system of five "great powers" prevailed over the Napoleonic Empire. France was reduced to the borders it had had before the Revolutionary-Napoleonic wars. Prussia was firmly installed on both banks of the Rhine, thus obtaining the part of Germany in which industrialization became important fifty years later. South Germany remained as reorganized under Napoleon. Poland was again partitioned as in 1795. The Russian tsar now had not only an enlarged share of Poland but also Finland and Bessarabia. The Austrians added Venetia to what they had held before 1796.

The union of the Dutch and Belgian Netherlands lasted only until 1831, when the kingdom of Belgium was established. Otherwise, the boundaries of 1815 lasted until the Italian war of 1859 which led to the unification of Italy.

so arranged that all important matters were decided by the four triumphant Great Powers. Europe was at peace, a treaty having been signed with the late enemy; France also was represented at the Congress by Talleyrand, now minister to Louis XVIII. Castlereagh, Metternich, and the tsar Alexander I spoke for their respective countries, Britain, Austria, and Russia; Prussia was represented by Hardenburg. Aristocrats of the Old Regime, they applied prerevolutionary diplomatic principles to the existing problem. They by no means wished to restore the territorial boundaries obtaining before the wars. They did desire, as they put it, to restore the "liberties of Europe," meaning the freedom of European states from domination by a single power. They thus sought a balance of power, which by an ingenious calculation of forces, with transfer of territory from one government to another, would distribute political power among a number of free and sovereign states. It was hoped that a proper balance would also produce a lasting peace.

There was in fact no long war between Great Powers for a hundred years after the Congress of Vienna, but the Congress made decisions against which the liberal and nationalist movements of the nineteenth century were soon to rebel. From the ruins of Napoleon's Grand Empire it set up the kingdom of the Netherlands (including both the Dutch and the Belgian regions), transferred the German area west of the Rhine to Prussia, revived the kingdom of Sardinia in northwest Italy, and assigned the rest of north Italy (Lombardy and Venetia) to Austria. In central Italy the pope restored himself as temporal ruler of the papal states, and various dukes reclaimed their small duchies. Two Bourbon dynasties, related to the French Bourbons, were restored in the kingdom of Naples (all southern Italy) and in Spain. Opposition to most of those regimes became apparent soon after 1815, except in the Rhineland. The Germans there, who before the French Revolution had lived in a hundred small states, were now willing to accept Prussian rule, and Prussia, formerly an East European state, now for the first time had a firm foothold in Western Europe.

In reconstructing Germany, the Congress made no attempt to put together again the Humpty Dumpty of the Holy Roman Empire. The pleas of the former princelings went unheeded. Except for the transfer of the Rhineland to Prussia, the French and Napoleonic reorganization of Germany was substantially confirmed. The rulers of Bavaria, Württemberg, and Saxony kept the royal crowns that Napoleon had bestowed on them. The German states, now thirty-nine in number, were joined in a loose confederation in which the members remained virtually sovereign. The Congress ignored the yearning of German nationalists for a great unified Fatherland; Metternich especially feared nationalistic agitation; and in any case the nationalists themselves had no practical answer to concrete questions, such as the institutions of government and the frontiers that a united Germany should have.[3] The Congress did declare, somewhat ineffectually, that in each of the German states there should be a representative legislative body.

---

[3] The map of Europe in 1815, which appears on the preceding pages, is often referred to in notes to Chapters 11 through 13 below, where the reference, however, is to pp. 412–413. Readers of this second half of the larger work should simply convert pp. 412–413 to pp. *xxviii–xxix* when wishing to see European boundaries as established in 1815.

The assembled diplomats almost came to blows on the question of Poland, or of what was to succeed Napoleon's Grand Duchy of Warsaw. The Russian tsar at this time expressed liberal views, and believed that the partitions of Poland had been a crime; he therefore wished to restore a reunited Poland with himself as its constitutional king. The Prussians were willing to agree, if only they were allowed to annex the kingdom of Saxony. Metternich, speaking for Austria, was alarmed at the possibility of such Russian and Prussian expansion. Castlereagh, speaking for Great Britain, opposed any plan that would bring the power of Russia, by way of Poland, so far into central Europe. Metternich and Castlereagh were on this matter supported by Talleyrand, who shrewdly used this rift between the victors to bring France back into the diplomatic circle as a power in its own right. On January 3, 1815, Castlereagh, Metternich, and Talleyrand signed a secret treaty, pledging themselves to go to war if necessary against Russia and Prussia. So, in the very midst of the peace conference, war again reared its head; and, in the very deliberations of the victors, one party among them allied itself with the vanquished.

No sooner had the news of the secret treaty leaked out than Alexander offered to compromise. He agreed to content himself with a much reduced Polish kingdom. The Congress therefore created a new Poland (called "Congress Poland," which lasted for fifteen years); Alexander became its king, and he gave it a constitution; it comprised much the same area as Napoleon's Grand Duchy, but it reached 250 miles farther west into Europe than had the Russian segment of the third partition of 1795. Some Poles still remained in Prussia and some in the Austrian Empire; Poland was not reunited. With the tsar thus content, Prussia too had to back down. It received only a part of Saxony, the rest remaining to the Saxon king. The addition of both Saxon and Rhenish territories brought the Prussian monarchy into the most advanced parts of Germany. The net effect was to shift the center of gravity of both Russia and Prussia farther west, Russia almost to the Oder River, Prussia to the borders of France.

With the solution of the Polish-Saxon question the main work of the Congress was completed. Other incidental matters were taken up. The Congress initiated international regulation of certain rivers. It issued a declaration against the Atlantic slave trade, which, however, remained ineffective, since the Continental powers were unwilling to grant the British navy the right to make searches at sea, and the British were unwilling to put their naval forces at the disposal of an international body. Committees of the Congress set to work to draft the Final Act.

The work of the Congress was interrupted by Napoleon's return from Elba. After Waterloo, and after Napoleon's second abdication, the allies made a new treaty with France, more severe than the first, since the French seemed to have shown themselves incorrigible in rallying to the Emperor. The new treaty imposed minor changes of the frontiers, an indemnity of 700 million francs, and an army of occupation.

The effect of the Hundred Days, as the episode following Napoleon's return from Elba is called, was to renew the dread of revolution, war, and aggression. Britain, Russia, Austria, and Prussia, after being almost at war with each other in January, again joined forces to get rid of the apparition from Elba, and in November 1815 they solemnly reconfirmed their alliance, adding a provision that no

Bonaparte should ever govern France. They agreed also to hold future congresses to review the political situation and enforce the peace. In addition, the tsar Alexander now devised a vague scheme which he called the Holy Alliance, by which all the powers should uphold Christian principles of charity and peace. The Holy Alliance, probably sincerely meant by Alexander as a condemnation of violence, soon came to signify, in the minds of liberals, a kind of unholy alliance of monarchies against liberty and progress.

The Peace of Vienna was the most far-reaching diplomatic agreement before the Peace of Paris which closed the First World War in 1919. It had its strong points and its weak ones. It produced a minimum of resentment in France, for the new French government accepted the new arrangements. It ended almost two centuries of colonial rivalry; for sixty or seventy years no colonial empire seriously challenged the British. Two other causes of friction in the eighteenth century—the control of Poland and the Austro-Prussian rivalry in Germany—were smoothed over for fifty years. A balance of power was restored, that is, a European state system in which a number of sovereign and independent states existed without fear of conquest or domination. Some details of the settlement broke down in 1830, and others in 1848, but not until 1914 was there a war in Europe that lasted longer than a few months, or in which all the great powers were involved.

With past issues the peace of 1815 dealt rather effectively; with future issues, not unnaturally, it was less successful. The treaty gave no satisfaction to nationalists and democrats. It was a disappointment to many liberals. The transfer of peoples from government to government, without consultation of their wishes, opened the way under nineteenth-century conditions to a good deal of subsequent trouble. The peacemakers were in fact hostile to both nationalism and democracy, the potent forces of the coming age; they regarded them, with reason, as leading to revolution and war.

Yet the settlement was a compromise. The forces of conservatism, controlling the governments, held down but did not crush those who opposed them. In many places—notably in France, but also in Italy, Germany, the Netherlands, and elsewhere—there were still active middle-aged persons who had favored the French Revolution in their youth, or who had worked for reorganization under Napoleon, or who had become more nationalistic under French domination. There were also many in the rising generation who shared in such sentiments.

XI.
Reaction versus Progress, 1815-1848

In the period of some thirty years preceding 1815 two "revolutions" had been taking place. One was the upheaval associated with the French Revolution and the Napoleonic empire. At bottom, it was mainly political, having to do with the organization of government, public power and authority, public finance, taxation, administration, law, individual rights, and the legal position of social classes. The other "revolution," a revolution in a more metaphorical sense, was primarily economic, having to do with the production of wealth, the techniques of manufacture, the exploitation of natural resources, the formation of capital, and the distribution of products to consumers. The political and the economic revolutions, in these years, to a surprising degree, went on independently of each other. Until 1815 the political revolution affected mainly the Continent, while the economic revolution was most active in England. The Continent, while renewing itself politically, remained economically less advanced than England. England, transformed economically, remained conservative in other respects. Hence it has been possible, in the preceding chapters, to deal with the French Revolution and its Napoleonic sequel without attending to the Industrial Revolution, as the economic changes then occurring in England are always called.

It may be (the matter is arguable) that the Industrial Revolution was more important than the French Revolution or any other. In a telescopic view of world

Chapter Emblem: A medal commemorating the Congress of Vienna, showing the victorious rulers of Austria, Russia, and Prussia.

history the two biggest changes experienced by the human race in the past ten thousand years may have been the agricultural or Neolithic revolution which ushered in the first civilizations, and the Industrial Revolution which has ushered in the civilization of the nineteenth and twentieth centuries. However that may be, it proves on closer examination that the economic and the political, the Industrial Revolution (or industrialization) and the other institutions of a society, cannot long be kept apart in an attempt at understanding. The Industrial Revolution occurred first in England, becoming evident about 1780, because of certain political characteristics of English society, because access to world markets had been gained by earlier commercial and naval successes, and because English life offered rewards to the individual for a spirit of risk taking and innovation. Nor can the effects of political and economic revolution, in England or elsewhere, be kept apart for the years after 1815.

With the defeat of Napoleon and signing of the peace treaty at Vienna in 1815, it seemed that the French Revolution was at last over. European conservatism had triumphed; since it frankly opposed the new "French ideas," it can appropriately be called "reaction." But the processes of industrialization, as they accelerated in England and spread to the Continent, worked against the politically conservative settlement. They greatly enlarged both the business and wage-earning classes, and so made it harder for monarchs and landed aristocrats to maintain their control over public power. Industrial development in the nineteenth century was often called "progress," and progress proved stronger than reaction.

Industrial society arose in England, Western Europe, and the United States, in the nineteenth century, within the system known as capitalism. In the twentieth century, since the Russian Revolution, industrial societies have been created in which capitalism is vehemently rejected. Industrialism and capitalism are therefore by no means the same. Yet all industrial societies use capital, which is defined as wealth that is not consumed but is used to produce more wealth, or future wealth. An automobile is a consumer's good; the automobile factory is the capital. What distinguishes a capitalist from a non-capitalist society is not the existence of capital, but the kinds of people who control it. The distinctions sometimes become blurred. But in one form of society the control of capital is through "private ownership" or institutions of private property, by which capital is owned by individuals or family trusts, or nowadays by foundations, pension funds, or corporations that are in turn owned by shareholders; in any case not by the state. In such societies, though ownership may be widespread, most capital is owned or at least controlled by relatively few people. In the other form of society productive capital in principle belongs to the public, and is in effect "owned" and controlled by the state or its agencies; such societies usually call themselves socialist, because the first socialists rejected the principle of private ownership of the means of production, that is, of capital. In these societies the control of capital, or decisions on saving, investment, and production, are also in the hands of relatively few.

In Europe the institutions of secure private property had been developed since the Middle Ages, and much that happened in the French Revolution was designed to protect property from the demands of the state. Possession of property was held to be the basis of personal independence and political liberty, and the expectation of keeping future profits inspired, in some, a willingness to commit their capital to new and uncertain ventures. There had been a commercial capitalism in Europe at least since the sixteenth century.[1] Industrialization in Europe was therefore capitalistic. Countries outside the West-European orbit, and industrializing later, faced a different problem. A country in which little capital had accumulated from the trade and agriculture of previous generations, and which had few capital-owners or enterprising individuals, could hardly industrialize by European methods. If it lacked the European background, in which various political, social, legal, and intellectual features were as important as the economic, it would have to achieve industrialization by other methods. This has usually meant that innovation, planning, decision making, control, and even domination would rest with the state.

So in the short run, within a few years, the Industrial Revolution in Western Europe favored the liberal and modernizing principles proclaimed in the French Revolution. In the middle run, or in half a century, it made Europe overwhelmingly more powerful than other parts of the world, leading to a world-wide European ascendancy in the form of imperialism. In the still longer run, by the twentieth century, it provoked a retaliation, in which other countries tried hastily to industrialize in self-protection, or to improve the condition of their peoples, desperately hoping to catch up with the West while loudly denouncing it as imperialistic and capitalistic. Of these newer industrial societies the Soviet Union and the Chinese People's Republic would be the most prominent.

51. THE INDUSTRIAL REVOLUTION IN BRITAIN

On the whole, from the beginning of history until about 1800, the work of the world was done with hand tools. Since then it has been increasingly done by machines. Before about 1800 power was supplied by human or animal muscle, reinforced by levers or pulleys, and supplemented by the force of running water or moving air. Since then power has been supplied by the human manipulation of more recondite forms of energy found in steam, electricity, the combustion of gases, and most recently within the atom. The process of shifting from hand tools to power machinery is what is meant by the Industrial Revolution. Its beginning cannot be dated exactly. It grew gradually out of the technical practices of earlier times. It is still going on, for in some countries industrialization is barely beginning, and even in the most highly developed it is still making advances. But the first country to be profoundly affected by industrialization was Great Britain, where its effects became manifest in the half-century following 1780.

It seems likely, despite the emphasis placed on revolutionary upheavals by historians, that people are habitually quite conservative. Workingmen do not put off their old way of life, move to strange and overcrowded towns, or enter the deadly rounds of mine and factory except under strong incentive. Well-to-do people, living in comfort on assured incomes, do not risk their wealth in new and untried ventures except for good reason. The shifting to modern machine production requires in any country a certain mobility of people and of wealth. Such mobility may be produced by state planning, as in the industrialization of the

[1] See pp. 108–114.

Soviet Union in recent times. In England a high degree of social mobility existed in the eighteenth century in consequence of a long historical development.

The Agricultural Revolution in Britain

The English Revolution of 1688, confirming the ascendancy of Parliament over the king, meant in economic terms the ascendancy of the more well-to-do property-owning classes.[2] Among these the landowners were by far the most important, though they counted the great London merchants among their allies. For a century and a half, from 1688 to 1832, the British government was substantially in the hands of these landowners—the "squirearchy" or "gentlemen of England." The result was a thorough transformation of farming, an Agricultural Revolution without which the Industrial Revolution could not have occurred.

Many landowners, seeking to increase their money incomes, began experimenting with improved methods of cultivation and stock raising. They made more use of fertilizers (mainly animal manure); they introduced new implements (such as the "drill seeder" and "horse-hoe"); they brought in new crops, such as turnips, and a more scientific system of crop rotation; they attempted to breed larger sheep and fatter cattle. An improving landlord, to introduce such changes successfully, needed full control over his land. He saw a mere barrier to progress in the old village system of open fields, common lands, and semicollective methods of cultivation. Improvement also required an investment of capital, which was impossible so long as the soil was tilled by numerous poor and custom-bound small farmers.

The old common rights of the villagers were part of the common law. Only an act of Parliament could modify or extinguish them. It was the great landowners who controlled Parliament, which therefore passed hundreds of "enclosure acts," authorizing the enclosure, by fences, walls, or hedges, of the old common lands and unfenced open fields. Land thus came under a strict regime of private ownership and individual management. At the same time small owners sold out or were excluded in various ways, the more easily since the larger owners had so much local authority as justices of the peace. Ownership of land in England, more than anywhere else in central or western Europe, became concentrated in the hands of a relatively small class of wealthy landlords, who let it out in large blocks to a relatively small class of substantial farmers. This development, though in progress throughout the eighteenth century, reached its height during the Napoleonic wars.

One result was greatly to raise the productivity of land and of farm labor. Fatter cattle yielded more meat, more assiduous cultivation yielded more cereals. The food supply of England was increased, while a smaller percentage of the population was needed to produce it. Labor was thus released for other pursuits. The greater number of the English country people became wage earners, working as hired men for the farmers and landlords, or spinning or weaving in their cottages for merchants in the towns. The English workingman (and woman) was dependent on daily wages long before the coming of the factory and the machine. English working people became mobile; they would go where the jobs were, or where the wages were slightly higher. They also became available, in that fewer

2 See p. 173.

of them were needed on the land to produce food. Such conditions hardly obtained except in Great Britain. On the Continent agricultural methods were less productive, and the rural workers were more established on the soil, whether by institutions of serfdom as in eastern Europe or by the possession of property or firm leaseholds as in France.[3]

Industrialism in Britain: Incentives and Inventions

Meanwhile, as the Agricultural Revolution ran its course in the eighteenth century and into the nineteenth, the British had conquered a colonial empire, staked out markets all over the Americas and Europe, built up a huge mercantile marine, and won command of the sea. The British merchant could sell more, if only more could be produced. He had the customers, he had the ships, and moreover he could obtain the capital with which to finance new ideas. The profit motive prompted the search for more rapid methods of production. The old English staple export, woolen cloth, could be marketed indefinitely if only more of it could be woven. The possibilities in cotton cloth were enormous. The taste of Europeans for cottons had been already formed by imports from Asia. By hand methods Europeans could not produce cotton in competition with the East. But the market was endless if cotton could be spun, woven, and printed with less labor, i.e., by machines. Capital was available, mobile, and fluid, because of the rise of banking, credit, and stock companies. Funds could be shifted from one enterprise to another. Wealthy landowners could divert some of their profits to industry. If an invention proved a total loss, as sometimes happened, or if it required years of development before producing any income, still the investment could be afforded. Only a country already wealthy from commerce and agriculture could have been the first to initiate the machine age. England was such a country.

These conditions induced a series of successful inventions in the textile industry. In 1733 a man named John Kay invented the fly shuttle, by which only one person instead of two was needed to operate a loom. The resulting increase in the output of weaving set up a strong demand for yarn. This was met in the 1760s by the invention of the spinning jenny, a kind of mechanized spinning wheel. The new shuttles and jennies were first operated by hand and used by domestic workers in their homes. But in 1769 Richard Arkwright patented the water frame, a device for the multiple spinning of many threads. At first it was operated by water power, but in the 1780s Arkwright introduced the steam engine to drive his spinning machinery. Thus requiring a considerable installation of heavy equipment, he gathered his engines, frames, and workers into large and usually dismal buildings, called "mills" by the English, or "factories" in subsequent American usage. Mechanical spinning now for a time overwhelmed the hand weavers with yarn. This led to the development of the power loom, which became economically practicable shortly after 1800. Weaving as well as spinning was therefore done increasingly in factories. These improvements in the finishing process put a heavy strain on the production of raw cotton. An ingenious Connecticut Yankee, Eli Whitney, while acting as a tutor on a plantation in Georgia, in ten days produced a cotton gin, which by speeding up the removal of seeds greatly increased the

3 See pp. 200–201.

output of cotton. The gin soon spread through the American South, where the almost decaying plantation economy was abruptly revived, becoming an adjunct to the Industrial Revolution in England. British imports of raw cotton multiplied fivefold in the thirty years following 1790. In value of manufactures, cotton rose from ninth to first place among British industries in the same years. By 1820 it made up almost half of all British exports.

The steam engine, applied to the cotton mills in the 1780s, had for a century been going through a development of its own.[4] Scientific and technical experiments with steam pressures had been fairly common in the seventeenth century, but what gave the economic impetus to invention was the gradual dwindling away of Europe's primeval stocks of timber. The wood shortage became acute in England about 1700, so that it was more difficult to obtain the charcoal needed in smelting iron, and smelters turned increasingly to coal. Deeper coal shafts could not be sunk until someone devised better methods of pumping out water. About 1702 Thomas Newcomen built the first economically significant steam engine, which was soon widely used to drive pumps in the coal mines. It consumed so much fuel in proportion to power delivered that it could generally be used only in the coal fields themselves. In 1763 James Watt, a technician at the University of Glasgow, began to make improvements on Newcomen's engine. He formed a business partnership with Matthew Boulton. Boulton, originally a manufacturer of toys, buttons, and shoe buckles, provided the funds to finance Watt's rather costly experiments, handmade equipment, and slowly germinating ideas. By the 1780s the firm of Boulton and Watt was eminently successful, manufacturing steam engines both for British use and for the export trade.

At first, until further refinements and greater precision could be obtained in the working of iron, the engines were so cumbersome that they could be used as stationary engines only, as in the new spinning mills of Arkwright and others. Soon after 1800 the steam engine was successfully used to propel river boats, notably on the Hudson in 1807, by Robert Fulton, who employed an imported Boulton and Watt engine. Experiments with steam power for land transportation began at the same time. As it was in the coal fields of England a century before that Newcomen's engine had been put to practical uses, so now it was in the coal fields that Watt's engine first became a "locomotive." Well before 1800 the mines had taken to using "rail ways," on which wagons with flanged wheels, drawn by horses, carried coal to canals or to the sea. In the 1820s steam engines were successfully placed on moving vehicles. The first fully satisfactory locomotive was George Stephenson's *Rocket,* which in 1829, on the newly built Liverpool and Manchester Railway, not only reached an impressive speed of sixteen miles per hour but met other more important tests as well. By the 1840s the era of railroad construction was under way in both Europe and the United States.

The Industrial Revolution in Great Britain in its early phase, down to 1830 or 1840, took place principally in the manufacture of textiles, with accompanying developments in the exploitation of iron and coal. The early factories were principally textile factories, and indeed mainly cotton mills; for cotton was an entirely new industry to Europe and hence easily mechanized, whereas the long established woolen trade, in which both employers and workers hesitated to abandon their customary ways, was mechanized more slowly. The suddenness of the

4 See p. 280.

change must not be exaggerated. It is often said that the Industrial Revolution was not a revolution at all. As late as the 1830s only a small fraction of the British working people were employed in factories. But the factory and the factory system were even then regarded as the coming mode of production, destined to grow and expand, mighty symbols of the irresistible march of progress.

Some Social Consequences of Industrialism in Britain

The Britain that emerged fundamentally unscathed and in fact strengthened from the wars with Napoleon was no longer the "merrie England" of days of yore. The island was becoming crowded with people, as was the lesser island of Ireland. The combined population of Great Britain and Ireland tripled in the century from 1750 to 1850, rising from about 10 million in 1750 to about 30 million in 1850. The growth was distributed very unevenly. Formerly, in England, most people had lived in the south. But the coal and iron, and hence the steam power, lay in the Midlands and the north. Here whole new cities rose seemingly out of nothing. In 1785 it was estimated that in England and Scotland, outside of London, there were only three cities with more than 50,000 people. Seventy years later, the span of one lifetime, there were thirty-one British cities of this size.

Preeminent among them was Manchester in Lancashire, the first and most famous of industrial cities of modern type. Manchester, before the coming of the cotton mills, was a rather large market town. Though very ancient, it had not been significant enough to be recognized as a borough for representation in Parliament. Locally it was organized as a manor. Not until 1845 did the inhabitants extinguish the manorial rights, buying them out at that time from the last lord, Sir Oswald Mosley, for £200,000 or about 1,000,000 dollars. In population Manchester grew from 25,000 in 1772 to 455,000 in 1851. But until 1835 there was no regular procedure in England for the incorporation of cities. Urban organization was more backward than in Prussia or France. Unless inherited from the Middle Ages, a city had no legal existence. It lacked proper officials and adequate tax-raising and lawmaking powers. It was therefore difficult for Manchester, and the other new factory towns, to deal with problems of rapid urbanization, such as provision of police protection, water and sewers, or the disposal of garbage.

The new urban agglomerations were drab places, blackened with the heavy soot of the early coal age, settling alike on the mills and the workers' quarters, which were dark at best, for the climate of the Midlands is not sunny. Housing for workers was hastily built, closely packed, and always in short supply, as in all rapidly growing communities. Whole families lived in single rooms, and family life tended to disintegrate. A police officer in Glasgow observed that there were whole blocks of tenements in the city, each swarming with a thousand ragged children who had first names only, usually nicknames—like animals, as he put it.

The distressing feature of the new factories was that for the most part they required unskilled labor only. Skilled workers found themselves degraded in status. Hand weavers and spinners, thrown out of work by the new machines, either languished in a misery that was the deepest of that of any class in the Industrial Revolution or else went off to a factory to find a job. The factories paid good wages by the standards for unskilled labor at the time. But these standards were very low, too low to allow a man to support his wife and children. This had

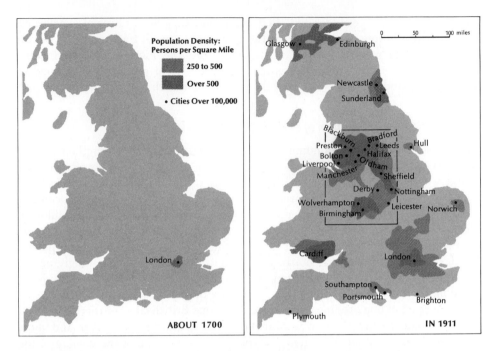

BRITAIN BEFORE AND AFTER THE INDUSTRIAL REVOLUTION

In 1700 England, Scotland, and Wales had only one city with a population of more than 100,000. In 1911 they had nearly thirty. The area within the small rectangle in the right-hand panel, roughly the Midlands, is almost exactly the area of Massachusetts.

generally been true for unskilled labor, in England and elsewhere, under earlier economic systems also. In the new factories the work was so mechanical that children as young as six years old were often preferred. Women, too, worked for less and were often more adept at handling a bobbin.

Hours in the factories were long, fourteen a day or occasionally more; and though such hours were familiar to persons who had worked on farms, or at domestic industry in rural households, they were more tedious and oppressive in the more regimented conditions that were necessary in the mills. Holidays were few, except for the unwelcome leisure of unemployment, which was a common scourge, because the short-run ups and downs of business were very erratic during this period of bewildering expansion. A day without work was a day producing nothing to live on, so that even where the daily wage was relatively attractive the worker's real income was chronically insufficient. Workers in the factories, as in the mines, were almost entirely unorganized. They were a mass of recently assembled humanity without traditions or common ties. Each bargained individually with his employer, who, usually a small businessman himself, facing a ferocious competition with others, often in debt for the equipment in his factory, or determined to save money in order to purchase more, held his "wages bill" to the lowest possible figure that he could manage.

The factory owners, the new "cotton lords," were the first industrial capitalists. They were often self-made men, who owed their position to their own intelligence, persistence, and foresight. They lived in comfort without ostentation or luxury, saving from each year's income to build up their factories and their machines. Hard-working themselves, they thought that landed gentlemen were usually idlers and that the poor tended to be lazy. They were usually honest, in a hard and exacting way; they would make money by any means the law allowed, but not beyond it. They were neither brutal nor knowingly hard-hearted. They gave to charitable and philanthropic causes. They believed that they did "the poor" a favor by furnishing them with work and by seeing to it that they worked diligently and productively. Most of them disapproved of public regulation of their business, though a few, driven by competition to expedients that they did not like, such as the employment of small children, would have accepted some regulation that fell on all competitors equally. It was a cotton magnate, the elder Robert Peel, who in 1802 pushed the first Factory Act through Parliament. This act purported to regulate the conditions in which pauper children were employed in the textile mills, but it was a dead letter from the beginning, since it provided no adequate body of factory inspectors. The English at this time, alone among the leading European peoples, had no class of trained, paid, and professional government administrators; nor did they yet want such a class, preferring self-government and local initiative. To have inspectors for one's affairs smacked of Continental bureaucracy. The fact that the older methods of economic regulation were obsolescent, actually unsuited to the new age, had the effect of discrediting the idea of regulation itself. The new industrialists wanted to be let alone. They considered it unnatural to interfere with business and believed that, if allowed to follow their own judgment, they would assure the future prosperity and progress of the country.

Classical Economics: "Laissez Faire"

The industrialists were strengthened in these beliefs by the emerging science of "political economy." In 1776 Adam Smith published his epochal *Wealth of Nations,* which criticized the older mercantilism, with its regulatory and monopolistic practices, and urged, though with moderation, that certain "natural laws" of production and exchange be allowed to work themselves out. Smith was followed by Thomas R. Malthus, David Ricardo, and the so-called Manchester School. Their doctrine was dubbed (by its opponents) laissez faire and in its elaborated form is still called the classical economics. It held, basically, that there is a world of economic relationships autonomous and separable from government or politics. It is the world of the free market, and is regulated within itself by certain "natural laws," such as the law of supply and demand or the law of diminishing returns. All persons should follow their own enlightened self-interest; each knows his own interest better than anyone else; and the sum total of individual interests will add up to the general welfare and liberty of all. Government should do as little as possible; it should confine itself to preserving security of life and property, providing reasonable laws and reliable courts, and so assuring the discharge of private contracts, debts, and obligations. Not only business, but education, charity, and personal matters generally should be left to private initiative. There should be no tariffs; free trade should reign everywhere, for the economic system is world-wide, unaffected by political barriers or national differences. As for the working-

£ MILLIONS
(CURRENT PRICES)

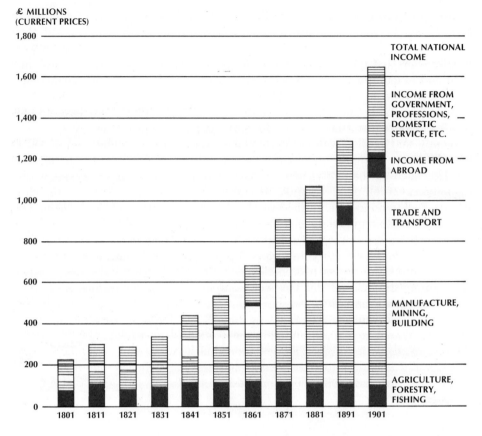

Source: P. Deane and W. A. Cole, *British Economic Growth*
(Cambridge, Eng.: Cambridge University Press, 1962), pp. 166-167.

THE INDUSTRIAL REVOLUTION IN BRITAIN (AS SHOWN BY SOURCES OF INCOME)

Despite uncertainties in such figures several things are apparent. British national income grew about eightfold in the nineteenth century. Incomes derived from agriculture, forestry, and so forth, remained about the same, but sank from one-third to one-sixteenth of all incomes. By 1851 half the national income came from manufacturing, trade, and transportation, and by 1901 three-quarters came from these sources. The category "income from abroad" refers to interest and dividends on loans and investments outside Great Britain, that is, from the export of capital, and this source of income, insignificant in the early years of the century, grew rapidly after the 1850s.

man, according to classical economists before about 1850, he should not expect to make more than a bare minimum living; an "iron law of wages" brings it about that as soon as the worker receives more than a subsistence wage he breeds more children, who eat up the excess, so that he reduces himself, and the working class generally, again to a subsistence level. The workingman, if discontented, should see the folly of changing the system, for this *is* the system, the natural system—there is no other. Political economy as taught in grim Manchester was not without reason called the "dismal science."

For working people in England the Industrial Revolution was a hard experience. It should be remembered, however, that neither low wages, nor the fourteen-hour day, nor the labor of women and children, nor the ravages of unemployment were anything new. All had existed for centuries, in England and western Europe, as agricultural and commercial capitalism replaced the more self-sufficient economies of the Middle Ages. The factory towns were in some ways better places to live than the rural slums from which many of their people came. Factory routine was psychologically deadening, but the textile mills were in some ways not worse than the domestic sweatshops in which manufacturing processes had previously been carried on. The concentration of working people in city and factory opened the way to improvement in their condition. It made their misery apparent; philanthropic sentiment was gradually aroused among the more fortunate. Gathered in cities, workers obtained more knowledge of the world. Mingling and talking together they developed a sense of solidarity, class interest, and common political aims; and in time they became organized, establishing labor unions by which to obtain a larger share of the national income.

Britain after the fall of Napoleon became the workshop of the world. Though factories using steam power sprang up in France, Belgium, New England, and elsewhere, it was really not until after 1870 that Great Britain faced any industrial competition from abroad. The British had a virtual monopoly in textiles and machine tools. The English Midlands and Scottish Lowlands shipped cotton thread and steam engines to all the world. British capital was exported to all countries, there to call new enterprises into being. London became the world's clearinghouse and financial center. Progressive people in other lands looked to Britain as their model, hoping to learn from its advanced industrial methods, and to imitate its parliamentary political system. Thus more foundations of the nineteenth century were laid.

52. THE ADVENT OF THE "ISMS"

The combined forces of industrialization and of the French Revolution led after 1815 to the proliferation of doctrines and movements of many sorts. These broke out in a general European revolution in 1848. As for the thirty-three years from 1815 to 1848, there is no better way of grasping their long-run meaning than to reflect on the number of still living "isms" that arose at that time.

So far as is known the word "liberalism" first appeared in the English language in 1819, "radicalism" in 1820, "socialism" in 1832, "conservatism" in 1835. The 1830s first saw "individualism," "constitutionalism," "humanitarianism," and "monarchism." "Nationalism" and "communism" date from the 1840s. Not until the 1850s did the English-speaking world use the word "capitalism" (French *capitalisme* is much older); and not until even later had it heard of "Marxism," though the doctrines of Marx grew out of and reflected the troubled times of the 1840s.

The rapid coinage of new "isms" does not in every case mean that the ideas they conveyed were new. Many of them had their origin in the Enlightenment, if not before. Men had loved liberty before talking of liberalism and been conservative without knowing conservatism as such. The appearance of so many "isms" shows rather that people were making their ideas more systematic. To the "philosophy" of the Enlightenment were now added an intense activism and a partisanship generated during the French Revolution. People were being obliged to reconsider and analyze society as a whole. The social sciences were taking form. An "ism" (excluding such words as "hypnotism" or "favoritism") may be defined as the conscious espousal of a doctrine in competition with other doctrines. Without the "isms" created in the thirty-odd years after the peace of Vienna it is impossible to understand or even talk about the history of the world since that event, so that a brief characterization of some of the most important is in order.[5]

Romanticism

One of the "isms" was not political. It was called "romanticism," a word first used in English in the 1840s to describe a movement then half a century old. Romanticism was primarily a theory of literature and the arts. Its great exponents included Wordsworth, Shelley, and Byron in England, Victor Hugo and Chateaubriand in France, Schiller and the Schlegels and many others in Germany. As a theory of art it raised basic questions on the nature of significant truth, on the importance of various human faculties, on the relation of thought and feeling, on the meaning of the past and of time itself. Representing a new way of sensing all human experience, it affected most thinking on social and public questions.

Possibly the most fundamental romantic attitude was a love of the unclassifiable—of moods or impressions, scenes or stories, sights or sounds or things concretely experienced, personal idiosyncrasies or peculiar customs which the intellect could never classify, box up, explain away, or reduce to an abstract generalization. The romantics, characteristically, insisted on the value of feeling as well as of reason. They were aware of the importance of the subconscious. They were likely to suspect a perfectly lucid idea as somehow superficial. They loved the mysterious, the unknown, the half-seen figures on the far horizon. Hence romanticism contributed to a new interest in strange and distant societies and in strange and distant historical epochs. Where the philosophes of the Enlightenment had deplored the Middle Ages as a time of intellectual error, the romantic generation looked back upon them with respect and even nostalgia, finding in them a fascination, a colorfulness, or a spiritual depth which they missed in their own time. The "Gothic," which rationalists thought barbarous, had a strong appeal for romantics. A Gothic Revival set in in the arts, of which one example was the British Parliament buildings, built in the 1830s.

In medieval art and institutions, as in the art and institutions of every age and people, the romantics saw the expression of an inner genius. The idea of original or creative genius was in fact another of the most fundamental romantic beliefs. A genius was a dynamic spirit that no rules could hem in, one that no analysis or classification could ever fully explain. Genius, it was thought, made its own rules and laws. The genius might be that of the individual person, such as the artist, writer, or Napoleon-like mover of the world. It might be the genius or spirit of an age. Or it might be the genius of a people or nation, the *Volksgeist* of Herder, an inherent national character making each people grow in its own distinctive way, which could be known only by a study of its history, and not by ratiocination.[6]

5 For some other "isms" important after 1850, see pp. 481–488.
6 See p. 402.

Here again romanticism gave a new impetus to study of the past. Politically romantics could be found in all camps, conservative and radical. Let us turn to the more purely political "isms."

Classical Liberalism

The first Liberals, calling themselves by that name (though Napoleon used that word for his own system, as has been seen[7]), arose in Spain among certain opponents of the Napoleonic occupation. The word then passed to France, where it denoted opposition to royalism after the restoration of the Bourbons in 1814. In England many Whigs became increasingly liberal, as did even a few Tories, until the great Liberal party was founded in the 1850s. Nineteenth-century, or "classical," liberalism varied from country to country, but it showed many basic similarities.

Liberals were generally men of the business and professional classes, together with enterprising landowners wishing to improve their estates. They believed in what was modern, enlightened, efficient, reasonable, and fair. They had confidence in man's powers of self-government and self-control. They set a high value on parliamentary or representative government, working through reasonable discussion and legislation, with responsible ministries and an impartial and law-abiding administration. They demanded full publicity for all actions of government, and to assure such publicity they insisted on freedom of the press and free rights of assembly. All these political advantages they thought most likely to be realized under a good constitutional monarchy. Outside of England they favored explicit written constitutions. They were not democrats; they opposed giving every man the vote, fearing the excesses of mob rule or of irrational political action. Only as the nineteenth century progressed did liberals gradually and reluctantly come to accept the idea of universal male suffrage. They subscribed to the doctrines of the rights of man as set forth in the American and French revolutions, but with a clear emphasis on the right of property, and in their economic views they followed the British Manchester School or the French economist J. B. Say. They favored lassez faire, were suspicious of the ability of government to regulate business, wanted to get rid of the guild system where it still existed, and disapproved of attempts on the part of the new industrial laborers to organize unions.

Internationally they advocated freedom of trade, to be accomplished by the lowering or abolition of tariffs, so that all countries might exchange their products easily with each other and with industrial England. In this way, they thought, each country would produce what it was most fitted for, and so best increase its wealth and standards of living. From the growth of wealth, production, invention, and scientific progress they believed that the general progress of humanity would ensue. They generally frowned upon the established churches and landed aristocracies as obstacles to advancement. They believed in the spread of tolerance and education. They were also profoundly civilian in attitude, disliking wars, conquerors, army officers, standing armies, and military expenditures. They wanted

7 See p. 393.

orderly change by processes of legislation. They shrank before the idea of revolution. Liberals on the Continent were usually admirers of Great Britain.

Radicalism, Republicanism, Socialism

Radicalism, at least as a word, originated in England, where about 1820 the Philosophical Radicals proudly applied the term to themselves. These Radicals in the 1820s included not only the few working-class leaders who were beginning to emerge but also many of the new industrial capitalists, who were still unrepresented in Parliament. They took up where such English "Jacobins" as Thomas Paine had left off a generation earlier, before the long crisis of the French wars had discredited all radicalism as pro-French.[8]

The Philosophical Radicals were a good deal like the French philosophes before the Revolution. They were followers of an elderly sage, Jeremy Bentham, who in prolific writings from 1776 to 1832 undertook to reform the English criminal and civil law, church, Parliament, and constitution. The English Radicals professed to deduce the right form of institutions from the very nature and psychology of man himself. They impatiently waved aside all arguments based on history, usage, or custom. They went to the "roots" of things. ("Radical" is from the Latin word for "root.") They wanted a total reconstruction of laws, courts, prisons, poor relief, municipal organization, rotten boroughs, and fox-hunting clergy. Their demand for the reform of Parliament was vehement and insistent. They detested the Church of England, the peerage, and the squirearchy. Many radicals would just as soon abolish royalty also; not until the long reign of Queen Victoria (1837–1901) did the British monarchy become undeniably popular in all quarters. Above all, radicalism was democratic; it demanded a vote for every adult Englishman. After the Reform Bill of 1832 the industrial capitalists generally turned into liberals, but the working-class leaders remained radical democrats, as will be seen.

On the Continent radicalism was represented by militant republicanism. The years of the First French Republic, which to liberals and conservatives signified horrors associated with the Reign of Terror, were for the republicans years of hope and progress, cut short by forces of reaction. Republicans were a minority even in France; elsewhere, as in Italy and Germany, they were fewer still, though they existed. Mostly the republicans were drawn from intelligentsia such as students and writers, from working-class leaders protesting at social injustice, and from elderly veterans, or the sons and nephews of veterans, to whom the Republic of '93, with its wars and its glory, was a living thing. Because of police repression, republicans often joined together in secret societies. They looked with equanimity on the prospect of further revolutionary upheaval, by which they felt that the cause of liberty, equality, and fraternity would be advanced. Strong believers in political equality, they were democrats demanding universal suffrage. They favored parliamentary government but were much less primarily concerned with its successful operation than were the liberals. Most republicans were bitterly anticlerical. Remembering the internecine struggle between the church and the republic during the French Revolution, and still facing the political activity of the Catholic clergy (for republicanism was most common in Catholic countries),

8 See pp. 358, 373.

they regarded the Catholic church as the implacable enemy of reason and liberty. Opposed to monarchy of any kind, even to constitutional monarchy, intensely hostile to church and aristocracy, conscious heirs of the great French Revolution, organized in national and international secret societies, not averse to overthrowing existing regimes by force, the more militant republicans were considered by most people, including the liberals, to be little better than anarchists.

Republicanism shaded off into socialism. Socialists generally shared the political attitudes of republicanism but added other views besides. The early socialists, those before the Revolution of 1848, were of many kinds, but all had certain ideas in common. All of them regarded the existing economic system as aimless, chaotic, and outrageously unjust. All thought it improper for owners of wealth to have so much economic power—to give or deny work to the worker, to set wages and hours in their own interests, to guide all the labors of society in the interests of private profit. All therefore questioned the value of private enterprise, favoring some degree of communal ownership of productive assets—banks, factories, machines, land, and transportation. All disliked competition as a governing principle and set forth principles of harmony, coordination, organization, or association instead. All flatly and absolutely rejected the laissez faire of the liberals and the political economists. Where the latter thought mainly of increasing production, without much concern over distribution, the early socialists thought mainly of a fairer or more equal distribution of income among all useful members of society. They believed that beyond the civil and legal equality brought in by the French Revolution a further step toward social and economic equality had yet to be taken.

One of the first socialists was also one of the first cotton lords, Robert Owen (1771–1858) of Manchester and the Scottish Lowlands. Appalled at the condition of the millhands, he created a kind of model community for his own employees, paying high wages, reducing hours, sternly correcting vice and drunkenness, building schools and housing and company stores for the cheap sale of workers' necessities. From such paternalistic capitalism in his early years he passed on to a long lifetime spent in crusading for social reforms, in which he was somewhat handicapped, not only by the opposition of industrialists, but by his unpopular radicalism in matters of religion.

Most of the early socialists were Frenchmen, spurred onward by the sense of an uncompleted revolution. One was a nobleman, the Count de Saint-Simon (1760–1825), who had fought in the War of American Independence, accepted the French Revolution, and in his later years wrote many books on social problems. He and his followers, who called themselves not socialists but Saint-Simonians, were among the first clear exponents of a planned society. They advocated the public ownership of industrial equipment and other capital, with control vested in the hands of great captains of industry or social engineers, who should plan vast projects like the digging of a canal at Suez, and in general coordinate the labor and resources of society to productive ends. Of a different type was Charles Fourier (1772–1837), a somewhat doctrinaire thinker who subjected all known institutions to a sweeping condemnation. His positive program took the form of proposing that society be organized in small units which he termed "phalansteries." Each of these he conceived to contain 1,620 persons, each doing the work suited to his natural inclination. Among the practical French no phalanstery was ever successfully organized. A number were established in the United States, still the land of Europe's utopian dream; the best known, since it was operated by literary people, was the Brook Farm "movement" in Massachusetts, which ran through a troubled existence of five years from 1842 to 1847. Robert Owen also, in 1825, had founded an experimental colony in America, at New Harmony, Indiana, on the then remote and unspoiled banks of the Wabash; it, too, lasted only about five years. Such schemes, presupposing the withdrawal of select spirits to live by themselves, really had little to say on the problems of society as a whole in an industrial age.

Politically the most significant form of antediluvian socialism—before the "deluge" of 1848—was the movement stirring among the working classes of France, a compound of revolutionary republicanism and socialism. The politically minded Paris workingmen had been republican since 1792. For them the Revolution, in the 1820s, 1830s, 1840s, was not finished but only momentarily interrupted. Reduced to political impotence, discriminated against in their rights in the law courts, obliged to carry identity papers signed by their employers, goaded by the pressures of industrialization as it spread to France, they developed a deep hostility to the owning classes of the bourgeoisie. They found a spokesman in the Paris journalist Louis Blanc, editor of the *Revue de progrès* and author of the *Organization of Work* (1839), one of the most constructive of the early socialist writings. He proposed a system of "social workshops," or state-supported manufacturing centers, in which the workers should labor by and for themselves without the intervention of private capitalists. Of this kind of socialism we shall hear more as the story unfolds.

As for "communism," it was at this time an uncertain synonym for socialism. A small group of German revolutionaries, mainly exiles in France, took the name for themselves in the 1840s. They would have been historically forgotten had they not included Karl Marx and Friedrich Engels among their members. Marx and Engels consciously used the word in 1848 to differentiate their variety of socialism from that of such utopians as Saint-Simon, Fourier, and Owen. But the word "communism" went out of general use after 1848, to be revived after the Russian Revolution of 1917, at which time it received a new meaning.

Nationalism: Western Europe

Nationalism, since it arose so largely in reaction against the international Napoleonic system, has already been discussed in the preceding chapter.[9] It was the most pervasive and the least crystallized of the new "isms." In western Europe—Britain, France, or Spain—where national unity already existed, nationalism was not a doctrine so much as a latent state of mind, easily aroused when national interests were questioned, but normally taken for granted. Elsewhere in Italy, Germany, Poland, the Austrian and Turkish empires—where peoples of the same nationality were politically divided or subject to foreign rule, nationalism was becoming a deliberate and conscious program. It was undoubtedly the example of the West, of Great Britain and France, successful and flourishing because they were unified nations, that stimulated the ambitions of other peoples to become unified nations too. The period after 1815 was in Germany a time of rising

9 See pp. 400–405.

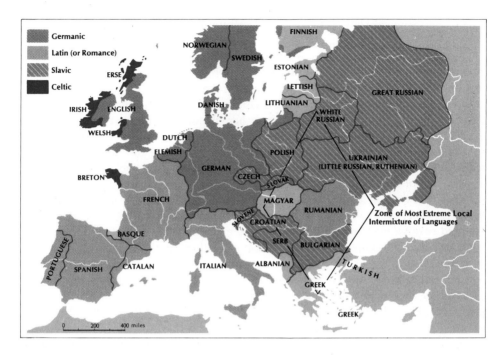

LANGUAGES OF EUROPE

There are three main European language-families—Germanic, Latin, and Slav. It will be seen that they cover most of Europe. Language areas are shown as they were in the first part of the twentieth century, at which time they had not changed much in over five centuries. The map cannot show local complications which have been a leading source of political trouble—such as the overlapping of adjoining languages, bilingual areas, and the existence of small language "pockets," as of Turkish in the Balkans, Greek in Asia Minor, Yiddish in Poland, or German in scattered parts of eastern Europe. In the extreme northwest is the "Celtic fringe," to which the Breton, Welsh, and Gaelic languages were pushed back in the early Middle Ages. For the area within the diamond-shaped zone no map on the present scale can give a realistic idea; the reader must consult an atlas. In any case, during the past decades, in Eastern Europe many language pockets have been wiped out through exchange, transportation, or extermination of peoples. (See map p. 822.)

agitation over the national question, in Italy of the Risorgimento or "resurgence," in eastern Europe of the Slavic Revival.

The movement was led by intellectuals, who often found it necessary to instill in their compatriots the very idea of nationality itself. They seized upon Herder's conception of the *Volksgeist* or national spirit, each applying it to his own people.[10] Usually they began with a cultural nationalism, holding that each people had a language, history, world view, and culture of its own, which must be preserved and perfected. They then usually passed on to a political national-ism, holding that in order to preserve this national culture, and to assure liberty and justice to its individual members, each nation should create for itself a sovereign state. Governing authorities, they held, should be of the same national-

10 See p. 402.

ity, i.e., language, as those they governed. All persons of the same nationality, i.e., language, should be encompassed within the same state.

Since such ideas could not be fully realized without the overthrow of every government in Europe east of France, thoroughgoing nationalism was inherently revolutionary. Outspoken nationalists were discountenanced or persecuted by the authorities and consequently formed secret societies in large numbers. The Carbonari, organized in Italy in the time of Napoleon, was the best known. There were many others—the *Veri Italiani*, the Apophasimenes, the Sublime and Perfect Masters, etc. In some regions Masonic lodges might serve the same purpose. In many of the societies nationalism was mixed with liberalism, socialism, or revolutionary republicanism in an as yet undifferentiated way. Members were initiated by a complex ritual intended to impress upon them the dire consequences of betraying the society's secrets. They used special grips and passwords and adopted revolutionary names to conceal their identity and baffle the police. They were usually so organized that the ordinary member knew the identity of only a few others, and never of the higher-ups, so that if arrested he could reveal nothing important. The societies kept busy, circulating forbidden literature and generally maintaining a revolutionary ferment. Conservatives dreaded them, but they were not really dangerous to any government that enjoyed the support of its people.

Best known of the nationalist philosophers in western Europe was the Italian Joseph Mazzini (1805–1872), who spent most of his adult life in exile in France and England. In his youth he joined the Carbonari, but in 1831 he founded a society of his own, called Young Italy, and he edited and smuggled into Italy copies of a journal of the same name. Young Italy was soon imitated by other societies of similar aim, such as Young Germany. In 1834 Mazzini organized a filibustering expedition against the kingdom of Sardinia, hoping that all Italy would rise and join him. Undeterred by its total failure, he continued to organize, to conspire, and to write. For Mazzini nationality and revolution were a holy cause in which the most generous and humane qualities were to find expression. He was a moral philosopher, as may be judged from the title of his most widely read book, *The Duties of Man*, in which he placed a pure duty to the nation intermediate between duty to family and duty to God.

To the Germans, divided and frustrated, nationality became almost an obsession. It affected everything from folklore to metaphysics. *Grimm's Fairy Tales*, for example, was first published in 1812. It was the work of the two Grimm brothers, founders of the modern science of comparative linguistics, who traveled about Germany to study the popular dialects and in doing so collected the folk tales that for generations had been current among the common people. They hoped in this way to find the ancient, native, indigenous "spirit" of Germany, deep and unspoiled in the bosom of the *Volk*. The same preoccupation with nationhood revealed itself in the philosophy of Hegel (1770–1831), possibly the most stupendous of all nineteenth-century thinkers.

To Hegel, with the spectacle of the Napoleonic years before him, it was evident that for a people to enjoy freedom, order, or dignity it must possess a potent and independent state. The state, for him, became the institutional embodiment of reason and liberty—the "march of God through the world," as he put it, meaning not an expansion in space through vulgar conquest, but a march through time and through the processes of history. Hegel conceived of reality itself as a process, a development having an inner logic and necessary sequence of its own. He thus broke with the more static and mechanical philosophy of the eighteenth century, with its fixed categories of unchangeable right and wrong. He became a philosopher of unfolding change. The pattern of change he held to be the "dialectic," or irresistible tendency of the mind to proceed by the creation of opposites. A given state of affairs (the "thesis") would in this view inevitably produce the conception of an opposite state of affairs (the "antithesis"), which would equally inevitably be followed by a reconciliation and a fusion of the two (the "synthesis"). Thus it could be thought that the very disunity of Germany, by producing the idea of unity, would inevitably bring about the creation of a German state.

The Hegelian dialectic was soon to be appropriated by Karl Marx to new uses, but meanwhile Hegel's philosophy, with other currents in Germany, made the study of history more philosophically meaningful than it had ever been before. History, the study of time process, seemed to be the very key with which to unlock the true significance of the world. Historical studies were stimulated, and the German universities became centers of historical learning, attracting scholars from many countries. Most eminent of the German historians was Leopold von Ranke (1795–1886), founder of the "scientific" school of historical writing. Ranke, too, though intellectually scrupulous to the last degree, owed much of his incentive to his national feeling. His first youthful work was a study of the *Latin and Teutonic Peoples;* and one of his main ideas, throughout his long life, was that Europe owed its unique greatness to the coexistence and interplay of several distinct nations, which had always resisted the attempts of any one nation to control the whole. By the latter Ranke really meant France—the France of Louis XIV and Napoleon. The Germans, said Ranke in 1830, had a mission from God to develop a culture and a political system entirely different from those of the French. They were destined to "create the pure German state corresponding to the genius of the nation." Whether Western constitutional, parliamentary, and individualist principles were suited to the national character of Germany seemed to Ranke very doubtful.

In economics Friedrich List, in his *National System of Political Economy* (1841), held that political economy as taught in England was suited only to England. It was not an abstract truth but a body of ideas developed in a certain historical stage in a certain country. List thus became a founder of the historical or institutional school of economics. The doctrine of free trade, he said, was designed to make England the world's industrial center by keeping other countries in the status of suppliers of raw material and food. But any country, he held, if it was to be civilized and develop its own national culture, must have cities, factories, industries, and capital of its own. It must therefore put up high tariffs (at least temporarily, in theory) for protection. List, it should be remarked, had developed his ideas during a sojourn in the United States, where Henry Clay's "American system" was in fact a national system of political economy.

Nationalism: Eastern Europe

In eastern Europe the Poles and the Magyars had long been active political nationalists, the Poles wishing to undo the partitions and reestablish their Polish state, the Magyars insisting on autonomy of their kingdom of Hungary within the Habsburg empire.[11] But for the most part nationalism in eastern Europe long remained more cultural than political. Centuries of development had tended to submerge the Czechs, Slovaks, Ruthenians, Rumanians, Serbs, Croats, Slovenes— and even the Poles and Magyars in lesser degree. Their upper classes spoke German or French and looked to Vienna or to Paris for their ideas. The native languages had remained peasant languages, and the cultures peasant cultures, barely known to civilized Europeans. It seemed that many of these languages would disappear.

But early in the nineteenth century the process began to reverse itself. Patriots began to demand the preservation of their historic cultures. They collected folk tales and ballads; they studied the languages, composing grammars and diction- aries, often for the first time; and they took to writing books in their mother tongues. They urged their own educated classes to give up "foreign" ways. They wrote histories showing the famous exploits of their several peoples in the Middle Ages. A new nationalism stirred the Magyars; in 1837 a national Hungarian theater was established at Budapest. In what was to become Rumania a former Transylvanian peasant youth named George Lazar began as early as 1816 to teach at Bucharest. He lectured in Rumanian (to the surprise of the upper classes, who preferred Greek), telling how Rumania had a distinguished history back to the Roman emperor Trajan. As for the Greeks, they entertained visions of restoring the medieval Greek empire (known to Westerners as the Byzantine Empire) in which persons of Greek language or Greek Orthodox religion should become the predominant people of the Balkans.

The most far-reaching of the east-European movements was the Slavic Revival. The Slavs included the Russians, Poles, and Ruthenians; the Czechs and Slovaks; and the South Slavs, consisting of the Slovenes, Croats, Serbs, and Bulgars. All branches of the Slavs began to come to life. In 1814 the Serb Vuk Karajich published a grammar of his native tongue and a collection of *Popular Songs and Epics of the Serbs;* he worked out a Serbian alphabet, translated the New Testa- ment, and declared that the dialect of Ragusa (now Dubrovnik) should become the literary language of all South Slavs. He was opposed by the Serbian clergy, who preferred to have writing confined to Slavonic, a purely learned language, like Latin; but he found much support outside Serbia, including that of the brothers Grimm. The Czechs had always been a more advanced people than the Serbs, but educated Czechs were usually half Germanized. In 1836 the historian Palacky published the first volume of his *History of Bohemia*, designed to give the Czechs a new pride in their national past. He first wrote his book in German, the common reading language of educated Czechs. But he soon recast it into Czech, significantly reentitling it a *History of the Czech People.* Among Poles the poet and revolutionary Adam Mickiewicz may be mentioned. Arrested by the Russians in 1823 for membership in a secret society, he was soon allowed by the tsarist government to pass into western Europe. From 1840 to 1844 he taught Slavic languages at the Collège de France, using his lecture platform as a rostrum to deliver eloquent pleas for the liberation of all peoples and overthrow of autoc- racy. He wrote epic poems on Polish historical themes and continued to be active among the revolutionary Polish exiles settled in France.

11 On the Poles, see pp. 235–237, 319–321, 401; on the Magyars, pp. 215, 258, 313.

Russia itself, which Poles and Czechs regarded as very backward, was slower to develop a pronounced national sense. Under Tsar Alexander I a Western or European orientation prevailed, but in Alexander's last years and after his death the doctrines of Slavophilism began to spread. Russian Slavophilism, or the idea that Russia possessed a way of life of its own, different from and not to be corrupted by that of Europe, was simply the application to Russia of the fundamental idea of the *Volksgeist*. Such views in Russia were at least as old as the opposition to the reforms of Peter the Great.[12] In the nationalistic nineteenth century they crystallized more systematically into an "ism," and they tended to merge into Pan-Slavism, which made substantially the same assertions for the Slavic peoples as a whole. But Pan-Slavism, before 1848, was no more than embryonic.

Other "Isms"

Liberalism, radical republicanism, socialism, and nationalism were after 1815 the political forces driving Europe onward toward a future still unknown. Of other "isms" less need be said. Conservatism, too, remained strong. Politically, on the Continent, conservatism upheld the institutions of absolute monarchy, aristocracy, and church and opposed the constitutional and representative government sought by liberals. As a political philosophy, conservatism built upon the ideas of Edmund Burke, who had held that every people must change its institutions by gradual adaptation, and that no people could suddenly realize in the present any freedoms not already well prepared for in the past.[13] This doctrine lacked appeal for those to whom the past had been a series of misfortunes. Conservatism sometimes passed into nationalism, since it stressed the firmness and continuity of national character. But nationalists at this time were more often liberals or republicans. "Monarchism" was conservative and even reactionary. Gone was the enlightened despotism of the last century, when kings had boldly irritated their nobles and defied their churches. After the thunders of the French Revolution aristocracy and monarchy huddled together, and their new watchword was to maintain "the throne and the altar."

Deeper than other "isms," a feeling shared in varying ways by people of all parties, was the profound current of humanitarianism. It consisted in a heightened sense of the reality of cruelty inflicted upon others. Here the thought of the Age of Enlightenment suffered no reversal. Torture was gone, and even backward governments showed no inclination to restore it. Conditions in prisons, hospitals, insane asylums, and orphanages improved. People began to be moved by the misery of pauper children, chimney sweeps, women in the mines, and black slaves. Russian serf owners and American slave owners began to show psychological signs of moral doubt. To degrade human beings, use them as work animals, torture them, confine them unjustly, hold them as hostages for others, tear apart their families, and punish their relatives were regarded by Europeans as foreign to true civilization, something distant, "Turkish" or "Asiatic," like the castration of eunuchs, the impressment of janissaries, or the burning of widows. The

---

12 See pp. 234–235, 315.
13 See p. 358.

Christian sense of the inviolability of the human person was now again, in a mundane way, beginning to relieve the sufferings of humanity.

53. THE DIKE AND THE FLOOD: DOMESTIC

It is time now to resume the narrative of political events, broken off at the close of the last chapter with the peace settlement of 1814–1815. The governments that defeated Napoleon wanted to assure themselves above all else that the disturbances of the past twenty-five years would not be renewed. In France the restored Bourbon king, Louis XVIII, aspired to keep his throne for himself and his successors. In Great Britain the Tory governing class hoped to preserve the old England that they had so valiantly saved from the clutches of Bonaparte. In Germany, Austria, Italy, and central Europe the chief aim of Metternich, who for another thirty-three years remained the mastermind of these regions, was to maintain a system in which the prestige of the Habsburg dynasty should be supreme. The aims of the tsar, Alexander, were less clear. He was feared by representatives of the other powers as a dreamer, a self-chosen world savior, a man who said he wanted to bring Christianity into politics, a crowned Jacobin, and even a liberal. It became one of Metternich's chief hopes to convert Alexander to conservatism.

The arrangements made by the victorious powers were in some ways moderate, at least when the provocations they had undergone in the late wars are considered. Partly by the tsar's insistence written constitutions existed after 1814 in France and in Russian or "Congress" Poland. Some of the rulers of south German states allowed a measure of representative government. Even the king of Prussia promised a representative assembly for his kingdom, though the promise was not kept. But it was difficult to maintain any kind of stability. The forces of the political right, the privileged classes (or in France the former privileged classes) denounced all signs of liberalism as dangerous concessions to revolution. Those of the political left—liberals, nationalists, republicans—regarded the newly installed regimes as hopelessly reactionary and inadequate. Statesmen were jittery on the subject of revolution, so that they met every sign of agitation with attempts at repression, which though they might drive agitation temporarily underground really only made it worse by creating additional grievances. A vicious circle was set endlessly revolving.

Reaction after 1815: France, Poland

In France Louis XVIII in 1814 granted an amnesty to the regicides of 1793. But the regicides, like all republicans, found the France of 1814 an uncomfortable place to live in, exposed as they were to the unofficial vengeance of counterrevolutionaries, and in 1815 most of them rallied to Napoleon when he returned from Elba. This exasperated the royalist counterrevolutionaries beyond all measure. A brutal "white terror" broke out. Upper-class youths murdered Bonapartists and republicans, Catholic mobs seized and killed Protestants at Marseilles and Toulouse. The Chamber of Deputies chosen in 1815 (by the tiny electorate of 100,000 well-to-do landowners) proved to be more royalist than the king—*plus royaliste que le roi.* The king himself could not control the mounting frenzy of reaction, which he was sensible enough to realize would only infuriate the revolutionary element still further, as in fact happened. In 1820 a fanatical workingman assassinated the king's nephew, the Duke de Berry. Those who said that all partisans of the French Revolution were criminal extremists seemed to be justified. The reaction deepened, until in 1824 Louis XVIII died and was succeeded by his brother Charles X. Not only was Charles X the father of the recently murdered Duke de Berry, but for over thirty years he had been the acknowledged leader of implacable counterrevolution. As the Count of Artois, youngest brother of Louis XVI, he had been among the first to emigrate in 1789. He was the favorite Bourbon among the most obstinate ex-seigneurs, nobles, and churchmen. Regarding himself as hereditary absolute monarch by the grace of God, he had himself crowned at Reims with all the romantic pomp of ages past, and proceeded to stamp out not only revolutionary republicanism but liberalism and constitutionalism as well.

In Poland, it will be recalled, the Vienna settlement created a constitutional kingdom, with Alexander as king, joined in merely personal union with the Russian empire. The new machinery did not work very well. The Polish constitution provided for an elected diet, a very wide suffrage by the standards of the day, the Napoleonic civil code, freedom of press and religion, and exclusive use of the Polish language. But the Poles discovered that Alexander, though favoring liberty, did not like to have anyone disagree with him. They could make little use of their much touted freedom in any actual legislation. The elected diet could not get along with the viceroy, who was a Russian. In Russia the serf-owning aristocracy viewed Alexander's idea of a constitutional kingdom in Poland with a jaundiced eye. They wanted no experimentation with liberty on the very borders of Russia. The Poles themselves played into the hands of their enemies. For the Poles were nationalist at least as much as they were liberal. They were dissatisfied with the boundaries accorded to Congress Poland. They dreamed of the vast kingdom that had existed before the First Partition and so agitated the interminable question of the Eastern Border, laying claim to huge territories in the Ukraine and White Russia.[14] At the University of Vilna professors and students began to join secret societies. Some members of these societies were revolutionaries aiming at driving out Alexander, reuniting with Prussian and Austrian Poland, and reconstituting an independent Polish state. It was in the discovery and breaking up of one such society, the Philarets of Vilna, that Adam Mickiewicz was arrested in 1823. Reaction and repression now struck the University of Vilna.

Reaction after 1815: The German States, Britain

In Germany those who had felt national stirrings during the Wars of Liberation were disillusioned by the peace treaty, which maintained the several German principalities about as Napoleon had left them and purposely united them only in a loose federation, or Bund. National ideas were most common in the numerous universities, where students and professors were more susceptible than most people to the doctrines of an eternal *Volksgeist* and a far-flung *Deutschtum.* National ideas, being a glorification of the German common people, carried with them a kind of democratic opposition to aristocrats, princes, and kings. Students

14 See map, p. 319.

in many of the universities in 1815 formed college clubs, called collectively the *Burschenschaft,* which, as centers of serious political discussion, were to replace the older clubs devoted to drinking and dueling. The *Burschenschaft,* a kind of German youth movement, held a nation-wide congress at Wartburg in 1817. Students listened to rousing speeches by patriotic professors, marched about in "Teutonic" costume, and burned a few reactionary books. This undergraduate performance was no immediate threat to any established state, but the nervous governments took alarm. In 1819 a theology student assassinated the German writer Kotzebue, known as an informer in the service of the tsar. The assassin received hundreds of letters of congratulation, and at Nassau the head of the local government barely escaped the same fate at the hands of a pharmacy student.

Metternich now chose to intervene. He had no authority in Germany except in that Austria was a member of the Germanic federation. He regarded all these manifestations of German national spirit, or of any demand for a more solidly unified Germany, as a threat to the favorable position of the Austrian Empire and to the whole balance of Europe. He called a conference of the principal German states at Carlsbad in Bohemia; the frightened conferees adopted certain resolutions, proposed by Metternich, which were soon enacted by the diet of the Bund. These Carlsbad Decrees (1819) dissolved the *Burschenschaft* and the equally nationalistic gymnastic clubs (some of whose members thereupon joined secret societies); and they provided for government officials to be placed in the universities to watch them and for censors to control the contents of books and of the periodical and newspaper press. The Carlsbad Decrees remained in force for many years, and they imposed an effective check on the growth of liberal and nationalist ideas in Germany.

Metternich was unable to persuade the south German rulers to retract the constitutions they had granted. The rulers here, in Bavaria, Württemberg, and elsewhere, found that with representative government they could rally popular support as well as assimilate the numerous new territories that they had obtained from Napoleon. But in general, throughout Germany, after 1820, repression of new or unsettling ideas was the rule. Still more so was this true of the Austrian Empire, which Metternich could more directly control.

Nor did Great Britain escape the dreary rounds of agitation and repression. As elsewhere, radicalism produced reaction, and vice versa. Britain after Waterloo was still a country of the old regime but one afflicted by the most advanced social evils. In 1815, at the close of the wars, the landed classes feared an inrush of imported agricultural products and consequent collapse of farm prices and rentals. The gentry who controlled Parliament enacted a new Corn Law, raising the protective tariff on imports of grains to the point where importation became impossible unless prices were very high. Landlords and their farmers benefited, but wage earners found the price of breadstuffs soaring out of reach. At the same time there was a postwar depression in industry. Wages fell and many were thrown out of work. These conditions naturally contributed to the spread of political radicalism, which looked first of all to a drastic reform of the House of Commons, in order that thereafter a radical program of social and economic legislation might be enacted.

A riot broke out in London in December 1816. In the following February the Prince Regent was attacked in his carriage. The government suspended habeas corpus and employed *agents provocateurs* to obtain evidence against the agitators. Industrialists of Manchester and the new factory towns, determined to force through the reform of parliamentary representation, took the chance offered by the distress of the working classes to organize mass meetings of protest. At Birmingham a crowd elected a mock member of Parliament. At sprawling Manchester 80,000 people staged an enormous demonstration at St. Peter's Fields in 1819; they demanded universal male suffrage, annual election of the House of Commons, and the repeal of the Corn Laws. Although perfectly orderly they were fired upon by soldiers; 11 persons were killed and about 400 wounded, including 113 women. Radicals called this episode the Peterloo massacre in derisive comparison with the battle of Waterloo. The frightened government thanked the soldiers for their brave upholding of the social order. Parliament rushed through the Six Acts (1819), which outlawed "seditious and blasphemous" literature, put a heavy stamp tax on newspapers, authorized the search of private houses for arms, and rigidly restricted the right of public meeting. A group of revolutionaries thereupon plotted to assassinate the whole cabinet at a dinner; they were caught in Cato Street in London in 1820—whence the name "Cato Street Conspiracy." Five of them were hanged. Meanwhile, for publishing the writings of Thomas Paine, Richard Carlisle spent seven years in prison.

"Our example," wrote the Duke of Wellington to a Continental correspondent in 1819, "will be of value in France and Germany, and it is to be hoped that the world will escape from the general revolution with which we all seem to be threatened."

In summary, reactionary policies entrenched themselves everywhere in the years following the peace. The reaction was due only in part to memories of the French Revolution. It was due even more to the living fear of revolution in the present. This fear, though exaggerated, was no mere hallucination. Sensing the rising flood, the established interests desperately built dikes against it in every country. The same is true of international politics at the time.

54. THE DIKE AND THE FLOOD: INTERNATIONAL

At the Congress of Vienna the powers agreed to hold meetings in the future to enforce the treaty and take up new issues as they arose. A number of congresses of the Great Powers resulted, which are of significance as an experimental step toward international regulation of the affairs of Europe. The congresses resembled, in a tentative and partial way, the League of Nations that arose after the First World War of 1914–1918, or the United Nations that arose during and after the war of 1939–1945. The powers had also, in 1815, in alarm after the return of Napoleon, subscribed to Alexander I's Holy Alliance, which became the popular term for the collaboration of the European states in the congresses.[15] The Holy Alliance, on the face of it a statement of Christian purpose and international concord, gradually became an alliance for the suppression of revolutionary and

[15] See p. 416 and map, pp. 412–413.

even liberal activity, following in that respect the trend of the governments which made it up.

The Congress of Aix-la-Chapelle, 1818

The first general postwar assemblage of the powers took place at the Congress of Aix-la-Chapelle (or Aachen) in 1818. The principal item on the agenda was to withdraw the allied army of occupation from France. The French argued that Louis XVIII would never be popular in France so long as he was supported by a foreign army. The other powers, since they all desired the French to forget the past and accept the Bourbons, withdrew their military forces without disagreement. They arranged also to have private bankers take over the French reparations debt (the 700 million francs imposed by the second Treaty of Paris); the bankers paid the allied governments, and the French in due time paid the bankers. On a few other smaller matters international collective action proved successful.

Tsar Alexander was still the most advanced internationalist of the day. He suggested at Aix-la-Chapelle a kind of permanent European union and even proposed the maintenance of international military forces to safeguard recognized states against changes by violence. Governments if thus reassured against revolution, he argued, would more willingly grant constitutional and liberal reforms. But the others demurred, especially the British foreign minister Lord Castlereagh. The British declared themselves willing to make international commitments against specified contingencies, such as a revival of aggression on the part of France. But they would assume no obligations to act upon indefinite and unforeseeable future events. They reserved the right of independent judgment in foreign policy. Concretely, the congress addressed itself to the problems of the Atlantic slave trade and of the recurring nuisance of the Barbary pirates. It was unanimously agreed that both should be suppressed. To suppress them required naval forces, which only the British possessed in adequate amount, and it meant also that naval captains must be authorized to stop and search vessels at sea. The continental states, always touchy on the subject of British sea power, refused to countenance any such uses of the British fleet. They feared for the freedom of the seas. As for the British, they would not even discuss placing British warships in an international naval pool or putting British squadrons under the authority of an international body. Nothing therefore was done; the slave trade continued, booming illicitly with the endless demand for cotton; and the Barbary pirates were not disposed of until the French occupied and annexed Algeria some years later. The growth of international institutions was blocked by the separate interests of the sovereign states.

Revolution in Southern Europe: Troppau, 1820

Scarcely had the Congress of Aix-la-Chapelle disbanded when revolutionary agitation came to a crisis in southern Europe. It was not that revolutionary or liberal sentiment was stronger here than in the north, in the sense of having more followers, but rather that the governments in question, those of Spain, Naples, and the Ottoman Empire, were inefficient, ignorant, flimsy, and corrupt. In 1820 the governments of Spain and Naples collapsed with remarkable ease before the demonstrations of the revolutionaries. The kings of both countries reluctantly took oaths to the Spanish constitution of 1812, itself modeled on the French revolutionary constitution of 1789–1791.[16]

Metternich considered Italy, since the ejection of Napoleon, to be within the legitimate sphere of influence of the Austrian Empire. He saw the insurrections as the first symptoms of a new revolutionary seizure against which Europe should be quarantined. It was a fact that revolutionary agitation was international, easily leaping across frontiers, because of the operations of secret societies and of political exiles, and because in any case the same ideas had been aroused in all countries by the French Revolution. Metternich therefore called a meeting of the Great Powers at Troppau, hoping to use the authority of an international congress to put down the revolution in Naples. The governments of Great Britain and France, not eager to play Austria's game, sent only observers to the congress. Metternich's main problem was, as usual, Alexander. What would be the attitude of the liberal tsar, the friend and patron of constitutions, toward the idea of a constitutional monarchy in Naples? At an inn in Troppau Metternich and Alexander met alone, and there held a momentous interview over the teacups. Metternich reviewed the horrors of revolutionism, the unwisdom of granting any concessions lest revolutionaries be encouraged. Alexander was already somewhat disillusioned by the ungrateful feelings of the Poles. He was troubled by rumors of disaffection among officers in his own army. He had always believed that constitutions should be granted by legitimate sovereigns, not extorted from them by revolutionaries, as had happened in Naples. He allowed himself to be persuaded by Metternich. He declared that he had always been wrong, and that Metternich had always been right; and he announced himself ready to follow Metternich's political judgment. The triumph of the Austrian chancellor was complete. The radical tsar now turned reactionary.

Thus fortified, Metternich drew up a document, the protocol of Troppau, for consideration and acceptance by the five Great Powers. It held that all recognized European states should be protected by collective international action, and in the interests of general peace and stability, from internal changes brought about by force. It was a statement of collective security against revolution. Neither France nor Great Britain accepted it. Castlereagh wrote to Metternich that if Austria felt its interests to be threatened in Naples it should intervene in its own name only. It was not the repression of the Neapolitan revolution that the Tories of 1820 objected to, so much as the principle of a binding international collaboration. Metternich could get only Russia and Prussia to endorse his protocol, in addition to Austria. These three, acting as the Congress of Troppau, authorized Metternich to dispatch an Austrian army into Naples. He did so; the Neapolitan revolutionaries were arrested or put to flight; the incompetent and brutal Ferdinand I was restored as "absolute" king; the demon of revolution was seemingly exorcised. Reaction won out. But the Congress of Troppau, ostensibly a Europe-wide international body, had in effect functioned as an antirevolutionary alliance of Austria,

16 See pp. 352–353.

Russia, and Prussia. A gap opened between the three Eastern autocracies and the two Western powers—even when the latter consisted of Tories and Bourbons.

Spain, Spanish America, the Near East: Verona, 1822

Thousands of revolutionaries and liberals fled from the terror raging in Italy. Many went to Spain, now dreaded by conservatives as the main seat of revolutionary infection. During the Napoleonic domination of Spain, a few Spanish Americans had seized the opportunity to launch the rebellions that led to wars of independence in both North and South America. In the years before 1815, Simón Bolívar and other leaders, long dissatisfied with Spanish colonial rule and influenced by the examples of the American and French revolutions, had temporarily established independent states. After major setbacks, these independence movements slowly recovered during the years after 1816. To crush the rebellions in America and regain absolute power in Spain became the twin objectives of the Spanish king.

The Near East also seemed about to ignite in conflagration. Alexander Ypsilanti, a Greek who had spent his adult life in the military service of Russia, in 1821 led a band of armed followers from Russia into Rumania (still a part of Turkey), hoping that all Greeks and pro-Greeks in the Turkish empire would join him. He expected Russian support, since the penetration of Turkey by the use of Greek Christians had long been a pet project of Russian foreign policy.[17] The possibility of a Turkish empire converted into a "Greek" empire and dependent on Russia was naturally unpleasant to Metternich. To deal with all these matters an international congress met at Verona in 1822.

Alexander, in shifting from liberal to reactionary views, had not changed his belief in the need of international government. Had pure power politics determined his decisions he would doubtless have favored Ypsilanti's Grecophile revolution. But he stood by the principle of international solidarity against revolutionary violence. He disowned Ypsilanti, who found less enthusiasm for Greek culture among the Rumanians and Balkan peoples than he had expected and was soon defeated by the Turks. As for intervention to repress the Greek uprising, the question did not arise, since the Turkish government proved quite able for a time to handle the matter itself.

Further to advance the cause of international solidarity Alexander urged that the Congress of Verona mediate between Spain and its revolting colonies. This was a euphemistic way of suggesting military intervention in Spanish America, following the principle of the protocol of Troppau. The British objected. They had penetrated the Spanish empire commercially for over a century. During the Napoleonic wars they had increased their exports to Latin America twentyfold.[18] This advantage they intended to retain, and even the Tory government favored the breakup of the Spanish empire into independent states, with which free trade treaties might be negotiated. Without at least benevolent neutrality from the British fleet no armed force could sail to America. The Spanish Americans therefore maintained their independence, thanks in part to the use made by the British of their sea power on this occasion.

17 See pp. 319–320.
18 See p. 399.

The new republics received strong moral support from the United States also. In December 1823 President James Monroe, in a message to Congress, announced the "Monroe Doctrine." It stated that attempts by European powers to return parts of America to colonial status would be viewed as an unfriendly act by the United States. The British foreign minister George Canning (who had just succeeded Castlereagh) had at first proposed a joint statement by Great Britain and the United States against the Eastern powers on the Spanish American question. President Monroe, at the advice of his secretary of state John Quincy Adams, decided instead to make a unilateral statement in the form of a message to Congress. They intended to aim their "doctrine" at Great Britain as well as the Continental states, since the British, with their command of the sea, were in fact the only power by which the independence of American states could in practice be threatened. Canning, having no such threats in mind, and concerned more with the Congress of Verona, accepted the line taken by the United States. Indeed, he declared with a flourish that he had "called the New World into existence to redress the balance of the Old." The Monroe Doctrine, at its inception, was a kind of counterblast to the Metternich doctrine of the protocol of Troppau. Where the latter announced the principle of intervention against revolution, the Monroe Doctrine announced that revolutions in America, if they resulted in regimes recognized by the United States, were outside the pale of attention of European powers. In any case the efficacy of the Monroe Doctrine long depended on the tacit cooperation of the British fleet.

The question of the revolution in Spain was settled in a different way. The Bourbon regime in France had no taste for a Spain in which revolutionaries, republicans, political exiles, and members of secret societies might be harbored. The French government proposed to the Congress of Verona that it be authorized to dispatch an army across the Pyrenees. The Congress welcomed the offer, and despite many dire predictions of ruin, arising from memories of Napoleon's disaster, a French army of 200,000 men moved into Spain in 1823. The campaign proved to be a military promenade through a cheering country. Not many Spanish liberals, constitutionalists, or revolutionaries could be found. The mass of the people saw the invasion as a deliverance from Masons, Carbonari, and heretics and shouted with satisfaction at the restoration of church and king. Ferdinand VII, unscrupulous and narrow-minded, repudiated his constitutional oath and let the vindictive ecclesiastics, grandees, and hidalgos have their way. The late revolutionaries were savagely persecuted, exiled, or jailed.

The End of the Congress System

After the Congress of Verona no more such meetings were held. The attempt at a formal international regulation of European affairs was given up. In the broadest retrospect, the congresses failed to make progress toward an international order because, especially after Alexander's conversion to conservatism, they came to stand for nothing except preservation of the status quo. They made no attempt at accommodation with the new forces that were shaping Europe. It was not the policy of the congresses to forestall revolution by demanding that governments institute reforms. They simply repressed or punished all revolutionary agitation. They propped up governments that could not stand on their own feet.

In any case the congresses never succeeded in subordinating the separate interests of the Great Powers. Perhaps Alexander's repudiation of Ypsilanti was a sacrifice of Russian advantage to international principle; but when the Austrian government intervened to crush the revolution in Naples, and when the French government crushed the revolution in Spain, though in both cases they acted with an international mandate, each was really promoting what it conceived to be its own interests. The interest of Great Britain was to pull away from the system entirely. As defined by Castlereagh and by Canning after him, it was to stand aloof from permanent international commitments, to preserve a free exercise of sea power and foreign policy, and to take a benevolent view toward revolution in other countries. Since France eventually pulled away also, the Holy Alliance ceased to be even ostensibly a European system and became no more than a counterrevolutionary league between the three east-European autocracies. With a majority of the five Great Powers highly illiberal, the cause of liberalism in Europe was advanced by the collapse of the international system. At the same time the collapse of the system opened the way to the uncontrolled nationalism of the sovereign states. "Things are getting back to a wholesome state again," wrote George Canning in 1822. "Every nation for itself and God for us all!"

Russia: The Decembrist Revolt, 1825

Alexander I, "the man who defeated Napoleon," the ruler who had led his armies from Moscow to Paris, who had frightened the diplomats by the Russian shadow that he threw over the Continent, and who yet in his way had been the great pillar of constitutional liberalism and international order, died at Taganrog in 1825. His death was the signal for revolution in Russia. Officers of the Russian army, during the campaigns of 1812–1815 in Europe, had become acquainted with many unsettling ideas. Secret societies were formed even in the Russian officer corps; their members held all sorts of conflicting ideas, some wanting a constitutional tsardom in Russia, some demanding a republic, some even dreaming of an emancipation of the serfs. When Alexander died it was for a time uncertain which of his two brothers, Constantine or Nicholas, should succeed him. The restless coteries in the army preferred Constantine, who was thought to be more favorable to innovations in the state. In December 1825 they proclaimed Constantine at St. Petersburg, having their soldiers shout "Constantine and Constitution!" The soldiers, it is said, thought that Constitution was Constantine's wife.

But the fact was that Constantine had long before abdicated in favor of Nicholas, who was the rightful heir. The uprising, known as the Decembrist revolt, was soon put down. Five of the mutinous officers were hanged; many others were condemned to forced labor or interned in Siberia. The Decembrist revolt was the first manifestation of the modern revolutionary movement in Russia—of a revolutionary movement inspired by an ideological program, as distinguished from the elemental mass upheavals of Pugachev or Stephen Razin. But the immediate effect of the Decembrist revolt was to clamp repression upon Russia more firmly. Nicholas I (1825–1855) maintained an unconditional and despotic autocracy.

Ten years after the defeat of Napoleon the new forces issuing from the French Revolution seemed to be routed, and reaction, repression, and political immobility seemed everywhere to have prevailed. The dike—a massive dike—seemed to be containing the flood.

55. THE BREAKTHROUGH OF LIBERALISM IN THE WEST: REVOLUTIONS OF 1830–1832

The dike broke in 1830, nor in western Europe was the stream thereafter stopped. The seepage, indeed, had already begun. By 1825 Spanish America was independent. The British and the French had pulled away from the congress system. The Greek nationalist movement against the Turks had broken out in the early 1820s.

With the defeat of Ypsilanti in 1821 the Greek nationalists turned somewhat away from the idea of a neo-Greek empire and more toward the idea of independence for Greece proper, the islands and peninsulas where Greek was the predominant language. Tsar Nicholas was more willing than Alexander to assist this movement. The governments of Great Britain and France were not inclined to let Russia stand as the only champion of Balkan peoples. Moreover, liberals in the West thought of the embattled Greeks as ancient Athenians fighting the modern oriental despotism of the Turkish empire.

The result was a joint Anglo-French-Russian naval intervention, which destroyed the Turkish fleet at Navarino Bay in 1827. Russia again, as often in the past, sent armies into the Balkans. A Russo-Turkish war and a great Near Eastern crisis followed, in the course of which the rival powers agreed in 1829 to recognize Greece as an independent kingdom. The Balkan states of Serbia, Wallachia, and Moldavia were also recognized as autonomous principalities within the badly shaken Ottoman Empire.[19] From the same crisis Egypt emerged as an autonomous region under Mehemet Ali. Egypt in time became a center of Arabic nationalism, which cut down Ottoman power in the south just as Balkan nationalism did in the north.

France, 1824–1830: The July Revolution, 1830

It was in 1830, and first of all in France, that the wall of reaction really collapsed. Charles X became king in 1824.[20] In the next year the legislative chambers voted an indemnity, in the form of perpetual annuities totaling 30 million francs a year, to those who as émigrés thirty-odd years before had had their property confiscated by the revolutionary state. Catholic clergy began to take over classrooms in the schools. A law pronounced the death penalty for sacrilege committed in church buildings. But the France of the restored Bourbons was still a free country, and against these apparent efforts to revive the Old Regime a strong opposition developed in the newspapers and in the chambers. In March 1830 the Chamber of Deputies, in which the bankers Laffitte and Casimir-Périer led the "leftist" opposition, passed a vote of no confidence in the government. The king, as was his legal right, dissolved the Chamber and called for new elections. The

19 See maps, pp. 412–413, 618.
20 See p. 439.

LIBERTY LEADING THE PEOPLE
by Eugène Delacroix (French, 1798–1863)

Delacroix, a founder of the romantic school of painting, painted this picture soon after the July Revolution in Paris in 1830 (see pp. 447–450). It well illustrates the idealistic conception of revolution which prevailed among revolutionaries before 1848, in sharp contrast to the "realistic," "scientific," or "materialistic" conception of revolution that set in after 1848 and was typified by Karl Marx. (See pp. 484–488.) Revolution is shown as a noble and moral act. The figures express determination and courage, but show no sign of hatred or even anger. They are not a class (note how the costume varies from the top hat to the semi-nude); they are the People, affirming the rights of man. Liberty, holding the tricolor aloft, is a composed and even rational goddess. Romantic though the painter was, he represents the insurgents as realizing an abstract idea—Liberty, or the Republic. It is to this idea that the half-recumbent and presumably wounded figure directs his gaze. Courtesy of the Louvre (Giraudon).

elections repudiated the king's policies. He replied on July 26, 1830, with four ordinances issued on his own authority. One dissolved the newly elected Chamber before it had ever met; another imposed censorship on the press; the third so amended the suffrage as to reduce the voting power of bankers, merchants, and industrialists and to concentrate it in the hands of the old-fashioned aristocracy; the fourth called for a new election on the new basis.

These July Ordinances produced on the very next day the July Revolution. The upper bourgeois class was of course desperate at being thus brazenly ousted from political life. But it was the republicans—the nucleus of revolutionary workingmen, students, and intelligentsia in Paris—that actually moved. For three days, from July 27 to 29, barricades were thrown up in the city, behind which a swarming populace defied the army and the police. Most of the army refused to fire. Charles X, in no mood to be made captive by a revolution like his long-dead brother Louis XVI, precipitately abdicated and headed for England.

Some of the leaders wished to proclaim a democratic republic. Working people hoped for better conditions of employment. The political liberals, supported by bankers, industrialists, various journalists, and intellectuals, had other aims. They had been satisfied in general with the constitutional charter of 1814; it was only to the policies and personnel of the government that they had objected, and they wished now to continue with constitutional monarchy, somewhat liberalized, and with a king whom they could trust. A solution to the deadlock was found by the elderly Marquis de Lafayette, the aging hero of the American and the French revolutions, who now came forward as symbol of national unity. Lafayette produced the Duke of Orleans on the balcony of the Paris Hôtel de Ville, embraced him before a great concourse of people, and offered him as the answer to France's need. The duke was a collateral relative of the Bourbons; he had also, as a young man, served in the republican army of 1792. The militant republicans accepted him, willing to see what would develop; and the Chamber of Deputies on August 7 offered him the throne, on condition that he observe faithfully the constitutional charter of 1814. He reigned, until 1848, under the title of Louis Philippe.

The regime of Louis Philippe, called the Orléanist, bourgeois, or July Monarchy, was viewed very differently by different groups in France and in Europe. To the other states of Europe and to the clergy and legitimists within France, it seemed shockingly revolutionary. The new king owed his throne to an insurrection, to a bargain made with republicans, and to promises made to a parliament. He called himself not king of France but king of the French, and he flew not the Bourbon lily but the tricolor flag of the Revolution. The latter produced an effect on the established classes not unlike that of the hammer and sickle of a later day. He cultivated a popular manner, wore sober dark clothing (the ancestor of the modern "business suit"), and carried an umbrella. Though in private he worked stubbornly to maintain his royal position, in public he adhered scrupulously to the constitution.

The constitution remained substantially what it had been in 1814. The main political change was one of tone; there would be no more absolutism, with its notion that constitutional guarantees could be abrogated by a reigning prince. Legally the main change was that the Chamber of Peers ceased to be hereditary, to the chagrin of the old nobility, and that the Chamber of Deputies was to be elected by a somewhat enlarged body of voters. Where before 1830 there had been

100,000 voters, there were now about 200,000. The right to vote was still based on the ownership of a considerable quantity of real estate. About one-thirtieth of the adult male population (the top thirtieth in the possession of real property) now elected the Chamber of Deputies. The beneficiaries of the new system were the upper bourgeoisie—the bankers, merchants, and industrialists. The big property owners constituted the *pays légal*, the "legal country," and to them the July Monarchy was the consummation and stopping place of political progress. To others, and especially to the radical democrats, it proved as the years passed to be a disillusionment and an annoyance.

Revolutions of 1830: Belgium, Poland, and Elsewhere

The immediate effect of the three-day Paris revolution of 1830 was to set off a series of similar explosions throughout Europe. These in turn, coming after the collapse of the Bourbons in France, brought the whole peace settlement of 1815 into jeopardy. It will be recalled that the Congress of Vienna had joined Belgium with the Dutch Netherlands to create a strong buffer state against a resurgent France and had also done what it could to prevent direct pressure of Russian power upon central Europe by way of Poland.[21] Both these arrangements were now undone.

The Dutch-Belgian union proved economically beneficial, for Belgian industry complemented the commercial and shipping activity of the Dutch, but politically it worked very poorly, especially since the Dutch king had absolutist and centralizing ideas. The Belgians, though they had never been independent, had always stood stiffly for their local liberties under former Austrian rulers (and Spanish before them); now they did the same against the Dutch. The Catholic Belgians disliked Dutch Protestantism; those Belgians who spoke French (the Walloons) objected to regulations requiring the use of Dutch. About a month after the July Revolution in Paris disturbances broke out in Brussels. The leaders asked only for local Belgian self-government, but when the king took arms against them they went on to proclaim independence. A national assembly met and drafted a constitution.

Nicholas of Russia wished to send troops to stamp out the Belgian uprising. But he could not get his forces safely through Poland. In Poland, too, in 1830, a revolution broke out. The Polish nationalists saw in the fall of the French Bourbons a timely moment for them to strike. They objected also to the appearance of Russian troops bound presumably to suppress freedom in western Europe. One incident led to another, until in January 1831 the Polish diet proclaimed the dethronement of the Polish king (i.e., Nicholas), who thereupon sent in a large army. The Poles, outnumbered and divided among themselves, could put up no successful resistance. They obtained no support from the West. The British government was unsettled by agitation at home. The French government, newly installed under Louis Philippe, had no wish to appear disturbingly revolutionary, and in any case feared the Polish agents who besought its backing as international firebrands and republicans. The Polish revolution was therefore crushed. Congress Poland disappeared; its constitution was abrogated, and it was merged into

21 See pp. 410–414.

the Russian empire. Thousands of Poles settled in western Europe, where they became familiar figures in republican circles. In Poland the engines of repression rolled. The tsar's government exiled some thousands to Siberia, began to Russify the Eastern Border, and closed the universities of Warsaw and Vilna. Since meanwhile it was too late for the tsar any longer to contemplate intervention in Belgium, it may be said that the sacrifice of the Poles contributed to the success of the west-European revolution of 1830, as it had done to that of the great French Revolution of 1789–1795.[22]

It was true enough, as Nicholas maintained, that an independent Belgium presented great international problems. Belgium for twenty years before 1815 had been part of France. A few Belgians now favored reunion with it, and in France the republican left, which regarded the Vienna treaty as an insult to the French nation, saw an opportunity to win back this first and dearest conquest of the First Republic. In 1831, by a small majority, the Belgian national assembly elected as their king the son of Louis Philippe, who, however, not wishing trouble with the British, forbade his son to accept it. The Belgians thereupon elected Leopold of Saxe-Coburg, a German princeling who had married into the British royal family and become a British subject. He was in fact the uncle of a twelve-year-old girl who was to be Queen Victoria. The British negotiated with Talleyrand, sent over by the French government (it was his last public service); and the result was a treaty of 1831 (confirmed in 1839) setting up Belgium as a perpetually neutral state, incapable of forming alliances and guaranteed against invasion by all five of the Great Powers. The aim intended by the Treaty of Vienna, to prevent the annexation of Belgium to France, was thus again realized in a new way. Internally Belgium presently settled down to a stable parliamentary system, somewhat more democratic than the July Monarchy in France but fundamentally offering the same type of bourgeois and liberal rule.

Revolutionary disturbances also took place in 1830 in Germany, Italy, Switzerland, Spain, and Portugal. To trace them in any detail is not necessary. In a word, a greater measure of liberalism was established in Switzerland; Spain entered a long period of tortuous parliamentary development confused by civil wars, which arose from a disputed succession to the throne; and in Italy and Germany the 1830 uprisings were quickly put down, showing only the continuance of a radical dissatisfaction still held in check by the authorities. It was in Great Britain that sweeping changes really came.

Reform in Great Britain

The three-day Paris revolution of 1830 had direct repercussions across the Channel. The quick results following on working-class insurrection gave radical leaders in England the idea that threats of violence might be useful. On the other hand, the ease and speed with which the French bourgeoisie gained the upper hand reassured the British middle classes, who concluded that they might unsparingly embarrass the government without courting a mass upheaval.

The Tory regime in England had in fact already begun to loosen up. A group of younger men came forward in the 1820s in the Tory party, notably George Can-

[22] See pp. 363–364 and map on p. 319.

ning, the foreign minister, and Robert Peel, son of one of the first cotton manufacturers.[23] This group was sensitive to the needs of British business and to the doctrines of liberalism.[24] They reduced tariff duties and liberalized the old Navigation Acts, permitting British colonies to trade with countries other than Britain. By repealing certain old statutes, they made it lawful for skilled workmen to emigrate from England, taking their skills with them to foreign parts, and for manufacturers to export machinery to foreign countries, even though English industrial secrets would thus be given away. By such measures they advanced the liberal conception of a freely exchanging international system; they moved toward freedom of trade. The Liberal Tories also undermined the legal position of the Church of England, forwarding the conception of a secular state, though such was hardly their purpose. They repealed the old laws (which dated from the seventeenth century) forbidding dissenting Protestants to hold public office except through a legal fiction by which they pretended to be Anglicans. They even allowed the Test Act of 1673 to be repealed and Catholic Emancipation to be adopted. Catholics in both Great Britain and Ireland received the same rights as others.[25] Capital punishment was abolished for about a hundred offenses. A professional police force was introduced, in place of the old-fashioned and ineffectual local constables. (It is after Robert Peel that London policemen came to be called "bobbies.") The new police were expected to handle protest meetings, angry crowds, or occasional riots without having to call for military assistance.

There were two things that the Liberal Tories could not do. They could not question the Corn Laws, and they could not reform the House of Commons. By the Corn Laws, which set the tariff on imported grain, and which was raised to new heights in 1815, the gentlemen of England protected their rent rolls; and by the existing structure of the House of Commons they governed the country, expecting the working classes and the business interests to look to them as natural leaders.

Never in the five hundred years of its history had the Commons been so unrepresentative. No new borough had been created since the Revolution of 1688. The boroughs, or urban centers having the right to elect members of Parliament, were heavily concentrated in southern England. With the Industrial Revolution, population was shifting noticeably to the north. The new factory towns were unrepresented. Of the boroughs, many had decayed over the centuries; some were quite uninhabited, and one was under the waters of the North Sea. In a few boroughs real elections took place, but in some of them it was the town corporation, and in others the owners of certain pieces of real estate, that had the right to name members of Parliament. Each borough was different, carrying over the local liberties of the Middle Ages. Many boroughs were entirely dominated by influential persons called borough-mongers by their critics. As for the rural districts, the "forty-shilling freeholders" chose two members of Parliament for each county, in a convivial assembly much influenced by the gentlefolk. It was estimated about 1820 that less than 500 men, most of them members of the House of Lords, really selected a majority of the House of Commons.

23 See p. 425.
24 See pp. 429–430.
25 See p. 169.

Some two dozen bills to reform the House of Commons had been introduced in the half-century preceding 1830. They had all failed to pass. In 1830, after the Paris revolution, the issue was again raised by the minority party, the Whigs. The Tory prime minister, the Duke of Wellington, the victor of Waterloo and a most extreme conservative, so immoderately defended the existing system that he lost the confidence even of some of his own followers. The existing methods of election in England, he declared, were more perfect than any that human intelligence could contrive at a single stroke. After this outburst a Whig ministry took over the government. It introduced a reform bill. The House of Commons rejected it. The Whig ministry thereupon resigned. The Tories, fearing popular violence, refused to take the responsibility for forming a cabinet. The Whigs resumed office and again introduced their reform bill. This time it passed the Commons but failed in the House of Lords. An angry roar went up over the country. Crowds milled in the London streets, rioters for several days were in control at Bristol, the jail at Derby was sacked, and Nottingham castle burned. Only the passage of the bill, it seemed, could prevent an actual revolution. Using this argument the Whigs got the king to promise to create enough new peers to change the majority in the House of Lords.[26] The Lords yielded rather than be swamped, and in April 1832 the bill became law.

The Reform Bill of 1832 was a very English measure. It adapted the English or medieval system rather than following new ideas let loose by the French Revolution. On the Continent, where constitutions existed at all (as in France), the idea was that each representative should represent roughly the same number of voters, and that voters should qualify to vote by a flat uniform qualification, usually the payment of a stated amount of property taxes. The British held to the idea that members of the House of Commons represented boroughs and counties, in general without regard to size of population (with exceptions); in other words, no attempt was made to create equal electoral districts. The qualification for voting was enormously simplified, but it still remained rather complex. The franchise, or right to vote, depended on whether one lived in a borough or in a county. It was defined also very largely in terms of rents, because in England, with the high concentration of landownership in the old landowning class, many important people did not own any land at all.

In a borough, under the new law, a man could vote for a member of Parliament if he occupied premises for which he paid £10 annual rental. In a county (a rural area or a small town not considered a borough), a man could vote if he paid £10 annual rental for land held on a long-term sixty-year lease; but he had to pay as high as £50 rental for land occupied on a shorter-term lease in order to be eligible to vote. If he himself owned the land, he could vote if its annual rental value was £2 a year (the old forty-shilling freehold). Thus the vote was nicely distributed according to evidences of economic substance, reliability, and permanence. The total effect on the size of the electorate was to raise the number of voters in the British Isles from about 500,000 to about 813,000. Some persons actually lost their votes, namely, the poorer elements in the handful of old boroughs which had been fairly democratic, like the borough of Westminster in greater London.

The most important thing was not the increased size of the electorate but its

[26] See note, p. 187.

redistribution by region and by class. The Reform Bill reallocated the seats in the House of Commons. Fifty-six of the smallest older boroughs were abolished, their inhabitants thereafter voting as residents of their counties. Thirty other small boroughs kept the right to send only one burgess to Parliament instead of the historic two. The 143 seats thus made available were given to the new industrial towns. Here it was the £10-householders who voted, i.e., the middle classes—factory owners and businessmen and their principal employees; doctors, lawyers, brokers, merchants, and newspaper people; relatives and connections of the well-to-do.

The Reform Bill of 1832 was more sweeping than the Whigs would have favored except for their fear of revolution. It was more conservative than the democratic radicals would have accepted, except for their belief that the suffrage might be widened in the future. Great Britain in 1830 was probably nearer to real revolution than any country of Europe—for the revolutions of 1830 on the Continent were in reality only insurrections and readjustments. In Britain a distressed mass of factory workers, and of craft workers thrown out of employment by factory competition, was led by an irate manufacturing interest, grown strong by industrial changes and determined no longer to tolerate its exclusion from political life. Had these elements resorted to general violence a real revolution might have occurred. Yet there was no violent revolution in Britain. The reason probably lies first of all in the existence of the historic institution of Parliament, which, erratic though it was before the Reform Bill, provided the means by which social changes could be legally accomplished and continued, in principle, to enjoy universal respect. Conservatives, driven to the wall, would yield; they could allow a revision of the suffrage because they could expect to remain themselves in public life. Radicals, using enough violence to scare the established interest, did not thereafter face a blank wall; they could expect, once the breach was made, to carry some day a further democratization of Parliament and with it their social and economic program by orderly legislation.

Britain after 1832

But the Reform Bill of 1832 was in its way a revolution. The new business interests, created by industrialization, took their place alongside the old aristocracy in the governing elite of the country. The aristocratic Whigs who had carried the Reform Bill gradually merged with formerly radical industrialists and with a few Liberal Tories to form the Liberal party. The main body of the Tories, joined by a few old Whigs and even a few former radicals, gradually turned into the Conservative party. The two parties alternated in power at short intervals from 1832 to the First World War, this being the classic period in Great Britain of the Liberal-Conservative two-party system.

In 1833 slavery was abolished in the British Empire. In 1834 a new Poor Law was adopted. In 1835 the Municipal Corporations Act, second only to the Reform Bill in basic importance, modernized the local government of English cities; it broke up the old local oligarchies and brought in uniform electoral and administrative machinery, enabling city dwellers to grapple more effectively with the problems of urban life. In 1836 the House of Commons allowed the newspapers to report how its members voted—a long step toward publicity of government proceedings was thus taken. Meanwhile an ecclesiastical commission reviewed the affairs of the Church of England; financial and administrative irregularities were corrected, together with the grosser inequalities between the income of upper and lower clergy, all of which had made the church formerly a kind of closed preserve for the landed gentry.

The Tories, thus assaulted in their immemorial strongholds of local government and the established church, carried a counteroffensive into the strongholds of the new liberal manufacturing class, namely, the factories and the mines. Tories became champions of the industrial workers. Landed gentlemen, of whom the most famous was Lord Ashley, later seventh Earl of Shaftesbury, took the lead in publicizing the social evils of a rapid and indeed ruthless industrialization. They received some support from a few humanitarian industrialists; indeed, the early legislation tended to follow practices already established by the best or strongest business firms. A Factory Act of 1833 forbade the labor of children less than nine years old in the textile mills. It was the first effective piece of legislation on the subject, for it provided for paid inspectors and procedures for enforcement. An act of 1842 initiated significant regulation in the coal mines; the employment underground of women and girls, and of boys under ten, was forbidden.

The greatest victory of the working classes came in 1847 with the Ten Hours Act, which limited the labor of women and children in all industrial establishments to ten hours a day. Thereafter men commonly worked only ten hours also, since the work of men, women, and young people was too closely coordinated for the men to work alone. The great Liberal, John Bright, Quaker and cotton magnate, called the Ten Hours Act "a delusion practiced on the working classes." To regulate the hours of labor was contrary to the accepted principles of laissez faire, economic law, the free market, freedom of trade, and individual liberty for employer and workman. Yet the Ten Hours Act stood, and British industry continued to prosper.

Gathering their strength, the Whig-liberal-radical combination established in 1838 an Anti–Corn Law League. Wage earners objected to the Corn Laws because the tariff on grain imports kept up the price of food. Industrial employers objected to them because, in keeping up food prices, they also kept up wages and cost of production in England, thus working to England's disadvantage in the export trade. Defenders of the Corn Laws argued that protection of agriculture was necessary to maintain the natural aristocracy of the country (most land being owned by peers and gentry, as has been seen), but they also sometimes used more widely framed economic arguments, affirming that Britain should preserve a balanced economy as between industry and farming, and avoid becoming too exclusively dependent on imported food. The issue became a straight contest between the industrialists, acting with working-class support, and the aristocratic and predominantly Tory landowning interest. The Anti–Corn Law League, whose headquarters were at Manchester, operated like a modern political party. It had plenty of money, supplied by large donations from manufacturers and small ones from laboring people. It sent lecturers on tour, agitated in the newspapers, and issued a stream of polemical pamphlets and educational books. It held political teas, torchlight processions, and open-air mass meetings. The pressure proved irresistible and received a final impetus from a famine in Ireland. It was a Tory

Grand placement d'actions.

government, headed by Sir Robert Peel, which in 1846 yielded before so vociferous a demand.

The repeal of the Corn Laws in 1846 stands as a symbol of the change that had come over England. It reaffirmed the revolutionary consequences of the Reform Bill of 1832. Industry was now a governing element in the country. Free trade was henceforth the rule. Great Britain, in return for the export of manufactures, became deliberately dependent on imports for its very life. It was committed henceforth to an international and even world-wide economic system. The first to undergo the Industrial Revolution, possessing mechanical power and methods of mass production, the British could produce yarn and cloth, machine tools and railroad equipment, more efficiently and more cheaply than any other people. In Britain, the workshop of the world, people would pour increasingly into mine, factory, and city, live by selling manufactures, coal, shipping, and financial services to the other peoples of the earth, and obtain raw cotton, rare ores, meat, cereals, and thousands of lesser but still vital necessities from the rest of the earth in exchange. The welfare of Britain depended on the maintenance of a freely exchanging world-wide economic system.

It depended also, more than ever, on British control of the sea, which was rarely mentioned by the civilian-minded Anti–Corn Law League, but which, firmly established in the long duel with Napoleon, was now an assumed postulate of economic discussion. No one understood this better than Lord Palmerston, a flamboyant Anglo-Irish Whig aristocrat, who by risky and audacious moves that alarmed his colleagues and threw Queen Victoria into consternation, came forward as the very British bulldog in defense of Britain's name. For example, in 1850 a Moroccan Jew known as Don Pacifico, who was a British subject, got into trouble in Greece because of certain debts owed to him by the Greek government. Though the claim was not above question, Palmerston unloosed the thunders of the British fleet. He sent a squadron to the Piraeus, the port of Athens, and forbade Greek vessels the use of their own harbor until the matter was settled. On another occasion, in 1856, when Chinese authorities arrested a Chinese ship called the *Arrow*, which, though without due right, was flying the British flag, Palmerston again called on the navy, which proceeded to bombard Canton and precipitated the Second Anglo-Chinese War. In other connections, as a good mid–nineteenth-century liberal, Palmerston favored movements for national independence,

BIG INVESTMENTS
by Honoré Daumier (French, 1808–1879)

The Revolution of 1830, romanticized by Delacroix, was in fact followed by a period of moneymaking and business ferment (as well as genuine economic development) made famous in the novels of Balzac and the graphic art of Daumier. This lithograph of 1837 shows a financier, with bundles of stock certificates piled beside him, offering to sell shares in factories, foundries, breweries, etc., to a skeptical client. Daumier was a satirist and caricaturist of bourgeois society. Where Rembrandt in the seventeenth century could portray businessmen with a high seriousness (as on p. 158), artists since the 1830s have been generally alienated from such subjects. Courtesy of the Bibliothèque Nationale, Paris.

including that of the Confederate States of America, expecting them to result in the further extension of free trade.

56. TRIUMPH OF THE WEST-EUROPEAN BOURGEOISIE

In both Great Britain and France (as also in Belgium) the revolutionary agitation of 1830–1832 ushered in a period of ascendancy for the bourgeois or propertied classes. The reigning liberal doctrine was the "stake in society" theory: those should govern who have something to lose. In the France of the July Monarchy (1830–1848) about one adult male in thirty could vote, in the Britain of the first Reform Bill (1832–1867) about one in eight. In Britain virtually the whole middle class was now enfranchised, in France only the most well-to-do. In Britain the continuation of the Tory landed interests in politics somewhat blunted the edge of capitalist and managerial rule, resulting in the passage of significant legislation for the protection of industrial labor. In France the aristocratic landed interest, weaker and less public spirited than in England in any case, lost much of its influence by the revolution of 1830. France under Louis Philippe was a more purely bourgeois country than Great Britain, and less was done to relieve the condition of labor.

In general, the decades following 1830 may be thought of as a kind of golden age of the west-European bourgeoisie. It left its mark on Europe in many ways. For one thing, western Europe continued to accumulate capital and build up its industrial plant. National income was constantly rising, but a relatively small share went to the laboring class, and a relatively large share went to owners of capital. This meant that less was spent on consumers' goods—housing, clothing, food, recreation—and that more was saved and available for reinvestment. New stock companies were constantly formed, and the law of corporations was amended, allowing for the extension of corporate enterprise to new fields. The factory system spread from Britain to the Continent and within Britain from the textile industry to other lines of production. The output of iron, a good index to economic advancement in this phase of industrialism, rose about 300 percent in Great Britain between 1830 and 1848 and about 65 percent in France between 1830 and 1845. (All the German states combined, at the latter date, produced about a tenth as much iron as Great Britain, and less than half as much as France.) Railroad building set in in earnest after 1840. In 1840 Samuel Cunard put four steamships in regular transatlantic service. Much capital was exported; as early as 1839 an American estimated that Europeans (mainly British) owned $200,000,000 worth of stocks in American companies. Such investments financed the purchase of British and other goods and helped to rivet together a world economic system, in which western Europe and especially England took the lead, with other regions remaining in a somewhat subordinate status.

The Frustration and Challenge of Labor

The bourgeois age had the effect also of estranging the world of labor. The state in Britain and France was as near as it has ever been to what Karl Marx was soon to call it—a committee of the bourgeois class. Already in France people spoke worriedly of the *prolétaires,* those at the bottom of society, who had nothing to lose. Republicans in France, radical democrats in Britain, felt cheated and imposed upon in the 1830s and 1840s. They had in each country forced through a virtual revolution by their insurrections and demonstrations and then in each country had been left without the vote. Some lost interest in representative institutions. Excluded from government they were tempted to seek political ends through extragovernmental, which is to say revolutionary or utopian, channels. Social and economic reforms seemed to the average worker far more important, as a final aim, than mere governmental innovations. Workers were told by respected economists that they could not hope to change the system in their own favor. They were tempted, therefore, to destroy the system, to replace it utterly with some new system conceived mainly in the minds of thinkers. They were told by the Manchester School, and by its equivalent in France, that the income of labor was set by ineluctable natural laws, that it was best and indeed necessary for wages to remain low, and that the way to rise in the world was to get out of the laboring class altogether, by becoming the owner of a profitable business and leaving working people about where they were.[27]

The reigning doctrine emphasized the conception of a labor market. The worker sold labor, the employer bought it. The price of labor, or wage, was to be agreed upon by the two individual parties. The price would naturally fluctuate according to changes in supply and demand. When a great deal of a certain kind of labor was required the wage would go up, until new persons moved into the market offering more labor of this type, with the result that something like the old wage would again be established. When no labor was needed none should be bought, and persons who could not sell labor might then subsist for a time by poor relief. The new Poor Law of 1834 was especially repugnant to the British working classes. It corrected crying evils in the old system, which had pauperized and demoralized millions of people. But the new law followed the stern precepts of the dismal science; its main principle was to safeguard the labor market by making relief more unpleasant than any job. It granted relief only to persons willing to enter a workhouse, or poorhouse; and in these establishments the sexes were segregated and life was in other ways made noticeably less attractive than in the outside world. The workers considered the new law an abomination. They called the workhouses "bastilles." They resented the whole conception of a labor market, in which labor was to be bought and sold (or remain unsold) like any other commodity.

In the long run it would be the increase of production in Europe that was to relieve the condition of the workers. Meanwhile there were two means of escape. One was to improve the position of labor in the market. This led to the formation of labor unions for control of the labor supply and collective bargaining with employers. Such unions, illegal in France, were barely legal in Great Britain after 1825, though it was still illegal in both countries to strike. The other means of escape was to repudiate the whole idea of a market economy and of the capitalist system. It was to conceive of a system in which goods were to be produced for use, not for sale; and in which working people should be compensated according

[27] See pp. 425–427, 429.

to need, not according to the requirements of an employer. This was the basis of most forms of nineteenth-century socialism.[28]

Socialism and Chartism

Socialism spread rapidly among the working classes after 1830. In France it blended with revolutionary republicanism. There was a revival of interest in the great Revolution and the democratic Republic of 1793. Cheap reprints of the writings of Robespierre began to circulate in the working-class quarters of Paris. Robespierre was now seen as a people's hero. The socialist Louis Blanc, for example, who in 1839 published his *Organization of Work*, recommending the formation of "social workshops," also wrote a long history of the French Revolution, in which he pointed out the equalitarian ideals that had inspired the National Convention in 1793. In Britain, as befitted the different background of the country, socialistic ideas blended in with the movement for further parliamentary reform. This was advanced by the working-class group known as the Chartists, from the People's Charter which they drafted in 1838. Between the British Chartists and the French socialists there was considerable coming and going. One Chartist, the Irish-born journalist Bronterre O'Brien, translated a French book on the "conspiracy of Babeuf" of 1796, which itself was a source and inspiration of the rising socialism of France.[29]

Chartism was far more of a mass movement than the French socialism of the day. Only a few Chartists were clearly socialists in their own minds. But all were anticapitalistic. All could agree that the first step must be to win working-class representation in Parliament. The Charter of 1838 consisted of six points. It demanded (1) the annual election of the House of Commons by (2) universal suffrage for all adult males, through (3) a secret ballot and (4) equal electoral districts; and it called for (5) the abolition of property qualifications for membership in the House of Commons, which perpetuated the old idea that Parliament should be composed of gentlemen of independent income, and urged instead (6) the payment of salaries to the elected members of Parliament, in order that people of small means might serve. A convention composed of delegates sent by labor unions, mass meetings, and radical societies all over the country met in London in 1839. "Convention" was an ominous word, with French revolutionary and even terrorist overtones; some members of this British convention regarded it as the body really representing the people, and favored armed violence and a general strike, while others stood only for moral pressure upon Parliament.

A petition bearing over a million signatures, urging acceptance of the Charter, was submitted to the House of Commons. The violent and revolutionary wing, or "physical force" Chartists, precipitated a wave of riots which were effectively quelled by the authorities. In 1842 the petition was again submitted. This time, according to the best estimate, it was signed by 3,317,702 persons. Since the entire population of Great Britain was about 19 million it is clear that the Charter, whatever the exact number of signatures, commanded the explicit adherence of half the adult males of the country. The House of Commons nevertheless rejected the petition by 287 votes to 49. It was feared, with reason, that political democ-

28 See pp. 431–432.
29 See pp. 372–373.

racy would threaten property rights and the whole economic system as they then existed. The Chartist movement gradually died down in the face of firm opposition by the government and the business classes, and was weakened by mutual fears and disagreements among its own supporters. It had not been entirely fruitless; for without popular agitation and the publicizing of working-class grievances, the Mines Act of 1842 and the Ten Hours Act of 1847 might not have been enacted. These measures in turn alleviated the distress of industrial workers and kept alive a degree of confidence in the future of the economic system. Chartism revived briefly in 1848, as will be seen in the next chapter; but in general, in the 1840s, British working people turned from political agitation to the forming and strengthening of labor unions, by which they could deal directly with employers without having to appeal to the government. Not until 1867 was the suffrage extended in Great Britain, and it took about eighty years to realize the full program of the Charter of 1838, except for the annual election of Parliament, for which there soon ceased to be any demand.

It is not easy to summarize the history of Europe between 1815 and 1848. Among all the forces set free by the French and Industrial revolutions—liberalism, conservatism, nationalism, republicanism, democracy, socialism—no stabilization had been achieved. No international system had been created; Europe had rather fallen into two camps, composed of a West in which liberal conceptions moved forward, and an East in which three autocratic monarchies held sway. Western Europe favored the principles of nationality; governments in central and eastern Europe still opposed them. The West was growing collectively richer, more liberal, more bourgeois. Middle-class people in Germany, central Europe, and Italy (as well as in Spain and Portugal) did not enjoy the dignities and emoluments that they enjoyed in Great Britain or France. But the West had not solved its social problem; its whole material civilization rested upon a restless and sorely tried working class. Everywhere there was repression, in varying degree, and everywhere apprehension, more in some places than in others; but there was also hope, confidence in the progress of an industrial and scientific society, and faith in the unfinished program of the rights of man. The result was the general Revolution of 1848.

XII.
Revolution and the Reimposition of Order, 1848-1870

ears haunting the established classes of Europe for thirty years came true in 1848. Governments collapsed all over the Continent. Remembered horrors appeared again, as in a recurring dream, in much the same sequence as after 1789 only at a much faster rate of speed. Revolutionaries milled in the streets, kings fled, republics were declared, and within four years there was another Napoleon. Soon thereafter came a series of wars.

Never before or since has Europe seen so truly universal an upheaval as in 1848. While the French Revolution of 1789 and the Russian Revolution of 1917 both had immediate international repercussions, in each of these cases a single country took the lead. In 1848 the revolutionary movement broke out spontaneously from native sources from Copenhagen to Palermo and from Paris to Budapest. Contemporaries sometimes attributed the universality of the phenomenon to the machinations of secret societies, and it is true that the faint beginnings of an international revolutionary movement existed before 1848; but the fact is that revolutionary plotters had little influence upon what actually happened, and the

Chapter Emblem: A medal showing St. Paul's Church at Frankfurt, then a new building in the neoclassic style, where the German National Assembly met in 1848–1849.

nearly simultaneous fall of governments is quite understandable from other causes. Many people in Europe wanted substantially the same things—constitutional government, the independence and unification of national groups, an end to serfdom and manorial restraints where they still existed. With some variation, there was a common body of ideas among politically conscious elements of all countries. Some of the powers that the new forces had to combat were themselves international, notably the Catholic church and the far-spreading influence of the Habsburgs, so that resistance to them arose independently in many places. In any case, only the Russian empire and Great Britain escaped the revolutionary contagion of 1848, and the British received a very bad scare.

But the Revolution of 1848, though it shook the whole Continent, lacked basic driving strength. It failed almost as rapidly as it succeeded. Its main consequence, in fact, was to strengthen the more conservative forces that viewed all revolution with alarm. Revolutionary ideals succumbed to military repression. To some extent the governments of the 1850s and 1860s, while hostile to revolution, satisfied some of the aims of 1848, notably in national unification and constitutional government with limited representation, but they did so in a mood of calculated realism, and while reasserting their own authority. The repressed Revolution of 1848 also left a legacy of class fears and class conflict, in which prophets of a new society also became more realistic, as when Karl Marx, branding earlier forms of socialism as "utopian," offered his own views as hard-headed and "scientific."

57. PARIS: THE SPECTER OF SOCIAL REVOLUTION IN THE WEST

The July Monarchy in France was a platform of boards built over a volcano. Under it burned the repressed fires of the republicanism put down in 1830, which since 1830 had become steadily more socialistic.[1]

Politics in the July Monarchy became increasingly more unreal. So few interests were represented in the Chamber of Deputies that the most basic issues were seldom debated. Even most of the bourgeois class had no representation. Graft and corruption were more common than they should have been, as economic expansion favored stockjobbing and fraud by business promoters and politicians in combination. A strong movement set in to give the vote to more people instead of to only one man in thirty. Radicals wanted universal suffrage and a republic, but liberals asked only for a broadening of voting rights within the existing constitutional monarchy. The king, Louis Philippe, and his prime minister, Guizot, instead of allying with the latter against the former, resolutely and obtusely opposed any change whatsoever.

The "February" Revolution in France

Reformers, against the king's expressed wishes, planned a great banquet in Paris for February 22, 1848, to be accompanied by demonstrations in the streets. The government on February 21 forbade all such meetings. That night barricades were built in the working-class quarters. These consisted of paving blocks, build-

1 See pp. 449–450, 458–460.

ing stones, or large pieces of furniture thrown together across the narrow streets and intersections of the old city, and constituting a maze within which insurgents prepared to resist the authorities. The government called out the National Guard, which refused to move. The king now promised electoral reform, but republican firebrands took charge of the semimobilized working-class elements, which held a demonstration outside the house of Guizot. Someone shot at the guards placed around the house; the guards replied, killing twenty persons. The republican organizers put some of the corpses on a torch-lit cart and paraded them through the city, which, armed and barricaded, soon began to swarm in an enormous riot. On February 24 Louis Philippe, like Charles X before him, abdicated and made for England. The February Revolution of 1848, like the July Revolution of 1830, had unseated a monarch in three days.

The constitutional reformers hoped to carry on with Louis Philippe's young grandson as king, but the republicans, now aroused and armed, poured into the Chamber of Deputies and forced the proclamation of the Republic. Republican leaders set up a provisional government of ten men, pending election by all France of a Constituent Assembly. Seven of the ten were "political" republicans, the most notable being the poet Lamartine. Three were "social" republicans, the most notable being Louis Blanc. A huge crowd of workers appeared before the Hôtel de Ville, or city hall, demanding that France adopt the new socialist emblem—the red flag. They were dissuaded by the eloquence of Lamartine, and the tricolor remained the republican standard.

Louis Blanc urged the Provisional Government to push through a bold economic and social program without delay. But since the "social" republicans were in a minority in the Provisional Government (though probably not among Paris republicans generally), Louis Blanc's ideas were very much watered down in the application. He wanted a Ministry of Progress to organize a network of "social workshops," the state-supported and collectivist manufacturing establishments that he had projected in his writings. All that was created was a Labor Commission, with limited powers, and a system of shops significantly entitled "national" rather than "social." The National Workshops, as they are always called in English (though "workshop" suggests something more insignificant than Louis Blanc had in mind), were agreed to by the Provisional Government only as a political concession, and no significant work was ever assigned them to do, for fear of competition with private enterprise and dislocation of the economic system. Indeed, the man placed in charge of them admitted that his purpose was to prove the fallacies of socialism. Meanwhile the Labor Commission was unable to win public acceptance for the ten-hour day, which the British Parliament had enacted the year before.

The National Workshops became in practice only an extensive project in unemployment relief. Men of all trades, skilled and unskilled, were set to work digging on the roads and fortifications outside of Paris. They were paid two francs a day. The number of legitimate unemployed increased rapidly, for 1847 had been a year of depression and the revolution prevented the return of business confidence. Other needy persons also presented themselves for remuneration, and soon there were too many men for the amount of "work" made available. From 25,000 enrolled in the workshops by the middle of March, the number climbed to 120,000 by mid-June, by which time there were also in Paris another 50,000 whom the bulging workshops could no longer accommodate. In June there were probably almost 200,000 essentially idle but able-bodied men in a city of about a million people.

The Constituent Assembly, elected in April by universal male suffrage throughout France, met on May 4. It immediately replaced the Provisional Government with a temporary executive board of its own. The main body of France, a land of provincial bourgeois and peasant landowners, was not socialist in the least. The new temporary executive board, chosen by the new Constituent Assembly in May, included no "social" republicans. All five of its members, of whom Lamartine was the head, were known as outspoken enemies of Louis Blanc. Blanc and the socialists could no longer expect even the grudging and insincere concessions that they had so far obtained.

The battle lines were now drawn, after only three months of revolution, somewhat as they had been drawn in 1792 after three years.[2] Paris again stood for a degree of revolutionary action in which the rest of the country was not prepared to share. Revolutionary leaders in Paris, in 1848 as in 1792, were unwilling to accept the processes of majority rule or slow parliamentary deliberation. But the crisis in 1848 was more acute than in 1792. A larger proportion of the population were wage earners. Under a system of predominantly merchant capitalism, in which machine industry and factory concentration were only beginning, the workers were tormented by the same evils as the more industrialized working classes of England. Hours were if anything longer, and pay less, in France than in Great Britain; insecurity and unemployment were at least as great; and the feeling that a capitalist economy held no future for the laboring man was the same. In addition, where the English workingman shrank from the actual violation of Parliament, the French workingman saw nothing very sacrilegious in the violation of elected assemblies. Too many regimes in France since 1789, including those preferred by the comfortable classes, had been based on insurrectionary violence for the French workingman to feel much compunction over using it for his own ends.

The "June Days" of 1848

On the one hand stood the nationally elected Constituent Assembly. On the other, the National Workshops had mobilized in Paris the most distressed elements of the working class. Tens of thousands had been brought together where they could talk, read journals, listen to speeches, and concert common action. Agitators and organizers naturally made use of the opportunity thus presented to them. Men in the workshops began to feel desperate, to sense that the social republic was slipping from them perhaps forever. On May 15 they attacked the Constituent Assembly, drove its members out of the hall, declared it dissolved, and set up a new provisional government of their own. They announced that a social revolution must follow the purely political revolution of February. But the National Guard, a kind of civilian militia, turned against the insurgents and restored the Constituent Assembly. The Assembly, to root out socialism, prepared to get rid of the National Workshops. It offered those enrolled in them the alternatives of enlistment in the army, transfer to provincial workshops, or being put out of Paris

[2] See pp. 362–363.

by force. The whole laboring class in the city began to resist. The government proclaimed martial law, the civilian executive board resigned, and all power was given to General Cavaignac and the regular army.

There followed the "Bloody June Days"—June 24–26, 1848—three days during which a terrifying class war raged in Paris. Over 20,000 men from the workshops took to arms (more would doubtless have done so had not the government continued to pay wages in the workshops during the insurrection), and they were joined by other unnumbered thousands from the working-class districts of the city. Half or more of Paris became a labyrinth of barricades defended by determined men and equally resolute women. Military methods of the time made it possible for civilians to shoot it out openly with soldiers; small arms were the main weapons, and armies had no armored vehicles or even any very devastating artillery. The soldiers found it a difficult operation, even several generals being killed, but after three days the outcome was in doubt no longer. Ten thousand persons had been killed or wounded. Eleven thousand insurgents were taken prisoner. The Assembly, refusing all clemency, decreed their immediate deportation to the colonies.

The June Days sent a shudder throughout France and Europe. Whether the battle in Paris had been a true class struggle, how large a portion of the laboring class had really participated (it was large in any case), how much they had fought for permanent objectives, and how much over the temporary issue of the workshops—all these are secondary questions. It was widely understood that a class war had in fact broken out. Militant workers were confirmed in a hatred and loathing of the bourgeois class, in a belief that capitalism existed in the last analysis by the callous shooting of laboring men in the streets. People above the laboring class were thrown into a panic. They were sure that they had narrowly escaped a ghastly upheaval. The very ground of civilized living seemed to have quaked. After June 1848, wrote a Frenchwoman of the time, society was "a prey to a feeling of terror incomparable to anything since the invasion of Rome by the barbarians."

Nor were the signs in England much more reassuring. There the Chartist agitation was revived by the February Revolution in Paris.[3] "France is a Republic!" cried the Chartist Ernest Jones; the Chartist petition was again circulated and was soon said to have 6 million signatures. Another Chartist convention met, considered by its leaders to be the forerunner of a Constituent Assembly as in France. The violent minority was the most active; it began to gather arms and to drill. The old Duke of Wellington swore in 70,000 special constables to uphold the social order. Clashes occurred at Liverpool and elsewhere; in London the revolutionary committee laid plans for systematic arson and organized men with pickaxes to break up the pavements for barricades. Meanwhile the petition, weighing 584 pounds, was carried in three cabs to the House of Commons, which estimated that it contained "only" 2 million signatures and again summarily rejected it. The revolutionary menace passed. One of the secret organizers in London proved to be a government spy; he revealed the whole plan at the critical moment, and the revolutionary committee was arrested on the day set for insurrection. Most Chartists had in any case refused to support the militants, but the truculent minority of radical workers and journalists had a deeper sense of

3 See pp. 460–461.

envenomed class consciousness. The word "proletarian" was imported from France. "Every proletarian," wrote the Chartist editor of *Red Revolution,* "who does not see and feel that he belongs to an enslaved and degraded class is a *fool.*"

The specter of social revolution thus hung over western Europe in the summer of 1848. Doubtless it was unreal; in all probability there could have been no successful socialist revolution at the time. But the specter was there, and it spread a sinking fear among all who had something to lose. This fear shaped the whole subsequent course of the Second Republic in France and of the revolutionary movements that had by this time begun in other countries as well.

The Emergence of Louis Napoleon Bonaparte

In France, after the June Days, the Constituent Assembly (keeping General Cavaignac as a virtual dictator) set about drafting a republican constitution. It was decided, in view of the disturbances just passed, to create a strong executive power in the hands of a president to be elected by universal male suffrage. It was decided also to have this president elected immediately, even before the rest of the constitution was finished. Four candidates presented themselves: Lamartine, Cavaignac, Ledru-Rollin—and Louis Napoleon Bonaparte. Lamartine stood for a somewhat vaguely moral and idealistic republic, Cavaignac for a republic of disciplined order, Ledru-Rollin for somewhat chastened "social" ideas. What Bonaparte stood for was not so clear. He was, however, elected by an avalanche of votes in December 1848, receiving over 5,400,000, to only 1,500,000 for Cavaignac, 370,000 for Ledru-Rollin, and a mere 18,000 for Lamartine.

Thus entered upon the European stage the second Napoleon. Born in 1808, Louis Napoleon Bonaparte was the nephew of the great Napoleon. His father, Louis Bonaparte, was at the time of his birth the king of Holland. When Napoleon's own son died in 1832 Louis Napoleon assumed the headship of the Bonaparte family. He resolved to restore the glories of the empire. With a handful of followers he tried to seize power at Strasbourg in 1836 and at Boulogne in 1840, leading what the following century would know as *Putsches.* Both failed ridiculously. Sentenced to life imprisonment in the fortress of Ham, he had escaped from it as recently as 1846 by simply walking off the grounds dressed as a stonemason. He expressed advanced social and political ideas, had probably joined the Carbonari in his youth, and had taken part in the Italian revolutionary uprising of 1830. He wrote two books, one called *Napoleonic Ideas,* claiming that his famous uncle had been misunderstood and checkmated by reactionary forces, and one called the *Extinction of Poverty,* a somewhat anticapitalistic tract like so many others of its time. But he was no friend of "anarchists," and in the spring of 1848, while still a refugee in England, he enrolled as one of Wellington's special constables to oppose the Chartist revolution. He soon returned to France. Compromised neither by the June Days nor by their repression, he was supposed to be a friend of the common people and at the same time a believer in order; and his name was Napoleon Bonaparte.

For twenty years a groundswell had been stirring the popular mind. It is known as the Napoleonic Legend. Peasants put up pictures of the emperor in their cottages, fondly imagining that it had been Napoleon who gave them the free ownership of their land. The completion of the Arch of Triumph in 1836 drove home the memory of imperial glories, and in 1840 the remains of the emperor were brought from St. Helena and majestically interred at the Invalides on the banks of the Seine. All this happened in a country where, government being in the hands of a few, most people had no political experience or political sense except what they had gained in revolution. When millions were suddenly, for the first time in their lives, asked to vote for president in 1848, the name of Bonaparte was the only one they had ever heard of. "How should I not vote for this gentleman," said an old peasant, "I whose nose was frozen at Moscow?"

So Prince Louis Napoleon became president of the republic, by an overwhelming and indubitable popular mandate, in which an army officer was his only even faintly successful rival. He soon saw the way the wind was blowing. The Constituent Assembly dissolved itself in May 1849 and was replaced by the Legislative Assembly provided for in the new constitution. It was a strange assembly for a republic. It may be recalled that in 1797 the first normal election in the First Republic had produced a royalist majority.[4] Now in the Second Republic, under universal male suffrage, the result was the same. Five hundred of the deputies, or two-thirds, were really monarchists, but they were divided into irreconcilable factions—the Legitimists, who favored the line of Charles X, and the Orléanists, who favored that of Louis Philippe. One-third of the deputies called themselves republicans. Of these, in turn, about 180 were socialists of one kind or another; and only about 70 were political or old-fashioned republicans to whom the main issue was the form of government rather than the form of society itself.

The president and the Assembly at first combined to conjure away the specter of socialism, with which republicanism itself was now clearly associated. An abortive insurrection of June 1849 provided the chance. The Assembly, backed by the president, ousted thirty-three socialist deputies, suppressed public meetings, and imposed controls on the press. In 1850 it went so far as to rescind universal male suffrage, taking the vote away from about a third of the electorate—naturally the poorest and hence most socialistic third. The Falloux Law of 1850 put the schools at all levels of the educational system under supervision of the Catholic clergy; for, as M. Falloux said in the Assembly, "lay teachers have made the principles of social revolution popular in the most distant villages," and it was necessary "to rally around religion to strengthen the foundations of society against those who want to divide up property." The French Republic, now actually an antirepublican government, likewise intervened against the revolutionary republic established by Mazzini in the city of Rome. French military forces were sent to Rome to protect the pope; they remained there twenty years.

To the conservatives Bonaparte knew that he was virtually indispensable. They were so sharply divided between two sets of monarchists—Legitimist and Orléanist—that each would accept any antisocialist regime rather than yield to the other. Bonaparte's problem was to win over the radicals. He did so by urging in 1851 the restoration of universal suffrage, which he had himself helped repeal in 1850. He now posed as the people's friend, the one man in public life who trusted the common man. He let it be thought that greedy plutocrats controlled the Assembly and hoodwinked France. He put his lieutenants in as ministers of war and of the interior, thus controlling the army, the bureaucracy, and the police. On

4 See p. 373.

December 2, 1851, the anniversary of Austerlitz, he sprang his coup d'état. Placards appeared all over Paris. They declared the Assembly dissolved and the vote for every adult Frenchman reinstated. When members of the Assembly tried to meet, they were attacked, dispersed, or arrested by the soldiers. The country did not submit without fighting. One hundred and fifty persons were killed in Paris, and throughout France probably 100,000 were put under arrest. But on December 20 the voters elected Louis Napoleon president for a term of ten years, by a vote officially stated as 7,439,216 to 646,737. A year later the new Bonaparte proclaimed the empire, with himself as emperor of the French. Remembering Napoleon's son, he called himself Napoleon III.

How the empire functioned will be seen below. Not only the republic was dead. The republic as republicans understood it, an equalitarian, anticlerical regime with socialist or at least antibourgeois tendencies, had been dead since June 1848. Feeble anyway, it was killed by its reputation for radicalism. Liberalism and constitutionalism were dead also. Bourgeois and property-owning monarchists were greater sticklers for constitutional liberalism than were the republicans or the Bonapartists or than town laborers or rural peasants. But the monarchists, hopelessly divided among themselves, were now pushed aside. For the first time since 1815 France ceased to have any parliamentary life. It was ruled by a dictatorship, more demagogic, more calculating, more hollow, and more modern than any that the first Napoleon had ever imagined.

58. VIENNA: THE NATIONALIST REVOLUTION IN CENTRAL EUROPE AND ITALY

The Austrian Empire in 1848

The Austrian Empire of the Habsburgs, with its capital at Vienna, was in 1848 the most populous European state except Russia. Its peoples, living principally in the three major geographical divisions of the empire, Austria, Bohemia, and Hungary, were of about a dozen recognizably different nationalities or language groups—Germans, Czechs, Magyars, Poles, Ruthenians, Slovaks, Serbs, Croats, Slovenes, Dalmatians, Rumanians, and Italians.[5] In some parts of the empire the nationalities lived in solid blocks, but in many regions two or more were interlaced together, the language changing from village to village, or even from house to house, in a way quite unknown in western Europe.

Germans, the leading people, occupied all of Austria proper and considerable parts of Bohemia, and were scattered also in small pockets throughout Hungary. The Czechs occupied Bohemia and the adjoining Moravia. The Magyars were the dominant group in the historic kingdom of Hungary, which contained a mixture of nationalities with a considerable number of Slavic peoples. Two of the most advanced parts of Italy also belonged to the empire—Venetia, with its capital at Venice, and Lombardy, whose chief city was Milan.

The Czechs, Poles, Ruthenians, Slovaks, Serbs, Croats, Slovenes, and Dalmatians in the empire were all Slavs; i.e., their languages were all related to one another and to the several forms of Russian. Neither the Magyars nor the Ruma-

[5] See maps, pp. 212, 412–413, 433; and pp. 211–216, 257–260, 310–311, 389–390, 414.

nians were Slavs. The Magyars, as national sentiment grew, prided themselves on the uniqueness of their language in Europe and the Rumanians on their linguistic affiliations with the Latin peoples of the West. Rumanians, Magyars, and Germans formed a thick belt separating the South Slavs (in later years called Yugoslavs) from those of the north. Germans and Italians within the empire were in continual touch with Germans and Italians outside. The peoples of the empire represented every cultural level known to Europe. Vienna, where the Waltz King Johann Strauss was reigning, recognized no peer except Paris itself. Milan was a great center of trade. Bohemia had long had a textile industry of importance, which was beginning to be mechanized in the 1840s; but 200 miles to the south a Croatian intellectual remarked, about the same time, that the first steam engine he ever saw was in a picture printed on a cotton handkerchief imported from Manchester. In 1848, some denied that any such people as the Ruthenians existed at all. Nor was it clear exactly what groups made up the South Slavs. No such word as Yugoslavia or Czechoslovakia had been invented, and Rumania was a term used only by professors.

Thus the empire ruled from Vienna included, according to political frontiers established seventy years later, in 1918, all of Austria, Hungary, and Czechoslovakia, with adjoining portions of Poland, Rumania, Yugoslavia, and Italy. But the political authority of Vienna reached far beyond the borders of the empire. Austria since 1815 had been the most influential member of the German confederation, for Prussia in these years was content to look with deference upon the Habsburgs. The influence of Vienna was felt throughout Germany in many ways, as in the enactment and enforcement of the Carlsbad Decrees mentioned in the last chapter.[6] It reached also through the length of Italy. Lombardy and Venetia were part of the Austrian Empire. Tuscany, ostensibly independent, was governed by a Habsburg grand duke. The kingdom of Naples or the Two Sicilies, comprising all Italy south of Rome, was virtually a protectorate of Vienna. The papal states looked politically to Vienna for leadership, at least until 1846, when the College of Cardinals elected a liberal-minded pope, Pius IX—the one contingency upon which Metternich confessed he had failed to reckon. In all Italy there was only one state ruled by a native Italian dynasty and attempting any consistent independence of policy—the kingdom of Sardinia (called also Savoy or Piedmont) tucked away in the northwest corner around Turin. Italy, said Metternich blandly, was only a "geographical expression," a mere regional name. He might have said the same of Poland, or even of Germany, though Germany was tenuously joined in the Bund, or loose confederation, of 1815.

These peoples since the turn of the century had all felt the flutters of the *Volksgeist*, persistent stirrings of a cultural nationalism, and among Germans, Italians, Poles, and Hungarians a good deal of political agitation and liberal reformism had been at work. Metternich, in Vienna, had discouraged such manifestations for over thirty years, ominously predicting that if allowed to break out they would produce the *bellum omnium contra omnes*—"the war of all against all." As a prophet he was not wholly mistaken, but if it is the business of statesmanship not merely to prophesy events but to control them it cannot be said that the regime of Metternich was very successful. The whole nationalities question was evaded. The fundamental problem of the century, the bringing of peoples

6 See p. 440.

into some kind of mutual and moral relationship with their governments—the problem of which nationalism, liberalism, constitutionalism, and democracy were diverse aspects—remained unconsidered by the responsible authorities of central Europe. All that Metternich offered was the idea that a reigning house, with an official bureaucracy, should rule benevolently over peoples with whom it need have no connection and who need have no connection with each other. They were the ideas of the eighteenth century, dating from before the French Revolution and best suited to an agricultural and localistic society.

The March Days

In March 1848, everything collapsed with incredible swiftness. At that time the diet of Hungary had been sitting for some months, considering constitutional reforms and, as usual, debating further means of keeping German influence out of Hungary. Then came news of the February Revolution in Paris. The radical party in the Hungarian diet was aroused. Its leader, Louis Kossuth, on March 3 made an impassioned speech on the virtues of liberty. This speech was immediately printed in German and read in Vienna, where restlessness was also heightened by the news from Paris. On March 13 workingmen and students rose in insurrection in Vienna, manned barricades, fought off soldiers, and invaded the imperial palace. So flabbergasted and terrified was the government that Metternich, to the amazement of Europe, resigned and fled in disguise to England.

The fall of Metternich proved that the Vienna government was entirely disoriented. Revolution swept through the empire and through all Italy and Germany. On March 15 rioting began in Berlin; the king of Prussia promised a constitution. The lesser German governments collapsed in sequence. On the last day of March a Pre-Parliament met to arrange the calling of an all-German national assembly. In Hungary, aroused by Kossuth's national party, the diet on March 15 enacted the March Laws, by which Hungary assumed a position of complete constitutional separatism within the empire, while still recognizing the Habsburg house. The harassed Emperor Ferdinand a few days later granted substantially the same status to Bohemia. At Milan between March 18 and 22 the populace drove out the Austrian garrison. Venice proclaimed itself an independent republic. Tuscany drove out its grand duke and also set up as a republic. The king of Sardinia, Charles Albert (who, stimulated by the Paris revolution, had granted a constitution to his small country on March 4) declared war on Austria on March 23 and invaded Lombardy-Venetia, hoping to bring that area under the house of Savoy. Italian troops streamed up from Tuscany, from Naples (where revolution had broken out as early as January), and even from the papal states (the new pope being in some sympathy with national and liberal aims) to join in an all-Italian war against the seemingly helpless Austrian government.

Thus in the brief span of these phenomenal March Days the whole structure based on Vienna went to pieces: the Austrian Empire had fallen into its main components, Prussia had yielded to revolutionaries, all Germany was preparing to unify itself, and war raged in Italy. Everywhere constitutions had been wildly promised by stupefied governments, constitutional assemblies were meeting, and independent or autonomous nations struggled into existence. Patriots everywhere demanded liberal government and national freedom—written constitutions, representative assemblies, responsible ministries, a more or less extended suffrage, restrictions upon police action, jury trial, civil liberty, freedom of press and assembly. And where it still existed—in Prussia, Galicia, Bohemia, Hungary—serfdom was declared abolished and the peasant masses became legally free from control by their local lords.

The Turning of the Tide after June

The revolution, as in France, surged forward until the month of June, and then began to ebb. For its steady reflux there are many reasons. The old governments had been only stunned in the March Days, not really broken. They merely awaited the opportunity to take back promises extorted by force. The force originally imposed by the revolutionaries could not be sustained. The revolutionary leaders were not really very strong. Middle-class, bourgeois, property-owning, and commercial interests were nowhere nearly as highly developed as in western Europe. The revolutionary leaders were to a large extent writers, editors, professors, and students, men of ideas rather than spokesmen for large positive interests. In Vienna, Milan, and a few other cities the working class was numerous and socialist ideas fairly common; but the workers were not as literate, organized, politically conscious, or irritated as in Paris or Great Britain. They were strong enough, however, to disquiet the middle classes; and especially after the specter of social revolution rose over western Europe, the middle-class and lower-class revolutionaries began to be afraid of each other. The liberated nationalities also began to disagree. The peasants, once emancipated, had no further interest in revolution. Nor were the peasants at this time conscious of nationality; nationalism was primarily a doctrine of the educated middle classes or of the landowning classes in Poland and Hungary. Since the old internationally minded aristocracy furnished the bulk of officers in the armies, and the peasants the bulk of the soldiers, the armies remained almost immune to nationalist aspirations. This attitude of the armies was decisive.

The tide first turned in Prague. The all-German national assembly met at Frankfurt-on-the-Main in May. Representatives from Bohemia had been invited to come to Frankfurt, since many Germans had always lived in Bohemia, and since Bohemia formed part of the confederation of 1815 as it had of the Holy Roman Empire before it. But the idea of belonging to a national German state, a Germany based on the principle that the inhabitants were Germans (which had not been the principle of the Holy Roman Empire or of the confederation of 1815) did not appeal to the Czechs in Bohemia. They refused to go to the all-German congress at Frankfurt. Instead, they called an all-Slav congress of their own. At Prague, in June 1848, this first Pan-Slav assembly met. Most of the delegates were from the Slav communities within the Austrian Empire, but a few came from the Balkans and non-Austrian Poland. Only one Russian was present, the anarchist revolutionary Michael Bakunin. Slavs generally did not at this time look with favor upon Russia, the oppressor of Poles; nor did the tsarist government, under Nicholas I, think well of Pan-Slavism, seeing in it a subversive popular agitation.

The spirit of the Prague congress was that of the Slavic Revival described in the last chapter;[7] the Czech historian Palacky was in fact one of its most active figures. The congress was profoundly anti-German, since the essence of the Slavic Revival was resistance to Germanization. But it was not profoundly anti-Austrian or anti-Habsburg. A few extremists, indeed, maintained that Slavdom should be the basis of political regeneration, and that the world therefore had no place for an Austrian empire. But the great majority at the Prague congress were Austroslavs. Austroslavism held that the many Slavic peoples, pressed on two sides by the population masses of Russians and Germans, needed the Austrian Empire as a political frame within which to develop their own national life. It demanded that the Slavic peoples be admitted as equals with the other nationalities in the Austrian Empire, enjoying local autonomy and constitutional guarantees.

The Germans of Bohemia, the Sudeten Germans, were of course attracted to the Frankfurt Assembly. They were eager to be included in the unified Germany about to be formed. As the Bohemian Czechs would be a minority in a German Germany, so the Bohemian Germans would be a minority in a Czech Bohemia. There was therefore friction among the mixed people of Bohemia and in Prague, a bilingual city.

Victories of the Counterrevolution, June–December

But the Emperor Ferdinand, and the advisers on whom he chose to rely, would have nothing to do with national movements, since they were also liberal, bristling with restrictions upon the powers of the state. All therefore were to be resisted. The first victory of the old government came at Prague. In that city a Czech insurrection broke out on June 12, at the time when the Slav congress was sitting, and made worse by local animosities between Czechs and Germans. Windischgrätz, the local army commander, bombarded and subdued the city. The Slav congress dispersed. The Habsburg army was in control.

The next victory of the counterrevolution came in north Italy in the following month. Only Lombardy-Venetia, of all parts of the empire, had declared independence from the Habsburgs during the upheavals of March. The diminutive kingdom of Sardinia had supported them and had declared war on Austria. Italians from all over the peninsula had flocked in to fight; and until after the June Days in Paris it seemed not impossible that republican France might intervene, to befriend fellow revolutionaries, as in 1796. But in France no radical or expansionist revolution succeeded. The Italians were left to themselves. Radetsky, the Austrian commander in Italy, overwhelmingly defeated the king of Sardinia at Custozza on July 25. The Sardinian king, Charles Albert, retreated into his own country. Lombardy and Venetia were restored with savage vengeance to the Austrian Empire.

The third victory of the counterrevolution came in September and October. The Hungarian radical party of Louis Kossuth was liberal and even democratic in many of its principles, but it was a Magyar nationalist party above all else. Triumphant in the March Days, it completely shook off the German connection. It moved the capital from Pressburg near the Austrian border to Budapest in the center of Hungary. It changed the official language of Hungary from Latin to

7 See pp. 435–437.

Magyar. Less than half the people of Hungary were Magyars, and Magyar is an extremely difficult language, quite alien to the Indo-European tongues of Europe. It soon became clear that one must be a Magyar to benefit from the new liberal constitution, and that the Magyars intended to denationalize and Magyarize all others with whom they shared the country. Slovaks, Rumanians, Germans, Serbs, and Croats violently resisted, each group determined to keep its own national identity unimpaired. The Croats, who had enjoyed certain Croatian liberties before the Magyar revolution, took the lead under Count Jellachich, the "ban," or provincial governor, of Croatia. In September Jellachich raised a civil war in Hungary, leading a force of Serbo-Croatians, supported by the whole non-Magyar half of the population. Half of Hungary, alarmed by Magyar nationalism, now looked to the Habsburgs and the empire to protect them. Emperor Ferdinand made Jellachich his military commander against the Magyars. Hungary dissolved into the war of all against all.

At Vienna the more clear-sighted revolutionaries, who had led the March rising, now saw that Jellachich's army, if successful against the Magyars, would soon be turned against them. They therefore rose in a second mass insurrection in October 1848. The emperor fled; never had the Viennese revolution gone so far. But it was already too late. The Austrian military leader Windischgrätz brought his intact forces down from Bohemia. He besieged Vienna for five days and forced its surrender on October 31.

With the recapture of Vienna the upholders of the old order took heart. Counterrevolutionary leaders—large estate holders, Catholic clergy, high-ranking army men—decided to clear the way by getting rid of the Emperor Ferdinand, considering that promises made in March by Ferdinand might be more easily repudiated by his successor. Ferdinand abdicated and on December 2, 1848, was succeeded by Francis Joseph, a boy of eighteen, destined to live until 1916 and to end his reign in a crisis even more shattering than that in which he began it.

Final Outburst and Repression, 1849

For a time in that first part of 1849 the revolution in many places seemed to blaze more fiercely than ever. Republican riots broke out in parts of Germany. In Rome someone assassinated the reforming minister of Pius IX. The pope fled from the city, and a radical Roman Republic was proclaimed under three Triumvirs, one of whom was Mazzini, who hastened from England to take part in the republican upheaval. In north Italy Charles Albert of Sardinia again invaded Lombardy. In Hungary, after the revived Habsburg authorities repudiated the new Magyar constitution, the Magyars, led by the flaming Kossuth, went on to declare absolute independence. But all these manifestations proved short-lived. German republicanism flickered out. Mazzini and his republicans were driven from Rome, and Pius IX was restored, by intervention of the French army.[8] The Sardinian king was again defeated by an Austrian army on March 23, 1849. In Hungary the Magyars put up a terrific resistance, which the imperial army and the anti-Magyar native irregulars could not overcome. The Habsburg authorities now renewed the procedures of the Holy Alliance. The new Emperor Francis Joseph invited the Tsar Nicholas to intervene. Over a hundred thousand Russian troops

8 See p. 468.

poured over the mountains into Hungary, soon defeated the Magyars, and laid the prostrate country at the feet of the court of Vienna. This was in August 1849.

The nationalist upheaval of 1848 in central Europe and Italy was now over. The Habsburg authority had been reasserted over Czech nationalists in Prague, Magyars in Hungary, Italian patriots in north Italy, and liberal revolutionists in Vienna itself. Reaction, or antirevolutionism, became the order of the day. Pius IX, the "liberal pope" of 1846, resumed the papal throne, disillusioned in his liberal ideas. The breach between liberalism and Roman Catholicism, which had opened wide in the first French Revolution, was made a yawning chasm by the revolutionary violence of Mazzini's Roman Republic and by the measures taken to repress it. Pius IX now reiterated the anathemas of his predecessors. He codified them in 1864 in the *Syllabus of Errors*, which warned all Catholics, on the authority of the Vatican, against everything that went under the names of liberalism, progress, and civilization. As for the nationalists in Italy, many were disillusioned with the firecracker methods of romantic republicans and inclined to conclude that Italy would be liberated from Austrian influence only by an old-fashioned war between established powers.

In the Austrian Empire, under Prince Schwarzenberg, the emperor's chief minister, the main policy was now to oppose all forms of popular self-expression, with a sophistication, in view of the events of 1848, that Metternich had never known, and with a candid reliance on military force. Constitutionalism was to be rooted out, as well as all forms of nationalism—Slavism, Magyarism, Italianism, and also Germanism, which would draw the sentiments of Austrian Germans from the Habsburg empire to the great kindred body of the German people. The regime came to be called the Bach system, after Alexander Bach, the minister of the interior. Under it, the government was rigidly centralized. Hungary lost the separate rights it had had before 1848. The ideal was to create a perfectly solid and unitary political system. Bach insisted on maintaining the emancipation of the peasants, which had converted the mass of the people from subjects of their landlords into subjects of the state. He drove through a reform of the legal system and law courts, created a free trading area of the whole empire with only a common external tariff, and subsidized and encouraged the building of highways and railroads. The aim, as in France at the same time under Louis Napoleon, was to make people forget liberty in an overwhelming demonstration of administrative efficiency and material progress. But some, at that time, would not forget. A liberal said of the Bach system that it consisted of "a standing army of soldiers, a sitting army of officials, a kneeling army of priests, and a creeping army of informers."

59. FRANKFURT AND BERLIN: THE QUESTION OF A LIBERAL GERMANY

The German States

Meanwhile, from May 1848 to May 1849, the Frankfurt Assembly was sitting at the historic city on the Main. It was attempting to bring a unified German state into being, one which should also be liberal and constitutional, assuring civil rights to its citizens and possessing a government responsive to popular will as manifested in free elections and open parliamentary debate. The failure to produce a democratic Germany was long one of the overshadowing facts of modern times.

The convocation of the Frankfurt Assembly was made possible by the collapse of the existing German governments in the March Days of 1848. These governments, the thirty-nine states recognized after the Congress of Vienna, were the main obstacles in the way of unification. The reigning princes and their ministers enjoyed a heightened political stature from political independence. The German states resisted the surrender of sovereignty to a united Germany just as national states in the next century were to resist the surrender of sovereignty to a United Nations. In another way Germany was a miniature of the political world. It consisted of both great and small powers. Its great powers were Prussia and Austria. Austria was the miscellaneous empire described above; Prussia after 1815 included the Rhineland, the central regions around Berlin, West Prussia, and Posen acquired in the partitions of Poland, and historic East Prussia. The former Polish areas were inhabited by a mixture of Germans and Poles.[9] Neither of these great powers could submit to the other or allow the other to dominate its lesser German neighbors. The small German powers, in turn, upheld their own independence in the balance between the two great ones.

This German "dualism," or polarity between Berlin and Vienna, had been somewhat abated under the common menace of the Napoleonic empire. The whole German question had lain dormant, so far as the governments were concerned, nor did it agitate the old aristocracies. In Prussia the Junkers, the owners of great landed estates east of the Elbe, were singularly indifferent to the all-German dream. Their political feeling was not German but Prussian. They were making a good thing of Prussia for themselves and could expect only to lose by absorption into Germany as a whole, for in Germany west of the Elbe the small peasant holding was the basis of society, and there was no landowning element corresponding to the Junkers. The rest of Germany looked upon Prussia as somewhat uncouth and Eastern; but this feeling, too, had been abated in the time of Napoleon, when patriots from all over Germany enlisted in the Prussian service.[10]

Berlin: Failure of the Revolution in Prussia

Prussia was illiberal but not backward. Frederick William III repeatedly evaded his promise to grant a modern constitution.[11] His successor, Frederick William IV, who inherited the throne in 1840, and from whom much was at first hoped by liberals, proved to be a somewhat cloudy and neomedieval romantic, equally determined not to share his authority with his subjects. At the same time the government, administratively speaking, was efficient, progressive, and fair. The universities and elementary school system surpassed those of western Europe. Literacy was higher than in England or France. The government followed in

9 See maps, pp. 218–219, 412–413; and see pp. 216–224, 236, 415.
10 See p. 404.
11 See p. 438.

mercantilist traditions of evoking, planning, and supporting economic life.[12] In 1818 it initiated a tariff union, at first with tiny states (or enclaves) wholly enclosed within Prussia. This tariff union, or *Zollverein,* was extended in the following decades to include almost all Germany.

On March 15, 1848, as noted above, rioting and street fighting broke out in Berlin. For a time it seemed as if the army would master the situation. But the king, Frederick William IV, a man of notions and projects, and erratically conscientious, called off the soldiers and allowed his subjects to elect the first all-Prussian legislative assembly. Thus though the army remained intact, and its Junker officers unconvinced, revolution proceeded superficially on its way. The Prussian Assembly proved surprisingly radical, since it was dominated by anti-Junker lower-class extremists from East Prussia. These men were supporting Polish revolutionaries and exiles who sought the restoration of Polish freedom. Their main belief was that the fortress of reaction was tsarist Russia—that the whole structure of Junkerdom, landlordism, serf-owning, and repression of national freedom depended ultimately on the armed might of the tsarist empire. (The subsequent intervention of Russia in Hungary indicated the truth of this diagnosis.) Prussian radicals, like many elsewhere, hoped to smash the Holy Alliance by raising an all-German or even European revolutionary war against Russia, to precipitate which they supported the claims of the Poles.

Meanwhile the radical-dominated Berlin Assembly granted local self-government to the Poles of West Prussia and Posen. But in those areas Germans and Slavs had long lived side by side. The Germans in Posen refused to respect the authority of Polish officials. Prussian army units stationed in Posen supported the German element. As early as April 1848, a month after the "revolution," the army crushed the new pro-Polish institutions set up in Posen by the Berlin Assembly. It was clear where the only real power lay. By the end of 1848, in Prussia as in Austria, the revolution was over. The king again changed his mind; and the old authorities, acting through the army, were again in control.

The Frankfurt Assembly

Meanwhile a similar story was enacted on the larger stage of Germany as a whole. The disabling of the old governments left a power vacuum. A self-appointed committee convoked a Pre-Parliament, which in turn arranged for the election of an all-German assembly. Bypassing the existing sovereignties, voters throughout Germany sent delegates to Frankfurt to create a federated superstate. The strength and weakness of the resulting Frankfurt Assembly originated in this manner of its election. The Assembly represented the moral sentiment of people at large, the liberal and national aspirations of many Germans. It stood for an idea. Politically it represented nothing. The delegates had no power to issue orders or expect compliance. Superficially resembling the National Assembly which met in France in 1789, the German National Assembly at Frankfurt was really in a very different position. There was no preexisting national structure for it to work with. There was no all-German army or civil service for the Assembly to take over. The Frankfurt Assembly, having no power of its own, became

[12] See pp. 112–114, 221–222, 314.

dependent on the power of the very sovereign states that it was attempting to supersede.

The Assembly met in May 1848. Its members with a handful of exceptions were not at all revolutionary. They were overwhelmingly professional people—professors, judges, lawyers, government administrators, clergy both Protestant and Catholic, and prominent businessmen. They wanted a liberal, self-governing, federally unified, and "democratic" though not equalitarian Germany. Their outlook was earnest, peaceable, and legalistic; they hoped to succeed by persuasion. Violence was abhorrent to them. They wanted no armed conflict with the existing German states. They wanted no war with Russia. They wanted no general international upheaval of the working classes. The example of the June Days in Paris, and of the Chartist agitation in Great Britain, coinciding with the early weeks of the Frankfurt Assembly, increased the dread of that body for radicalism and republicanism in Germany. The tragedy of Germany (and hence of Europe) lies in the fact that this German revolution came too late, at a time when social revolutionaries had already begun to declare war on the bourgeoisie, and the bourgeoisie was already afraid of the common man. It is the common man, not the professor or respectable merchant, who in unsettled times actually seizes firearms and rushes to shout revolutionary utterances in the streets. Without lower-class insurrection not even middle-class revolutions have been successful. The combination effected in France between 1789 and 1794, an unwilling and divergent combination of bourgeois and lower-class revolutionaries, was not and could not be effected in Germany in 1848. One form of revolutionary power—controlled popular turbulence—the Germans of the Frankfurt Assembly would not or could not use. Quite the contrary: when radical riots broke out in Frankfurt itself in September 1848 the Assembly undertook to repress them. Having no force of its own, it appealed to the Prussian army. The Prussian army put down the riots, and thereafter the Assembly met under its protection.

But the most troublesome question facing the Frankfurt Assembly was not social but national. What, after all, was this "Germany" which so far existed only in the mind? Where was the line really to be drawn in space? Did Germany include Austria and Bohemia, which belonged to the Bund of 1815 and had in former days belonged to the Holy Roman Empire?[13] Did it include all Prussia, although eastern Prussia had lain outside the Empire and did not now belong to the Bund? On the side toward Denmark, did it include the duchies of Schleswig and Holstein, which belonged to the Danish king, who was therefore himself, as ruler of Holstein, a member of the 1815 confederation? And if, as poets said, the Fatherland existed wherever the German tongue was spoken, what of the German communities in Hungary and Moravia, or along the upper Baltic and in the city of Riga, or in some of the Swiss cantons and the city of Zurich, or for that matter in Holland, which had left the Holy Roman Empire only two hundred years before—not long as time is measured in Europe.

These last and most soaring speculations, though they had already been launched by a few bold spirits, were put out of mind by the men of the Frankfurt Assembly. The other questions remained. The men at Frankfurt, eager to create a real Germany, naturally could not offer one smaller than the shadow Germany that they so much deplored. Most therefore were Great Germans; they thought

13 See maps, pp. 309, 412–413, 514.

that the Germany for which they were writing a constitution should include the Austrian lands, except Hungary. This would mean that the federal crown must be offered to the Habsburgs. Others, at first a minority, were Little Germans; they thought that Austria should be excluded, and that the new Germany should comprise the smaller states and the entire kingdom of Prussia. In that case the king of Prussia would become the federal emperor.

The desire of the Frankfurt Assembly to retain non-German peoples in the new Germany, at a time when these peoples also were feeling national ambitions, was another reason for its fatal dependency upon the Austrian and Prussian armies. The Frankfurt Assembly applauded when Windischgrätz broke the Czech revolution. It expressed its satisfaction when Prussian forces put down the Poles in Posen. On this matter the National Assembly at Frankfurt and the Prussian Assembly at Berlin did not agree. The men of Frankfurt, thinking the Prussian revolutionary assembly too radical and pro-Polish, and wanting no war with Russia, in effect supported the Prussian army and the Junkers against the Berlin revolution, without which the Frankfurt Assembly itself could never have existed.

A still clearer case arose over Schleswig-Holstein. These duchies belonged to the Danish king. Schleswig, the northern of the two, had a mixed population of Danes and Germans. The Germans in Schleswig rebelled in March 1848; and the Danes, who also had a constitutional upheaval at the time, proceeded to incorporate Schleswig integrally into their modernized Danish state. When the Frankfurt Assembly met, it found that the Pre-Parliament had already declared an all-German war upon Denmark in defense of fellow Germans in Schleswig. Having no army of its own, the Frankfurt Assembly invited Prussia to fight the war; and the revolutionary Prussian government in Berlin was at first able to persuade the Prussian generals to initiate a campaign. Great Britain and Russia prepared to intervene to keep control of the mouth of the Baltic out of German hands. The Prussian army simply withdrew from the war. Its officers had no desire to antagonize Russia or to advance the interests of nationalist revolutionaries in Germany. The Frankfurt Assembly, humiliated and helpless, was obliged to accept the armistice concluded by the Prussian generals. Radical socionationalistic riots broke out against the Junkers, the tsar, and the Frankfurt Assembly; and it was at this time that the Assembly called in Prussian forces for its own protection.

The Failure of the Frankfurt Assembly

By the end of 1848 the debacle was approaching. The nationalists had checkmated each other. Everywhere in central Europe, from Denmark to Naples and from the Rhineland to the Transylvanian forests, the awakening nationalities had failed to respect each other's aspirations, had delighted in each other's defeats, and by quarreling with each other had hastened the return of the old absolutist and nonnational order. At Berlin and at Vienna the counterrevolution, backed by the army, was in the saddle. At this very time, in December, the Frankfurt Assembly at last issued a Declaration of the Rights of the German People. It was a humane and high-minded document, announcing numerous individual rights, civil liberties, and constitutional guarantees, much along the line of the French and American declarations of the eighteenth century, but with one significant difference—the French and Americans spoke of the rights of man, the Germans of the rights of Germans. In April 1849 the Frankfurt Assembly completed its constitution. It was now clear that Austria must be excluded, for the simple reason that the restored Habsburg government refused to come in. The Danubian empire, as already seen, was as profoundly opposed to Germanism as to any other nationalistic movement. The Little Germans in the Assembly therefore had their way. The hereditary headship of a new German empire, a constitutional and federal union of German states minus Austria, was now offered to Frederick William IV, the king of Prussia.

Frederick William was tempted. The Prussian army officers and East-Elbian landlords were not. They had no wish to lose Prussia in Germany. The king himself had his scruples. If he took the proffered crown he would still have to impose himself by force on the lesser states, which the Frankfurt Assembly did not represent and could not bind, and which were in fact still the actual powers in the country. He could also expect trouble with Austria. He did not wish war. Nor was it proper for an heir to the Hohenzollerns to accept a throne circumscribed with constitutional limitations and representing the revolutionary conception of the sovereignty of the people. Declaring that he could not "pick up a crown from the gutter," he turned it down. It would have to be offered freely by his equals, the sovereign princes of Germany.

Thus all the work of the Frankfurt Assembly went for nothing. Most members of the Assembly, having never dreamed of using violence in the first place, concluded that they were beaten and went home. A handful of extremists remained at Frankfurt, promulgated the constitution on their own authority, urged revolutionary outbreaks, and called for elections. Riots broke out in various places. The Prussian army put them down—in Saxony, in Bavaria, in Baden. The same army drove the rump Assembly out of Frankfurt, and that was the end of it.

In summary, Germany in 1848 failed to solve the problem of its unification in a liberal and constitutional way. Liberal nationalism failed, and a less gentle kind of nationalism soon replaced it. The German movement of 1848, like so much else in German history, in the long run contributed to a fateful estrangement between Germany and the West. Thousands of disappointed German liberals and revolutionaries migrated to the United States, which came to know them as the "Forty-eighters." They brought to the new country, besides a ripple of revolutionary agitation, a stream of men trained in science, medicine, and music, and of highly skilled craftsmen like silversmiths and engravers.

The Prussian Constitution of 1850

In Prussia itself the ingenious monarch undertook to placate everybody by issuing a constitution of his own, one that should be peculiarly Prussian. It remained in effect from 1850 to 1918. It granted a single parliament for all the miscellaneous regions of Prussia. The parliament met in two chambers. The lower chamber was elected by universal male suffrage, not along the individualist or equalitarian principles of the West, but by a system that in effect divided the population into three estates—the wealthy, the less wealthy, and the general run of the people. Division was made according to payment of taxes. Those few big taxpayers who together contributed a third of the tax returns chose a third of the members of district electoral colleges, which in turn chose deputies to the Prussian lower house. In this way one large property owner had as much voting power as hundreds of working people. Large property in Prussia in 1850 still meant mainly the landed estates of the East-Elbian Junkers, but as time went on it came to include industrial property in the Rhineland also. The Junkers likewise were not harmed by the final liquidation of serfdom. They increased the acreage of their holdings, as after the reforms of Stein;[14] and the former servile agricultural workers turned into free wage earners economically dependent on the great landowners.

For 1850 the Prussian constitution was fairly progressive. If the mass of the people could elect very few deputies under the indirect system described, the mass of the British people, until 1867 or even 1884, could elect no deputies to Parliament at all. But the Prussian constitution remained in force until 1918. By the close of the nineteenth century, with democratic advances making their appearance elsewhere, the electoral system in Prussia, remaining unchanged, came to be reactionary and illiberal, giving the great landowners and industrialists an unusual position of special privilege within the state.

60. THE NEW TOUGHNESS OF MIND: REALISM, POSITIVISM, MARXISM

The Revolution of 1848 failed not only in Germany but also in Hungary, in Italy, and in France. The "springtime of peoples," as it was called, was followed by chilling blasts of winter. The dreams of half a century, visions of a humane nationalism, aspirations for liberalism without violence, ideals of a peaceful and democratic republican commonwealth, were all exploded. Everywhere the cry had been for constitutional government, but only in a few small states—Denmark, Holland, Belgium, Switzerland, Sardinia—was constitutional liberty more firmly secured by the Revolution of 1848. Everywhere the cry had been for the freedom of nations, to unify national groups or rid them of foreign rule; but nowhere was national liberty more advanced in 1850 than it had been two years before. France obtained universal male suffrage in 1848, and kept it permanently thereafter; but it did not obtain democracy; it obtained a kind of popular dictatorship under Louis Napoleon Bonaparte. One accomplishment, however, was real enough. The peasantry was emancipated in the German states and the Austrian Empire. Serfdom and manorial restraints were abolished, nor were they reimposed after the failure of the revolution. This was the most fundamental accomplishment of the whole movement. The peasant masses of central Europe were thereafter free to move about, find new jobs, enter a labor market, take part in a money economy, receive and spend wages, migrate to growing cities—or even go to the United States. But the peasants, once freed, showed little concern for constitutional or bourgeois ideas. Peasant emancipation, in fact, strengthened the forces of political counterrevolution.

The most immediate and far-reaching consequence of the 1848 revolutions, or of their failure, was a new toughness of mind. Idealism was discredited. Revolutionaries became less optimistic, conservatives more willing to exercise repression. It was now a point of pride to be realistic, emancipated from illusions, willing to

14 See p. 405.

face facts as they were. The future, it was thought, would be determined by present realities rather than by imaginings of what ought to be. Industrialization went forward, with England still far in the lead, but spreading to the Continent and initiating the momentous transformation of Germany. The 1850s were a period of rising prices and wages, thanks in part to the gold rush in California. There was more prosperity than in the 1840s; the propertied classes felt secure, and spokesmen for labor turned from theories of society to the organizing of viable unions, especially in the skilled trades.

Materialism, Realism, Positivism

In basic philosophy the new mental toughness appeared as materialism, holding that everything mental, spiritual, or ideal was an outgrowth of physical or physiological forces. In literature and the arts it was called "realism." Writers and painters broke away from romanticism, which they said colored things out of all relation to the real facts. They attempted to describe and reproduce life as they found it, without intimation of a better or more noble world. More and more people came to trust science, not merely for an understanding of nature, but for insights into the true meaning of man and society. In religion the movement was toward skepticism, renewing the skeptical trend of the eighteenth century, which had been somewhat interrupted during the intervening period of romanticism.[15] It was variously held, not by all but by many, that religion was unscientific and hence not to be taken seriously; or that it was a mere historical growth among peoples in certain stages of development and hence irrelevant to modern civilization; or that one ought to go to church and lead a decent life, without taking the priest or clergyman too seriously, because religion was necessary to preserve the social order against radicalism and anarchy. To this idea the radical counterpart was of course that religion was a bourgeois invention to delude the people.

"Positivism" was another term used to describe the new attitude. It originated with the French philosopher Auguste Comte, who had begun to publish his numerous volumes on *Positive Philosophy* as long ago as 1830 and was still writing in the 1850s. He saw human history as a series of three stages, the theological, the metaphysical, and the scientific. The revolutions in France, he thought, both of 1789 and of 1848, suffered from an excess of metaphysical abstractions, empty words, and unverifiable high-flying principles. Those who worked for the improvement of society must adopt a strictly scientific outlook, and Comte produced an elaborate classification of the sciences, of which the highest would be the science of society, for which he coined the word "sociology." This new science would build upon observation of actual facts to develop broad scientific laws of social progress. Comte himself, and his closest disciples, envisaged a final scientific Religion of Humanity, which, stripped of archaic theological and metaphysical concerns, would serve as the basis for a better world of the future. More generally, however, "positivism" came to mean an insistence on verifiable facts, an avoidance of wishful thinking, a questioning of all assumptions, and a dislike of unprovable generalizations. Positivism in a broad sense, both in its demand for observation of facts and testing of ideas, and in its

15 See pp. 296, 300–301, 304, 428.

aspiration to be humanly useful, contributed to the growth of the social sciences as a branch of learning.

In politics the new toughness of mind was called by the Germans *Realpolitik.* This simply meant a "politics of reality." In domestic affairs it meant that people should give up utopian dreams, such as had caused the debacle of 1848, and content themselves with the blessings of an orderly, honest, hard-working government. For radicals it meant that people should stop imagining that the new society would result from goodness or the love of justice, and that social reformers must resort to the methods of politics—power and calculation. In international affairs *Realpolitik* meant that governments should not be guided by ideology, or by any system of "natural" enemies or "natural" allies, or by any desire to defend or promote any particular view of the world; but that they should follow their own practical interests, meet facts and situations as they arose, make any alliances that seemed useful, disregard tastes and scruples, and use any practical means to achieve their ends. The same men who, before 1848, had been not ashamed to express pacifist and cosmopolitan hopes now dismissed such ideas as a little soft-headed. War, which governments since the overthrow of Napoleon had successfully tried to prevent, was accepted in the 1850s as an obvious means sometimes necessary to achieve a purpose. It was not especially glorious; it was not an end in itself; it was simply one of the tools of the statesman. *Realpolitik* was by no means confined to Germany, despite its German name and despite the fact that the famous German chancellor, Bismarck, became its most famous practitioner. Two other tough-minded thinkers, each in his own way, were Karl Marx and Louis Napoleon Bonaparte.

Early Marxism

Karl Marx and Friedrich Engels were among the disappointed revolutionaries of 1848. Marx (1818–1883), son of a lawyer in the Prussian Rhineland, was a democratic-radical newspaperman, who had studied law and philosophy. Engels (1820–1893) was the son of a well-to-do German textile manufacturer who owned a factory at Manchester, which the young Engels went to England to manage. Marx and Engels met in Paris in 1844. There they began a collaboration in thinking and writing that lasted for forty years. In 1847 they joined the Communist League, a tiny secret group of revolutionaries, mainly Germans in exile in the more liberal western Europe. The League, according to Engels, was at first "not actually much more than the German branch of the French secret societies." It aspired to become international and worked by tactics of infiltration. It agitated like other societies during the Revolution of 1848, and issued a set of "Demands of the Communist Party in Germany," which urged a unified indivisible German republic, democratic suffrage, universal free education, arming of the people, a progressive income tax, limitations upon inheritance, state ownership of banks, railroads, canals, mines, etc., and a degree of large-scale, scientific, collectivized agriculture. It was such obscurely voiced radicalism that alarmed the Frankfurt Assembly. With the triumph of counterrevolution in Germany the Communist League was crushed.

It was for this League that Marx and Engels wrote their *Communist Manifesto,* which was published in January 1848. But there was as yet no Marxism, and Marxism played no role in the Revolution of 1848. As a historical force Marxism set in during the 1870s. Meanwhile, with the failure of the revolution, Engels returned to his factory at Manchester, and Marx also settled in England, spending the rest of his life in London, where, after long labors in the British Museum, he finally produced his huge work called *Capital,* of which the first volume was published in German in 1867.

Sources and Content of Marxism

Marxism may be said to have had three sources or to have merged three national streams: French revolutionism, the British Industrial Revolution, and German philosophy. Without the massive fact of the Great French Revolution standing at the opening of the nineteenth century it is doubtful whether anyone would have developed so improbable a doctrine as the abrupt and total renovation of human affairs by the Revolution. But revolution had in fact occurred; it therefore might occur again. What the bourgeois class had done, the workers could do too. And Marxism, along with all early forms of socialism, saw an unredeemed promise in the French Revolution, believing that social and economic equality should follow the civil and legal equality already won.[16] In addition, and in keeping with the general movement of romanticism, the concept of liberty began also to mean a more personal emancipation. Marx, especially in his youthful writings, developed the idea of psychological alienation, a state of mind produced when a human being becomes divorced from the object on which he works, through the historic process of mechanization and commercialization of labor.

The revolutionary outbreaks of 1848, coming within a few weeks of the publication of the *Communist Manifesto,* naturally confirmed Marx and Engels in their beliefs, and the actual class war that shook Paris in the June Days was taken by them as a manifestation of a universal class struggle. But Marx was no mere insurrectionary schemer, like the "revolution-makers," as he contemptuously called them. His mature thought was a system for producing revolution, but it showed how the future revolution must come by the operation of vast impersonal forces.

Engels, engaged in the Manchester cotton industry, possessed a personal knowledge of the new industrial and factory system in England. He was in touch with a few of the most radical Chartists, though he had no respect for Chartism itself as a revolutionary movement. In 1844 he published a revealing book on *The Condition of the Working Classes in England.* The depressed condition of labor, to which Marxism like all forms of socialism called emphatic attention, was an actual fact.[17] It was a fact that labor received a relatively small portion of the national income, and that much of the product of society was being reinvested in capital goods, which belonged as private property to private persons. Government and parliamentary institutions, also as a matter of fact, were in the hands of the well-to-do in both Great Britain and France. Religion was commonly held to be necessary to keep the lower classes in order. The churches at the time, as a matter of fact, took next to no interest in problems of the workers. At best, evangelical

16 See pp. 430–432.
17 See pp. 423–425, 458–460.

sects taught the poor that they must be patient. The family, as an institution, was in fact disintegrating among laboring people in the cities, through exploitation of women and children and the overcrowding in inadequate and unsanitary living quarters. All these facts were seized upon and dramatized in the *Communist Manifesto:* The worker is deprived of the wealth he has himself created! The state is a committee of the bourgeoisie for the exploitation of the people! Religion is a drug to keep the workingman quietly dreaming upon imaginary heavenly rewards! The worker's family, his wife and children, have been prostituted and brutalized by the bourgeoisie! It seemed to Marx and Engels that the uprooted workingman should be loyal to nothing—except his own class. Even country had become meaningless. The proletarian had no country. Workers everywhere had the same problems and faced everywhere the same enemy. Therefore "let the ruling classes tremble at a communist revolution. The proletarians have nothing to lose but their chains. They have a world to win. Workingmen of all countries, unite!" So closed the *Manifesto.*

It was from English sources that Marx also took over much of his economic theory. From British political economy he adopted the subsistence theory of wages, or Iron Law, which orthodox economists presently abandoned since wages did in fact begin to rise.[18] It held that the average workingman could never obtain more than a minimum level of living—of which the corollary, for those who wished to draw it, was that the existing economic system held out no future for the laboring class as a class. Marx likewise took over from orthodox economists the labor theory of value, holding that the value of any man-made object depended ultimately on the amount of labor put into it—capital being regarded as the stored up labor of former times. Orthodox economists soon discarded the labor theory of value, preferring the theory that value is determined psychologically by satisfaction of human wants or tastes. Marx, from the labor theory, developed his doctrine of surplus value. This was very intricate; but "surplus value" meant in effect that the workingman was being robbed. He received in wages only a fraction of the value of the product which his labor produced. The difference was "expropriated" by the bourgeois capitalists—the private owners of the factories and the machines. And since workers never received in wages the equivalent of what they produced, capitalism was constantly menaced by overproduction, the accumulation of goods that people could not afford to buy. Hence it ran repeatedly into crises and depressions and was obliged also to be constantly expanding in search of new markets. It was the depression of 1847, according to Marx, that had precipitated the Revolution of 1848; and with every such depression during the rest of his lifetime Marx hoped that the day of the great social revolution was drawing nearer.

What brought all these observations together in a unified and compelling doctrine was the philosophy of dialectical materialism. By dialectic, Marx meant what the German philosopher Hegel had meant,[19] that all things are in movement and in evolution, and that all change comes through the clash of antagonistic elements. The word itself, coming from the Greek, meant originally a way of arriving at a higher conclusion through debate. The implications of the dialectic,

18 See pp. 426, 582.
19 See p. 435.

for both Hegel and Marx, were that all history, and indeed all reality, is a process of development through time, a single and meaningful unfolding of events, necessary, logical, and deterministic; that every event happens in due sequence for good and sufficient reason (not by chance); and that history could not and cannot happen any differently from the way it has happened and is still happening today. This, it need hardly be said, cannot be demonstrated on any basis of knowable fact.

Marx differed from Hegel in one vital respect. Whereas Hegel emphasized the primacy of "ideas" in social change, Marx gave emphasis to the primacy of material conditions. By materialism, Marx meant that the basic element in society is economic. It is not primarily by having ideas that men create the social world in which they live. On the contrary, their form of society, especially their economic institutions, predisposes them to have certain ideas. At bottom, it is the "relations of production" (technology, invention, natural resources, property systems, etc.) that determine what kind of religions, philosophies, governments, laws, and moral values men accept. To believe that ideas precede and generate actualities was, according to Marx, the error of Hegel. Hegel had thought, for example, that the mind conceives the idea of freedom, which it then realizes in the Greek city-state, in Christianity, in the French Revolution, and in the kingdom of Prussia. Not at all, according to Marx: the idea of freedom, or any other idea, is generated by the actual economic and social conditions. Conditions are the roots, ideas the trees. Hegel had held the ideas to be the roots and the resulting actual conditions to be the trees. Or as Marx and Engels said, they found Hegel standing on his head and set him on his feet again.

The picture of historical development offered by Marx was somewhat as follows. Material conditions, or the relations of production, give rise to economic classes. Agrarian conditions produce a landholding or feudal class, but with changes in trade routes, money, and productive techniques a new commercial or bourgeois class arises. Each class, feudal and bourgeois, develops an ideology suited to its needs. Prevailing religions, governments, laws, and morals reflect the outlook of these classes. The two classes inevitably clash. Bourgeois revolutions against feudal interests break out—in England in 1642, in France in 1789, in Germany in 1848, though the bourgeois revolution in Germany proved abortive. Meanwhile, as the bourgeois class develops, it inevitably calls another class into being, its dialectical antithesis, the proletariat. The bourgeois is defined as the private owner of capital, the proletarian as the wage worker who possesses nothing but his own hands. The more a country becomes bourgeois, the more it becomes proletarian. The more production is concentrated in factories, the more the revolutionary laboring class is built up. Under competitive conditions the bourgeois tend to devour and absorb each other; ownership of the factories, mines, machines, railroads, etc. (capital) becomes concentrated into very few hands. Others sink into the proletariat. In the end the proletarianized mass simply takes over from the remaining bourgeois. It "expropriates the expropriators," and abolishes the old private property in the means of production. The social revolution is thus accomplished. It is inevitable. A classless society results, because class arises from economic differences which have been done away with. The state and religion, being outgrowths of bourgeois interests, also disappear. For a time, until all vestiges of bourgeois interests have been rooted out, or until the danger of counterrevolution against socialism has been overcome, there will be a "dictator-ship of the proletariat." After that the state will "wither away," since there is no longer an exploiting class to require it.

Meanwhile the call is to war. Bourgeois and proletarian are locked in a univer-sal struggle. It is really war, and as in all war all other considerations must be subordinated to it. Periods of social calm are not peace; they are merely inter-ludes between battles. The workers must not be allowed to grow soft or concilia-tory, any more than an army should be allowed to forget its primary function of fighting. Workers and labor unions must be kept in a belligerent and revolution-ary mood. They must never forget that the employer is their class enemy, and that government, law, morality, and religion are merely so much artillery directed against them. Morals are "bourgeois morals," law is "bourgeois law," government is an instrument of class power, and religion is a form of psychological warfare, a means of providing "opium" for the masses. Workers must not let themselves be fooled; they must learn how to detect the class interest underlying the most exalted institutions and beliefs. In this piece of military intelligence, ferreting out the ways of the enemy, they will be helped by intellectuals especially trained in explaining it to them. Like all fighting forces, the workers need a disciplined solidarity. Individuals must lose themselves in the whole—in their class. It is a betrayal of their class for workers to rise above the proletariat, to "improve themselves," as the bourgeois says. It is dangerous for labor unions merely to obtain better wages or hours by negotiation with employers, for by such little gains the war itself may be forgotten. It is likewise dangerous, and even treason-ous, for workers to put faith in democratic machinery or "social legislation," for the state, an engine of repression, can never be made into an instrument of welfare. Law is the will of the stronger (i.e., the stronger class); "right" and "justice" are thin emanations of class interest. We must hold, wrote Marx in 1875, to "the realistic outlook which has cost so much effort to instill into the party, but which has now taken root in it"; and we must not let this outlook be perverted "by means of ideological nonsense about 'right' and other trash common among the democrats and French Socialists."

The Appeal of Marxism: Its Strength and Weaknesses

The original Marxism was a hard doctrine, with both advantages and handicaps in the winning of adherents. One of its advantages was its claim to be scientific. Marx classified earlier and rival forms of socialism[20] as utopian: they rested on moral indignation, and their formula for reforming society was for men to become more just, or for the upper classes to be converted to sympathy for the lower. His own doctrine, Marx insisted, had nothing to do with ethical ideas; it was purely scientific, resting upon the study of actual facts and real processes, and it showed that socialism would be not a miraculous reversal but a historical continuation of what was already taking place. He also considered it utopian and unscientific to describe the future socialist society in any detail. It would be classless, with neither bourgeois nor proletarian; but to lay any specific plans would be idle dreaming. Let the revolution come, and socialism would take care of itself.

[20] See pp. 431–432.

Marxism was a strong compound of the scientific, the historical, the metaphysi-cal, and the apocalyptic. But some elements of Marxism stood in the way of its natural propagation. The working people of Europe were not really in the frame of mind of an army in battle. They hesitated to subordinate all else to the distant prospect of a class revolution. They were not exclusively class-people, nor did they behave as such. Enough of Christianity was still alive in them, and of older natural-law ideas, to inhibit the belief that morality was a class weapon, or right and justice "trash." They had national loyalties to country; they could with diffi-culty associate themselves emotionally with a world proletariat in an unrelenting struggle against their own neighbors.

The cure for the revolutionism of 1848 proved in time to be the admission of the laboring classes to a fuller membership in society. Wages generally rose after 1850, labor unions were organized, and by 1870 in the principal European coun-tries the workingman very generally had a vote. Through their unions, workers were often able to get better wages and working conditions by direct pressure upon employers. Having the vote, they gradually formed working-class parties, and as they proceeded to act through the state they had less inclination to destroy it. Marx's word for such maneuvers was "opportunism." Opportunism, the ten-dency of working people to better themselves by dealing with employers and by obtaining legislation through existing government channels, was the most danger-ous of all dangers to the Revolution. For in war people do not negotiate or pass laws; they fight. From Marxism the working classes absorbed much, including a watchful hostility to employers and a sense of working-class solidarity; but on the whole, as Marxism spread at the close of the nineteenth century it ceased to be really revolutionary.[21] Had the old Europe not gone to pieces in the twentieth-century wars, and had Marxism not been revived by Lenin and transplanted to Russia, it is probable that Marx's ideas would have been domesticated into the general body of European thought, and that much less would be said about them in this book.

61. BONAPARTISM: THE SECOND FRENCH EMPIRE, 1852–1870

We have seen how Louis Napoleon Bonaparte, elected president of the republic in 1848, in 1852 made himself emperor of the French with the title of Napoleon III.[22] Those willing to fight for the parliamentary and liberal institutions which he crushed in 1851 proved helpless. There is no doubt that he became "dictator" on a wave of popular acclaim.

Political Institutions of the Second Empire

Indeed the dubious title of first modern dictator fits Napoleon III far better than it fits Napoleon I. The new Napoleon was not at all like his great uncle. He was no soldier, no administrator, and though intelligent enough he had no especial distinction or force of mind. He was a politician. He had led *Putsches* against the

[21] See pp. 581–583.
[22] See pp. 467–469.

July Monarchy, for which he had been imprisoned. The first Napoleon came to power in the course of a war that he had not started. The second Napoleon made himself dictator in time of peace, by playing on social fears in a country divided by an abortive revolution. The first Napoleon, it is hardly too much to say, never in his life condescended to make a public speech. Louis Napoleon made them all the time; the political rostrum was his natural habitat. Public opinion was more of a force in 1850 than in 1800. Louis Napoleon recognized it as an opportunity, not merely as a nuisance. He appealed to the masses by promises and by pageantry; he cultivated, solicited, directed, and manufactured popular favor. He understood perfectly that a single leader exerts more magnetism than an elected assembly. And he knew that a Europe still shuddering over the June Days was hoping desperately for order in France.

He gloried in modern progress. Toward the changes coming over Europe the monarchs of the old school usually showed an attitude of timidity and doubt if not positive opposition. Napoleon III boldly offered himself as the leader in a brave new world. Like his uncle, he announced that he embodied the sovereignty of the people. He said that he had found a solution to the problem of mass democracy. In all the other great Continental states and in Great Britain, in 1852, universal suffrage was thought to be incompatible with intelligent government and economic prosperity. Napoleon III claimed to put them together. Like Marx and other "realists" after 1848 he held that elected parliamentary bodies, far from representing an abstract "people," only accentuated class divisions within a country. He declared that the regime of the restored Bourbons and the July Monarchy had been dominated by special interests, that the Republic of 1848 had first been violent and anarchic, then fallen into the hands of a distrustful assembly that robbed the laboring man of his vote, and that France would find in the empire the permanent, popular, and modern system for which it had been vainly searching since 1789. He affirmed that he stood above classes and would govern equally in the interests of all. In any case, like many others after 1848, he held that forms of government were less important than economic and social realities.

The political institutions of the Second Empire were therefore authoritarian, modeled on those of the Consulate of the first Bonaparte. There was a Council of State, composed of experts who drafted legislation and advised on technical matters. There was an appointive Senate with few significant functions. There was a Legislative Body elected by universal male suffrage. The elections were carefully managed. The government put up an official candidate for each seat whom all officeholders in the district were required to support. Other candidates might offer themselves for election, but there could be no political meetings of any kind, and if the independent candidate put up posters he had to use a different kind of paper from the official candidate. Few ventured in these circumstances to differ with the government.

The Legislative Body had no independent powers of its own. It could not initiate legislation but only consider what was submitted to it by the emperor. It had no control over the budget, for the emperor was legally free to borrow money as he saw fit. It had no power over the army or the foreign office or the making of war and peace. To publish speeches made in the legislative chamber was against the law. Any five members, by requesting a secret session, could exclude the public from the galleries. Parliamentary life sank toward absolute zero.

To captivate public attention and glorify the Napoleonic name the new emperor set up a sumptuous court at the Tuileries. Balked in the ambition to marry into one of the great dynasties, Napoleon III chose as his empress a young Spanish beauty, Eugénie, who was destined to outlive the empire by fifty years, dying in 1920. It was said to be a love match—a sure sign of popularized royalty. The court life of the empire was brilliant, gay, luxurious, and showy beyond anything known at the time in St. Petersburg or Vienna. The note of pageantry was further struck in the embellishment of the city of Paris. Baron Haussmann, one of the most creative of city planners, gave Paris much of the appearance that it has today. He built roomy railway stations with broad approaches, and he constructed a system of boulevards and public squares offering long vistas ending in fine buildings or monuments, as at the Place de l'Opéra. He also modernized the sewers and the water supply. The building program, like the expensive court, had the additional advantage of stimulating business and employment. And the cutting of wide avenues through the crooked streets and congested old houses would permit easier military operations against insurrectionists entrenched behind barricades, should the events of 1848 ever be repeated.

Economic Developments under the Empire

It was as a great social engineer that Napoleon III preferred to be known. In his youth he had tried to read the riddle of modern industrialism, and now, as emperor, he found some of his main backers in former Saint-Simonians, who called him their "socialist emperor." Saint-Simon, it may be recalled, had been among the first to conceive of a centrally planned industrial system.[23] But the Saint-Simonians of the 1850s shared in the new sense of being realistic, and their most signal triumph was the invention of investment banking, by which they hoped to guide economic growth through the concentration of financial resources. They founded a novel kind of banking institution, the *Crédit Mobilier*, which raised funds by selling its shares to the public, and with the funds thus obtained bought stock in such new industrial enterprises as it wished to develop. A land bank, or *Crédit Foncier*, was likewise established to lend funds to landowners for the improvement of agriculture.

The times were exceedingly favorable for expansion, for the discovery of gold in California in 1849, and in Australia soon afterward, together with the newly organized credit facilities, brought a substantial increase in the European money supply, which had a mildly inflationary effect. The steady rise of prices and all money values encouraged company promotion and investment of capital. Railway mileage, increasing everywhere in the Western world, increased in France from 3,000 to 16,000 kilometers in the 1850s. The demand for rolling stock, iron rails, auxiliary equipment, and building materials for stations and freight houses kept the mines and factories busy. The railway network was rationalized, fifty-five small lines in France being merged into six big regional trunks. Iron steamboats replaced wooden sailing ships. Between 1859 and 1869 a French company built the Suez Canal, which it continued to own for almost a century, though the British government after 1875 was the principal stockholder.

---

23 See p. 431.

Large corporations made their appearance, in railroads and banking first of all. In 1863 the law granted the right of "limited liability," by which a stockholder could not lose more than the par value of his stock, however insolvent or debt-burdened the corporation might become. This encouraged investment by persons of small means, and by capitalists large and small in enterprises of which they knew very little; thus the wealth and savings of the country were more effectively mobilized and put to work. Stocks and shares became more numerous and diversified. The Stock Exchange boomed. Financiers—those whose business was to handle money, credit, and securities—assumed a new eminence in the capitalistic world. A good many people became very rich, richer perhaps than anyone had ever been in France before.

The emperor aspired also to do something for the workingman, within the limits of the existing system. The land bank was of some use to the more substantial peasants. Jobs were plentiful and wages good, by the ideas of the day, at least until the temporary depression of 1857. The emperor had a plan, as did some of the Saint-Simonians, for organizing forces of workers in military fashion and setting them to clear and develop uncultivated land. Not much was done in this direction. More was accomplished in the humanitarian relief of suffering. Hospitals and asylums were established, and free medicines were distributed. The outlines of a social-service state began somewhat vaguely to appear. Meanwhile the workers were building up unions. All combinations of workingmen had been prohibited during the French Revolution, and the Le Chapelier Law of 1791 was deemed to be still in force.[24] Gradually the ambiguous legal position of labor unions was clarified. In 1864 it even became legal for organized workers to go on strike. Large labor units, or unions, and large business units, or corporations, were thus legalized at the same time. Napoleon III hardly did enough for labor to rank as a working-class hero, but he did enough to be suspected as "socialistic" by many middle-class people of the day.

Later dictatorships, bent like the Second Empire on a program of economic development, were usually highly protectionist, unwilling to face open competition with the rest of the world. Napoleon III believed in freedom of international trade. He had a project for a tariff union with Belgium, which some Belgians also supported. Belgium was already well industrialized, and a Franco-Belgian union, especially since Belgium had the coal that France lacked, would have formed a trading area of very great strength. But the plan was blocked by private interests in both countries, and strongly opposed by both Great Britain and the German Zollverein. The emperor then turned to an all-around reduction of import duties. Since the repeal of the Corn Laws in 1846 the free traders were in power in England.[25] They were eager to abolish trade barriers between Britain and France. Napoleon III, overriding opposition in his Legislative Body, concluded a free trade treaty with Great Britain in 1860. He set aside 40 million francs of government funds to assist French manufacturers in making adjustments to British competition; but this sum was never spent in full, and it has hence been concluded that French industry was able to compete successfully with the more intensively mechanized industry of Britain. The Anglo-French treaty was accom-

24 See p. 355.
25 See p. 457.

panied by lesser trade agreements with other countries. It looked, in the 1860s, as if Europe might actually be about to enter the promised land of freedom of trade.

Internal Difficulties and War

But by 1860 the empire was running into trouble. It took a few years to overcome the depression of 1857. By his free trade policy the emperor made enemies among industrialists in certain lines. The Catholics did not like his policy in Italy.[26] After 1860 opposition mounted. The emperor granted more leeway to the Legislative Body. The 1860s are called the decade of the Liberal Empire—all such terms being relative. How the empire would have fared had purely internal causes been left free scope we shall never know. Louis Napoleon actually ruined himself by war. His empire evaporated on the battlefield in 1870. But he was at war long before that.

"The empire means peace," he had assured his audiences in 1852: *l'empire, c'est la paix*. But war is after all the supreme pageantry (or was then); France was the strongest country of Europe, and the emperor's name was Napoleon. Less than a year and a half after the proclamation of the empire France was at war with a European state for the first time since Waterloo. The enemy was Russia, and the war was the Crimean War. Napoleon III did not alone instigate the Crimean War. Many forces in Europe after 1848 made for war; but Napoleon III was one of these forces. In 1859 the new Napoleon was fighting in Italy, from 1862 to 1867 in Mexico, and in 1870 in France itself, in a war with Prussia which he could easily have avoided. These wars form part of the story of the following chapter.[27]

It is enough to say here that in 1870 the Second Empire went the way of the First, into the limbo of governments tried and discarded by the French. It had lasted eighteen years, exactly as long as the July Monarchy, and longer than any other regime known in France, up to that time, since the fall of the Bastille. Not until the 1920s and 1930s, when dictators sprouted all over Europe, did the world begin to suspect what Louis Napoleon had really been, an omen of the future rather than a bizarre reincarnation of the past. It is only right to add that some, like Alexis de Tocqueville, suspected it even then.

26 See p. 507.
27 See pp. 504–506, 507, 516–518; for Mexico, see pp. 610–611.

Early Industrialism and Social Classes

Industrialization, as it appeared first in England in the nineteenth century, rested on a combination of coal and iron, of which the steam engine was the most portentous offspring. Steam engines provided power to the textile mills, and when put on wheels they revolutionized transportation. In the factories a new kind of wage-earning working class was assembled. The railway train, powered by steam, running on rails at first made of wood, then of iron, then of steel, carried people and goods at a speed and in a volume never known in the past. It made possible the concentration of population in cities, both gigantic cities such as London, and clusters of smaller cities in which manufacturing processes were carried on. In this urban world, while polite architecture ran through a series of classical, Gothic, Renaissance, and other revivals, more utilitarian structures of a novel kind were built of iron, and then of structural steel. The new habitat provided luxury for a few, comfort for some, and misery for all too many.

Class conflict therefore raged throughout the nineteenth century, but most acutely in the first half. One difficulty was that, though there had long been talk of the progress of science and invention, the actual difficulties of industrialization had been unforeseen. As the first people to undergo the Industrial Revolution, the English had no experience on which to draw. The English imagination dwelt by preference on rural rather than urban themes, especially in the early part of the century, and under the influence of literary romanticism. Government until 1832 was in the hands of a landed aristocracy and country gentry, made conservative in their politics by the French Revolution. Priding themselves on their English liberties, and fearing anything like Continental bureaucracy, the English only gradually endowed their government with adequate powers of regulation, inspection, enforcement, and police.

After 1850 some of the more favorable consequences of modern industry and technology became apparent. While poverty remained chronic, and the working class struggled to better itself, the middle classes grew in numbers and enjoyed new amenities and conveniences. The following pages illustrate the life of social classes in England, and also in France, in this new Age of Iron. The medium here is part of the message, since the nineteenth-century innovations of lithography, photography, and low-cost printing for a wide market are to be observed.

At the left, this piece of popular art (a song-book cover) points up the exciting contrast between new and old. An express train rushes at night, on a high bridge, with the city behind it, through an English countryside illuminated by the moon.

Above: The newly organized London police, in the 1840s, await the arrival of a Chartist procession. Between 1832 and 1848 the Chartists organized mass demonstrations in the vain attempt to democratize the electoral laws and so obtain legislation designed to favor the working classes. The government introduced a more modern and better disciplined police force as a measure of crowd control, and to avoid the kind of chaotic confrontation shown on the following page. The men are in a kind of civilian uniform complete with stovepipe hats.

Upper left: The "Peterloo Massacre" of 1819, as caricatured by Cruikshank. A peaceable crowd in St. Peter's Fields, Manchester, was fired upon and dispersed by the yeomanry, a militia of nonprofessional part-time soldiers, mostly rural people out of sympathy with modern cities.

Lower left: These primitive trains, about 1840, are running on wooden rails with "guidance wheels" at an apparently crazy angle to help keep them on the track.

Above: London, or rather one of its poorer quarters, as seen by the French artist Gustave Doré about 1880. The omnipresent railroad is in the background, while in the foreground the mass housing, with the little yards, or rather pens, evokes the atmosphere of a prison.

497

Upper left: A workers' meeting in Paris, as seen by the painter Jean Béraud in 1884. The audience is probably hearing some socialist speeches.

Lower left: The future King Edward VII, then Prince of Wales, with his wife, comfortably installed in box seats, observes the new Bessemer steel-making process at Sheffield in 1875.

Above: The Bon Marché department store in Paris about 1880. The new era is evident in the vast expanse, the proliferation of merchandise, and the presence of affluent women, who have come downtown with their children to shop.

500

Buildings of cast iron and glass, appearing about 1850, represented the most significant technical innovation in architecture in centuries. The department store on the preceding page was of this kind. At the left, above, is the famous Crystal Palace in Hyde Park, London, built to house the Great Exhibition of 1851. The world's fair, or industrial exposition, was another product of the revolution in transportation.

Lower left: The Café de la Rotonde in Paris about 1860. The new French café was designed to be large, airy, open, cosmopolitan, suitable for ladies, and not necessarily alcoholic.

Above: The Eiffel Tower, built for the Paris exposition of 1889, with elevators to carry visitors to the top 984 feet above the ground, long remained the world's highest structure, and still stands as a symbol of nineteenth-century civilization. It was at first criticized as ungainly and vulgarly colossal. A later generation, accustomed to an architecture of concrete slabs and oblong cages, sees its graceful curves and the delicate tracery of its four immense legs.

XIII.
The Consolidation of Large Nation-States, 1859-1871

O nly a dozen years, from 1859 to 1871, were enough to see the formation of a new German empire, a unified kingdom of Italy, a Dual Monarchy of Austria-Hungary, drastic internal changes in tsarist Russia, the triumph of central authority in the United States, the creation of a united Dominion of Canada, and the modernizing or "Europeanization" of the empire of Japan. All these disparate events reflected profound changes brought in by the railroad, steamship, and telegraph, which made the communication of ideas, exchange of goods, and movement of people over wide areas more frequent and easier than ever before. Politically, all represented the advancing principle of the nation-state.

62. BACKGROUNDS: THE IDEA OF THE NATION-STATE

Before 1860 there were two prominent nation-states—Great Britain and France. Spain, united on the map, was internally so miscellaneous as to belong to a different category. Portugal, Switzerland, the Netherlands, and the Scandinavian

Chapter Emblem: Medallion to celebrate the Prussian defeat of Austria in 1866, and featuring the King of Prussia, William I, who later became the first German Emperor.

countries were nation-states, but small and peripheral. The characteristic political organizations were small states comprising fragments of a nation, such as were strewn across the middle of Europe—Hanover, Baden, Sardinia, Tuscany, or the Two Sicilies—and large sprawling empires made up of all sorts of peoples, distantly ruled from above by dynasties and bureaucracies, such as the Romanov, Habsburg, and Ottoman domains.[1] Except for recent developments in the Americas the same mixture of small nonnational states and of large nonnational empires was to be found in most of the rest of the world.

Since 1860 or 1870 a nation-state system has prevailed. The consolidation of large nations became a model for other peoples large and small. In time, in the following century, other large peoples undertook to establish nation-states in India, Pakistan, Indonesia, and Nigeria. Small and middle-sized peoples increasingly thought of themselves as nations, entitled to their own sovereignty and independence; the result, also accomplished in the following century, was the appearance of such states as Czechoslovakia, the Turkish Republic, Israel, and the Republic of Ireland. Some of these sovereignties comprise fewer people than a large modern city. The idea of the nation-state has served both to bring people together into larger units and to break them apart into smaller ones. In the nineteenth century, outside the disintegrating Ottoman Empire, from which Greece, Serbia, Bulgaria, and Rumania became independent, and in which an Arabic national movement also began to stir, the national idea served mainly to create larger units in place of small ones. The map of Europe, from 1871 to 1918, was the simplest it has ever been before or since.[2]

About the idea of the nation-state and the movement of nationalism much has been said already in this book. Earlier chapters have described the ferment of national ideas and movements stirred up by the French Revolution and by the Napoleonic domination of Europe, the nationalist agitation and repression of the years after 1815, and the frustration and failure of patriotic aspirations in Germany, Italy, and central Europe in the Revolution of 1848.[3] For many in the nineteenth century, nationalism, the winning of national unity and independence and the creation of the nation-state, became a kind of secular faith.

A nation-state may be thought of as one in which supreme political authority somehow rests upon and represents the will and feeling of its inhabitants. There must be a people, not merely a swarm of human beings. The people must basically will and feel something in common. They must sense that they belong—that they are members of a community, participating somehow in a common life, that the government is their government, and that outsiders are "foreign." The outsiders or foreigners are usually (though not always) those who speak a different language. The nation is usually (though not always) composed of all persons sharing the same speech. A nation may also possess a belief in common descent or racial origin (however mistaken), or a sense of a common history, a common future, a common religion, a common geographical home, or a common external menace. Nations take form in many ways. But all are alike in feeling themselves to be communities, permanent communities in which individual persons, together

---

[1] See map, pp. 412–413.
[2] See map, pp. 520–521.
[3] See pp. 345, 357–358, 400–405, 432–451, 469–481.

with their children and their children's children, are committed to a collective destiny on earth.

In the nineteenth century governments found that they could not effectively rule, or develop the full powers of state, except by enlisting this sense of membership and support among their subjects. The consolidation of large nation-states had two distinguishable phases. Territorially, it meant the union of preexisting smaller states. Morally and psychologically it meant the creation of new ties between government and governed, the admission of new segments of the population to political life, through the creation or extension of liberal and representative institutions. This happened even in Japan and in tsarist Russia. National consolidation in the nineteenth century favored constitutional progress. Although there was considerable variation in the real power of the new political institutions and in the extent of self-government actually realized, parliaments were set up for the new Italy, the new Germany, the new Japan, the new Canada; and the movement in Russia was in the same direction. In Europe, some of the aims which the revolutionists of 1848 had failed to achieve were now realized by the established authorities.

They were realized, however, only in a series of wars. To create an all-German or an all-Italian state, as the revolutions of 1848 had already shown, it was necessary to break the power of Austria, render Russia at least temporarily ineffective, and overthrow or intimidate those German and Italian governments which refused to surrender their sovereignty. In the United States, to maintain national unity as understood by President Lincoln, it was necessary to repress the movement for Southern independence by force of arms. For forty years after 1814 there had been no war between established powers of Europe. Then in 1854 came the Crimean War, in 1859 the Italian War, in 1864 the Danish War, in 1866 the Austro-Prussian War, and in 1870 the Franco-Prussian War. Concurrently the Civil War raged in the United States. After 1871, for forty-three years there was again no war between European powers.

The Crimean War, 1854–1856

Before moving on to the first of the national consolidation movements, the Italian, we must examine the Crimean War which, though seemingly remote and unconnected, helped to make possible the success of the European national movements. Its chief significance in the story of the present chapter is that it seriously weakened both Austria and Russia, the two powers most bent on preserving the peace settlement of 1815 and on preventing national changes. It was also the first war covered by newspaper correspondents, and the first in which women, led by Florence Nightingale, established their position as army nurses.

The pressure of Russia upon Turkey was an old story. Every generation saw its Russo-Turkish war.[4] In the last Russo-Turkish war, to go back no further, that of 1828–1829, the Tsar Nicholas I protected the independence newly won by Greece and annexed the left bank of the mouth of the Danube. Now, in 1853, Nicholas again made demands upon the still large but decaying Ottoman Empire, moving in on the two Danubian principalities, Wallachia and Moldavia (later to be

4 See pp. 229–230, 318–320, 385, 406, 444, 447.

known as Rumania), with military forces.[5] The dispute this time ostensibly involved the protection of Christians in the Ottoman Empire, including the foreign Christians at Jerusalem and in Palestine. Over these Christians the French also claimed a certain protective jurisdiction. The French had for centuries been the principal Western people in the Near East: they had often furnished money and advisers to the sultan, they carried on a huge volume of trade, they staffed and financed Christian missions, and they were continually talking of building a Suez canal. Napoleon III had especial reason to resent the Tsar Nicholas, who regarded him as a revolutionary adventurer. Napoleon III encouraged the Turkish government to resist Russian claims to protect Christians within Turkey. War between Russia and Turkey broke out late in 1853. In 1854 France joined the side of the Turks, as did Great Britain, whose settled policy was to uphold Turkey and the Near East against penetration by Russia. The two Western powers were soon joined by a diminutive and somewhat ridiculous ally, which had no visible interest in the issues—the small mountain kingdom of Sardinia, which entered the war mainly for the purpose of raising the Italian question at the peace conference.

The British fleet successfully blockaded Russia in both its Baltic and Black Sea outlets. French and British armies invaded Russia itself, landing in the Crimean peninsula, to which all the important fighting was confined. The Austrian Empire had its own reasons not to wish Russia to conquer the Balkans and Constantinople, or to see Britain and France master the situation alone; Austria therefore, though not yet recovered from the upheaval of 1848–1849, mobilized its armed forces at a great effort to itself and occupied Wallachia and Moldavia, which the Russians evacuated under this threat of attack by a new enemy. Tsar Nicholas died in 1855, and his successor Alexander II sued for peace.

A congress of all the great powers made peace at Paris in 1856. By the treaty the powers pledged themselves jointly to maintain the "integrity of the Ottoman Empire." The Russian tide ebbed a little. Russia ceded the left bank of the mouth of the Danube to Moldavia and gave up its claim to the special protection of Christians in the Turkish empire. Moldavia and Wallachia (united as "Rumania" in 1858), together with Serbia, were recognized as self-governing principalities under protection of the European powers. It was agreed that Russia should maintain no warships on the Black Sea, and that the Danube should be an international river open to commercial shipping of all nations. At the Congress of Paris all seemed harmonious. There seemed to be such a thing as Europe, undertaking collective obligations, protecting small states, rationally and peaceably conducting its affairs.

But trouble was in the making. Napoleon III needed glory. The Italians wanted some kind of unified Italy. The Prussians, who had done nothing in the Crimean War, and were only tardily invited to the Congress of Paris, feared that their status as a great power might be slipping away. Napoleon III, the Italian nationalists, the Prussians, all stood to gain by change. Change in central Europe and Italy meant a tearing up of the Treaty of Vienna of 1815, long guarded by Metternich and unsuccessfully challenged by the revolutionaries of 1848. Now, after the Crimean War, the forces opposing change were very weak. It was the Russian and Austrian empires that had stood firmly for the status quo. But these

[5] See maps, pp. 412–413, 618.

two powers, which had most seriously attempted to uphold the Vienna settlement, could do so no longer. The first proof came in Italy.

63. CAVOUR AND THE ITALIAN WAR OF 1859: THE UNIFICATION OF ITALY

Italian Nationalism: The Program of Cavour

In Italy there had long been about a half dozen sizable states, together with a few very small ones. Several of them had dissolved in the Italian movements that accompanied the wars of the French Revolution. All had been reorganized, first by Napoleon and then by the Congress of Vienna. In the northwest lay Sardinia, called also Savoy or Piedmont; its royal house was the only native Italian dynasty in Italy. East of it lay Lombardy, and east of that, Venetia. Since 1814 Lombardy and Venetia belonged to the Austrian Empire. South of Lombardy, in the northwest corner of the "leg" of the peninsula, was the duchy of Tuscany with its capital at Florence. The smaller duchies of Modena, Parma, and Lucca filled the interstices between Tuscany and the northern states. Across the middle of the peninsula were spread the papal states, the hereditary temporal possession of the Roman See. Further south, comprising half of all Italy, lay the large kingdom of Naples or the Two Sicilies, ruled since 1735 by a branch of the Bourbons. The governments of these states were generally content with their separate independence. But the governments were remote from their peoples.

There was a widespread disgust in Italy with the existing authorities and a growing desire for a liberal national state in which all Italy might be embodied and which might resurrect the Italian grandeur of ancient times and of the Renaissance. This sentiment, the dream of an Italian Risorgimento, or resurgence, had become very heated at the time of the French Revolution and Napoleon, then had been transformed into a moral purpose by the writings of Mazzini.[6] Mazzini, who had invested the cause of Italian unity with almost a holy character, had seen his hopes for a unified republican Italy elevated for a brief moment and then blasted in the general debacle of 1848. In the stormy events of 1848 the pope had been frightened off by the radical romantic republicanism of Mazzini, Garibaldi, and other firebrands and could no longer be expected to support the cause of Italian nationalism. And in the same events the kingdom of Sardinia had failed in its vow to oust Austria from the Italian peninsula without the aid of any outside great power.[7]

These lessons were not lost on the prime minister of Sardinia, which was ruled since 1848 as a constitutional monarchy and was now under King Victor Emmanuel. This prime minister of Sardinia after 1852 was Camillo di Cavour, one of the shrewdest political tacticians of that or any age. Cavour was a liberal of Western type. He tried to make Sardinia a model of progress, efficiency, and fair government that other Italians would admire. He worked hard to plant constitutional and parliamentary practices in Sardinia. He favored the building of railroads and docks, the improvement of agriculture, and emancipation of trade. He

6 See p. 434.
7 See pp. 471–472, 473, 474–475.

followed a strongly anticlerical policy, cutting down the number of religious holidays, limiting the right of church bodies to own real estate, abolishing the church courts—all without negotiation with the Holy See. A liberal and constitutional monarchist, a loyal servant of the house of Savoy, a wealthy landowner in his own right, he had no sympathy for the revolutionary and republican nationalism of Mazzini. To him it did not seem that Italy would be united by the methods of conspiracy and secret societies, by hortatory literature smuggled in from political exiles, or by the proclamation of idealistic radical republics, as in 1848, which alarmed the most influential people in the country.[8]

Cavour shared in that new toughness of mind described in the last chapter. He embraced a "politics of reality." He did not approve of republicans but was willing to work with them surreptitiously. He did not idealize war but was willing to make war to unify Italy under the Sardinian king. With unruffled calculation, he took Sardinia into the Crimean War, sending troops to Russia, in the hope of winning a place at the peace table and raising the Italian question at the Congress of Paris. It was evident to him that against one great power one must pit another, and that the only way to get Austria out of Italy was to use the French army. It became his master plan deliberately to provoke war with Austria, after having assured himself of French military support.

It was not difficult to persuade Napoleon III to collaborate. The Bonapartes looked upon Italy as their ancestral country, and Napoleon III, in his adventurous youth, had traveled in conspiratorial Italian circles and even participated in an Italian insurrection in 1831. Now, as emperor, in his role of apostle of modernity, he entertained a "doctrine of nationalities" which held the consolidation of nations to be a forward step at the existing stage of history. To fight reactionary Austria for the freedom of Italy would also mollify liberal opinion in France, which in other ways Napoleon was engaged in suppressing. The last note in persuasion was furnished by an Italian republican named Orsini, who in 1858, finding the French emperor too slow to make up his mind, attempted to assassinate him with a bomb. Napoleon III reached a secret agreement with Cavour. In April 1859, Cavour tricked Austria into a declaration of war. The French army poured over the Alps.

There were two battles, Magenta and Solferino, both won by the French and Sardinians. But Napoleon III was now in a quandary. The Prussians began to mobilize on the Rhine, not wishing France to create an Italian sphere of influence for itself. In Italy, with the defeat of the Austrians, revolutionary agitation broke out all over the peninsula, as it had a decade before—and the French emperor was no patron of popular revolution. The revolutionaries overthrew or denounced the existing governments and clamored for annexation to Sardinia. In France, as elsewhere, the Catholics, fearful that the pope's temporal power would be lost, upbraided the emperor for his godless and unnecessary war. The French position was indeed odd, for while the bulk of the French army fought Austria in the north, a detachment of it was still stationed in Rome, sent there in 1849 to protect the pope against Italian republicanism.[9] Napoleon III, in July 1859, at the height of his victories, stupefied Cavour. He made a separate peace with the Austrians.

8 See p. 475.
9 See p. 468.

The Franco-Austrian agreement gave Lombardy to Sardinia but left Venetia within the Austrian Empire. It offered a compromise solution to the Italian question, in the form of a federal union of the existing Italian governments, to be presided over by the pope. This was not what Cavour, or the Sardinians, or the more fiery Italian patriots wanted. Revolution continued to spread. Tuscany, Modena, Parma, and Romagna drove out their old rulers. They were annexed to Sardinia, after plebiscites or general elections in these regions had shown an overwhelming popular favor for this step. Since Romagna belonged to the papal states the pope excommunicated the organizers of the new Italy. Undeterred, representatives of all north Italy except Venetia met at the Sardinian capital of Turin in 1860 in the first parliament of the enlarged kingdom. The British government hailed these events with enthusiasm, and Napoleon III also recognized the expanded Sardinian state, in return for the transfer to France of Nice and Savoy, where plebiscites disclosed enormous majorities for annexation to France.

The Completion of Italian Unity

There were now, in 1860, a north Italian kingdom, the papal states in the middle, and the kingdom of the Two Sicilies still standing in the south. The latter was being undermined by revolutionary agitation, as often in the past.[10] A Sardinian republican, Giuseppe Garibaldi, brought matters to a head. Somewhat like Lafayette, Garibaldi was a "hero of two worlds," who had fought for the independence of Uruguay, lived in the United States, and been one of the Triumvirs in the short-lived Roman Republic of 1849. He now organized a group of about 1,150 personal followers—"Garibaldi's Thousand," or the Red Shirts—for an armed expedition to the south. Cavour, unable openly to favor such filibustering against a neighboring state, connived at Garibaldi's preparations and departure. Garibaldi landed in Sicily and soon crossed to the mainland. Revolutionists hastened to join him, and the government of the Two Sicilies, backward and corrupt, commanding little loyalty from its population, collapsed before this picturesque intrusion.

Garibaldi now prepared to push from Naples up to Rome. Here, of course, he would meet not only the pope but the French army, and the international scandal would reverberate throughout the globe. Cavour decided that so extreme a step must be averted, but that Garibaldi's successes must at the same time be used. Anticipating Garibaldi, a Sardinian army entered the papal states, carefully avoiding Rome, and proceeded onward into Naples. The Sardinians conquered the

10 See pp. 442-444, 471.

NATION BUILDING, 1859-1867

In eight years from 1859 to 1867 Italy was unified (except for the city of Rome, annexed in 1870), the Habsburg government tried to solve its nationalities problem by creating a Dual Monarchy of Austria-Hungary, the United States affirmed its unity by defeating the Southern secessionist movement, and the Dominion of Canada was formed to include all British North America (with dates shown for accession of provinces) except Newfoundland and Labrador, which were added in 1949.

UNIFICATION OF ITALY, 1859-1870

KINGDOM OF SARDINIA
PIEDMONT
LOMBARDY
•Turin •Milan
VENETIA
•Venice
PARMA
MODENA
Florence•
TUSCANY
PAPAL STATES
ROME
SARDINIA
NAPLES
SICILY

FORMATION OF DUAL MONARCHY OF AUSTRIA-HUNGARY, 1867

AUSTRIA
Vienna •
•Budapest
HUNGARY

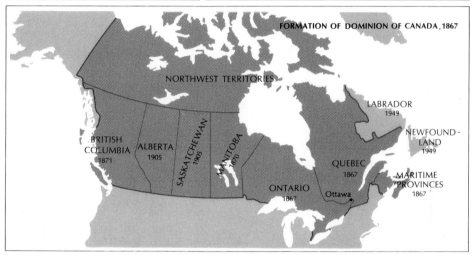

FORMATION OF DOMINION OF CANADA, 1867

NORTHWEST TERRITORIES
LABRADOR
1949
BRITISH COLUMBIA
1871
ALBERTA
1905
SASKATCHEWAN
1905
MANITOBA
1870
NEWFOUND-LAND
1949
QUEBEC
1867
MARITIME PROVINCES
1867
ONTARIO
1867
Ottawa•

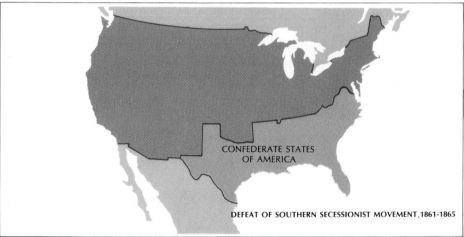

CONFEDERATE STATES OF AMERICA

DEFEAT OF SOUTHERN SECESSIONIST MOVEMENT, 1861-1865

kingdom which Garibaldi had hoped to make a republic. The conquest was peaceful; for Garibaldi, though somewhat disposed to bargain, finally yielded. The chief of the Red Shirts, the foe of kings, consented to ride in an open carriage with Victor Emmanuel through the streets of Naples amid cheering thousands. Plebiscites held in the Two Sicilies showed an almost unanimous willingness to join with Sardinia. In the remainder of the papal states, except for Rome and its environs, plebiscites were held also, with the same result. A parliament representing all Italy except Rome and Venetia met in 1861, and the Kingdom of Italy was formally proclaimed, with Victor Emmanuel II as king "by grace of God and the will of the nation." Venetia was added in 1866, as a prize for Italian aid to Prussia in a war against Austria, and Rome was annexed in 1870 after the withdrawal of French troops in the Franco-Prussian War of 1870.[11]

So Italy was "made," as the phrase of the time expressed it. It had been made by the long high-minded apostolate of Mazzini, the audacity of Garibaldi, the cold policy of Cavour, by war and insurrection, by armed violence endorsed by popular vote.

Persistent Problems after Unification

Very little was settled or ended by unification. Even territorially, the more pronounced nationalists refused to believe that Italian unity was completed. They looked beyond, to regions of mixed population where Italians were numerous or preponderant—to the Trentino, to Trieste, to certain Dalmatian islands, or to Nice and Savoy. They saw in these regions an *Italia irredenta,* "an unredeemed Italy," awaiting in its turn the day of incorporation. "Irredentism" even passed into the English language as a word signifying a vociferous demand, on nationalist grounds, for annexation of regions beyond one's own frontiers.

The occupation of Rome in 1870 by the Italian government opened the rift between church and state still wider. The pope, deprived of territories he had held for a thousand years, renewed his condemnations and chose to remain in lifelong seclusion in the Vatican. His successors followed the same policy until 1929. Hence good Italian patriots were bound to be anticlerical, and good Catholics were bound to look upon the Italian state with unfriendly eyes. The regional differences between northern and southern Italy did not disappear with unification. The north looked upon the agrarian south, the land of priest, landlord, and impoverished peasant, as disgracefully backward. Lawlessness in Sicily and Naples did not disappear with the overthrow of the Bourbons.

The new Italy was parliamentary but not democratic. At first the vote was only given to some 600,000 persons out of more than 20 million. Not until 1913 was the suffrage significantly broadened. Meanwhile parliamentary life, confined to a few, was somewhat unrealistic and frequently corrupt. With the mass of the population excluded from the vote, the revolutionary agitation continued unabated after the unification. Garibaldi himself, in the 1860s, made two more attempts to seize Rome by violence. In general, the revolutionary movement shifted from the older republican nationalism to the newer forms of Marxian socialism, anarchism, or syndicalism.

But the dream of ages was realized. Italy was one. The period that seemed so

11 See pp. 515–516, 517, 594.

shameful to patriots, the long centuries that had elapsed since the Renaissance, were now terminated in the glories of a successful Risorgimento.

64. BISMARCK: THE FOUNDING OF A GERMAN EMPIRE

To play upon the divisions among the Germans, keeping them in rivalry with each other and dependent upon outside powers, had been the policy of France ever since the Reformation and of Russia since it began to take part in the affairs of Europe. The pulverization of the Germanic world was in fact a kind of negative prerequisite to the development of modern history as we know it, for without it the economic and cultural leadership of Europe would hardly have become concentrated along the Atlantic seaboard, or a great military empire have arisen in Russia and spread along the Baltic and into Poland.

Gradually, as we have seen, the Germans became dissatisfied with their position. They became nationalistic.[12] Many German thinkers held that Germany was different from the West, destined some day to work out a peculiarly German way of life and political system of its own. To the Slavs the Germans felt immeasurably superior. German philosophy, as shown most clearly in Hegel, took on a certain characteristic tone. It pronounced individualism to be Western; it skipped lightly over individual liberty; it tended to glorify group loyalties, collectivist principles, and the state. It made a great to-do about History, which in the thought of Hegel, and after him Marx, became a vast force almost independent of human beings. History was said to ordain, require, necessitate, condemn, justify, or excuse. What one did not like could be dismissed as a mere historical phase, opening into a quite different and more attractive future. What one wanted, in the present or future, could be described as historically necessary and bound to come.

The German States after 1848

In 1848 a series of revolutions unseated the several governments of Germany. At the Frankfurt Assembly a group composed essentially of private citizens undertook to organize a united Germany by constitutional methods. They failed because they had no power. Hence after 1848 the Germans began to think in terms of power, developing a somewhat extreme admiration for *die Macht*. The men of Frankfurt failed also, perhaps, because they were insufficiently revolutionary. The Germans were a sober, orderly, and respectful people. They were still attached emotionally to their several states. What happened in Italy, a revolutionary extermination of all the old governments except that of Sardinia, could not happen in Germany.[13]

After the failure of the 1848 revolution German nationalists and liberals were confused. By 1850 the old states were restored—Austria and Prussia, the kingdoms of Hanover, Saxony, Bavaria, and Württemberg, together with about thirty other states ranging in size down to the free cities of Hamburg and Frankfurt. The loose confederation of 1815, linking all these states together, was restored

[12] See pp. 400–404, 434–435.
[13] See pp. 434–435.

also.[14] But within this framework great economic and social changes were occurring. Between 1850 and 1870 the output of both coal and iron in Germany multiplied sixfold. In 1850 Germany produced less iron than France, in 1870 more. Germany was overcoming the economic and social lag which had characterized it for 300 years. A *Zollverein*, or tariff union, initiated by Prussia in 1818, had come to include almost all Germany outside of Austria and Bohemia and provided a large measure of economic unity. The German cities were growing, bound together by railroad and telegraph, requiring larger supporting areas on which to live. Industrial capitalists and industrial workingmen were becoming more numerous. With the advantages of unity more obvious than ever, with the ideals of 1848 badly compromised, with an exaggerated respect for the state and for power, and with a habit of accepting the successful event as the "judgment of history," the Germans were ripe for what happened. They did not unify themselves by their own exertions. They fell into the arms of Prussia.

Prussia in the 1860s: Bismarck

Prussia had always been the smallest and most precarious of the great powers. Ruined by Napoleon, it had risen again. It owed its international influence and internal character to its army. Actually it had fought rather fewer wars than other great powers, but, with its army in being, it had followed a program of expansion by conquest or diplomacy. The taking of Silesia in 1740, of parts of Poland in the 1770s and 1790s, of the Rhineland in 1815 by an international bargain were the highlights of Prussian growth.[15] After 1850 those who controlled the destinies of Prussia were apprehensive. Their state had been shaken by revolution. In the Crimean War and at the Congress of Paris they were hardly more than spectators. Italy was unified without any Prussian saying yes or no. It seemed as if the hard-won and still relatively recent position of Prussia might be waning.

Since 1815 the population of Prussia had grown from 11 to 18 million, but the size of the army had not changed. Merely to enforce existing principles of conscription would therefore almost double the army. But this would require increased financial appropriations. After 1850 Prussia had a parliament.[16] It was a parliament, to be sure, dominated by men of wealth; but some of the wealthy Prussians, notably the capital owners of the Rhineland, were liberals who wished the parliament to have control over government policies. These men did not like professional armies and considered the Prussian Junkers, from whom the officer corps was recruited, as their main rivals in the state. The parliament refused the necessary appropriations. The king at this juncture, in 1862, appointed a new chief minister, Otto von Bismarck.

Bismarck was a Junker from old Brandenburg east of the Elbe. He cultivated the gruff manner of an honest country squire, though he was in fact an accomplished man of the world. Intellectually he was far superior to the rather slow-witted landlord class from which he sprang, and for which he often felt an impatient contempt. He shared in many Junker ideas. He advocated, and even felt, a kind of stout Protestant piety. Although he cared for the world's opinion, it never deterred him in his actions; criticism and denunciation left him untouched. He was in fact obstinate. He was not a nationalist. He did not look upon all

---

[14] See pp. 411–414, 480 and map, p. 514.
[15] See maps, pp. 218–219.
[16] See pp. 480–481.

Germany as his Fatherland. He was a Prussian. His social affinities, as with the Junkers generally, lay to the East with corresponding landowning elements of the Baltic provinces and Russia.[17] The West, including the bulk of Germany, he neither understood nor trusted; it seemed to him revolutionary, turbulent, free-thinking, materialistic. Parliamentary bodies he considered ignorant and irresponsible as organs of government. Individual liberty seemed to him disorderly selfishness. Liberalism, democracy, socialism were repugnant to him. He preferred to stress duty, service, order, and the fear of God. The idea of forming a new German union developed only gradually in his mind and then as an adjunct to the strengthening of Prussia.

Bismarck thus had his predilections, and even his principles. But no principle bound him, no ideology seemed to him an end in itself. He became the classic practitioner of *Realpolitik*. The time came when the Junkers thought him a traitor to his class, when even the king was afraid of him, when he outraged and then mollified the august house of Habsburg, when he made friends with liberals, democrats, and even socialists, and in turn made enemies of them. First he made wars, then he insisted upon peace. Enmities and alliances were to him only matters of passing convenience. The enemy of today might be the friend of tomorrow. Far from planning out a long train of events, then following it step by step to a grand consummation, he seems to have been practical and opportunistic, taking advantage of situations as they emerged and prepared to act in any one of several directions as events might suggest.

In 1862, as minister president, it was his job, or duty, to outface the liberals in the Prussian parliament. For four years, from 1862 to 1866, Bismarck waged this "constitutional struggle." The parliament refused to vote the proposed taxes. The government collected them anyway. The taxpayers paid them without protest—it was the orderly thing to do, and the collectors represented public authority. The limitations of Prussian liberalism, the docility of the population, the respect for officialdom, the belief that the king and his ministers were wiser than the elected deputies, all clearly revealed themselves in this triumph of military policy over the theory of government by consent. The army was enlarged, reorganized, retrained, and reequipped. Bismarck fended off the showers of abuse from the liberal majority in the chamber. The liberals declared that the government's policy was flagrantly unconstitutional. The constitution, said Bismarck, could not have been meant to undermine the state. The government, said the liberals, was itself undermining Prussia, for the rest of Germany hoped to find in Prussia, as Italy had found in Sardinia, a model of political freedom. What the Germans admired in Prussia, replied Bismarck coldly, was not its liberalism but its power. He declared that the Prussian boundaries as set in 1815 were unsound, that Prussia must be prepared to seize favorable opportunities for further growth.[18] And he added one of his most memorable utterances: "Not by speeches and majority votes are the great questions of the day decided—that was the great error of 1848 and 1849—but by blood and iron."

Bismarck's Wars: The North German Confederation, 1867

A favorable opportunity was not long in presenting itself. The Schleswig-Holstein question arose again. We have seen how it had arisen in 1848, and how even the

17 See map, p. 202.
18 See maps, pp. 219, 514.

THE GERMAN QUESTION, 1815–1871

From 1815 to 1866 there were thirty-nine states in Germany (of which only the largest are shown) joined in the Confederation of 1815. At the Frankfurt Assembly in 1848 (see p. 478) two groups developed: the Great Germans who adhered to the idea of an all-German union, including the Austrian lands except Hungary; and the Little Germans who were willing to exclude Austria and its empire. Bismarck was a Little German but a Great Prussian. He (1) enlarged Prussia by conquest in 1866, (2) joined Mecklenburg, Saxony, etc., with his enlarged Prussia in a North German Confederation of 1867, (3) combined this in turn with Bavaria, Württemberg, etc., to form the German empire of 1871, (4) conquered Alsace-Lorraine from France, and (5) ejected Austria. The boundaries of Bismarckian Germany remained unchanged until 1918. (See also maps, pp. 218–219, 412–413, 686–687.)

mild men of Frankfurt had insisted, to the point of war, upon the incorporation of the two duchies into their German union.[19] Now in 1863 the story was repeated. The Danes, engaged in a process of national consolidation of their own, wished to make Schleswig an integral part of Denmark. The population of Schleswig was part Dane and part German. The diet of the German confederation, unwilling to see Germans thus annexed outright to Denmark, called for an all-German war upon the Danes, just as the revolutionary Frankfurt Assembly had done. Bismarck had no desire to support or strengthen the existing German confederation. He wanted not an all-German war but a Prussian war. To disguise his aims he acted jointly with Austria. In 1864 Prussia and Austria together went to war with Denmark, which they soon defeated. It was Bismarck's intention to annex both Schleswig and Holstein to Prussia, gaining whatever other advantages might present themselves from future trouble with Austria. He arranged a provisional occupation of Schleswig by Prussia, and of Holstein by Austria. Disputes soon arose over rights of passage, the keeping of internal order, and other problems with which occupying forces are commonly afflicted. While pretending to try to regulate these disputes he allowed them to ripen.

He now proceeded to discredit and isolate Austria. The British government was at the time following a policy of nonintervention in the affairs of the Continent. The Russian empire was in no position for action; it was divided internally by a reform program then at its height; it was in a mood of hostility to Austria, because of events of the Crimean War, and well disposed toward Prussia and Bismarck, because Bismarck in 1863 took care to support it against an uprising of Russian Poles. To win over the new kingdom of Italy Bismarck held out the lure of Venetia. As for France, Napoleon III was embarrassed by domestic discontents and had his army committed to adventures in Mexico. In addition, Bismarck charmed him at a confidential interview at Biarritz, where vague oral intimations of French expansion were exchanged, and the two men seemed to agree to a needed modernization of the map of Europe. To weaken Austria within Germany, Bismarck presented himself as a democrat. He proposed a reform of the German confederation, recommending that it have a popular chamber elected by universal male suffrage. He calculated that the mass of the German people were wedded neither to the well-to-do capitalistic liberals, nor to the existing government structures of the German states, nor to the house of Habsburg. He would use "democracy" to undermine all established interests that stood in his way.

Meanwhile the occupying powers continued to quarrel over Schleswig-Holstein. Austria finally raised the matter formally in the German federal diet, one of whose functions was to prevent war between its members. Bismarck declared that the diet had no authority, accused the Austrians of aggression, and ordered the Prussian army to enter Holstein. The Austrians called for federal sanctions in the form of an all-German force to be sent against Prussia. The result was that Prussia, in 1866, was at war not only with Austria but with most of the other German states. The Prussian army soon proved its superiority. Trained to an unprecedented precision, equipped with the new needle-gun, by which the infantryman could deliver five rounds a minute, brought into the zone of combat by an imaginative strategy that made use of the new railroads, commanded by the skill

[19] See p. 479.

of von Moltke, the Prussian army overthrew the Austrians at the battle of Sadowa (or Königgrätz) and defeated the other German states soon thereafter. The Austro-Prussian, or Seven Weeks' War, was amazing in its brevity. Bismarck hastened to make peace before the other European powers could realize what had happened.

Prussia annexed outright, together with Schleswig-Holstein, the whole kingdom of Hanover, the duchies of Nassau and Hesse-Cassel, and the free city of Frankfurt. Here the old governments simply disappeared before the axe of the "red reactionary." The German federal union disappeared likewise. In its place, in 1867, Bismarck organized a North German Confederation, in which the newly enlarged Prussia joined with twenty-one other states, all of which combined it greatly outweighed. The German states south of the river Main—Austria, Bavaria, Baden, Württemberg, and Hesse-Darmstadt—remained outside the new organization, with no kind of union among themselves. Meanwhile the kingdom of Italy annexed Venetia.

For the North German Confederation Bismarck produced a constitution. The new structure, though a federal one, was much stronger than the now defunct Confederation of 1815. The king of Prussia became its hereditary head. Ministers were responsible to him. There was a parliament with two chambers. The upper chamber, as in the United States, represented the states as such, though not equally. The lower chamber, or Reichstag, was deemed to represent the people and was elected by universal male suffrage. Such flirting with democracy seemed madness to both conservative Junker and liberal bourgeois. It was indeed a bold step, for only France at the time illustrated universal suffrage in Europe on a large scale, and in the France of Napoleon III neither old-fashioned conservatives nor genuine liberals could take much satisfaction. As for Great Britain, where voting rights were extended in this same year, 1867, they were still given to less than half the adult male population. Bismarck sensed in the "masses" an ally of strong government against private interests. He negotiated even with the socialists, who had arisen with the industrialization of the past decade, and who, in Germany at this time, were mainly followers of Ferdinand Lassalle. The Lassallean socialists, unlike the Marxian, believed it theoretically possible to improve working-class conditions through the action of existing governments. To the great annoyance of Marx, then in England (his *Capital* first appeared in 1867), the bulk of the German socialists reached an understanding with Bismarck. In return for a democratic suffrage they agreed to accept the North German Confederation. Bismarck, for his part, by making use of democratic and socialist sentiment, won popular approval for his emerging empire.

The Franco-Prussian War, 1870

It was clear that the situation was not yet stable. The small south German states were left floating in empty space; they would sooner or later have to gravitate into some orbit or other, whether Austrian, Prussian, or French. In France there were angry criticisms of Napoleon III's foreign policy. French intervention in Mexico had proved a fiasco.[20] A united Italy had been allowed to rise on France's

---

[20] See pp. 610–611.

borders. And now, contrary to all principles of French national interest observed by French governments for hundreds of years, a strong and independent power was being allowed to spread over virtually the whole of Germany. Everywhere people began to feel that war was coming between France and Prussia. Bismarck played on the fears of France felt in the south German states. South Germany, though in former times often a willing satellite to France, was now sufficiently nationalistic to consider such subservience to a foreign people disgraceful. To Bismarck it seemed that a war between Prussia and France would frighten the small south German states into a union with Prussia, leaving only Austria outside—which was what he wanted. To Napoleon III, or at least to some of his advisers, it seemed that such a war, if successful, would restore public approval of the Bonapartist empire. In this inflammable situation the responsible persons of neither country worked for peace.

Meanwhile a revolution in Spain had driven the reigning queen into exile, and a Spanish provisional government invited Prince Leopold of Hohenzollern, the king of Prussia's cousin, to be constitutional king of Spain. To entrench the Prussian royal house in Spain would naturally be distasteful to France. Three times the Hohenzollern family refused the Spanish offer. Bismarck, who could not control such family decisions, but who foresaw the possibility of a usable incident, deviously persuaded the Spanish to issue the invitation still a fourth time. On July 2, 1870, Paris heard that Prince Leopold had accepted. The French ambassador to Prussia, Benedetti, at the direction of his government, met the king of Prussia at the bathing resort of Ems, where he formally demanded that Prince Leopold's acceptance be withdrawn. It was withdrawn on July 12. The French seemed to have their way. Bismarck was disappointed.

The French government went still further. It instructed Benedetti to approach the king again at Ems and demand that at no time in the future would any Hohenzollern ever become a candidate for the Spanish throne. The king politely declined any such commitment and telegraphed a full report of the conversation to Bismarck at Berlin. Bismarck, receiving the telegram, which became famous as the "Ems dispatch," saw a new opportunity, as he put it, to wave a red flag before the Gallic bull. He condensed the Ems telegram for publication, so reducing and abridging it that it seemed to newspaper readers as if a curt exchange had occurred at Ems, in which the Prussians believed that their king had been insulted, and the French that their ambassador had been snubbed. In both countries the war party demanded satisfaction. On July 19, 1870, on these trivial grounds, and with the ostensible issue of the Spanish throne already settled, the irresponsible and decaying government of Napoleon III declared war on Prussia.

Again the war was short. Again Bismarck had taken care to isolate his enemy in advance. The British generally felt France to be in the wrong. They had been alarmed by French operations in Mexico, which suggested an ambition to recreate a French American empire. The Italians had long been awaiting the chance to seize Rome; they did so in 1870, when the French withdrew their troops from Rome for use against Prussia. The Russians had been awaiting the chance to upset the clause of the Peace of 1856 which forbade them to keep naval vessels in the Black Sea. They did so in 1870.

The War of 1870, like the others of the time, failed to become a general European struggle. Prussia was supported by the south German states. France had no allies. The French army proved to be technically backward compared with the Prussian. War began on July 19; on September 2, after the battle of Sedan, the principal French army surrendered to the Germans. Napoleon III was himself taken prisoner. On September 4 an insurrection in Paris proclaimed the Third Republic. The Prussian and German forces moved into France and laid siege to the capital. Though the French armies dissolved, Paris refused to capitulate. For four months it was surrounded and besieged.

The German Empire, 1871

With their guns encircling Paris, the German rulers or their representatives assembled at Versailles. The château and gardens of Versailles, since Louis XVI's unceremonious departure in October 1789, had been little more than a vacant monument to a society long since dead. Here, in the most sumptuous room of the palace, the resplendent Hall of Mirrors, where the Sun King had once received the deferential approaches of German princes, Bismarck on January 18, 1871, caused the German Empire to be proclaimed. The king of Prussia received the hereditary title of German emperor. The other German rulers (excepting, to be sure, the ruler of Austria, and those whom Bismarck had himself dethroned) accepted his imperial authority. Ten days later the people of Paris, shivering, hungry, and helpless, opened their gates to the enemy. France had no government with which Bismarck could make peace. It was not at all clear what kind of government the country wanted. Bismarck insisted on the election of a Constituent Assembly by universal suffrage. He demanded that France pay the German Empire a war indemnity of five billion gold francs (then an enormous and unprecedented sum) and cede to it the border region of Alsace and most of Lorraine. Though the Alsatians spoke German, most of them felt as Frenchmen, having shared in the general history of France since the seventeenth century. There was strong local protest at the transfer to Germany, and the French never reconciled themselves to this cold-blooded amputation of their frontier. The peace dictated by Bismarck was embodied in the treaty of Frankfurt of May 10, 1871. Thereafter, as will be seen, the French Constituent Assembly gradually proceeded to construct the Third Republic.[21]

The consolidation of Germany transformed the face of Europe. It reversed the dictum not only of the Peace of Vienna but even of the Peace of Westphalia.[22] The German Empire, no sooner born, was the strongest state on the continent of Europe. Rapidly industrialized after 1870, it became more potent still. Bismarck, by consummate astuteness, by exploiting the opportunities offered by a Europe in flux, and with no more fighting than that involved in a few weeks in three short wars, had brought about what European statesmen of many nationalities had long said should at all costs be prevented. He outwitted everybody in turn, including the Germans. The united all-German state that issued from the nationalist movement was a Germany conquered by Prussia. Prussia, with its annexations of 1866, embraced almost all Germany north of the Main. Within the empire it had about two-thirds of the area. In Prussia the liberals capitulated before Bismarck's unanswerable success. In 1867 the Prussian parliament passed

[21] See pp. 564–565.
[22] See p. 142, and map, pp. 140–141.

an "indemnity act"; the gist of it was that Bismarck admitted to a certain high-handedness during the constitutional struggle but that the parliament legalized the disputed tax collections *ex post facto,* agreeing to forgive and forget, in view of the victory over Austria and its consequences. Thus liberalism withered away before nationalism.

The German Empire received substantially the constitution of the North German Confederation. It was a federation of monarchies, each based in theory on divine or hereditary right. At the same time, in the Reichstag elected by universal male suffrage, it rested on a kind of mass appeal and was in a sense democratic. Yet the country's ministers were responsible to the emperor and not to the elected chamber. Moreover, it was the rulers who joined the empire, not the peoples. There were no popular plebiscites as in Italy. Each state kept its own laws, government, and constitution. The people of Prussia, for example, remained for Prussian affairs under the rather illiberal constitution of 1850,[23] while in affairs of the Reich, or empire, they enjoyed an equal vote by universal suffrage. The emperor, who was also the king of Prussia, had legal control over the foreign and military policy of the empire. The German Empire in effect served as a mechanism to magnify the role of Prussia, the Prussian army, and the East-Elbian Prussian aristocracy in world affairs.

65. THE DUAL MONARCHY OF AUSTRIA-HUNGARY

The Habsburg Empire after 1848

Bismarck united Germany, but he also divided it, for he left about a sixth of the Germans outside his German Empire. These Germans of Austria and Bohemia had now to work out a common future with the dozen other nationalities in the Danubian domain.

The clumsiness of the old Habsburg multinational empire is clear enough, but more impressive is its astonishing capacity to live and to survive. Prussia and France, in the 1740s, had tried unsuccessfully to dismember it. Smashed four different times by the French between 1796 and 1809, it outlived this crisis, and after 1815, under Metternich, it guided the counsels of Europe.[24] Broken up in

[23] See pp. 480–481.
[24] See pp. 257–261, 373–374, 384, 386, 388–390, 438–447.

EUROPE, 1871

The new features on this map, as compared to the Europe of 1815 (see pp. 412–413), are the existence of a unified German Empire and a unified Kingdom of Italy. The German domain was enlarged by the incorporation of Schleswig (in the neck of the Danish peninsula) and the annexation from France of Alsace and parts of Lorraine, the regions respectively around Strassburg (French Strasbourg) and Metz on the map. From 1871 to 1914 Europe had fewer separate states, fewer land frontiers, and a simpler political geography than at any other time in its history. Except for the voluntary separation of Norway and Sweden in 1905 there were no changes in this period outside the Balkans. (See map, p. 661.)

NORTH CAPE

WHITE SEA • Archangel

FINLAND

L. Ladoga

• Helsingfors   • St. Petersburg

• Riga

Warsaw

POLAND

Orenburg •

• Moscow

R U S S I A N   E M P I R E

• Vilna

Don R.

Ural R.

Volga R.

• Astrakhan

Kiev •

Dnieper R.

Rostov •

Dniester R.

BESSARABIA

Pruth R.

• Odessa

SEA OF AZOV

CRIMEA

C A S P I A N   S E A

C A U C A S I A

• Baku

RUMANIA (Autonomous)

• Sevastopol

DOBRUJA

BLACK SEA

AUSTRIA-HUNGARY

SERBIA

MONTENEGRO (Independent)

BULGARIA

Danube R.

Sinope •

• Tabriz

MACEDONIA

• Constantinople

O T T O M A N   E M P I R E

Tigris R.

PERSIA

DARDANELLES

AEGEAN SEA

• Smyrna

M E S O P O T A M I A

• Baghdad

Euphrates R.

• Athens

GREECE (Independent)

SYRIA

CYPRUS (Britain)

CRETE (Turkish)

ARABIA

SEA

0   100   200   300 miles

1848, restored by the intervention of Russia in 1849, dislocated by its effort at mobilization in 1855, attacked by Napoleon III in 1859 and by Bismarck in 1866, it still continued to hold together and disappeared finally only in 1918 in the cataclysm of the First World War.[25] But the events of the 1850s and 1860s greatly altered its character.

The essential question, in a nationalist age, was how the Habsburg government would react to the problems raised by national self-expression. The nationalities did not wish to destroy the empire. Among the Hungarians after 1848–1849, only a handful of extreme radicals dreamed of a Hungary entirely independent. Most of them desired constitutional autonomy for Hungary but were not prepared to sever the link with Vienna. Slav opinion, at the Slav Congress of Prague in 1848, went basically no further than Austroslavism.[26] The peoples of the empire, while increasingly insistent on certain national rights—such as a degree of local self-government, and schools, law courts, and administration in their own language—felt an underlying need for the large political structure which the empire gave.

By Habsburg, in this period, one means primarily Francis Joseph, who as emperor from 1848 to 1916 reigned even longer than his famous contemporary, Queen Victoria. Francis Joseph, like many others, could never shake off his own tradition. His thoughts turned on his house and on its rights. Buffeted unmercifully by the waves of change, he cordially disliked everything liberal, progressive, or modern. He allied himself with the Catholic hierarchy and the Vatican, which also, for decades after 1848, and for understandable reason, set itself bluntly against compromise with the new age. Personally, Francis Joseph was incapable of enlarged views, ambitious projects, bold decisions, or persevering action. And he lived in a pompous dream world, surrounded in the imperial court by great noblemen, high churchmen, and bespangled personages of the army.

Yet the government was not idle; it was, if anything, too fertile in devising new deals and new dispensations. Various expedients were tried after 1849, but none was tried long enough to see if it would work. For several years the ruling idea was centralization—to govern the empire through the German language and with German efficiency, maintaining the abolition of serfdom as accomplished in 1848 (and which required a strong official control over the landlords if it was to work in practice) and favoring the building of railroads and other apparatus of material progress.[27] This Germanic and bureaucratic centralization was distasteful to the non-German nationalities, and especially to the Magyars. It is important to say Magyars, not Hungarians, because the Magyars composed less than half the very mixed population of Hungary within its then existing borders. Nevertheless the Magyars, as the strongest of the non-German groups, and hence the most able to maintain a political system of their own, felt the Germanic influence as most oppressive. In the war of 1859 the Magyars sympathized with the Italians.

The Compromise of 1867

In 1867 a compromise was made, known as the *Ausgleich*. It was essentially a bargain between the Germans of Austria-Bohemia and the Magyars of Hungary.

[25] See pp. 469–475, 505–506, 507–508, 513–516, 675.
[26] See pp. 472–473.
[27] See p. 475.

It worked to the common disadvantage of the Slavs. Both Germans and Magyars looked upon the Slavs somewhat as many whites in the United States then looked upon blacks, seeing in them a people who had shown no aptitude for civilization except under tutelage. In fact the word "slave" in many languages (German *Sklave*) had originated from the word "Slav." As Count Beust, the Austrian negotiator, put it in 1867, the idea of the Compromise was that each people, Germans and Magyars, should thereafter govern its own barbarians in its own way.

The Compromise created a Dual Monarchy, of a kind unparalleled in Europe. West of the river Leith was the Empire of Austria, east of it the Kingdom of Hungary. The two were now judged exactly equal. Each had its own constitution and its own parliament, to which in each country the governing ministry was henceforth to be responsible. The administrative language of Austria would be German, of Hungary, Magyar. Neither state might intervene in the other's affairs. The two were joined by the fact that the same Habsburg ruler should always be emperor in Austria and king in Hungary. Yet the union was not personal only; for, though there was no common parliament, delegates of the two parliaments were to meet together alternately in Vienna and Budapest, and there was to be a common ministry for finance, foreign affairs, and war. To this common ministry of Austria-Hungary both Austrians and Hungarians were to be appointed.

In effect, the Compromise treated Austria as a kind of German nation-state and Hungary as a Magyar nation-state. It furnished each with parliamentary and constitutional organs, by which the leading nationality was made to feel a sense of participation in government. But the Germans formed less than half the people of Austria, as did the Magyars of Hungary. Austria included the Slovenes, Czechs, Poles, and Ruthenians (and a few Italians); Hungary the Slovaks, the Croats and Serbs, and the Transylvanians, who were essentially Rumanians.[28] All these peoples felt aggrieved.

Both Austria and Hungary, under the Dual Monarchy, were in form constitutional parliamentary states, although the principle of ministerial responsibility was not consistently honored. Neither was democratic. In Austria, after much juggling with voting systems, a true universal male suffrage was instituted in 1907. In Hungary, when the First World War came in 1914, still only a quarter of the adult male population had the vote. Socially, the great reform of 1848, the abolition of serfdom, was not allowed to lead on to upsetting conclusions. The owners of great landed estates, especially in Hungary (but also in parts of the Austrian Empire) remained the unquestionably dominant class. They were surrounded by landless peasants, an agrarian proletariat, composed partly of lower classes of their own nationality, and partly of entire peasant peoples, like the Slovaks and Serbs, who had no educated or wealthy class of their own. National and social questions therefore came together. For some nationalities, and for none more than the Magyars, not only a national but a social and economic ascendancy was at stake. Landlordism became the basic social issue. A landowning class, educated and civilized, faced a peasant mass that was generally ignorant, rude, and left out of the advancing civilization of the day.

[28] See maps, pp. 433, 520–521.

66. LIBERALIZATION IN TSARIST RUSSIA: ALEXANDER II

Tsarist Russia after 1856

For Russia also the Crimean War set off a series of changes. The ungainly empire, an "enormous village" as it has been called, stretching from Poland to the Pacific, had proved unable to repel a localized attack by France and Great Britain, into which neither of the Western powers had put anything like its full resources. Alexander II (1855–1881), who became tsar during the war, was no liberal by nature or conviction. But he saw that something drastic must be done. The prestige of western Europe was at its height. There the most successful and even enviable nations were to be found. The reforms in Russia therefore followed, at some distance, the European model.

Imperial Russia was a political organization very difficult to describe. Its own subjects did not know what to make of it. Some, called Westernizers in the mid–nineteenth century, believed Russia destined to become more like Europe. Others, the Slavophiles, believed Russia to be entrusted with a special destiny of its own, which imitation of Europe would only weaken or pervert.

That Russia differed from Europe at least in degree was doubted by nobody. The leading institution was the autocracy of the tsar. This was not exactly the absolutism known in the West. In Russia certain very old European conceptions were missing, such as the idea that spiritual authority is independent of even the mightiest prince or the old feudal idea of reciprocal duties between king and subject.[29] The notion that men have rights, claims for justice at the hands of power, which no one in Europe had ever expressly repudiated, was in Russia a somewhat doctrinaire importation from the West. The tsardom did not rule by law; it ran the country by ukase, police action, and the army. The tsars, since Peter and before, had built up their state very largely by importing European technical methods and technical experts, often against strong objection by native Russians of all classes, upon whom the new methods were, when necessary, simply forced. More than any state in Europe, the Russian empire was a machine superimposed upon its people without organic connection—bureaucracy pure and simple. But as the contacts with Europe were joined, many Russians acquired European ideas of a kind in which the autocracy was not interested—ideas of liberty and fraternity, of a just and classless society, of individual personality enriched by humane culture and moral freedom. Many people, with such sentiments, found themselves chronically critical of the government and of Russia itself. The government, massive though it seemed, was afraid of such people. Any idea arising outside of official circles seemed pernicious, and the press and the universities were as a rule severely censored.

A second fundamental institution, which had grown up with the tsardom, was legalized bondage or serfdom. The bulk of the population were serfs dependent upon masters. Russian serfdom was more onerous than that found in east-central Europe until 1848.[30] It resembled the slavery of the Americas in that serfs were "owned"; they could be bought and sold and used in other occupations than agriculture. Some serfs worked the soil, rendering unpaid labor service to the

[29] See pp. 13, 24–25. On Russia in the sixteenth and seventeenth centuries, see pp. 224–235.
[30] See pp. 227, 317–318.

gentry. Others could be used by their owners in factories or mines or rented out for such purposes. Others were more independent, working as artisans or mechanics, and even traveling about or residing in the cities, but from their earnings they had to remit certain fees to the lord, or return home when he called them. The owners had a certain paternalistic responsibility for their serfs, and in the villages the gentry constituted a kind of personal local government. The law, as in the American South, did little or nothing to interfere between gentry and servile mass, so that the serf's day-to-day fortunes depended on the personality or economic circumstances of his owner.

By the mid–nineteenth century both conservative and liberal Russians were agreeing that serfdom must some day end. Serfdom was in any case ceasing to be profitable; some two-thirds of all the privately owned serfs (i.e., those not belonging to the tsar or state) were mortgaged as security for loans at the time of Alexander II's accession. Increasingly serfdom was recognized as a bad system of labor relations, making the muzhiks into illiterate and stolid drudges, without incentive, initiative, self-respect, or pride of workmanship, and also very poor soldiers for the army.

Educated Russians, full of Western ideas, were estranged from the government, from the Orthodox church, which was an arm of the tsar, and from the common people of their own country. They felt ill at ease in a mass of ignorance and obscurantism and a pang of guilt at the virtual slavery on which their own position rested. Hence arose, at about the time under discussion, another distinctive feature of Russian life, the "intelligentsia." In Russia it was thought so exciting to be educated, to have ideas, to subscribe to magazines, or engage in critical conversation that the intelligentsia sensed themselves as a class apart. They were made up of students, university graduates, and persons who had a good deal of leisure to read. Such people, while not very free to think, were more free to think than to do almost anything else. The Russian intelligentsia tended to sweeping and all-embracing philosophies. They believed that intellectuals should play a large role in society. They formed an exaggerated idea of the direct influence of thinkers upon the course of historical change. Their characteristic attitude was one of opposition. Some, overwhelmed by the mammoth immobility of the tsardom and of serfdom, turned to revolutionary and even terroristic philosophies. This only made the bureaucrats more anxious and fearful, and the government more fitfully repressive.

The Emancipation Act of 1861 and Other Reforms

Alexander II, on becoming tsar, attempted to enlist the support of the liberals among the intelligentsia. He gave permission to travel outside of Russia, eased the controls on the universities, and allowed the censorship to go relatively unenforced. Newspapers and journals were founded, and those written by Russian revolutionaries abroad, like the *Polar Star* of Alexander Herzen in London, penetrated more freely into the country. The result was a great outburst of public opinion, which was agreed at least on one point, the necessity of emancipating the peasants. This was in principle hardly a party question. Alexander's father, Nicholas I, had been a noted reactionary, who abhorred Western liberalism and is memorable for having organized, as the "Third Section" of his chancellory, a system of secret political police until then unparalleled in Europe for its arbitrary and inquisitorial methods. Yet Nicholas I had taken serious measures to alleviate serfdom. Alexander II, basically conservative on Russian affairs, proceeded to set up a special branch of the government to study the question. The government did not wish to throw the whole labor system and economy of the country into chaos, nor to ruin the gentry class without which it could not govern at all. After many discussions, proposals, and memoranda, an imperial ukase of 1861 declared serfdom abolished and the peasants free.

By this great decree the peasants became legally free in the Western sense. They were henceforth subjects of the government, not subjects of their owners. It was hoped that they would be stirred by a new sense of human dignity. As one enthusiastic official put it shortly after emancipation: "The people are erect and transformed; the look, the walk, the speech, everything is changed." The gentry lost their old quasi-manorial jurisdiction over the villages. They could no longer exact forced and unpaid labor or receive fees arising from servitude.

It is important to realize what the Act of Emancipation did and did not do. Roughly (with great differences from region to region) it allocated about half the cultivated land to the gentry and half to the former serfs. The latter had to pay redemption money for the land they received and for the fees which the gentry lost. The Russian aristocracy was far from weakened; in place of a kind of human property largely mortgaged anyway, they now had clear possession of some half the land, they received the redemption money, and were rid of obligations to the peasants.

The peasants, on the other hand, now owned some half the arable land in their own right—a considerable amount by the standards of almost any European country. They did not, however, possess it according to the principles of private property or independent farming that had become prevalent in Europe. The peasant land, when redeemed, became the collective property of the ancient peasant village assembly, or *mir*. The village, as a unit, was responsible to the government for payment of the redemption and for collection of the necessary sums from its individual members. The village assembly, in default of collection, might require forced labor from the defaulter or a member of his family; and it could prevent peasants from moving away from the village, lest those remaining bear the whole burden of payment. It could (as in the past) assign and reassign certain lands to its members for tillage and otherwise supervise cultivation as a joint concern. To keep the village community intact, the government presently forbade the selling or mortgaging of land to persons outside the village. This tended to preserve the peasant society but also to discourage the investment of outside capital, with which equipment might be purchased, and so to retard agricultural improvement and the growth of wealth. Not all peasants within the village unit were equal. As in France before the Revolution, some had the right to work more land than others. Some were only day laborers. Others had rights of inheritance in the soil (for not all land was subject to reassignment by the commune) or rented additional parcels of land belonging to the gentry. These lands they worked by hiring other peasants for wages. These more substantial peasants, as agricultural entrepreneurs, resembled farmers of the type found in France or the United States. None of the Russian peasants, however, after the emancipation, possessed full individual freedom of action. In their movements and obligations, as in their thoughts, they were restricted by their villages as they had once been restricted by their lords.

Alexander II proceeded to overhaul and westernize the legal system of the country. With the disappearance of the lord's jurisdiction over his peasants a new system of local courts was needed in any case, but the opportunity was taken to reform the courts from bottom to top. The arbitrariness of authority and defenselessness of the subject were the inveterate evils. They were greatly mitigated by the edict of 1864. Trials were made public, and private persons received the right to be represented in court by lawyers of their own choosing. All class distinctions in judicial matters were abolished, although in practice peasants continued to be subject to harsh disadvantages. A clear sequence of lower and higher courts was established. Requirements were laid down for the professional training of judges, who henceforth received stated salaries and were protected from administrative pressure. A system of juries on the English model was introduced.

While thus attempting to establish a rule of law, the tsar also moved in the direction of allowing self-government. He hoped to win over the liberals and to shoulder the upper and middle classes with some degree of public responsibility. He created, again by an edict of 1864, a system of provincial and district councils called zemstvos. Elected by various elements, including the peasants, the zemstvos gradually went into operation and took up matters of education, medical relief, public welfare, food supply, and road maintenance in their localities. Their great value was in developing civic sentiment among those who took part in them. Many liberals urged a representative body for all Russia, a Zemsky Sobor or Duma, which, however, Alexander II refused to concede. After 1864 his policy became more cautious. A rebellion in Poland in 1863 inclined him to take advice from those who favored repression. He began to mollify the vested interests that had been disgruntled by the reforms and to whittle down some of the concessions already granted. But the essence of the reforms remained unaffected.

Revolutionism in Russia

The autocrat who thus undertook to liberalize Russia barely escaped assassination in 1866, had five shots fired at him in 1873, missed death by half an hour in 1880 when his imperial dining room was dynamited, and in 1881 was to be killed by a bomb. The revolutionaries were not pleased with the reforms, which if successful would merely strengthen the existing order. Dissatisfied intelligentsia in the 1860s began to call themselves "nihilists": they believed in "nothing"—except science— and took a cynical view of the reforming tsar and his zemstvos. The peasants, saddled with heavy redemption payments, remained basically unsatisfied, and intellectuals toured the villages fanning this discontent. Revolutionaries developed a mystic conception of the revolutionary role of the Russian masses. They reminded the peasants of the vast rebellions of Stephen Razin and Pugachev, in which they saw a native Russian revolutionary tradition.[31] Socialists, after the failure of socialism in Europe in the Revolution of 1848, came in many cases to believe, as Alexander Herzen wrote, that the true and natural future of socialism lay in Russia, because of the very weakness of capitalism in Russia and the

[31] See pp. 228, 317–318.

existence of a kind of collectivism already established in the village assemblies or communes.

More radical than Herzen were the anarchist Bakunin and his disciple Nechaiev. In their *People's Justice* these two called for terrorism not only against tsarist officials but against liberals also. As they wrote in their *Catechism of a Revolutionist*, the true revolutionary "is devoured by one purpose, one thought, one passion—the revolution. . . . He has severed every link with the social order and with the entire civilized world. . . . Everything which promotes the success of the revolution is moral, everything which hinders it is immoral." Terrorism (which is really to say assassination) was rejected by many of the revolutionaries, especially by those who in the 1870s took up the scientific socialism of Karl Marx. To Marx it did not seem that frantic violence would advance an inevitable social process. But other groups, recognizing the inspiration of men like Bakunin and Nechaiev, organized secret terroristic societies. One of these, the People's Will, determined to assassinate the tsar. In an autocratic state, they held, there was no other road to justice and freedom.

Alexander II, alarmed by this underground menace, which of course did not escape the attention of the police, again turned for support to the liberals. The liberals, who were themselves threatened by the revolutionaries, had become estranged from the government by its failure to follow through with the reforms of the early 1860s. Now, in 1880, to rally support, the tsar again relaxed the autocratic system. He abolished the dreaded Third Section or secret police set up by his father, allowed the press to discuss most political subjects freely, and encouraged the zemstvos to do the same. Further to associate representatives of the public with the government, he proposed, not exactly a parliament, but two nationally elected commissions to sit with the council of state. He signed the edict to this effect on March 13, 1881, and on the same day was assassinated, not by a demented individual acting wildly and alone, but by the joint efforts of the highly trained members of the People's Will.

Alexander III, upon his father's death, abandoned the project for elected commissions and during his whole reign, from 1881 to 1894, reverted to a program of brutal resistance to liberals and revolutionaries alike. The new regime established by peasant emancipation, judicial reform, and the zemstvos was nevertheless allowed to continue. How Russia finally received a parliament in 1905 is explained below in the chapter on the Russian Revolution. At present it is enough to have seen how even tsarist Russia, under Alexander II, shared in a liberal movement that was then at its height. The abolition of serfdom, putting both aristocracy and peasant more fully on a money economy, opened the way for capitalistic development within the empire. And between the two confining walls of autocracy and revolutionism—equally hard and unyielding—European ideas of law, liberty, and humanity inserted themselves in a tentative way.

67. THE UNITED STATES: THE AMERICAN CIVIL WAR

The history of Europe, long interconnected with that of the rest of the world, by the early twentieth century became merged with it entirely. Similarly the development of non-European regions, long a collection of separate stories, was to fuse into a single world-wide theme, to which later chapters of this book are largely devoted. It is no great leap at this point to pass to a treatment of areas overseas (as seen from Europe), some of which underwent in the 1860s the same process of national consolidation, or attempted consolidation, already traced in Italy and Germany, Austria, Hungary, and the Russian empire. In particular, foundations were laid for two new "powers" like those of Europe—the United States of America and the Empire of Japan. The huge Dominion of Canada was also established.

Growth of the United States

As in the time of the American Revolution and Napoleon, the history of the United States in the nineteenth century reflected that of the European world of which it formed a part. The most basic fact, besides territorial expansion, was rapid growth. This was so obvious as to lead a French observer in the 1830s, Alexis de Tocqueville, to make a famous prediction: that within a century the United States would have 100 million people and would, along with Russia, be one of the two leading powers of the world. By 1860, with 31 million, the United States was almost as populous as France and more so than Great Britain.

The growth in numbers was due to a prolific birth rate, but also to the arrival of immigrants, who became prolific in their turn. The immigrants—except for an uncounted, because illegal, importation of slaves—came almost entirely from Europe, and before 1860 almost entirely from Great Britain, Ireland, and Germany. The immigrants did not desire to surrender their native ways. Some brought skills that the new country greatly needed, but immigration also presented a true social problem, obliging peoples to live together without common tradition. On the whole, it appears that the older Americans accepted the reshaping of their country rather calmly, with anti-foreign movements occasionally surfacing but then quickly subsiding. Few concessions were made. English was the language of the public schools, the police, law courts, local government, and public notices and announcements. Usually the immigrant had to know some English to hold a job. On the other hand no one was exactly forced to become "Americanized"—the new arrivals were free to maintain churches, newspapers, and social gatherings in their own tongues. The fact that the English, Scots, and Irish already spoke English, and that the Germans readily learned it, alleviated the language issue. The immigrants did not constitute minorities in the European sense. They were more than willing to embrace American national attitudes as formed in the eighteenth century—the national traditions of republicanism and self-government, of individual liberty, free enterprise, and unbounded opportunity for self-improvement. The old America impressed itself on the new, being somewhat impressed itself in the process. In this sense a new nationality was being consolidated.

The Estrangement of North and South

But at the same time the nation was falling to pieces. North and South became completely estranged. The Industrial Revolution had contrary effects on the two regions. It turned the South into an economic associate of Great Britain. The

South became the world's chief producer of raw cotton for the Lancashire mills. The Southerners, living by the export of a cash crop, and producing virtually no manufactures, wished to purchase manufactured goods as cheaply as possible. Hence they favored free trade, especially with Great Britain. In the North, the Industrial Revolution led to the building of factories. Northern factory owners, usually backed by their workers, demanded protection from the inflow of British goods, with which no other country at the time could easily compete. The North therefore favored a high tariff, which the South declared to be ruinous.

More fundamental was the difference in the status of labor. As the demand for raw cotton reached astronomical magnitudes the South fell more deeply under the hereditary curse of the Americas—the slave and plantation system.[32] In the nineteenth century slavery increasingly revolted the moral conscience of the white man's world. It was abolished in the British colonies in 1833, in the French colonies in 1848, and in the Latin American republics at different dates in the first half of the century. Similarly, serfdom was abolished in the Habsburg possessions in 1848 and in Russia in 1861. The American South could not, and after about 1830 no longer even wished to shake the system off. The South was the Cotton Kingdom whose "peculiar institution" was unfree labor of blacks. Whites were hurt by the system as well as blacks. Few free men could prosper alongside a mass of subservient and virtually uncompensated labor. The incoming Europeans settled overwhelmingly in the North, the South remaining more purely "Anglo-Saxon"—except that in its most densely peopled areas some half of the people were of African descent.

In the movement westward, common in North and South, the pressure in the South came mainly from planters wishing to establish new plantations, in the North from persons hoping to set up small farms and from businessmen bent on founding new towns, building railroads, and creating markets. As once France and Great Britain had fought for control beyond the Alleghenies so now North and South fought for control beyond the Mississippi. In 1846 the United States made war upon Mexico by methods at which Bismarck would not have blushed. The North widely denounced the war as an act of Southern aggression, but was willing enough to take the ensuing conquests, which comprised the region from Texas to the Pacific. The first new state created in this region, California, prohibited slavery. Since 1820 the United States had held together precariously by the "Missouri Compromise," under which new states, as set up in the West, were admitted to the Union in pairs, one "slave" and one "free," so that a rough equality was maintained in the Senate and in the presidential electoral vote. With the creation of California this balance of power was upset in favor of the North, so that in return, by the "compromise of 1850," the North agreed to enforce the laws on runaway slaves to the satisfaction of the South. But the new strictness toward fugitive slaves ran against mounting sentiment in the North. Attempts to arrest blacks in the free states and return them to slavery aroused abolitionist sentiment to a higher pitch. The abolitionists, a branch of the humanitarian movement then sweeping the European world, and somewhat resembling the radical democrats who came forward in Europe in 1848, demanded the immediate and total elimination of slavery, without concession, compromise, or compen-

[32] See pp. 242–243.

sation for the property interests of the slave owners. Abolitionists denounced the Union itself as the unholy accomplice in a social abomination.

By 1860 a sense of "sectionalism" had developed in the South not different in principle from the nationalism felt by many peoples in Europe. In their proud insistence on states' rights and constitutional liberties, their aristocratic and war-like codes of ethics, their demand for independence from outside influence and for freedom in ruling their own subject people, the Southern whites suggested nothing in Europe so much as the Magyars of the Austrian Empire. They now wondered whether their way of life could be safely maintained within the Union which they had helped to create. They sensed Northerners as outsiders, unsympathetic, foreign, hostile, and the South as potentially an independent and distinct nation. They were aware that within the Union they were increasingly a minority; for where in 1790 North and South had been approximately equal, by 1860 the North had outrun the South in population, mainly because of the stream of migration from Europe. The incipient nationalism of the South was of the type of the small nation struggling against the great empire. In the North, nationalism was a sentiment in favor of maintaining the whole existing territory of the United States. Northerners by 1860, with a few exceptions, refused to admit that any state of the Union could withdraw, or secede, for any reason.

In 1860 the new Republican party elected Abraham Lincoln president. It advanced a program of free Western lands for small farmers, a higher tariff, transcontinental railroad building, and economic and capitalistic development on a national scale. The new party's radical wing, to which Lincoln himself did not belong, was vehemently abolitionist and anti-Southern in sentiment. Southern leaders, after the election of Lincoln, brought about the formal withdrawal of their states from the United States of America and the creation of the Confederate States of America reaching from Virginia to Texas. Lincoln ordered the armed forces to defend the territory of the United States, and the resulting Civil War, or war of Southern independence, lasting for four years and involving battles as great as those of Napoleon, was the most harrowing struggle of the nineteenth century with the exception of the Taiping rebellion in China.[33]

European governments, while never recognizing the Confederacy, were partial to the South. The United States stood for principles still considered revolutionary in Europe, so that, while the European working classes generally favored the North, the upper classes were willing enough to see the North American republic end in collapse and failure. In addition, Great Britain and France saw in the breakup of the United States the same advantages that they had formerly seen in the breakup of the Spanish empire.[34] In the Confederate States the British, and the French to a lesser degree, expected to find another free trade country, supplying western Europe with raw materials and buying its manufactures; in short, they saw not a competitor like the North, but a complementary partner to the industry of the Old World. It was likewise during the American Civil War that a French army sent by Napoleon III invaded Mexico to create a puppet empire under an Austrian archduke.[35] Thus the only serious attempt to ignore the Monroe Doc-

[33] See pp. 632–633.
[34] See pp. 188, 444–445.
[35] See pp. 610–611.

trine, violate the independence of Latin America, and revive European colonialism in the Americas occurred at the time when the United States was in dissolution.

But the North won the war and the Union was upheld. The Mexicans rid themselves of their unwanted emperor. Tsar Alexander II sold Alaska to the United States. The war ended the idea of the Union as a confederation of member states from which members might withdraw at will. In its place triumphed the idea that the United States was a national state, composed not of member states but of a unitary people irrevocably bound together. This doctrine was written explicitly into the Fourteenth Amendment to the Constitution, which pronounced all Americans to be citizens not only of their several states but of the United States and forbade any state to "deprive any person of life, liberty or property without due process of law"—"due process" to be determined by authority of the national government. The new force of central authority was felt first of all in the South. President Lincoln, using his war powers, issued the Emancipation Proclamation in 1863, abolishing slavery in areas engaged in hostilities against the United States. The Thirteenth Amendment in 1865 abolished slavery everywhere in the country. No compensation was paid to the slave owners, who were therefore ruined. The legal authority of the United States was thus used for an annihilation of individual property rights without parallel (outside of modern communism) in the history of the Western world; for neither the nobility in the French Revolution, nor the Russian serf owners in 1861, nor the slave owners of the West Indies in the nineteenth century, nor the owners of businesses nationalized by twentieth-century socialists in western Europe had to face such a total and overwhelming loss of property values as the slave owners of the American South.

After the Civil War: Reconstruction; Industrial Growth

The assassination of Lincoln in 1865 by a fanatical Southern patriot strengthened those radical Republicans who said that the South must be drastically reformed. With the old Southern upper class completely ruined, Northerners of many types poured into the defeated country. Some came to represent the federal government, some to dabble in local politics, some to make money, and a great many out of democratic and humanitarian impulses, to teach the distressed ex-slaves the elements of reading and writing or of useful trades. Blacks in the South voted, sat in legislatures, occupied public office. This period, called Reconstruction, may be compared to the most advanced phase of the French Revolution, in that "radical republicans" undertook to press liberty and equality upon a recalcitrant country, under conditions of emergency rule and under the auspices of a highly centralized national government with a mobilized army. The Southern whites strenuously objected, and the Northern radicals discredited themselves and gradually lost their zeal. Reconstruction was abandoned in the 1870s, and, by what Europeans would call a counterrevolution, the Southern whites gradually regained control.

The Northern business interests—financiers, bankers, company promoters, railway builders, manufacturers—expanded greatly with the wartime demand for munitions and military provisioning. They received protection by the Morrill tariff of 1861. In the next year, partly as a war measure, the Union Pacific Railroad was incorporated, and in 1869, at a remote spot in Utah, the last spike was driven in the first railroad to span the American continent. The Homestead Act, providing farms to settlers on easy conditions, and the granting of public lands to certain colleges (ever since called "land-grant colleges"), largely for the promotion of agricultural sciences, encouraged the push of population and civilization into the West. Vast tracts of land were given by the government to subsidize railway building. With the destruction of the Southern slaveholders, who before the war had counterbalanced the rising industrialists, it was now industry and finance that dominated national politics in the increasingly centralized United States. The Fourteenth Amendment, for many years, was mainly interpreted not to protect the civil rights of individual persons, but the property rights of business corporations against restrictive legislation by the states. The shift of political power from the states to the federal government accompanied and protected the shift of economic enterprise from local businesses to far-flung and continent-embracing corporations. As in France under Napoleon III, there was a good deal of corruption, fraud, speculation, and dishonestly or rapaciously acquired wealth; but industry boomed, the cities grew, and the American mass market was created. On Fifth Avenue in New York, and in other Northern cities, rose the pretentious and gaudy mansions of the excessively rich.

In short, the American Civil War, which might have reduced English-speaking America to a scramble of jealously competing minor republics, resulted instead in the economic and political consolidation of a large nation-state, liberal and democratic in its political principles, and committed enthusiastically to private enterprise in its economic system.

68. THE DOMINION OF CANADA, 1867

North of the United States, at the time of the Civil War, lay a number of British provinces unconnected with one another, and each in varying degree dependent on Great Britain. The population had originated in three great streams. One part was French, settled in the St. Lawrence valley since the seventeenth century. A second part was made up of descendants of United Empire Loyalists, old seaboard colonists who, remaining faithful to Britain, had fled from the United States during the American Revolution.[36] They were numerous in the Maritime Provinces and in Upper Canada, as Ontario was then called.[37] A third part consisted of recent immigrants from Great Britain, men and women of the working classes who had left the home country to improve themselves in America.

The French firmly resisted assimilation to the English-speaking world around them. Their statute of freedom was the Quebec Act of 1774, which had been denounced as "intolerable" by the aroused inhabitants of the Thirteen Colonies, but which put the French civil law, French language, and French Catholic church under the protection of the British Crown.[38] The French looked with apprehension upon the stream of immigrants, English-speaking and Protestant, which be-

[36] See p. 336.
[37] See map, p. 509.
[38] See p. 333.

gan to flow into Canada about 1780 and thereafter never stopped. There was constant irritation between the two nationalities.

The British government tried various expedients. In 1791 it created two provinces in the St. Lawrence and Great Lakes region—a Lower Canada to remain French, and an Upper Canada to be English. They received the same form of government as that enjoyed by the Thirteen Colonies before their break from the empire. Each colony, that is, had a locally elected assembly with certain powers of taxation and lawmaking, subject to veto by the British authorities, as represented either by the governor or by the London government itself. For many years there was no objection to these arrangements. The War of 1812, in which the United States embarked on the conquest of Canada, aroused a national sentiment among both French and English in that country, together with a willingness to depend politically upon Great Britain for military security. But the internal political differences continued. In Lower Canada the French feared the English-speaking minority. In Upper Canada the old aristocracy of United Empire Loyalists, who had carved the province from the wilderness, hesitated to share control with the new immigrants from Great Britain. Between the provinces there were grievances also, since Lower Canada stood in the way of Upper Canada's outlet to the sea. In 1837 a superficial rebellion broke out in both provinces. It was put down virtually without bloodshed.

Lord Durham's Report

In Great Britain at this time the reforming Whigs were busily renovating many ancient English institutions.[39] Some of them had definite views on the administration of colonies. In general, they held that it was not necessary to control a region politically in order to trade with it. This was an aspect of the free trade doctrine, separating economics from politics, business from power. The Whig reformers were rather indifferent to empire, unconcerned with military, naval, or strategic considerations. A few even thought it natural for colonies, when mature, to drop away entirely from the mother country. Whigs, liberals, and radicals all wished to economize on military expenditure, to relieve British taxpayers by cutting down British garrisons overseas.

After the Canadian insurrection of 1837 the Whig government sent out the Earl of Durham as governor. Durham, one of the framers of the parliamentary Reform Bill of 1832, published his views on Canadian affairs in 1839. Durham's Report has ever since been regarded as one of the classic documents in the rise of the British Commonwealth of Nations. He held that in the long run French separatist feeling in Canada should be extinguished and all Canadians brought to feel a common citizenship and national character. He therefore called for the reuniting of the two Canadas into one province. To consolidate this province he proposed an intensive development of railways and canals. In political matters he urged the granting of virtual self-government for Canada and the introduction of the British system of "responsible government," in which the elected assembly should control the executive ministers in the province, the governor becoming a kind of legal and ceremonial figure like the king in Great Britain.

[39] See pp. 454–457.

Most of Durham's Report was accepted immediately, and a united Canada was given the machinery of self-government in 1840. The British army was withdrawn. The Canadians undertook to maintain their own military establishment, still regarded as necessary, since the era of the famous undefended frontier between Canada and the United States had not yet dawned. The Webster-Ashburton treaty of 1842 put an end to the long dispute over the Maine border. But as late as 1866 the Canadians had to repel armed invaders from the United States, when several hundred Irish Americans, members of the Fenians, an Irish republican secret society, staged a Garibaldi-like attempt to detach Canada from the British Empire. Local Canadian forces proved sufficient to this threat.

The principle of responsible government was established in the late 1840s, the governors of Canada allowing the elected assembly to adopt policies and appoint or remove ministers as it chose. Responsible government, still confined to internal matters, worked satisfactorily from the beginning. But one feature of the new plan, the union of the two Canadas, began to produce friction as the English-speaking immigration continued. The French were afraid of being outnumbered in their own country. Many Canadians therefore turned to the idea of a federation, in which the French and English areas might each conduct its own local affairs, while remaining joined for larger purposes in a superior government.

Founding of the Dominion of Canada

Federalism in Canada was thus partly a decentralizing idea, aimed at satisfying the French element by a redivision into two provinces, and in part a plan for a new centralization or unification, because it contemplated bringing all the provinces of British North America into union with the St. Lawrence and Great Lakes region, to which alone the term Canada was then applied. While British North Americans discussed federation the Civil War was disrupting the United States. In the face of this unpleasant example, the British North Americans formed a strong union in which all powers were to rest in the central government except those specifically assigned to the provinces. The federal constitution, drafted in Canada by Canadians, was passed through the British Parliament in 1867 as the British North America Act, which constitutionally established the Dominion of Canada.

The new dominion received a common parliament, in which the majority party controlled a responsible ministry according to British principles of cabinet government. The original provinces were Quebec and Ontario, formed from the old Canada, and Nova Scotia and New Brunswick, which joined on the understanding that a railroad be built to connect them with Quebec. The old Hudson's Bay Company, founded in 1670, transferred its rights of government over the vast Northwest to the dominion in 1869. From these territories the province of Manitoba was created in 1870 and British Columbia in 1871. To link them solidly with the rest of the dominion the Canadian Pacific Railway was completed in 1885. It made possible the development of the prairies, where the provinces of Saskatchewan and Alberta were added in 1905.

The Dominion of Canada, though not large in population, possessed from the beginning a significance beyond the mere number of its people. It was the first example of successful devolution, or granting of political liberty, within one of the

European colonial empires. It embodied principles which Edmund Burke and Benjamin Franklin had vainly recommended a century before to keep the Thirteen Colonies loyal to Great Britain. The dominion after 1867 moved forward from independence in internal matters to independence in such external affairs as tariffs, diplomacy, and the decisions of war and peace. It thus pioneered in the development of "dominion status," working out precedents later applied in Australia (1901), New Zealand (1907), the Union of South Africa (1910), and in the 1920s, temporarily, in Ireland. By the middle of the twentieth century the same idea, or what may be called the Canadian idea, was even applied to the worldwide problem of colonialism as it affected non-European peoples, notably in India, Pakistan, Ceylon, and the former British colonies in Africa, until all these peoples chose to become republics, though still loosely and voluntarily joined together and to Great Britain in a Commonwealth of Nations.

More immediately, in America, the founding of the dominion, a solid band of self-governing territory stretching from ocean to ocean, stabilized the relations between British North America and the United States. The United States regarded its northern borders as final. The withdrawal of British control from Canadian affairs furthered the United States conception of an American continent entirely free from European political influence.

69. JAPAN AND THE WEST

The Japanese, when they allowed the Westerners to discover them, were a highly civilized people living in a complex society. They had many large cities, they enjoyed the contemplation of natural scenery, they went to the theater, and they read novels. With their stylized manners, their fans and their wooden temples, their lacquer work and their painting on screens, their tiny rice fields and their curious and ineffectual firearms, they seemed to Europeans to be the very acme of everything quaint. This feeling is immortalized in *The Mikado* of Gilbert and Sullivan, first performed in 1885. Not long thereafter the idea of Japanese quaintness, like the idea of the Germans as an impractical people given mainly to music and metaphysics, had to be revised. The Europeans, in "opening" Japan, opened up more than they knew.

In 1853, the American Commodore Perry forced his way with a fleet of naval vessels into Yedo Bay, insisted upon landing, and demanded of the Japanese government, somewhat peremptorily, that it engage in commercial relations with the United States and other Western powers. In the next year the Japanese began to comply, and in 1867 an internal revolution took place, of which the most conspicuous consequence was a rapid westernizing of Japanese life and institutions. But if it looked as if the country had been "opened" by Westerners, actually Japan had exploded from within.

Background: Two Centuries of Isolation, 1640–1854

For over two centuries Japan had followed a program of self-imposed isolation. No Japanese was allowed to leave the islands or even to build a ship large enough to navigate the high seas. No foreigner, except for handfuls of Dutch and Chinese, was allowed to enter. Japan remained a sealed book to the West. The contrary is not quite so true, for the Japanese knew rather more about Europe than Europeans did about Japan. The Japanese policy of seclusion was not merely based upon ignorance. Initially, at least, it was based on experience.

The first Europeans—three Portuguese in a Chinese junk—are thought to have arrived in Japan in 1542. For about a century thereafter there was considerable coming and going. The Japanese showed a strong desire to trade with the foreigners, from whom they obtained clocks and maps, learned about printing and shipbuilding, and took over the use of tobacco and potatoes. Thousands also adopted the Christian religion as preached to them by Spanish and Portuguese Jesuits. Japanese traveled to the Dutch Indies and even to Europe. The Japanese in fact proved more receptive to European ideas than other Asian peoples. But shortly after 1600 the government began to drive Christianity underground; in 1624 it expelled the Spaniards, in 1639 the Portuguese, and in 1640 all Europeans except for a few Dutch merchants who were allowed to remain at Nagasaki under strict control. From 1640 to 1854 these few Dutch at Nagasaki were the only channel of communication with the West.[40]

The reasons for self-seclusion, as for its abandonment later, arose from the course of political events in Japan. The history of Japan showed an odd parallel to that of Europe. In Japan, as in Europe, a period of feudal warfare was followed by a period of government absolutism, during which civil peace was kept by a bureaucracy, an obsolescent warrior class was maintained as a privileged element in society, and a commercial class of native merchants grew wealthier, stronger, and more insistent upon its position.

When the first Europeans arrived the islands were still torn by the wars and rivalries of the numerous clans into which the Japanese were organized. Gradually one clan, the Tokugawa, gained control, taking over the office of "shogun." The shogun was a kind of military head who governed in the name of the emperor, and the hereditary Tokugawa shogunate, founded in 1603, lasted until 1867. The early Tokugawa shoguns concluded from a good deal of evidence that the Europeans in Japan, both merchants and missionaries, were engaging in feudal or interclan politics and even aspiring to dominate Japan by helping Christian or pro-European Japanese to get into power. The first three Tokugawa shoguns, to establish their own dynasty, to pacify and stabilize the country, and to keep Japan free from European penetration, undertook to exterminate Christianity and adopted the rigid policy of nonintercourse with the rest of the world.

Under the Tokugawa Japan enjoyed peace, a long peace, for the first time in centuries. The Tokugawa shoguns completed the detachment of the emperor from politics, building him up as a divine and legendary being, too august and too remote for the hurly-burly of the world. The emperor remained shut in at Kyoto on a modest allowance furnished by the shoguns. The shoguns established their own court and government at Yedo (later called Tokyo); and as Louis XIV brought nobles to Versailles, or Peter the Great forced his uncouth lords to build town houses in St. Petersburg, so the shoguns required the great feudal chieftains and their men-at-arms to reside at least part of the year in Yedo.

The shoguns administered the country through a kind of military bureaucracy

40 See p. 157.

or dictatorship. This formidable instrument of state watched over the great lords (called daimyo), who, however, retained a good deal of feudal authority over their subjects in the regions most distant from Yedo. The great lords and their armed retainers (the samurai), having no further fighting to occupy them, turned into a landed aristocracy which spent a good deal of its time in Yedo and other cities. As a leisure class, they developed new tastes and standards of living and hence needed more income, which they obtained by squeezing the peasants, and which they spent by buying from the merchants.

The merchant class greatly expanded by catering to the government and the gentry. Japan in the seventeenth century passed on to a money economy. Many lords fell seriously into debt to the merchants. Many samurai, like lesser nobles in France or Poland at the time, were almost ridiculously impoverished, hard-pressed to keep up appearances, with nothing except social status to distinguish them from commoners. The law, as in Europe under the Old Regime, drew a sharp line between classes. Nobles, merchants, and peasants were subject to different taxes and were differently punished for different offenses. What was a crime for a commoner would be excusable for a samurai; or what in a samurai would be a punishable breach of honor would be accepted in a common person. The samurai had the right to carry two swords as a mark of class and could in theory cut down an impudent commoner without arousing further inquiry. In practice the shoguns repressed violence of this kind, but there was much less development of law and justice than in the European monarchies of the Old Regime. Economically the merchants and artisans prospered. By 1723 Yedo was a city with 500,000 people; by 1800 with over 1,000,000, it was larger than London or Paris, and twenty times as large as the largest city in the United States. After 1800 some merchants were able to purchase the rank of samurai for money. The old class lines were beginning to blur.

Though deliberately secluded, the economic and social life of Japan was thus by no means static. The same is true of its intellectual life. Buddhism, the historic religion, lost its hold on many people during the Tokugawa period, so that Japan in its way underwent, like the West, a "secularization" of ideas. As a code of personal conduct there was a new emphasis on Bushido, the "way of the warrior," a kind of nonreligious moral teaching which exalted the samurai virtues of honor and loyalty. With the decline of Buddhism went also a revival of the cult of Shinto, the "way of the gods," the ancient indigenous religion of Japan, which held, among much else, that the emperor was veritably the Son of Heaven. There was much activity in the study and writing of history, arousing, as in Europe, an acute interest in the national past. History, like Shinto, led to a feeling that shoguns were usurpers and that the emperor, obscurely relegated to Kyoto, was the true representative of everything highest and most lasting in the life of Japan.

Meanwhile, through the crack left open at Nagasaki, Western ideas trickled in. The shogun Yoshimune in the mid–eighteenth century permitted the importation of Occidental books, except those relating to Christianity. A few Japanese learned Dutch and began to decipher Dutch books on anatomy, surgery, astronomy, and other subjects. In 1745 a Dutch-Japanese dictionary was completed. For European manufactures also—watches, glassware, velvets, woolens, telescopes, barometers—there came to be an eager demand, satisfied as much as possible by the methodical Dutch. Nor were the Japanese wholly uninformed about politics in the West. While the most assiduous Westerner could learn nothing of the internal affairs of Japan, an educated Japanese could, if he wished, arrive at some idea of the French Revolution, or know who was president of the United States.

The Opening of Japan

When Perry in 1853 made his unwanted visit he therefore had many potential allies within Japan. There were nobles, heavily in debt, unable to draw more income from agriculture, willing to embark upon foreign trade and to exploit their property by introducing new enterprises. There were penurious samurai, with no future in the old system, ready and willing to enter upon new careers as army officers or civil officials. There were merchants hoping to add to their business by dealing in Western goods. There were scholars eager to learn more of Western science and medicine. There were patriots fearful that Japan was becoming defenseless against Western guns. Spiritually the country was already adrift from its moorings, already set toward a course of national self-assertion, restlessly susceptible to hazily understood new ideas. Under such pressures, and from downright fear of a bombardment of Yedo by the Americans, which if it would not subdue Japan would at least ruin the declining prestige of the shogunate, the shogun Iesada in 1854 signed a commercial treaty with the United States. Similar treaties were soon signed with the Europeans.

In the following years were sown the seeds of much later misunderstanding between Japan and the West. The whites in those days—European and American—were somewhat trigger-happy in the discharge of naval ordnance against backward peoples. The Japanese, a proud and elaborately civilized nation, soon found that the whites considered them backward. They found, for example, as soon as they learned more of the West by reading and travel, that the treaties they signed in the 1850s were not treaties between equals as understood in the West. These first treaties provided that Japan should maintain a low tariff on imports and not change it except with the consent of the foreign powers. To give outsiders a voice in determining tariff policy was not the custom among sovereign states of the West. The early treaties also provided for extraterritoriality. This meant that Europeans and Americans residing in Japan were not subject to Japanese law but remained under the jurisdiction of their respective homelands as represented by consular officials. Such extraterritorial provisions had long been established in Turkey and were currently taking root in China.[41] Europeans insisted upon them in countries where European principles of property, debt, or security of life and person did not prevail. At the same time, of course, no civilized state ever permitted a foreign power to exercise jurisdiction within its borders. Extraterritoriality was a mark of inferiority, as the Japanese soon discovered.

A strong antiforeign reaction developed after 1854. It was at first led by certain nobles of the western islands, the lords of Choshu and Satsuma, who had never been fully subordinated to the shogun at Yedo, and who now dreamed of overturning the Tokugawa shogunate and leading a national revival with the emperor as its rallying point. Their first idea was to check Western penetration (as two and a half centuries before) by driving the Westerners out. But in 1862 some

41 See pp. 210, 633–636.

Englishmen unintentionally violated a small point of Japanese etiquette. One of them was killed. The British government demanded punishment for the offending Japanese who were followers of the lord of Satsuma. The shogun proved unable to arrange this, and the British navy thereupon itself sailed up and bombarded the capital of Satsuma. In the same year the lord of Choshu, who commanded the straits of Shimonoseki with some ancient artillery, ordered it to fire on passing vessels. The British, French, Dutch, and United States governments immediately protested, and, when the embarrassed shogun proved unable to discipline Choshu, they dispatched an allied naval force to Shimonoseki. The forts and shipping of Choshu were destroyed, and an indemnity of $3,000,000 was imposed. These incidents were remembered in Japan long after they were forgotten in Europe and the United States. It was likewise remembered that the Western powers, discovering that the shogun was not the supreme ruler of the country, sent a naval expedition to Kyoto itself and required the emperor to confirm the treaties signed by the shogun and to reduce import duties, under threat of naval bombardment.

The Meiji Era (1868–1912): The Westernization of Japan

The lords of Choshu and Satsuma now concluded that the only way to deal with the West was to adopt the military and technical equipment of the West itself. They would save Japan for the Japanese by learning the secrets of the Western power. First they forced the resignation of the shogun, whose prestige had long been undermined anyway, and who had now discredited himself first by signing undesirable treaties with the West and then failing to protect the country from outrage. The last shogun abdicated in 1867. The reformers declared the emperor restored to his full authority. It was their intention to use the plenitude of imperial power to consolidate and fortify Japan for its new position in the world. In 1868 a new emperor inherited the throne; his name was Mutsuhito, but according to Japanese custom a name was given to his reign also, which was called Meiji. The Meiji era (1868–1912) was the great era of the westernization of Japan.

Japan turned into a modern national state. Feudalism was abolished, most of the great lords voluntarily surrendering into the emperor's hands their control over samurai and common people. "We abolish the clans and convert them into prefectures," declared one imperial decree. The legal system was reorganized and equality before the law introduced, in the sense that all persons became subject to the same rules regardless of class. In part with the hope of getting rid of extraterritoriality, the reformers recast the criminal law along Western lines, deleting the bizarre and cruel punishments which Europeans considered barbaric. A new army was established, modeled mainly on the Prussian. The samurai in 1871 lost his historic right to carry two swords; he now served as an army officer, not as the retainer of a clannish chief. A navy, modeled on the British, followed somewhat later. Control of money and currency passed to the central government, and a national currency, with decimal units, was adopted. A national postal service began to function and above all a national school system, which soon brought a high rate of literacy to Japan. Buddhism was discouraged, and the property of Buddhist monasteries was confiscated. Shinto was the cult favored by the government. Shinto gave a religious tincture to national sentiment and led to a renewed veneration of the imperial family. In 1889 a constitution was promulgated. It confirmed the civil liberties then common in the West and provided for a parliament in two chambers, but it stressed also the supreme and "eternal" authority of the emperor, to whom the ministers were legally responsible. In practice, in the new Japan, the emperor never actively governed. He remained aloof, as in the past; and political leaders, never fully responsible to the parliament, tended to govern freely in what they conceived to be the interests of the state.

Industrial and financial modernization went along with and even preceded the political revolution. In 1858 the first steamship was purchased from the Dutch. In 1859 Japan placed its first foreign loan, borrowing 5 million yen by a bond issue floated in England. In 1869 the first telegraph connected Yokohama and Tokyo. The first railroad, between the same two cities, was completed in 1872. In 1870 appeared the first spinning machinery. Foreign trade, almost literally zero in 1854, was valued at $200 million a year by the end of the century. The population rose from 33 million in 1872 to 46 million in 1902. The island empire, like Great Britain, became dependent on exports and imports to sustain its dense population at the level of living to which it aspired.

The westernization of Japan still stands as the most remarkable transformation ever undergone by any people in so short a time. It recalls the westernizing of Russia under Peter over a century before, though conducted somewhat less brutally, more rapidly, and with a wider consent among the population. For Japan, as formerly for Russia, the motive was in large measure defense against Western penetration, together with an admiration for Western statecraft and an ambition to become a "power."[42] What the Japanese wanted from the West was primarily science, technology, and organization. They were content enough with the innermost substance of their culture, their moral ideas, their family life, their arts and amusements, their religious conceptions, though even in these they showed an uncommon adaptability. Essentially it was to protect their internal substance, their Japanese culture, that they took over the external apparatus of Western civilization. This apparatus—science, technology, machinery, arms, political and legal organization—was the part of Western civilization for which other peoples generally felt a need, which they hoped to adopt without losing their own spiritual independence, and which therefore, though sometimes rather scornfully dismissed as materialistic, became the common ground for the interdependent worldwide civilization that emerged at the close of the nineteenth century.

In brief, to conclude a long chapter, the world between 1850 and 1870, revolutionized economically by the railroad and steamship, was revolutionized politically by the formation of large and consolidated nation-states. These states at the time all embodied certain liberal and constitutional principles, or at least the machinery of parliamentary and representative government. But the whole earth had also become an arena in which certain mighty beings, called nations or powers, were to act. The Great Powers in 1871 were Great Britain, Germany, France, Austria-Hungary, and Russia. Britain had produced a daughter nation in Canada. Whether Italy was to be called a Great Power was not yet clear. No one knew what Japan would do. All agreed that the United States would one day play a large role in international politics, but the time was not yet.

[42] See pp. 224–235.

XIV.
European
Civilization,
1871-1914

alf a century elapsed between the period of national consolidation described in the last chapter and the outbreak of the First World War in 1914. In this half-century Europe in many ways reached the climax of the modern phase of its civilization, and also exerted its maximum influence upon peoples outside Europe. The present chapter will attempt a description of European civilization in these years, the next chapter an account of the world-wide ascendancy which Europe enjoyed at this time.

For Europe and the European world the years 1871 to 1914 were marked by hitherto unparalleled material and industrial growth, international peace, domestic stability, the advance of constitutional, representative, and democratic government, and continued faith in science, reason, and progress. But in these very years, in politics, economics, and basic thinking there were forces operating to undermine the liberal premises and tenets of this European civilization. Most of the present chapter will be devoted to the continuing triumphs of liberalism, but the signs of its transformation and wane will be pointed out too.

Chapter Emblem: A painting called "The Last of England," dated 1852, by Ford Madox Brown, showing two emigrants looking back from their departing ship.

70. THE "CIVILIZED WORLD"

Materialistic and Nonmaterialistic Ideals

With the extension of the nation-state system Europe was politically more divided than ever. Its unity lay in the sharing by all Europeans of a similar way of life and outlook, which existed also in such "European" countries as the United States, Australia, and New Zealand. Europe and its offshoots constituted the "civilized world." Other regions—Africa, China, India, the up-country of Peru—were said to be "backward." (They are today referred to as "less developed.") Europeans were extremely conscious and inordinately proud of their civilization in the half-century before 1914. They believed it to be the well-deserved outcome of centuries of progress. Feeling themselves to be the most advanced branch of mankind in the important areas of human endeavor, they assumed that all peoples should respect the same social ideals—that so far as they were unwilling or unable to adopt them they were backward, and that so far as they did adopt them they became civilized in their turn.

These ideals of civilization were in part materialistic. If Europeans considered their civilization to be better in 1900 than in 1800, or better in 1900 than the ways of non-Europeans at the same time, it was because they had a higher standard of living, ate and dressed more adequately, slept in softer beds, and had more satisfactory sanitary facilities. It was because they possessed ocean liners, railroads, and streetcars, and after about 1880 telephones and electric lights. But the ideal of civilization was by no means exclusively materialistic. Knowledge as such, correct or truthful knowledge, was held to be a civilized attainment—scientific knowledge of nature, in place of superstition or demonology; geographical knowledge, by which civilized people were aware of the earth as a whole with its general contours and diverse inhabitants. The ideal was also profoundly moral, derived from Christianity, but now secularized and detached from religion. An Englishman, Isaac Taylor, in his *Ultimate Civilization* published in 1860, defined this moral ideal by listing the contrasting "relics of barbarism" which he thought were due to disappear—"Polygamy, Infanticide, Legalized Prostitution, Capricious Divorce, Sanguinary and Immoral Games, Infliction of Torture, Caste and Slavery." The first four of these had been unknown to the approved customs of Europe at least since the coming of Christianity. Torture went out of use about 1800, even in the illiberal European states, and legalized caste and slavery in the course of the nineteenth century. But there were few non-European peoples, in 1860, among whom two or three of Taylor's "relics" could not be found.

There are certain other indices, more purely quantitative, worked out by sociologists to show the level of advancement of a given society. One of these is the death rate, or number of persons per thousand of population who die each year. In England, France, and Sweden the "true" death rate (or death rate regardless of the proportion of infants and old people, who are most susceptible to death) is known to have fallen from about 25 before 1850, to 19 in 1914 and 18 in the 1930s. Indeed, before the Second World War, it stood seemingly stabilized at about 18 in all countries of northwestern Europe, the United States, and the British dominions. Death rates in countries not "modern" run over 40 even in favorable times. A closely related index is infant mortality, which fell rapidly after 1870 in all countries affected by medical science. Thus a woman under civilized conditions had to go through pregnancy and childbirth less often to produce the same number of surviving children. Another index is life expectancy, or the number of years of age which a person has an even chance of attaining. In England the expectation of life at birth rose from 40 years in the 1840s to 59 in 1933 and 69 in 1970. In India in 1931 it was less than 27 years. It had risen to about 42 in 1970. Still another index is the literacy rate, or proportion of persons above a certain age (such as ten) able to read and write. In northwestern Europe by 1900 the literacy rate approached 100. In some countries it still does not rise very far above zero. A further basic index is the productivity of labor, or amount produced by one worker in a given expenditure of time. This is difficult to compute, especially for earlier periods for which statistical data are lacking. In the 1930s, however, the productivity of a farmer in Denmark was over ten times that of a farmer in Albania. All northwestern Europe was above the European average in this respect with the exception of Ireland, whereas Ireland, Spain, Portugal, Italy, and all eastern Europe were below it.

The essence of civilized living doubtless is in the intangibles, in the way in which people use their minds, and in the attitudes they form toward others or toward the conduct and planning of their own lives. The intangibles, however, are not always agreed upon by persons of different culture or ideology. On the quantitative criteria there is less disagreement; all, with few exceptions, wish to lower the death rate, raise the literacy rate, and increase the productivity of human exertion. Even if we apply quantitative or sociological indices alone, we can say that after 1870 there was in fact, and not merely in the opinion of Europeans, a civilized world of which Europe was the center.

The "Zones" of Civilization

Or rather, a certain region of Europe was the center. For there were really two Europes, an inner zone and an outer. A Frenchman writing in the 1920s, describing the two Europes that had risen since 1870, called the inner zone the "Europe of steam," and bounded it by an imaginary line joining Glasgow, Stockholm, Danzig, Trieste, Florence, and Barcelona. It included not only Great Britain but Belgium, Germany, France, northern Italy, and the western portions of the Austrian Empire. Virtually all heavy European industry was located in this zone.

TRAIN IN THE SNOW
by Claude Monet (French, 1840–1926)

With the Impressionists, and notably with Claude Monet, some of the conventions of Western painting since the Renaissance began to fade. Emphasis shifted from the representation of objects to the perception of them as experienced through the eye. Solid masses melted into the play of light under a variety of atmospheric conditions. The railway age, which developed rapidly in Monet's youth, furnished many subjects to excite his imagination. In this picture the solid iron of the locomotive merges into the indeterminate grays of a dull day in winter. The chill and the low visibility are conveyed as much as the visual images themselves. Courtesy of the Musée Marmottan, Paris (Giraudon). Permission S.P.A.D.E.M. 1970 by French Reproduction Rights, Inc.

Here the railway network was thickest. Here was concentrated the wealth of Europe, in the form both of a high living standard and of accumulations of capital. Here likewise were almost all the laboratories and all the scientific activity of Europe. Here, in the same zone, lay the strength of constitutional and parliamentary government and of liberal, humanitarian, socialist, and reformist movements of many kinds. In this zone the death rate was low, life expectancy high, conditions of health and sanitation at their best, literacy almost universal, productivity of labor very great. To the same zone, for practical purposes, belonged certain regions of European settlement overseas, especially the northeastern part of the United States.

The "outer zone" included most of Ireland, most of the Iberian and Italian peninsulas, and all Europe east of what was then Germany, Bohemia, and Austria proper. The outer zone was agricultural, though the productivity of agriculture, per farm worker or per acre, was far less than in the inner zone. The people were poorer, more illiterate, and more likely to die young. The wealthy were landlords, often absentees. The zone lived increasingly after 1870 by selling grain, livestock, wool, or lumber to the more industrialized inner zone but was too poor to purchase many manufactured products in return. To obtain capital it borrowed in London or Paris. Its social and political philosophies were characteristically imported from Germany and the West. It borrowed engineers and technicians from the first zone to build its bridges and install its telegraph systems and sent its youth to universities in the first zone to study medicine or other professions. Many areas of European settlement overseas, for example in Latin America and the southern part of the United States, may also be thought of as belonging to this outer zone.

Beyond the European world lay a third zone, the immense reaches of Asia and Africa, all "backward" by the standards of Europe, with the exception of the recently Europeanized Japan, and all destined, with the exception of Japan, to become heavily dependent upon Europe in the half-century after 1870. Much of the world's history since 1870 could be written as the story of relations among these three zones; but it is necessary in all human things to guard against formulas that are too simple.

71. BASIC DEMOGRAPHY: THE INCREASE OF THE EUROPEANS

European and World Population Growth, 1650–1975

All continents except Africa grew enormously in population in the three centuries following 1650, but it was Europe that grew the most. There is little doubt that the proportion of Europeans in the world's total reached its maximum for all time between 1850 and the Second World War. Estimates are given in the following table, beginning with 1650.

The causes of sudden rise in world population after 1650 are not known. Some of them must obviously have operated in Asia as well as Europe. All students agree in attributing the increase to falling death rates rather than to increasing birth rates. Populations grew because more people lived longer, not because more

ESTIMATED POPULATION OF THE WORLD BY CONTINENTAL AREAS

	1650	1750	1850	1900	1950	1975
	MILLIONS					
Europe	100	140	266	401	532	667
United States and Canada	1	1	26	81	166	237
Australasia-Oceania	2	2	2	6	13	21
Predominantly "European"	103	143	294	488	711	925
Latin America	12	11	33	63	162	323
Africa	100	95	95	120	217	399
Asia	330	479	749	937	1,396	2,349
Predominantly "Non-European"	442	585	877	1,120	1,775	3,071
World Total	545	728	1,171	1,608	2,486	3,996
	PERCENTAGES					
Europe	18.3	19.2	22.7	24.9	21.5	16.6
United States and Canada	.2	.1	2.3	5.1	6.7	5.9
Australasia-Oceania	.4	.3	.2	.4	.5	.5
Predominantly "European"	18.9	19.6	25.2	30.4	28.7	23.0
Latin America	2.2	1.5	2.8	3.9	6.5	8.0
Africa	18.3	13.1	8.1	7.4	8.7	10.0
Asia	60.6	65.8	63.9	58.3	56.1	59.0
Predominantly "Non-European"	81.1	80.4	74.8	69.6	71.3	77.0
World Total	100.0	100.0	100.0	100.0	100.0	100.0

SOURCE: Figures for 1650–1900 are from A. N. Carr-Saunders, *World Population* (Oxford: Oxford University Press, 1936), p. 42. Those for 1950 and 1975 are from the *United Nations Demographic Yearbook*. Neither source attempts a breakdown between "Europeans" and "non-Europeans," which as presented here is significant only in very rough outline for comparative purposes. Figures for the U.S.S.R. are divided in the table between Europe and Asia. Population of the United States and Canada before the eighteenth century, and of Australasia before the nineteenth, was of course almost entirely non-European. Distinctions are further blurred when it is remembered that millions of Europeans (i.e., Russians) have long lived in the Asian parts of the U.S.S.R., that there are almost 4 million whites in South Africa, that the population of the United States has always been of both European and African descent, and that Latin America is so mixed that it could as accurately be placed, especially on cultural grounds, in the European category. For world population in the twentieth century, see also pp. 934–936.

were born. It is probable that a better preservation of civil order reduced death rates in both Asia and Europe. In Europe the organized sovereign states, as established in the seventeenth century, put an end to a long period of civil wars, stopping the chronic violence and marauding, with the accompanying insecurity of agriculture and of family life, which were more deadly than wars fought by armies between governments. Similarly, the Tokugawa kept peace in Japan, and the Manchu dynasty brought a long period of order to China. The British rule in India, and that of the Dutch in Java, by curbing famine and violence, allowed the populations to mount very rapidly. Only in Africa, where the slave trade removed over 10 million persons of the childbearing ages in three or four centuries, and where slave raiding led to intertribal warfare and the disruption of African cultures, did the growth of population fail to keep pace with the world's average. The fate of the American aborigines was somewhat the same.

In Europe, sooner than in Asia, other causes of growth were at work beyond the maintenance of civil peace. They included the liberation from certain endemic diseases, beginning with the subsiding of bubonic plague in the seventeenth century and the retreat of smallpox in the eighteenth; the improvement of agricultural output, beginning notably in England about 1750; the improvement of transportation, which, by road, canal, and railroad, made localized famine a thing of the past since food could be moved into areas of temporary shortage; and, last, the development of machine industry, which allowed large populations to subsist in Europe by trading with peoples overseas.

Consequently, while it seems that the death rate fell in Asia as well as in Europe after 1650, it fell much more substantially in Europe, and since the European birth rate long remained at a high level, the result was a tremendous swelling of population. Approximate figures are given in the preceding table. Asia, by these estimates, increased less than threefold in population between 1650 and 1900, but Europe increased fourfold, and the total number of Europeans, including the descendants of Europeans who migrated to other continents, increased almost fivefold. In 1650 the Europeans comprised only about a fifth of the world's population. In 1900 the proportion of "Europeans" on all continents was approaching a third of the human race. Since 1900 this proportion has been falling. But the ascendancy of European civilization, or roughly of the white races, in the two or three centuries after about 1650, was due in some measure to merely quantitative growth.

Stabilization of European Population

This advantage of a higher growth rate began to disappear in the middle of the twentieth century. As early as 1910 it was possible to anticipate that the population of Europe, or, more accurately, of the most advanced "inner zone," would soon grow less rapidly, because the children being born about 1910, who would become the parents of 1940, were not sufficiently numerous to maintain growth at the birth rates which then existed. At the same time death rates began to fall dramatically in Asia. With a large population base to begin with, non-Europeans by the mid–twentieth century were multiplying faster than Europeans.

Stabilization and relative decline of European population followed from a fall in the birth rate. We have seen how the persistence of high birth rates, while death rates fell, accounted for a long period of rapid expansion. But European birth rates began to fall about 1880. As early as 1830 they began noticeably to drop in France, with the result that France, long the most populous European state, was surpassed in population by Russia in the eighteenth century, by Germany about 1870, by the British Isles about 1895, and by Italy about 1930. France, once thought to be decadent for this reason, was in fact only the leading country in a population cycle through which the European countries seemed to pass. The birth rate, which had fallen below 30 per 1,000 in France in the 1830s, fell to that level in Sweden in the 1880s, in England in the 1890s, and in Germany, Bohemia, and the Netherlands between 1900 and 1910. After the Second World

War there was a temporary rise, but by 1970 the birth rate seemed stabilized at about 17 per 1,000 in most European countries and in the Soviet Union, as well as in the United States.

The reduced birth rate is not a mere dry statistical item, nor does it affect populations merely in the mass. It is one of the indices of modern civilization, first appearing in that inner European zone in which the other indices were also highest, and thence spreading outward in a kind of wave. Concretely, a low birth rate means that families average from two to four children, where in former times, or today under conditions not "modern," families are commonly found to consist of ten children or even more. The low birth rate means the small family system, than which few things are more fundamental to modern life. The principal means used to hold down the birth rate, or to limit the family, is the practice of contraception. But the true causes, or reasons why parents wish to limit their families, are deeply embedded in the codes of modern society.

Historical demographers have detected a "European family pattern" as far back as the seventeenth century. It was a pattern in which, in comparison to other societies, Europeans married later, and a larger number never married at all. Late marriage shortened the number of years during which a woman bore children, and enabled young people to acquire skills or accumulate savings (as in tools and household goods) before setting up new families. The effect was a less explosive population growth, and less extreme poverty, than occurred in some other parts of the world. Evidence indicating the practice of contraception can be found in the eighteenth century among the upper classes, by study of the number and spacing of their children. The practice seems to have spread to other social classes during the French Revolution. The Code Napoleon then required that inheritances be divided among all sons and daughters. The French peasants, many of them owners of land, began to limit themselves to two or three children, in order that all children (by inheritance, marriage, and dowries) might remain in as high an economic and social position as their parents. It was thus economic security and the possession of a social standard that led to the reduced birth rate in France.

In the great cities of the nineteenth century, in which standards of life for the working classes often collapsed, the effect might at first be a proliferation of offspring. But life in the city, under crowded conditions of housing, also set a premium on the small family. There were many activities in the city that people with many children could only with difficulty enjoy. After about 1880 child labor became much less frequent among the working classes. When children ceased to earn part of the family income parents tended to have fewer of them. About the same time governments in the advanced countries began to require universal compulsory schooling. The number of years spent in education, and hence in economic dependency upon parents, grew longer and longer, until it became common even for young adults to be still engaged in study. Each child represented many years of expense for its parents. The ever rising idea of what it was necessary to do for one's children, and the desire of parents to give them every possible advantage in a competitive world, were probably the most basic causes of voluntary limitation of the family. Hardly less basic was the desire to lighten the burdens upon mothers. The small family system, together with the decline of infant mortality, since they combined to free women from the interminable bear-ing and tending of infants, probably did more than anything else to improve the position of civilized women.

But the effects of the small family system upon total population became mani-fest only slowly. More people lived on into the middle and older age groups, and the fall of the birth rate was gradual, so that in all the leading countries total numbers continued to rise, except in France, which hardly grew between 1900 and 1945. The persistent note was one of superabundant increase. In five genera-tions, between 1800 and 1950, some 200 million "Europeans" grew into 700 mil-lion. Since productivity increased even more rapidly, the standard of living for most of these "Europeans" rose in spite of the increase of numbers, and there was no general problem of overpopulation.

Growth of Cities and Urban Life

Where did so many people go? Some stayed in the rural areas where most people had always lived. Rural populations in the "inner zone" became more dense, turning to the more intensive agriculture of truck gardening or dairy farming, leaving products like wool and cereal grains to be raised elsewhere and then imported. But it is estimated that of every seven persons added to the western European population only one stayed on the land. Of the other six, one left Europe altogether and five went to the growing cities.[1]

The modern city is mostly the child of the railroad, for with the railroads it became possible for the first time to concentrate manufacturing in large towns, to which bulky goods such as foods and fuel could now be moved in great volume. The growth of cities between 1850 and 1914 was phenomenal. In England two-thirds of the people lived in places of 20,000 or less in 1830; in 1914 two-thirds lived in places of 20,000 or more. Germany, the historic land of archaic towns carried over from the Middle Ages, rivaled England after 1870 in modern indus-trial urbanization. Whereas in 1840 only London and Paris had a million people, the same could be said by 1914 of Berlin, Vienna, St. Petersburg, and Moscow.[2] Some places, like the English Midlands and the Ruhr valley in Germany, became a mass of contiguous smaller cities, vast urban agglomerations divided only by municipal lines.

The great city set the tone of modern society. City life was impersonal and anonymous; people were uprooted, less tied to home or church than in the coun-try. They lacked the country person's feeling of deference for aristocratic families. They lacked the sense of self-help characteristic of older rural communities. The hungry, the jobless, the miserable could expect little comfort from neighbors. It was in the city that the daily newspaper press, which spread rapidly in the wake of the telegraph after 1850, found its most habitual readers. The so-called yellow or sensational press appeared about 1900. Articulate public opinion was formed in the cities, and city people were on the whole disrespectful of tradition, recep-tive to new ideas, having in many cases deliberately altered their own lives by moving from the country or from smaller towns. That socialism spread among the

[1] See Appendix III for the growth of cities and the map on p. 424 for England.
[2] And, outside Europe, of New York, Chicago, Philadelphia, Rio de Janeiro, Buenos Aires, Calcutta, Tokyo, and Osaka.

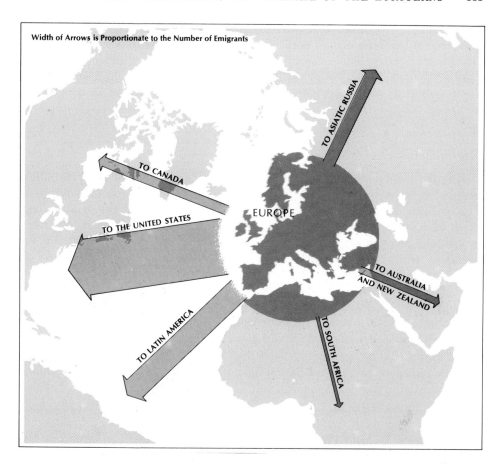

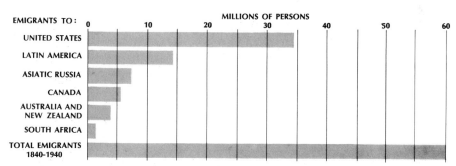

MIGRATION FROM EUROPE, 1840–1940

Over 60 million people left Europe in the century preceding the Second World War,
distributing themselves as shown in the diagram above. (See figures on p. 552.) About
half went to the United States. This huge wave of settlement built up, outside of Europe,
populous "European" countries which produced foods and raw materials for Europe
and borrowed capital and bought manufactures from Europe, thus helping to support
the increasingly dense European population and to build up a world-wide economic
system.

industrial masses of European cities is hardly surprising. It is less often realized that some of the more blatant nationalism that arose after 1870 was stimulated by city life, for people felt increasingly detached from all institutions except the state. At the same time city life, by its greater facilities for schooling, reading, and discussion, made for a more alert and informed public opinion of an enlightened kind.

Migration from Europe, 1840–1940

During the same period in which the cities were rising, approximately 60 million people left Europe altogether, of whom possibly a fifth sooner or later returned. This Atlantic Migration—aptly so called, because all crossed the ocean except those who moved from European to Asiatic Russia—towers above all other historical migrations in magnitude, and possibly also in significance, for it was the means by which earlier colonial offshoots of Europeans were transformed into new Europes alongside the old. All parts of Europe contributed, as is shown in the table below, which comprises the years from 1846 to 1932. Before 1846 the movement had scarcely begun, though over a million immigrants had entered the United States at that time since the close of the Napoleonic wars. After 1932 it was greatly reduced, except into Soviet Asia.

The British and Irish (inseparable in the statistical records) went to the British dominions and to the United States. The Italians divided between the United States and Latin America. Spaniards settled overwhelmingly in the Spanish Amer-

MIGRATION FROM EUROPE,* 1846–1932

FROM:		
	Great Britain and Ireland	18,000,000
	Italy	10,100,000
	Russia†	9,200,000
	Austria-Hungary	5,200,000
	Germany	4,900,000
	Spain	4,700,000
	Portugal	1,800,000
	Sweden	1,200,000
	Norway	850,000
	Poland‡	640,000
	France	520,000
	Denmark	390,000
	Finland	370,000
	Switzerland	330,000
	Holland	220,000
	Belgium	190,000
	Total	58,610,000

* Carr-Saunders, *World Population*, pp. 49 and 56.
† Including 7 million from European to Asiatic Russia up to 1914 only. It is thought that 3 million went from European to Asiatic parts of the U.S.S.R. between 1926 and 1939.
‡ 1920–1932 only. Previous Polish emigration included under Russia, Germany, and Austria-Hungary.

ican republics, and Portuguese in Brazil. The Germans moved overwhelmingly to the United States, though some went to Argentina and Brazil. The new countries received the following influxes of people:

IMMIGRATION INTO OTHER COUNTRIES
FROM EUROPE*

TO:	United States	34,000,000
	Asiatic Russia (to 1914 only)	7,000,000
	Argentina	6,400,000
	Canada	5,200,000
	Brazil	4,400,000
	Australia	2,900,000
	Cuba	860,000
	South Africa	852,000
	Uruguay	713,000
	New Zealand	594,000

* Carr-Saunders, *World Population*, p. 49.

The extraordinary preponderance of the United States is apparent. At the same time, it is well to rectify the impressions of most Americans on the subject. Almost half the European migration was directed elsewhere than to the United States. Asiatic Russia was second only to the United States in the receipt of new settlers. Germany was by no means a chief source of emigration, especially in proportion to total national population from which emigrants came. Canada received fewer immigrants than Argentina, Australia fewer than Brazil, New Zealand fewer than Uruguay. The new worlds were not peculiarly Anglo-Saxon.

The exodus from Europe was due to a remarkable and temporary juxtaposition of causes. One fundamental cause, or precondition, was that before 1914 the new countries welcomed immigration. Hands were wanted to farm the land, build houses, dig in the mines. This was least true of Australia and New Zealand, which preferred to limit themselves to English-speaking settlers, and which also pioneered as social democracies, becoming models, even before 1900, of legislation to protect the working classes. One result was that no inrush of outsiders to compete for jobs at low wages was desired. A similar combination of national preferences and labor protectionism led to laws restricting immigration in the United States in 1921 and 1924. Thereafter immigrants could enter only under quotas, and the quotas were lowest for eastern and southern Europe from which most emigration was then forthcoming.

In Europe there were many conditions propelling emigrants outward. Physically, the steamship made it easier and cheaper to cross the sea, and the railroad helped people to get to the ports as well as to distribute themselves after landing in the new countries. Economically, people in the mass could for the first time afford a long journey. People migrated to improve their material circumstances; but the great crests in the wave of emigration coincided with crests in the business cycle in Europe, when jobs in Europe were plentiful and wages at their highest. Of the opposite case, of actual flight from economic ruin or starvation, the emigration from Ireland after 1846 is the best example. After the revolutions of 1848 a certain number left Europe for political reasons, and, later on, to avoid compulsory military service. The best example of flight from actual persecution is that of the Jews of Russia and Russian Poland, of whom a million and a half moved to the United States in the fifteen years preceding the First World War.

But perhaps most basic in the whole European exodus was the underlying liberalism of the age. Never before (nor since) had people been legally so free to move. Old laws requiring skilled workmen to stay in their own countries were repealed, as in England in 1824.[3] The old semicommunal agricultural villages, with collective rights and obligations, holding the individual to his native group, fell into disuse except in Russia. The disappearance of serfdom allowed the peasant of eastern Europe to change his residence without obtaining a lord's permission.[4] Governments permitted their subjects to emigrate, to take with them their savings of shillings, marks, kronen, or lire, and to change nationality by becoming naturalized in their new homes. The rise of individual liberty in Europe, as well as the hope of enjoying it in America, made possible the great emigration. For so huge a mass movement the most remarkable fact is that it took place by individual initiative and at individual expense. Individuals and family groups (to borrow the metaphor of one authority) detached themselves atom by atom from the mass of Europe, crossed the seas on their own, and reattached themselves atom by atom to the accumulating mass of the New World.

72. THE WORLD ECONOMY OF THE NINETEENTH CENTURY

How did the swelling population of Europeans manage to feed itself? How, in fact, did it not merely feed itself but enjoy an incomparably higher standard of living in 1900 than in 1800? By science, industry, transportation, and communications. And by organization—in business, finance, and labor.

The "New Industrial Revolution"

The Industrial Revolution entered upon a new phase. The use of steam power, the growth of the textile and metallurgical industries, and the advent of the railroad had characterized the early part of the century. Now, after 1870, new sources of power were tapped, the already mechanized industries expanded, new industries appeared, and industry spread geographically.

The steam engine itself was refined and improved. By 1914 it still predominated over other power machinery, but electricity with its incomparable advantages came into use. The invention of the internal combustion (or gasoline) engine and the diesel engine gave the world automobiles, airplanes, and submarines in the two decades before 1914; the advent of the automotive and aviation industries made oil one of the most coveted of natural resources. In the new chemical industries industrial research laboratories were replacing the individual inventor. Chemists discovered new fertilizers, and from coal tar alone produced a bewildering array of new products ranging from artificial food flavors to high explosives. With the latter the first great tunnels were built, the Mount Cenis in 1873, the Simplon in 1906—both in the Alps; and great new canals, the

---

3 See p. 452.
4 See pp. 472, 481.

CLASSIC LANDSCAPE
by Charles Sheeler (American, 1883–1965)

This landscape depicts the River Rouge plant of the Ford Motor Company in 1931, but it also symbolizes what has been called the Second Industrial Revolution, in which electricity, the internal combustion engine, and the automobile were important, and industry spread beyond its original centers in Britain and Western Europe. The picture is "classic" in its clear delineation, its array of familiar mathematical forms, and the universality of its message. The plant seems rational and precise, but the absence of human beings is to be noted; it is as if the machine had a life of its own and could do without human hands. The sharp shadows suggest bright sunshine, despite the smoke pouring from the tall chimney. When the picture was painted no one was alarmed about atmospheric pollution. Courtesy of Mrs. Edsel B. Ford.

Suez in 1869, the Kiel in 1895, the Panama in 1914. Chemistry made possible the production of synthetic fabrics like rayon which revolutionized the textile industry. Electricity transformed all indoor and outdoor lighting. There was a communications revolution too. The telephone appeared in the 1870s. Marconi brought the continents closer together, successfully transmitting wireless signals across the Atlantic in 1901. The moving picture and the radio modestly presented themselves before 1914. Medicine ran a tongue-twisting alphabetical gamut from anesthetics to x-rays; yellow fever was overcome. Vastly improved processes for refining iron ore made possible a great expansion in the production of steel, the key product of the new industrial age; aluminum and other metal alloys were also being produced. Railroad mileage multiplied; the European network, including the Russian, increased from 140,000 miles in 1890 to 213,000 in 1914.

In the new phase of the Industrial Revolution machine industry spread geographically from Britain and Belgium, the only truly industrial countries in 1870, to France, Italy, Russia, Japan, and, most markedly, to Germany and the United States. In Europe industrial production was concentrated in the "inner zone." Three powers alone—Britain, Germany, and France—accounted in 1914 for more than seven-tenths of all European manufactures and produced over four-fifths of all European coal, steel, and machinery. Of the major European powers Germany was now forging ahead. To use steel alone as a criterion, in 1871 Germany was producing annually three-fifths as much steel as Britain; by 1900 it was producing more, and by 1914 it was producing twice as much as Britain—but only half as much as the new industrial giant, the United States. By 1914 American steel output was greater than that of Germany, Britain, and France combined. Britain, the pioneer in mechanization, was being outstripped in both the old world and the new. The three European powers increased their industrial production by about 50 percent in the two decades before 1914, but the United States had a far higher annual growth rate from 1870 to 1913, 4.3 percent as compared to the next leading powers, Germany with 2.9 percent, Britain with 2.2 percent, and France with 1.6 percent.[5] By 1914 the United States had moved ahead of Europe in the mechanization of agriculture, in manufactures, and in coal and steel production, in which it was producing over two-fifths of the world's output. The Americans were pioneering also in assembly-line, conveyor-belt techniques for the mass production of automobiles and all kinds of consumer goods.

Free Trade and the European "Balance of Payments"

It was Britain in the mid–nineteenth century, then the workshop of the world, that had inaugurated the movement toward free trade. It will be recalled that in 1846, by the repeal of the Corn Laws, the British embarked upon a systematic free trade policy, deliberately choosing to become dependent upon overseas imports for their food.[6] France adopted free trade in 1860.[7] Other countries soon followed. It is true that by 1880 there was a movement back to protective tariffs, except in Britain, Holland, and Belgium. But the tariffs were impediments rather

5 *The New Cambridge Modern History*, Volume XII, rev. ed. (Cambridge: Cambridge University Press, 1968), p. 40.
6 See pp. 456–457.
7 See pp. 491–492.

than barriers, and until 1914 the characteristic of the economic system was the extreme mobility of goods across political frontiers. Politically, Europe was more than ever nationalistic; but economic activity, under generally liberal conditions in which business was supposed to be free from the political state, remained predominantly international and globe-encircling.

Broadly speaking, the great economic accomplishment of Europe before 1914 was to create a system by which the huge imports used by industrial Europe could be acquired and paid for. All European countries except Russia, Austria-Hungary, and the Balkan states imported more than they exported. It was the British again that had led in this direction. Britain had been a predominantly importing country since the close of the eighteenth century. That is to say, despite the expanding export of cotton manufactures and other products of the Industrial Revolution, Britain consumed more goods from abroad than it sent out. Industrialization and urbanization in the nineteenth century confirmed the same situation. Between 1800 and 1900 the value of British exports multiplied eightfold, but the value of imports into Great Britain multiplied tenfold, and in the decade before 1914 the British had an import surplus of about three-quarters of a billion dollars a year. Great Britain and the industrial countries of Europe together (roughly Europe's "inner zone"), at the beginning of the twentieth century, were drawing in an import surplus, measured in dollars, of almost $2 billion every year (the dollar then representing far more goods than it came to represent later). The imports into Europe's inner zone consisted of raw materials for its industries and of food and amenities for its people.

How were the imports paid for? How did Europe enjoy a favorable "balance of payments" despite an unfavorable balance of trade in commodities? Export of European manufactures paid for some imports, and even most, but not all. It was the so-called invisible exports that made up the difference, that is, shipping and insurance services rendered to foreigners, and interest on money lent out or invested, all bringing in foreign exchange. Shipping and insurance were important. An Argentine merchant in Buenos Aires, to ship hides to Germany, might employ a British vessel; he would pay the freight charges in Argentine pesos, which might be credited to the account of the British shipowner in an Argentine bank; the British shipowner would sell the pesos to someone, in England or elsewhere in Europe, who needed them to buy Argentine meat. The far-flung British merchant marine thus earned a considerable amount of the food and raw materials needed by Britain. To insure themselves against risks of every conceivable kind people all over the world turned to Lloyds of London. With the profits drawn from selling insurance the British could buy what they wished. Governments or business enterprises borrowed money in Europe, mainly in England; the interest payments, putting foreign currencies into European and British hands, constituted another invisible export by which an excess of imports could be financed. But the lending of money to foreigners is only part of a larger phenomenon, the export of capital.

The Export of European Capital

The migration of millions of Europeans had the effect of creating new societies, basically European in character, which both purchased manufactures from Europe and produced the food, wool, cotton, and minerals that Europe needed. It could not have had this effect if Europe had exported people only, especially people of such small means as most emigrants were. Europe also exported the capital necessary to get the new settlers and the new worlds into production.

The export of capital meant that an older and wealthier country, instead of using its whole annual income to raise its own standard of living, or to add to its own capital by expanding or improving its houses, factories, machinery, mines, transportation, etc., diverted some of its income to expanding or improving the houses, factories, machinery, mines, and transportation of foreign countries. It meant that British, French, Dutch, Belgian, Swiss, and eventually German investors in the desire to increase their income bought the stocks of foreign business enterprises and the bonds of foreign businesses and government; or they organized companies of their own to operate in foreign climes; or their banks granted loans to banks in New York or Tokyo, which then lent the funds to local users. Capital arose in Europe to some extent from the savings of quite small people, especially in France, where peasants and modest bourgeois families were notably thrifty. But most capital accumulated from savings by the well-to-do. The owners of a business concern, for example, instead of spending the concern's income by paying higher wages, took a portion of it in profits or dividends, and instead of spending all this on their own living, reinvested part of it in domestic or foreign enterprises. The gap between rich and poor was thus one cause of the rapid accumulation of capital, though the accumulation of capital, in the nineteenth century, produced in turn a steady rise of living standards for the working classes. In a sense, however, the common people of western Europe, by foregoing the better housing, diet, education, or pleasures that a more democratic or consumer-oriented society might have planned for them, made possible the export of capital and hence the financing and building up of other regions of the world.

The British were the chief exporters of capital, followed at some distance by the French, and at the close of the century by the Germans. As early as the 1840s half the annual increase of wealth in Great Britain was going into foreign investments. By 1914 the British had $20 billion in foreign investments, the French about $8.7 billion, the Germans about $6 billion. A quarter of all the wealth owned by the inhabitants of Great Britain consisted in 1914 of holdings outside the country. Almost a sixth of the French national wealth lay in investments outside of France. All three countries had given hostages to fortune, and fortune proved unkind, for in the First World War the British lost about a quarter of their foreign investments, the French about a third, the Germans all.

These huge sums, pouring out from Europe's inner zone for a century before 1914, at first went mainly to finance the Americas and the less affluent regions of Europe.[8] No country except Great Britain completely built its railways with its own resources. In the United States the railway system was built very largely with capital obtained from England. In central and eastern Europe British companies often constructed the first railways, then sold out to native operating companies or to governments which subsequently ran them. In the Argentine Republic the British not merely financed and built the railways, but continued thereafter to operate and own them. In addition, up to 1914 the British sold about

[8] The penetration of European capital into Asia and Africa, after about 1890, is considered in the following chapter.

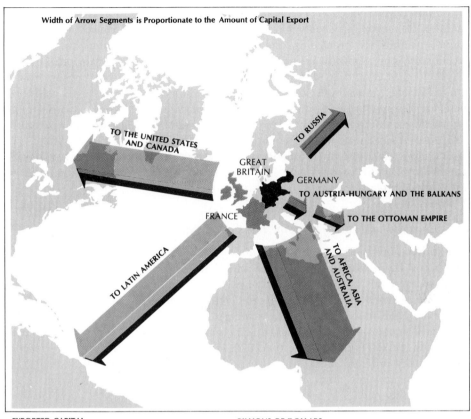

Width of Arrow Segments is Proportionate to the Amount of Capital Export

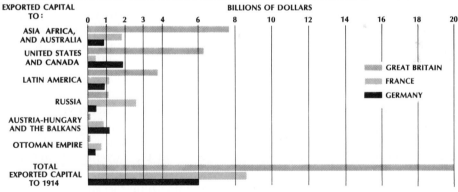

EXPORT OF EUROPEAN CAPITAL TO 1914

In 1914 the British, French, and Germans held upwards of $30 billion in foreign and colonial loans and investments, distributed as shown on the map. Dutch investments, especially in the Netherlands Indies, together with Swiss, Belgian, and Scandinavian holdings, would add several billion dollars more. Proceeds from such investments helped Europeans to pay for the excess of their imports over exports. New and undeveloped countries were built up by capital borrowed from Europe. British capital predominated in the overseas world, while the less advanced regions of eastern Europe and the Near East were financed mainly from Germany and France. Much of the investment shown on this map was lost or expended in the First World War. See pp. 678, 684.

75 million tons of coal a year to South America to keep the railways going, not to mention items for replacement and upkeep of equipment. Docks, warehouses, mines, plantations, processing and manufacturing establishments all over the world were similarly built up with capital drawn from Europe. European capital also helped emigrants in the new countries to live in a civilized fashion. In the United States, for example, state and local governments very commonly sold their bonds in Europe, to build roads, pave streets, or construct school systems for the westward-moving population. A few of these American bonds proved a partial or total loss to European investors. On the whole, by 1914, the United States had paid back a good deal of its indebtedness. Even so, in 1914, Americans still owed about $4 billion to Europeans—a sum three times as large as the national debt of the United States at the time.

An International Money System: The Gold Standard

The international economy rested upon an international money system, based in turn upon the almost universal acceptance of the gold standard. England had adopted the gold standard in 1816, when the pound sterling was legally defined as the equivalent of 113 grains of fine gold. Western Europe and the United States adopted an exclusively gold standard in the 1870s. A person holding any "civilized" money—pounds, francs, dollars, marks, etc.—could turn it into gold at will, and a person holding gold could turn it into any money. The currencies were like so many different languages all expressing the same thing. All had substantially the same value, and until 1914 the exchange rates between currencies remained highly stable. It was assumed that no civilized country's currency ever "fell"; such things might happen in Turkey or China, or in the French Revolution, but not in the world of practical men, modern progress, and civilized affairs.

The important currencies were all freely exchangeable. A Frenchman, selling silks to a German, and hence receiving German marks, could turn the marks into francs, pounds sterling, or dollars. That is, he was not obliged to buy from Germany or spend his money in Germany but could use the proceeds of his German sale to buy French, British, or American goods or services as he chose. Trade was multilateral. A country needing imports from another country, such as American cotton, did not have to sell to that country to obtain them; it could sell its own goods anywhere and then import according to its needs.

It was the acceptance of the gold standard, and the fact that all important countries possessed a sufficient share of gold to support their currencies, that made possible so fluid an interchange. At the same time the gold standard had less wholesome effects. It was hard on countries that lacked gold. And it produced a gradual fall of prices, especially between 1870 and 1900, because (until the gold discoveries in South Africa, Australia, and Alaska in the 1890s) the world's production of gold lagged behind the expanding production of industrial and agricultural goods. Persistently declining prices were a hardship to those who habitually worked with borrowed money—many farmers, many businessmen, and debtor nations as a whole. A famous speech of William Jennings Bryan in the United States in 1896, declaring that mankind should not be crucified "upon this cross of gold," expressed a restlessness that was world-wide. But falling prices were an advantage to the wage-earning class, which generally improved its position in these years, and also to the wealthy, the owners and lenders of capital, the bankers and financiers, who so long as prices were falling were repaid in money of more value than that which they had lent.

The center of the global economic and financial system was London. The London banks came forward in consequence of the defeat of Napoleon, the older financial centers in Amsterdam having been ruined in the Revolutionary and Napoleonic wars. It may be recalled also that the victors in 1815 imposed upon France an indemnity of 700 million francs, which in 1818 was taken over by a syndicate of private bankers; the London banks played a leading part in this affair and so developed their connections with many government treasuries.[9] In the Crimean War of 1854–1856, with England at war with Russia, the London banks floated loans for the Russian government—so independent were business and politics at the time. The early adoption of the gold standard in England meant that many people, British and foreign, kept their funds in the form of sterling on deposit in London, where quantities of available capital therefore accumulated.

The banks, too, grew up in the financing of the British export trade, itself borne on the tide of the Industrial Revolution. A small Lancashire manufacturer, for example, might receive an order for a gross of scissors from an unknown merchant in Trieste. He would draw a bill or "sight draft" against the Trieste merchant, and take this bill to a financial institution known as an acceptance house. The acceptance house, which in the course of its business had acquired a microscopic knowledge of the credit of thousands of individuals and firms in all parts of the world, would then "discount" the bill, giving cash to the Lancashire manufacturer and collecting from the Trieste merchant through international banking channels. In this way the bank took a burden off the British manufacturer, and extended short-term credit to foreigners for the purchase of British goods. Many acceptance houses gradually went into the business of long-term foreign lending also. London became the apex of a pyramid which had the world for its base. It was the main center of exchange of currencies, the clearinghouse of the world's debts, the depository from which all the world borrowed, the banker's bank, the insurance man's resort for reinsurance, as well as the world's shipping center and the headquarters of many international corporations.

A World Market: Unity, Competition—and Insecurity

Never had the earth been so unified economically, with each region playing its due role in a global specialization. Western Europe, and in 1870 mainly Great Britain, was the world's industrial workshop. Other parts of the earth supplied its many needs. An English economist marveled in 1866 that Britain now had its granaries in Chicago and Odessa, its forests in Canada and the Baltic, its sheep farms in Australia, and its gold and silver mines in California and Peru, while drinking tea brought from China and coffee from East Indian plantations. The same could have been said of most of Europe's "inner zone" by the time of the First World War.

A true world market had been created. Goods, services, money, capital, people moved back and forth almost without regard to national boundaries. Articles

9 See p. 442.

were bought and sold at uniform world prices. Dealers in wheat, for example, followed prices in Minneapolis, Liverpool, Buenos Aires, and Danzig as reported by telegraph and cable from day to day. They bought where it was cheapest, and sold where it was dearest. In this way the world's wheat supply was distributed roughly according to need or ability to pay. The worker of Milan, if the Italian crop was poor and prices high, was fed from another source. On the other hand, the Italian wheat grower would in this case feel the pinch of world competition. The world market, while it organized the world into a unified economic system, at the same time brought distant regions into competition for the first time. The producer—whether businessman, factory employee, farmer, or coffee planter—had no secure outlet for his product, as had generally been true in the past. He was in competition not only with the man across the street or down the road, but with the world.

The creation of an integrated world market, the financing and building up of countries outside of Europe, and the consequent feeding and support of Europe's increasing population were the great triumphs of the nineteenth-century system of unregulated capitalism. The system was intricate, with thousands and even millions of individuals and business firms supplying each other's wants without central planning. But it was extremely precarious, and the position of most people in it was exceedingly vulnerable. Region competed against region, and person against person. A fall of grain prices in the American Middle West, besides ruining a few speculators, might oblige the Prussian or Argentine wheat grower to sell at a price at which he could not live. A factory owner might be driven out of business if his competitor successfully undersold him or if a new commodity made his own product obsolete. The workingman, hired only when needed by an employer, faced unemployment when business slackened, or the permanent disappearance of his job by the next labor-saving invention. The system went through cycles of boom and depression, the most notable example of the latter being the long depression that set in about 1873 and lasted to about 1893. It rested on expansion and on credit; but sometimes people could not pay their debts, so that credit collapsed, and sometimes expansion failed to keep pace with expectations, and anticipated profits proved to be losses. To combat the essential insecurity of private capitalism, all manner of devices were resorted to. Governments adopted protective tariffs on the one hand and social insurance and welfare legislation on the other; trade unionism and socialist movements grew; business mergers took place. These and other measures, to which we shall return, signalized the gradual decline in the years after 1880 of nineteenth-century unregulated, laissez-faire capitalism.

Changes in Organization: Big Business

A great change came over capitalism itself about 1880 or 1890. Formerly characterized by a very large number of very small units, small businesses run by individuals, partnerships, or small companies, it was increasingly characterized by large and impersonal corporations. The attractions of the "limited liability" corporation as a form of business organization and as a means of encouraging investment arose from laws, enacted by most countries in the nineteenth century, which limited the individual investor's personal loss in the event of a bankruptcy to the amount of his shares of stock in the enterprise. The corporation, in its modern form appearing first with the railroads, became the usual form of organization for industry and commerce. As machinery grew more complicated only a large pool of capital could finance it. And as corporations grew in size and number, relying on the sale of stock and the issue of bonds, the influence of banking and financial circles was enhanced. Financiers, using not so much their own money as the savings of others, had a new power to create or to extinguish, to stimulate, discourage, or combine corporate enterprises in various industries. Industrial capitalism brought finance capitalism with it.[10]

Corporate organization made it possible to concentrate economic processes under unified management. In retail commerce, large department stores appeared about 1890 in the United States and France. In industry, steel offers a good example. Steel became in any case a big business when heavy blast furnaces were introduced. It was not safe for the steel business, or for the blast furnaces, to rely for iron and coal on independent producers who might sell to whomsoever they pleased. The steel works therefore began to operate mines of their own or to buy out or otherwise reduce coal and iron mines to subsidiary status. Some, to assure their markets, began to produce not merely steel but steel manufactures as well—steel ships, railway equipment, naval and military ordnance. Thus entire processes from mining to finished product became concentrated in a "vertical" integration. By "horizontal" integration concerns at the same level combined with each other to reduce competition and to protect themselves against fluctuations in prices and in markets. Some fixed prices, some agreed to restrict production, some divided up markets among themselves. They were called trusts in the United States, cartels in Europe. They were common in many of the new industries at the close of the century, such as chemicals, aluminum, and oil. In steel such combinations produced the great interests of Krupp in Germany, Schneider-Creusot in France, Vickers-Armstrong in Great Britain. It was in the United States that such big business developed furthest, headed by "captains" of industry and "titans" of finance. Andrew Carnegie, by origin a poor Scottish immigrant boy, produced more steel than all England; in 1901 he sold out to an even more colossal organization, the United States Steel Corporation, formed by the financier J. P. Morgan. It was in the United States, too, that concern over monopoly and the power of big business in general was felt most strongly; antitrust legislation, beginning with the Sherman Act of 1890, was enacted but never with any substantial effect.

Many of the new combinations were beneficial in making the ups and downs of business less erratic, and so providing more stable prices and more continuous and secure employment. Generally they reduced the costs of production; but whether the savings went into higher profits, higher wages, or lower prices depended on numerous factors. Some trusts were more greedy than others or confronted with only weakly organized or unorganized labor. In any case, for good or ill, decisions rested with management and finance. A new kind of private power had arisen, which its critics liked to call "feudal." Since no economic system had ever been so centralized up to that time, never in fact had so few people exercised so much economic power over so many. The middle class, with the rise of great corporations, came typically to consist of salaried employees; the salaried man

[10] See pp. 490–491, 532–533.

might spend a lifetime with the same company, and feel toward it, in its disputes with labor or government, a loyalty not unlike that of a lord's retainer in feudal times. The laboring class was less amenable; labor attempted to organize unions capable of dealing with increasingly gigantic employers. It also after about 1880 played an increasingly decisive role in the politics of all advanced nations.

73. THE ADVANCE OF DEMOCRACY: THIRD FRENCH REPUBLIC, UNITED KINGDOM, GERMAN EMPIRE

In the years from 1815 to 1870 European political life had been marked by liberal agitation for constitutional government, representative assemblies, responsible ministries, and guarantees of individual liberties. In the years from 1871 to 1914, even where these liberal objectives were not fully achieved but remained as goals, the most notable political development was the democratic extension of the vote to the working class—the adoption of universal male suffrage, which in turn meant for the first time the creation of mass political parties and the need for political leaders to appeal to a wide electorate. The extension of the suffrage in these years did not take place because of popular agitation as in the days of the Chartists or of the radical reformers in France. Governments for a variety of reasons extended the suffrage on their own. Often democratization took place in a continuing monarchical and aristocratic framework, but almost everywhere by 1914 the machinery at least of democratic self-government was being established. In addition, to counter the growing strength of socialism after 1871, and for humanitarian reasons, governments were also assuming responsibility for the so-cial and economic problems arising from industrialism. The welfare state in its modern form was taking shape.

France: The Establishment of the Third Republic

In France the democratic republic was not easily established, and its troubled early years left deep cleavages within the country. It will be recalled that in September 1870, when the empire of Napoleon III revealed its helplessness in the Franco-Prussian War, insurrectionaries in Paris, as in 1792 and 1848, again pro-claimed the Republic.[11] A provisional government of national defense sought desperately to continue the war, but the cause was hopeless. By January 1871, a bitter siege of Paris came to an end and an armistice was signed. Bismarck, insisting that only a properly constituted government could make peace, per-mitted the election, by universal male suffrage, of a National Assembly which was to consider his peace terms and draft a constitution for the new French state. When the elections were held in February, it was found, as in 1848 (and, indeed, 1797), that republicanism was so distrusted by the French people as a whole, and most especially in the provinces and rural areas, that a free election brought monarchist elements into power.[12] Republicanism was still thought to be vio-lent—bellicose in its foreign policy, turbulent in its political workings, unfriendly to the church, and socialistic or at least equalitarian in its views of property and

11 See p. 518.
12 See pp. 373, 465.

private wealth. The new Assembly contained only about 200 republicans out of more than 600 deputies.

But the Paris republicans, who had defended France when Napoleon III failed to do so, who for four months had been besieged, starved, and frozen by the Germans, and who still refused to make peace on the harsh terms imposed by Bismarck and about to be accepted by the Assembly, refused to recognize the latter's authority. A civil war broke out between the National Assembly, now sitting at Versailles, and the city of Paris, where a revolutionary municipal council or "Commune" was set up. Paris, so lately attacked by German soldiers, was now attacked by French.

The Paris Commune, which lasted from March to May 1871, seemed to be another explosion of social revolution. Actually, it was in essence a revival of the Jacobinism of 1793. It was fiercely patriotic and republican, anti-German, opposed to wealthy bourgeois, aristocrats, and clergy, in favor of government controls upon prices, wages, and working conditions, but still not socialist in any sweeping or systematic way. Among its leaders, however, there were a few of the new international revolutionary socialists, who saw in a Jacobin or democratic republic a step toward their new order. Marx in England, and others elsewhere, hopefully read into the Commune the impending doom of the bourgeoisie. This was precisely what more conservative elements feared. To many of the French middle and peasant class, and to people like them all over Europe, it seemed that the "Communards" were wild and savage destroyers of nineteenth-century civilization. The fighting in Paris was atrocious beyond anything known in any preceding French revolution. The Communards, in final desperation, burned a number of public buildings and put to death the archbishop of Paris, whom they held as a hostage. The forces of the National Assembly, when finally triumphant, were determined to root out the inveterate revolutionism of Paris. Some 330,000 persons were denounced, 38,000 arrested, 20,000 put to death, and 7,500 deported to New Caledonia. The Third Republic was born in an atmosphere of class hate and social terror.

The form of government for the new regime still had to be established. The monarchist majority in the Assembly was itself evenly divided between those who favored a restoration of the Bourbon family and those who favored the Orléanist. In the end, even after they were reconciled, the Bourbon candidate alienated everyone by his stiff insistence on a return to the white flag of the Bourbons. The monarchists checkmated each other. Meanwhile, after extended discussion of various constitutional projects, the Assembly adopted in 1875 not a constitution, but certain constitutive laws. By a margin of one vote, a resolution indirectly amounting to the establishment of a republic was passed. The new laws provided for a president, a parliament in two chambers, and a council of ministers, or cabinet, headed by a premier. The Senate was to be elected by a complicated and indirect system of election, the Chamber of Deputies by universal, direct, male suffrage.

Within two years, in 1877, the role of the president, the ministers, and the parliament was further clarified as a result of an unsuccessful attempt by an early president, Marshal MacMahon, to dismiss a premier of whom he did not approve but who had the backing of the Chamber. MacMahon proceeded to dissolve the Chamber and to hold new elections, but the example of Napoleon III's transformation of the Second Republic into a personal dictatorship was still fresh. The elections vindicated the principle of parliamentary primacy and of the responsibility of the premier and his cabinet to the legislature, a responsibility which in France meant generally but not exclusively to the lower house. The true executive in republican France was to be the premier and his cabinet, themselves held strictly to account by a majority of the legislature. Unfortunately, that majority, in a parliament where a dozen or so parties were represented, was always difficult to form and could be created only by unstable, temporary, shifting party alliances, coalitions, or blocs. No president, and indeed no premier, could henceforth dissolve the Chamber in order to hold new elections and consult the country as could be done in Britain. Actually, under the Third Republic the substantial machinery of state—ministries, prefectures, law courts, police, army, all under highly centralized control—was carried over virtually untouched as in all upheavals since the time of Napoleon I. France in the nineteenth century, so volatile in appearance, in effect underwent less extensive reorganization than any other leading country in Europe.

Troubles of the Third French Republic

Yet the Third Republic was precarious. The government had changed so often since 1789 that all forms of government seemed to be transitory. Questions which in other countries were only party questions became in France questions of "regime"—monarchy versus republic. Many people, especially those influenced by the upper classes, the Catholic clergy, and the professional army officers, continued to feel a positive aversion to the republic. On the other hand, the unmerciful and vindictive repression of the Commune made many middle-class people sympathetic to the republicans. Many turned republican simply because no other form of government established itself, or because it was the form of government that divided the country the least. As republicanism took in wider elements of society, it became less revolutionary and less fearsome. In 1879, for the first time, republicans won control of both houses of the government. In the 1880s their radicalism hardly went further than the founding of a democratic and compulsory school system at government expense and the passage of anticlerical legislation intended to curb church influence in education.

For over a quarter of a century, however, republican energies had to be expended in defense of republican institutions in order to ensure the survival of the regime. An initial crisis arose in 1886–1889, when General Boulanger gathered around him an incongruous following that included not only Bonapartists, monarchists, and aristocrats but also extreme radical republicans, who wished a war of revenge against Germany, and workers disgruntled over their general lot. Boulanger became a popular figure and seemed for a moment about to seize power as a dictator. But the menace collapsed in a comical failure as the general lost heart at the crucial hour and fled into exile. Meanwhile, in the 1880s and 1890s scandals and revelations of corruption in high republican circles provided ammunition for the antirepublicans. Moreover, the hope that unsympathetic French Catholics would rally to the republic, as urged by French prelates and by Pope Leo XIII in 1892, was shattered by the Dreyfus Affair, which in the late 1890s rocked the country and indeed the world.

In 1894 Captain Dreyfus, a Jewish army officer, was found guilty of treason by a military court and deported to Devil's Island. Evidence accumulated showing his innocence and pointing to the guilt of another officer, a Major Esterhazy, an adventurer known to be riddled with gambling debts. But the army refused to reopen the case, unwilling to admit it had erred; a staff officer, Major Henry, even forged documents to confirm Dreyfus' guilt. Meanwhile anti-Semites, royalists, traditionalists, militarists, and most of the "best" people fought the reopening of the case, deeming it unpatriotic to shake the nation's confidence in the army and wishing also to disgrace the republican regime. The partisans of Dreyfus stubbornly upheld him, both because they believed in justice and because they wished to discredit their adversaries. The country was deeply split. Finally, in 1899, Dreyfus was pardoned, and in 1906, fully exonerated. In the aftermath of the affair the left republicans and socialists revenged themselves by blocking the promotions of antirepublican officers and by anticlerical legislation. In 1905, in a series of laic laws, they "separated" church and state, ending the close relationship established under Napoleon's concordat a century earlier.

The Strength and Weakness of the Republic

The Third Republic, when the First World War came in 1914, a test which it was successfully to meet, had lasted over twice as long as any French regime since 1789. Born unwanted and accidentally, though it still had its opponents, it now commanded the loyalty of the overwhelming mass of the French people. What it had done, since 1870, was to domesticate democratic republicanism in Europe. Republicanism, one of the most militant of revolutionary movements down to 1870, had been shown in France to be compatible with order, law, parliamentary government, economic prosperity, and a mutual tolerance between classes, to the extent at least that they no longer butchered each other in the streets. Industrial workers were in many ways less well off than in England or Germany, but there were fewer of them; and for most people France in these years was a pleasant country, full of painters, writers, scholars, and scientists, full of bankers, bourgeois and well-established farmers, a country living comfortably and unhurriedly on the savings of generations, and one in which, in a close-knit family group, the average man could plan securely for his own and his children's future.

But the very comforts and values of bourgeois France were not those that would equip it for leadership in the modern age of technology and industrial power. Though substantial economic progress was made, the country lagged behind Germany in industrial development; the French entrepreneur showed little inclination to take the business risks needed for industrial growth. Politically, the fragmentation of political parties, itself a democratic reflection of a divided public opinion, and the distrust for historic reasons of a strong executive power led to the rise and fall of numerous short-lived ministries—no fewer than fifty in the years between 1871 and 1914. Ministerial instability was to be a chronic symptom of the Third Republic both before and after 1914; continuity of government policy was, however, generally maintained because of stability in certain key ministries and because of the permanent civil service.

French labor remained a steady source of discontent. Although French workers benefited from some labor legislation in the two decades after 1890, they continued to feel frustrated at the failure to establish a "social republic." Socialist representation in the Chamber grew. However, the most important single party of the republic, the Radicals, or Radical Socialists, were in actuality radical republicans—patriotic, anticlerical, spokesmen for the small shopkeepers and the lesser propertied interests; they drew the line at the advanced social legislation that labor expected from them, and on occasion their leaders even took positive steps to prevent unionization and to suppress strikes. Since some of these Radicals had started out as socialists, the distrust of French workers for all politicians and even for political processes was intensified. But the difficulties of the republic went deeper. The political energies of the republican statesmen had gone into liquidating the past, into curbing the political strength of the monarchists, the church, and the army; by the turn of the century, even before these older issues were fully resolved, the republic was compelled to meet the challenge of labor and to face other domestic and international pressures that were to try it sorely. The Third Republic was to weather the crisis of the First World War but not that of the Second.

The British Constitutional Monarchy

The British constitutional monarchy in the half-century before 1914 was the great exemplar of reasonable, orderly, and peaceable self-government through parliamentary methods. For over sixty years, spanning two-thirds of the nineteenth century, Victoria reigned (1837–1901) and gave her name to a distinguished era of material progress, literary accomplishment, and political stability. The two great parties, Liberal and Conservative, the heirs roughly of the Whigs and Tories, took form in the 1850s, the former producing its great leader in William E. Gladstone, the latter, a series of leaders of whom the most colorful was Benjamin Disraeli.

The advance toward an equalitarian political democracy in Britain was more cautious and slower than in France. The Reform Bill of 1832 had granted the vote to about an eighth of the adult male population. The democratic Chartist agitation of the 1830s and 1840s came to nothing.[13] In 1867, in response to continued

[13] See pp. 460–461, 466–467.

SUNDAY AFTERNOON ON THE ISLAND OF LA GRANDE JATTE
by Georges Seurat (French, 1859–1891)

This picture of sunny calm, painted in 1886, suggests something of the well-being brought to a great many people by the European civilization of the late nineteenth century. Whether boating, or idly fishing, or quietly sitting and watching, or strolling alone or in pairs or in families with their children, the figures seem to live in a peaceable world which a later age of war, speed, and mechanical amusements has made to seem far away. Technically this is one of the most remarkable pictures ever painted. The artist, an impressionist, created it without the use of lines by filling the canvas with thousands of minute dots of the primary colors, which so blur and mix in the eye as to produce the forms and hues of nature. As a result it seems to be a picture of light itself, with an actual shimmer on the water, an astonishing "grassiness" in the grass, with shadows that seem to be real shadows, and distant figures looking really distant as if seen through the intervening air. Courtesy of The Art Institute of Chicago.

demand for a wider suffrage, the Second Reform Bill was passed, Conservatives as well as Liberals outdoing one another in an effort to satisfy the country and to win new political strength for their own party. The bill, adopted under Disraeli's Conservative ministry, extended the suffrage from about 1 million eligible voters to about 2 million, or over a third of the adult males in the United Kingdom, reaching down far enough to include most workingmen in the cities. The Conservative critic Lord Derby called it a "leap in the dark." In 1884, under Liberal auspices, the suffrage was again broadened, this time in the rural areas, adding some 2 million additional voters and enfranchising over three-fourths of all adult males in the country. The suffrage still excluded agricultural workers who did not have a fixed residence, servants living with employers, and such people as unmarried grown sons who lived in the homes of their parents. Not until 1918 did Great Britain adopt universal male suffrage, as generally understood; and at that time women over thirty were given the vote too.

Despite the extension of the suffrage, the leadership of the country at the turn of the century was still in the hands of the upper and wealthier classes. Until 1911 the government paid no salaries to members of the House of Commons, who therefore, in both great parties, were usually gentlemen with private incomes, possessing the same family background and education. An attitude of sportsmanship and good feeling was characteristic of British politics. The two parties alternated in power at regular intervals, each indulgent toward the other, carrying over and developing rather than reversing the policies of its predecessor in office. Both parties sought support where they could find it, the Liberals leaning somewhat more on the industrial and commercial interests, the Conservatives on the landed aristocracy; both sought and succeeded in winning their share of the new working-class vote. It was in these years that both parties, when parliamentary reversals occurred, increasingly appealed to the country in general elections; the traditional crown and cabinet basis of British parliamentary government was being transformed into crown, cabinet, and country.

The Liberals were usually the more willing to pioneer, the first of the four ministries of Gladstone being especially notable in this respect. Gladstone in this first ministry (1868–1874) developed the principle of state-supported public education under the Forster Education Act of 1870, introduced the secret ballot, formally legalized labor unions, promoted competitive examinations for civil service posts, reorganized the upper judiciary, eliminated the purchase and sale of commissions in the army (a form of property in office), and by abolishing religious tests enabled persons not members of the Church of England to graduate from Oxford and Cambridge. The Conservative party, less sensitive to pressure from business interests for a laissez-faire policy in economic matters and continuing the tradition of early Tory reformers, took the initiative in further labor legislation. Under Disraeli's second ministry (1874–1880), the existing acts regulating public sanitation and conditions in mines and factories were extended and codified, safety measures were enacted to protect sailors, and the first attempt to regulate housing conditions for the poorer classes was initiated. But the Liberals, it must be added, protected the workers' interests too. In Gladstone's second ministry (1880–1885) workingmen were assured of compensation for injuries not of their own responsibility, and in 1892, before the formation of his fourth ministry (1892–1894), Gladstone campaigned to shorten labor hours and to extend employers' liability in accidents.

British Political Changes after 1900

At the turn of the century important changes were discernible on the British political scene. Labor emerged as an independent political force, the Labour party itself being organized shortly after 1900.[14] The rise of labor had a deep impact upon the Liberal party, and indeed upon liberalism itself. With many persons insisting that protective measures be taken to counteract the poor health, low income, and economic insecurity of the British working people, the Liberals abandoned their traditional position of laissez faire and sponsored a policy of government intervention and social legislation in behalf of the workingman. The Liberals, though they acted in part for humanitarian reasons, were aware that with the emergence of the Labour party workingmen who customarily had voted for them might readily transfer their allegiance.

In control of the government from 1906 to 1916, with Herbert Asquith as prime minister and David Lloyd George as chancellor of the exchequer during most of this time, the Liberals put through a spectacular program of social welfare. Sickness, accident, old-age, and a degree of unemployment insurance were adopted, and a moderate minimum wage law was enacted. Labor exchanges, or employment bureaus, were set up over the country. Restrictions on strikes and other trade union activities were removed. To meet the costs of the new program as well as of other government expenditures, Lloyd George's budget of 1909 called for progressive income and inheritance taxes: the wealthier the taxpayer, the higher the rate at which he was taxed. He was in effect advancing the then novel idea of using taxation to modify the extremes of wealth and poverty. It was a "war budget," he said, intended "to wage war against poverty." Its fiscal measures were directed primarily at the landed aristocracy, and it aroused great opposition, especially in the House of Lords, where the contest over the budget led to a further constitutional curtailment of the power of the upper house. The Parliament Act of 1911 deprived the Lords of all veto power in money matters and of all but a two-year delaying veto on action of the Commons in other legislation. At this time, too, the government voted to pay salaries to members of the House of Commons, making it possible for workers and others without independent incomes to take seats in Parliament. This last measure was enacted to circumvent a court ruling, the Osborne Judgment of 1909, that trade unions could not pay the salaries of workingmen elected to Parliament.

The Liberal party was embracing a program of positive state intervention in social and economic matters that the older liberalism, nurtured on the doctrines of laissez faire and the Manchester School, would not have accepted. With the Liberals actively seeking the support of labor and altering much in their traditional program, the Conservatives in the twentieth century tended to become the party of industry as well as of landed wealth and to replace the Liberals as the champions of economic liberalism and laissez faire. In the next generation, after

---

[14] See p. 579.

the First World War, the Conservatives were to remain one of the two major parties of the country; the Liberals were to be far outstripped by the Labour party.

Meanwhile, despite its gains, labor was not pacified. Real wages showed a tendency to fall after 1900, and great coal and railway strikes broke out in 1911 and 1912. The British capacity to survive crises without violence, while still conspicuous, was being strained. An even more serious threat came from Ireland.

The Irish Question

Britain suffered from one of the worst minorities questions in Europe—the Irish question. After 1801 Britain was known as the United Kingdom of Great Britain and Ireland, Ireland having been incorporated into the United Kingdom as a defensive measure against pro-French sympathies in Ireland during the wars of the French Revolution.[15] The Irish representatives who sat in Parliament were generally obstructionist in their tactics. The Irish had many substantial grievances, among which two were conspicuous. The Irish peasant was defenseless against his landlord, far more so, for example, than the French peasant before 1789; and the Irish people, though predominantly Catholic, were obliged to pay tithes to the established Church of Ireland (an Anglican sister church to the Church of England), which also owned a good deal of the land.

Gladstone, in his first ministry, disestablished the Church of Ireland. He also initiated measures to protect the Irish farm tenant. By 1900, under Conservative auspices, Irish tenants were being assisted by the British government to buy out their landlords—often Englishmen or Anglicized and absentee Irishmen. The Irish also wanted home rule, or a parliament of their own. Gladstone, in trying to give it to them in 1886, split his Liberal party, part of which went along with the Conservatives, not wishing political division of the British Isles. Home rule was finally granted to Ireland in 1914. But the Ulstermen, Presbyterians of north Ireland, objected vehemently to inclusion in an autonomous Ireland, in which they would be outnumbered by the Catholics of the south. The latter, however, insisted with equal vehemence on the inclusion of Ulster, not wishing a political division of Ireland.

The Ulstermen, backed by British Conservatives, started arming and drilling to resist the act of Parliament that authorized home rule. Great Britain, in 1914, was about to see a civil war on its own doorstep. It suffered from something of the insoluble nationalistic disputes that afflicted Austria-Hungary. During the First World War home rule was suspended, and after considerable violence on both sides Catholic Ireland (Eire) received dominion status in 1922, but eventually dissolved all ties with Britain. Ulster remained in the United Kingdom and was dominated by Protestants, so that its Catholic minority remained discontented. No satisfactory solution had yet been found to the "Irish question."

Bismarck and the German Empire, 1871–1890

The German Empire, as put together by Bismarck in 1871 with William I, king of Prussia, as Kaiser, was a federation of monarchies, a union of twenty-five German

[15] See pp. 330–331, 374.

states, in which the weight of monarchical Prussia, the Prussian army, and the Prussian landed aristocracy was preponderant. It developed neither the strong constitutionalism of England nor the democratic equality that was characteristic of France. To win popular support for his projects, Bismarck exploited existing democratic and socialist sentiment and provided that members of the Reichstag, the lower chamber, be elected by universal male suffrage.[16] Remaining chancellor of the united empire for some twenty years, from 1871 to 1890, he usually tried to have a majority in the Reichstag on his side, but he recognized no dependence on a majority in principle, holding to the doctrine that it was the emperor and his chancellor who were to govern the country. Moreover, in practice, the legislative powers of the lower house were severely restricted, and the upper chamber, representing the princes and not the people, and favored by the government, tended to be more important. Despite the nature of the empire, the Prussian conservatives, the East-Elbian Junker landlords, were at first by no means enthusiastic over Bismarck's unified Germany.[17] They opposed his democratic concessions and were left horrified when in 1872 he undertook to extinguish what was left of their manorial jurisdiction over their peasants.

Bismarck in the 1870s therefore leaned not on the Conservatives but on the National Liberals. With their aid he put through a number of economic and legal measures designed to consolidate the unity of the new empire. Bismarck's first serious conflict developed with the Catholic church. At the very time that he was bent on subordinating all groups within the state to the sovereign power of the new empire, the church had spoken out. In 1864 in the *Syllabus of Errors*, it denounced the encroachment of all governments on educational and church affairs; in 1870 the new dogma of papal infallibility made it incumbent on Catholics to accept unreservedly the pope's pronouncements in matters of faith and morals.[18] To many, the implication was that the new empire could not count on the undivided loyalty of its Catholic citizens. To defend Catholic interests and those of the south German states where Catholicism predominated, Catholic elements had organized the strong Center party, which now upheld the church pronouncements. In 1871 Bismarck launched the so-called *Kulturkampf,* or "battle for modern civilization." The Liberals joined in eagerly. Like nineteenth-century liberals elsewhere (Gladstone's campaign against Anglican privilege and the French laic laws have just been mentioned), they were strongly anticlerical and disapproved of the influence of organized churches in public and private life. Laws were put through imposing restrictions upon Catholic worship and education, the Jesuits were expelled, and many Catholic bishops throughout Germany were arrested or went into exile. But Bismarck gradually concluded that the anti-Catholic legislation was fruitless, that he had overestimated the danger to the state of organized Catholicism, and that he needed the support of the Center party for other parts of his program.

In 1879, with the support of the Center and Conservative parties but to the dismay of many of his erstwhile Liberal allies, Bismarck abandoned free trade and adopted a protective tariff that provided needed revenues for the government and gave satisfaction both to agricultural and industrial interests. Meanwhile, the

---

[16] See pp. 516, 519.
[17] See pp. 476, 512–513.
[18] See p. 594.

country's rapid and spectacular industrial expansion had stimulated the growth of the German working class, and to Bismarck's alarm, socialism was spreading.

The German Social Democratic party had been founded in 1875 by a fusion of Marxian socialists and the reformist followers of Ferdinand Lassalle on an essentially moderate program which Marx had denounced. But even a moderate socialism was mistrusted by Bismarck. He shared in the European horror at the recent Paris Commune, he feared socialism as anarchy, and he knew that socialism was in any case republican, and in that alone a potentially revolutionary movement in an empire of monarchies. Two radical attempts on the emperor's life (in neither case by Social Democrats) provided him with all the excuse he needed. In 1878, having already made peace with the Catholics, he set out to exterminate socialism. Antisocialist laws from 1878 to 1890 prohibited socialist meetings and socialist newspapers. For twelve years socialism was driven underground. But repression was not his only weapon; he turned also to another tactic. Bismarck sought to persuade the workers to place their faith in him and the German Empire rather than in Marx and the prophets of socialism. To that end, in the 1880s, he initiated an extensive program of social legislation. Workingmen were insured by the state against sickness, accident, and incapacity in old age. "Our democratic friends," said Bismarck, "will pipe in vain when the people see princes concerned with their well-being." In social insurance imperial Germany was, from whatever motives, years ahead of more democratic England, France, and the United States.

Bismarck failed to kill socialism. The number of socialists elected to the Reichstag was greater in 1890 than in 1878—for Bismarck's antisocialist campaign, in deference to the then current standards of civilized government, never suppressed the voter's freedom to vote as he chose. It seems, however, that Bismarck by the later 1880s was more apprehensive than ever of social revolution that would destroy his empire and contemplated some kind of coup d'état in which the Reichstag would be throttled. He never reached this point because in 1890, at the age of seventy-five, he was obliged by the new emperor, William II, to retire.

The German Empire after 1890: William II

William I died in 1888 and was succeeded by his son Frederick III who, incurably ill of cancer, died some three months after his accession. Frederick's son, William II, the last king of Prussia and the last German Kaiser, began his reign (1888–1918) as a young man of twenty-nine, full of startling ideas about his personal power and privileges. He was uncomfortable in the presence of an elder statesman who had made the German Empire, who had been his grandfather's aide and adviser, and whom he regarded partly with veneration and partly as an old fogy. William soon quarreled with Bismarck over continuation of the antisocialist laws and over matters of foreign affairs. When Bismarck forbade his ministers to meet with the emperor on policy matters unless he was present, William resolved that he, and not Bismarck, would rule the empire, and in 1890 he ordered Bismarck to resign, "dropping the pilot," in the celebrated phrase. Under the four chancellors who succeeded Bismarck, it was William who dominated policy.

After 1890 Germany embarked upon what was termed a "new course." In foreign affairs this meant a more aggressive and ambitious colonial, naval, and diplomatic policy, as will appear in the next two chapters. In domestic affairs it meant a more conciliatory attitude toward the masses. The antisocialist laws were dropped, and the system of social security legislation was enlarged and codified. But no democratic adjustment seemed possible. William II believed in the divinely ordained prerogatives of the house of Hohenzollern, and the empire still rested on the power of the federated princes, on the Junkers, the army, and the new industrial magnates. But the Social Democrats, the Progressive party, and other democratic forces were growing in strength. They demanded, for Prussia, a reform of the illiberal constitution of 1850,[19] and for the Reich, real control over the federal chancellor by the majority party in the Reichstag. In the election of 1912 the Social Democrats reached a new high by polling four and a quarter million votes, about one-third of the total, and by electing 110 members to the Reichstag, in which they now formed the largest single party; yet they were excluded from the highest posts of government. Even had war not come in 1914, it is clear that the imperial Germany created by Bismarck was moving toward a constitutional crisis in which political democracy would be the issue.

Developments Elsewhere; General Observations

Of political developments in other European states before 1914, something has already been said in the preceding chapter. Italy had become a constitutional monarchy in the 1860s and completed its unification by the forceful seizure of Rome in 1870.[20] Despite parliamentary forms, Italian political life in substance was characterized by unstable, opportunistic maneuvers and alliances manipulated by party chieftains, the best known of whom were Francesco Crispi, Agostino Depretis, and Giovanni Giolitti, moderate liberals who maintained themselves in office for long periods of time by shuffling and balancing political coalitions and by controlling elections in a form of parliamentary politics that received the name *trasformismo*. Giolitti, who headed five cabinets in all, governed with few interruptions from 1903 to 1914. The liberal leaders were anticlerical, and the quarrel with the papacy over the seizure of the papal territories remained unsettled. The popes refused to recognize the Italian kingdom and forbade Catholics to participate in its affairs or even to vote in elections. Catholics voted nonetheless and in 1907 bishops in each diocese were permitted to relax the ban, as they increasingly did.

Industry had begun to make an appearance in the northern cities like Milan. More as a matter of expediency than out of any democratic impulse, the government moved to extend the franchise to the working classes. The narrow suffrage of 1861 was broadened, first in 1882, and then in 1912, when the new reform increased the number of eligible voters from three to eight million, or virtually universal male suffrage. Because of illiteracy and political inertia not all of the newly enfranchised hastened to exercise their voting privilege. The social problem remained serious, too, despite some modest social legislation. Poverty and illiteracy, especially in the agrarian south, were grievous problems and radical unrest appeared in the industrial cities. In 1900 Victor Emmanuel's son and successor Humbert was assassinated. The first manifestations of an antiparliamentary ideol-

[19] See pp. 480–481.
[20] See pp. 508–510, 517, 594.

ogy, chauvinistic nationalism, and explosive irrationalism appeared in the writings and political activism of literary men like Gabriele d'Annunzio and Filippo Marinetti, the latter publishing in 1909 the manifesto of a violently nihilistic movement he called "futurism." The machinery of political democracy was established in Italy but there could be no assurances about the direction Italian parliamentary democracy was taking.

In the Dual Monarchy of Austria-Hungary, created by the Compromise of 1867, Austria and Hungary were each in form constitutional parliamentary states.[21] In theory, the Emperor-King Francis Joseph ruled through ministries responsible to the legislature in each state. However, in the important sphere of matters affecting the empire as a whole, such as foreign affairs and military questions, there was little parliamentary restraint on the emperor. Here he had virtually final authority; moreover, in all matters he still had broad powers to govern by decree, which he exercised. As in Germany, the tide of socialism was held back both by repressive laws and by social insurance and benevolent legislation. The most serious problem in the empire remained not socialism but agitation by the various subject nationalities, the Czechs and other Slavic peoples. Political democracy took a different course in Austria than in Hungary. In the former, partly as an effort to placate nationalist sentiment, universal male suffrage was introduced in 1907. In the latter it was bitterly and successfully resisted by the Magyars, who saw in it a weapon that could be employed by the Slavs to contest and destroy their preponderance. Austria itself, despite the democratic suffrage, was ruled very much like the German Empire, with the legislature able to debate and criticize but not control policy.

Of other countries it can be said that the political forms of democracy showed signs of advancing everywhere. Universal male suffrage was adopted in Switzerland in 1874, in Belgium in 1893 (though plural voting was still permitted), in the Netherlands in 1896; and in the next few years in Norway and Sweden (Norway was peacefully separated in 1905 from Sweden). In southern Europe, besides Italy, universal suffrage was introduced in Spain, Greece, Bulgaria, Serbia, and after the revolt of 1908, in Turkey. Although both Spain and Portugal were beset by civil wars, constitutional forms were eventually adopted in both countries, universal male suffrage being introduced in Spain in 1890 and a liberal suffrage in Portugal under a republic in 1911. Even tsarist Russia, after the Revolution of 1905, received a Duma, or national parliament, elected on a wide franchise but on an indirect and undemocratic class basis, and with narrow powers.[22] Among states west of the Russian empire, only Hungary and Rumania had a highly restricted suffrage on the eve of the First World War. The vote for women was considerably slower in arriving. Women voted before 1914 only in certain western states of the United States, in Australia, New Zealand, Finland, and Norway. Not until after the First World War did female suffrage begin to make significant advances.

The progress of representative and democratic institutions did not mean an end to the rule of monarchs, landed aristocrats, and other minority interests. For one thing, with the exception of France and Switzerland, Europe remained monarchical. Second, despite the growing importance of parliaments, parliamentary control

[21] See pp. 522–523.
[22] See p. 702.

over political life was far from guaranteed; emperors and kings still ruled through their chancellors and prime ministers. Of the major world powers it was mainly in the United States (at least for whites), Britain, and France that democratic and popular control was something of a reality. But the extension of the suffrage, by the relaxation of property qualifications, had a dynamic of its own and was altering the framework of politics everywhere; mass political parties, including socialist parties and confessional, or religious-oriented parties, were replacing the older, narrowly oligarchic political organizations, and support now had to be sought on a wider electoral basis. In almost all Europe, and in many of the outlying areas peopled by European descendants, democracy was advancing, even within the older framework. By 1871, most European nations, with the notable exception of Russia, had already won written constitutions, guarantees of personal freedom, parliamentary and representative institutions, and limitations on absolutism; in the years between 1871 and 1914 the most significant new political factor was the advance of male suffrage.

74. THE ADVANCE OF DEMOCRACY: SOCIALISM AND LABOR UNIONS

The artisan and laboring classes had never viewed with much pleasure the rise of capitalism or of "bourgeois" liberalism. They had always been doubtful of free competition, unrestrained private enterprise, the Manchester School, laissez faire, the laws of supply and demand, the free market for goods and labor, the idea of an economy independent of states and governments. These were the ideas of middle-class liberals, not of radical democrats. Popular leaders had opposed them in the French Revolution in 1793. The English Chartists had been outspokenly anticapitalistic, and on the Continent the ideas of socialism had been spreading. In 1848 there was a strong movement among the working classes for a "social" republic, and, though the social revolution failed in 1848, the force of it was enough to terrify the possessing classes and shape the philosophy of Karl Marx.[23] With the advent of the ballot, workers pressed for social legislation and used their political power to gain a greater measure of social democracy.

But in addition, before and after obtaining the ballot, working people resorted to other devices for the improvement of their position. Against the owners of capital, who controlled the giving of jobs, there were two principal lines of action. One was to abolish the capitalists, the other to bargain with them. The former led to socialism, the latter to the formation of labor unions. Socialism, in logic, meant the extinction of the private employer as such.[24] Trade unionism, in logic, meant that the workingman had every reason to keep his employer prosperously in business in order that bargaining with him might produce more results. The working-class movement thus contained an internal contradiction which was never completely resolved.

Middle-class and educated people who took up the workers' cause, the "intellectuals" of the movement—Karl Marx, Friedrich Engels, Louis Blanc, Ferdinand Lassalle, and thousands of less famous names—tended more to socialism than to

[23] See pp. 458–461, 463–467, 483–484.
[24] See pp. 431–432, 460.

unionism. They thought of society as a whole, they saw the economic system as a system, they thought of the future in long-run terms, and their time scale allowed generously for whole historical epochs to come and go. The actual workingman, put to work at an early age, barely educated if at all, with the waking hours of his adult life spent on a manual job, was inclined to keep his attention more on unionism than on socialism. To earn a shilling more every week beginning next week, to be spared the nervous strain and physical danger of constant exposure to unprotected machinery, to have fifteen minutes more every day for lunch, were likely to seem more tangible and important than far-reaching but distant plans for a reconstructed society. The worker looked on the intellectual as an outsider, however welcome; the intellectual looked on the worker as shortsighted and timid, however much in need of help.

After the failures of 1848 the socialist and trade union movements diverged for a generation. The 1850s, compared with the hungry '40s, were a time of full employment, rising wages, and increasing prosperity for all classes. Workers set to organizing unions, socialist thinkers to perfecting their doctrines.

The Trade Union Movement and Rise of British Labor

Organizations of wage workers, or labor unions in the modern sense (as distinguished from medieval craft guilds), had long maintained a shadowy and sporadic existence, as in the old French journeymen's associations.[25] But they had always been extralegal, frowned upon or actually prohibited by governments. French revolutionaries in the Le Chapelier Act of 1791, British Tories in the Combination Act of 1799, had been as one in forbidding workers to unite. It was the rise of "bourgeois" liberalism, so insensitive to the worker in most ways, that first gave legal freedom to labor unions. The British unions received a tacit recognition from the Liberal Tories in 1825 and explicit recognition from Gladstone's Liberal ministry in 1871. French unions were recognized by Napoleon III in 1864, then restrained in the reaction caused by the Commune, then fully legalized in 1884. In Germany Bismarck negotiated with labor leaders to find support against the vested interests that stood in his way.

The prosperity of the 1850s favored the formation of unions, for workers can always organize most easily when employers are most in need of their services. The craft union—or union of skilled workers in the same trade, such as carpenters—was at first the typical organization. It was most fully developed in England, where a "new model" unionism was introduced by the Amalgamated Society of Engineers (i.e., machinists) in 1851. It was the policy of the "new model" union officials to take the unions out of politics, to forget the semisocialism of the Chartists, to abandon Robert Owen's grandiose idea of "one big union" for all workers, and to concentrate on advancing the interests of each separate trade. The new leaders proposed to be reasonable with employers, avoid strikes, accumulate union funds, and build up their membership. In this they were very successful; the unions took root; and the two governing parties in England, reassured by the unexpected moderation of working-class spokesmen, combined to give the town workman the vote in 1867.

[25] See pp. 354, 491.

In the 1880s, and especially with the great London dock strike of 1889, which closed the port of London for the first time since the French Revolution, unions of unskilled workers began to form. Industrial unionism, or the joining in one union of all workers in one industry, such as coal or transportation, regardless of the skill or job of the individual worker, began to take shape at the same time. In some cases the older skilled unionists joined with unskilled laborers who worked beside them. Thus gradually arose, for example, the Transport Workers Union, which half a century later was to give a foreign secretary to the government in the person of Ernest Bevin. By 1900 there were about 2,000,000 union members in Great Britain, compared with only 850,000 in Germany and 250,000 in France.

It was largely because British workers were so far advanced in trade unionism, and so successful in forcing collective bargaining upon their employers, that they were much slower than their Continental counterparts in forming a workers' political party. By the 1880s, when avowed socialists were already sitting in French, Belgian, and German parliaments, the only corresponding persons in Britain were a half-dozen "Lib-Labs," as they were called, laboring men elected on the Liberal ticket. The British Labour party was formed at the turn of the century by the joint efforts of trade union officials and middle-class intellectuals.[26] Where on the Continent the labor unions were often led, and even brought into being, by the socialist political parties, in Britain it was the labor unions that brought into being, and subsequently led, the Labour party. Hence for a long time the Labour party was less socialistic than working-class parties on the Continent. Its origin and rapid growth were due in large measure to a desire to defend the unions as established and respectable institutions. The unions were threatened in their very existence by a ruling of the British courts in 1901, the Taff Vale decision, which held a union financially responsible for business losses incurred by an employer during a strike. The shortest and most orderly strike, by exhausting a union's funds, might ruin the union. The year before, steps had been taken to bring together the unions and all other existing labor and socialist organizations into a labor representation committee, in preparation for the elections of 1900; the effort was not very successful and only two of the fifteen labor candidates were returned. But the Taff Vale decision unified all ranks and precipitated the formation of the modern Labour party. In the election of 1906 the new Labour party sent twenty-nine members to Parliament, which thereupon overruled the Taff Vale decision by new legislation. The social legislation put through Parliament by the Liberal party government in the next few years, in good part under pressure from labor, has already been described.[27]

European Socialism after 1850

As for socialism, which had so frightened the middle and upper classes in 1848, it seemed in the 1850s to go into abeyance. Karl Marx, after issuing the *Communist Manifesto* with Engels in 1848, and agitating as a journalist in the German revolution of that year, withdrew to the secure haven offered by England, where, after years of painstaking research, he published the first volume of his *Capital* in 1867. This work, of which the succeeding volumes were published after his death, gave

[26] See p. 581.
[27] See pp. 571–572.

body, substance, and argument to the principles announced in the *Manifesto*.[28] Marx, during more than thirty years in London, scarcely mixed with the labor leaders then building up the English unions. Hardly known to the English, he associated mainly with political exiles and temporary visitors of numerous nationalities.

In 1864 there took place in London the first meeting of the International Working Men's Association, commonly known as the First International. It was sponsored by a heterogeneous group, including the secretary of the British carpenters' union, Robert Applegarth; the aging Italian revolutionary, Mazzini; and Karl Marx. With the union officials absorbed in union business, leadership in the Association gradually passed to Marx, who used it as a means of publicizing the ideas about to appear in his *Capital*. At subsequent annual congresses, at Geneva, Lausanne, Brussels, and Basel, Marx built up his position. He made the Mazzinians unwelcome, and he denounced the German Lassalleans for their willingness to cooperate with Bismarck, arguing that it was not the business of socialists to cooperate with the state but to seize it. His sharpest struggle was with the Russian Bakunin. With his background in tsarist Russia, Bakunin believed the state to be the cause of the common man's afflictions; he was hence an "anarchist," holding that the state should be attacked and abolished. To Marx anarchism was abhorrent; the correct doctrine was that the state—tsarist or bourgeois —was only a product of economic conditions, a tool in the class struggle, a weapon of the propertied interests, so that the true target for revolutionary action must be not the state but the capitalist economic system. Marx drove Bakunin from the International in 1872.

Meanwhile members of the First International watched with great excitement the Paris Commune of 1871, which they hoped might be the opening act of a European working-class upheaval. Members of the International infiltrated the Commune, and the connection between the two, though rather incidental, was one reason why the French provisional government repressed the Commune with such terrified ferocity. But the Commune actually killed the First International. The Commune had been bloody and violent, an armed rebellion against the democratically elected National Assembly of France. Marx praised it as a stage in the international class war. He even saw in it a foretaste of what he was coming to call the "dictatorship of the proletariat." He thus frightened many possible followers away. Certainly British trade unionists, sober and steady men, could have nothing to do with such doings or such doctrines. The First International faded out of existence after 1872.

But in 1875, at the Gotha conference, Marxian and Lassallean socialists effected enough of a union to found the German Social Democratic party, whose growth thereafter, against Bismarck's attempts to stop it, has already been noted. About 1880 socialist parties sprouted up in many countries. In Belgium, highly industrialized, a Belgian Socialist party appeared in 1879. In the industrial regions of France some workingmen were attracted to Jules Guesde, a self-taught worker, former Communard, and now a rigid Marxist, who held it impossible to emancipate the working class by compromise of any sort; others followed the "possibilist" Dr. Brousse, who thought it possible for workers to arrive at socialism through parliamentary methods; still others supported Jean Jaurès, who elo-

28 See pp. 484–485.

quently linked social reform to the French revolutionary tradition and the defense of republican institutions. Not until 1905 did the socialist groups in France form a unified Socialist party. In England, in 1881, H. M. Hyndman founded a Social Democratic Federation on the German model and with a Marxist program; it never had more than a handful of members. In 1883 two Russian exiles in Switzerland, Plekhanov and Axelrod, recent converts to Marxism, founded the Russian Social Democratic party, from which the communism of the following century was eventually to be derived. The socialist parties all came together to establish an international league in 1889, known as the Second International, which thereafter met every three years and lasted until 1914.

Revisionist and Revolutionary Socialism, 1880–1914

The new socialist parties of the 1880s were all Marxist in inspiration. Marx died in 1883. Marxism or "scientific socialism," by the force of its social analysis, the mass of Marx's writings over forty years, and an attitude of unyielding hostility to competing socialist doctrines, had become the only widely current form of systematic socialism. Strongest in Germany and France, Marxism was relatively unsuccessful in Italy and Spain, where the working class, less industrialized anyway, more illiterate, unable to place its hopes in the ballot, and habituated to an excitable insurrectionism in the manner of Garibaldi, turned more frequently to the anarchism preached by Bakunin.

Nor was Marxism at all successful in England; workers stood by their trade unions, and middle-class critics of capitalism followed the Fabian Society, established in 1883. The Fabians (so called from the ancient Roman general Fabius Cunctator, the "delayer," or strategist of gradual methods) were very English and very un-Marxist. George Bernard Shaw, H. G. Wells, and Sidney and Beatrice Webb were among early members of the Society. For them socialism was the social and economic counterpart to political democracy, as well as its inevitable outcome. They held that no class conflict was necessary or even existed, that gradual and reasonable and conciliatory measures would in due time bring about a socialist state, and that improvement of local government, or municipal ownership of such things as waterworks and electric lighting, were steps toward this consummation. The Fabians, like the trade union officials, were content with small and immediate satisfactions. They joined with the unions to form the Labour party. At the same time, by patient and detailed researches into economic realities, they provided a mass of practical information on which a legislative program could be based.

The Marxist or Social Democratic parties on the Continent grew very rapidly. Marxism turned into a less revolutionary "parliamentary socialism"—except indeed for the Russian Social Democratic party, since Russia had no parliamentary government. For the growth of socialist parties meant that true workingmen, and not merely intellectuals, were voting for socialist candidates for the Reichstag, Chamber of Deputies, or whatever the lower house of parliament might be called; and this in turn meant that the psychology and influence of labor unions within the parties were increased. The workers, and their union officials, might in theory consider themselves locked in an enormous struggle with capital; but in practice their aim was to get more for themselves out of their employers' business. They might believe in the internationalism of the workers' interests; but in practice, acting through the parliaments of national states, they would work for orderly legislation benefiting the workers of their own country only—social insurance, factory regulation, minimum wages, or maximum hours. Nor was it possible to deny, by the close of the century, that Marx's anticipations (based initially on conditions of the 1840s) had not come true, at least not yet; the bourgeois was getting richer, but the proletarian was not getting poorer. Real wages—or what the wage earner's income would actually buy, even allowing for the losses due to unemployment—are estimated to have risen about 50 percent in the industrialized countries between 1870 and 1900. The increase was due to the greater productivity of labor through mechanization, the growth of the world economy, the accumulation of capital wealth, and the gradual fall in prices of food and other items that the workers had to buy.

Repeatedly, but in vain, the Second International had to warn its component socialist parties against collaboration with the bourgeoisie. Marxism began in the 1890s to undergo a movement of revisionism, led in France by Jean Jaurès, socialist leader in the Chamber of Deputies, and in Germany by Eduard Bernstein, Social Democratic member of the Reichstag and author in 1898 of *Evolutionary Socialism*, an important tract setting forth the new views. The revisionists held that the class conflict might not be absolutely inevitable, that capitalism might be gradually transformed in the workers' interest, and that now that the workers had not only the vote but a political party of their own, they could obtain their ends through democratic channels, without revolution and without any dictatorship of the proletariat. Most socialists or social democrats followed the revisionists.

This tendency to "opportunism"[29] among Marxists drove the really revolutionary spirits into new directions. Thus there arose revolutionary syndicalism, of which the main intellectual exponent was a Frenchman, Georges Sorel. "Syndicalism" is simply the French word for trade unionism (*syndicat*, a union), and the idea was that the workers' unions might themselves become the supreme authoritative institutions in society, replacing not only property and the market economy, but government itself. The means to this end was to be a stupendous general strike, in which all workers in all industries should simultaneously stop work, thus paralyzing society and forcing acceptance of their will. Syndicalism made most headway where the unions were weakest, as in Italy, Spain, and France, since here the unions had the least to lose and were most in need of sensational doctrines to attract members. Its strongest base was in the French General Confederation of Labor, founded in 1895.

Among orthodox Marxists there was also a revival of Marxist fundamentals in protest against revisionism. In Germany Karl Kautsky arraigned the revisionists as compromisers who betrayed Marxism for petty-bourgeois ends. In 1904 he and other rigorists prevailed upon the Second International to condemn the political behavior of the French socialist Alexandre Millerand who in 1899 had accepted a ministerial post in a French cabinet. Socialists might use parliaments as a forum, the International ruled, but socialists who entered the government itself were unpardonably identifying themselves with the enemy bourgeois state. Not until the First World War did socialists henceforth join the cabinet of any European

29 See p. 488.

country. In the Russian Social Democratic party the issue of revisionism came to a head in 1903, at a party congress held in London—for the most prominent Russian Marxists were mainly exiles. Here a group led by Lenin demanded that revisionism be stamped out. Lenin won a majority, at the moment at least, and hence the uncompromising Marxists were called Bolsheviks (from the Russian word for majority), while the revisionist or conciliatory Russian Marxists, those willing to work with bourgeois liberals and democrats, were subsequently known as Mensheviks or the "minority" group.[30] But in 1903 the Russian Marxists were considered very unimportant.

In general, in Europe's "inner zone," by the turn of the century, most people who called themselves Marxists were no longer actively revolutionary. As revolutionary republicanism had quieted down in the Third French Republic, so revolutionary Marxism seemed to have quieted down into the milder doctrines of social democracy. What would have happened except for the coming of war in 1914 cannot be known; possibly social revolutionism would have revived, since real wages no longer generally rose between 1900 and 1914, and considerable restlessness developed in labor circles, punctuated by great strikes. But in 1914 the working class as a whole was in no revolutionary mood. Workers still sought a greater measure of social justice, but the social agitation so feared or hoped for in 1848 had subsided. There seem to have been three principal reasons: capitalism had worked well enough to raise the workers' living standard above what they could remember of their fathers' or grandfathers'; workers had the vote and so felt that they participated in the state, could expect to benefit from the government, and had little to gain by its overthrow; and third, they had their interests watched over by organized and increasingly powerful unions, by which a larger share in the national income could be demanded and passed on to them.

75. SCIENCE, PHILOSOPHY, THE ARTS, AND RELIGION

Faith in the powers of natural science has been characteristic of modern society for over three centuries, but never was there a time when this faith spread to so many people, or was held so firmly, so optimistically, and with so few qualms or mental reservations as in the half-century preceding the First World War. Science lay at the bottom of the whole movement of industrialization; and if science became positively popular after about 1870, in that persons ignorant of science came to look upon it as an oracle, it was because it manifested itself to everybody in the new wonders of daily life. Hardly had the world's more civilized regions digested the railroad, the steamship, and the telegraph when a whole series of new inventions already described[31] had begun to unfold itself. In thirty years following 1875 the number of patents tripled in the United States, quadrupled in Germany, and multiplied in all the civilized countries. The scientific and technical advance was as completely international (though confined mainly to the "inner zone") as any movement the world has ever seen. Never had the rush of scientific invention been so fundamentally useful, so helpful to the constructive labors and serious problems of mankind, and in that sense human.

[30] See pp. 697–698.
[31] See pp. 554–556.

In more basic scientific thinking important changes set in about 1860 or 1870. Up to that time, generally speaking, the underlying ideas had been those set forth by Isaac Newton almost two centuries before.[32] The law of universal gravitation reigned unquestioned, and with it, hardly less so, the geometry of Euclid and a physics that was basically mechanics. The ultimate nature of the universe was thought to be regular, orderly, predictable, and harmonious; it was also timeless, in that the passage of ages brought no change or development. By the end of the epoch considered here, that is, by 1914, the old conceptions had begun to yield on every side.

The Impact of Evolution

In impact upon general thinking the greatest change came in the new emphasis upon biology and the life sciences. Here the great symbolic date is the publication by Charles Darwin of the *Origin of Species* in 1859. Evolution, after Darwin, became the order of the day. Evolutionary philosophies, holding that the way to understand anything was to understand its development, were not new in 1859. Hegel had introduced the evolutionary conception into metaphysics; and he and Marx, into theories of human society.[33] The idea of progress, taken over from the Age of Enlightenment, was a kind of evolutionary philosophy; and the great activity in historical studies, under romantic and nationalistic auspices, had made people think of human affairs in terms of a time process.[34] In the world of nature, the rise of geology after 1800 had opened the way to evolutionary ideas, and venturesome biologists had allowed themselves to speculate on an evolutionary development of living forms. What Darwin did was to stamp evolution with the seal of science, marshaling the evidence for it and offering an explanation of how it worked. In 1871, in his *Descent of Man*, he applied the same hypotheses to human beings.

By evolution, Darwin meant that species are mutable; that no species is created to remain unchanged once and for all; and that all species of living organisms, plant and animal, microscopic or elephantine in dimensions, living or extinct, have developed by successive small changes from other species that went before them. An important corollary was that all life was interrelated and subject to the same laws. Another corollary was that the whole history of living things on earth, generally held by scientists in Darwin's time to be many millions of years, was a unified history unfolding continuously in a single meaningful process of evolution.

Darwin thought that species changed, not by any intelligent or purposeful activity in the organism, but essentially by a kind of chance. Individual organisms, through the play of heredity, inherited slightly different characteristics, some more useful than others in food getting, fighting, or mating; and the organisms that had the most useful characteristics tended to survive, so that their characteristics were passed on to offspring, until the whole species gradually changed. Certain phrases, not all of them invented by Darwin, summed up the theory. There was a "struggle for existence" resulting in the "survival of the

[32] See pp. 279–282.
[33] See pp. 435, 485–487.
[34] See pp. 296, 304, 402, 434.

fittest" through "natural selection" of the "most favored races"—races meaning not human races but the strains within a species. The struggle for existence referred to the fact that, in nature, more individuals were born in each species than could live out a normal life span; the "fittest" were those individual specimens of a species having the most useful characteristics, such as fleetness in deer or ferocity in tigers; "natural" selection meant that the fittest survived without purpose in themselves or in a Creator; the "favored races" were the strains within a species having good survival powers.

Darwin's ideas precipitated a great outcry. Scientists rushed to defend and churchmen to attack him. The biologist T. H. Huxley became the chief spokesman for Darwin—"Darwin's bulldog." He debated with, among others, the bishop of Oxford. Darwin was denounced, with less than fairness, for saying that men came from monkeys. It was feared that all grounds of human dignity, morality, and religion would collapse. Darwin himself remained complacent on this score. Under civilized conditions, he said, the social and cooperative virtues were useful characteristics assisting in survival, so that "we may expect that virtuous habits will grow stronger, becoming perhaps fixed by inheritance." Much of the outburst against Darwin was somewhat trivial, nor were those who attacked him generally noted for spiritual insight; yet they were not mistaken in sensing a profound danger.

That Darwinism said nothing of God, Providence, or salvation was not surprising; no science ever did. That evolution did not exactly square with the first chapter of Genesis was disturbing but not fatal; much of the Old Testament was already regarded as symbolic, at least outside certain fundamentalist circles. Even the idea that man and the animals were of one piece was not ruinous; the animal side of human nature had not escaped the notice of theologians. The novel and upsetting effect of evolutionary biology was to change the conception of nature. Nature was no longer a harmony, it was a scene of struggle, "nature red in tooth and claw." Struggle and elimination of the weak were natural, and as means toward evolutionary development they might even be considered good. There were no fixed species or perfected forms, but only an unending flux. Change was everlasting; and everything seemed merely relative to time, place, and environment. There were no norms of good and bad; a good organism was one that survived where others perished; adaptation replaced virtue; outside of it there was nothing "right." The test was, in short, success; the "fit" were the successful; and here Darwinism merged with that toughness of mind, or *Realpolitik*, which came over Europe at the same time from other causes.[35]

Such at least were the implications if one generalized from science, carrying over scientific findings into human affairs, and the prestige of science was so great that this is precisely what many people wished to do. With the popularization of biological evolution, a school known as Social Darwinists actively applied the ideas of the struggle for existence and survival of the fittest to human society. Social Darwinists were found all over Europe and the United States. Their doctrines were put to various uses, to show that some peoples were naturally superior to others, such as whites to blacks, or Nordics to Latins, or Germans to Slavs (or vice versa), or non-Jews to Jews; or that the upper and middle classes, comfort-

[35] See p. 483.

able and contented, deserved these blessings because they had proved themselves "fitter" than the shiftless poor; or that big business in the nature of things had to take over smaller concerns; or that some states, such as the British or German Empire, were bound to rise; or that war was morally a fine thing, proving the virility and survival value of those who fought.

Anthropology and Psychology

The newer life sciences, such as anthropology and psychology, developed very rapidly in the latter part of the nineteenth century. Their effect upon the civilization of the day was not unlike that of Darwinism. Both accepted biological evolution. Both, as the price of being truly scientific, eschewed standards of right and wrong and set themselves to finding out and explaining the mere facts of human behavior.

Anthropology set itself the task of studying the physical and cultural characteristics of all branches of mankind. Physical anthropologists became interested in the several human "races," some of which they considered might be "favored" in the Darwinian sense, that is, superior in inheritance and survival value. It was often concluded, even by scientists at the time, that the whites were the most competent race, and among the whites the Nordics, Teutons, or Germans and Anglo-Saxons. The public, more or less exaggerating such ideas, became more race conscious than Europeans had ever been before. On the other hand the cultural anthropologists, surveying all manner of primitive or complex societies with scientific disinterest, seemed sometimes to teach a more deflating doctrine. Scientifically, it seemed, no culture or society was "better" than any other, all being adaptations to an environment, or merely a matter of custom—of the *mores,* as people said in careful distinction from "morals." The effect was again a kind of relativism or skepticism—a negation of values, a belief that right and wrong were matters of social convention, psychological conditioning, mere opinion, or point of view. We are describing, let it be repeated, not the history of science itself but the effects of science upon European civilization at the time.

The impact of anthropology was felt keenly in religion too. Sir James Frazer (1854–1941) in his multivolumed *The Golden Bough* could demonstrate that some of the most sacred practices, rites, and ideas of Christianity were not unique but could be found among primitive societies, and that, moreover, only the thinnest of lines divided magic from religion. Anthropology, Darwinian evolution, and other developments went far to upset traditional religious beliefs.

Psychology, as a science of human behavior, led to thoroughly upsetting implications about the very nature of man. It was launched in the 1870s as a natural science by the German physiologist Wilhelm Wundt (1832–1920), who developed various new experimental techniques. The Russian Ivan Pavlov (1849–1036) conducted a famous series of experiments in which he "conditioned" dogs to salivate automatically at the ringing of a bell once they had become accustomed over a period of time to associate the sound with the serving of their food. Pavlov's observations were important; they implied that a great part of animal behavior, and presumably human behavior, could be explained on the basis of conditioned responses. In the case of human beings these would be responses which men have been trained to make automatically by virtue of their environment and upbringing and which they do not make through choice or conscious reasoning.

Most significant of all the developments in the study of human behavior was the work of Sigmund Freud (1856–1939) and those influenced by him. Freud, a Viennese physician, founded psychoanalysis at the turn of the century. He came to believe that certain forms of emotional disturbance like hysteria were traceable to earlier forgotten episodes of patients' lives. After first trying various techniques such as hypnosis, which he soon abandoned, he employed free association, or free recall. If patients could be helped to bring these suppressed experiences into conscious recall, the symptoms of illness would often disappear. From these beginnings Freud and his followers explored the role that the unconscious played in all human behavior, he himself stressing the sexual drive. In one of his most famous books, *The Interpretation of Dreams* (1900), he stressed dreams as a key to understanding the unconscious; elsewhere he related his findings to religion, education, art, and literature. Freud and Freudian ideas had great influence on the social and behavioral sciences, and a good deal of the Freudian vocabulary later entered into everyday language and popular culture. In its deepest significance psychoanalysis, by revealing the wide areas of human behavior outside conscious control, suggested that human beings were not essentially rational creatures at all.

The New Physics

The revolution in biology of the nineteenth century, together with the developments in psychology and anthropology, were soon to be matched and surpassed by the revolution in physics. In the late 1890s physics was on the threshold of a revolutionary transformation. Like Newtonian mechanics in the seventeenth century and Darwinian evolution in the nineteenth, the new physics represented one of the great scientific revolutions of all time. There was no single work comparable to Newton's *Principia* or Darwin's *Origin of Species* unless Albert Einstein's theory of relativity, propounded in a series of scientific papers in 1905 and 1916, might be considered as such. Instead there was a series of discoveries and findings, partly mathematical and then increasingly empirical, that threw new light on the nature of matter and energy. In Newtonian physics the atom, the basic unit of all matter, which the Greeks had hypothesized in ancient times, was like a hard, solid, unstructured billiard ball, permanent and unchanging; and matter and energy were separate and distinct. But a series of discoveries from 1896 on profoundly altered this view. In 1896 the French scientist Antoine Henri Becquerel discovered radioactivity, observing that uranium emitted particles or rays of energy. In the years immediately following, from the observations and discoveries of the French scientists Pierre and Marie Curie and the Englishmen J. J. Thomson and Lord Rutherford, there emerged the notion that atoms were not simple but complex, and, moreover, that various radioactive atoms were by nature unstable, releasing energy as they disintegrated. The German physicist Max Planck demonstrated in 1900 that energy was emitted or absorbed in specific and discrete units or bundles, each called a quantum; moreover, energy was not emitted smoothly and continuously as previously thought, nor was it as distinguishable from matter as once supposed. In 1913, the Danish physicist Niels Bohr postulated an atom consisting of a nucleus of protons surrounded by electrically charged units, called electrons, rotating around the nucleus, each in its orbit, like a minuscule solar system.

With radioactivity scientists were being brought back to the idea long rejected, the favored view of the alchemists, that matter was transmutable; in a way undreamed of even by the alchemists, it was convertible into energy. This the German-born Jewish scientific genius Albert Einstein (1879–1955) expressed in a famous formula $e = mc^2$. From his theory of relativity emerged also the profoundly revolutionary notion that time, space, and motion were not absolute in character but were all relative to the observer and the observer's own movement in space. In later years, in 1929 and in 1954, Einstein brought together into one common set of laws, as Newton formerly had done, a unified field theory, an explanation of gravitation, electromagnetism, and subatomic behavior. Difficult as it was to grasp, and a great deal was still the subject of scientific controversy, it modified much that had been taken for granted since Newton. The Newtonian world was being replaced by a four-dimensional world, a kind of space-time continuum; and in mathematics, non-Euclidean geometries were being developed. It turned out, too, that neither cause and effect nor time and space nor Newton's law of universal gravitation meant very much in the subatomic world nor indeed in the cosmos when objects moved with the speed of light. It was impossible, as the German scientist Werner Heisenberg demonstrated a little later, in 1927, by his principle of uncertainty, or indeterminacy, to ascertain simultaneously both the position and the velocity of the individual electron. On these foundations established before the First World War there developed the new science of nuclear physics and the tapping of the atom's energy. The atom was soon discovered to be even more complex than conceived of before 1914, and its potentialities even greater.

Trends in Philosophy and the Arts

The step from pure science to philosophy is a long one, but one that many were prepared to take. Not only was the faith in science widespread but it was widely held that science was the only means of certain knowledge, and that anything unknowable to science must remain unknowable forever—a doctrine called agnosticism, or the acknowledgment of ignorance. Herbert Spencer (1820–1903) in England and Ernst Haeckel (1834–1919) in Germany were widely read popularizers of agnosticism; both also pictured a universe governed by Darwinian evolution. For Spencer especially, all philosophy could be unified, organized, and coordinated through the doctrine of evolution; this doctrine he applied not only to all living things but to sociology, government, and economics as well. The evolution of society, he felt, was toward the increasing freedom of the individual, the role of governments being merely to maintain freedom and justice; they were not to interfere with natural social and economic processes, nor to coddle the weak and unfit. Yet, like Darwin himself, Spencer believed that altruism, charity, and good will as individual ethical virtues were themselves useful and laudable products of evolutionary development.

These latter views were not shared by another of the serious writers of the age, also much influenced by evolutionary ideas, the German philosopher Friedrich Nietzsche (1844–1900). More a philosopher of art than of science, and drawing from many intellectual currents of the century, Nietzsche was an unsystematic and unclear thinker to whom it is easy to do less than justice. It is evident, however, that his opinion of mankind was a low one, and that from a background of evolutionary thinking he developed some kind of doctrine of a Superman, a noble being who, in a final triumph of world history, should issue from, lead, dominate, and dazzle the multitude. Qualities of humility, patience, brotherly helpfulness, hope, and love, in short the specifically Christian virtues, Nietzsche described as a slave morality concocted by the weak to disarm the strong. Qualities of courage, love of danger, intellectual excellence, and beauty of character he considered much better. Such views, for better or worse, were actually a new form of classical paganism. Nietzsche was neither much read nor much respected by his contemporaries, who considered him unbalanced or even insane; but he nevertheless expressed with unshrinking frankness many ideas implied in the outlook of his day.

As in the sciences, so in works of creative imagination—pure literature and the fine arts—the changes at the dawn of the twentieth century ushered in the contemporary age. Some writers, like Zola in France or Ibsen in Scandinavia, turned to the portrayal of social problems, producing a realistic literature dealing with industrial strife, strikes, prostitution, divorce, or insanity. Freudian and other views of psychology slowly made themselves felt in works of fiction; the new novels were often more lifelike than the old even though they added little to one's faith in human nature. The arts followed the intellectual developments of the age, reflecting, as they do today, attitudes of relativism, irrationalism, social determinism, and interest in the subconscious. On the other hand, never had artist and society been so far apart. The painter Gauguin, an extreme case, fled to the South Seas, went primitive, and reveled in the stark violence of tropical colors. Others became absorbed in technicalities or mere capricious self-expression. Art at its extreme fringe became incomprehensible, and the average person was deprived of a means (as old as the cave paintings of the Stone Age) of perceiving, seizing, and enjoying the world about him. After the First World War, and on into the present, the same trends of subjectivism in the arts attracted a wider, if still skeptical, audience. People read books without punctuation (or with peculiar punctuation), listened to music called atonal and deliberately composed for effects of discord and dissonance, and studied intently abstract or "nonobjective" paintings and sculpture to which the artists themselves often refused even to give titles.

The problem of communication remained serious. The arts suffered from the specialization of the modern world. The artist was not thought of as a collective spokesman or creator of something for common use but as a specialist plying his own trade and pursuing his own concerns. Society itself was divided into busy, self-centered groups, unable to communicate except on superficial matters, and hence in the long run less able to work in common.

The Churches and the Modern Age

Religion, too, was displaced. It was now a long time since almost everyone had looked to religion for guidance. But religion was more threatened after 1860 or 1870 than ever in the past, because never before had science, or philosophies drawing upon science, addressed themselves so directly to the existence of life and of man. Never before had so many of the fundamental premises of traditional religion been questioned or denied. Darwinian evolution had challenged the traditional picture of Creation, and anthropologists had questioned the uniqueness of the most sacred Christian tenets. There developed also the "higher" criticism of the Bible, an effort to apply to the Scriptures the techniques of scholarship long applied to secular documents, to incorporate archeological discoveries, and to reconstruct a naturalistic, historical account of ancient religious times. The movement, going back at least to the seventeenth century,[36] now took on significant proportions and was applied both to the Old Testament and the New. In the case of the Old Testament the patient scrutiny of style and language cast doubt on the validity of certain prophecies; and in the New the inconsistencies of the several Gospel sources were made patent. The German theologian David Friedrich Strauss (1808–1874), one such critical scholar, was the author of a widely discussed *Life of Jesus,* in which many miraculous and supernatural episodes were reverently but firmly explained away as "myth." The sensitive French historian and man of letters Ernest Renan (1823–1892) in a somewhat similar vein wrote on the origins of Christianity and on the life of ancient Israel. The ordinary person's long-established articles of faith were being further undermined. Moreover, the whole tenor of the time, its absorption in material progress, likewise kept people away from church; and the wholesale uprooting, the movement from country to city, often broke religious ties.

The Protestant churches were less successful than the Catholic in protecting their membership from the disintegrating effects of the age. Church attendance among Protestants became increasingly casual, and the doctrines set forth in

36 See pp. 287–288.

PAINTING #198 (AUTUMN)
by Vasily Kandinsky (Russian, then in Germany and France, 1866–1944)

What is loosely called modern art dates from the early twentieth century. Where the Impressionists continued to represent objects while losing interest in objective representation, in the next generation many painters gave up the objects themselves, thus launching various nonobjective or "abstract" styles. This "Painting #198" was done in 1914 by Kandinsky, one of the first practitioners of purely abstract painting. Since it is meant to convey color, without reference to physical objects, it does not lend itself to the kind of reproduction here used. Color at this time had a deep and vital meaning for Kandinsky, though he later turned to the invention of geometric or linear images as well. For the commonly perceived world of external objects he substituted a universe of his own. "To create a body of artistic work," he said, "is to create a world." Or again, speaking of nature, "it is not enough to see it; we must live it." With such sentiments Kandinsky shared in the antirationalist or vitalistic philosophies of the period. Courtesy of The Solomon R. Guggenheim Museum. Permission A.D.A.G.P. 1970 by French Reproduction Rights, Inc.

sermons seemed increasingly remote. Protestant laymen traditionally trusted their own private judgment and regarded their clergy as their own agents, not as authoritative teachers placed above them. Protestants also had always set special emphasis on the Bible as the source of religious belief; and as doubts accumulated on the literal truth of Biblical narratives there seemed no other source on which to rely.

Protestants tended to divide between modernists and fundamentalists. The fundamentalists, as they were called in the United States, in an effort to defend the literal word of Scripture were often obliged to deny the most indubitable findings of science. The modernists were willing enough to be scientific and to interpret much of the Bible as allegory, but only with difficulty could they recapture any spirituality or urgent feeling of Christian truth. Most Protestant churches were slow to face the social problems and wholesale injustices produced by the economic system, though a group of "Christian socialists" developed, notably within the Church of England. And as education and the care of orphans, aged, sick, and insane persons passed to the state, Protestant groups had less to do in the relief of suffering and upbringing of the young. Protestantism, to the regret of many Protestants, became increasingly a customary observance by people whose minds were elsewhere. Not until after the First World War could a strong Protestant revival be discerned, with a reaffirmation of basic doctrines by thinkers like Karl Barth, and a movement on the part of divergent Protestant churches to combine.

The Roman Catholic church proved more resistant to the trends of the age. We have seen how Pope Piux IX (1846–1878), after being driven from Rome by republicans in 1848, gave up his inclinations to liberalism.[37] In 1864, in the *Syllabus of Errors*, he denounced as erroneous a long list of widely current ideas, including the faith in rationalism and science, and he vigorously denied that the head of the church "should reconcile and align himself with progress, liberalism,

[37] See p. 475.

COMPOSITION WITH THE ACE OF CLUBS
by Georges Braque (French, 1882–1963)

This painting, of about the same date as the preceding one by Kandinsky, represents a quite different direction in modern art. It is one of the great works of the Cubist movement. Where the Kandinsky painting presents color without line and seeks to express life and feeling, Braque and the Cubists break up the visual world into lines and planes, in a more analytic and intellectual fashion. Objects recede or disappear, not into an impressionist blur nor a burst of color, but into a carefully contrived and almost mathematical pattern. In the new movement, it made sense to "see" things from more than one direction at a time, as the mind conceives them. Perception is not enough; as Braque once wrote, "the senses deform, but the mind forms." In any case, innovative artists after 1900 turned away from the main concerns of Western painting since the Renaissance: realistic representation of persons, places, or objects; natural color; illusionistic three-dimensional volume; a humanly occupied space with perspectives, horizons, location, and distance as seen by the eye from a single fixed viewpoint. Courtesy of the Musée d'Art Moderne, Paris (Service Photographique). Permission A.D.A.G.P. 1970 by French Reproduction Rights, Inc.

593

and modern civilization." The *Syllabus* was in form a warning to Catholics, not a matter of dogma incumbent upon them to believe. In dogma, the Immaculate Conception of the Virgin Mary was announced as dogmatic truth in 1854; a century later, in 1950, the bodily assumption of Mary into heaven was proclaimed. Thus the Catholic church reaffirmed in a skeptical age, and against Christian modernists, its faith in the supernatural and miraculous.

Pius IX also convened an ecumenical church council which met at the Vatican in 1870. It was the first such council since the Council of Trent some 300 years before.[38] The Vatican Council proclaimed the dogma of papal infallibility, which holds that the pope, when speaking *ex cathedra* on matters of faith and morals, speaks with a final and supernatural authority that no Catholic may question or reject. The Vatican Council, and the acceptance of papal infallibility by Catholics, was only the climax of centuries of development within the church. In brief, as the world grew more national, Catholicism became more international. As state sovereignty and secularism grew, Catholic clergy looked increasingly to the spiritual powers of Rome for protection against alien forces. Much in the past 300 years had made Catholics distrustful of their own governments or of non-Catholics in their midst—the Protestantism and the state churches of the sixteenth century, the Jansenist movement of the seventeenth, the anticlericalism of enlightened despotism in the eighteenth, the hostility to the church shown by the French Revolution, and by liberalism, republicanism, and socialism in the nineteenth century. By 1870 the net effect was to throw Catholics into the arms of the Holy See. Ultramontanism, the unconditional acceptance of papal jurisdiction, prevailed over the old Gallican and other national tendencies within the church.

In 1870, while the 600 prelates of the Vatican Council were sitting, the new Italian state unceremoniously entered and annexed the city of Rome.[39] The pope's temporal power thus disappeared. It is now widely agreed that with the loss of local temporal interests the spiritual hold of the papacy on Catholics throughout the world has been enhanced. The popes long refused, however, to recognize the loss of Rome; and each pope in turn, from 1870 to 1929, adopted a policy of self-imprisonment in the Vatican grounds. By the Lateran treaty of 1929 the papacy finally recognized the Italian state, and Italy conceded, along with much else, the existence of a Vatican City about a square mile in area, as an independent state not legally within Italy at all. The papacy thus gained that independence from national or secular authority deemed necessary by Catholics to the performance of its role.

Pius IX's successor, Leo XIII (1878–1903), carried on the counteroffensive against irreligion, and instituted a revival of medieval philosophy as represented by Thomas Aquinas.[40] But Leo XIII is chiefly remembered for formulating Catholic social doctrine, especially in the encyclical *Rerum Novarum* ("of modern things") of 1891, to which subsequent pontiffs have adhered, and from which various movements of Catholic socialism are derived. *Rerum Novarum* upheld private property as a natural right, within the limits of justice; but it found fault with capitalism for the poverty, insecurity, and even degradation in which many

38 See pp. 84–85.
39 See p. 517.
40 See p. 38.

of the laboring classes were left. It declared that much in socialism was Christian in principle; but it criticized socialism insofar as (like Marxism) it was materialistic and antireligious. The pope therefore recommended that Catholics, if they wished, form socialist parties of their own, and that Catholic workingmen form labor unions under Catholic auspices. Since the 1830s there had been individual Catholics and Catholic clergy who were socialists, or at least severe critics of the then emerging social order; these were encouraged by the encyclical of 1891, and Catholic (or Christian, as they were often called) socialist parties and labor unions began to appear at the turn of the century. The Roman church thus undertook to free itself from dependency upon capitalism. At the same time it took steps to insure that a future society, if socialist, might be Catholic also.

As for Judaism, the Jews were a small minority, but their condition had always been a kind of barometer reflecting changes in the atmosphere of Europe as a whole. In the nineteenth century the basic trend was toward "emancipation" and "assimilation." Science and secularism had the same dissolving effect upon Orthodox Judaism as upon traditional Christianity. Reform Judaism grew up as the Jewish counterpart to "modernism" in other faiths. Individual Jews increasingly gave up their old distinctive Jewish way of life. In society at large, the prevalence of liberalism allowed them to act as citizens and to enter business or the professions like everybody else. Jews were thus freed from old legal discriminations that had been imposed on them for centuries.

Toward the end of the century two tendencies, counter to assimilation, became evident. One, a cultural and political nationalism, originated with Jews themselves, some of whom feared an assimilation that would lead to a loss of Jewish identity and perhaps even the disappearance of Judaism itself. The other countertendency, or barrier to assimilation, was the rise of anti-Semitism, noticeable in many quarters by 1900. Racist theories, dislike for Jewish competitors in business and the professions, socialist scorn for Jewish capitalists like the Rothschilds, upper-class fears of Jewish revolutionaries and Marxists, together with a growth of ethnic nationalism, which held that France should be purely French and Latin, Germany purely German and Nordic, or Russia purely Russian and Slav, all combined to raise an anti-Semitic hue and cry. In Russia there were actual pogroms, or massacres of Jews. In France the Dreyfus case, dragged out from 1894 to 1906, revealed unsuspected depths of anti-Semitic fury. Many Jews were forced by such hostility into a new sense of Jewish identity. The Hungarian-born Jewish journalist Theodor Herzl was one. Appalled by the turbulence of the Dreyfus affair in civilized France, which he observed firsthand as a reporter for a Vienna newspaper, he founded modern, or political, Zionism when he organized the first international Zionist congress at Basel in 1897. Zionists hoped to establish a Jewish state in Palestine, in which Jews from all the world might find refuge, although there had been no independent Jewish state there since ancient times.

Many Jews, wishing civic assimilation yet despairing of obtaining it, began to sympathize with the Jewish nationalist movement, looking to Zionism and a Jewish renascence as a way to maintain their own dignity. Others insisted that Judaism was a religious faith, not a nationality by itself; that Jews and non-Jews within the same country shared in exactly the same nationality, citizenship, and political and social outlook. Liberals and democrats were of the same opinion. On the integration of Jews into the larger community the traditions of the Enlightenment, the American and French revolutions, the empire of Napoleon I, and the liberalism of the nineteenth century all agreed.

76. THE WANING OF CLASSICAL LIBERALISM

The net effect of the political, economic, and intellectual trends described above was twofold. There was a continued advance of much that was basic to liberalism and at the same time a weakening of the grounds on which liberalism had firmly rested ever since the seventeenth and eighteenth centuries. A third effect might be noted too. Even where the essentials of liberalism persisted, in program and doctrine it underwent important changes; liberalism persisted but the classical type of liberalism was in eclipse.

Classical liberalism, the liberalism in its heyday in the nineteenth century, went back at least as far as John Locke in the seventeenth century and the philosophes of the eighteenth and found its highest nineteenth-century expression in the writings of men like John Stuart Mill and in the political outlook of men like William Gladstone. Classical liberalism had as its deepest principle the liberty of the individual person.[41] Man, or each specimen of mankind, according to liberals, was or could become a freestanding human being. "Man" meant for them any member of the human race, *homo sapiens,* though in practice, except for a few like Mill, they were thinking of adult males. The very principle of liberalism, however, with its stress on the autonomy of the individual, contributed to the still small but growing movement of women's rights.

The individual, in this view, was not simply formed by race, class, church, nation, or state but was ultimately independent of all such things. Individuals did not have such and such ideas because they belonged to such and such a group, but were capable of the free use of reason or of thinking things out independently, apart from their own interests, prejudices, or subconscious drives. And, since this was so, people of different interests could reasonably and profitably discuss their differences, make compromises, and reach solutions by peaceable agreement. It was because they thought all persons potentially reasonable that liberals favored education. They opposed all imposition of force upon the individual, from physical torture to mental indoctrination.

In religion, liberals thought each individual should adopt any faith or no faith as he or she chose, and that churches and clergy should play little or no part in public affairs. In politics, they thought that governments should be constitutional and limited in power, with individuals governing themselves through their chosen representatives, with issues presented, discussed, and decided by the use of intelligence, both by the voters in election campaigns and by elected deputies in parliamentary debate. The will of a majority, or larger number of individuals, was taken as decisive, with the understanding that the minority might become a majority in its turn through individual changes of opinion. At first distrustful of democracy, fearing the excesses of popular rule, and eager to limit political power and the suffrage to the propertied classes, in the course of the nineteenth century

41 See pp. 429–430.

liberals had accepted the democratic principle of universal male suffrage. In economics, liberals thought of the whole world as peopled by individuals doing business with one another—buying and selling, borrowing and lending, hiring and firing—without interference from governments and without regard to religion or politics, both of which were thought to impose superficial differences upon the underlying uniformity of mankind. The practical consequences of liberalism were toleration, constitutionalism, laissez faire, free trade, and an international or non-national economic system. It was thought that all peoples would progress to these same ends.

There never was a time, even in one country, when all liberal ideas were simultaneously triumphant. Pure liberalism has never existed except as a doctrine. Advancing in one way, liberalism would be blocked or reversed in another. On the whole, Europe before 1914 was predominantly liberal. But signs of the wane of liberalism set in clearly about 1880; some, like the changing conceptions of human behavior, have already been mentioned.

The Decline of Nineteenth-Century Liberalism: Economic Trends

The free economy produced many hardships. The workingman tossed by the ups and downs of a labor market, the producer tossed by those of a world commodity market, alike clamored for protection against exposure. A severe depression in 1873 sent prices and wages into collapse, and the economy did not fully recover until 1893. European farmers, both small French farm owners and big Junker landlords of East Germany, demanded tariff protection: they could not compete with the American Middle West or the steppes of South Russia, both opened up by rail and steamship, and both of which after 1870 poured their cereals at low prices into Europe. The revival of tariffs and decline of free trade, very marked in Europe about 1880, thus began with the protection of agricultural interests. Industry soon demanded the same favors. In Germany the Junkers and the rising Rhineland industrialists joined forces in 1879 to extort a tariff from Bismarck. The French in 1892 adopted a high tariff to shelter both manufacturing and agricultural interests. The United States, rapidly industrializing, also put up protective tariffs beginning in the 1860s, the earliest of all.

The Industrial Revolution was now definitely at work in other countries than Great Britain. There was an increasing resistance to buying manufactures from England, selling only raw materials and foodstuffs in return. Everywhere there was a revival of the arguments of the German economist Friedrich List, who a half-century before, in his *National System of Political Economy* (1840), had branded free trade as a system mainly advantageous to the British and declared that no country could become strong, independent, or even fully civilized if it remained a semi-rustic supplier of unfinished goods.[42] With Germany, the United States, and Japan manufacturing for export, a nationalist competition for world markets set in, contributing also to the drive for colonies and the phenomena of imperialism described in the next chapter. The new imperialism was another sign of the waning of liberalism, which had been largely indifferent to colonies.

In all these respects the division between politics and economics, postulated by

[42] See p. 435.

liberals, began to fade. A kind of neomercantilism arose, recalling the attempts of governments in the seventeenth and eighteenth centuries to subordinate economic activity to political ends. A better term is economic nationalism, which became noticeable by 1900. Nations struggled to better themselves by tariffs, by trade rivalries, and by internal regulation, without regard to the effect upon other nations. And for the individual worker or businessman also, in purely economic matters, it now made a great difference to what nation he belonged, by what government he was backed, and under what laws he lived.

It was of course to protect themselves against insecurity and abuse as individuals that workers formed labor unions. It was likewise to protect themselves against the uncertainties of uncontrolled markets that business interests began to merge, to concentrate in large corporations, or to form monopolies, trusts, or cartels. The rise of big business and organized labor undermined the theory and practice of individual competition to which classical liberalism had been attached. Organized labor, socialist parties, universal male suffrage, and a sensitivity to social distress all obliged political leaders to intervene increasingly in economic matters. Factory codes became more detailed and better enforced. Social insurance, initiated by Bismarck, spread to other countries. Governments regulated the purity of food and drugs. The social service state developed, a state assuming responsibility for the social and economic welfare of the mass of its own subjects. The "new" liberalism, that of the Liberals in England of the David Lloyd George era, of the Republican President Theodore Roosevelt and the Democratic President Woodrow Wilson in the United States, accepted the enlarged role of the government in social and economic matters. Both Theodore Roosevelt and Wilson, and others, sought also to reestablish economic competition by government action against monopolies and trusts. The new liberals were generally less well disposed toward business than toward workers and the depressed classes; the improvement of the workers' lot would vindicate the old humanitarian concern of liberalism with the dignity and worth of the individual person. The welfare state, remote as it was from the older liberalism, was the direction taken by the new liberals. Others, liberal and otherwise, viewed with concern the growing power of governments and centralized authority and were apprehensive for individual liberties.

Intellectual and Other Currents

Liberalism, both old and new, was undermined also by many developments in the field of thought described earlier in this chapter—Darwinian evolution, the new psychology, trends in philosophy and the arts. Paradoxically, this great age of science found that man was not a rational animal. Darwinian theory implied that man was merely a highly evolved organism whose faculties were merely adaptations to an environment. Psychology seemed to teach that what was called reason was often only rationalization, or a finding of alleged "reasons" to justify material wants or emotional and unconscious needs, and that conscious reflection dominated only a narrow part of human behavior. Ideas themselves were said to be the products of conditioning. There were English ideas or Anglo-Saxon ideas, or bourgeois or progressive or reactionary ideas. In politics, some believed that parties or nations with conflicting interests could never reasonably agree on a program common to both, since neither could ever get beyond the limitations of its own outlook. It became common to dismiss the arguments of an adversary without further thought and without any expectation that thought could overcome difficulties. This insidious "anti-intellectualism" was destructive to liberal principles. If, because of prior conditioning, it was impossible for anyone to change his mind, then there was no hope of settling matters by persuasion.

From the view that man was not essentially a rational being, which in itself was only a scientific attempt at a better understanding of human behavior, it was but a short step deliberately to reject reason and to emphasize and cultivate the irrational, to stress the will, intuition, impulse, and emotion, and to place a new value on violence and conflict. A philosophy of "realism," a kind of unrealistic faith in the constructive value of struggle and a tough-minded rejection of ideas and ideals, spread. It was not new. Marxism, since the 1840s, had taught that class war, latent or open, was the motivating power of history. Now Nietzsche rejected the ordinary virtues in favor of courage and daring; and the Social Darwinists glorified the successful and the dominant in all phases of human activity as the "fit" in the perpetual struggle for existence. Other thinkers embraced a frank irrationalism. Georges Sorel, the philosopher of syndicalism, in his *Reflections on Violence* in 1908, declared that violence was good irrespective of the end accomplished (so much did he hate existing society), and that workers should be kept alert in the class war through believing in the "myth" of a future general strike. They should believe in such a strike, with its attendant debacle of bourgeois civilization, even though it was known to be only a "myth." The function of thought, in this philosophy of the social myth, was to keep people agitated and excited and ready for action, not to achieve any correspondence with rational or objective truth. Such ideas passed into the fascism and other activist movements of the twentieth century.

Thus the end of the nineteenth century, the greatest age of peace in Europe's history, abounded in philosophies glorifying struggle. Men who had never heard a shot fired in anger solemnly announced that world history moved forward by violence and antagonism. They said not merely that struggle existed (which would have been a purely factual statement) but that struggle was a positive good through which progress was to be accomplished. The popularity of struggle was due not only to the intellectuals but in part to actual historical events. People remembered that before 1871 certain weighty questions had been settled by force, that the movements of social revolution in 1848 and in the Paris Commune of 1871 had been put down by the military, and that the unity of Italy and Germany, as well as of the United States, had been confirmed by war. In addition, after 1871, all continental European states maintained large standing armies, the largest ever maintained until then in time of peace.

In economic and political matters, even in England, the homeland of liberalism, there were numerous signs between 1900 and 1914 that the older liberalism was on the wane. Joseph Chamberlain led a movement to return to tariff protection (to repeal, so to speak, the repeal of the Corn Laws); it failed at the time, but was strong enough to disorient the Conservative party in 1906. The Liberal party abandoned its traditional laissez-faire policy in sponsoring the labor legislation of the years following 1906. The new Labour party required its members in Parliament to vote as directed by the party, thus initiating a system of party solidarity, eventually copied by others, that hardened the lines of opposition, denied that individuals should freely change sides, and hence reduced the practical significance of parliamentary discussion. The Irish nationalists had long used unparliamentary methods; in 1914, when Parliament at last enacted Irish home rule, the anti-Irish and Conservative interests prepared to resist parliamentary action by force. The suffragettes, as women pioneering for female suffrage were called, despairing of ever getting the men to listen to reason, resorted to amazingly "un-English" and unreasonable arguments. They chained themselves to public buildings, smashed the store fronts in Bond Street, threw acids into mailboxes, and broke porcelains in the British Museum. When arrested they went on hunger strikes, threatening self-starvation, to which the police replied by "forcible feeding" through tubes lowered into their stomachs. And in 1911 and 1912 great railway and coal strikes disclosed the sheer power of organized labor.

Still, it is the persistence of liberalism rather than its wane that should be emphasized at the close of a chapter on European civilization in the half-century before 1914. Tariffs existed, but goods still circulated freely in world trade. Nationalism was heightened, but there was nothing like totalitarianism. Racist ideas were in the air, but they had little political importance. Anti-Semitism was sometimes vocal; but all governments except the Russian protected the rights of Jews, and the years from 1848 to 1914 were in fact the great period of Jewish integration into general society. The laissez-faire state was disappearing, but social legislation continued the humanitarian strain that had always been the essence of liberalism. A few advanced revolutionaries preached social catastrophism, but social democrats and laboring men were overwhelmingly revisionist, loyal to parliamentary procedures and to their existing states. Doctrinaires exalted the grim beauty of war, but all governments down to 1914 tried to prevent war among the great powers. And there was still a supreme faith in progress.

XV.
Europe's World Supremacy

European civilization, as described in the last chapter, spread to the whole earth after about 1870. The large nation-states whose consolidation was described in the chapter before last, and now equipped with the overwhelming new powers of science and industry, gained empires for themselves throughout the globe. The history of Europe—as of Asia, Africa, and America—became more involved in the history of the world.

For a while the most active of the imperial nation-states were located in Europe, and the forty years preceding the First World War were the years of Europe's world supremacy. With the rise of the United States the term "Western" came into use, signifying European in an expanded sense. The arrival of Japan made the term "Western" inappropriate for some purposes, and later the industrialization of the Soviet Union created similar verbal embarrassments, so that by the mid–twentieth century it was customary to speak of "developed" parts of the earth, alongside which others were seen as "developing" or "less developed." There even came to be a "Third World," which had no geographic identity of its

Chapter Emblem: A medal commemorating the opening of the Suez Canal in 1869.

own, but which did not wish to be identified with either the Western or the Soviet form of modern society. All these terms represented efforts to deal with the same basic reality, namely, a bifurcation between modern and traditional societies, rich countries and poor ones, or between the powerful and the weak.

For the first time in human history, by 1900, it was possible to speak of a world civilization. All countries were drawn into a world economy and a world market. The attributes of modernity, where they existed at all, were much the same everywhere—modern science, modern weapons of warfare, machine industry, fast communications, industrial organization, efficient forms of taxation and law enforcement, and of public hygiene, sanitation, and medicine.

But not all peoples participated in this global evolution on equal terms. It was the Europeans (or "Westerners") who reaped the greatest rewards. Under the impact of modernity both tribal societies and massive old civilizations began to come apart. Scientific ideas changed ways of thinking everywhere, as they had done in Europe. In India, China, or Africa the native industries often suffered, and many people found it harder than ever to subsist even at a low level. The building of railways in China, for example, threw boatmen, carters, and innkeepers out of work. In India, the hand spinners and weavers of cotton could not compete in their own villages with the machine-made products of Lancashire. In parts of Africa, native tribes that had lived by owning herds of cattle, moving from place to place to obtain grazing lands, found white farmers or plantation or mine owners occupying their country and were often forced by the white man's law to give up their migratory habits. Peoples of all races began to produce for export—rubber, raw cotton, jute, petroleum, tin, gold—and hence were exposed to the rise and fall of world prices. A depression tended to become a world depression, dragging all down alike.

Imperialism, or the colonialism of the late nineteenth century, may be briefly defined as the government of one people by another. European imperialism proved to be transitory. It was a phase in the world-wide spread of the industrial and scientific civilization which had originated in Europe's "inner zone."[1] That it was not the last phase became clear as the twentieth century unfolded. The subordinated peoples, forcibly introduced to the West by imperialism, came to feel a need for modernizing and industrializing their own countries and for the aid of Western science, skill, and capital; but they wished to get rid of imperialists, govern themselves, and control the conditions under which modernization and borrowing should take place. In opposition to European empires, subject peoples began to assert ideas learned from Europe—ideas of liberty and democracy, and of an anticapitalism that passed easily into socialism. Many such ideas were derived from the French and American revolutions, or from Marxism, or the whole record of Europe itself.

The present chapter deals only with the imperialist phase of the global transformation. By one of the ironics of history, the imperialist rivalries of the European powers, while representing Europe's world supremacy, also contributed to the disaster of the First World War, and so to the collapse of such supremacy as Europe had enjoyed.

---

1 See pp. 152, 544.

77. IMPERIALISM: ITS NATURE AND CAUSES

European civilization had always shown a tendency to expand. In the Middle Ages Latin Christendom spread by conquest and conversion to include the whole area from Spain to Finland. Then came the age of overseas discoveries and the founding of colonial empires, whose struggles filled the seventeenth and eighteenth centuries, and of which the Europeanization of the Americas was the most far-reaching consequence. At the same time European culture spread among the upper classes of Russia. The defeat of Napoleon left only one of the old colonial empires standing in any strength, namely, the British. For sixty years after 1815 there were no significant colonial rivalries. In many circles there was an indifference to overseas empire. Under principles of free trade, it was thought unnecessary to exercise political influence in areas in which one did business. Actually, in these years, the French moved into Algeria, the British strengthened their Indian empire, the Dutch developed Java and the neighboring islands more intensively, and the Western powers "opened" Japan and began to penetrate China. But there was no overt conflict among Europeans, and no systematic program, doctrine, or "ism."

Rather suddenly, about 1870 or 1880, colonial questions came again to the fore. In the short space of two decades, by 1900, the advanced countries partitioned most of the earth among themselves. A world map by 1900 showed their possessions in some eight or ten colors.

The New Imperialism

The new imperialism differed both economically and politically from the colonialism of earlier times. The older empires had been maritime and mercantile. European traders, in India, Java, or Canton, had simply purchased the wares brought to them by native merchants as produced by native methods. They operated on a kind of cash-and-carry basis. European governments had had no territorial ambitions beyond the protection of way stations and trading centers. To these generalizations America had been an exception. It had neither native states which Europeans respected, nor native industries in which Europeans were interested. Europeans therefore developed territorial claims, and invested capital and brought in their own methods of production and management, especially in the then booming sugar islands of the West Indies.[2]

Under the new imperialism Europeans were by no means content simply to purchase what native merchants provided. They wanted goods of a kind or in a quantity that preindustrial handicraft methods could not supply. They moved into the "backward" countries more thoroughly. They invested capital in them, setting up mines, plantations, docks, warehouses, factories, refineries, railroads, river steamships, and banks. They built offices, homes, hotels, clubs, and cool mountain resorts suitable for white men in the tropics. Taking over the productive life of the country, they transformed large elements of the local population into the wage employees of foreign owners and so introduced the class problems of industrial Europe in a form accentuated by racial difference. Or they lent money

[2] See pp. 242–243.

to native rulers—the khedive of Egypt, the shah of Persia, the emperor of China—to enable them to hold up their tottering thrones or simply to live with more pleasure and magnificence than they could pay for from their usual revenues. Europeans thus developed a huge financial stake in governments and economic enterprises outside the pale of Western civilization.

To secure these investments, and for other reasons, in contrast to what had happened under the older colonialism, the Europeans now aspired to political and territorial domination. Some areas became outright "colonies," directly governed by white men. Others became "protectorates": here the native chief, sultan, bey, rajah, or prince was maintained and guaranteed against internal upheaval or external conquest. A European "resident" or "commissioner" usually told him what to do. In other regions, as in China or Persia, where no single European state could make good its claims against the others, they arranged to divide the country into "spheres of influence," each European power having advisory privileges and investment and trade opportunities within its own sphere. The sphere of influence was the vaguest of all forms of imperial control; supposedly, it left the country independent.

An enormous differential opened up, about 1875, between the power of European and non-European states. Queen Elizabeth had dealt with the Great Mogul with genuine respect. Even Napoleon had pretended to regard the shah of Persia as an equal. Then came the Industrial Revolution in Europe, iron and steel ships, heavier naval guns, more accurate rifles. Democratic and nationalistic movements produced large and solid European peoples, united in the service of their governments as no "backward" people ever was. Seemingly endless wealth, with modern administration, allowed governments to tax, borrow, and spend almost without limit. The civilized states loomed as enormous power complexes without precedent in the world's history. At the same time it so happened that all the principal non-European empires were in decay. They were receiving a minimum of support from their own subjects. As in the eighteenth century the disintegration of the Mogul empire had enabled the British to take over in India,[3] so in the nineteenth century the decrepitude of the sultan of Turkey, the sultan of Zanzibar, the shah of Persia, the emperor of China, and the shogun of Japan made European intervention easy. Only the Japanese were able to revolutionize their government in time to ward off imperialist penetration. Even the Japanese, thanks to early treaties, remained unfree to determine their own tariff policy until after 1900.[4]

So great was the difference in the sheer mechanics of power that usually a mere show of force allowed the whites to impose their will. A garrison of only 75,000 white troops long held India for the British. Numerous sporadic little wars were constantly fought—Afghan wars, Burmese wars, Zulu wars—which passed unnoticed by Europeans in the home country and were no more like true war than the operations of the United States army against the Indians of the western plains. The Spanish-American War of 1898 and the Boer War of 1899 were also wars of colonial type, fought between entirely unequal parties. Often a show of naval strength was enough. It was the classic age of the punitive or minatory bombardment. We have seen how the American Commodore Perry threatened to bombard

---

[3] See pp. 263, 331.
[4] See pp. 539–540.

Tokyo in 1854.[5] In 1856 the British consul at Canton, to punish acts of violence against Europeans, called upon the local British admiral to bombard that Chinese city. In 1863 the British bombarded Satsuma, and in 1864 an allied force including Americans bombarded Choshu—precipitating revolution in Japan.[6] Similarly, Alexandria was bombarded in 1882 and Zanzibar in 1896. The usual consequence was that the local ruler signed a treaty, reorganized his government, or accepted a European (usually British) adviser.

Incentives and Motives

Behind the aggressiveness lay many pressures. Europeans could not maintain, for themselves in Europe, the style of life to which they had become accustomed, except by bringing the rest of the world within their orbit. But many other needs felt in Europe drove men into distant and savage places. Catholic and Protestant groups sent growing numbers of missionaries to regions increasingly remote and wild. The missionaries sometimes got into trouble with the natives, and some were even killed. Public opinion in the home countries, soon learning of such events by ocean cable, might clamor for political action to suppress such vestiges of barbarism. Similarly, science required scientific expeditions for geographical exploration, or for botanical, zoological, or mineral discoveries, or for astronomical or meteorological observations. Wealthy persons traveled more, now that travel was so easy; they hunted tigers or elephants, or simply went to see sights. It seemed only reasonable, at the close of the nineteenth century, that all civilized persons wherever they might choose to go should enjoy the security of life and limb and the orderly procedures that only European supervision could provide.

Economically, European life required material goods, many of which only tropical regions could supply. Even the working classes now drank tea or coffee every day. After the American Civil War Europe relied for its cotton increasingly on Africa and the East. Rubber and petroleum became staple needs. The lowly jute, which grew only in India, was used to make burlap, twine, carpets, and the millions of jute bags employed in commerce. The lordly coconut tree had innumerable common uses, which led to its intensive cultivation in the Dutch Indies. Various parts of it could be eaten, or manufactured into bags, brushes, cables, ropes, sails, or doormats or converted into copra and coconut oil, which in turn went into the making of candles, soap, margarine, and many other products.

Industrial countries also attempted to sell their own products, and one of the reasons given by imperialists, in support of imperialism, was the urgent necessity of finding new markets. The industrialization of Germany, the United States, Japan, and other countries, after about 1870, meant that they competed with each other and with Great Britain for foreign trade. The slowly declining price level after 1873 meant that a business firm had to sell more goods to turn over the same amount of money. Competition was more intense. The advanced countries raised tariffs to keep out each other's products. It was therefore argued that each industrial country must develop a colonial empire dependent on itself, an area of "sheltered markets," as the phrase went in England, in which the home country

[5] See pp. 536, 539.
[6] See pp. 539–540.

would supply manufactured goods in return for raw materials. The idea was to create a large self-sufficient trading unit, embracing various climates and types of resources, protected if necessary from outside competition by tariffs, guaranteeing a market for all its members and wealth and prosperity for the home country. This phase of imperialism is often called neomercantilism, since it revived in substance the mercantilism of the eighteenth and earlier centuries.[7]

Purely financial considerations also characterized the new imperialism. Money invested in "backward" countries, by the close of the nineteenth century, brought a higher rate of return than if invested in the more civilized ones. For this there were many reasons, including the cheap labor of non-European regions, the heavy and unsatisfied demand for non-European products, and the greater risk of losses in half-unknown areas where European ideas of law and order did not prevail. By 1900 western Europe and the northeastern United States were equipped with their basic industrial apparatus. Their railway networks and first factories were built. Opportunities for investment in these countries became stabilized. At the same time, these countries themselves accumulated capital seeking an outlet. In the mid-century most exported capital was British-owned. By the close of the century more French, German, American, Dutch, Belgian, and Swiss investors were investing or lending outside their own borders. In 1850, most exported capital went to build up Europe, the United States, Canada, Australia, or the Argentine—the white man's world. By 1900 more of it was going to the undeveloped regions. This capital was the property of small private savers or of large banking combinations. Investors preferred "civilized" political control over the parts of Asia, Africa, or Latin America in which their railroads, mines, plantations, government loans, or other investments were situated. Hence the profit motive, or desire to invest "surplus" capital, promoted imperialism.

This analysis was put forward by critics like the English socialist J. A. Hobson, who wrote an influential book on imperialism in 1903, and later by Lenin, in his *Imperialism, the Highest Stage of World Capitalism,* written in 1916. They ascribed imperialism primarily to the accumulation of surplus capital and condemned it on socialist grounds. Argued Hobson especially, if more of the national income went to workers as wages, and less of it to capitalists as interest and dividends, or if wealthy people were more heavily taxed and the money used for social welfare, there would be no surplus of capital and no real imperialism. Since the working class, if this were done, would also have more purchasing power, it would be less necessary to look endlessly for new markets outside the country. But the "surplus capital" explanation of imperialism was not entirely convincing. That investors and exporters were instrumental in the rise of imperialism was of course very true. That imperialism arose essentially from the capitalists' pressure to invest abroad was more doubtful. Perhaps even more basic was Europe's need for imports—only by enormous imports could Europe sustain its dense population, complex industry, and high standard of living. It was the demand for such imports—cotton, cocoa, coffee, copper, or copra drawn from "the colonies"—that made investment in the colonies financially profitable. Moreover, non-Europeans themselves often asked for the capital, glad though the European lenders were to lend it at high rates. In 1890 this might mean merely that a shah or sultan wanted

[7] See pp. 112–115, 239–244.

to build himself a new palace, but the need of non-Europeans for Western capital was basic, nor was it to decline as the world became more democratic. Lastly, the imperialism of some countries, notably Russia and Italy, which had little capital and few modern-type capitalists of their own, could not reasonably be attributed to pressure for lucrative foreign investments.

For the British, however, the capitalistic incentive was of great importance. We have seen how the British, in 1914, had $20 billion invested outside of Great Britain, a quarter of all their wealth.[8] About half, or $10 billion, was invested in the British Empire. Only a tenth of French foreign investments was in French colonies. French investment in the colonial world in general, however, including Egypt, Suez, South Africa, and Asia in addition to the French colonies, amounted to about a fifth of all French foreign investments. Only an infinitesimal fraction of German foreign investment in 1914 was in German colonies, which were of slight value. A fifth of German foreign investments, however, was placed in Africa, Asia, and the Ottoman Empire. These sums are enough to suggest the pressures upon the European governments to assert political influence in Africa, Turkey, or China.

In addition, French investors (including small bourgeois and even affluent peasants) had in 1914 a huge stake in the Russian empire. Russia, an imperial power with respect to adjoining countries in the Balkans and Asia, occupied an almost semicolonial status with respect to western Europe. The tsardom in its last twenty years, not unlike the Ottoman sultanate or the Manchu dynasty, was kept going by foreign loans, predominantly French. The French in 1914 had lent over $2 billion to Russia, more than to all colonial regions combined. For these huge outlays the motivation was at least as much political as economic. The French government often urged French banks to buy Russian bonds. The aim was not merely to make a profit for bankers and savers, but to build up and hold together a military ally against Germany.

Politics went along with economics in the whole process of imperialist expansion. National security, both political and economic, was as important an aim as the accumulation of private wealth. So, too, was the growing concern in many quarters over the economic security and welfare of the working classes. The ideas of the British statesman Joseph Chamberlain (1836–1914) illustrated how these motives entered into imperialist thinking.

Chamberlain, father of Neville Chamberlain who was to be prime minister of Britain in the years just prior to the Second World War, began as a Birmingham manufacturer, the type of man who a generation before would have been a staunch free trader and upholder of laissez faire. Discarding the old individualism, he came to believe that the community should and could take better care of its members, and, in particular, that the British community (or empire) could advance the welfare of Britons. As mayor of Birmingham he introduced a kind of municipal socialism, including public ownership of utilities. As colonial secretary from 1895 to 1903, he preached Britain's need for "a great self-sustaining and self-protecting empire" in an age of rising international competition—a world-wide British trading area, developed by British capital, which would give a secure source of raw materials and food, markets for exports, and a steady level of profits, wages, and employment.

[8] See p. 558.

Chamberlain saw with misgivings the tendencies toward independence in Canada, New Zealand, and the Australian Commonwealth. For these dominions he favored complete self-government, but he hoped that, once assured of virtual independence, they would reknit their ties with each other and with Great Britain. Such a reintegration of the empire he called "imperial federation." Britain and its dominions, in Chamberlain's view, should pool their resources not only for military defense but also for economic well-being. The dominions had already levied tariffs against British manufactures in order to build up their own. Chamberlain, to favor British exports, urged the dominions to charge a lower duty on British wares than on the same wares coming from foreign countries. In return, he even proposed that Great Britain adopt a protective tariff, so that it might then favor Canadian or Australian goods by imposing on them a lower rate. His plan was to bind the empire together by economic bonds, making it a kind of tariff union, or system of "imperial preference." Since Britain imported mainly meat and cereals from the dominions, Chamberlain was obliged to recommend a tariff even upon these—to "tax the people's food," repudiating the very ark of the covenant of Free Trade upon which the British economy had rested for half a century.[9] The proposal was rejected. Chamberlain died in 1914, his goal unaccomplished. But after the First World War the British Empire, or Commonwealth of Nations, followed closely along the lines he had mapped out.[10]

Whether the economic welfare and security of the European working classes was advanced by imperialism is still debated. It is probable that the workingman in western Europe did benefit from imperialism. Socially conservative imperialists were joined in this belief by thinkers of the extreme Left. Marx himself, followed by Lenin, thought that the European worker obtained higher real wages through the inflow of low-priced colonial goods. To Marxists this was unfortunate, for it gave European workers a vested interest in imperialism, made the European proletariat "opportunistic" (i.e., unrevolutionary), and blocked the formation of a true international world proletariat of all races.

Another imperialist argument much heard at the time held that European countries must acquire colonies to which surplus population could migrate without altogether abandoning the native land. It seemed unfortunate, for example, that so many Germans or Italians emigrating to the United States should be lost to the fatherland. This argument was purely specious. No European country after 1870 acquired any colony to which European families in any numbers wished to move. The millions who still left Europe, up to 1914, persisted in heading for the Americas, where in the circumstances no European colony could be founded.[11]

The competitive nature of the European state system introduced other almost exclusively political elements. The European states had to guard their security against each other. They had to keep some kind of balance among themselves, in the overseas world as in Europe. Hence, as in the scramble for Africa, one government often hurriedly annexed territory simply for fear that another might do so first. Or again, colonies came to have an intangible but momentous value in symbolism and prestige. To have colonies was a normal criterion of greatness. It

9 See pp. 457, 556–557.
10 See p. 761.
11 See map, p. 551.

was the sign of having arrived as a Great Power. Britain and France had had colonies for centuries. Therefore the new powers formed in the 1860s—Germany, Italy, Japan, and in a sense the United States—had to have colonies also.

Imperialism as Crusade

Imperialism arose from the commercial, industrial, financial, scientific, political, journalistic, intellectual, religious, and humanitarian impulses of Europe compounded together. It was an outthrust of the whole white man's civilization. It would bring civilization and enlightened living to those who still sat in darkness. Faith in "modern civilization" had become a kind of substitute religion. Imperialism was its crusade.

So the British spoke of the White Man's Burden, the French of their *mission civilisatrice*, the Germans of diffusing *Kultur*, the Americans of the "blessings of Anglo-Saxon protection." Social Darwinism and popular anthropology taught that white races were "fitter" or more gifted than colored.[12] Others argued, more reasonably, that the backwardness of non-Europeans was due to historical and hence temporary causes, but that for a long period in the future the civilized whites must keep a guardianship over their darker protégés. In the psychology of imperialism there was much that was not unworthy. Young men of good family left the pleasant lands of Devonshire or Poitou to spend long and lonely years in hot and savage places, sustained by the thought that they were advancing the work of humanity. It was a good thing to bring clearer ideas of justice to barbaric peoples, to put down slave raiding, torture, and famine, to combat degrading superstitions or fight the diseases of neglect and filth. But these accomplishments, however real, went along all too obviously with self-interest and were expressed with unbearable complacency and gross condescension to the larger part of the human race. As Rudyard Kipling wrote in 1899:

> *Take up the White Man's burden—*
> *Send out the best ye breed—*
> *Go bind your sons to exile,*
> *To serve your captives' need;*
> *To wait in heavy harness,*
> *On fluttered folk and wild—*
> *Your new-caught sullen peoples,*
> *Half devil and half child.*

78. THE AMERICAS

After the general considerations above, let us examine each of the earth's great regions in turn, and first the Americas where we must begin our discussion earlier in the century, before the age of the "new imperialism."

In America the breakup of the Spanish and Portuguese empires in the first quarter of the nineteenth century, during and after the Napoleonic wars, left the vast tract from Colorado to Cape Horn very unsettled. Most of the people were

12 See p. 586.

Indian or a mixture of Indian and white (*mestizo*), with clusters here and there of pure European stock, which the nineteenth-century immigration was greatly to increase.[13] Except in inaccessible spots, the Spanish culture and language predominated. In Brazil the culture was Portuguese, and the country, though independent after 1822, remained a monarchy or "empire" until 1889, when it became a republic. In the former Spanish domains the disappearance of royal control left a large number of flaccid and shifting republics, chronically engaged in border disputes with one another. Fortunately for these republics, at the time of independence in the 1820s, European imperialism was at a low ebb. We have seen how the Congress of Verona considered ways of returning them to Spain but was opposed by Great Britain; and how the United States, in 1823, supplemented the British action by announcing the Monroe Doctrine.[14] But it was by the United States that one of the new republics was first threatened from the outside.

The United States and Mexico

Mexico, on becoming independent of Spain, reached almost to the Mississippi and the Rocky Mountains. Hardly was it independent when land seekers from the United States swarmed over its northeastern borders. They brought with them their slaves, to grow the cotton so voraciously demanded in industrial England. The Mexican Republic did not allow slavery. The newcomers proclaimed their own republic, which they called Texas. Agitation developed for annexation to the United States. Mexico objected, but in 1845 the United States annexed Texas. A war followed, in which Mexico lost to the United States not only Texas but the whole region from Texas to the California coast. As is usual in such affairs, the loser preserved a longer memory than the winner. It soon seemed only natural in the United States to possess these regions; in Mexico many decades had to pass before the wound was healed. Mexico had lost half its territory within the first generation of its independence. It was argued at the time that the United States had far better facilities than Mexico for civilizing the region.

The next threat to Mexico came from Europe. Political leaders in Mexico, at a time of internal disorders, contracted large loans in Europe on exorbitant terms, the European leaders rightly estimating Mexican credit to be highly unsound. When the liberal leader Juárez (a pure-blooded Indian, at least racially "non-European") repudiated the loans, the European bondholders demanded satisfaction from their governments. The United States was paralyzed by the Civil War. Great Britain, France, and Spain, which had never recognized the Monroe Doctrine, in 1861 sent combined military forces to Veracruz. The British proposed seizure of the customs houses in Mexican ports, and appropriation of the customs revenues to pay off the debt (an expedient introduced in China three years before); but the French had more ambitious designs. Unknown both to the British, who wanted only to collect debts, and to the Spanish, who dreamed of setting up a new Bourbon monarchy in Mexico, the Emperor Napoleon III had a secret project for establishing a French satellite state in Mexico, which French capital and exports might subsequently develop. He planned to create a Mexican

13 See pp. 106–108.
14 See pp. 444–445.

empire with the Austrian archduke Maximilian as its figurehead emperor. The British and Spanish disapprovingly withdrew their forces. The French army proceeded into the interior. Maximilian reigned for some years, but Napoleon III gradually concluded that conquest of Mexico was impossible, or too expensive. It further appeared, by 1865, that the United States was not going to collapse after all, as expected and even hoped for by the European governing classes. The United States protested strongly to the French government. The French withdrew, Maximilian was captured and shot, and Juárez and the Mexican liberals came back to power.

United States pressure, before 1870, had thus in turn both despoiled and protected the adjoining part of Latin America. This ambivalent situation became characteristic of the New World. As the United States became a great power the Monroe Doctrine became an effective barrier to European territorial ambitions. Latin America never became subject to imperialism as completely as did Asia and Africa. On the other hand, the United States became the imperialist power feared above all others south of the border. It was the *Yanqui* menace, the Colossus of the North.

In the 1870s in the course of its turbulent politics, both natives of Mexico and foreign residents were obliged to pay forced loans to rival leaders. The State Department at Washington demanded that American citizens be reimbursed by the Mexican government. The double standard characteristic of imperialism—one standard for civilized and one for uncivilized states—became clear in the exchange of notes. The Mexican government, now under Porfirio Díaz, attempted to lay down the principle that "foreigners locating in a country accepted the mode of life of the people . . . and participated not only in the benefits of such residence but also in the adversities. Foreigners should enjoy the same guarantees and the same legal protection as natives, but no more." The Mexicans observed that the United States had never recognized the claims of foreigners for losses sustained in its Civil War. The United States, under President Hayes, held on the other hand that citizens of advanced states, operating in more primitive regions, should continue to enjoy the security of property characteristic of their home countries. When on another occasion the United States sent troops to the border, and the Mexicans objected, the secretary of state remarked on "the volatile and childish character of these people and their incapacity to treat a general question with calmness and without prejudice." Mexico retorted that the United States had "disregarded all the rules of international law and practice of civilized nations and treated the Mexicans as savages, as Kaffirs of Africa."

It was, in fact, a principle of international law in the nineteenth century that civilized states might not intervene in each other's affairs but had the right of intervention in "backward" countries. In the dispute of 1877 the United States classified Mexico as backward, "volatile and childish." What the Mexicans objected to was being treated like "savages and Kaffirs," and not like a civilized nation. They differed on which of the two standards should apply.

United States Imperialism in the 1890s

The 1890s saw a crescendo of imperialism both in Europe and in the United States. In 1895, in a resounding restatement of the Monroe Doctrine, President

Cleveland forbade the British to deal directly with Venezuela in a boundary dispute affecting British Guiana. The British were obliged to accept international arbitration. When, however, the adjacent Colombia faced a revolution in the Isthmus of Panama the United States supported the revolutionaries and, consulting nobody, recognized Panama as an independent republic. Here the United States leased and fortified a Canal Zone, and proceeded to build the Panama Canal. Panama became in effect what Europeans would call a protectorate of the United States.

Meanwhile what was left of the old Spanish American empire, confined to Cuba and Puerto Rico, was agitated by revolutionary disturbances looking to independence. Sympathies in the United States lay with the revolutionaries. Every sign of the new imperialism showed itself unmistakably. Americans had $50 million invested in Cuba. They bought the bonds issued by Cuban revolutionaries in New York. Cuban sugar, whose production was interfered with by political troubles, was necessary to the famed American standard of living. An orderly and amenable Cuba was vital to American strategic interests in the Caribbean, in the soon to be built canal, and in the Pacific. The barbarity of the Spanish authorities was deplored as an outrage to modern civilization. The newspapers, especially the new "yellow" press, roused the American public to a fury of moral indignation and imperial self-assertion. The climax came when an American warship, the *Maine,* sank under mysterious circumstances in Havana harbor.

The United States easily won the ensuing war with Spain in 1898. Puerto Rico was annexed outright, as were the Philippine Islands on the other side of the world. Cuba was set up as an independent republic, subject to the Platt Amendment, a series of provisions by which the United States obtained the right to oversee Cuba's relations with foreign powers, and to intervene in Cuba in matters of "life, property, individual liberty" and "Cuban independence." Thus the United States obtained another protectorate in the Caribbean. The right of intervention in Cuba was exercised several times in the following two decades, until the growth of Cuban nationalism and subsiding of American imperialism led to abrogation of the Platt Amendment in 1934. Later, after the Second World War, the Philippines formally received independence in 1946 and Puerto Rico became a self-governing commonwealth in 1952.

It was under President Theodore Roosevelt, the peppery "hero of San Juan hill," that the imperial greatness of the United States was most emphatically trumpeted. He announced in 1904 that weakness or misbehavior "which results in a general loosening of the ties of civilized society may . . . require intervention by some civilized nation," and that the Monroe Doctrine might force the United States "to the exercise of an international police power." In the following year Santo Domingo fell into such financial disorder that European creditors were alarmed. To forestall any pretext for European intervention, the United States sent a financial administrator to Santo Domingo, reformed the economy of the country, and impounded half the customs receipts to pay its debts. Roosevelt declared—in what came to be known as the "Roosevelt Corollary" to the Monroe Doctrine—that, since the United States would not permit European states to intervene in America to collect debts, it must itself assume the duty of intervention to safeguard the investments of the civilized world. The Monroe Doctrine, initially a negative warning to Europe, now stood with the new corollary as a positive notice of supervision of all America by the United States. A quarter of a century of "dollar diplomacy" followed, in which the United States repeatedly intervened, by military or other means, in the Caribbean and Mexico. But the Roosevelt Corollary, like the Platt Amendment, created so much bad feeling in Latin America that the Washington government finally repudiated it.

The story of the Hawaiian Islands was as typical of the new imperialism as any episode in the history of any of the European empires. Known originally to outsiders as the Sandwich Islands, these spots of land long enjoyed isolation in the vastnesses of the mid-Pacific. The growth of navigation in the nineteenth century introduced them to the world. Sailors, whalers, missionaries, and vendors of rum and cloth filled Honolulu by 1840. The native ruler, confused and helpless in the new situation, almost accepted a British protectorate in 1843 and in 1875 did accept a virtual protectorate by the United States, which guaranteed Hawaiian independence against any third party, obtained trading privileges, and acquired Pearl Harbor as a naval base. American capital and management entered the island. They created huge sugar and pineapple industries, entirely dependent on export to, and investment by, the United States. In 1891, when Queen Liliuokalani came to the throne, she tried to check westernization and Americanization. The American interests, endangered by her nativist policies, overthrew the queen and set up an independent republic, which soon sought annexation to the United States. It was the story of Texas reenacted. For several years the issue hung in the balance because of lingering disapproval in the United States for such strong-arm methods. But with Japan revealing imperial designs in 1895, the rush of the other powers into China, the Spanish-American War, acquisition of the Philippines, and plans for the Panama Canal, the United States "accepted its destiny" in the Pacific, and annexed the Hawaiian Republic by joint resolution of Congress in 1898. Hawaii became a state in the American union in 1959.

79. THE DISSOLUTION OF THE OTTOMAN EMPIRE

The Ottoman Empire in the 1850s

Of all parts of the non-European world, the Ottoman, or Turkish, Empire was the nearest to Europe, and with it Europeans had for centuries had close relations. It had for long extended from Hungary and the Balkan peninsula to the south Russian steppes and from Algeria to the Persian Gulf. The empire was not at all like a European state. Immense in extent, it was a congeries of religious communities. Most of its people were Muslim, including both orthodox Muslims and such reform sects as Druses and Wahabis; some were Jews who had always lived in the Near East; many were Christian, principally Greek Orthodox. The Turks were the ruling class and Islam the dominant religion. Only Muslims, for example, could serve in the army; non-Muslims were known as *raya*, the "flock" or "herd"—they paid the taxes. Persons of different religion lived side by side, each under the laws, courts, and customs of his own religious group. Religious officials—patriarchs, bishops, rabbis, imams, ulemas—were responsible to the Turkish government for their own people, over whom therefore they had a great deal of authority.[15]

Western Europeans had their own special rights. Roman Catholic clergy, living mainly in Palestine, looked to the pope in religion and to France for a mundane protector. Western merchants enjoyed the regime of the "capitulations," or special rights granted by the Ottoman government in numerous treaties going back to the sixteenth century. By the capitulations Turkey could not levy a tariff of more than 8 percent on imported goods. Europeans were exempt from most taxes. Cases involving two Europeans, civil or criminal, could be settled only in a court held by a European consul under European law. Disputes between a European and an Ottoman subject were settled in Turkish courts, but in the presence of a European observer.

The Ottoman Empire, in short, completely lacked the European idea of nationalism or national unity. The European idea of sovereignty and a uniform law for all its peoples were also absent, as was the idea of the secular state, or of law and citizenship separated from religion. The empire had fallen behind Europe in scientific, mechanical, material, humanitarian, and administrative achievements.

Turkey was the "sick man of Europe," and its long decline constituted the Eastern Question. Since the loss of Hungary in 1699 the Ottoman Empire had entered on a long process of territorial disintegration. That the empire lasted another two centuries was due to the European balance of power.[16] But by the 1850s the empire was falling away at the edges. Russia had advanced in the Crimea and the Caucasus. Serbia was autonomous, Greece independent, and Rumania recognized as a self-governing principality. The French occupied Algeria. A native Arab dynasty, the Sauds, of the Wahabi reform sect, ruled over much of Arabia. A former Turkish governor of Egypt, Mehemet Ali, had established his family as hereditary khedives in the Nile valley.[17] Notwithstanding these changes, the Ottoman Empire in the 1850s was still huge. It encompassed not only the Turkish or Anatolian peninsula (including Armenia and territory south of the Caucasus) but also the central portion of the Balkan peninsula from Constantinople to the Adriatic where many Christians of Slavic nationality lived, Tripoli (Libya) in North Africa, and the islands of Crete and Cyprus. Egypt and Arabia, though autonomous, were still under the nominal suzerainty of the sultan.

The Crimean War of 1854–1856 opened a new phase in Ottoman history as in that of Europe.[18] We have seen how this war was followed by the consolidation of great nation-states in Europe, and how even the United States, Canada, and Japan consolidated or modernized themselves at the same time. The Turks tried to do the same between 1856 and 1876.

In the Crimean War the Turks were on the winning side, but the war affected them as it affected Russia, the loser. Exposing their military and political weakness, it pointed up the need of organization. The outcome of the war was taken to prove the superiority of the political system of England and France. It was

---

[15] See pp. 209–210.

[16] See pp. 213, 236, 318–320, 447.

[17] See p. 447. The Egyptian ruler, as viceroy under the Ottoman Empire, did not adopt the title of "khedive" until 1867; he was called "sultan" from 1914 to 1922; and thereafter "king" until the overthrow of the monarchy in 1952.

[18] See pp. 504–506.

therefore on Western lines that Turkish reformers wished to remodel. It was not merely that they wished to defend themselves against another of the periodic wars with Russia. They wished also to avoid being periodically saved from Russia by the West, a process which if continued could lead only to French or British control of Turkey.

Attempts at Reform and Revival, 1856–1876

In 1856 the Ottoman government issued the Hatt-i Humayun, the most far-reaching Turkish reform edict of the century. Its purpose was to create an Ottoman national citizenship for all persons in the empire. It abolished the civil authority of religious hierarchs. Equality before the law was guaranteed as was eligibility to public office without regard to religion. The army was opened to Christians and Muslims alike and steps were even taken to include both in nonsegregated military units. The edict announced a reform of taxes, security of property for all, abolition of torture, and reform of prisons. It promised to combat the chronic evils of graft, bribery, and extortion by public officials.

For twenty years there were serious efforts to make the reform decree of 1856 a reality. Western and liberal ideas circulated freely. Newspapers were founded. Writers called for a national Turkish revival, threw off the old Persian style in literature, composed histories of the Ottomans, translated Montesquieu and Rousseau. Foreign loans entered the country. Railroads joined the Black Sea and the Danube. Abdul Aziz (1861–1876), the first sultan to travel in Europe, visited Vienna, London, and the great Paris world's fair of 1867. But powerful resistance developed against such radical changes. Also, the best efforts of the Turkish reformers miscarried. There were too few Turks with skill or experience in the work required. Abdul Aziz took to spending his borrowed money somewhat too freely for purposes of the harem. In 1874 the Ottoman government, having recklessly overborrowed, repudiated half its debt.

A new and more determined reforming minister, Midhat Pasha, goaded by opposition and desperate at the weight of inertia, deposed Abdul Aziz in 1876, deposed the latter's nephew three months later, and set up Abdul Hamid II as sultan. The new sultan at first briskly went along with the reform movement, proclaiming a new constitution in 1876. It declared the Ottoman Empire to be indivisible, and promised personal liberty, freedom of conscience, freedom of education and the press, and parliamentary government. The first Turkish parliament met in 1877. Its members earnestly addressed themselves to reform. But they reckoned without Abdul Hamid, who in 1877 revealed his true intentions. He got rid of Midhat, packed off the parliament, and threw away the constitution.

Repression after 1876

Abdul Hamid reigned for thirty-three years, from 1876 to 1909. For all this time he lived as a terrified animal, fighting back blindly and ferociously against forces that he could not understand. Once when a consignment of dynamos reached the Turkish customs it was held up by fearful officials, because the contents were declared to make several hundred revolutions per minute. Again, chemistry books for use in the new American college were pronounced seditious, because their chemical symbols might be a secret cipher. The sultan sensed that tampering with the old Ottoman way would lead to ruin. He dreaded any moves to check his own whim or power. He was thrown into a panic by Turkish reformers and western-izers, who became increasingly terroristic in the face of his opposition. Driven away by Abdul Hamid, some tens of thousands of Young Turks, the activists of the reform era before 1876, or their children and successors, lived in exile in Paris, London, or Geneva, plotting their return to Turkey and vengeance upon Abdul the Damned. The sultan was frightened also by agitation among his non-Turkish subjects. Nationalist Armenians, Bulgars, Macedonians, and Cretans defied and taunted the Ottoman authorities, which responded with the Bulgarian massacres of 1876 and the Armenian massacres of 1894. These horrible butcheries of thousands of peasants by Ottoman troops came as a shock to a Europe unused to such violence. Lastly, and with good reason, Abdul Hamid lived in a creeping fear of the designs of the imperialist European powers upon his dissolving empire.

A thoroughly reformed, consolidated, and modernized Ottoman Empire was the last thing that European governments desired. They might wish for humanitarian reforms in Turkey, for more efficiency and honesty in Turkish government and finance, and even for a Turkish parliamentary system. Such demands were eloquently expressed by liberals like Gladstone in England. But no one wanted what Turkish reformers wanted, a reinvigorated Ottoman Empire that could deal with Europe politically as an equal.

The Russo-Turkish War of 1877–1878: The Congress of Berlin

In Russia, since the time of Catherine II, many had dreamed of installing Russia on the shores of the Bosporus.[19] Constantinople they called Tsarigrad, the Imperial City, which Orthodoxy was to liberate from the infidel. Crusading motives, in a nationalist and imperialist age, reappeared anew in the form of Pan-Slavism.[20] This was now a doctrine preached by leading Russians, including the novelist Dostoevski, the poet Tyutchev, and the publicist Danilevsky. Danilevsky's *Russia and Europe*, published in 1871, predicted a long war between Europe and Russia, to be followed by a grand federation of the East, in which not only all Slavs, but Greeks, Hungarians, and parts of Asiatic Turkey would be included under Russian control. This type of Pan-Slavism was favored and patronized by the Russian government, because it diverted attention from internal and revolutionary troubles. As for the Slav peoples of the Ottoman Empire, they were willing to use Russian Pan-Slavism as a means of combating their Turkish rulers. Insurrection against the Turks broke out in Bosnia in 1875, in Bulgaria in 1876. In 1877 Russia declared war on Turkey. Russia was again on the move against the Ottoman Empire for the sixth time in a hundred years.

The British, who had fought Russia over Turkey in 1854, were prepared to do so again. A number of recent developments added to their apprehension. The Suez Canal was completed in 1869. It was within the territory of the Ottoman Empire. It restored the Near East to its ancient position as a crossroads of world trade. The British also took alarm when Russia, in 1870, in the confusion of the Franco-Prussian War, repudiated a clause in the treaty of 1856 and began to

19 See pp. 504–505.
20 On earlier Pan-Slavism, see p. 472.

build a fleet on the Black Sea. In 1874 Benjamin Disraeli, a Conservative and an imperialist, became prime minister of Great Britain. By a sudden coup in the following year he was able to buy up, from the almost bankrupt khedive of Egypt, 44 percent of the shares of the Suez Canal Company. In 1876, in a dramatic affirmation of imperial splendor, he had Queen Victoria take the title of empress of India. British commercial and financial interests in India and the Far East were growing, and the Suez Canal, of which the British government was now the principal stockholder, was becoming the "lifeline" of empire. But the Ottoman state, and hence the whole Near East, was now collapsing before the Russians, whose armies advanced rapidly through the Balkans in 1877, reached Constantinople, and forced the Turks to sign a treaty, the treaty of San Stefano. By this treaty Turkey ceded to Russia Batum and Kars on the south side of the Caucasus Mountains, gave full independence to Serbia and Rumania, promised reforms in Bosnia, and granted autonomy to a new Bulgarian state, whose boundaries were to be very generously drawn, and which everyone expected to be dominated by Russia. England seethed with a popular clamor for war against Russia. The outcry gave the word "jingoism" to the language:

> *We don't want to fight, but by jingo, if we do,*
> *We've got the men, we've got the ships, we've*
> *got the money too.*

It now appeared that the weakness of Turkey, its inability to fend off foreigners from its borders, would precipitate at least an Anglo-Russian and possibly a general European war. But war was averted by diplomacy. Bismarck assembled a congress of all the European great powers at Berlin. Once again Europe attempted to assert itself as a unity, to restore life to the much-battered Concert of Europe by dealing collectively with the common problem presented by the Eastern Question. The immediate need was to mediate between the Russians and Turks and to placate the British. To prevent any single power from gaining unequal advantage, and to win the acceptance of all powers for the arrangements agreed to, it was deemed necessary to give something to all, or almost all. The congress in effect initiated a partition of the Ottoman domain. It kept peace in Europe at the expense of Turkey. The European balance now both protected and dismembered Turkey at the same time.

The Russians were persuaded at Berlin to give up the treaty of San Stefano that they had imposed on the Turks, but they still obtained Batum and Kars and won independence for the Serbs and Rumanians. Montenegro, too, was recognized as an independent state. They compromised on Bulgaria, which was divided into three zones with varying degrees of autonomy, all still nominally within the Ottoman Empire. Austria-Hungary was authorized by the congress to "occupy and administer" Bosnia (but not annex it) in the interests of civilization and in compensation for the spread of Russian influence in the Balkans. To the British (Disraeli boasted he brought home "peace with honor") the Turks ceded Cyprus, a large island not far from the Suez Canal. The French were told that they might expand from Algeria into Tunisia. To the Italians (who counted least) it was more vaguely hinted that some day, somehow, they might expand across the Adriatic into Albania. As Bismarck put it, "the Italians have such a large appetite

THE DISSOLUTION OF THE OTTOMAN EMPIRE, 1699–1914

Beginning in 1699, with the loss of Hungary to the House of Austria, the Ottoman Empire entered upon a long process of territorial disintegration which lasted for over 200 years. Dates shown are those at which territories dropped away. In general, regions lost from 1699 to the fall of Napoleon, 1812–1815, were annexed directly by Austria and Russia. European territories lost in the nineteenth century emerged as independent states, owing to the rise of nationalism and the balance among the great European powers. In the Arabic world, reaching from Algeria to the Persian Gulf, regions lost before the First World War were absorbed into European colonial empires; those lost in the First World War (1918) were at first mostly assigned to France and Britain as mandates, but after the Second World War emerged as independent Arabic states. During the First World War Britain, France, Italy, Russia, and Greece took steps to partition Turkey proper, but a Turkish nationalist movement blocked these designs and established a Turkish republic (see pp. 669, 749–750).

and such poor teeth." Germany took nothing. Bismarck said he was the "honest broker," with no interest except in European peace.

The treaty of Berlin of 1878 dispelled the immediate threat of war. But it left many continuing problems for later statesmanship to deal with, problems which, because they were not dealt with successfully, became a principal cause of the First World War thirty-six years later. Neither the Balkan nationalists nor the Russian Pan-Slavs were satisfied. The Turks, both reactionaries like Abdul Hamid and the revolutionary Young Turks in exile, were indignant that peace had been made by further dismemberment of their territory. The demonstrated weakness of Turkey was a constant temptation to all concerned. In the years before 1914 German influence grew. Germans and German capital entered Turkey, projecting, and partially completing, a great Berlin to Bagdad railway to be accompanied by the exploitation of Near Eastern natural resources. The railroad was all but completed before 1914 despite the protests and representations of the Russians, the French, and particularly the British, who saw in it a direct threat to their empire in India.

Egypt and North Africa

For Egypt, technically autonomous within the Ottoman Empire, the 1850s and 1860s were a time of progress in the Western sense as they had been for the empire as a whole. The Egyptian government modernized its administration, court system, and property law, cooperated with the French in building the Suez Canal, encouraged shipping on the Red Sea, and let British and French interests construct railroads. Between 1861 and 1865, while the American South was unable to export raw cotton, the annual export of Egyptian cotton rose from 60 million to 250 million pounds. Egypt more than Turkey was drawn into the world market, and the khedive more than the sultan became a Western type of man. The khedive Ismail built himself a fine new opera house in Cairo, where, in 1871, two years after the opening of the Suez Canal, Verdi's *Aïda,* written at the khedive's request, was resoundingly performed for the first time.

Such improvements cost a good deal of money, borrowed in England and France. The Egyptian government was soon in financial straits, only temporarily relieved by the sale of Canal shares to Disraeli. By 1879 matters reached the point where Western banking interests forced the abdication of Ismail and his replacement by Tewfik, who, with a childlike fascination for the new Western marvels, soon let himself become thoroughly enmeshed by his creditors. This led to nationalistic protests within Egypt, headed by Colonel Arabi. In a pattern repeated in many parts of the colonial world, especially in Manchu China, the nationalists opposed both the foreigners and their own government, charging it with being a mere front for foreign interests. Arabi's movement, an early expression of Arab nationalism, led to riots in Alexandria, where Europeans had to flee aboard British and French shipping in the harbor. A British squadron then unceremoniously bombarded Alexandria. British troops (the French, though invited to take part, refused) disembarked in 1882 at Suez and Alexandria, defeated Arabi, and took Tewfik under their protection. The military intervention of 1882 was said by the British to be temporary, but British troops remained there for a long time, through two world wars and well into the twentieth century, not leaving until 1956.

Egypt became a British protectorate. The British protected the khedive from discontent within his own country, from the claims of the Ottoman Porte, and from the rival attentions of other European powers. The British resident from 1883 to 1907, an exceptionally capable administrator named Evelyn Baring, the first Earl of Cromer, did much to reconstruct the economy of the country, reform its taxation, ease the burdens on the peasants and raise their productivity, while encouraging the growth of raw materials wanted by England and assuring regular payment of interest to British, French, and other holders of Egyptian bonds.

The French strenuously objected when the British stayed on so long in Egypt. It had long been the French who had the greatest investments in the Near East, and Near Easterners who were at all westernized—Egyptian, Syrian, Turkish—overwhelmingly preferred the French language and culture to the English. The French, harboring deep suspicion of British designs in Egypt, compensated themselves by building a North African empire farther west. They developed Algeria, assumed a protectorate over Tunisia, and began to penetrate Morocco. Upon these French advances the British, and soon the Germans, looked with unmitigated disfavor. Rivalry for the spoils of the Ottoman Empire thus created enmity among the Great Powers and constituted a fertile source of the war scares, fears, and diplomatic maneuvers that preceded the First World War. These are related in the following chapter.

The dissolution of the Ottoman Empire became indistinguishable from the whole chronic international crisis before 1914. It is enough to say here, to keep the fate of the Ottoman Empire in focus, that Abdul Hamid's frantic policies came to nothing and that the Young Turks won control of the Ottoman government in 1908. They forced the restoration of the constitution of 1876 and introduced many reforms. In the midst of the revolutionary disturbances of 1908 Bulgaria proclaimed its full independence and Austria annexed Bosnia. In the Turco-Italian War of 1911–1912 Italy took Libya and the Dodecanese Islands from the Turks. In two successive Balkan Wars (1912–1913) Turkey lost nearly all its territory in Europe to Bulgaria, Serbia, Greece, and Albania, the latter becoming an independent state in 1912.[21] Finally, when all Europe became involved in war in 1914, Russia again declared war on Turkey, and the Turks came into the war on the side of Germany, whose political and economic influence in the empire had been steadily growing. During the war, with British aid, the Arabs detached themselves from the empire, becoming eventually independent Arab states. Egypt, too, ended all connections with the empire. In 1923 a Turkish republic was proclaimed. It was confined to Constantinople and the Anatolian peninsula, where the bulk of the true Turkish people lived. The new republic proceeded to undergo a thorough nationalist and secular revolution.[22]

80. THE PARTITION OF AFRICA

South of Mediterranean Africa lay the Sahara, and south of that lay Black Africa, the Dark Continent for Europeans. For centuries Europeans knew only its coasts —the Gold Coast, Ivory Coast, Slave Coast—to which from an inexhaustible interior had come shackled processions of captive slaves, as well as the swelling waters of enormous rivers, like the Nile and the Congo, whose sources in the dim hinterland were a subject of romantic speculation. The population was black, except that Arabic-speaking whites were found on the east coast; and in the southern part of the continent (at the time of the founding of the Union of South Africa in 1910) about 1.1 million Europeans lived along with about 5 million

21 See p. 660.
22 See pp. 749–750.

blacks. The native peoples were agricultural or pastoral, without written language or enduring political states but with bold and remarkable art forms and a memory of great kingdoms in earlier times.

The Opening of Africa

Missionaries, explorers, and individual adventurers first opened this world to Europe. The historic pair, Livingstone and Stanley, well illustrate the drift of events. Long before the imperialist age, in 1841, the Scot David Livingstone arrived in southeast Africa as a medical missionary. He gave himself to humanitarian and religious work, with a little occasional trading and much travel and discovery, but without political or true economic aims. Exploring the Zambesi River, he was the first white man to look upon the Victoria Falls. Fully at home in inner Africa, safe and on friendly terms with its native people, he was quite content to be let alone. But the hectic forces of modern civilization sought him out. Word spread in Europe and America that Dr. Livingstone was lost. The New York *Herald*, to manufacture news, sent the roving journalist H. M. Stanley to find him, which he did in 1871. Livingstone soon died, deeply honored by the natives. Stanley was a man of the new era. Seeing vast possibilities in Africa, he went to Europe to solicit backers. In 1878 he found a man with the same ideas, who happened to be a king, Leopold II, king of the Belgians.

Leopold, for all his royalty, was at heart a promoter. China, Formosa, the Philippines, and Morocco had in turn attracted his fancy, but it was the central African basin of the Congo that he decided to develop. Stanley was exactly the man he was looking for, and the two founded at Brussels, with a few financiers, an International Congo Association in 1878. It was a purely private enterprise; the Belgian government and people had nothing to do with it. All Africa inland from the coasts was considered to be, like America in the time of Columbus, a *terra nullius*, without government and claimed by nobody, wide open to the first civilized persons who might arrive. Stanley, returning to the Congo in 1882, in a year or two concluded treaties with over 500 chiefs, who in return for a few trinkets or a few yards of cloth put their crude marks on the mysterious papers and accepted the blue-and-gold flag of the Association.

Since the Dark Continent was still innocent of internal frontiers, no one could tell how much ground the Association might soon cover by these methods. The German explorer Karl Peters, working inland from Zanzibar, was signing treaties with the chiefs of East Africa. The Frenchman Brazza, departing from the west coast and distributing the tricolor in every village, was claiming on the Congo River itself a territory larger than France. The Portuguese aspired to join their ancient colonies of Angola and Mozambique into a trans-African empire, for which they required a generous portion of the interior. Britain supported Portugal. In every case the home governments in Europe were still hesitant over involvement in the African wilds, but they were pushed on by small organized minorities of colonizing enthusiasts, and they faced the probability that if they missed the moment it would be too late.

Bismarck, who personally thought African colonies an absurdity, but was sensitive to the new pressures, called another conference at Berlin in 1885, this time to submit the African question to international regulation. Most European states, as

PRE-COLONIAL AFRICA: SITES AND PEOPLES

This map is meant to show Africa before penetration by the Europeans in the nineteenth century. It does not refer to any particular date. Names in brown designate ancient or medieval centers, like the Ghana and Mali empires, which no longer existed in modern times. Even the most extensive African kingdoms had indefinite and shifting boundaries which are hard to indicate on a map. Bantu peoples were moving toward the southern tip of the continent in the nineteenth century, at the time when Europeans began to move northeastward into the interior from the Cape.

well as the United States, attended. The Berlin conference attempted to do two things: to set up the territories of the Congo Association as an international state, under international auspices and restrictions; and to draft an international code governing the way in which European powers wishing to acquire African territory should proceed.

The Congo Free State, which in 1885 took the place of the International Congo

Association, was not only an international creation but embodied, in principle, what were to be known after the First World War as international mandates or international trusteeships for "backward" peoples. The Berlin conference specified that the new state should have no connection with any power, including Belgium. It delegated the government to Leopold. It drew the boundaries, making the Congo Free State almost as large as the United States east of the Mississippi, and it added certain specific provisions: the Congo River was internationalized, persons of all nationalities should be free to do business in the Congo state, there should be no tariff levied on imports, and the slave trade should be suppressed. Leopold in 1889 reassembled the signatory powers in a second conference, held at Brussels. The Brussels conference took further steps to root out the slave trade, which remained a stubborn though declining evil, because the Muslim world was several generations behind the Christian in abolishing slavery. The Brussels conference also undertook to protect native rights, correct certain glaring abuses, and reduce the traffic in liquor and firearms.

This attempt at internationalism failed, because Europe had no international machinery by which the hard daily work of executing general agreements could be carried out. Leopold went his own way in the Congo. His determination to make it commercially profitable led him to unconscionable extremes. Europe and America demanded rubber, and the Congo was at the time one of the world's few sources of supply. The Congo people, among the least advanced in Africa, and afflicted by the disease and enervation of a lowland equatorial climate, could be made to tap enough rubber trees only by inhuman severity and compulsion. The trees themselves were destroyed without thought of replacement. Leopold, by ravaging its resources and virtually enslaving its people, was able to draw from the Congo a princely income to be spent in Brussels, but he could never make the enterprise self-supporting. Consumed with debt, he borrowed another 25 million francs from the kingdom of Belgium, agreeing that Belgium should inherit the Congo on his death if the debt was unpaid. In 1908, the reluctant Belgians thus found themselves heirs to some "tropical gardens" to which they had been consistently indifferent. The Free State became the Belgian Congo, and under Belgian administration the worst excesses of Leopold's regime were removed.

The Berlin conference of 1885 had also laid down, for expansion in Africa, certain rules of the game—a European power with holdings on the coast had prior rights in the back country; occupation must not be on paper only, through drawing lines on a map, but must consist in real occupation by administrators or troops; and each power must give proper notice to the others as to what territories it considered its own. A wild scramble for "real occupation" quickly followed. In fifteen years the entire continent was parceled out. The sole exceptions were Ethiopia and, technically, Liberia, founded in 1822 as a colony for emancipated American slaves and virtually a protectorate of the United States ever since.

Everywhere a variant of the same process was repeated. First, somewhere in the wilderness, would appear a handful of white men, bringing their inevitable treaties—sometimes printed forms. To get what they wanted, the Europeans commonly had to ascribe powers to the chief which by the customs of the tribe he did not possess—powers to convey sovereignty, sell land, or grant mining concessions. Thus the Africans were baffled at the outset by foreign legal conceptions.

Then the Europeans would build up the position of the chief, since they themselves had no influence over the people. This led to the widespread system of "indirect rule," by which colonial authorities acted through the existing chiefs and tribal forms. There were many things that only the chief could arrange, such as security for isolated Europeans, porter services, or gangs of workmen to build roads or railroads.

Labor was the overwhelming problem. For pure slavery Europeans now had an abhorrence, and they abolished it wherever they could. But the African, so long as he lived in his traditional way, did not react like the free wage earner postulated in civilized business and economics. He had little sense of individual gain and almost no use for money. He worked rather sporadically according to European ideas; work, continuous and laborious work, was in many African societies left to the women. The result was that Europeans all over Africa resorted to forced labor. For road building, systems like the French *corvée* before the Revolution reappeared. Or the chief would be required to supply a quota of able-bodied men for a certain length of time, and frequently he did so gladly to raise his own importance in the eyes of the whites. More indirect methods were also used. The colonial government might levy a hut tax or a poll tax, payable only in money, to obtain which the native would have to seek a job. Or the new government, once installed, might allocate so much land to Europeans as private property (another foreign conception) that the local tribe could no longer subsist on the lands that remained to it. Or the whole tribe might be moved to a reservation, like Indians in the United States. In any case, while the women tilled the fields or tended the stock at home, the men would move off to take jobs under the whites for infinitesimal pay. The men then lived in "compounds," away from family and tribal kindred; they became demoralized; and the labor they gave, unintelligent and unwilling, would scarcely have been tolerated in any more civilized community. In these circumstances everything was done to uproot the Africans, and little was done to benefit them. The old tribal or village society collapsed, and nothing replaced it.

Conditions improved with the twentieth century, as traditions of enlightened colonial administration were built up. Colonial officials even came to serve as buffers or protectors of the natives against the white man's interest. Throughout, it was part of the ethos of imperialism to put down slavery, tribal warfare, superstition, disease, and illiteracy. Slowly a westernized class of Africans grew—chiefs and the sons of chiefs, Catholic priests and Protestant ministers, warehouse clerks and government employees. Young men from Nigeria or Uganda appeared as students at Oxford, the University of Paris, or universities in the United States. Westernized Africans usually resented both exploitation and paternalism. They showed signs of turning nationalistic, like their counterparts in the Ottoman Empire and Asia. If they wanted westernization, it was at a pace and for a purpose of their own. As the twentieth century progressed, nationalism in Africa grew more vocal and more intense.

Friction and Rivalry between the Powers

Meanwhile, in the fifteen years from 1885 to 1900, the Europeans in Africa came dangerously near to open blows. The Portuguese annexed huge domains in

Angola and Mozambique. The Italians took over two barren tracts, Italian Somaliland and Eritrea on the Red Sea. They then moved inland, in quest of more imposing possessions, to conquer Ethiopia and the headwaters of the Nile. Some 80,000 Ethiopians, however, slaughtered and routed 20,000 Italians in pitched battle at Adowa in 1896. It was the first time that native Africans successfully defended themselves against the whites, and it discouraged invasion of Ethiopia by the Italians (or other Europeans) for forty years. Italy and Portugal, like the Congo Free State and Spain (which retained a few vestiges of former days), were able to enjoy sizable holdings in Africa because of mutual fears among the principal contenders. The principal contenders were Great Britain, France, and Germany. Each preferred to have territory held by a minor power rather than by one of its significant rivals.

The Germans were latecomers in the colonial race, which Bismarck entered with reluctance. By the 1880s all the usual imperialist arguments were heard in Germany, though most of them, such as the need of new markets, of outlets for emigration, or for the investment of capital, had little or no application in tropical Africa. The Germans established colonies in German East Africa, and in the Cameroons and Togo on the west coast, along with a desert area that came to be called German Southwest Africa. It did not escape the notice of German imperial planners that some day the Congo and the Portuguese colonies might be joined with German East Africa and the Cameroons in a solid German belt across the African heartland. The French controlled most of West Africa, from Algeria across the Sahara and the Sudan to various points on the Guinea coast. They also occupied Obok on the Red Sea, and after the Italian defeat in 1896 their influence in Ethiopia grew. French planners therefore dreamed of a solid French belt across Africa from Dakar to the Gulf of Aden. The French government in 1898 dispatched Captain J. B. Marchand with a small party eastward from Lake Chad, to hoist the tricolor far away on the upper Nile, in the southern part of the Sudan, which no European power as yet "effectively" occupied.

The two presumptive east-and-west belts, German and French, were cut (presumptively) by a north-and-south belt, projected in the British imperial imagination as an "Africa British from the Cape to Cairo." From the Cape of Good Hope Cecil Rhodes pushed northward into Rhodesia. Kenya and Uganda in the midcontinent were already British. In Egypt, a British protectorate since 1882, the British began to support old Egyptian claims to the upper Nile. The first venture proved a disaster, when in 1885 a British officer, "Chinese Gordon," leading an Egyptian force, was killed by aroused Muslims at Khartoum. In the following decade British opinion turned imperialist in earnest. Another British officer, General Kitchener (with a young man named Winston Churchill under his command), again started southward up the Nile and defeated the local Muslims in 1898 at Omdurman. He then pushed on further upstream. At a place called Fashoda he met Marchand.

The ensuing Fashoda crisis brought Britain and France to the verge of war. Already at odds over Egypt and Morocco,[23] the two governments used the encounter at Fashoda to force a showdown. It was a test of strength, not only for their respective plans for all Africa, but for their relative position in all imperialist

23 See pp. 619–620.

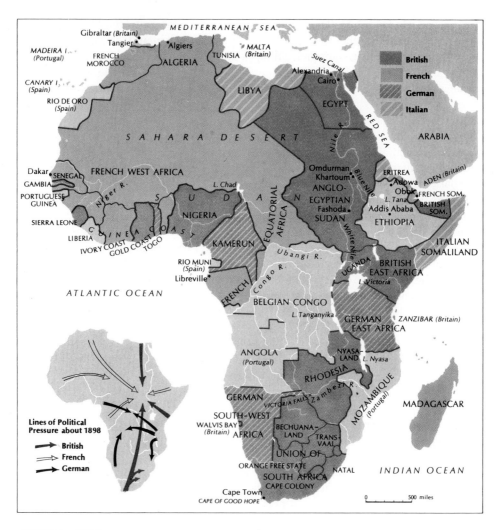

AFRICA, 1914

The map shows the recognized holdings of the Powers in 1914. The inset suggests the directions of political pressure about 1898. These pressures led to the Fashoda crisis in 1898 and the Boer War in 1899. In 1898 the British and German governments held secret discussions on the possible partitioning of the Portuguese colonies, which, however, never came to pass since the British greatly preferred to have the Portuguese colonies remain in the hands of Portugal.

and international issues. Both at first refused to yield. The British virtually threatened to fight. The French, fearful of their insecurity against Germany in Europe, at last decided not to take the risk. They backed down and recalled Marchand from Fashoda. A wave of hatred for the British swept over France.

The British no sooner won this Pyrrhic victory than they became involved in more unpleasantness at the other end of the African continent. In 1890 Cecil Rhodes had become prime minister of the Cape Colony. He was a principal sponsor of the Cape-to-Cairo dream. Two small independent neighboring republics, the Transvaal and the Orange Free State, stood in his way. Their people were Afrikaners—Dutch who had originally settled the Cape in the seventeenth century, then after 1815, when England annexed the Cape of Good Hope, had made the "great trek" to escape from British rule. The Boers, as the English called them, from the Dutch word for "farmer," were simple, obstinate, and old-fashioned. They thought slavery not ungodly and disliked promoters, fortune hunters, footloose adventurers, mining-camp people, and other Uitlanders.

The discovery of diamonds and gold in the Transvaal brought the issue to a head. British capital and British people poured in. The Transvaal refused to pass legislation needed by the mining corporations and their employees. In 1895 Rhodes, attempting to precipitate revolution in the Transvaal, sent a party of armed irregulars, under Dr. Jameson, over its borders. This Jameson Raid was a failure, but in Europe a great cry went up against British bullying of a small inoffensive republic. The German emperor, William II, dispatched a famous telegram to Paul Kruger, president of the Transvaal, congratulating him on his driving off the invaders "without having to call for the support of friendly powers"— i.e., Germany. Three years later the British Empire went to war with the two Boer republics. It took another three years to subdue them. Once conquered and brought within the British Empire they were left with their self-governing institutions, and in 1910 they were joined with the Cape Colony and the predominantly English Natal into the Union of South Africa, which received a semi-independence along the lines of the Dominion of Canada.

The Fashoda crisis and the Boer War, coming in rapid succession, revealed to the British the bottomless depths of their unpopularity in Europe. All European governments and peoples were pro-Boer; only the United States, involved at the time in a similar conquest of the Philippines, showed any sympathy for the British. The British, after the Boer War, began to rethink their international position, as will soon be seen.

As in the case of the Ottoman Empire, rivalry between the Great Powers over the spoils of Africa embittered international relations and helped prepare the way for the First World War. The rivalry over Morocco involving France and Germany entered into the general prewar crisis and will be related in the following chapter. As for Africa as a whole, there was little territorial change after the Boer War, although in 1911 Italy took Libya from the Turks. In 1914 the Germans were excluded from their short-lived empire. Had the Germans won the First World War, the map of Africa would probably have been greatly revised, but since they lost it the only change was to assign the German colonies, under international mandate, to the French and British. With this change, and except for Italy's ephemeral conquest of Ethiopia in 1935, the map of Africa remained what the brief years of partition had made it until the spectacular end of the European empires after the Second World War.[24]

[24] See pp. 874–881, and map, p. 877.

81. IMPERIALISM IN ASIA: THE DUTCH, THE BRITISH, AND THE RUSSIANS

The Dutch East Indies and British India

British India and the Dutch East Indies, in the half-century before the First World War, were the world's ideal colonies. They illustrated the kind of empire that all imperialists would have wished to have, and a glance at them suggests the goal toward which imperialism was logically moving.

Whereas all countries of western Europe showed a surplus of imports, receiving more goods from the rest of the world than they sent out, India and Indonesia invariably, year after year and decade after decade, showed a surplus of exports, sending out far more goods than they took in. This export surplus was the hallmark of the developed colonial area, geared closely into the world market, with low purchasing power for the natives and kept going by foreign investment and management. Both regions, in addition, were so large as to have a good deal of internal business—commerce, insurance, banking, transportation—which never appeared in the statistics for world trade, but which, being dominated by Europeans, added immeasurably to their profits. Both had rich and varied natural resources, tropical in character, so that they never competed with the products of Europe—though India even before 1914 showed tendencies to industrialization. In both regions the people were adept and quick to learn. But they were divided by religion and language, so that, once conquered, they were relatively easy for Europeans to govern. Neither region before the First World War had any self-government at the highest levels. Both were ruled by a civil service, honest and high-minded by its own lights, in which the most illustrious, most influential, and best paying positions were reserved for Europeans. Hence upper-class families in England and the Netherlands valued their empires as fields of opportunity for their sons—somewhat as they had formerly valued an established church. In both India and Indonesia the governments were more or less benevolent despotisms, which, by curbing warfare, plague, and famine, at least allowed the population to grow in numbers. Java, with 5 million people in 1815, had 48 million in 1942. India's population in the same years probably grew from less than 200 million to almost 400 million. Finally, as the last virtue of a perfect colony, no foreign power directly challenged the British in India or the Dutch in their islands.

The Dutch in 1815 occupied little more than the island of Java itself.[25] In the following decades the British moved into Singapore, the Malay peninsula, and north Borneo, and made claims to Sumatra. The French in the 1860s appeared in Indochina. The Germans in the 1880s annexed eastern New Guinea and the Marshall and Solomon islands. Ultimately it was the mutual jealousy of these three that preserved the Dutch position. The Dutch, however, took the initiative themselves. To forestall occupation by other Europeans, and to put down native pirates and find raw materials that the world demanded, the Dutch spread their rule over the whole 3,000-mile extent of the archipelago. They created an empire, in place of the old chain of trading posts concerned only with buying and selling. Revolts were suppressed in 1830, 1849, and 1888; not till the twentieth century was northern Sumatra or the interior of Celebes brought under control. For some

25 See p. 157.

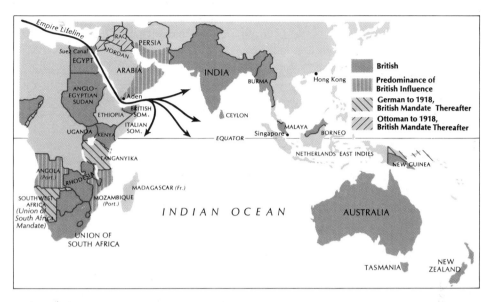

"THE BRITISH LAKE," 1918

This small map shows almost half the surface of the earth. All the most important parts of the British Empire are visible except Canada and the United Kingdom itself. All shores of the Indian Ocean are shown to be British, except for French Madagascar, the politically weak Portuguese, Italian, and Dutch colonies, and the Arabian and Persian coasts, in which British influence was strong. It is easy to see why the Mediterranean and the Suez Canal, leading from Europe into this half-world, were called the lifeline of the British Empire.

decades the Dutch exploited their huge empire by a kind of forced labor, the "culture system," in which the authorities required farmers to deliver, as a kind of tax, stated amounts of stated crops, such as sugar or coffee. After 1870 a freer system was introduced. The Dutch also, as an important matter of policy, favored instruction in the Malay and Javanese languages, not in Dutch. This preserved the native cultures from westernizing disintegration but at the same time meant that Western ideas of nationalism and democracy entered more slowly.

In India, in 1857, the British faced a dangerous rebellion, commonly called the Indian Mutiny, as if it had been a revolt of undisciplined soldiers only. The Indian army, with its sepoys, was the only organization through which Indians could exert any collective pressure. The proportion of sepoys in the army was high in 1857 (about five-sixths) because British units had been withdrawn for the Crimean War and for action in China. Many Indians, outside the army, had been restless for decades. Rulers had been conquered and dethroned. Landowners had lost their property and been replaced by new ones more friendly to the British. Religious sentiments were inflamed. The British too obviously regarded Indian beliefs as repulsive; they had outlawed suttee, or widow burning, suppressed the Thugs, a small sect of holy assassins, and one British officer even declared that in ten years the government would abolish caste. The Muslims were agitated by Wahabi fundamentalism. Mysterious propaganda circulated over India. It infiltrated the sepoys, announcing to Muslim soldiers that certain newly issued cartridges were greased with the fat of a pig and to Hindus that the same cartridges were greased with the fat of a cow. Since for Hindus the cow was sacred, and for Muslims to touch pork was profane, much agitation was produced. The sepoys mutinied in the Ganges valley; and with them the other injured interests, including the far-faded Great Mogul and his court, rose against the British.

The British put down the rebellion, aided by the fact that western and southern India took no part in it. But the uprising persuaded the British to a radically new course of policy, pursued basically until the end of the Indian empire almost a century later. The British East India Company and the Mogul empire were both finally and forever done away with. British authorities ruled directly. But the British concluded that they must rule India with and through the Indians themselves, not against them. This in practice meant a collaboration between the imperial power and the Indian upper classes. The British began to shelter Indian vested interests. They supported the Indian landlords and became more indulgent toward Indian "superstition." Where before 1857, when they conquered an Indian state, they had simply abolished it and incorporated its territories, after the Mutiny they kept the remaining Indian states as protectorates. States existing in 1857, such as Hyderabad and Kashmir and over 200 others, with their galaxy of rajahs and maharajahs, carried on to the end of British rule in 1947. It was largely to provide a fitting summit for this mountain of Indian royalty that Queen Victoria was proclaimed empress of India in 1877.

India had been a considerable manufacturing country by preindustrial standards. Indian merchants had once been important throughout the Indian Ocean, and before 1800 Indian exports to Europe had included many textiles and other finished goods.[26] The native crafts collapsed before modern industrialism reinforced by political power. "India," observed a British expert in 1837, "can never again be a great manufacturing country, but by cultivating her connection with England she may be one of the greatest agricultural countries in the world." Free trade (made possible by military superiority, usually overlooked by the economists) turned Britain into the world's workshop and India into a supplier of raw materials. Indian exports, in the latter part of the nineteenth century, consisted increasingly in raw cotton, tea, jute, oilseeds, indigo, and wheat. The British shipped their manufactures in return. Business in India boomed; India came to have the densest railway network outside of Europe and North America. It is important to note, however, as a commentary on dealing with poor countries, that Britain in 1914 did far more trading with the 6 million people of Australia and New Zealand than with the 315 million impoverished people of India.

The British, in contrast to the Dutch, decided in 1835 to favor instruction in English, not in the native languages. The historian Macaulay, one of the commission to make this recommendation, branded the Indian languages as vehicles of barbarous and unenlightened ideas—a bar to progress. The British also, after the Mutiny, admitted Indians to the civil service and to governors' councils—sparingly indeed, but more than the Dutch in Indonesia. There were also many Indian businessmen. A class of westernized Indians grew up, speaking perfect English, and often educated in England. They demanded more of a role in the affairs of their country. In 1885 the predominantly Hindu Indian National Con-

26 See p. 242.

gress was organized; in 1906, the All-India Muslim League. Muslim separatism, while favored by the British and sometimes even blamed upon them, was natural to India and exploited by some Indian leaders. Nationalism spread. It became increasingly anti-British, and radical nationalism turned also against the Indian princes, capitalists, and businessmen, as accomplices in imperialism, and so took on the color of socialism. In the period of the First World War, under nationalist pressure, the British granted more representation to Indians, especially in provincial affairs, but the movement toward self-rule was never fast enough to overcome the basic anti-British feeling of the Indian peoples.

Conflict of Russian and British Interests

While no outsider yet threatened the British in India, British statecraft discerned in the northern sky a large cloud which was clearly approaching. The Russian empire had occupied northern Asia since the seventeenth century.[27] About 1850 Russian pressure on inner Asia was resumed. It was a type of imperialism in which neither the demand for markets nor for raw materials, nor for the investment of capital, counted for much. In these matters Russia was itself semicolonial with respect to the West. The Russians had, like the Westerners, a sense of spreading their type of civilization; but Russian expansion was distinctively political in that most of the initiative came from the government. Russia was an ice-bound empire, craving "warm-water ports." It was a landlocked empire, so that whichever way it turned it moved toward one ocean or another. The ocean was the domain of the Westerners, and in particular the British. In the large picture, Russia pushed by land against the Ottoman Empire, Persia, India, and China, all of which the British (and others) reached by sea. In 1860, on the shores of the Sea of Japan, the Russians founded Vladivostok, the farthest-flung of all Slavic cities, whose name meant Lord of the East. But their advance in the mid-century was mainly in the arid and thinly settled regions of western Asia. The British had already fought two Afghan wars to keep Afghanistan as a no man's land between Russia and India. In 1864 the Russians took Tashkent, in Turkestan. A decade later they touched India itself but were kept away by an Anglo-Russian agreement, which allotted a long tongue of land to Afghanistan and so separated the Indian and Russian empires by twenty miles—the new frontier, in the high Pamirs, on the Roof of the World, was to be sure, scarcely adapted to military operations.

Russian advances in Turkestan, east of the Caspian, increased the pressure on Persia, which had long felt the same pressure west of the Caspian, where cities like Tiflis and Baku, now Russian, had once been Persian. If Tiflis and Turkestan could fall to the Russian empire, there was no reason why Persia should not do so next—except that Persia had a seacoast and so might also be available for occupancy by the British. In 1864 a British company completed the first Persian telegraph as part of the line from Europe to India. Other British investments and interests followed. Oil became important about 1900. In 1890, to bolster the Persian government against Russia, the British granted it a loan—taking the customs in Persian Gulf ports as collateral. In 1900 the Russian government granted the same favor, making its own loan to Persia, and appropriating as

[27] See pp. 225–226.

security all Persian customs except those of the Gulf. Russian ships appeared in the Persian Gulf in 1900, a demonstration soon countered by a state visit to Persia of the Viceroy of India, Lord Curzon. Clearly Persia was losing control of its own affairs, falling into zones, turning ripe for partition. A Persian nationalist revolution, directed against all foreigners and against the subservient government of the shah, broke out in 1905 and led to the assembly of the first parliament but hardly settled the question of Persian independence. In 1907 the British recognized a Russian "sphere of influence" in northern Persia, the Russians a British sphere in the south.[28]

Imperial ambitions had deepened the hostility between Great Britain and Russia, with disputes over Persia and the Indian borderlands adding fuel to the quarrel they had long waged over the Ottoman Empire. We have seen how the struggle for Africa had at the same time estranged Britain from France and indeed from all Europe.

82. IMPERIALISM IN ASIA: CHINA AND THE WEST

China before Western Penetration

But the biggest bone of imperialist contention was offered by China. On this bone every Great Power without exception tried to bite. The Manchu dynasty held a suzerainty over the whole area affected by Chinese civilization, from the mouth of the Amur River (as far north as Labrador) to Burma and Indochina (as far south as Panama), and from the ocean westward into Mongolia and Tibet. In the old Chinese view China was the world itself, the Middle Kingdom between the upper and nether regions. The Europeans were outlandish barbarians. A few had trickled through to China since the European Middle Ages. But the Chinese people persistently wanted nothing to do with them.

China was moving into an upheaval of its own even before Western influence became of any importance. For 2,000 years the country had seen dynasties come and go in a kind of cycle. The Manchu dynasty in the nineteenth century was clearly nearing its end. It was failing to preserve order or to curb extortion. About 1800 a White Lotus Society revolted and was suppressed. In 1813 a Heavenly Reason Society attempted to seize Peking. In the 1850s a Muslim rebellion set up a temporary independent state in the southwest. Greatest of all the upheavals was the Taiping Rebellion of 1850, in which as many as 20 million people, approximately the population of Great Britain at the time, are thought to have perished. Except that some fragmentary Christian ideas, obtained from missionaries, were expressed by some of the Taipings, the rebellion was due entirely to Chinese causes. The rebels attacked the Manchus, who had come from Manchuria two centuries before, as corrupt foreigners ruling over China. Their grievances were poverty, extortion, rack-renting, and absentee landlords. The Taipings at first set up a state in south China, and their armies were at first disciplined, but the fighting lasted so long that both the Taiping leaders and the Manchu commanders sent against them got out of control, and much of the country sank into chronic banditry and disorder. It was in this period that China's war lords, men

[28] See p. 658.

controlling armed forces but obeying no government, appeared. The Manchus managed to put down organized Taiping resistance after fourteen years, with some European assistance, led by the British General Gordon, the "Chinese Gordon" who later died at Khartoum. But it is clear that Chinese social confusion, agrarianism, and nationalism (the latter at first only anti-Manchu) antedated the impact of European imperialism.

Into this distracted China the Europeans began to penetrate about 1840. It became their policy to extort concessions from the Manchu empire but at the same time to defend the Manchu empire against internal opposition, as was shown by the exploits of Gordon. This was because they needed some kind of government in China with which they could make treaties, legalizing their claims and binding upon the whole country.

The Opening of China to the West

The modern phase of Chinese relations with the West was inauspiciously opened by the Opium War of 1841. We have already observed how, though Europeans wanted Chinese products, the Chinese had no interest in buying European products in return. Trade therefore was difficult, and the British East India Company had for decades solved the problem of getting Chinese tea for Europe by shipping Indian-grown opium in return, since opium was one available commodity for which a Chinese demand existed.[29] When the Chinese government attempted to control the inflow of opium the British government went to war. Fifteen years later, in 1857, Britain and France combined in a second war upon China to force the Chinese to receive their diplomats and deal with their traders. The Chinese proving contumacious, 17,000 French and British soldiers entered Peking and deliberately burned the emperor's very extensive Summer Palace, an appalling act of vandalism from which soldiers brought back so much loot—vases, tapestries, porcelain, enamels, jades, wood carvings—as to set a fashion in Europe and America for Chinese art.

From the first of these wars arose the treaty of Nanking (1842), from the second the treaties of Tientsin (1857), whose terms were soon duplicated in still other treaties signed by China with other European powers and with the United States. The resulting complex of interlocking agreements imposed certain restric-

[29] See pp. 242, 333.

IMPERIALISM IN ASIA, 1840–1914

Boundaries and possessions are as of 1914. During these years the British and Dutch filled out their holdings in India and the East Indies, in each case moving outward from establishments founded long before. The Russians, who had long occupied Siberia, pressed southward in Central Asia, founded Vladivostok in 1860, and penetrated Manchuria at the close of the century. The French built an empire in Indochina, while the United States acquired the Philippines, and the Germans, as latecomers, were confined to miscellaneous parts of the western Pacific. The Japanese won control of Korea and replaced the Russians as the chief outside influence in Manchuria. Meanwhile all obtained special rights and concessions in China. A bid for such concessions by Italy was refused.

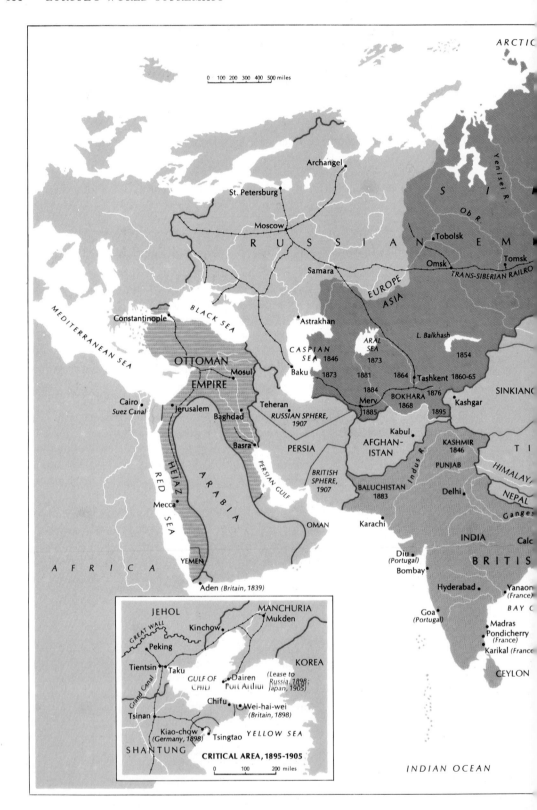

0   100 200 300 400 500 miles

ARCTIC

S I   E M

Yenisei R.

Archangel

Ob R.

St. Petersburg

Tobolsk

Moscow

R U S S I A N

Samara   EUROPE   Omsk   Tomsk

ASIA   TRANS-SIBERIAN RAILRO

Constantinople   BLACK SEA   Astrakhan

L. Balkhash

MEDITERRANEAN SEA   CASPIAN   ARAL   1854
                                           SEA   SEA
                                           1846   1873

OTTOMAN   Baku   1873   1881   1864   Tashkent 1860-65
          Mosul   1884   1876   SINKIANG
EMPIRE   BOKHARA
          Teheran   Mery   1868   Kashgar
Cairo   Jerusalem   RUSSIAN SPHERE,   1885   1895
Suez Canal   Baghdad   1907
                                                Kabul
                              Basra   PERSIA   AFGHAN-   KASHMIR   T I
                                                ISTAN   1846
                                           BRITISH   PUNJAB   HIMALAY
                                           SPHERE,   NEPAL
HEJAZ   1907   BALUCHISTAN   Delhi
          RED   ARABIA   1883   Ganges
Mecca   SEA   OMAN   Karachi   INDIA   Calc
                                                Diu   BRITIS
AFRICA   YEMEN   (Portugal)
                                                Bombay
          Aden (Britain, 1839)   Hyderabad   Yanaon
                                                                    (France)
                                           Goa   BAY C
          JEHOL   MANCHURIA   (Portugal)
                         Mukden   Madras
GREAT WALL   Kinchow   Pondicherry
                                                             (France)
Peking   Karikal (France
Tientsin   Taku   KOREA
          GULF OF   Dairen   (Lease to   CEYLON
          CHILI   Port Arthur   Russia, 1898;
                              Japan, 1905)
          Chifu
Tsinan   Wei-hai-wei
                (Britain, 1898)
Kiao-chow   Tsingtao   YELLOW SEA
(Germany, 1898)
SHANTUNG   **CRITICAL AREA, 1895-1905**

0   100   200 miles

INDIAN OCEAN

tions on China, or conferred certain rights upon foreigners, which came to be known as the "treaty system." To the British in 1842 the Chinese ceded Hong Kong outright. They opened over a dozen cities, including Shanghai and Canton, to Europeans as "treaty ports." In these cities Europeans were allowed to make settlements of their own, immune to all Chinese law. Europeans traveling in the Chinese empire remained subject only to their own governments, and European and American gunboats began to police the Yangtse River. The Chinese likewise paid large war indemnities, though it was they themselves who suffered most of the damages. They agreed to levy no import duty over 5 percent and so became a free trade market for European products. To administer and collect the customs a staff of European experts was introduced. Money from the customs, collected with a new efficiency, on a swelling volume of imports, went in part to the British and French in payment of the indemnities, but part remained with the Manchu government, which, as noted, the Europeans had no desire to overthrow.

Annexations and Concessions

While China was thus permeated at the center like an aging cheese, by extraterritorial and other insidious privileges for Europeans, whole slabs of it were cut away at the outer rim. The Russians moved down the Amur River, established their Maritime Province, and founded Vladivostok in 1860. The Japanese, now sufficiently westernized to behave like Europeans in such matters, in 1876 recognized the independence of Korea. The British annexed Burma in 1886. The French in 1883 assumed a protectorate over Annam despite Chinese protests; they soon combined five areas—Annam, Cochin China, Tonkin, Laos, and Cambodia—into French Indochina. (The first three were known also as Vietnam, a word not familiar in the West until after the Second World War.) These outlying territories had never, it is true, been integral parts of China proper; but it was with China that they had had their most important political and cultural relations and to the Chinese emperor that they had paid tribute.

Japan, whose modernization has been described already, lost little time in developing an imperialistic urge.[30] An expansionist party already looked to the Chinese mainland and to the south. Japanese imperialism first revealed itself to the rest of the world in 1894, when Japan went to war with China over disputes in Korea. The Japanese soon won, equipped as they were with modern weapons, training, and organization. They obliged the Chinese to sign the treaty of Shimonoseki in 1895, by which China ceded Formosa and the Liaotung peninsula to Japan and recognized Korea as an independent state. The Liaotung was a tongue of land reaching down from Manchuria to the sea; at its tip was Port Arthur. Manchuria was the northeastern part of China itself.

This sudden Japanese triumph precipitated a crisis in the Far East. No one had realized how strong Japan had become. All were astounded that a people who were not "European," i.e., white, should show such aptitude for modern war and diplomacy. It was to be supposed that Japan had designs on Manchuria.

Now it so happened that Russia, not long before, in 1891, had begun to build the Trans-Siberian Railway, whose eastern terminus was to be Vladivostok, the "Lord of the East." Manchuria extended northward in a great hump between

30 See pp. 536–541.

central Siberia and Vladivostok. The Russians, whether or not they ever dominated Manchuria themselves, could not allow its domination by another Great
Power. It happened also that Germany was at this time looking for a chance to
enter the Far Eastern arena, and that France had formed an alliance with Russia,
whose good will it was eager to retain.[31]

Russia, Germany, and France therefore registered an immediate joint demurrer
with the Tokyo Foreign Office. They demanded that Japan give up the Liaotung
peninsula. The Japanese hesitated; they were indignant, but they yielded. The
Liaotung went back to China.

In China many alert people were humiliated at the defeat by the Japanese
whom they had despised. The Chinese government, at last facing the inevitable,
began madly to plan westernization. Huge loans were obtained from Europe—
the customs being pawned as security, following the pattern well established in
Turkey, Persia, and Santo Domingo. But the European powers did not wish
China to become consolidated too soon. Nor had they forgotten the sudden
apparition of Japan. The result was a frantic scramble for further concessions in
1898.

It seemed in 1898 as if the Chinese empire in its turn would be partitioned.
The Germans extorted a ninety-nine-year lease on Kiaochow Bay, plus exclusive
rights in the Shantung peninsula. The Russians took a lease on the Liaotung
peninsula from which they had just excluded Japan; they thus obtained Port
Arthur and rights to build railroads in Manchuria to interlock with their Trans-
Siberian system. The French took Kwangchow and the British Wei-hai-wei,
in addition to confirming their sphere of influence in the Yangtse valley. The
Italians demanded a share but were refused. The United States, fearing that all
China might soon be parceled out into exclusive spheres, announced its policy of
the Open Door. The idea of the Open Door was that China should remain
territorially intact and independent, and that powers having special concessions
or spheres of influence should maintain the 5 percent Chinese tariff and allow
businessmen of all nations to trade without discrimination. The British supported
the Open Door, as a means of discouraging actual annexations by Japan or
Russia, which, as the only Great Powers adjacent to China, were the only ones
that could dispatch real armies into its territory. The Open Door was a program
not so much of leaving China to the Chinese, as of assuring that all outsiders
should find it literally "open."

If the reader will imagine what the United States would be like if foreign
warships patrolled the Mississippi as far as St. Louis, if foreigners came and went
throughout the country without being under its laws, if New York, New Orleans,
and other cities contained foreign settlements outside its jurisdiction, but in
which all banking and management were concentrated, if foreigners determined
the tariff policy, collected the proceeds, and remitted much of the money to their
own governments, if the western part of the city of Washington had been burned
(the Summer Palace), Long Island and California annexed to distant empires
(Hong Kong and Indochina), and all New England were coveted by two immediate neighbors (Manchuria), if the national authorities were half in collusion
with these foreigners and half victimized by them, and if large areas of the
country were the prey to bandits, guerrillas, and revolutionary secret societies

[31] See pp. 655–656.

NORTHEAST CHINA AND ADJOINING REGIONS, 1895–1914

This area has long been one of the world's trouble zones. Note how Vladivostok is shut off from the ocean by the Japanese islands and Korea, and almost shut off from the mass of Russia by the intervening bulk of Manchuria. Manchuria, which began to be industrialized about 1900, became an object of dispute between China, to which it belonged historically, the Russian empire, to which it had strategic value and offered an access to the open ocean, and the Japanese empire, which found in it an outlet for commercial and military expansion and a buffer against Russia. Manchuria was dominated by the Russians from 1898 to 1905, by the Japanese from 1905 to 1945, and again by the Russians from 1945 to 1950, when they handed over their concessions and privileges to the Chinese Communist government. Korea was dominated by Japan after its victories over China in 1895 and over Russia in 1905. After World War II, Korea was promised independence but was divided at the 38th parallel into a Russian occupation zone and an American zone. After the Korean War (1950–1953, see pp. 917–919) the country remained divided at roughly the same parallel with a Communist regime in the north and a Western-sponsored regime in the south.

conspiring against the helpless government and occasionally murdering some of the foreigners—then he can understand how observant Chinese felt at the end of the last century, and why the term "imperialism" came to be held by so many of the world's peoples in abomination.

One Chinese secret society, its name somewhat literally translated as the Order of Literary Patriotic Harmonious Fists, and so dubbed the Boxers by the amused Westerners, broke out in insurrection in 1899. The Boxers pulled up railway tracks, fell upon Chinese Christians, besieged the foreign legations, and killed about 300 foreigners. The European powers, joined by Japan and the United States, sent a combined international force against the insurgents, who were put down. The victors imposed still more severe controls on the Chinese government and inflicted an indemnity of $330 million. Of this the United States received $24 million, of which, in 1924, it canceled the balance that was still due. On the other hand, as a consequence of the Boxer Rebellion, the Manchu officials strove desperately to strengthen themselves by westernization, while at the same time the revolutionary movement in China, aiming at expulsion of Manchus and foreigners alike, spread rapidly throughout the country, especially in the south, under the leadership of Sun Yat-sen.

83. THE RUSSO-JAPANESE WAR AND ITS CONSEQUENCES

Meanwhile Russia and Japan opposed each other's intrigues in Manchuria and Korea. The Japanese felt a need for supplying their new factories with raw materials and markets on the Asian mainland, for employment for their newly westernized army and navy, and for recognized status as a Great Power in the Western sense. The Russian government needed an atmosphere of crisis and expansion to stifle criticism of tsarism at home; it could not abide the presence of a strong power directly on its East Asian frontier; it could use Manchuria and Korea to strengthen the exposed outpost of Vladivostok, which was somewhat squeezed against the sea and landlocked by Japanese waters. The Russians had

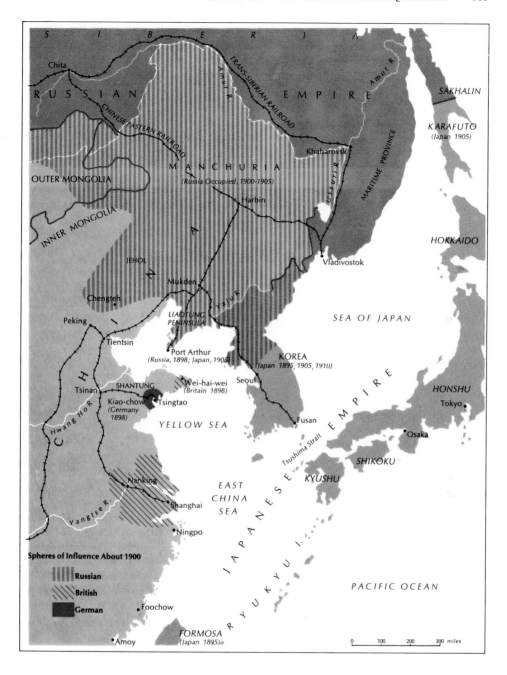

obtained a concession from China to build the Chinese Eastern Railway to Vladivostok across the heart of Manchuria. A railway, in Manchuria, implied special zones, railway guards, mining and timber rights, and other auxiliary activities. The Japanese saw the fruits of their successful war of 1895 against China greedily enjoyed by their rival. In 1902 Japan signed a military alliance with Great Britain. We have seen how the British were alarmed by their diplomatic isolation after

Fashoda and the Boer War, and how for many years, in the Far East, the Middle East, and the Near East, they had been expecting to have trouble with Russia. The Anglo-Japanese military alliance lasted twenty years.

War broke out in 1904, undeclared, by Japanese naval attack on Russian installations at Port Arthur. Both sides sent large armies into Manchuria. The battle of Mukden, in the number of men engaged, which was 624,000, was the largest battle that human experience had thus far witnessed. Military observers were present from all countries, anxiously trying to learn what the next war in Europe would be like. The Russians sent their Baltic fleet around three continents to the Far East, but to the world's amazement the Russian fleet was met and destroyed at Tsushima Strait by the new and untested navy of Japan. Russian communications by sea were thereby broken, and since the Trans-Siberian Railway was unfinished, and since the Japanese also won the battle of Mukden, Russia was beaten.

At this point the president of the United States, Theodore Roosevelt, stepped upon the scene. With an outpost in the Philippines and growing interests in China, it was to the American advantage to have neither side win too overwhelming a victory in the Far East. The most imperially minded of all American presidents offered his mediation, and plenipotentiaries of the two powers met at Portsmouth, New Hampshire. By the treaty of Portsmouth, in 1905, Japan recovered from Russia what it had won and lost in 1895, namely, Port Arthur and the Liaotung peninsula, a preferred position in Manchuria, which remained nominally Chinese, and a protectorate in Korea, which remained nominally independent, although a few years later in 1910, it was annexed by Japan. Japan also received from Russia the southern half of the island of Sakhalin. Much of what Russia lost to Japan in 1905 was regained forty years later at the end of the Second World War.

The Russo-Japanese War was the first war between Great Powers since 1870. It was the first war fought under conditions of developed industrialism. It was the first actual war between westernized powers to be caused by competition in the exploitation of undeveloped countries. Most significant of all (except for the Ethiopian rout of the Italians), it was the first time that a nonwhite people had defeated a white people in modern times. Asians had shown that they could learn and play, in less than half a century, the game of the Europeans.

The Japanese victory set off long chains of repercussions in at least three different directions. For one thing, the Russian government, frustrated in its foreign policy in East Asia, shifted its attention back to Europe, where it resumed an active role in the affairs of the Balkans. This contributed to a series of international crises in Europe, of which the result was the First World War. Second, the tsarist government was so weakened by the war, both in prestige and in actual military strength, and opinion in Russia was so disgusted at the clumsiness and incompetency with which the war had been handled, that the various underground movements were able to come to the surface, producing the Revolution of 1905. This in turn was a prelude to the great Russian Revolution twelve years later, of which Soviet communism was the outcome. Third, news of Japan's victory over Russia electrified those who heard of it throughout the non-European world. The fact that Japan was itself an imperialist power was overlooked in the excited realization that the Japanese were not white. Only half a century ago the

Japanese, too, had been "backward"—defenseless, bombarded, and bulldozed by the Europeans. The moral was clear. Everywhere leaders of subjugated peoples concluded, from the Japanese precedent, that they must bring Western science and industry to their own countries, but that they must do it, as the Japanese had done, by getting rid of control by the Europeans, supervising the process of modernization themselves, and preserving their own native national character. Nationalist revolutions began in Persia in 1905, in Turkey in 1908, in China in 1911. In India and Indonesia many were stirred by the Japanese achievement. In the face of rising agitation, the British admitted an Indian to the Viceroy's executive Council in 1909, and in 1916 the Dutch created a People's Council, to include Indonesian members, in the Indies. The self-assertion of Asians was to grow in intensity after the First World War.

The Japanese victory and Russian defeat can therefore be seen as steps in three mighty developments, the First World War, the Russian Revolution, and the Revolt of Asia. These three together put an end to Europe's world supremacy and almost to European civilization; or at least they so transmuted them as to make the world of the twentieth century far different from that of the nineteenth.

The British in India

The British presence in India, reaching over three centuries, spanned the whole period from the early trading empires to the latest phases of European imperialism. In the seventeenth century the Indian subcontinent was held together by a Muslim empire whose ruler was known in Europe as the Great Mogul. His revenues, in 1605, were some twenty times greater than those of the King of England. The Europeans were for a long time only handfuls of foreigners operating out of small coastal stations. After 1700 the Mogul authority fell to pieces, leaving a disorganized situation in which the British emerged as the supreme power throughout the country.

India in the nineteenth century represented, in its fullest form, the European imperialism that by 1900 reached throughout Asia and Africa. Parts of it were ruled by the British directly, parts through the rajahs and maharajahs of native states. British power prevented internal warfare and subordinated the conflicts between Hindus and Muslims. Peace generally prevailed except for the great Mutiny, or rebellion, of 1857, which was quickly suppressed. The British introduced their own ideas of law, government, civil service, and education. With food production increased by irrigation and famine relieved by transport of provisions by railroad, population grew very rapidly.

The British invested a great deal of capital in India, in railroads, coal mines, and tea plantations. There was also much development of Indian capital, especially in the new jute, cotton, and steel industries. As the railroad opened the interior to the cheaper products of Lancashire, the old handicraft and village industries were destroyed, to be symbolically revived by Gandhi and his spinning wheel in the 1920s, and in fact replaced by an extensive development of modern manufactures. India moved into the twentieth century as a land of violent contrasts, of endless villages interrupted by teeming cities, with staggering problems of poverty and overpopulation, yet also as an important industrial country with a heavy involvement in world trade.

The British, throughout their rule in India, lived very much to themselves, occasionally mixing with the Indian upper classes but avoiding intimate or even equal relationships. For many Indians, nevertheless, English became a second language, used both for contacts with the Western world and as a common medium among themselves. A modern Indian upper class, largely English-speaking, grew up with the development of business, government, and the professions. It ultimately took the lead in the national movement against foreign rule. But historic divisions within the country, between Hindu and Muslim, dating back to the Mogul empire and before, brought it about that upon the British withdrawal, in 1947, what had formerly been known as India became the separate states of India and Pakistan. Later Bangladesh was formed by secession from Pakistan.

The gorgeous East, as Milton called it, had been fabled in Europe for its riches since ancient times. Above, right, we see the weighing of the Great Mogul on his birthday, upon
which he was to receive an equal weight in gold and jewels. The picture is from an
English geography of 1782. As the French "Encyclopédie" put it at about this time:
"The most solemn day of the year was when the emperor was weighed in golden bal-
ances in the presence of the people; on that day he received over 50 millions in
presents."

At the left is the English factory at Surat, near Bombay, in the early seventeenth
century. A "factory" was only a trading center where the agents, or factors, of the East
India Company stored their goods.

644

645

646

Calcutta, now the largest city in India, is far from being one of the oldest. It was founded by the English East India Company in 1690, and acquired many Western-style buildings in the two following centuries. At the left above is the Old Court House; at the right the early nineteenth-century Government House, with a large British lion astride the neoclassic gate. At the left an English lady is carried in a palanquin, and in both pictures important persons ride by in carriages, surveyed at a distance by some of the plain people of India, one of them with a bullock cart. The two cultures never really merged.

Darjeeling, in the mountains 300 miles north of Calcutta, grew up after 1840 as a cool retreat for Britons in refuge from the Indian heat. At the left is the "big loop" of the Darjeeling Railway, a substantial feat of engineering, by which the imperial rulers were able to make the journey more comfortably. The clouds probably obscure a view of the Himalayas for which Darjeeling is famous.

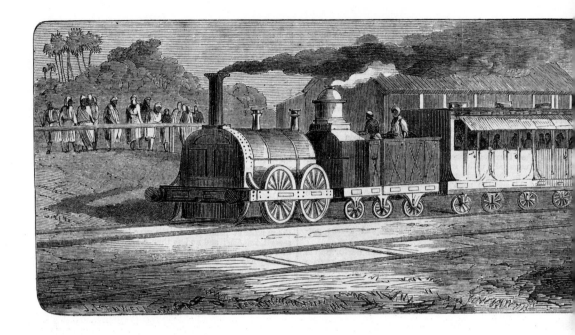

The railroad also had a transforming impact on India as a whole. By carrying goods it brought the interior into the world market, breaking up old native industries while creating new ones, and by transporting persons it drew together the members of diverse religions, castes, and linguistic groups. A passenger train of 1863 appears above. In its crowded coaches Indians who in former times would have kept scrupulously apart, for fear of pollution, had to rub elbows together, and on long journeys even eat together and breathe the same tainted air. Such proximity, together with the increasing adoption of English, produced a new basis for Indian unity which in the end was to make the British position untenable.

At the right, before the track is laid, a team of elephants hauls the first locomotive into Indore in Central India.

Above left: Queen Victoria is proclaimed Empress of India at Bombay in 1877. The neo-Gothic canopy, built for the occasion, under which an effigy of the queen is enthroned, seems incongruous in the circumstances. It reminds us, together with the more permanent church in the background, that the British maintained their own ways with supreme confidence, making few concessions to the alien culture over which they presided.

In the nineteenth century the traveling Englishwoman became legendary for her indomitability. At the right, two of them go on a jungle picnic. The pith helmets of their escorts, and the bearer carrying the refreshments in his head, may be taken as symbols of the heyday of empire.

The two scenes depicted in the drawings above represent the administration of justice, with a British magistrate at the left, a native magistrate at the right. They seem much alike, and their purpose may be to show how under British rule the Indian judicial system was brought up to British standards of legal procedure.

Many Indians received a thoroughly English education. At the right is Jawaharlal Nehru at Harrow about 1905. Nehru, born in 1889 of Brahmin parents, his father a wealthy lawyer, was educated at home by English tutors, then sent to Harrow and Cambridge. He joined Gandhi in the independence movement in the 1920s, and served as first prime minister of independent India from 1947 until his death in 1964. British India dug its own grave, or prepared its own successors.

653

XVI.
The First
World War

Somewhere before 1914 Europe went off its course. Europeans believed themselves to be heading for a kind of high plateau, full of a benign progress and more abundant civilization, in which the benefits of modern science and invention would be more widely diffused, and even competitive struggle worked out somehow for the best. Instead, Europe stumbled in 1914 into disaster. It is not easy to see exactly where Europe went astray, at what point, that is, the First World War became inevitable, or (since the human mind does not know what is truly inevitable) so overwhelmingly probable that only the most Olympian statesmanship could have avoided it.

84. THE INTERNATIONAL ANARCHY

After 1870 Europe lived in a repressed fear of itself. The great questions of the mid-century had been settled by force. The German Empire was only the strongest and most obvious of the new structures which armed power had reared. Never had the European states maintained such huge armies in peacetime as at the beginning of the twentieth century. One, two, or even three years of compul-

Chapter Emblem: A German medal to celebrate the sinking of the Lusitania in 1915, showing the Cunard Line as a skeleton selling tickets, under an inscription, "Business First."

sory military service for all young men became the rule. In 1914 each of the Continental Great Powers had not only a huge standing army but millions of trained reserves among the civilian population. Few people wanted war; all but a few sensational writers preferred peace in Europe, but all took it for granted that war would come some day. In the last years before 1914 the idea that war was bound to break out sooner or later probably made some statesmen, in some countries, more willing to unleash it.

Rival Alliances: Triple Alliance versus Triple Entente

Political diagnosticians, from Richelieu to Metternich, had long thought that an effective union of Germany would revolutionize the relationships of Europe's peoples. After 1870 their anticipations were more than confirmed. Once united (or almost united), the Germans entered upon their industrial revolution. Manufacturing, finance, shipping, population grew phenomenally. In steel, for example, of which Germany in 1865 produced less than France, by 1900 Germany produced more than France and Great Britain combined. Germans felt that they needed and deserved a "place in the sun," by which they vaguely meant some kind of acknowledged supremacy like that of the British. Neither the British nor the French, the leaders of modern Europe since the seventeenth century, could share wholeheartedly in such German aspirations. The French had the chronic grievance of Alsace and Lorraine, annexed to Germany in 1871. The British as the years passed saw German salesmen appear in their foreign markets, selling goods often at lower prices and by what seemed ungentlemanly methods; they saw Germans turn up as colonial rivals in Africa, the Near East, and the Far East; and they watched other European states gravitate into the Berlin orbit, looking to the mighty German Empire as a friend and protector to secure or advance their interests.[1]

Bismarck after 1871 feared that in another European war his new German Empire might be torn to pieces. He therefore followed, until his retirement in 1890, a policy of peace. We have seen him as the "honest broker" at the Berlin Congress of 1878, helping to adjudicate the Eastern Question, and again offering the facilities of Berlin in 1885 to regulate African affairs. To isolate France, divert it from Europe, and keep it embroiled with Britain, he looked with satisfaction on French colonial expansion. He took no chances, however; in 1879 he formed a military alliance with Austria-Hungary, to which Italy was added in 1882. Thus was formed the Triple Alliance, which lasted until the First World War. Its terms were, briefly, that if any member became involved in war with two or more powers its allies should come to its aid by force of arms. To be on the safe side, Bismarck signed a "reinsurance" treaty with Russia also; since Russia and Austria were enemies (because of the Balkans), to be allied to both at the same time took considerable diplomatic finesse. After Bismarck's retirement his system proved too intricate, or too lacking in candor, for his successors to manage. The Russo-German agreement lapsed. The French, faced by the Triple Alliance, soon seized the opportunity to form their own alliance with Russia, the Franco-Russian Alliance signed in 1894. In its time this was regarded as politically almost impossible.

---

[1] See map, p. 657.

The French Republic stood for everything radical, the Russian empire for everything reactionary and autocratic. But ideology was thrown to the winds, French capital poured into Russia, and the tsar bared his head to the *Marseillaise.*

The Continent was thus divided by 1894 into two opposed camps, the German-Austrian-Italian against the Franco-Russian. For a time it seemed that this rigid division might soften. Germany, France, and Russia cooperated in the Far Eastern crisis of 1895.[2] All were anti-British at the time of Fashoda and the Boer War.[3] The Kaiser, William II, outlined tempting pictures of a Continental league against the global hegemony of England and her empire.

Much depended on what the British would do. They had long prided themselves on a "splendid isolation," going their own way, disdaining the kind of dependency that alliance with others always brings. Fashoda and the Boer War came as a shock. British relations with France and Russia were very bad. Some in England, including Joseph Chamberlain, therefore thought that a better understanding with Germany was to be sought. Arguments of race, in this race-conscious age, made Englishmen and Germans feel akin.[4] But politically it was hard to cooperate. The Kaiser's Kruger Telegram of 1896 was a studied insult.[5] Then in 1898 the Germans decided to build a navy.

A new kind of "race" now entered the picture, the naval competition between Germany and Great Britain. British sea power for two centuries had been all too successful. The American Admiral Mahan, teaching at the Naval War College, and taking his examples largely from British history, argued that sea power had been the foundation of Britain's greatness, and that in the long run sea power must always choke off and ruin a power operating on the land. Nowhere were Mahan's books read with more interest than in Germany. The German naval

---

2 See pp. 636–637.

3 See pp. 626–627.

4 The will of Cecil Rhodes, who died in 1902, illustrates this point. Rhodes left most of his fortune (£ 6 million) to establish scholarships at Oxford to be awarded to students in the United States, as an Anglo-Saxon country, the British dominions and colonies, and Germany. The German Rhodes Scholarships were suspended from 1914 to 1930 and again after 1938. The same feeling that Germans were racially akin was common in the United States also; a prominent example of this viewpoint was President Theodore Roosevelt.

5 See p. 627.

ANGLO-GERMAN INDUSTRIAL COMPETITION, 1898 AND 1913

This diagram really shows two things: first, the huge increase in world trade in the last fifteen years before the First World War, shared in by all countries; and second, the fact that German exports grew more rapidly than British. The exports of both countries together, as shown on the diagram, multiplied no less than threefold in these fifteen years. The increase, while due in small part to a slight rise of prices, was mainly due to a real increase in volume of business. If the reader will compare the shaded bands within the large arrows he will see that, for the countries shown, British exports about doubled, but those of Germany multiplied many times. In 1913 total German exports about equaled the British, but German exports to the United States and Russia greatly exceeded the British. Note how the Germans even gained in exports to British India, where the liberalism of British policy freely admitted competitive goods. In merchant marine, though the Germans doubled their tonnage, the British continued to enjoy an overwhelming lead.

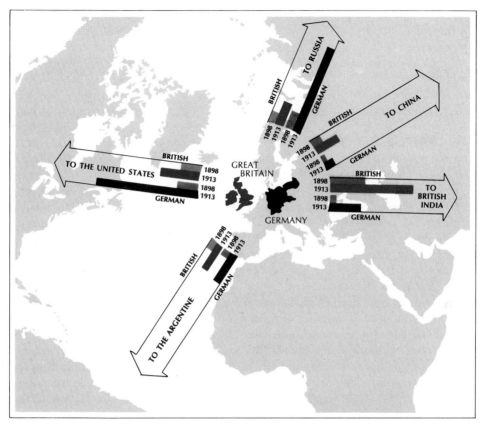

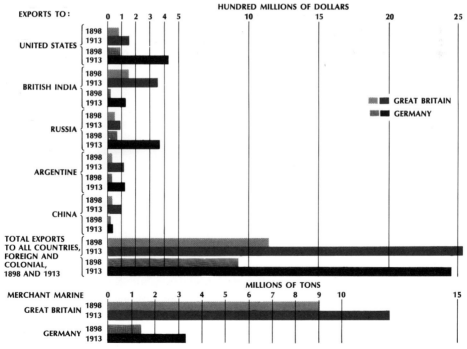

program, mounting rapidly after 1898, in a few years became a source of concern to the British, and by 1912 was felt as a positive menace. The Germans insisted that they must have a navy to protect their colonies, secure their foreign trade, and "for the general purposes of their greatness." The British held with equal resolution that England, as a densely populated industrial island, dependent even for food upon imports, must at all costs control the sea in both peace and war. They adhered stubbornly to their traditional policy of maintaining a navy as large as the next two combined. The naval race led both sides to enormous and increasing expenditures. In the British it produced a sense of profound insecurity, driving them as the years passed ever more inescapably into the arms of Russia and France.

Slowly and cautiously the British emerged from their diplomatic isolation. In 1902 they formed a military alliance with Japan against their common enemy, Russia.[6] The decisive break came in 1904, from which may be dated the immediate series of crises issuing in the World War ten years later.

In 1904 the British and French governments agreed to forget Fashoda and the accumulated bad feeling of the preceding twenty-five years. The French recognized the British occupation of Egypt, and the British recognized the French penetration of Morocco. They also cleared up a few lesser colonial differences and agreed to support each other against protests by third parties. There was no specific alliance; neither side said what it would do in the event of war; it was only a close understanding, an *entente cordiale*. The French immediately tried to reconcile their new friend to their ally, Russia. After defeat by Japan the Russians proved amenable. The British, increasingly uncertain of German aims, proved likewise willing. In 1907 Britain and Russia, the inveterate adversaries, settled their differences in an Anglo-Russian Convention. In Persia, the British recognized a Russian sphere of influence in the north, the Russians a British sphere in the south and east. By 1907 England, France, and Russia were acting together. The older Triple Alliance faced a newer Triple Entente, the latter somewhat the looser, since the British refused to make any formal military commitments.

The Crises in Morocco and the Balkans

The Germans, who already felt encircled by the alliance of France and Russia, naturally watched with concern the drift of England into the Franco-Russian camp. The Entente Cordiale was barely concluded when the German government decided to test it, to find out how strong it really was, or how far the British would really go in support of France. The French, now enjoying British backing, were taking over more police powers, concessions, and loans in Morocco. In March 1905 William II disembarked from a German warship at Tangier, where he made a startling speech in favor of Moroccan independence. To diplomats everywhere this carefully staged performance was a signal: Germany was attempting not primarily to keep France out of Morocco, nor even to reserve Morocco for itself, but to break up the new understanding between France and England. The Germans demanded and obtained an international conference at Algeciras (at which the United States was represented), but the conference,

6 See p. 640.

which met in 1906, supported the French claims in Morocco, only Austria voting with Germany. The German government had thus created an incident and been rebuffed. The British, disturbed by German diplomatic tactics, stood by the French all the more firmly. French and British army and naval officers now began to discuss common plans. Distrust of Germany also inclined the British to bury the hatchet with Russia in the next year. The German attempt to break the Entente simply made it more solid.

In 1911 came a second Morocco crisis. A German gunboat, the *Panther*, arrived at Agadir "to protect German interests." It soon developed that the move was a holdup: the Germans offered to make no further trouble in Morocco if they could have the French Congo. The crisis passed, the Germans obtaining some trifling accessions in Africa. But a member of the British cabinet, David Lloyd George, made a rather inflammatory speech on the German menace.

Meanwhile a series of crises rocked the Balkans. Here at the opening of the twentieth century the situation was very confused. The Ottoman Empire, in an advanced state of dissolution, still held a band of territory from Constantinople westward to the Adriatic.[7] South of this band lay an independent Greece. North of it, on the Black Sea side, lay an autonomous Bulgaria and an independent Rumania. In the center and west of the peninsula, north of the Turkish belt, was the small, landlocked independent kingdom of Serbia, adjoined by Bosnia-Herzegovina, which belonged legally to Turkey but had been "occupied and administered" by Austria since 1878. Within the Austro-Hungarian Empire, adjoining Bosnia on the north, lay Croatia and Slovenia.

Serbs, Bosnians, Croats, and Slovenes all spoke basically the same language, the main difference being that Serbs and Bosnians wrote with the eastern or Cyrillic alphabet, the Croats and Slovenes with the western or Roman. With the Slavic Revival and general growth of nationalism these peoples came to feel that they were really one people, for which they took the term South Slavs or Yugoslavs. We have seen how when the Dual Monarchy was formed in 1867, the Slavs of the Habsburg empire were kept subordinate to the German Austrians and to the Magyars. By 1900 the most radical Slav nationalists within the empire had concluded that the Dual Monarchy would never grant them equal status, that it must be broken up, and that all South Slavs should form an independent state of their own. Concretely, this meant that an element of the Austro-Hungarian population, namely, the Croatian and Slovenian nationalists, wished to get out of the empire and join with Serbia across the border. Serbia became the center of South Slav agitation. The Serbs conceived of their small kingdom as the Sardinia of a South Slav Risorgimento, the nucleus around which a new national state could be formed, at the expense of Austria-Hungary, which, to repeat, contained Croatia-Slovenia within its own frontiers and "occupied" Bosnia.

This brew was brought to a boil in 1908 by two events. First, the Young Turks, whose long agitation against Abdul Hamid has been noted, managed in that year to carry through a revolution.[8] They obliged the sultan to restore the liberal-parliamentary constitution of 1876. They showed, too, that they meant to stop the dissolution of the Ottoman Empire, by taking steps to have delegates from Bulgaria and Bosnia sit in the new Ottoman parliament. Second, Russia, its foreign

[7] See maps, pp. 433, 618, and 661.
[8] See pp. 615–619.

policy in the Far East ruined by the Japanese war, turned actively to the Balkan and Turkish scene. Russia, as always, wanted control at Constantinople. Austria wanted full annexation of Bosnia, the better to discourage Pan-Yugoslav ideas. But if the Young Turks really modernized and strengthened the Ottoman Empire, Austria would never get Bosnia, nor the Russians Constantinople.

The Russian and Austrian foreign ministers, Isvolsky and Aehrenthal, at a conference at Buchlau in 1908 came to a secret agreement: they would call an international conference, at which Russia would favor Austrian annexation of Bosnia, and Austria would support the opening of the Straits to Russian warships. Austria, without waiting for a conference, proclaimed the annexation of Bosnia without more ado. This infuriated the Serbs, who had marked Bosnia for their own. Meanwhile, that same year, the Bulgarians and the Cretans broke finally with the Ottoman Empire, Bulgaria becoming fully independent, Crete uniting with Greece. Isvolsky was never able to realize his plans for Constantinople. His partners in the Triple Entente, Britain and France, refused to back him; the British in particular were evasive on plans for opening the Straits to the Russian fleet. The projected international conference was never called. In Russia itself public opinion knew nothing of Isvolsky's secret deal. The known fact in Russia was that the Serbs, the little Slav brothers of Russia, had had their toes rudely stepped on by the Austrians by the annexation of Bosnia.

This "first Balkan crisis" presently passed. The Russians, weakened by the Japanese war and by recent revolution,[9] accepted the Austrian *fait accompli*. Russia protested but backed down. Austrian influence in the Balkans seemed to be growing. And South Slav nationalism was frustrated and inflamed.

In 1911 Italy declared war on Turkey, from which it soon conquered Tripoli and the Dodecanese Islands. With the Ottomans thus embarrassed, Bulgaria, Serbia, and Greece joined forces in their own war against Turkey, hoping to annex certain Balkan territories to which they believed they had a right. Turkey was soon defeated, but the Bulgarians claimed more of Macedonia than the Serbs would yield, so that the first Balkan war of 1912 was followed in 1913 by a second, in which Serbia, Greece, Rumania, and Turkey turned upon and defeated Bulgaria. Albania also, a mountainous region on the Adriatic, mainly Muslim, and known as the wildest place in all Europe, was the subject of angry discord. The Serbs occupied part of it in the two Balkan wars, but the Greeks also claimed a part, and it had also on several occasions been vaguely promised to Italy.[10] Russia supported the Serbian claim. Austria was determined to shut off the Serbs from access to the sea, which they would obtain by annexation of Albanian territory. An agreement of the great powers, to keep the peace, conjured up an independent kingdom of Albania. This confirmed the Austrian policy, kept Serbia from the sea, and aroused vehement outcries in both Serbia and Russia. But Russia again backed down. Serbian expansionism was again frustrated and inflamed.

The third Balkan crisis proved to be the fatal one. It was fatal because two others had gone before it, leaving feelings of exasperation in Austria, desperation in Serbia, and humiliation in Russia.

9 See pp. 638–640, 699–701.
10 See p. 617.

THE BALKANS, 1878 AND 1914

The Ottoman Empire, under the blows of Austria and Russia, had been receding from Europe since 1699 (see map, p. 618). The Congress of Berlin of 1878 undertook to stabilize the situation by recognizing Rumania, Serbia, and Montenegro as independent monarchies, and northern Bulgaria as an autonomous principality within the Ottoman Empire. The ambitions of these new states (and of Greece, independent since 1829), together with the discontents of all non-Turkish peoples remaining under Ottoman rule, led to successive altercations culminating in the Balkan wars of 1912–1913. Albania then became independent, and Serbia, Bulgaria, and Greece contiguous. Austrian and Russian pressures meanwhile continued; in 1908 Austria annexed Bosnia, where the South Slav population was related to the Serbs. In Bosnia, at Sarajevo, six years later, the assassination of an Austrian archduke by a South Slav patriot precipitated the First World War.

The Sarajevo Crisis and the Outbreak of War

On June 28, 1914, a young Bosnian revolutionary, a member of the Serbian secret society called "Union or Death," and commonly known as the Black Hand, acting with the knowledge of certain Serbian officials, assassinated the heir to the Habsburg empire, the Archduke Francis Ferdinand, in the streets of Sarajevo, the Bosnian capital, in the Austrian Empire. The world was shocked at this terrorist outrage and at first sympathized with the protests of the Austrian government. Francis Ferdinand, who would soon have become emperor, was known to favor some kind of transformation of Austria-Hungary, in which a more equal place might be given to the Slavs; but the reformer who makes a system work is the most dangerous of all enemies to the implacable revolutionary, and it is perhaps for this reason that the archduke was killed by the Black Hand.

The Austrian government was determined to make an end to the South Slav separatism that was gnawing its empire to pieces. It decided to crush the independence of Serbia, the nucleus of South Slav agitation, though not to annex it, since there were now thought to be too many Slavs within the empire already. The Austrian government consulted the German to see how far it might go with the support of its ally. The Germans, issuing their famous "blank check," encouraged the Austrians to be firm. The Austrians, thus reassured, dispatched a drastic ultimatum to Serbia, demanding among other things that Austrian officials be permitted to collaborate in investigating and punishing the perpetrators of the assassination. The Serbs counted on Russian support, even to the point of war, judging that Russia could not again yield in a Balkan crisis, for the third time in six years, without losing its influence in the Balkans altogether. The Russians in turn counted on France; and France, terrified at the possibility of being some day caught alone in a war with Germany, and determined to keep Russia as an ally at any cost, in effect gave a blank check to Russia. The Serbs rejected the critical item in the Austrian ultimatum as an infringement on Serbian sovereignty, and Austria thereupon declared war upon Serbia. Russia prepared to defend Serbia and hence to fight Austria. Expecting that Austria would be joined by Germany, Russia rashly mobilized its army on the German as well as the Austrian frontier. Since the power which first mobilized had all the advantages of a rapid offensive, the German government demanded an end to the Russian mobilization on its border and, receiving no answer, declared war on Russia on August 1, 1914. Convinced that France would in any case enter the war on the side of Russia, Germany also declared war on France on August 3.

The German decisions were posited on a reckless hope that Great Britain might not enter the war at all. England was bound by no formal military alliance. Even the French did not know for certain, as late as August 3, whether the British would join them in war. The British clung to scraps of their old proud isolation; they hesitated to make a final choice of sides; and as the foreign secretary, Sir Edward Grey, repeatedly explained, in England only Parliament could declare war, so that the foreign office could make no binding promise of war in advance. It has often been said that, had the German government known as a positive fact that England would fight, the war might not have come. Hence the evasiveness of British policy is made a contributing cause of the war. In reality, the probability that England would fight was so great that to underestimate it, as the Germans did, was an act of supreme folly. The British were deeply committed to France, especially through naval agreements. As the German High Seas Fleet grew, the British had been obliged to concentrate naval forces in the North Sea. They had therefore had to withdraw forces from the Mediterranean. In 1914, by agreement with France, the French fleet was concentrated in the Mediterranean, watching over British interests, while the British fleet attended to French interests in the north. The French Channel coast was therefore open to German naval attack, unless the British defended it. Sir Edward Grey accepted this moral obligation, but what swept the British public was the invasion of Belgium. The German plan to crush France quickly was such that it could succeed only by crossing Belgium. When the Belgians protested, the Germans invaded anyway, violating the treaty of 1839 which had guaranteed Belgian neutrality. England declared war on Germany on August 4.

The mere narration of successive crises does not explain why the chief nations of

Europe became locked in combat over the murder of an imperial personage within a few days. Among more obvious general causes, the alliance system may be singled out. Europe was divided into two camps. Every incident tended to become a test of strength between the two. A given incident, such as German intervention in Morocco, or the assassination of Francis Ferdinand, could not be settled on its own merits, merely by the parties concerned; however it was dealt with, one of the two camps was deemed to have lost or gained and hence to have lost or gained in influence in other incidents, of perhaps greater purport, that would arise in the future. Each power felt that it must stand by its allies whatever the specific issue. This was because all lived in the fear of war, of some nameless future war in which allies would be necessary. The Germans complained of being "encircled" by France and Russia. They dreaded the day when they might have to face a war on two fronts. Willing to accept even a European-wide war to break their threatened "encirclement" by the Entente powers, they were obliged to hold to their one ally, Austria-Hungary, which was in turn able to sell its support at its own price. The French dreaded a coming conflict with Germany, which in forty years had far surpassed France in population and industrial strength; they were obliged to cling to their ally Russia, which therefore could oblige the French to yield to Russian wishes. As for Russia and Austria, they were both tottering empires. Especially after 1900, the tsarist regime suffered from endemic revolutionism, and the Habsburg empire from chronic nationalistic agitation. Authorities in both empires became desperate. Like the Serbs, they had little to lose and were therefore reckless. It was Russia that drew France and hence England into war in 1914, and Austria that drew in Germany. Seen in this light, the tragedy of 1914 is that the most backward or politically bankrupt parts of Europe, through the alliance system, dragged the more advanced parts automatically into ruin.

The German Empire, too, faced an internal crisis. The Social Democrats became the largest party in the Reichstag in 1912. Their sentiments for the most part were antimilitarist and antiwar. But the German imperial government recognized no responsibility to a majority in the chamber. Policy was determined by men of the old unreconstructed upper class, in which army and navy interests, now reinforced by the new business interests, were very strong; and even moderates and liberals shared in the ambition to make Germany a world power, the equal of any. The perplexities the ruling groups faced at home, the feeling that their position was being undermined by the Social Democrats, may have made them less unwilling to view war as a way out. And while it is not true that Germany started the war, as its enemies in 1914 popularly believed, it must be granted that its policies had for some years been rather peremptory, arrogant, devious, and obstinate. In a broad sense, the failure of Europe to assimilate the consolidated industrial Germany which arose after 1870, and which therefore made its bid for world-power status relatively late, was a distant and basic cause of the war.

The alliance system was only a symptom of deeper trouble. In a word, the world had an international economy but a national polity. Economically, each European people now required habitual contact with the world as a whole. Each people was to that extent dependent, and insecure. Industrial countries were especially vulnerable, relying as they did on import of raw materials and food, and on export of goods, services, or capital in return. There was, however, no world state to police the world-wide system, assuring participation in the world econ-

WORLD WAR I

Land fighting in the First World War was confined to the areas shown by the darker horizontal shading. The huge battles on the Western Front, which in expenditure of manpower exceeded those of the Second World War in the West, for four years swayed back and forth over the small area indicated, less than a hundred miles wide.

omy to all nations under all conditions. Each nation had to take care of itself. Hence came much of the drive for imperialism, in which each Great Power tried to stake out part of the world system for itself. And hence also came the quest for allies and for binding alliances. The alliances, in a world that was in the strict sense anarchic (and seemed likely to remain so), were a means by which each nation attempted to bolster up its security; to assure that it would not be cut off, conquered, or subjected to another's will; to obtain some hope of success in the competitive struggle for use of the world's goods.

85. THE ARMED STALEMATE

The First World War lasted over four years, from 1914 to the end of 1918, the United States entering with effective result in the last year. Germany and its allies were called the Central Powers, while the Entente governments were termed the Allies. The war was appalling in its human costs; on the Western Front, more men were used and killed in the First World War than in the Second.

At first a short war, as in 1870, was universally expected. The German General Staff had its plans ready for a two-front struggle against France and Russia. The disadvantage of fighting on two fronts was offset by the possession of good rail lines, which allowed the rapid shuttling of troops from one front to the other. The German war plan, known as the Schlieffen Plan, rested upon this fact. The idea was first to defeat France by the rapid wheeling motion of a tremendous army through Belgium and then to turn at more leisure against Russia, whose great size and less developed railways would make its deployment much slower.

The War on Land, 1914–1916

On August 3, 1914, the Germans launched 78 infantry divisions in the West. They were opposed by 72 French divisions, 5 British, and 6 Belgian. The Germans swept irresistibly forward. The Schlieffen Plan seemed to be moving like clockwork. The civilian authorities made plans for the conquest and annexation of large parts of Europe. Then a hitch occurred: the Russians were fulfilling the terms of their alliance; the 10 billion francs invested by Frenchmen in Russia now paid their most significant dividend. The Russians pushed two armies into Germany, penetrating into East Prussia. Moltke withdrew forces from the German right wing in France, on August 26, for service in the east. The Germans moved on, but their striking arm was weakened, and their lines of communication were already overextended. Joffre, the French commander, regrouping his forces, with strong support from the relatively small British contingent, and at exactly the right moment, ordered a counterattack. The ensuing battle of the Marne, fought from September 5 to 12, changed the whole character of the war. The Germans were obliged to retreat. The hope of felling France at a single blow was ended. Each side now tried to outflank and destroy the other until the battle lines extended to the sea. The Germans failed to win control of the Channel ports; French and British communications remained uninterrupted. For these reverses the great victories meanwhile won by the Germans in the east, though of gigantic proportions (the battles of Tannenberg and the Masurian Lakes, at which 225,000 Russians were captured), were in the long run small consolation.

In the West the war of movement now settled into a war of position. The armies on the Western Front became almost immobile. The units of horse cavalry —the uhlans, hussars, and lancers that had pranced off to war in high spirits—disappeared from the field. Since aviation was barely beginning, and motor transport was still new (the armies had trucks, but no self-propelled guns, and no tanks until very late in the war), the basic soldier more than ever was the man on foot. The most deadly new weapon was the machine gun, which made it impossible for foot soldiers to advance across open fields without overwhelming artillery preparation. The result was a long stalemate of war in the trenches in which the indispensable infantry sought protection.

In 1915 the Germans and Austro-Hungarians put their main effort into an attempt to knock out Russia. They pressed far into the tsarist empire. The Russian losses were enormous—2 million killed, wounded, or captured in 1915 alone. But at the end of the year the Russian army was still fighting. Meanwhile the British and French, hoping to open up communications with Russia, launched a naval attack on Turkey, aiming at Constantinople by way of the Dardanelles. They poured 450,000 men into the narrow peninsula of Gallipoli, of whom 145,000 were killed or wounded. After almost a year the enterprise was given up as a failure.

In 1916 both sides turned again to northern France in an attempt to break the deadlock. The Allies planned a great offensive along the river Somme, while the Germans prepared one in the neighborhood of Verdun. The Germans attacked Verdun in February. The French commander, Joffre, put in General Pétain to defend it but resisted committing his main reserves, holding them for the coming offensive on the Somme. Pétain and his troops, held to minimum numbers, thus had to take the full weight of the German army. The battle of Verdun lasted six months, it drew the horrified admiration of the world, and it became a legend of determined resistance ("they shall not pass"), until the Germans finally abandoned the attack because they sustained almost as many casualties as the French—330,000 to 350,000—so that their purpose was baffled. While the inferno still raged at Verdun the Allies opened their offensive on the Somme in July. They brought up unheard of amounts of artillery, and the newly raised British army was present in force. The idea was to break through the German line simply by stupendous pressure; on both sides, Allied and German, the art of generalship had sunk to an all-time low. Despite a weeklong artillery bombardment the British lost 60,000 men on the first day of the attack. In a week they had advanced only a mile along a six-mile front. In a month they had advanced only two miles and a half. The battle of the Somme, lasting from July to October, cost the Germans about 500,000 men, the British 400,000, and the French 200,000. Nothing of any value had been gained. It was, indeed, at the Somme that the British first used the tank, an armored vehicle with caterpillar tracks that could crash through barbed wire, lunge over trenches, and smash into machine gun nests; but the tanks were introduced in such small numbers, and with such skepticism on the part of many commanders, that they had no effect on the battle.

The War at Sea

With land armies thus helpless, both sides looked to the sea. The long preponderance of British sea power, and the more recent Anglo-German naval race, would now be tested. The British, with French aid, imposed a strict naval blockade. International law at the time placed goods headed for a country at war into two classes. One class was called "contraband"; it included munitions and certain specified raw materials which might be used in the manufacture of military equipment. The other class, including foodstuffs and raw cotton, was defined as "noncontraband." A country was supposed, by international law, to be able to import noncontraband goods even in wartime. These terms of wartime law had been set forth as recently as 1909 at an international conference held in London. The purpose was to make it impossible for a sea power (that is, the British) to starve out an enemy in wartime, or even to interfere with normal civilian production. The jealousy of Continental Europe for British sea power was an old story.

Such law, if observed, would make the blockade of Germany entirely ineffective, and the Allies did not observe it. To starve out the enemy and ruin his economy was precisely their purpose. Economic warfare took its place alongside armed attack as a military weapon, as in the days of Napoleon.[11] The Allies announced a new international law. The distinction between contraband and noncontraband was gradually abolished. The British navy (aided by the French) proceeded to stop all goods of whatever character destined for Germany or its allies. Neutrals, among whom the Americans, Dutch, and Scandinavians were the ones mainly affected, were not allowed to make for German ports at all.

The United States protested vehemently against these regulations. It defended the rights of neutrals. It reasserted the distinction between contraband and noncontraband, claimed the right to trade with other neutrals, and upheld the "freedom of the seas." Much mutual bad feeling resulted between the American and British governments in 1915 and 1916. But when the United States entered the war it adopted the Allied position, and its navy joined in enforcing exactly the same regulations. International law was in fact changed. In the Second World War the very words "contraband" and "freedom of the seas" were never heard.

The Germans countered with an attempt to blockade England. A few isolated German cruisers were able for some time to destroy British shipping in the several oceans of the world. But the Germans relied mainly on the submarine, against which the British naval power at first seemed helpless. The submarine was an unrefined weapon; a submarine commander could not always tell what kind of ship he was attacking, nor could he remove passengers, confiscate cargo, escort the vessel, or indeed do much except sink it. Citing British abuses of international law in justification, the German government in February 1915 declared the waters surrounding the British Isles to be a war zone, in which Allied vessels would be torpedoed and neutral vessels would be in grave danger. Three months later the liner *Lusitania* was torpedoed off the Irish coast. About 1,200 persons were drowned, of whom 118 were American citizens. The *Lusitania* was a British ship; it carried munitions of war manufactured in the United States for Allied use; and the Germans had published ominous warnings in the New York papers that Americans should not take passage upon it. Americans then believed that they should be able to sail safely, on peaceable errands, on the ship of a belligerent power in wartime. The loss of life shocked the country. President Wilson informed the Germans that another such act would be considered "deliberately unfriendly." The Germans, to avoid trouble, refrained for two years from making full use of their submarines. For two years the Allied use of the sea was only partly impeded.

11 See pp. 397–399.

Allied access to the sea was confirmed by the one great naval engagement of the war, the battle of Jutland. The German admirals became restless at seeing their newly built navy skulking behind minefields on the German shores, yet they could not presume to challenge the superior British Grand Fleet, posted watchfully at Scapa Flow. They hoped, however, to decoy smaller formations of British ships, destroy them one by one, and perhaps eventually obtain enough of a naval balance in the North Sea to loosen the British blockade, by which Germany was slowly being strangled. They were themselves, however, trapped into a major engagement in which the British Grand Fleet of 151 ships took them by surprise. After a few hours of furious combat the Germans were able to withdraw into mined waters. They had lost less tonnage and fewer men than the British. They had proved themselves to be dangerously proficient in naval combat. But they had failed to undermine the British preponderance at sea.

Diplomatic Maneuvers and Secret Agreements

With no military solution in sight, both sides looked about for new allies. The Ottoman Empire, fearing Russia, had joined Germany and Austria-Hungary as early as October 1914. Bulgaria, being anti-Serb, had done the same in 1915.

The leading new prospect was Italy, which, though formally a member of the Triple Alliance, had long ago drifted away from it. Both sides solicited the Italian government, which bargained imperturbably with both. The Italian public was divided. Both Catholic and socialist leaders recommended staying at peace, but extreme nationalists saw a chance to obtain their *irredenta*, the border regions in which Italians lived, but which had not been incorporated in the time of Cavour.[12] The Italian government cast its lot with the Allies in the secret treaty of London of 1915. It was agreed that if the Allies won the war Italy would receive (from Austria) the Trentino, the south Tyrol, Istria and the city of Trieste, and some of the Dalmatian islands, and that in a partition of the Ottoman Empire Italy should have small pieces of Asia Minor. If Britain and France took over Germany's African colonies, Italy should receive territorial increases in Libya and Somaliland. The treaty of London, in short, carried on the most brazen prewar practices of territorial expansionism. It must be remembered that the Allies were desperate. Italy, thus bought, and probably against the will of most Italians, opened up a front against Austria-Hungary in May 1915.

Each side tampered with minorities and discontented groups living within the domains of the other. The Germans promised an independent Poland, to embarrass Russia. They stirred up local nationalism in the Ukraine. They raised up a pro-German Flemish movement in Belgium. They persuaded the Ottoman sultan, as caliph, to proclaim a holy war in North Africa, hoping that irate Muslims would drive the British from Egypt and the French from Algeria. This had no success. German agents worked in Ireland, and one Irish nationalist, Sir Roger Casement, landed in Ireland from a German submarine, precipitating the Easter Rebellion of 1916, which was suppressed by the British.

To Americans the most amazing of similar activities was the famous Zimmermann telegram. In 1916 an American military force had crossed the Mexican border in pursuit of bandits, against protests by the Mexican government. Rela-

12 See p. 510.

tions between the United States and Germany were also deteriorating. In January 1917 the German state secretary for foreign affairs, Arthur Zimmermann, dispatched a telegram of instructions to the German minister at Mexico City. He was to tell the Mexican president that if the United States went to war with Germany, Germany would form an alliance with Mexico, enabling Mexico to get back its "lost territories." These territories referred to the region conquered by the United States from Mexico in 1848—Texas, New Mexico, and Arizona. (California was not mentioned by Zimmermann, who was no doubt somewhat vague on the exact history and location of these Alsace-Lorraines of America.) Zimmermann's telegram was intercepted and decoded by the British, and passed on by them to Washington. Printed in the newspapers, it shocked public opinion in the United States.

The Allies were more successful than the Germans in appealing to nationalist discontent, for the obvious reason that the most active national minorities were within the lands of their enemies. They were able to promise restoration of Alsace-Lorraine to France without difficulty. They promised independence to the Poles, though with some difficulty as long as the tsarist monarchy stood. It was easier for them to favor national independence for Czechs, Slovaks, and Yugoslavs, since an Allied victory would dissolve the Austro-Hungarian monarchy.

The Allies likewise made plans for a final partition of the Ottoman Empire, which still reached from Constantinople through the Near East into Arabia and modern Iraq. Britain and France were so dependent on Russia that they gave up their age-old opposition to Russian domination of the Straits. By a secret treaty of 1915 they agreed that, upon an Allied victory, Russia might proceed to the annexation of Constantinople, along with the whole Bosporus, the Sea of Marmara, and the Dardanelles. The British also aroused the hopes of Arabs for independence from Turkey. Colonel T. E. Lawrence led an insurrection in the Hejaz against the Turks; and the emir Hussein of Hejaz, with British support, in 1916 took the title of king of the Arabs, with a kingdom reaching from the Red Sea to the Persian Gulf. Zionists saw in the impending Ottoman collapse the opportunity to realize their dream for Palestine.[13] Since Palestine was an Arab country (and had been for over 1,000 years) the Zionist program conflicted with British plans to sponsor Arab nationalism. Nevertheless, in the Balfour note of 1917, the British government promised to support the idea of a "Jewish homeland" in Palestine. As for the rest of the Ottoman Empire, another agreement of 1916, made at the time when Hussein became king in Arabia, divided it into spheres of influence: Mesopotamia was to go to Britain, Syria and southeastern Asia Minor to France, Armenia and Kurdistan to Russia. Small portions were reserved for Italy.

Meanwhile the British and French easily took over the German colonies in Africa. Early in the war the British foreign secretary, Sir Edward Grey, revealed to Colonel House, President Wilson's personal emissary, that the Allies did not intend that Germany should ever get its colonies back.

In China, too, the third important area of imperialist competition, the war accelerated the tendencies of preceding years. The Japanese saw their own opportunity in the self-slaughter of the Europeans. Japan had also been allied to Britain since 1902. In August 1914 Japan declared war on Germany. It soon overran the German concessions in China and the German islands in the Pacific, the Marshalls

13 See pp. 595–596.

and Carolines. In January 1915 Japan presented its Twenty-One Demands on China, a secret ultimatum most of which the Chinese were obliged to accept. Japan thereby proceeded to turn Manchuria and north China into an exclusive protectorate.

As for the Germans, their war aims were even more expansionist, and more menacing to existing boundaries in Europe itself. Early in September 1914, when a quick victory seemed within grasp, Bethmann-Hollweg, who remained chancellor until the summer of 1917, drew up a list of German war aims which stayed unaltered until the end of hostilities. The plans called for an enlarged German Empire dominating all central Europe, and annexations or satellites in both western and eastern Europe. In the east, Lithuania and other parts of the Baltic coast were to become German dependencies, large sections of Poland were to be directly annexed, and the remainder joined with Austrian Galicia to form a German-dominated Polish state. In the west, Belgium was to become a German dependency to provide more direct access to the Atlantic, and French Lorraine with its rich iron ore was to be added to the already German parts of Alsace-Lorraine. Colonial adjustments, including the acquisition of most of central Africa from coast to coast, were also projected. The political map of Europe and of colonial Africa would thus be transformed.

All these developments, especially the Allied negotiations, whether accomplished facts or secret agreements, affecting Europe, Asia, or Africa, became very troublesome later at the peace conference. They continued some of the most unsettling tendencies of European politics before the war. It does not appear that the Allies, until driven by Woodrow Wilson, gave any thought to means of controlling anarchic nationalism or of preventing war in the future. As president of the United States, Wilson for a long time could see little to choose between the warring alliances, though his personal sympathies were with England and France. In 1916 he attempted to mediate, entering into confidential discussions with both sides; but both still hoped to win on their own terms, so that negotiation was fruitless. Wilson judged that most Americans wished to remain uninvolved, and in November 1916 he was reelected to a second term, on the popular cry, "he kept us out of war." Wilson urged a true neutrality of thought and feeling, or a settlement, as he said, that should be a "peace without victory."

As of the end of 1916, it is hard to see how the First World War would have turned out, had not two new sets of forces been brought in.

86. THE COLLAPSE OF RUSSIA AND THE INTERVENTION OF THE UNITED STATES

The Withdrawal of Russia: Revolution and the Treaty of Brest-Litovsk

The first victim of the First World War, among governments, was the Russian empire. As the Russo-Japanese War had led to the Revolution of 1905 in Russia, so the more ruinous conflict in Europe led to the far greater Revolution of 1917. The story of the Russian Revolution is told in the following chapter. It is enough to say here that war offered a test that the tsarist government could not meet. Bungling, dishonest, and secretive, incapable of supplying the materiel required for modern fighting, driving hordes of peasants into battle in some cases even without rifles, losing men by the millions yet offering no goal to inspire sacrifice, the tsarist regime lost the loyalty of all elements of its people. In March 1917 the troops in St. Petersburg mutinied, while strikes and riots desolated the city. The Duma, or Russian parliament, used the occasion to press its demands for reform. On March 15 Nicholas II abdicated. A Provisional Government took over, made up of liberal noblemen and middle-class leaders, generally democrats and constitutionalists, with at first only one socialist. The Provisional Government remained in office from March to November 1917. Its members, who shared in the liberalism of western Europe, believed that a liberal and parliamentary regime could not succeed in Russia unless the German Empire were defeated. They took steps, therefore, to prosecute the war with a new vigor. In July 1917 an offensive was opened in Galicia, but the demoralized Russian armies again collapsed.

The mass of the Russian people were wearied of a war in which they were asked to suffer so much for so little. Nor did the Russian peasant or workingman feel any enthusiasm for the westernized intellectuals and professional men who manned the Provisional Government. The ordinary Russian, so far as he had any politics, was drawn to one or another of numerous forms of socialism, Marxist and non-Marxist. The Russian Marxist party, the Social Democrats, was divided between Menshevik and Bolshevik factions, the latter being the more extreme. The Bolshevik leaders had for some time lived as exiles in western Europe. Their principal spokesman, V. I. Lenin, with a few others, had spent the war years in Switzerland. In April 1917 the German government offered safe passage to Lenin through Germany to Russia. A railway car full of Bolsheviks, carefully "sealed" to prevent infection of Germany, was thus hauled by a German train to the frontier, whence it passed on to St. Petersburg, or Petrograd, as the city was renamed during the war. The aim of the Germans in this affair, as in the sending of Roger Casement to Ireland in a submarine, was of course to use a kind of psychological warfare against the enemy's home front. It was to promote rebellion against the Provisional Government and thus at last to eliminate Russia.

The position of the Provisional Government became rapidly more untenable, from many causes, until by November 1917 the situation was so confused that Lenin and the Bolsheviks were able to seize power. The Bolsheviks stood for peace with Germany, partly to win popular favor in Russia, and partly because they regarded the war impartially, as a struggle between capitalist and imperialist powers which should be left to exhaust and destroy each other for the benefit of socialism. On December 3, 1917, a peace conference opened between the Bolsheviks and the Germans at Brest-Litovsk. Meanwhile the peoples within the western border of the old Russia—Poles, Ukrainians, Bessarabians, Estonians, Latvians, Finns—with German backing, proclaimed their national independence. The Bolsheviks, since they would not or could not fight, were obliged to sign with Germany a treaty to which they vehemently objected, the treaty of Brest-Litovsk of March 3, 1918. By this treaty they acknowledged the "independence," or at least the loss to Russia, of Poland, the Ukraine, Finland, and the Baltic provinces.

For the Germans the treaty of Brest-Litovsk represented their maximum success during the First World War; it accomplished some of the war aims formulated at the beginning of hostilities. Not only had they neutralized Russia; they also now dominated eastern Europe through puppets placed at the head of the new independent states. They relieved the effects of the naval blockade by draw-ing considerable quantities of foodstuffs from the Ukraine, though less than they expected. A certain number of German troops remained in the East to preserve the new arrangements. But it was no longer a two-front war. Masses of the German army were shifted from east to west. The High Command, under Hin-denburg and Ludendorff since August 1916, prepared to concentrate for a last blow in France to end the war in 1918.

The year 1918 was essentially a race to see whether American aid could reach Europe soon enough, in sufficient amount, to offset the added strength which Germany drew from the collapse of Russia. In March of that year the Germans, beginning with gas attacks and a bombardment by 6,000 artillery pieces, opened a formidable offensive before which the French and British both recoiled. On May 30, 1918, the Germans again stood at the Marne, thirty-seven miles from Paris. At this time there were only two American divisions in action, though the United States had been at war over a year. At this point in the story there are therefore two open questions: how the United States entered the war, and the length of time required for the build-up of its forces overseas.

The United States and the War

We have seen how President Wilson clung persistently to neutrality. The Ameri-can people were divided. Many had been born in Europe or were the children of immigrants. Those of Irish origin were anti-British; those of German origin were often sympathetic to Germany. On the other hand, since the time of the Spanish-American and Boer Wars, a noticeable current of friendliness to the English had been running, more than ever before in American history. The sale of war mate-rials to the Allies, and the purchase of the bonds of Allied governments, had given certain limited though influential circles a material interest in an Allied victory. The idealism of the country was on the side of England and France, so far as it was not isolationist. An Allied victory would clearly advance the cause of democ-racy, freedom, and progress far more than a victory of the German Empire. On the other hand, England and France were suspected of somewhat impure mo-tives, and they were allied with the Russian autocracy, the reactionary and brutal tsardom.

The fall of tsarism made a great impression. Democratic and progressive men now came forward even in Russia. No one had ever heard of Lenin or foresaw the Bolshevik Revolution. It seemed in the spring of 1917 that Russia was struggling along the path that England, France, and America had already taken. An ideo-logical barrier had dropped away, and the demand for American intervention to safeguard democracy became more insistent.

The Germans gave up the attempt to keep the United States out. Constricted ever more tightly by the blockade, and failing to get a decision on land, the German government and High Command listened more readily to the submarine experts, who declared that if given a free hand they could force British surrender in six months. It was the chief example in the First World War of the claim that one branch of the service could win the war alone. Civilian and diplomatic members of the government objected, fearing the consequences of war with the United States. They were overruled; it was a good example of the way in which, in Germany, the army and navy had taken the highest policy into their hands. Unrestricted submarine warfare was to be resumed on February 1, 1917. It was foreseen that the United States would declare war, but the German High Command believed that this would make no immediate difference. They estimated in 1917 (correctly) that between the time when the United States entered a European war and the time when it could take part with its own army about a year must intervene. Meanwhile, the planners said, in six months they could force Britain to accept defeat.

On January 31, 1917, the Germans notified Wilson of the resumption of unrestricted submarine attacks. They announced that they would sink on sight all merchant vessels found in a zone around the British Isles or in the Mediterranean. Wilson broke off diplomatic relations and ordered the arming of American freighters. Meanwhile, the publication of the Zimmermann telegram convinced many Americans of German aggressiveness. German secret agents also had been at work in America, fomenting strikes and causing explosions in factories engaged in the manufacture of munitions for the Allies. In February and March several American ships were sunk. Americans regarded all these activities as an interference with their rights as neutrals. Wilson at last concluded that Germany was a menace. Having made his decision, Wilson saw a clear-cut issue between right and wrong, and he obtained a rousing declaration of war from Congress, on April 6, 1917. The United States went to war "to make the world safe for democracy."

At first the German campaign realized and even exceeded the predictions of its sponsors. In February 1917 the Germans sank 540,000 tons of shipping, in March 578,000 tons, in April, as the days grew longer, 874,000 tons. Something akin to terror, with difficulty concealed from the public, seized on the government in London. Britain was reduced to a mere six-weeks' reserve of food. Gradually countermeasures were developed—mine barrages, hydrophones, depth charges, airplane reconnaissance, and most of all the convoy. It was found that a hundred or more freighters together, though all had to steam at the pace of the slowest, could be protected by a sufficient concentration of warships to keep submarines away. The United States navy, which, unlike the army, was of considerable size and ready for combat, supplied enough additional force to the Allies to make convoying and other antisubmarine measures highly effective. By the end of 1917 the submarine was no more than a nuisance. For the Germans the great plan produced the anticipated penalty without the reward—its net result was only to add America to their enemies.

On the Western Front in 1917, while the Americans desperately got themselves ready for the war they had entered, the French and British continued to hold the line. The French, finding in General Nivelle a commander who still believed in the breakthrough, launched an offensive so unsuccessful and so bloody that mutiny spread through the French army. Pétain then replaced Nivelle and restored discipline to the exhausted and disillusioned soldiers, but he had no thought of further attack. "I am waiting for the Americans and the tanks," he said. The British then assumed the main burden. For three months late in 1917 they fought the dismal battle of Passchendaele. They advanced five miles, near Ypres, at a cost of 400,000 men. At the very end of 1917 the British surprised the Germans with a raid by 380 tanks, which penetrated deep into the German lines, but were obliged to withdraw, since no reserve of fresh infantry was at hand to exploit their success. Meanwhile the Austro-Hungarians, strongly reinforced by German troops, overwhelmed the Italians at the disastrous battle of Caporetto. The Central Powers streamed into northern Italy, but the Italians, with British and French reinforcements, were able to hold the line. The net effect of the campaigns of 1917, and of the repulse of the submarine at the same time, was to reemphasize the stalemate in Europe, incline the weary Allies to await the Americans, and give the Americans what they most needed—time.

The Americans made good use of the time given them. Conscription, democratically entitled selective service, was adopted immediately after the declaration of war. The United States army, whose professionals in 1916 numbered only 130,000, performed the mammoth feat of turning over 3.5 million civilians into soldiers. With the navy, the United States came to have over 4 million in its armed services (which may be compared with over 12 million in the Second World War). Aid flowed to the Allies. To the loans already made through private bankers were added some $10 billion lent by the American government itself. The Allies used the money mainly to buy food and munitions in the United States. American farms and factories, which had already prospered by selling to the Allies during the period of neutrality, now broke all records for production. Civilian industry was converted to war uses; radiator factories turned out guns, and piano factories airplane wings. Every possible means was employed to build up ocean shipping, without which neither American supplies nor American armies could reach the theater of war. Available shipping was increased from 1 million to 10 million tons. Civilian consumption was drastically cut. Eight thousand tons of steel were saved in the manufacture of women's corsets, and 75,000 tons of tin in the making of children's toy wagons. Every week people observed meatless Tuesday, and sugar was rationed. Daylight-saving time, invented in Europe during the war, was introduced to save coal. By such means the United States made enormous stocks available for its Allies as well as itself, though for some items, notably airplanes and artillery ammunition, the American armies, when they reached France, drew heavily on British and French manufactures.

The Final Phase of the War

The Germans, as we have seen, victorious in the East, opened a great final offensive in the West in the spring of 1918, hoping to force a decision before American participation turned the balance forever. To oppose it, a unity of command was at last achieved, for the first time, when a French general, Ferdinand Foch, was made commander in chief of all Allied forces in France, with the national commanders subordinate to him, including Pershing for the Americans. In June the Germans first made contact with American troops in significant force, meeting the Second Division at Château-Thierry. The German position was so favorable that civilians in the German government thought it opportune to make a last effort at a compromise peace. The military, headed by Hindenburg and Ludendorff, successfully blocked any such attempts; they preferred to gamble on one final throw. The German armies reached their farthest advance on July 15 along the Marne. There were now nine American divisions in the Allied line. Foch used them to spearhead his counterattack on July 18. The badly overstrained Germans began to falter. Over 250,000 American troops were now landing in France every month. The final Allied offensive which opened in September, with American troops in the Argonne occupying an eastern sector, proved more than the Germans could withstand. The German High Command notified its government that it could not win the war. The German foreign office made peace overtures to President Wilson. An armistice was arranged, and on November 11, 1918, firing ceased on the Western Front.

Since Germany's allies had surrendered during the preceding weeks, the war, or at least the shooting war in western Europe, was now over. The horror it brought to individual lives cannot be told by statistics, which drily report that almost 10 million men had been killed, and 20 million wounded. Each of the European Great Powers (except Italy) lost from 1 million to 2 million in killed alone. The United States, with some 330,000 casualties of all types (of whom 115,000 died) lost in the entire war fewer men than the main combatants had lost in such a single battle as Verdun or Passchendaele.[14] American assistance was decisive in the defeat of Germany. But it came so late, when the others had been struggling for so long, that the mere beginnings of it were enough to turn the scale. On the date of the armistice there were 2 million American soldiers in France, and another 1 million were on the way. But the American army had really been in combat only four months. During the whole year 1918, out of every hundred artillery shells that were fired by the three armies, the French fired 51, the British 43, and the Americans only 6.

87. THE COLLAPSE OF THE AUSTRIAN AND GERMAN EMPIRES

The war proved fatal to the German and Austro-Hungarian empires, as to the Russian. The subject Habsburg nationalities, or the "national councils" representing them in the Western capitals, obtained increasing recognition from the Allies, and in October declared their independence. The last Austrian emperor, Charles I, abdicated on November 12, and on the next day Austria was proclaimed a republic, as was Hungary in the following week. Before any peace conference could convene, the new states of Czechoslovakia, Yugoslavia, an enlarged Rumania, a republican Hungary, and a miniature republican Austria were in existence by their own action.

The German Empire stood solid until the closing weeks. Liberals, democrats, and socialists had lately begun to press for peace and democratization. Yet it was the High Command itself that precipitated the debacle. In the last years of the war dictatorial powers had become concentrated in the hands of General Ludendorff, and in September 1918 only he and his closest military associates realized that the German cause was hopeless. On September 29, at supreme headquarters at Spa in Belgium, Ludendorff informed the Kaiser that Germany must ask for

---

[14] Of the 115,000 American deaths only 50,000 represented men killed in battle, the remainder representing mainly deaths by disease. The great influenza epidemic of 1918, which brought death to over 20 million people, civilians and military alike, in all parts of the world, probably accounted for 25,000 deaths in the American army.

peace. He urged that a new government be formed at Berlin, reflecting the majority in the Reichstag, on democratic parliamentary principles.

In calling for immediate peace negotiations, he seems to have had two ideas in mind. First, he might win time to regroup his armies and prepare a new offensive. Or if collapse became unavoidable, then the civilian or democratic elements in Germany would be the ones to sue for peace.

The liberal Prince Max of Baden was found to head a cabinet in which even socialists were included. In October various reforms were enacted, the Bismarckian system was ended, and Germany became a liberal constitutional monarchy. For Ludendorff the changes were not fast enough. What was happening was essentially simple. The German military caste, at the moment of Germany's crisis, was more eager to save the army than to save the empire. The army must never admit surrender; that was an affair for small men in business suits. Emperor, High Command, officers, and aristocrats were unloading frantically upon civilians.

President Wilson unwittingly played into their hands. Speaking now as the chief of the Allied coalition, the one to whom peace overtures were first made, he insisted that the German government must become more democratic. It may be recalled how Bismarck, after defeating France in 1871, demanded a general election in France before making peace.[15] Wilson, unlike Bismarck, really believed in democracy; but in a practical way his position was the same. He wanted to be sure that he was dealing with the German people itself, not with a discredited elite. He wanted it to be the real Germany that applied for and accepted the Allied terms. In Germany, as realization of the military disaster spread, many people began to regard the Kaiser as an obstacle to peace. Or they felt that Germany would obtain better terms if it appeared before the Allies as a republic. Even the officer corps, to halt the fighting before the army disintegrated, began to talk of abdication. Sailors mutinied at Kiel on November 3, and councils of workers and soldiers were formed in various cities. The socialists threatened to withdraw from the newly formed cabinet (i.e., go into opposition and end the representative nature of the new government) unless William II abdicated. A general strike, led by minority socialists and syndicalists, began on November 9. "Abdication," Prince Max told the emperor, "is a dreadful thing, but a government without the socialists would be a worse danger for the country." William II abdicated on November 9, and slipped across the frontier into Holland, where despite cries to try him as a "war criminal" he lived quietly until his death in 1941. Germany was proclaimed a republic on the same day. Two days later the war stopped.

The fall of the empire in Germany, with the consequent adoption of the republic, did not arise from any basic discontent, deep revolutionary action, or change of sentiment in the German people. It was an episode of the war. The republic (soon called the Weimar Republic) arose because the victorious enemy demanded it, because the German people craved peace, because they wished to avoid forcible revolution, and because the old German military class, to save its face and its future strength, wished at least temporarily to be excused. When the war ended, the German army was still in France, its discipline and organization

15 See p. 578.

still apparently unimpaired. No hostile shot had been fired on German soil. It was said later, by some, that the army had not been defeated, that it had been "stabbed in the back" by a dissolving civilian home front. This was untrue; it was the panic-stricken Ludendorff who first cried for "democracy." But the circumstances in which the German republic originated made its later history, and hence all later history, very troubled.

88. THE ECONOMIC AND SOCIAL IMPACT OF THE WAR

Effects on Capitalism: Government-Regulated Economies

European society was forced by the First World War into many basic changes that were to prove more lasting than the war itself. First of all, the war profoundly affected capitalism as previously known. Essential to the older capitalism (or economic liberalism, or free private enterprise) had been the idea that government should leave business alone, or at the most regulate certain general conditions under which businessmen went about their affairs. Before 1914 governments had increasingly come into the economic field. They had put up tariffs, protected national industries, sought for markets or raw materials by imperialist expansion, or passed protective social legislation to benefit the wage-earning classes. During the war all belligerent governments controlled the economic system far more minutely. Indeed, the idea of the "planned economy" was first applied in the First World War. For the first time (with such rare and archaic precedents as the French dictatorship of 1793)[16] the state attempted to direct all the wealth, resources, and moral purpose of society to a single end.

Since no one had expected a long war, no one had made any plans for industrial mobilization. Everything had to be improvised. By 1916 each government had set up a system of boards, bureaus, councils, and commissions to coordinate its war effort. The aim was to see that all manpower was effectively utilized, and that all natural resources within the country, and all that could possibly be imported, were employed where they would do the most good. In the stress of war free competition was found to be wasteful and undirected private enterprise too uncertain and too slow. The profit motive came into disrepute. Those who exploited shortages to make big profits were stigmatized as "profiteers." Production for civilian use, or for mere luxury purposes, was cut to a minimum. Businessmen were not allowed to set up or close down factories as they chose. It was impossible to start a new business without government approval, because the flotation of stocks and bonds was controlled, and raw materials were made available only as the government wished. It was equally impossible to shut down a business engaged in war production; if a factory was inefficient or unprofitable the government kept it going anyway, making up the losses, so that in some cases management came to expect government support. Here too the tests of competition and profitableness were abandoned. The new goal was coordination or "rationalization" of production in the interests of the country as a whole. Labor was discouraged from protesting against hours or wage rates, and the big unions

16 See pp. 367–369.

generally agreed to refrain from strikes. For the upper and middle classes it became embarrassing to show their comforts too openly. It was patriotic to eat meagerly and to wear old clothes. War gave a new impetus even to the idea of economic equality, if only to enlist rich and poor alike in a common cause.

Military conscription was the first step in the allocation of manpower. Draft boards told some men to report to the army, granting exemptions to others to work safely in war industries. Given the casualty rates at the front, state determination over individual life could hardly go farther. With the insatiable need for troops, drawing in men originally exempted or at first rejected as physically inadequate, great numbers of women poured into factories and offices, and in Britain even into newly organized women's branches of the armed forces. Women took over many jobs which it had been thought only men could do. Since their invasion proved to be permanent, the labor force of all countries was enlarged, women's place in society was revolutionized, the institution of marriage and the relations of husband and wife were transformed, and the lives, liberty, and outlook of millions of individual women were turned outward from the home. It was a process that would be intensified during the Second World War and in the years that followed. During the war governments did not directly force men or women to drop one job and take another. There was no systematic labor conscription except in Germany. But by influencing wage scales, granting draft exemptions, forcing some industries to expand and others to contract or stand still, and propagandizing the idea that work in an arms factory was patriotic, the state shifted vast numbers of workers to war production. Impressed or "slave" labor was not used in the First World War nor were prisoners of war obliged to give labor service, though there were some abuses of these rules of international law by the Germans, who were possibly the least scrupulous and certainly the most hard pressed.

Governments controlled all foreign trade. It was intolerable to let private citizens ship off the country's resources at their own whim. It was equally intolerable to let them use up foreign exchange by importing unneeded goods, or to drive up prices of necessities by competing with one another. Foreign trade became a state monopoly, in which private firms operated under strict licenses and quotas. The greatest of the exporting countries was the United States, whose annual exports rose from $2 billion to $6 billion between 1914 and 1918. The endless demand for American farm and factory products naturally drove up prices, which, however, were fixed by law in 1917, for the most important items.

As for the European Allies, which even before the war had exported less than they imported, and were now exporting as little as possible, they could make purchases in the United States only by enormous loans from the American government. British and French citizens, under pressure from their own governments, sold off their American stocks and bonds, which were bought up by Americans. The former owners received pounds sterling or francs from their own governments, which in return took and spent the dollars paid by the new American owners. In this way the United States ceased to be a debtor country (owing some $4 billion to Europeans in 1914), and became the world's leading creditor country, to which by 1919 Europeans owed about $10 billion.

The Allies controlled the sea, but they never had enough shipping to meet rising demands, especially with German submarines taking a steady though fluctuating toll. Each government set up a shipping board, to expand shipbuilding at any cost and to assign available shipping space to whatever purposes—troop movements, rubber imports, foodstuffs—the government considered most urgent in view of overall plans. Control and allocation eventually became international under the Interallied Shipping Council, of which the United States was a member after entering the war. In England and France, where all manufactures depended on imports, government control of shipping and hence of imports was itself enough to give control over the whole economy.

Germany, denied access to the sea and also to Russia and western Europe, was obliged to adopt unprecedented measures of self-sufficiency. The oil of Rumania and grain of the Ukraine, which became available late in the war, were poor substitutes for the world trade on which Germany had formerly depended. The Germans went with less food than other belligerents. Their government controls became more thorough and more efficient, producing what they called "war socialism." In Walter Rathenau they found a man with the necessary ideas. He was a Jewish industrialist, son of the head of the German electrical trust. One of the first to foresee a long war, he launched a program for the mobilization of raw materials. Early in the war it seemed that Germany might be soon defeated by lack of nitrogen, necessary to make explosives. Rathenau sweepingly requisitioned every conceivable natural source, including the very manure from the farmers' barnyards, until German chemists succeeded in extracting nitrogen from the air. The German chemical industry developed many other substitute products, such as synthetic rubber. German production was organized into War Companies, one for each line of industry, with private business firms working under close government supervision.

The other belligerent governments also replaced competition between individual firms and factories with coordination. "Consortiums" of industrialists in France allocated raw materials and government orders within each industry. The War Industries Board did the same in the United States. In Britain, similar methods became so efficient that by 1918, for example, the country produced every two weeks as many shells as in the whole first year of the war and turned out seventy times as much heavy artillery.

Inflation, Industrial Changes, Control of Ideas

No government, even by heavy taxes, could raise all the funds it needed except by printing paper money, selling huge bond issues, or obliging banks to grant it credit. The result, given heavy demand and acute shortages, was rapid inflation of prices. Prices and wages were regulated but were never again so low as before 1914. The hardest hit by this development were those whose money income could not easily be raised—people living on "safe" investments, those drawing annual salaries, professional people, government employees. These classes had been one of the most stabilizing influences in Europe before the war. Everywhere the war threatened their status, prestige, and standard of living. The huge national debts meant higher taxes for years to come. The debt was most serious when it was owed to a foreign country. During the war the Continental Allies borrowed from

Britain, and they and the British both borrowed from the United States. They thereby mortgaged their future. To pay the debt, they were bound for years to export more than they imported—or, roughly, to produce more than they consumed. It may be recalled that in 1914 every advanced European country habitually imported more than it exported.[17] That fact, basic to the European standard of life, was now threatened with reversal.

Moreover, with Europe torn by war for four years, the rest of the world speeded up its own industrialization. The productive capacity of the United States increased immensely. The Japanese began to sell in China, in India, in South America the cotton textiles and other civilian goods which these countries for the time being could not obtain from Europe. The Argentine and Brazil, unable to get locomotive parts or mining machinery from England, began to manufacture them themselves. In India the Tata family, a group of wealthy Parsees controlling $250 million of native Indian capital, developed numerous manufacturing enterprises, one of which became the largest iron and steel works in the British Empire. With Germany entirely out of the world market, with Britain and France producing desperately for themselves, and with the world's shipping commandeered for war uses, the position of western Europe as the world's workshop was undermined. After the war Europe had new competitors. The economic foundations of the nineteenth century had slipped away. The age of European supremacy was in its twilight.

All the belligerent governments during the war attempted to control ideas as they did economic production. Freedom of thought, respected everywhere in Europe for half a century, was discarded. Propaganda and censorship became more effective than any government, however despotic, had ever been able to devise. No one was allowed to sow doubt by raising any basic questions.

It must be remembered that the facts of the prewar crises, as related above, were then largely unknown. People were trapped in a nightmare whose causes they could not comprehend. Each side wildly charged the other with having started the war from pure malevolence. The long attrition, the fruitless fighting, the unchanging battle lines, the appalling casualties were a severe ordeal to morale. Civilians, deprived of their usual liberties, working harder, eating dull food, seeing no victory, had to be kept emotionally at a high pitch. Placards, posters, diplomatic white papers, schoolbooks, public lectures, solemn editorials, and slanted news reports conveyed the message. The new universal literacy, the mass press, the new moving pictures, proved to be ideal media for the direction of popular thinking. Intellectuals and professors advanced complicated reasons, usually historical, for loathing and crushing the enemy. In Allied countries the Kaiser was portrayed as a demon, with glaring eyes and abnormally bristling mustaches, bent on the mad project of conquest of the world. In Germany people were taught to dread the day when Cossacks and Senegalese should rape German women and to hate England as the inveterate enemy which inhumanly starved little children with its blockade. Each side convinced itself that all right was on its side and all wrong, wickedness, and barbarity on the other. An inflamed opinion helped to sustain men and women in such a fearsome struggle. But when it came time to make peace the rooted convictions, fixed ideas, profound aversions, hates, and fears became an obstacle to political judgment.

17 See p. 557.

89. THE PEACE OF PARIS, 1919

The late ally, Russia, was in the hands of Bolsheviks, ostracized like a leper colony, and taking no part in international relations. The late German and Austro-Hungarian empires were already defunct, and more or less revolutionary regimes struggled to establish themselves in their places. New republics already existed along the Baltic coast, in Poland, and in the Danube basin but without effective governments or acknowledged frontiers. Europe east of France and Italy was in a state approaching chaos, with revolution on the Russian style threatening. Western Europe was wrenched out of all resemblance to its former self. The Allied blockade of Germany continued. In these circumstances the victors assembled in Paris, in the bleak winter of 1919, to reconstruct the world. During 1919 they signed five treaties, all named after Paris suburbs—St.-Germain with Austria, Trianon with Hungary, Neuilly with Bulgaria, Sèvres with Turkey (1920), and most especially, with Germany, the Treaty of Versailles.

The world looked with awe and expectation to one man—the president of the United States. Wilson occupied a lone eminence, enjoyed a universal prestige. Victors, vanquished, and neutrals admitted that American intervention had decided the conflict. Everywhere people who had been long tried, confused, bereaved, were stirred by Wilson's thrilling language in favor of a higher cause, of a great concert of right in which peace would be forever secure and the world itself at last free. Wilson reached Europe in January 1919, visiting several Allied capitals. He was wildly acclaimed, and almost mobbed, greeted as the man who would lead civilization out of its wasteland.

The Fourteen Points and the Treaty of Versailles

Wilson's views were well known. He had stated them in January 1918 in his Fourteen Points—principles upon which, after victory, peace was to be established. The Fourteen Points demanded an end to secret treaties and secret diplomacy (or in Wilsonian language, "open covenants openly arrived at"); freedom of the seas "alike in peace and in war"; removal of barriers and inequalities in international trade; reduction of armaments by all powers; colonial readjustments; evacuation of occupied territory; self-determination of nationalities and a redrawing of European boundaries along national lines; and, last but not least, an international political organization to prevent war. On the whole, Wilson stood for the fruition of the democratic, liberal, progressive, and nationalistic movements of the century past, for the ideals of the Enlightenment, the French Revolution, and of 1848. As Wilson saw it, and as many believed, the World War should end in a new type of treaty. There was thought to be something sinister about peace conferences of the past, for example, the Congress of Vienna of 1815.[18] The old diplomacy was blamed for leading to war. Lenin in his own way and for his own purposes was saying this in Russia too. It was felt that treaties had too long been wrongly based on a politics of power, or on unprincipled deals and bargains made without regard to the people concerned. Democracy having defeated the Central Powers, people hoped that a new settlement, made in a

[18] See pp. 410–416.

democratic age, might be reached by general agreement in an atmosphere of mutual confidence. There was a real sense of a new era.

Wilson had had some difficulty, however, in persuading the Allied governments to accept his Fourteen Points. The French demanded a guarantee of German payment for war damages. The British vetoed the freedom of the seas "in peace and war"; it was naval rivalry that had estranged them from Germany, and they had fought the war to preserve British command of the sea. But with these two reservations the Allies expressed their willingness to follow Wilson's lead. The Germans who asked for the armistice believed that peace would be made along the lines of the Fourteen Points with only the two modifications described. The socialists and democrats now trying to rule Germany thought also that, having overthrown the Kaiser and the war lords, they would be treated by the victors with some moderation, and that a new democratic Germany would reemerge into the place in the world which they considered to be due it.

Twenty-seven nations assembled at Paris in January 1919, but the full or plenary sessions were unimportant. Matters were decided by conferences among the Big Four—Wilson himself, Lloyd George for England, Clemenceau for France, Orlando for Italy. The conjunction of personalities was not a happy one. Wilson was sternly and stubbornly righteous; Lloyd George, a fiery and changeable Welshman; Clemenceau, an aged patriot, the "tiger of France," who had been not exactly young in the War of 1870 (he was born in 1841); Orlando, a passing phenomenon of Italian politics. None of them was especially equipped for the task in hand. Clemenceau was a pronounced nationalist, Lloyd George had always been concerned with domestic reforms, Orlando was by training a professor like Wilson, and Wilson, a former college president, lacked concrete knowledge or intimate feeling for peoples other than his own. However, they democratically represented the governments and peoples of their respective countries, and thus spoke with an authority denied to professional diplomats of the old school.

Wilson first fought a hard battle for a League of Nations, a permanent international body in which all nations, without sacrificing their sovereignty, should meet together to discuss and settle disputes, each promising not to resort to war. Few European statesmen had any confidence in such a League. But they yielded to Wilson, and the covenant of the League of Nations was written into the treaty with Germany. In return, Wilson had to make concessions to Lloyd George, Clemenceau, Orlando, and the Japanese. He was thus obliged to compromise the idealism of the Fourteen Points. Probably compromise and bargaining would have been necessary anyway, for such general principles as national self-determination and colonial readjustment invariably led to difference of opinion in concrete cases. Wilson allowed himself to believe that, if a League of Nations were established and operating, faults in the treaty could later be corrected at leisure by international discussion.

The great demand of the French at the peace conference was for security against Germany. On this subject the French were almost rabid. The war in the West had been fought almost entirely on their soil. To trim Germany down more nearly to French size, they proposed that the part of Germany west of the Rhine be set up as an independent state under Allied auspices. Wilson and Lloyd George objected, sagely observing that the resulting German resentment would only lead to another war. The French yielded, but only on condition that they obtain their security in another way, namely, by a promise from both Britain and the United States to join them immediately if they were again attacked by the Germans. An Anglo-French-American guarantee treaty, with these provisions, was in fact signed at Paris. France obtained control over the Saar coal mines for fifteen years; during that time, a League commission would administer the Saar territory and in 1935 a plebiscite would be held. Lorraine and Alsace were returned to France. German fortifications and troops were banned from a wide belt in the Rhineland. Allied troops would occupy the Rhineland for fifteen years to assure German compliance with the treaty.

In the east the Allies wished to set up strong buffer states against Bolshevism in Russia. Sympathies with Poland ran very high. Those parts of the former German Empire that were inhabited by Poles, or by mixed populations of Poles and Germans—Posen and West Prussia—were assigned to the new Polish state. This gave Poland a corridor to the sea, but at the same time cut off the bulk of Germany from East Prussia.[19] Danzig, an old German town, became a free city, belonging to no country. Memel also was internationalized; it was soon seized by Lithuania. Upper Silesia, a rich mining country, went to Poland after a disputed plebiscite. In Austria and among the Sudeten Germans of Bohemia, now that there was no longer a Habsburg empire (whose existence had blocked an all-German union in 1848 and in the time of Bismarck),[20] a feeling developed for annexation to the new German republic. But the feeling was unorganized, and in any case the Allies naturally refused to make Germany bigger than it had been in 1914. Austria remained a dwarf republic, and Vienna a former imperial capital cut off from its empire—a head severed from its body, and scarcely more capable of sustaining life. The Bohemian Germans became disgruntled citizens of Czechoslovakia.

Germany lost all its colonies. Wilson and the South African General Smuts, to preserve the principle of internationalism against any imputation of raw conquest, saw to it that the colonies were actually awarded to the League of Nations. The League, in turn, under "mandates," assigned them to various powers for administration. In this way France and Great Britain divided the best of the African colonies; the Belgian Congo received a slight enlargement; and the Union of South Africa took over German Southwest Africa. In the colonial world, Italy got nothing. Japan received the mandate for the German Pacific islands north of the equator, Australia for German New Guinea and the Solomon Islands, New Zealand for German Samoa. The Japanese claimed rights over the German concessions in China. The Chinese at the Paris conference tried to get all special concessions and extraterritorial rights in China abolished.[21] No one listened to such proposals. By a compromise, Japan received about half the former German rights. The Japanese were dissatisfied. The Chinese walked out of the conference.

The Allies took over the German fleet, but the German crews, rather than surrender it, solemnly scuttled it at Scapa Flow. The German army was limited to 100,000. Since the Allies forbade conscription, or the annual training of successive groups of young civilians, the army became exclusively professional, the officer class retained political influence in it, and the means used by the Allies to demili-

---

[19] See maps, pp. 319, panel 4, and 686–687.
[20] See pp. 477–480, 511–516.
[21] See pp. 633–638.

tarize Germany served if anything the contrary purpose. The treaty forbade Germany to have any heavy artillery, aviation, or submarines. Wilson saw his plan for universal disarmament applied to Germany alone.

The French, even before the armistice, had stipulated that Germany must pay for war damages. The other Allies made the same demand. Wilson, at the conference, was stupefied at the size of the bills presented. The Belgians suggested, for their own share, a sum larger than the entire wealth of all Belgium according to officially published Belgian statistics. The French and British proposed to charge Germany with the entire expenses, including war pensions, incurred by them during the war. Wilson observed that "total" reparation, while not strictly unjust, was absolutely impossible, and even Clemenceau noted that "to ask for over a trillion francs would lead to nothing practical." The insistence on enormous reparations was in fact largely emotional. No one knew or considered how Germany would pay, though all dimly realized that such sums could only be made up by German exports, which would then compete with the Allies' own economic interests. The Germans, to avoid worse, even offered to repair physical damages in Belgium and France, but were brusquely refused on the ground that the Belgians and French would thereby lose jobs and business. No total at all was set for reparations in the treaty; it was made clear that the sum would be very large, but it was left for a future commission to determine. The Allies, maddened by the war, and themselves loaded with fantastic debts to the United States, had no desire in the matter of reparations to listen to economic reason and regarded the reparations as simply another means of righting a wrong and of putting off the dangers of a German revival. As a first payment on the reparations account the treaty required Germany to surrender most of its merchant marine, make coal deliveries, and give up all property owned by German private citizens abroad. This last proviso ended Germany's prewar career as an exporter of capital.

It was with the specific purpose of justifying the reparations that the famous "war guilt" clause was written into the treaty. By this clause Germany explicitly "accepted the responsibility" for all loss and damage resulting from the war "imposed upon them (the Allies) by the aggression of Germany and her allies." The Germans themselves felt no such responsibility as they were now obliged formally to accept. They considered their honor as a people to be impugned. The "war guilt" clause gave a ready opening to agitators in Germany and made even moderate Germans regard the treaty as something to be escaped from as a matter of self-respect.

The Treaty of Versailles was completed in three months. The absence of the Russians, the decision not to give the Germans a hearing, and the willingness of Wilson to make concessions in return for obtaining the League of Nations, made it possible to dispose of intricate matters with considerable facility. The Germans, when presented with the completed document in May 1919, refused to sign. The Allies threatened a renewal of hostilities. A government crisis ensued in Berlin. No German wished to damn himself, his party, or his principles, in German eyes, by putting his name to a document which all Germans regarded as outrageous. A combination drawn from the Social Democratic and Catholic parties finally consented to shoulder the hateful burden. Two abashed and virtually unknown representatives appeared at the Hall of Mirrors at Versailles, and signed the treaty for Germany in the presence of a large concourse of Allied dignitaries.

The other treaties drafted by the Paris conference, in conjunction with the Versailles treaty, laid out a new map for eastern Europe and registered the recession of the Russian, Austrian, and Turkish empires. Seven new independent states now existed: Finland, Estonia, Latvia, Lithuania, Poland, Czechoslovakia, and Yugoslavia. Rumania was enlarged by adding areas formerly Hungarian and Russian; Greece was enlarged at the expense of Turkey. Austria and Hungary were now small states, and there was no connection between them. The Ottoman Empire presently disappeared: Turkey emerged as a republic confined to Constantinople and Asia Minor, Syria and Lebanon went to France as mandates of the League of Nations, Palestine and Iraq to Great Britain on the same basis.[22] The belt of states from Finland to Rumania was regarded as a *cordon sanitaire* (sanitary zone) to prevent the westward expansion of communism. The creation of Yugoslavia realized the aims of the South Slav or Pan-Serb movement which had set off the fatal crisis of 1914. The fact, however, that Italy received Trieste and some of the Dalmatian Islands (in keeping with the secret treaty of 1915) left the more ambitious Yugoslavs discontented.

Significance of the Paris Peace Settlement

The most general principle of the Paris settlement was to recognize the right of national self-determination, at least in Europe. Each people or nation, as defined by language, was in principle set up with its own sovereign and independent national state. Nationalism triumphed in the belief that it went along naturally with liberalism and democracy. It must be added that the peacemakers at Paris had little choice in this matter, for the new states had already declared their independence. Since in eastern Europe the nationalities were in many places intermixed, and since the peacemakers did not contemplate the actual movement and exchange of populations to sort them out, each new state found alien minorities living within its borders or could claim that people of its own kind still lived in neighboring states under foreign rule. There were Hungarians in Czechoslo-

---

[22] The secret of 1916 (p. 669) promising the Straits to Russia lapsed with the Revolution, neither the Bolsheviks nor the Allies recognizing an agreement made with the tsarist government.

EUROPE, 1923

The map shows European boundaries between the two World Wars, after the Peace of Versailles and certain other agreements. Comparison with the language map (p. 433) will suggest how the principle of nationality was recognized. Germany returned Alsace-Lorraine to France and lost the region around Danzig (the "Polish corridor") to Poland—essentially the area taken by Prussia in the First Partition of 1773 (see map, p. 218. In place of the Austro-Hungarian empire we find the "succession states," Austria, Hungary, Czechoslovakia, Yugoslavia, and Rumania. Poland regained its independence, and Finland and the three Baltic states, Estonia, Latvia, and Lithuania, emerged from the tsarist empire. Most of Ireland became a "free state" in the British Commonwealth of Nations, only Ulster remaining in the United Kingdom.

These boundaries lasted until 1938–1940, when, as the Second World War began, the Germans annexed Austria and parts of Czechoslovakia, and the Russians annexed (or re-annexed) the Baltic states, while both Germans and Russians occupied Poland.

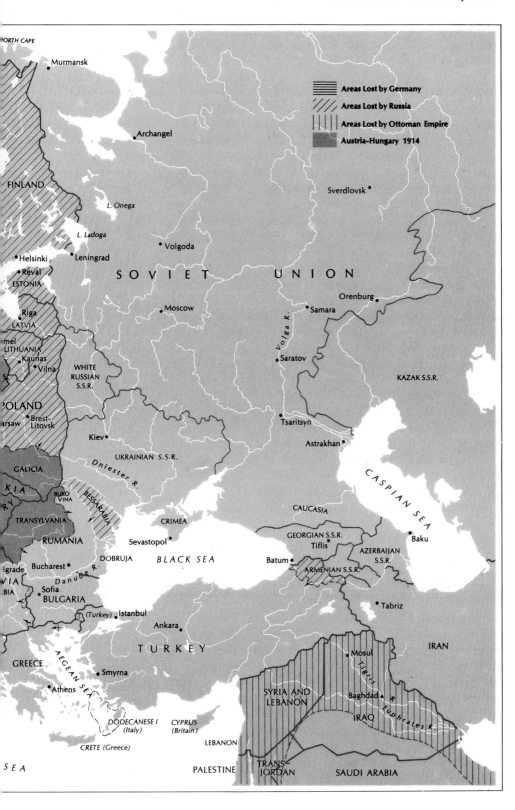

vakia, Ruthenians in Poland, Poles in Lithuania, Bulgars in Rumania—to cite only a few examples. Hence minority problems and irredentism troubled eastern Europe, as they had before 1914. Eventually it was the complaint of Germans in Czechoslovakia that they were an oppressed minority, together with the irredentist demand of Germany to join these outlying brothers to the Fatherland, that produced the Munich crisis preceding the Second World War.[23]

The Treaty of Versailles was designed to put an end to the German menace. It was not a successful treaty. The wisdom of it has been discussed without end, but a few comments can safely be made. For practical purposes, with respect to Germany, the treaty was either too severe or too lenient. It was too severe to conciliate and not severe enough to destroy. Possibly the victors should have dealt more moderately with the new German republic, which professed their own ideals, as the monarchical victors over Napoleon, in 1814, had dealt moderately with the France of the restored Bourbons, regarding it as a regime akin to their own. As it was, the Allies imposed upon the German republic about the same terms that they might have imposed upon the German Empire. They innocently played the game of Ludendorff and the German reactionaries; it was the Social Democrats and liberals who bore the "shame" of Versailles. The Germans from the beginning showed no real intention to live up to the treaty. On the other hand, the treaty was not sufficiently disabling to Germany to destroy its economic and political strength. Even the degree of severity that it incorporated soon proved to be more than the Allies were willing to enforce. The treaty makers at Paris in 1919, working hastily and still in the heat of war, under pressure from press and propaganda in their own countries, drafted a set of terms which the test of time showed that they themselves did not in the long run wish to impose. As the years passed, many people in Allied countries declared various provisions of the Versailles treaty to be unfair or unworkable. The loss of faith by the Allies in their own treaty only made easier the task of those German agitators who demanded its repudiation. The door was opened for Adolf Hitler.

Even at the beginning the Allies showed doubts. Lloyd George, in the last weeks before signature, tardily called for certain amendments, though in vain; for in 1919 British opinion shifted somewhat from fear of Germany to the fear of Bolshevism, and already the idea of using Germany as a bulwark against communism was expressed. The Italians disliked the whole settlement from the beginning; they observed that the spoils of Africa and the Near East went only to France and Great Britain. The Chinese were also dissatisfied. The Russians, when they reentered the international arena some years later, found a situation that they did not like and had had no part in making. They objected to being faced with a *cordon sanitaire* from Finland to Rumania and soon remembered that most of this territory had once belonged to the Russian empire.

The United States never ratified the Treaty of Versailles at all. A wave of isolationalism and disgust with Europe spread over the country; and this feeling, together with some rational criticism of the terms, and a good deal of party politics, caused the Senate to repudiate Wilson's work. The Senate likewise refused to make any advance promises of military intervention in a future war between Germany and France, and hence also declined to ratify the Anglo-French-American guarantee treaty on which Wilson had persuaded Clemenceau

23 See pp. 797–799.

to rely. The French considered themselves duped, deprived both of the Rhineland and of the Anglo-American guarantee. They raised more anguished cries over their insecurity. This led them to try to hold Germany down while it was still weak, in turn raising many further complications.

The League of Nations was established at Geneva. Its mere existence marked a great step beyond the international anarchy before 1914. Wilson's vision did not die. But the United States never joined; Germany was not admitted until 1926, or Russia until 1934. The League could handle and dispatch only such business as the Great Powers were willing to allow. It was associated with a west-European ascendancy that no longer corresponded to the facts of the world situation. Its convenant was part of the Versailles treaty, and many people in many countries, on both sides in the late war, saw in it, not so much a system for international adjudication, as a means for maintaining a new status quo in favor of Britain and France.

The First World War dealt a last blow to the ancient institutions of monarchy and aristocratic feudalism. Thrones toppled in Turkey, in Russia, in Austria-Hungary, in the German Empire and the individual German states; and with the kings went the courtly retainers and all the social preeminence and special advantage of the old landed aristocracies. The war was indeed a victory for democracy, though a bitter one. It carried further a process as old as the French and American revolutions. But for the basic problems of modern civilization, industrialism and nationalism, economic security and international stability, it gave no answer.

XVII.
The Russian
Revolution
and the
Soviet Union

o less powerful than the First World War as a force shaping the twentieth century has been the revolution in Russia, of which the decisive step was the seizure of power by the Bolshevik party in November 1917. The Russian Revolution of 1917 can be compared in its magnitude only with the French Revolution of 1789. Both originated in deep-lying and distant causes, and both made their repercussions felt in many countries for many years. The present chapter will set forth the revolutionary process in Russia over half a century. We shall begin with the old regime before 1900, pass through the two revolutions of 1905 and 1917, and survey the Union of Soviet Socialist Republics down to 1939, at which time a new order had been consolidated under Joseph Stalin, a form of "planned economy" successfully realized, and the last of the original revolutionaries, or Old Bolsheviks, either silenced or put to death.

The comparison of the Russian Revolution to the French is enlightening in many ways. Both were movements of liberation, the one against "feudalism" and "despotism," the other against "capitalism" and "imperialism." Neither was a strictly national movement dealing with merely domestic troubles; both addressed their message to all the world. Both attracted followers in all countries. Both aroused a strong reaction on the part of those whose view of life was endan-

Chapter Emblem: One of a series of bronze medals issued by the Leningrad mint in honor of Lenin and the Russian Revolution of 1917.

gered. And both showed the same pattern of revolutionary politics: a relative unity of opinion so long as the problem was to overthrow the old regime, followed by disunity and conflict over the founding of the new, so that one set of revolutionaries eliminated others, until a small, organized, and determined minority (Jacobin democrats in 1793, Bolshevik communists in 1918) suppressed all opposition in order to defend or advance the revolutionary cause; and in short order (within a matter of months in France, years in Russia), many of the most intensely revolutionary leaders were themselves suppressed or liquidated.

The differences are equally deserving of notice. Relatively speaking, or compared in general civilization with other European countries, Russia in 1900 was in the rear, and France in 1780 in many ways in the lead. The main strength of the French Revolution lay in the middle classes, who soon managed to prevail over more extreme pressures. In the Russian Revolution middle-class people were also active, especially at first, but they proved unable to cope with mass discontents, and succumbed to a more radical party which appealed to workers and peasants. In France, so to speak, the revolution just "happened," in that ordinary people from many walks of life unexpectedly found themselves in a revolutionary situation, and even the Jacobin dictatorship was improvised by men who had spent their lives thinking of other things. In Russia professional revolutionaries worked for the revolution long in advance, and the dictatorship of the Bolsheviks realized the plans and preparations of twenty years. In France the revolution was followed by a reaction in which émigrés returned, dispossessed classes reappeared in politics, and even the Bourbons were restored. The French Revolution was followed by a century of uneasy compromise. The Russian Revolution effectively wiped out its opposition; no once discredited class ever came back, few émigrés returned, no Romanovs regained their throne. The Russian Revolution was in this sense more immediately successful.

The repercussions of the Russian Revolution were the more far-reaching because of the very ambivalence of Russia itself. Since the days of Peter the Great and before, it had always faced toward both Europe and Asia. It was European, yet it was also outside Europe, and even opposed to it. If about 1900 it was the least developed of the major European countries, it was at the same time the most developed, industrialized, or modernized part of the non-European world. Its revolution could win sympathy on the Left in Europe because it reinforced the old European socialist objections to capitalism. It aroused the interests of submerged peoples in other continents because it also denounced imperialism (i.e., the possession of colonies by Europeans), affirming that imperialism was merely the "highest stage" of capitalism, and that both must be overthrown together. The Soviet Union, once established, came to occupy an intermediate position between the West and the Third World. In the West it could long be feared or admired as the last word in social revolution. In the Third World it suggested new beginnings, a new way to become modern without being capitalistic or European, a step in a world-wide rebellion against European supremacy. The Russian Revolution thus not only produced communism and hence fascism in Europe, but added strength to the revolt of Asia, as explained in the following chapters.

Although professional revolutionaries worked for revolution in Russia, they did not "cause" it. Lenin and the Bolsheviks did not bring about the Russian Revolution. They captured it after it had begun. They boarded the ship in midstream. The Russian Revolution, like all great revolutions, originated in a totality of previous history and in the prolonged dissatisfaction of many kinds of people.

90. BACKGROUNDS

Russia after 1881: Reaction and Progress

We have seen in earlier chapters how the tsarist autocracy arose, how it ruled as a machine superimposed upon its subjects, how the upper class became westernized while the masses sank further into serfdom, and how an intelligentsia developed, divorced both from the work of government and the activities of the people.[1] It has been explained in Chapter XIII how Alexander II freed the serfs in 1861 and created provincial and district councils or zemstvos, elected mainly by landowners, which attended to such matters as roads, schools, and hospitals.[2]

In 1881 Alexander II was assassinated by members of the People's Will. His son, Alexander III (1881–1894), tried to stamp out revolutionism and to silence even peaceable criticism of the government. Revolutionaries and terrorists were driven into exile. The People's Will as an organized group became extinct. Jews were subjected to pogroms, by far the worst of any (until then) in modern times. For the first time the empire adopted a program of systematic Russification. Poles, Ukrainians, Lithuanians, Caucasians, the scattered German communities, the various Muslim groups, all faced the prospect of forcible assimilation to the Great Russian culture. The philosopher and chief official of this movement was Pobiedonostsev, procurator of the Holy Synod, or layman head, under the tsar, of the Russian Orthodox Church. Pobiedonostsev saw in the West something alien and doomed. Drawing on such old enemies of the French Revolution as Edmund Burke, he attacked Western rationalism and liberalism in his writings, declared that Slavs had a peculiar national character of their own, and dreamed of turning Holy Russia into a kind of churchly community, in which a disciplined clergy should protect the faithful from the insidious influences of the West.

This is not, however, what happened. In the closing decades of the nineteenth century Russia became more than ever before a part of European civilization. Almost overnight it presented Europe with great works of literature and music that Europeans could understand. The Russian novel became known throughout the Western world. All could read the novels of Tolstoy (1828–1910) without a feeling of strangeness; and if the characters of Turgenev (1818–1883) and of Dostoevski (1821–1881) behaved more queerly, the authors themselves were obviously within the great European cultural family. The melodies of Tchaikovsky (1840–1893) and songs of Rimsky-Korsakov (1844–1908) became familiar throughout Europe and America; if they sometimes seemed hauntingly wild, distant, or sad, they still betrayed no more than the usual amount of national idiosyncrasy. Russians also contributed to the sciences, notably chemistry. They were considered to be especially talented in the more abstruse intellectual exercises, such as higher mathematics, physics, or chess.

[1] See pp. 224–235, 315–322, 524–528.
[2] See pp. 525–528.

Russia also, from the 1880s, began to pass through the Industrial Revolution and take its place as an integral part of the world economic system. European capital entered the country, financing railways, mines, and factories (as well as government and the army) until by 1914 Europeans had about the same amount invested in Russia as in the United States, some four billion dollars in each case.[3] In 1897, under the reforming ministry of Count Witte, Russia adopted the gold standard, making its currency readily convertible with all others. In the quarter-century between 1888 and 1913 the Russian railway mileage more than doubled, the miles of telegraph wires multiplied fivefold, the number of post offices trebled, and the number of letters carried by the mails multiplied seven times. Although still industrially undeveloped by Western standards, without, for example, any machine tool industry or chemical plants, Russia was industrializing rapidly. Exports rose in value from 400 million rubles in 1880 to 1.6 billion in 1913. Imports, though smaller, grew more rapidly, quintupling in the same period. They consisted of such items as tea and coffee and of the machines and industrial goods made in western Europe. For a long time after the Revolution, the Soviet Union conducted less foreign trade than did the Russian empire on the eve of the First World War. The Soviet regime, to keep control over its own economic system, tried to depend as little as possible on outside markets and sources of supply.

Industrialization, in Russia as in all countries, brought an increase both of the business and of the wage-earning classes, or, in socialist terminology, of the bourgeoisie and of the proletariat. Though growing, they were still not numerous by standards of the West. Factory workers, laboring for eleven or more hours a day, for low wages under hard conditions, were in somewhat the same position as in England or France before 1850.[4] Unions were illegal, and strikes prohibited. Nevertheless, great strikes in the 1890s called attention to the misery of the new industrial workers. There was one distinctive feature to the Russian proletariat. Russian industry was heavily concentrated; half of Russia's industrial workers were employed in factories employing over 500 persons. It was easier for workers under such circumstances to be organized economically and at the proper time to be mobilized politically. As for the Russian business and capitalist class, it was relatively the weaker because of several features in the situation. Ownership of much of Russia's new industrial plant was in foreign hands. Much was owned by the tsarist government itself; Russia already had the largest state-operated economic system in the world. Moreover, in Russia (unlike the United States at the time) the government itself was a heavy borrower from Europe; hence it was less dependent financially on its own people and more able to maintain an absolutist regime.

Nevertheless, the rising business and professional classes, reinforced by enterprising landowners, were strong enough to form a liberal segment of public opinion, which emerged in 1905 as the Constitutional Democratic party (the K.D.'s or "Cadets"). Many of those who were active in the provincial zemstvos also became Constitutional Democrats. They were liberals, progressives, or constitutionalists in the Western sense, thinking less about the troubles of factory

---

[3] See pp. 558–560, 607.
[4] See pp. 423–424, 458–461, 463–467.

workers and peasants than about the need of a nationally elected parliament to control the policies of state.

Russia remained predominantly agricultural. Its huge exports were mainly farm and forest products. The peasants formed four-fifths of the population. Free from their former lords since 1861, they lived in their village communes or *mirs*.[5] In most communes the land was divided and redivided among peasant households by agreement of the village community, nor could anyone leave without communal permission. The peasants still carried a considerable burden. Until 1906 they paid redemption money arising from the Emancipation of 1861, and even after that other forms of onerous payments. They also paid high taxes, for the government defrayed the interest on its foreign loans from taxes raised at home. The constantly rising export of cereals (also used to pay off debts contracted by Russia in the West) tended to keep food from the farmer's table; many a peasant raised the best wheat for sale and ate black bread himself. The farm population, in short (as in other countries in similar stages of their development), bore a considerable share of the costs of industrialization.

Under such pressures, and because of their crude methods of cultivation, the peasants were forever demanding more land. "Land hunger" was felt both by individual families and by the *mirs*. The Emancipation had turned over roughly half the land to peasant ownership, individual and collective; and in the following half-century the peasants added to their share by buying from nonpeasant owners. The *mirs* were by no means obsolescent. They were in fact flourishing; they acquired far more land by purchase than did individual buyers, and perhaps half or more of the peasants valued communal security above the uncertain pleasures of private property. The exceptions were the minority of more enterprising and wealthier peasants, later called the kulaks. Such a one was Leon Trotsky's father, who, a hard-working, plain, and illiterate man, owned or leased the equivalent of a square mile of land, employed scores of field hands at harvest time, and permanently maintained a large domestic staff. That such a "big farmer" could afford so many employees suggests the poverty in which the bulk of the peasants lived. Not all of the well-to-do peasants were as affluent as Trotsky's father, but the big farmers stood out conspicuously from the mass, by whom they were not liked.

The Emergence of Revolutionary Parties

The peasants were the ancient source of revolutionary disturbance in Russia. Fables about Pugachev and Stephen Razin circulated in peasant legend.[6] After the Emancipation the peasants continued to believe that they had some kind of rights in *all* the land of former estates on which they had formerly been serfs—not merely in the portion that had been allotted to peasant possession. They demanded (and obtained) credit from the government to buy from the big landowners or former masters. Their land hunger could not be appeased. They remained jealous of the landed aristocrat's very existence. In Russia, as elsewhere in Europe, and unlike the United States, the rural population was divided into

5 See pp. 525–527.
6 See pp. 228, 317.

two sharply distinct classes, on the one hand the peasants of all types, who worked the soil, and on the other the gentry who resided upon it. The two never intermarried. They differed not merely economically but in speech, dress, and manners, and even in the looks of their faces and hands. But in the last three decades of the nineteenth century the Russian peasants were notably quiet, insurrectionism seemingly having subsided.

The other traditional source of revolutionary disturbance lay among the intelligentsia.[7] In the conditions in which the Russian empire had grown up, many of the best and purest spirits were attracted to violence. Revolutionary intelligentsia (as distinguished from those who were simply liberal or progressive) yearned for a catastrophic overthrow of the tsardom. Since the days of the Decembrists[8] they had formed secret organizations, comprising a few hundreds or thousands of members, engaged in outwitting the tsarist police, by whom they were bafflingly interpenetrated. For example, at a Bolshevik party congress held in 1913, out of twenty-two delegates present, no less than five, unknown to the others, were government spies.

The revolutionary intelligentsia, since there was normally little that they could do, spent their time in vehement discussion and interminable refinement of doctrine. By 1890 the terrorism and nihilism of the 1870s were somewhat passé. The great question was where these willing officers of a revolutionary movement could find an army. Disputation turned upon such topics as whether the peasants or the new factory workers were the true revolutionary class, whether the peasants were potentially proletarian or incurably petty bourgeois, whether Russia was bound to experience the same historical process as the West, or whether it was different; and, specifically, whether Russia had to go through capitalism or might simply skip the capitalist stage in reaching the socialist society.

Most of the revolutionary intelligentsia were "populists." Some had once belonged to the now broken People's Will. Some continued to approve of terrorism and assassination as morally necessary in an autocratic country. They generally had a mystical faith in the vast inchoate might of the Russian people, and since most Russians were peasants, the populists were interested in peasant problems and peasant welfare. They believed that a great native revolutionary tradition existed in Russia, of which the peasant rebellion of Pugachev, in 1773, was the chief example.[9] The populists admired the Russian communal village or *mir*, in which they saw the European socialist idea of a "commune" represented. They read and respected Marx and Engels (indeed, a populist first translated the *Communist Manifesto* into Russian); but they did not believe that an urban proletariat was the only true revolutionary class. They did not believe that capitalism, by creating such a proletariat, had inevitably and logically to precede socialism. They said that, in Russia, the horrors of capitalism could be skipped. They addressed themselves to the plight of the farmer and the evils of landlordism, favored strengthening the *mir* and equalizing the shares of all peasants in it, and, since they did not have to wait for the prior triumph of capitalism in Russia, they thought that revolution might come quite soon. This populist sentiment crystallized in the founding in 1901 of the Social Revolutionary party.

[7] See p. 525.
[8] See pp. 446–447.
[9] See pp. 317–318.

Two populists, Plekhanov and Axelrod, fleeing to Switzerland in the 1870s, there became converted to Marxism. In 1883 they founded in exile the organization from which the Russian Social Democratic or Marxist party was to grow. A few Marxists began to declare themselves (though not publicly) in Russia itself. When the youthful Lenin met his future wife Krupskaya in 1894, she already belonged to a circle of argumentative Marxists. The fact that the peasants in the 1890s were disappointingly quiescent, while machine industry, factory labor, and strikes were developing rapidly, turned many of the revolutionary intelligentsia, though only a minority, from populism to Marxism. To Plekhanov and Axelrod were added, as young leaders, Lenin (1870–1924), Trotsky (1879–1940), Stalin (1879–1953), and others.

Of these it was Lenin who, after Marx, was to be claimed by communism as a father. Lenin was a short almost rotund man, with a small man's bounding quickness and intense, penetrating gaze. High cheekbones and somewhat slanting eyes showed an Asiatic strain on the paternal side; Russian friends at first said that he looked "like a Kalmuck." His hair receded in early youth, leaving a massive forehead, behind which a restless mind was inexhaustibly at work. Even in his twenties he was called the Old One. He was of upper-middle-class origin, son of an inspector of schools who rose in the civilian bureaucracy to a rank equivalent to major general. His boyhood was comfortable and even happy, until the age of seventeen, when his elder brother, a student at St. Petersburg, became somewhat incidentally involved in a plot to assassinate Alexander III, for which he was put to death by order of the tsar himself. Because of the blot on the family record it became impossible for Lenin to continue with his law studies. He soon joined the ranks of professional revolutionaries, having no other occupation and living precariously from the party funds, which came mainly from the donations of well-to-do sympathizers.

Arrested as a revolutionary, he spent three years of exile in Siberia. Here the tsarist government treated educated political prisoners with an indulgence not later shown by the Soviet regime. Lenin and most of the others lived in cottages of their own or boarded with local residents. No labor was required of them. They borrowed books from Europe; met and visited with one another; debated, played chess, went hunting, meditated, and wrote. They chafed, however, at being cut off from the mainstream of Russian political life back home. Lenin, his term over, proceeded in 1900 to western Europe, where except for short secret trips to Russia he remained until 1917. His intellectual vigor, irresistible drive, and shrewdness as a tactician soon made him a force in the party. Genius has been called the faculty for everlasting concentration upon one thing. Lenin, said his one-time close associate Axelrod, "for twenty-four hours of the day is taken up with the revolution, has no thoughts but thoughts of revolution, and even in his sleep dreams of nothing but revolution."

In 1898 the Marxists in Russia, spurred on by émigrés, founded the Social Democratic Labor party. They were not more revolutionary than the larger group of Social Revolutionaries. They simply had a different conception of the revolution. First of all, as good Marxists, they were more inclined to see the revolution as an international movement, part of the dialectical process of world history in which all countries were involved. Russia for them was no different from other countries except that it was less advanced. They expected the world revolution to break out first in western Europe. They particularly admired the German Social Democratic party, the largest and most flourishing of all the parties that acknowledged the fatherhood of Marx.[10]

If the Social Democrats were more oriented to Europe than the Social Revolutionaries, it was because so many of their spokesmen lived there in exile. They tended to think that Russia must develop capitalism, an industrial proletariat, and the modern form of class struggle before there could be any revolution. Seeing in the urban proletariat the true revolutionary class, they looked upon all peasantry with suspicion, ridiculed the *mir,* and abhorred the Social Revolutionaries. "Marxism," said Lenin, "has forever shaken itself loose from the nonsensical patter of the populists and anarchists to the effect that Russia can escape a capitalist development." (Russian Marxists were on this point more Marxist than Marx and Engels, both of whom, when urged, refused to pronounce on the merits of the *mir* or on the need of capitalism as a precondition to socialism in Russia.) Like Marx himself, the Russian Marxists disapproved of sporadic terrorism and assassination. For this reason, and because their doctrine seemed somewhat academic and their revolution rather conditional and far in the future, the Marxists were for a time actually favored by the tsarist police, who regarded them as less dangerous than the Social Revolutionaries.

Split in the Social Democrats: Bolsheviks and Mensheviks

The Russian Marxists held a second party congress in Brussels and London in 1903, attended by émigrés like Lenin and delegates from the underground in Russia, and by Social Democrats and members of lesser organizations. The purpose of the congress was to unify all Russian Marxism, but in fact it split it forever. The two resulting factions called themselves Bolsheviks, or majority men, and Mensheviks, or minority men. Lenin was the main author of the split and hence the founder of Bolshevism. Although he obtained his majority after one participating organization, the Jewish Bund, had seceded in indignation, and by calling for surprise votes on tactical issues, and although after 1903 it was usually the Mensheviks who had the majority, Lenin clung proudly and stubbornly to the term Bolshevism, with its favorable connotation of a majority in his support. For a number of years after 1903 the Social Democrats remained at least formally a single Marxist party, but they were irreconcilably divided into two wings. In 1912 the Bolshevik wing organized itself as a separate party.

Bolshevism, or Leninism, originally differed from Menshevism mainly on matters of organization and tactics. Russian Marxists referred to each other as "hards" and "softs." The "hards" were attracted to Lenin, the "softs" repelled by him. Lenin believed that the party should be a small revolutionary elite, a hard core of reliable and zealous workers. Those who wished a larger and more open party, with membership for mere sympathizers, became Mensheviks. Lenin insisted upon a strongly centralized party, without autonomy for national or other component groups. He demanded strong authority at the top, by which the central committee would determine the doctrine (or "party line") and control personnel

[10] See pp. 574, 580–581.

at all levels of the organization. The Mensheviks favored a greater degree of influence by the membership as a whole. Lenin thought that the party would strengthen itself by purges, expelling all who developed deviations of opinion. The Mensheviks favored covering up or bridging over all but the most fundamental disagreements. The Mensheviks came to recommend cooperation with liberals, progressives, and bourgeois democrats. Lenin regarded such cooperation as purely tactical and temporary, never concealing that in the end the Bolsheviks must impose their views through a dictatorship of the proletariat. The Mensheviks, in short, came to resemble the Marxists of western Europe, so far as that was possible under Russian conditions.[11] Lenin stood for the rigid reaffirmation of Marxian fundamentals—dialectical materialism and irreconcilable class struggle.

If we ask what Leninism added to the original Marxism,[12] the answer is not easy to find. Lenin accepted Marx's governing ideas: that capitalism exploited the workers, that it necessarily produced and preceded socialism, that history was logically predetermined, that class struggle was the law of society, that existing forms of religion, government, philosophy, and morals were weapons of the ruling class. He did, however, develop and transform into a first-rank element of Marxism certain theories of "imperialism" and of the "uneven development of capitalism" that had been propounded in only general terms by Marx and Engels. In the Marxist-Leninist view, "imperialism" was exclusively a product of monopoly capitalism, that is, capitalism in its big business, "highest," and "final" stage, which develops differently and at different times in each country. Monopoly capitalism is bent on exporting surplus capital and investing it in underdeveloped areas for greater profits.[13] The unceasing drive for colonies and markets in a world already almost completely partitioned leads inevitably to international "imperialist" wars for the "redistribution" of colonies, as well as to intensified national colonial struggles for independence; both provide new revolutionary opportunities for the proletariat.

In other respects, Lenin roundly denounced all who attempted to "add" anything to the fundamental principles of Marx. Nothing infuriated him so much as revisionist efforts to tone down the class struggle, or hints that Marxism might in the last analysis perhaps find room for some kind of religion. As he wrote in 1908: "From the philosophy of Marxism, cast of one piece of steel, it is impossible to expunge a single basic premise, a single essential part, without deviating from objective truth, without falling into the arms of bourgeois-reactionary falsehood." Lenin was a convert. He discovered Marxism; he did not invent it. He found in it a theory of revolution which he accepted without reservation as scientific and on which he was more outspokenly dogmatic even than Marx himself. His powers of mind, which were very great, were spent in demonstrating how the unfolding events of the twentieth century confirmed the analysis of the master.

But it was by his powers of will that Lenin was most distinguished, and if Leninism contributed little to Marxism as a theory it contributed a great deal to it as a movement. Lenin was an activist. He was the supreme agitator, a field commander in the class war, who could dash off a polemical pamphlet, dominate

11 See pp. 581–583.
12 See pp. 483–488.
13 See pp. 606–607.

a party congress, or address throngs of workingmen with equal ease. Beside him, Marx and Engels seem almost to be mere recluses or sociologists. Marx and Engels had preferred to believe that the dictatorship of the proletariat, when it came, would represent the wishes of the great majority in a society in which most people had become proletarians. Lenin more frankly foresaw the possibility that the proletarian dictatorship might represent the conscious wishes of a small vanguard and might have to impose itself on great masses by an unshrinking use of force.

Above all, Lenin developed Marx's idea of the role of the party. He drew on the rich experience of pre-Marxist revolutionaries in Russia—the mysterious use of false names, invisible ink, secret ciphers, forged passports, and hidden rendezvous—the whole conspiratorial wonderland which, when it existed to a lesser degree in the West before 1848, drew Marx's scorn and laughter. Lenin's conception of the party was basically Marx's, reinforced by his own experience as a Russian. The party was an organization in which intellectuals provided leadership and understanding for workers, who could not see for themselves. For trade unionism, concerned only with the day-to-day demands of workingmen, Lenin had even less patience than Marx. "The unconscious growth of the labor movement," he wrote, "takes the form of trade unionism, and trade unionism signifies the mental enslavement of the workers to the bourgeoisie." The task of intellectuals in the party, the elite, or experts, was to make the trade unions and the working class "conscious" and hence revolutionary. Armed with "objective" knowledge, known to be correct, the party leadership naturally could not listen to the subjective opinions of others—the passing ideas of laborers, of peasants, of mistaken party subordinates, or of other parties pretending to know more than Marx himself. The idea that intellectuals supply the brains and workers the brawn, that an elite leads while the toilers meekly follow, is understandable enough in view of the Russian background, which had created on the one hand a painfully self-conscious intelligentsia, and on the other a repressed working class and peasantry deprived of all opportunity for political experience of their own. It was one of the most distinctive traits of Leninism and one of the most foreign to the democratic movement of the West.

Leninism accomplished the marriage of Russian revolutionary traditions with the Western doctrine of Marxism. It was an improbable marriage, whose momentous offspring was to be communism. But at the time, when Bolshevism first appeared in 1903, it had little or no effect. A real revolution broke out in Russia in 1905. It took the revolutionary émigrés almost entirely by surprise.

91. THE REVOLUTION OF 1905

Background and Revolutionary Events

The almost simultaneous founding at the turn of the century of the Constitutional Democratic, Social Revolutionary, and Social Democratic parties was clearly a sign of mounting discontent. None of these was as yet a party in the Western sense, organized to get men elected to office, for there were no elections in Russia above the provincial zemstvo level. All three parties were propaganda agencies, made up of leaders without followers, intellectuals who followed various lines of thought. All, even those who became Constitutional Democrats, were watched by the police and obliged to do most of their work underground. At the same time, after 1900, there were signs of growing popular unrest. Peasants were trespassing on lands of the gentry and even rising in local insurrections against landlords and tax collectors. Factory workers sporadically refused to work. But with these popular movements none of the new parties had formed any solid links.

The government refused to make concessions of any kind. The tsar, Nicholas II, who had mounted the throne in 1894, was a man of narrow outlook. To the Little Father all criticism seemed merely childish. Tutored in his youth by Pobiedonostsev,[14] he regarded all ideas questioning autocracy, Orthodoxy, and Great Russian nationalism as un-Russian. That persons in the government should be controlled by interests outside the government—the mildest liberalism or most orderly democracy—seemed to the tsar, the tsarina, and the leading officials to be a monstrous aberration. Autocracy, for them, was the best and only, as it was the God-given, form of government for Russia.

The chief minister, Plehve, and the circles at court, hoped that a short successful war with Japan would create more attachment to the government. The war went so badly that its effect was the reverse.[15] Critics of the regime (except for the handful of the most internationalist Marxists) were sufficiently patriotic to be ashamed at the ease with which Russia was defeated by an upstart and Asian power. As after the Crimean War, there was a general feeling that the government had exposed its incompetence to all the world. Liberals believed that its secret methods, its immunity to criticism or control, had made it sluggish, torpid, obstinate, and inefficient, unable either to win a war or to lead the economic modernization that was taking place in Russia. But there was little that the liberals could do.

The police had recently allowed a priest, Father Gapon, to go among the St. Petersburg factory workers and organize them, hoping thus to counter the propaganda of revolutionaries. Father Gapon took up their grievances in all seriousness. They believed, as simple peasants only recently transplanted to the city, that if only they could reach the ear of the Little Father, the august being high above all hard capitalists and stony officials, he would hear their complaints with shocked surprise and rectify the evils that afflicted Russia. They drew up a petition, asking for an eight-hour day, a minimum daily wage of one ruble (fifty cents), a repudiation of bungling bureaucrats, and a democratically elected Constituent Assembly to introduce representative government into the empire. Unarmed, peaceable, respectful, singing "God save the Tsar," a crowd of 200,000— men, women, and children—gathered before the tsar's Winter Palace one Sunday in January 1905. But the tsar had fled, and his officials were afraid. Troops marched up and shot down the demonstrators in cold blood, killing several hundred.

"Bloody Sunday" in St. Petersburg snapped the moral bond upon which all stable government rests. The horrified workers saw that the tsar was not their

---

[14] See p. 692.
[15] See pp. 638–640.

friend. The autocracy stood revealed as the force behind the hated officials, the tax collectors, the landlords, and the owners of the industrial plants. A wave of political strikes broke out. Social Democrats (more Mensheviks than Bolsheviks) appeared from the underground or from exile to give revolutionary direction to these movements. Councils or "soviets" of workers were formed in Moscow and St. Petersburg. The peasants, too, in many parts of the country spontaneously began to erupt, overrunning the lands of the gentry, burning manor houses and doing violence to their owners. Social revolutionaries naturally tried to take this movement in charge. The liberal Constitutional Democrats, professors, engineers, businesspeople, lawyers, leaders in the provincial zemstvos founded forty years before, tried also to seize leadership or at least use the crisis to force the government's hand. All agreed on one demand—that there should be more democratic representation in the government.

The tsar yielded grudgingly and as little as possible. In March 1905 he promised to call to office men "enjoying the confidence of the nation." In August (after the ruinous battle of Tsushima) he agreed to call a kind of Estates General, for which peasants, landowners, and city people should vote as separate classes. Still the revolution raged unchecked. The St. Petersburg Soviet, or workers' council, led mainly by Mensheviks (Lenin had not yet reached Russia), declared a great general strike in October. Railroads stopped, banks closed, newspapers ceased to appear, and even lawyers refused to go to their offices. The strike spread to other cities and to the peasants. With the government paralyzed, the tsar issued his October Manifesto. It promised a constitution, civil liberties, and a Duma to be elected by all classes alike, with powers to enact laws and control the administration.

The tsar and his advisers intended to divide the opposition by releasing the October Manifesto, and in this they succeeded. The Constitutional Democrats, with a Duma promised, allowed themselves to hope that social problems could henceforth be dealt with by parliamentary methods. Liberals were now afraid of revolutionaries; industrialists feared the strength shown by labor in the general strike, and landowners demanded a restoration of order among the peasants. Aroused peasants and workers were not yet satisfied; the former still wanted more land and less taxation, the latter a shorter working day and a living wage. The several branches of revolutionary intellectuals worked upon the continuing popular agitation, hoping to carry matters forward until the tsarist monarchy was abolished and a socialist republic established with themselves at its head. They believed also (and correctly) that the October Manifesto was in any case a deception, which the tsar would refuse to adhere to as soon as revolutionary pressure was removed. The soviets continued to seethe, local strikes went on, and there were mutinies among soldiers at Kronstadt and sailors in the Black Sea fleet.

But the government was able to maintain itself. With the middle-class liberals now inactive or demanding order, the authorities arrested the members of the St. Petersburg Soviet. Peace was hastily made with Japan, and reliable troop units were recalled from the Far East. The revolutionary leaders fled back to Europe, or again went underground, or were caught and sent to prison or to Siberia; executions were carried out in the countryside.

The Results of 1905: The Duma

The chief apparent result of the Revolution of 1905 was to make Russia, at least ostensibly, into a parliamentary type of state, like the rest of Europe. The promised Duma was convoked. For ten years, from 1906 to 1916, Russia had at least the superficial attributes of a semiconstitutional monarchy.

But Nicholas II soon showed that he did not intend to yield much. He drew the teeth of the new Duma before the creature could even be born, by announcing in advance, in 1906, that it would have no power over foreign policy, the budget, or government personnel. His attitude toward constitutional monarchy continued until 1917 to be entirely negative; the one thing that tsarism would not allow was any real participation in government by the public. Within this "public" the two extreme fringes were equally impervious to liberal constitutionalism. On the right, stubborn upholders of pure autocracy and the Orthodox church organized the Black Hundreds, terrorizing the peasantry and urging them to boycott the Duma. On the left, in 1906, the Social Revolutionaries and both the Bolshevik and Menshevik wings of the Social Democrats likewise refused to recognize the Duma, urged workers to boycott it, and refused to put up any candidates for election.

The short-lived first Duma was elected in 1906 by a system of indirect and unequal voting, in which peasants and workers voted as separate classes, and with proportionately far less representation than was granted to the landlords. In the absence of socialist candidates, workers and peasants voted for all sorts of people, including the liberal Constitutional Democrats (the "Cadets"), who obtained a sweeping majority. The Cadets, when the Duma met, found themselves still fighting for the bare principle of constitutional government. They demanded true universal male suffrage and the responsibility of ministers to a parliamentary majority. The tsar's response was to dismiss the Duma after two months. The Cadets fled to Viborg in autonomous Finland, which the tsarist police generally let alone. It is significant that these constitutional liberals and democrats, in council at Viborg, again appealed for a general strike and nonpayment of taxes— that is, for mass revolution. But real revolutions are not easy to start, and nothing happened.

A second Duma was elected in 1907, with the government trying to control the elections through suppression of party meetings and newspapers, but since Social Revolutionaries and Mensheviks now consented to take part, some eighty-three socialists were elected. The Cadets, becoming fearful of the revolutionary left, concluded that constitutional progress must be gradual and showed a willingness to cooperate with the government. But the Duma came to an abrupt end when the government denounced and arrested some fifty socialists as revolutionaries bent only on destruction. A third Duma, elected after an electoral change that gave increased representation to the landed propertied class and guaranteed a conservative majority, managed to hold several sessions between 1907 and 1912, as did a fourth Duma from 1912 to 1916. The deputies, by following the lead of the government, by addressing themselves only to concrete issues, by losing themselves in committee work, and by avoiding the basic question of where supreme power lay, kept precariously alive a modicum of parliamentary institutions in the tsarist empire.

The Stolypin Reforms

Some officials believed that the way to checkmate the revolutionaries, and strengthen the hold of the monarchy, was for the government, while keeping all controls in its own hands, to attract the support of reasonable and moderate people by a program of reforms. One of these was Peter Stolypin, whom the tsar retained as his principal minister from 1906 to 1911. It was Stolypin who dissolved the first two Dumas. But it was not his policy merely to stand still. His aim was to build up the propertied classes as friends of the state. He believed, perhaps rightly, that a state actively supported by widespread private property had little to fear from doctrinaire intellectuals, conspirators, and émigrés. As he said in a speech to the Third Duma in 1908: "The government has placed its wager, not on the needy and the drunken, but on the sturdy and the strong—on the sturdy individual proprietor who is called upon to play a part in the reconstruction of our Tsardom."

Stolypin therefore favored and broadened the powers of the provincial zemstvos, in which the larger landowners took part in administering local affairs. For the peasantry he put through legislation more sweeping than any since the Emancipation.

Seeing in the *mir* the source of communal agrarian restlessness, Stolypin hoped to replace this ancient institution with a regime of private individual property. He abolished what was left of the redemption payments for which the *mirs* had been collectively responsible.[16] He allowed each peasant to sell his share of the communal rights and to leave the commune at will. He authorized peasants to buy land freely from the communes, from each other, or from the gentry. He thus favored the rise of the class of "big farmers," the later kulaks, men who obtained control of large tracts, worked them with hired help, and produced cash crops for the market. These were "the sturdy and the strong" upon whom Stolypin pinned his hopes. At the same time, by allowing peasants to sell out and leave the *mir* (it would generally be the worst farmers or most improvident persons who did so), he hastened the formation of a migratory wage-earning class, which would either seek work from the big farmers or go off to take jobs in the city. The creation of a mobile labor force, and of a food supply raised by big farmers for the market, would thus advance the industrialization of Russia.

The Stolypin policy was successful. Between 1907 and 1916, 6.2 million families out of 16 million who were eligible applied for legal separation from the *mir*. There was no mistaking the trend toward individual property and independent farming. But the results of the Stolypin program must not be exaggerated. The *mir* was far from broken. A vast majority of peasants were still involved in the old system of common rights and communal restrictions. The land shortage was still acute in the agricultural areas where yields were highest. Land hunger and poverty continued in the countryside. There were kulaks, to be sure, to be resented and envied, but the largest landed proprietors were still the gentry. About 30,000 landlords owned nearly 200 million acres of land, and another 200 million acres made up other large landed estates.

Stolypin was not left long to carry on his program. The tsar gave him only an unwilling support. Reactionary circles disliked his tampering ways and his West-

16 See pp. 525–527.

ern orientation. Social Revolutionaries naturally cried out against dissolution of the communes. Even Marxists, who should in theory have applauded the advance of capitalism in Russia, feared that Stolypin's reforms might do away with agrarian discontent. "I do not expect to live to see the revolution," said Lenin in these years. Stolypin was shot dead while attending the theater in Kiev, in the presence of the tsar and tsarina, in 1911. The assassin, a member of the terrorist wing of the Social Revolutionaries, is thought also to have been a secret agent of the reactionary tsarist police. It may be added that Stolypin's predecessor, Plehve, and about a dozen other high officials within the past few years had similarly died at the hands of assassins.

But all in all, violent and half barbaric though it still was, the Russian empire on the eve of the First World War was moving in a Western direction. Its industries were growing, its railways expanding, its exports almost half as great in value as those of the United States. It had a parliament, if not a parliamentary government. Private property and individualist capitalism were spreading to new layers of the people. There was a guarded freedom of the press, illustrated, for example, by the legal and open establishment of the Bolshevik party paper, *Pravda*, in St. Petersburg in 1912. It is not possible to say how far this development might have gone, for it was menaced on both the right and the left by obstinate and obscurantist reactionaries upholding the absolute tsardom and by revolutionaries whom nothing but the end of tsardom and wholesale transformation of society could appease. But both extremes were discouraged. The desperation of extreme reactionaries in the government, the feeling that they might in any case soon lose their position, perhaps made them the more willing to precipitate a European war by armed support of Serbian nationalists. As for the revolutionary parties, and especially the Bolsheviks, they were losing in membership on the eve of the war, their leaders lived year after year in exile, dreaming of the great days of 1905 which stubbornly failed to repeat themselves and sometimes pessimistically admitting, as Lenin did, that there might be no revolution in their time.

92. THE REVOLUTION OF 1917

End of the Tsardom: The Revolution of March 1917

War again put the tsarist regime to a test that it could not meet. In this war, more "total" than any had ever been, willing cooperation between government and people was indispensable to success. This essential prerequisite the tsarist empire did not have. National minorities, Poles, Jews, Ukrainians, Caucasians, and others, were disaffected. As for the socialists, who in every other European parliament voted for funds to finance the war, the dozen otherwise disunited socialists in the Duma refused to do so and were promptly jailed.[17] The ordinary workingman and peasant marched off with the army, but without the sense of personal conviction felt by common people in Germany and the West. More decisive was the attitude of the middle class. Because they patriotically wished Russia to win, the glaring mismanagement of the government was the more intolerable to them.

17 See pp. 702, 730–731.

The disasters with which the war opened in 1914, at Tannenberg and the Masurian Lakes, were followed by the advance of the Central Powers into Russia in 1915, at the cost of 2 million Russian soldiers killed, wounded, or captured.[18]

At the war's outbreak middle-class people, as in all countries, offered their assistance to the government.[19] The provincial zemstvos formed a union of all zemstvos in the empire to facilitate the mobilization of agriculture and industry. Business groups at Petrograd (St. Petersburg lost its Germanic name at this time) formed a Commercial and Industrial Committee to get the factories into maximum production. The government distrusted these signs of public activity arising outside official circles. On the other hand, organized in this way, middle-class people became conscious of their own strength and more critical of the bureaucracy. Some officials in the war ministry itself were known to be at heart pro-German, reactionaries who feared the liberalism of England and France, with which Russia was allied.

Life at court was bizarre even for Russia. The tsarina Alexandra, German by origin, looked upon all Russians outside her own circle with contempt, incited her husband to play the proud and pitiless autocrat, and took advice from a self-appointed holy man, the mysterious Rasputin. She was convinced that Rasputin possessed supernatural and prophetic powers, because he had apparently cured her young son, the tsarevitch, of hemophilia. Rasputin, by his influence over her, had a voice in appointments to high office. All who wished an audience with the imperial pair had to go through him. Patriotic and enlightened persons of all classes vainly protested. In these circumstances, and given the military defeats, the union of zemstvos and other such war-born bodies complained not merely of faults of administration but of fundamental conditions in the state. The government responded by holding them at arm's length. The tsarist regime, caught in a total war, was afraid of the help offered by its own people.

During the war, in September 1915, the Duma was suspended. It was known that reactionaries—inspired by the tsarina, Rasputin, and other sinister forces—expected that a victory in the war would make it possible to kill liberalism and constitutionalism in Russia. The war thus revived all the basic political issues that had been latent since the Revolution of 1905. The union of zemstvos demanded the assembly of the Duma. The Duma reassembled in November 1916 and, conservative though it had always been, expressed loud indignation at the way affairs were conducted. Among all elements of the population, dissatisfaction with the course of the war and with the government's ineptitude mounted. In December Rasputin was assassinated by nobles at the court. The tsar began to consider repression and again adjourned the Duma. Machine guns were issued to the police. Members of the Duma, and of the new extragovernmental bodies, concluded that the situation could be saved only by force. It is when moderate persons, normally concerned with their own business, come to such conclusions that revolution becomes a political possibility. The shift of moderates and liberals, their need of a coup d'état to save themselves from reactionaries, likewise raised the long failing prospects of the minority of professional revolutionaries.

Again it was the workers of Petrograd who precipitated the crisis. Food had

18 See p. 666.
19 See p. 678.

become scarce, as in all the belligerent countries. But the tsarist administration was too clumsy and too demoralized by graft to institute the controls that had become usual elsewhere, such as maximum prices and ration cards. It was the poorest who felt the food shortage most keenly. On March 8, 1917, food riots broke out, which soon developed, doubtless with the help of revolutionary intellectuals, into political insurrections. Crowds shouted, "Down with the tsar!" Troops within the city refused to fire on the insurgents; mutiny and insubordination spread from unit to unit. Within a few days a Soviet of Workers' and Soldiers' Deputies, on the model of 1905, had been organized in Petrograd.

Middle-class leaders, with the government now helpless, demanded dismissal of the ministry and formation of a new one commanding the confidence of a majority of the Duma. The tsar retaliated by disbanding the Duma. The Duma set up an executive committee to take charge until the situation clarified. There were now two new authorities in the city: one, the Duma committee, essentially moderate, constitutionalist, and relatively legal; the other, the Petrograd Soviet, representing revolutionary forces arising by spontaneous upsurge from below. The Petrograd Soviet (or workers' "council") was to play in 1917 a role like that of the Paris Commune of 1792, constantly pushing the supposedly higher and more nationwide authority to the left. The Soviet became the public auditorium and administrative center of the working-class upheaval. Since it was generally socialist in its outlook, all the factions of doctrinaire socialists—Social Revolutionaries, Mensheviks, Bolsheviks—tried to win it over and utilize it for their own ends.

The Duma committee, under pressure from the Petrograd Soviet, on March 14 set up a Provisional Government under Prince Lvov. The Duma liberals, as a concession to the Soviet, admitted one socialist to the new government, Alexander Kerensky, a moderate, legal-minded Social Revolutionary, and they furthermore consented to demand the abdication of Nicholas II. The tsar was then at the front. He tried to return to his palace near Petrograd, but the imperial train was stopped and turned back by troops. The army, fatefully, was taking the side of the Revolution. The very generals in the field, unable to vouch for the loyalty of their men, advised abdication. Nicholas yielded; his brother the grand duke declined to succeed him; and on March 17, 1917, Russia became a republic.

The Bolshevik Revolution: November 1917

The Provisional Government, following the best precedents of European revolutions, called for elections by universal male suffrage to a Constituent Assembly, which was to meet late in the year and prepare a constitution for the new regime. It tried also to continue the war against Germany. In July an offensive was mounted but the demoralized armies were quickly routed. Pending final decision by the Constituent Assembly, the Provisional Government promised wholesale redistribution of land to the peasants but took no action. Meanwhile, the peasants, driven by the old land hunger, were already overrunning the rural districts, burning and looting. At the front the armies melted away; many high officers refused to serve the republic, and masses of peasant soldiers simply turned their backs and went home, unwilling to be absent while farmlands were being handed out. The Petrograd Soviet, opposing the Provisional Government, called for speedy termination of the war. Fearing reactionary officers, it issued on March 14 its Order No. 1, entrusting command within the army to committees elected by both officers and men. Discipline collapsed.

The Revolution was thus already well advanced when Lenin and the other Bolsheviks arrived in Petrograd in the middle of April.[20] They immediately took sides with the Petrograd Soviet against the Provisional Government, and with similar soviets that had sprung up in other parts of the country. In July an armed uprising of soldiers and sailors, which the Bolshevik central committee disapproved of as premature, was put down. The Bolsheviks were blamed, and Lenin had to flee to Finland. But as a bid for popular support the Provisional Government named the socialist Kerensky as its head in place of Prince Lvov in an uneasy coalition of moderate socialists and liberals. Kerensky's middle position was next threatened from the right. The newly appointed military commander, General Kornilov, dispatched a force of cavalry to restore order. Not only conservatives but liberals wished him success in the hope that he would suppress the soviets. Kornilov's movement was defeated, but with the aid of the Bolsheviks, who rallied with other socialists, and of revolutionary-minded soldiers in the city who offered armed resistance. Radicals denounced liberals as accomplices in Kornilov's attempt at counterrevolution, and both camps blamed Kerensky for having allowed the plot to be hatched under his government. Both liberals and moderate socialists abandoned Kerensky, and he had to form a government of uncertain political support. Meanwhile the food shortage worsened, with transport disarranged and the farm population in turmoil, so that workers in the city listened more willingly to the most extreme speakers.

The Bolsheviks adapted their program to what the most aroused elements in a revolutionary people seemed to want. Lenin concentrated on four points: first, immediate peace with the Central Powers; second, redistribution of land to the peasants; third, transfer of factories, mines, and other industrial plants from the capitalists to committees of workers in each plant; and, fourth, recognition of the soviets as the supreme power instead of the Provisional Government. Lenin, though a rigid dogmatist on abstract questions, was a flexible and bold tactician; and his program in 1917 was dictated more by the immediate situation in Russia than by considerations of theoretical Marxism. What was needed was to win over soldiers, peasants, and workers by promising them "peace, land, and bread." With this program, and by infiltration and parliamentary stratagems, as well as by their accuracy as political prophets—predicting the Kornilov counterrevolution and "unmasking" the trend of middle-way liberals to support it—the Bolsheviks won a majority in the Petrograd Soviet and in soviets all over the country.

Lenin thereupon raised the cry, "All power to the Soviets!" to crush Kerensky and forestall the coming Constituent Assembly. Kerensky, to broaden the base on which he stood, and unable to wait for the Constituent Assembly, convoked a kind of preparliament representing all parties, labor unions, and zemstvos. Lenin and the Bolsheviks boycotted his preparliament. Instead they called an all-Russian Congress of Soviets.

20 See pp. 696–699.

Lenin now judged that the hour had come for the seizure of power. The Bolsheviks themselves were divided, many like Zinoviev and Kamenev opposing the move, but Lenin was backed by Trotsky, Stalin, and a majority of the party Central Committee. Troops garrisoned in Petrograd voted to support the soviets, which the Bolsheviks now controlled. On the night of November 6–7, 1917, the Bolsheviks took over telephone exchanges, railway stations, and electric lighting plants in the city. A warship turned its guns on the Winter Palace, where Kerensky's government sat. The latter could find almost no one to defend it. The hastily assembled Congress of Soviets pronounced the Provisional Government defunct and named in its place a Council of People's Commissars, of which Lenin became the head. Trotsky was named commissar for foreign affairs, Stalin commissar for nationalities. Kerensky fled, eventually arriving in the United States, where he lived until 1970.

At the Congress of Soviets Lenin introduced two resolutions. One called upon the belligerent governments to negotiate a "just democratic peace," without annexations and without indemnities; the second forthwith, and without compensation, abolished "all landlord property." Although determined to establish a proletarian dictatorship, the Bolsheviks knew the importance of the Russian peasants. The millions of acres belonging to the large estates that were now expropriated provided a base of support for the new regime without which it could hardly have survived.

Thus was accomplished the Bolshevik or November Revolution.[21] But the long awaited Constituent Assembly remained to be dealt with. It met in January 1918. Thirty-six million persons had voted for it. Of these, 9 million had voted for Bolshevik deputies, showing that the Bolshevik program, launched less than a year before by a small band of émigrés, had a widespread mass appeal. But almost 21 million had voted for Kerensky's party, the agrarian-populist, native Russian, peasant-oriented Social Revolutionaries. However, said Lenin, "to hand over power to the Constituent Assembly would again be compromising with the malignant bourgeoisie." The Assembly was broken up on the second day of its sessions; armed sailors dispatched by the people's commissars simply surrounded it. The dissolution of the Constituent Assembly was a frank repudiation of majority rule in favor of "class rule"—to be exercised for the proletariat by the Bolsheviks. The dictatorship of the proletariat was now established. Two months later, in March 1918, the Bolsheviks renamed themselves the Communist party.

The New Regime: The Civil War, 1918–1922

In these same months the Communists, or Bolsheviks, made the peace of Brest-Litovsk with Germany, surrendering to Germany control over the Baltic provinces, Poland, and the Ukraine. The conquests of two centuries were thus abandoned; not since the days of Peter the Great had the Russian frontier been so far from central Europe. To Lenin it made no difference. He was convinced that the events that he had just mastered in Russia were the prelude to a general up-

---

21 Also known as the October Revolution, since according to the Julian calendar, used in Russia until 1918, the events described took place in October.

heaval; that the war, still raging in the west, would bring all Europe to the inevitable proletarian or Marxist revolution; that Imperial Germany was therefore doomed; and that Poles, Ukrainians, and others would soon emerge, like the Germans themselves, as free socialist peoples. In any case, it was largely by promising peace that Lenin had won enough backing to overthrow Kerensky, who on this deep popular demand had delayed too long, waiting for England and France to release Russia from its treaty obligations as an ally. But real peace did not come, for the country sank immediately into civil war.

Not only old tsarist reactionaries, and not only liberals, bourgeois, zemstvo men, and Constitutional Democrats, but all types of anti-Leninist socialists as well, Mensheviks and Social Revolutionaries, scattered in all directions to organize resistance against the regime of soviets and people's commissars, and they obtained aid from the Western Allies. Both sides competed for the support of the peasants.

As for the new regime, the oldest of its institutions was the party, founded as a wing of the Social Democrats in 1903; the next oldest were the soviets, dating from 1905 and 1917; and then came the Council of People's Commissars set up on the day of the coup d'état. The first institution founded under the new order was a political police, an Extraordinary All-Russian Commission of Struggle Against Counterrevolution, Speculation, and Sabotage, commonly known from its Russian initials as the Cheka and in later years, without basic change of methods or purpose, under such successive names as the OGPU, the NKVD, the MVD, and the KGB. It was established on December 7, 1917. In January 1918 the Red Army was founded, with Leon Trotsky as war commissar and virtually its creator. In July a constitution was promulgated.

In social policy the Bolsheviks at first adopted no long-range plans, contenting themselves with a mixture of principle and expediency known as "war communism." They nationalized some of the largest industrial enterprises but left the bulk under the control of workers' committees. The pressing problem was to find food, which had ceased to move through any normal channels. The peasants, very much as in the French Revolution under similar conditions—worthless money, insecure property titles, unruly hired men, armed marauding, and a doubtful future—were producing less food than usual, consuming it themselves, or hoarding it on their own farms. The response of the government and city workers was also much as in 1793. The new government levied requisitions, required the peasants to make stated "deliveries," and invited labor unions to send armed detachments into the country to procure food by force. Since it was naturally the big farmers who had the surplus, they came into disrepute as starvers of the people. Class war broke out, rabid, ferocious, and elemental, between farmers who feared that their very subsistence as well as their property would be taken away, and city people, often supported by hungry agricultural laborers, who were driven to desperation by famine. Many peasants, especially the larger farmers, therefore rallied to anti-Bolshevik political leaders.

Centers of resistance developed on every side. In the Don valley a small force assembled under Kornilov and Denikin, with many army officers, gentry landowners, and expropriated business people taking part in it. The Social Revolutionaries gathered followers on the middle Volga. At Omsk a disaffected group proclaimed the independence of Siberia. As a military organization the most significant was a force of some 45,000 Czechs, who had deserted or been captured from the Austro-Hungarian armies and had then been organized as a Czech Legion to fight on the side of Russia and the Allies. After the November Revolution and the peace of Brest-Litovsk, these Czechs decided to leave Russia by way of the Trans-Siberian Railroad, return to Europe by sea, and resume fighting on the Western Front. When Bolshevik officials undertook to disarm them they allied with the Social Revolutionaries on the Volga.

The Allied governments believed that Bolshevism was a temporary madness that with a little effort could be stopped. They wished above all to bring Russia back into the war against Germany. So long as the war in Europe lasted, they could not reach Russia by the Black or Baltic Sea. A small Allied force took Murmansk and Archangel in the north. But for Allied military intervention the best opening was in the Far East, through Vladivostok. The Japanese, who had declined military aid to their Allies in any other theater, received this proposal with enthusiasm, seeing in the ruin of the Russian empire a rare opportunity to develop their sphere of influence in East Asia. It was agreed that an interallied military force should land at Vladivostok, cross Siberia, join with the Czechs, break up Bolshevism, and fall upon the Germans in eastern Europe. For this ambitious scheme Britain and France could supply no soldiers, engaged as they were on the Western Front; the force turned out to be American and Japanese, or rather almost purely Japanese, since Japan contributed 72,000 men and the United States only 8,000. They landed at Vladivostok in August 1918.

The civil war lasted until 1920, or even later in some places. It became a confused melee in which the Bolsheviks struggled against dissident Russians and against foreign intervention. They fought in the Ukraine first against the Germans, and then against the French, who occupied Odessa as soon as the war ended in Europe. They reconquered the Ukraine, Armenia, Georgia, and Azerbaidzhan, which had declared their independence; put to flight a hundred thousand "Whites" under Wrangel in the south; and fought off Admiral Kolchak, who, with a White army in Siberia, proclaimed himself ruler of all Russia. In 1920, the Bolsheviks carried on a war with the new republic of Poland, which was scarcely organized when it set out to recover the huge Ukrainian and White Russian territories that had been Polish before 1772.[22] British, French, and American troops remained at Archangel until the end of 1919, the Japanese at Vladivostok until the end of 1922.

But the anti-Bolshevik forces could never unite. The anti-Communist Russians represented every hue of the political spectrum from unregenerate tsarists to left-wing Social Revolutionaries. Many of the rightist anti-Bolsheviks openly antagonized the peasants by proceeding to restore expropriated landed estates in areas they occupied; many engaged in vindictive reprisals in a kind of "white terror." The Allies themselves could not agree, the French sent troops to the Ukraine and gave aid to the Poles, but the British and Americans wanted to be rid of all military entanglements as soon as the armistice with Germany was signed. Leon Trotsky, on the other hand, forged in the crucible of the civil wars the hard and solid metal of the Red Army, recruiting it, organizing it, restoring its discipline,

22 See map, p. 319.

equipping it as best he could, assigning political commissars to watch it, and assuring that trustworthy officers occupied its high command. The Bolsheviks could denounce the foreign intervention and appeal to national patriotism; and they could win peasant support by the distribution of land. By 1922 the Bolsheviks, or Communists, had established themselves up to the frontiers of the former tsarist empire in every direction except on the European side. There the band of Baltic states in the *cordon sanitaire* remained independent; Rumania had acquired Bessarabia, the new Rumanian frontier reaching now almost to Odessa; and Poland, as a result of the war of 1920, retaining a frontier farther east than the Allies themselves had intended. Russia had lost thousands of square miles of territory and buffer areas acquired over the centuries by the tsars. They were to remain lost until the Second World War. But peace was won and the regime stood.

It was during these civil wars that the Red Terror broke out in Russia. Like the famous Terror in France in 1793, it was in part a response to civil and foreign war. Before the Bolshevik Terror, the old Jacobin Terror paled. They differed as the cruelty and violence endemic in the old Russia differed from the more humane or law-abiding habits of western Europe. Thousands were shot merely as hostages (a practice unknown to Europe for some centuries); and other thousands without even the summary formalities of revolutionary tribunals. The Cheka was the most formidable political police that had yet appeared. The Bolshevik Terror was aimed at the physical extermination of all who opposed the new regime. A bourgeois class background would go far to confirm the guilt of the person charged with conspiring against the Soviet state. As a chief of the Cheka said: "The first questions you should put to the accused person are, To what class does he belong, what is his origin, what was his education, and what is his profession? These should determine the fate of the accused. This is the essence of the Red Terror." But a working-class background made little difference. In 1918 a young woman named Fanny Kaplan shot at Lenin and wounded him. She deposed that she had favored the Constituent Assembly, that her parents had emigrated to America in 1911, that she had six working-class brothers and sisters; and she admitted that she had intended to kill Lenin. She was of course executed, as were others in Petrograd. When the sailors at Kronstadt, who were among the first adherents won by the Bolsheviks, rose in 1921, objecting to domination of the soviets by the party (threatening a kind of leftist renewal of the revolution, like the Hébertists who had opposed Robespierre), they were branded as petty-bourgeois and shot down by the thousands. The Terror struck at the revolutionists themselves quite as much as it did the bourgeoisie; it was to continue to do so long after the Revolution was secured.

The Terror succeeded in its purpose. Together with the victories of the Red Army, it established the new regime. Those "bourgeois" who survived took on the protective coloration of "toilers." No bourgeois as such ever again presumed to take part in the politics of Russia. Mensheviks and other socialists fleeing to Europe told appalling stories of the human toll taken by Lenin. Horrified European socialists repudiated communism as an atrocious, Byzantine, Asiatic perversion of Marxism. But, at whatever cost, Lenin and his followers were now able to start building the socialist society as they understood it.

93. THE UNION OF SOVIET SOCIALIST REPUBLICS

Government: The Nationalities and Federalism

With the end of the civil wars and foreign intervention, and with the termination of the war with Poland, it became possible in 1922 to establish the Union of Soviet Socialist Republics. Its first members were four in number: the Russian Soviet Federated Socialist Republic, the Ukrainian Soviet Socialist Republic, the White Russian Soviet Socialist Republic, and the Transcaucasian Soviet Socialist Republic.[23] In the new Union, which geographically replaced the old Russian empire, the name Russia was not officially used. The guiding conception was a blend of the national and the international: to recognize nationality by granting autonomy to national groups, while holding these groups together in a higher union and allowing new groups to enter regardless of historic frontiers. In 1922 the expectation of world revolution was still alive. The constitution, formally adopted in 1924, pronounced the founding of the U.S.S.R. to be "a decisive step by way of uniting the workers of all countries into one World Soviet Socialist Republic." It made the Union, in principle, fluid and expansible, declared that any member republic might secede (none ever has) and that newly formed soviet socialist republics might join. When, in connection with the Second World War, the U.S.S.R. took back territories detached from tsarist Russia after the First World War—Bessarabia from Rumania, Karelia from Finland, parts of White Russia and the Ukraine from Poland, and Estonia, Latvia, and Lithuania after two decades of independence—these territories were sovietized and added to the Union as republics on a footing of legal equality with the old ones.

The federal principle in the U.S.S.R. was designed to answer the problem of nationalism. The tsardom, in its last decades, had tried to deal with this problem

[23] The original Russian and Transcaucasian federal republics were subsequently reorganized to create additional soviet republics, so that by the constitution of 1936 the S.S.R.'s were eleven in number, to which five more were added in 1940; the Karelo-Finnish S.S.R. lost this status, however, in 1956. There have come to be fifteen soviet republics in the U.S.S.R., with population figures in 1940 and as estimated for 1974, as follows:

	1940	1974 (est.)
Russian S.F.S.R.	109,000,000	132,900,000
Ukrainian S.S.R.	40,000,000	48,600,000
White Russian (Byelorussian) S.S.R.	10,000,000	9,300,000
Armenian S.S.R.	1,250,000	2,700,000
Georgian S.S.R.	3,500,000	4,900,000
Azerbaidzhan S.S.R.	3,200,000	5,500,000
Uzbek S.S.R.	6,300,000	13,300,000
Turkmen S.S.R.	1,200,000	2,400,000
Tadzhik S.S.R.	1,500,000	3,300,000
Kazakh S.S.R.	6,100,000	13,900,000
Kirghiz S.S.R.	1,500,000	3,200,000
ADDED IN 1940:		
Karelo-Finnish S.S.R.	500,000	———
Moldavian S.S.R.	2,500,000	3,800,000
Lithuanian S.S.R.	2,900,000	3,300,000
Latvian S.S.R.	2,000,000	2,500,000
Estonian S.S.R.	1,100,000	1,400,000
TOTAL U.S.S.R.	192,550,000	251,000,000

by systematic Russification. The nationalities had resisted, and nationalist discontent had been one of the forces fatally weakening the empire. Nationalism, or the demand that national groups should have their own political sovereignty, had not only broken up the Austro-Hungarian empire but "Balkanized" central and eastern Europe. In 1922 the U.S.S.R., occupying a sixth of the world's land area, was adjoined on the west by a Europe which in one twenty-seventh of the world's land surface contained twenty-seven independent states.

A hundred languages were spoken in the Soviet Union, and fifty distinct nationalities were recognized within its borders. Many of these were extremely small, splinter groups or isolated communities left by the ebb and flow of mankind in inner Asia over thousands of years. Many were very primitive, without political consciousness. All recognized nationalities received a cultural autonomy, or the right to use their own language, have their own schools, wear their own dress, and follow their own folkways without interference. Indeed, the Soviet authorities favored the growth of cultural nationalism. Some fifty languages were reduced to writing for the first time, and the new regime encouraged the singing of national songs, performance of dances, and collection of folklore. Administratively the nationalities were put on various levels, with varying degrees of separate identity according to their size, degree of civilization, or importance. Some constituted only "national districts," others "autonomous regions," still others "autonomous republics" within a federated soviet republic. The most important were the federated soviet republics themselves. The second constitution, adopted in 1936, created an upper legislative house, the Soviet (or Council) of Nationalities, to which each Union republic sent twenty-five delegates, each "autonomous republic" eleven, each "autonomous region" five, and each "national district" one. In practice, the Russian S.F.S.R., with over half the population and three-quarters of the territory of the Union, predominated over the others. When to the Russian were added the Ukrainian (or Little Russian) and White Russian republics, whose people were not very different from the Great Russians, the overwhelmingly Russian and Slavic character of the Union became marked.

The federal structure undoubtedly gave some dignity, self-respect, and sense of equal cooperation to many of the numerous minorities. Yet political rights were severely limited by the centralization of authority in the hands of the federal government and the Communist party, as well as by the overwhelming Slavic preponderance. There was no substance to the formal claim that each constituent republic was sovereign, had the right to secede, and had the right to conduct its own foreign affairs, on the basis of which the Soviets demanded sixteen (and received three) votes in the United Nations when it was formed in 1945. Moreover, there was evidence in the Second World War that separatism had not wholly died down, remaining especially alive in the Ukraine. Four autonomous republics and one autonomous region were officially dissolved for separatist as well as collaborationist activities. Grievances persisted on the part of many minorities on political and even on cultural grounds; the Soviet Jews in later years had many complaints. Yet, on balance, the Soviets accomplished much to prevent the disintegration of their multinational state by granting the nationalities a measure of political and cultural self-expression while on fundamental matters consolidating central authority and control within the communist framework as a whole.

THE UNION OF SOVIET SOCIALIST REPUBLICS

The U.S.S.R. is over 5,000 miles long and covers one-sixth of the land area of the globe, including 42 percent of Europe and 43 percent of Asia, though the conventional distinction between Europe and Asia is not officially recognized in the Soviet Union. It is the only state that immediately adjoins so many important political regions—Europe in the west, the Near and Middle East in the south, China along a long frontier, Japan

across a narrow sea, and the United States on the side toward Alaska and the Aleutian Islands. The Union has fifteen member republics, of which the Russian is by far the largest, embracing more than three-fourths of the territory and over half the population. Most of it lies farther north than Lake Superior, but around Tashkent, in the latitude of New York and Chicago, cotton and citrus fruits are grown.

Government: Parallelism of State and Party

Government in the Union, and in each component republic, followed a pattern worked out during the Revolution and written into the constitution of 1924 and the later constitution promulgated in 1936. Its chief feature was a system of parallelism. On the one hand was the state; on the other, paralleling the state but technically not part of it, was the party. There was a close interlocking relationship between the two.

On the side of the state, the distinctive institution was the council or soviet. Here elections took place, and authority proceeded from the bottom upward to the top. Under the constitution of 1924 only "toilers" had the right to vote. Surviving bourgeois, private traders, "persons using the labor of others to make a profit," as well as priests, were excluded from the suffrage. An indirect system of elections prevailed. In each village and town the voters chose a local soviet; the local soviet elected delegates to a provincial soviet, which in turn sent delegates to a soviet of the republic (Russian or other); the soviets of these republics sent delegates to a Union-wide Congress of Soviets, the supreme law-enacting body of the country. Soviets at all levels chose executive officials; the Congress of Soviets chose the Council of People's Commissars, or ministry.

In the constitution of 1936 a more direct democratic procedure was introduced—for the state side of the parallelism. Voters henceforth directly elected members of the higher soviets, a secret ballot was adopted, and no class was any longer denied the vote. A bicameral parliament was created, with an upper chamber, the Soviet of Nationalities, and a lower chamber, a Soviet of the Union, in which there was one representative for every 300,000 persons in the whole country. The Supreme Soviet, with its two chambers, chose a smaller body, the Presidium, to function while the chambers were not in session. The chairman of the Presidium served as "president," or nominal head, of the U.S.S.R. The Presidium supervised the Council of People's Commissars or Council of Ministers, as it came to be called after 1946, which the Supreme Soviet continued to elect. The chairman of the Council of Ministers was in Western terms the premier or prime minister. On the state side, as set forth in the constitution, especially the constitution of 1936, the government embodied many seemingly democratic features.

Yet alongside the state, at all levels and in all localities, was the party. Only one party was allowed, the Communist, though nonparty members might be elected to the soviets or to other official positions. In the party, authority began at the top and proceeded downward. At its apex stood the Central Committee, whose membership varied from about seventy in the 1930s to more than double that in later years. The Central Committee worked through an executive secretariat headed by a general secretary and through an Orgburo and a Politburo, subcommittees handling, respectively, matters of party organization and party policy. The Central Committee itself, or an inside group within it, and especially the general secretary, determined the membership of the Committee and of its subcommittees. It likewise assigned, transferred, and gave orders to party members through the successive lower levels of its organization. Although party congresses were held every few years before the Second World War, they generally simply registered decisions already made by the Central Committee. Actually it was the

Politburo[24] of about a dozen men that dominated the Central Committee. Power and authority flowed downward and outward, as in an army, or as in a highly centralized government agency or large private corporation in the West, except that the party was not subject to any outside control. Discipline was likewise enforced in ways not used in liberal countries, the fearsome machinery of the secret police being available for use in extreme cases against party members as well as those outside.

The number of party members, men and women, which could not have been more than 70,000 at the time of the Revolution, rose to about 2 million by 1930, 3 million by 1940, 8 million by 1960, and 15 million by the late 1970s. The Leninist ideal of a small, compact, and manageable party, made up of faithful and zealous workers who willingly carried out orders, the ideal on which the Bolsheviks had separated from the Mensheviks in 1903, continued to characterize the Communist party in the Soviet Union. Old Bolsheviks, those who had been members in the lean years before 1917, long continued to occupy the seats in the Politburo and other important party positions. The problem, once it was clear that the Revolution had come to stay, was to prevent an inrush of careerists, persons who simply wished to belong to the new governing elite, old Mensheviks, Social Revolutionaries, or even former bourgeois now flying Communist colors. A party of 2 million members, though small in contrast to the population of the U.S.S.R., still represented an enormous growth for the party itself, in which for each old member (who had joined before 1917) there were thousands of new ones. To preserve party unity under the new conditions strict uniformity was enforced. Members made an intensive study of the principles of Marxism-Leninism, embraced dialectical materialism as a philosophy and even a kind of religion, learned how to take orders without question or compunction, and to give authoritative leadership, assistance, or explanations of policy to the mass of nonparty members among whom they worked. The bottom of the party structure consisted of small nuclei or cells. In each factory, in each mine, in each office, in each class at the universities and technical schools, in each labor union, in each at least of the larger villages, one, two, or a dozen of the local people (factory workers, miners, office workers, students, etc., as the case might be) belonged to the party and imparted party views and party momentum to the whole.

The function of the party, in Marxist terms, was to carry out the dictatorship of the proletariat. It was to lead the people as a whole to the realization of socialism and, in day-to-day affairs, to coordinate the ponderous mechanism of government and make it work. Party members were present at all levels. The same men sat, in the party, in the Politburo of the Central Committee, and, in the state, in the Council of People's Commissars. At the next lower level, in the soviets of the Union and of the component republics, party members were numerous. Lower down, party members became more rare. In a small rural soviet there might be no one belonging to the party at all; the village councilmen would receive instructions, exhortations, or "pep talks" from itinerant party members. In any event, throughout the whole structure, the party decided what the state should do.

The role of the party in the U.S.S.R. has been called, at its best, a "vocation of

[24] For a time, during the years from 1952 to 1966, it was called the Presidium.

leadership." Those joined it who were willing to work hard, to devote themselves to party matters day and night, to absorb and communicate the party policy (or "line"), to go where they were sent, to attend meetings, speak up, and remain until all others had left for home, to perceive and explain the significance of small passing events for the future of Russia or the world revolution, to master intricate technical details of farming, manufacturing, or the care of machinery, so that others would look to them willingly for advice. The party was a specially trained elite whose members were in constant touch with each other. It was the thin stream of lifeblood which, circulating through all the diverse tissues of the U.S.S.R.—the multitudinous republics, soviets, bureaus, army, industrial and other enterprises owned under socialism by the state—kept the whole complex body unified, organic, functioning, and alive.

To the country as a whole the party undoubtedly represented the vocation of leadership. The corollary was that more than ninety-five out of a hundred persons were condemned to be followers, and while it is perhaps true (as apologists for the system have said) that under any system true leadership is exercised by a tiny fraction of people, the difference between Communist and non-Communist in the U.S.S.R. became a clear matter of social status. As the years passed, by the 1930s, many Communists in the U.S.S.R. were less of the type of revolutionary firebrand than of the successful and the efficient man or woman in any social system. They represented the satisfied, not the dissatisfied. Frequently they enjoyed material privileges, such as access to the best jobs, better housing, special food coupons, or priorities on trains. They worked faithfully for recognition and promotion in the party. They developed a bourgeois concern for the advantages of their own children. They became a new vested interest. Within the party, members had to be not so much leaders as followers. A homogeneous and monolithic organization was desired, presenting a solid front to the far more numerous but unorganized outsiders. Within the party, from time to time, a great deal of difference of opinion and open discussion was tolerated (indeed, since there was only one party all political questions were intraparty disputes), but in the end the entire membership had to conform. The party favored a certain initiative of action, and a certain fertility of mind in inventing ways to get things done, but it did not favor, and in fact repressed, originality, boldness, or freedom of thought or action.

The New Economic Policy, 1921–1927

By 1920 "war communism," as we have seen, had hopelessly antagonized the peasants, who, it was estimated, were cultivating only 62 percent as much land as in 1914.[25] This fact, together with a severe drought and the breakdown of transportation, produced a great famine. Four or five million people died. The ravages of eight years, of the World War, the Revolution, the civil wars, the Terror, had left the country in ruins, its productive facilities thrown back by decades as compared with the point reached in 1914. The rising of the Kronstadt sailors in 1921 revealed profound disillusionment in the revolutionary ranks themselves. Lenin concluded that socialization had advanced too fast. He openly advocated a

[25] See p. 709.

compromise with capitalism, a strategic retreat. The New Economic Policy, or Nep, adopted in 1921, lasted until 1927. Most of the decade of the 1920s saw a relaxation of tempo for most people in the U.S.S.R.

Under the Nep, while the state controlled the "commanding heights" of the economy, maintaining state ownership of the basic productive industries, it allowed a great deal of private trading for private profit. The basic problem was to restore trade between town and country. The peasant would produce nothing beyond the needs of his own subsistence unless he could exchange his surplus for city-made wares such as clothing or tools. The city people had to be fed from the country if they were to turn out factory products or even continue to live in the city. Under the Nep, peasants were allowed to sell their farm products freely. Middlemen were allowed to buy and sell farm products and manufactured articles at will, to whom they pleased, at market prices, and at a profit to themselves. The Nep therefore favored the big individualist farmer or kulak. Indeed, rural changes initiated before 1914 were still at work;[26] peasant families consolidated millions of acres as private property in 1922, 1923, and 1924. Correspondingly, other peasants became "proletarians," wage-earning hired hands. The Nep also favored the sprouting of a new-rich commercial class, neobourgeois who ate expensive dinners in the restaurants of Moscow, and whose very existence seemed to explode the dream of a classless society. Under the Nep the worst damages of war and revolution were repaired. But there was no real progress, for in 1928 Russia was producing only about as much grain, raw cotton, cattle, coal, and oil as in 1913, and far less than it presumably would have produced (given the rate of growth before 1913) had there been no revolution.

Stalin and Trotsky

Lenin died in 1924 prematurely at the age of fifty-four after a series of paralyzing strokes that left him incapacitated in the last two years of his life. His embalmed remains were put permanently on view in the Kremlin; Petrograd was renamed Leningrad; a leader cult was built up around his name and image; the party presented him as a deified equal of Marx himself; and it became necessary for all schools of communist thought to claim unflinching fidelity to the Leninist tradition. Actually, in his own lifetime, the Old Bolsheviks had never regarded Lenin as infallible. They had often differed with him and with each other. As he lay dying, and after his death, his old companions and contemporaries, men in their prime, carrying on the feuding habits of the émigré days, fought with each other for control of the party in Lenin's name. They disputed over Lenin's intentions. Had he secretly thought of the Nep as a permanent policy? If not, how would he have modified it, and, most especially, how soon? Quietly, behind the scenes, as secretary of the party, without much attention to broader problems, a hitherto relatively modest member named Joseph Stalin, of whom Lenin had never had an enthusiastic opinion, was drawing all the strings of party control into his own hands. More openly and vociferously Leon Trotsky, who as war commissar in the critical years had been only less conspicuous than Lenin himself, raised the basic issues of the whole nature and future of the movement.

26 See p. 703.

Trotsky, in 1925 and 1926, inveighed against the lassitude that had descended upon socialism.[27] The Nep with its tolerance of bourgeois and kulaks excited his contempt. He developed his doctrine of "permanent revolution," an incessant drive for proletarian objectives on all fronts in all parts of the world. He stood forth as the exponent of world revolution, which many in the party were beginning to discard in favor of first building socialism in one country. He denounced the tendency to bureaucratic ossification in the party and urged a new movement of the masses to give it life. He called for more forceful development of industry and for the collectivization of agriculture, which had figured in Communist manifestos ever since 1848.[28] Above all, he demanded immediate adoption of an overall plan, a central control and operation of the whole economic life of the country.

Trotsky failed to carry the party with him. He was charged with leftist deviationism, machinations against the Central Committee, and inciting to public discussion of issues outside the party. Stalin wove his web. At a party congress in 1927, 854,000 members dutifully voted for Stalin and the Central Committee and only 4,000 for Trotsky. Trotsky was first exiled to Siberia, then banished from the U.S.S.R.; he lived first in Turkey, then France, then Mexico, writing and propagandizing for the "permanent revolution," stigmatizing developments in the U.S.S.R. as "Stalinism," a monstrous betrayal of Marxism-Leninism, organizing an underground against Stalin as he had done in former days against the tsar. He was murdered in Mexico in 1940 under mysterious circumstances, presumably by a Soviet agent or sympathizer.

94. STALIN: THE FIVE-YEAR PLANS AND THE PURGES

Economic Planning

Hardly had the party expelled Trotsky when it appropriated certain fragments of his program. In 1928 it launched the First Five-Year Plan, aimed at rapid industrialization and the collectivization of agriculture. "Planning," or the central planning of a country's whole economic life by government officials, was to become the distinctive feature of Soviet economics and the one that was to have the greatest influence in the rest of the world.

In retrospect, it seems strange that the Communists waited ten years before adopting a plan. The truth seems to be that the Bolsheviks had only confused ideas of what to do after their seizure of power. Marxism for the most part gave only general hints. Marxism was primarily an analysis of existing or bourgeois society. It was also a theory of class war. But to portray any details of a future society, or specify what should be done after the class war had been won by the proletariat, was according to Marx and Engels sheer utopian fantasy. The bourgeoisie, to be sure, would be destroyed; there would be "social ownership of the

---

[27] For communists, though not for socialists, the terms "communism" and "socialism" are almost interchangeable, since Russian Communists regard their own system as true socialism and all other socialism as opportunistic, reactionary, or false. Communism is also defined, in the U.S.S.R., as a future state of society toward which socialism, i.e., Soviet socialism, is the intermediate stage.

[28] See p. 483.

means of production," and no "exploitation of man by man"; everyone would work, and there would be neither leisure class nor unemployment. This was not much to go on in the operation of a modern industrial system.

One great constructive idea had been mapped out, most clearly by Engels. *Within* each private enterprise, Engels had observed, harmony and order reigned; it was only *between* private enterprises that capitalism was chaotic. In the individual factory, he noted, the various departments did not compete with each other; the shipping department did not purchase from the production department at prices fluctuating according to daily changes in supply and demand; the output of all departments was planned and coordinated by management. In a larger way, the great capitalist mergers and trusts, controlling many factories, prevented blind competition between them, assigned specific quotas to each, anticipated, coordinated, and stabilized the work of each plant and each person by an overall policy. With the growth of large corporate enterprise, observed Engels, the area of economic life under free competition was constantly reduced, and the area brought under rational planning was constantly enlarged. The obvious next step, according to Engels and other socialists, was to treat *all* the economic life of a country as a single factory with many departments, or a single enormous monopoly with many members, under one unified, vigorous, and far-seeing management.

During the First World War the governments of belligerent countries had in fact adopted such centralized controls.[29] They had done so not because they were socialistic, but because in time of war people were willing to give up their usual liberties and willing to do as they were told by the government, and because all else was subordinated to a single overwhelming and undisputed social purpose—victory. The "planned society" therefore made its first actual (though incomplete) appearance in the First World War. It was partly from socialist doctrine as exemplified by Engels, partly from experience of the war, and in even larger measure from the irresistible pressure to meet the continuing chronic problems of the country by raising its productive level that Stalin and the party in Russia gradually developed the idea of a plan. The war experience was especially valuable for the lessons it gave on technical questions of economic planning, such as what kind of bureaus to set up, what kind of forecasts to make, and what kind of statistics to collect.

In the U.S.S.R. it was decided to plan for five years into the future, beginning with 1928. The aim of the plan was to strengthen and enrich the country, make it militarily and industrially self-sufficient, lay the groundwork for a true workers' society, and overcome the Russian reputation for backwardness. As Stalin said in a speech in 1929: "We are becoming a country of metal, a country of automobiles, a country of tractors. And when we have put the U.S.S.R. in a motor car and the *muzhik* in a tractor . . . we shall see which countries may then be 'classified' as backward and which as advanced."

The First Five-Year Plan was declared fulfilled in 1932, and a Second Five-Year Plan was launched, lasting until 1937. The Third, inaugurated in 1938, was interrupted by the war with Germany in 1941. New plans were introduced after 1945.[30]

[29] See pp. 677–679.
[30] See p. 854.

The First Five-Year Plan (like its successors) listed the economic goals to be achieved. It was administered by an agency called the Gosplan. Within the frame of general policy set by the party, the Gosplan determined how much of every article the country should produce, how much of the national effort should go into the formation of capital, and how much into producing articles for daily consumption, what wages all classes of workers should receive, and at what prices all goods should be exchanged. At the bottom level, in the individual factory, the local management drew up its "requirements," or estimates of what it would need, in raw material, machinery, trained workers, plant facilities, and fuel, if it was to deliver the planned quantity of its product at a stated date. These estimates were passed up the planning ladder (or, thousands of such estimates up thousands of ladders) until they reached the Gosplan, which, balancing them against each other and against other needs as seen at the top, determined how much steel, coal, etc., should be produced, and in what qualities and grades; how many workers should be trained in technical schools and in what particular skills; how many machines should be manufactured and how many spare parts; how many new freight cars should be constructed and which lines of railway track needed repair; and how, where, when, and to whom the steel, coal, technicians, machines, and rolling stock should be made available. The plan, in short, undertook to control, by conscious management, the flow of resources and manpower which under free capitalism was regulated by shifts in demand and supply, through changes in prices, wage levels, profits, interest rates, or rent.

The system was exceedingly intricate. It was not easy to have the right number of ball bearings, for example, arrive at the right place at the right time, in exact correspondence to the amounts of other materials or to the number of workers waiting to use them. Sometimes there was overproduction, sometimes underproduction. The plan was often amended as it was applied in action. Countless reports, checkups, and exchanges of information were necessary. A huge class of white-collar office workers came into existence to handle the paperwork. The plan achieved some of its goals, exceeded a few, and failed in some.

The primary objective of the First Five-Year Plan was to build up the heavy industry, or capital wealth, of the U.S.S.R. The aim was to industrialize without the use of foreign loans.[31] Russia in 1928 was still chiefly an agricultural country. The world offered hardly any case of a country shifting from agriculture to industry without borrowing capital from abroad. Great Britain, the original home of the Industrial Revolution, was the best example, although even there, in the eighteenth century, a great deal of capital invested in England was owned by the Dutch. An agricultural country could industrialize from its own resources only by drawing upon agriculture itself. An agricultural revolution had been prerequisite to an industrial revolution in England.[32] By enclosure of land, the squeezing out of small independent farmers, and the introduction of scientific cultivation, under the auspices of a growing class of wealthy landowners, England had both increased its production of food and released many of the rural population to find employment in industry. The First Five-Year Plan called for a similar agricultural

---

[31] The Bolsheviks had repudiated the entire debt of the tsarist empire. Their credit in capitalist countries was therefore not good, so that, in addition to fearing dependence upon foreign lenders, they were in any case for a long time unable to borrow large sums.

[32] See pp. 419–421.

revolution in Russia, without benefit to landlords and under the auspices of the state.

The Collectivization of Agriculture

The plan, as originally conceived, called for the collectivization of only one-fifth of the farm population, but it was suddenly revised in the winter of 1929 to include the immediate collectivization of the greater part of the peasantry. The plan set up collective farms, averaging a few thousand acres apiece, which were considered to be the property not of the state but of the peasants collectively who resided on them. Individual peasants were to pool their privately owned fields and livestock in these collectives. Those peasants who possessed fields or stock in considerable amount, the prosperous peasants or kulaks, resisted surrendering them to the new collectives. The kulaks were therefore liquidated as a class. Zealous detachments of Communists from the cities often used more violence than the plan envisaged; poor peasants turned upon rich ones; hundreds of thousands of kulaks and their families were killed and many more transported to labor camps in remote parts of the Soviet Union. The trend that had gone on since Stolypin and indeed since the Emancipation, building up a class of property-owning, labor-hiring, and "bourgeois" peasants, was now abruptly reversed. Politically, the obstinate obstruction of individualistic farmers was removed, and the peasantry was converted into a class more nearly resembling the proletariat of Marxian doctrine, a class of people who as individuals owned no capital and employed no labor, and so were better able to feel the advantages of a proletarian state. The year 1929, not 1917, was the great revolutionary year for most people in Russia.

Collectivization was accomplished at the cost of village class war in which the most capable farmers perished, and at the cost also of a wholesale destruction of livestock. The big farmers slaughtered their horses, cattle, pigs, and poultry rather than give them up. Even middling and small farmers did the same, caring nothing about animals that were no longer their own, or naïvely expecting that under collectivism the state would soon furnish a new supply. The ruinous loss of animals was the worst unforeseen calamity of the First Five-Year Plan. Agricultural disorder, together with two summers of bad weather, was followed in 1932 by temporary but deadly famine in southeast Russia that took the lives of an estimated 2 million to 3 million persons; the government meanwhile refused to cut back on export quotas because they were needed to pay for industrial imports under the Five-Year Plan. Agriculture long remained the weakest sector of the Soviet economy.

By introducing thousand-acre units in place of very small ones, collectivization made it possible to apply capital to the soil. Formerly the average peasant had been far too poor to buy a tractor and his fields too tiny and dispersed for him to use one, so that only a few rare kulaks had employed any machinery. In the course of the First Five-Year Plan hundreds of Machine Tractor Stations were organized throughout the country. Each, in its region, maintained a force of tractors, harvesting combines, expert agronomists, etc., which were dispatched from one collective farm to another by local arrangement. The application of capital increased the output per peasant. It was also much easier administratively for higher authorities to get control over the agricultural surplus (products not consumed by the village itself) from a single collective farm than from numerous small and unorganized peasants. Each collective was assigned a quota on which it contracted in advance to make delivery. Members of the collective could sell in a free market any products they raised beyond this quota; but meanwhile the government knew the quantity of agricultural produce it could count on, either to feed the cities and other regions that did not produce their own food, or for export in the world market to pay for imports of machinery from the West. By 1939 all but a negligible fraction of the peasantry were collectivized. Although collectivization failed to increase agricultural output, it accomplished the goal of insuring state control over agricultural production. Simultaneously, it made possible the success of industrialization by augmenting the supply of industrial workers. Since the villages needed less labor, 20 million people moved from country to city between the years 1926 and 1939 and were available for jobs in the new industries.

It was the peasants who bore the burden of collectivization. Not only had they been subjected to violence and expropriation, but the new collectives threw the peasant back into something like the *mir,* condemning him to the rounds of communal living, robbing him of the chance to make any decisions of his own. By obliging peasants to make "deliveries" below market prices, it even revived some features of the type of serfdom and forced labor that had prevailed a century before over most of eastern Europe. On the other hand, although the collectives varied widely in their degree of prosperity, it is probable that by 1939 a great many of the rural people were better housed and better fed than they had been before the Revolution. Kulaks who might have remembered better conditions had not survived.

The Growth of Industry

While the agricultural base was being revolutionized, industrialization went rapidly forward. At first there was considerable dependence on the capitalist countries. Engineers and other technicians from western Europe and the United States took service in the Soviet Union. Much machinery was at first imported. But the world-wide depression that set in about 1931, bringing a catastrophic fall of agricultural prices, meant that foreign-made machines became more costly in terms of the cereals that were the chief Soviet export. The international situation also deteriorated. Both Japan and Germany in the 1930s showed an increasing hostility to the U.S.S.R. From the beginning the Five-Year plans had as one of their objectives the industrial and military self-sufficiency of the country. The Second Five-Year Plan, launched in 1933, though in some ways less ambitious than the first, showed an even greater determination to cut down imports and achieve national self-sufficiency, especially in the heavy industry that was basic to war production.

No ten years in the history of any Western country ever showed such a rate of industrial growth as the decade of the first two plans in the Soviet Union. In Great Britain industrialization had been gradual; in Germany and the United States it had been more rapid, and in each country there had been decades in which output of coal or iron doubled; but in the U.S.S.R., from 1928 to 1938, production of iron and steel expanded four times and that of coal three and a half times. In 1938 the U.S.S.R. was the world's largest producer of farm tractors and railway locomotives. Four-fifths of all its industrial output came from plants built in the preceding ten years. Two plants alone, at the new cities of Magnitogorsk in the Urals and Stalinsk 1,000 miles farther east, produced as much iron and steel as the whole Russian empire in 1914. In 1939 the U.S.S.R. was surpassed in gross industrial output only by the United States and Germany.

The plans called for a marked development of industry east of the Urals, and so brought a modernization of life for the first time to inner Asia, in a way comparable only to the movement of machine industry into the once primitive Great Lakes region of the American Middle West. Pittsburghs, Clevelands, and Detroits rose in the old Turkestan and Siberia. Copper mines were opened in the Urals and around Lake Balkhash, lead mines in the Far East and in the Altai Mountains. New grain-producing regions were developed in Siberia and in the Kazakh S.S.R., whence grain was shipped westward to Russia proper, or southward to the Uzbek S.S.R., which was devoted mainly to cotton. Tashkent, the Uzbek capital, formerly a remote town of bazaars and caravans, grew to be a city of over half a million, a center of cotton culture, copper mining, and electrical industries, connected with the north by the newly built Turksib Railway. The Kuznetsk basin, 2,000 miles inland from every ocean, was found to possess coal deposits of high grade. Kuznetsk coal and the iron ores of the Urals became complementary, though separated by a thousand miles, somewhat like Pennsylvania coal and Minnesota iron in the United States. The opening of all these new areas, requiring the movement of food to Uzbekstan in exchange for cotton, or of Ural iron to the new Kuznetsk cities, demanded a revolution in transportation. The railroads in 1938 carried five times as much freight as in 1913.

These astounding developments were enough to change the relative economic strength of the world's peoples with respect to one another. It was significant that inner Asia was for the first time turning industrial. It was significant, too, that although the U.S.S.R. had less foreign trade than had the Russian empire, it had more trade than the old Russia with its Asian neighbors, with which it formed new and close connections. The Russia that went to war with Germany in 1941 proved to be a different antagonist from the Russia of 1914. Industrialization in the Urals and in Asia enabled the U.S.S.R. (with a good deal of Allied assistance) to survive the German occupation and destruction of the older industrial areas in the Don valley. The new "socialist fatherland" proved able to absorb the shock and strike back. A great deal of the increased industrial output had gone to equip and modernize the Red Army.

At the same time, the degree of industrialization of the U.S.S.R. should not be exaggerated. It was phenomenal because it started from so little. Qualitatively, by Western criteria, standards of production were low. Many of the hastily constructed, new plants were shoddy and suffered from rapid depreciation. In efficiency, as shown by output per worker employed, the U.S.S.R. continued to lag behind the West. In intensity of modernization, as shown by output of certain items in proportion to the whole population, it also lagged. Per capita of its huge population, in 1937, the U.S.S.R. produced less coal, electricity, cottons, woolens, leather shoes, or soap than did the United States, Britain, Germany, France, or even Japan, and less iron and steel than any of them except Japan. Production of

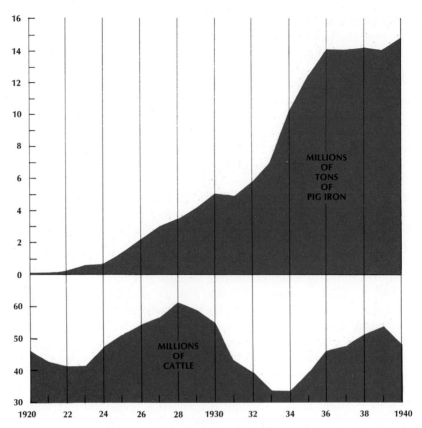

Source: B. R. Mitchell, *European Historical Statistics* (New York: Columbia University Press, 1975), pp. 316, 396.

PIG IRON AND CATTLE IN THE SOVIET UNION, 1920–1940

If pig iron is taken as a measure of industrial activity and number of cattle as a similar indication for agriculture, the chart reveals clearly what happened in the twenty years after the Revolution—an enormous build-up of heavy industry at the expense of food supplies. Iron mines and forges, in the disorganization of the Revolution and civil war, were producing almost nothing in 1920. By the late 1920s, output of pig iron regained the pre-Revolutionary level, but the great upsurge came with the Second Five-Year Plan. By 1940 Russia produced more pig iron than Germany, and far more than Britain or France. Numbers of cattle grew in the 1920s, but fell catastrophically during the collectivization of agriculture after 1929, and by 1940 hardly exceeded the figure for 1920. Since 1940 the industrial development of the Soviet Union has been impressive, but agricultural production has continued to be a problem.

paper is revealing because paper is used in so many "civilized" activities—in books, newspapers, magazines, schools, correspondence, placards, maps, pictures, charts, business and government records, and household articles and amenities. Where the United States about 1937 produced 103 pounds of paper per person, Germany and Great Britain each 92, France 51, and Japan 17, the U.S.S.R. produced only 11.

Social Costs and Social Effects of the Plans

Industrialization in Russia, as formerly in other countries, was put through at great sacrifice on the part of the people. It was not merely that kulaks lost their lives, or that others, whose numbers have never been known, were found to be enemies of the system and sent off to correctional labor camps. All were required to accept a program of austerity and self-denial, going without the better food, housing, and other consumers' goods that might have been produced, in order that the capital wealth and heavy industry of the country might be built up. As much as a third of the national income was reinvested in industry every year—twice as much as in the England of 1914, though probably not more than in the England of 1840. The plan required hard work and low wages. People looked to the future, to the time when, the basic industries having been built, better housing, better food, better clothing, and more leisure would follow. Morale was sustained by propaganda. One of the chief functions of party members was to explain why sacrifices were necessary. In the late 1930s life began to ease; food rationing was abolished in 1935, and a few more products of light industry, such as dishes and fountain pens, began to appear in Soviet retail stores. Living standards were at least up to those of 1927 with prospects brighter for raising them. But the need for war preparations, as the world again approached chaos, again drove back the vision of the Promised Land.

Socialism, as realized in the plans, did away with some of the evils of unrestrained free enterprise. There was no unemployment. There was no cycle of boom and depression. There was no misuse of women and children as in the early days of industrialism in the West. There was no absolute want or pauperization, except for political undesirables and except for temporary conditions of famine. There was a minimum below which no one was supposed to fall. On the other hand, there was no economic equality. Marxism, indeed, had never seen complete equality of income as a principal objective. While there was no handful of very rich people, as in the West (where the income of the rich came from property), the differences in income were nevertheless very great. High government officials, managers, engineers, and favored intellectuals received the highest rewards. People with large incomes, by buying government bonds or accumulating personal possessions, could build up little fortunes for themselves and their children. They could not, however, under socialism, own any industrial capital.

Competition persisted. In 1935 a miner named Stakhanov greatly increased his daily output of coal by devising improvements in his methods of work. He also greatly increased his wages, since Soviet workers were paid at piece rates. His example proved contagious; workers all over the country began to break records of all kinds. The government publicized their achievements, called them Stakhanovites and "labor heroes," and pronounced the movement to be "a new and higher stage of socialist competition." In labor circles in the United States such straining to increase output would be called a speed-up, and piecework wages had long been anathema to the organized labor of all countries. Nor was management free from competitive pressure. A factory manager who failed to show the net income (or "profit") upon which the plan counted, or who failed to meet his quota of output, might lose not only his job but his social status or even his life. Poor management was often construed as sabotage. Poor use of the men and resources allocated to a factory was considered a betrayal of Soviet workers and a waste of the property of the nation. The press, not otherwise free, freely denounced whole industries or individual executives for failures to meet the plan.

Foreign observers often found the distinctive feature of the new system to lie in this kind of competition or emulation, or in a feeling that everybody was busily toiling and struggling to create a socialist fatherland. Workers, it seemed, had a real belief that the new industrial wonders were their own. People rejoiced at every new advance as a personal triumph. It became a national pastime to watch the mounting statistics, the fulfilling of quotas or hitting of "targets." Newspaper readers read no comic strips; they read eagerly about the latest doings (or mis-doings) on the economic front. Never had there been such unalloyed delight in material and mechanical progress, not even in America in the Gilded Age. No class difference was felt between labor and management. There was apparently little envy, since differences of income, being socialistic, were regarded as neces-sary and fair. In creating this solidarity, so far as it existed, the U.S.S.R. offered one of its most serious challenges to the private enterprise and private capitalism of the West.

How real this feeling was, how much of it was spontaneous, and how much was inculcated by a watchful and dictatorial government, are questions on which there has been much difference of opinion. There is no doubt that solidarity was purchased at the price of totalitarianism.[33] The government supervised every-thing. There was no room for skepticism, eccentricity of thought, or any basic criticism that weakened the will to achieve. As in tsarist times, no one could leave the country without special permission, which was given far more rarely than before 1914. There was only one party. There were no free labor unions, no free press, no freedom of association, and at best only an irritable tolerance for reli-gion. Art, literature, and even science became vehicles of political propaganda. Dialectical materialism was the official philosophy. Conformity was the ideal, and the very passion for solidarity made for fear and suspicion of all who might go astray. As for the number of people sacrificed to the Juggernaut—liquidated bourgeois, liquidated kulaks, purged party members, disaffected persons sen-tenced to long terms in labor camps—a precise figure is difficult to arrive at, but it certainly reached many millions over the years.

The Purge Trials of the 1930s

In 1936 socialism was judged to have proved so successful that a new constitution for the U.S.S.R. was proclaimed. It enumerated, as rights of Soviet citizens, not merely the usual civil liberties of Western democracy but the rights to steady employment, rest, leisure, economic security, and a comfortable old age. All forms of racism were condemned. It reorganized the soviet republics and granted equal and direct universal suffrage, as explained above.[34] The new constitution of 1936 was favorably commented upon in the West, where it was hoped that the Russian Revolution, like former revolutions, had at last turned into more peace-able and quiet channels. It was nonetheless apparent that the Communist party

33 On totalitarianism, see pp. 786–789.
34 See p. 716.

remained the sole governing group in the country, that Stalin was tightening his dictatorship, and that the party was racked by internal troubles.

It was natural that the complex and multifarious operations of the Five-Year plans should produce divergences of opinion among the men who carried them out. The party elders, however, were engaged not merely in discussions of policy but in the older game of the seizure of power. On the right, led by Bukharin, was a group that believed in more gradual methods of collectivizing the peasants. More important was the element described as leftist. Its mastermind and rallying point was the exiled Trotsky. Probably there was some kind of secret Trotskyist machine within the U.S.S.R. and within the party, even if there is no evidence for the charge that some Trotskyists had intrigued with Germans and other foreigners to overthrow and replace Stalin. As early as 1933 the party underwent a drastic purge, in which a third of its members were expelled. Even faithful associates of Stalin were appalled at his growing ruthlessness. Serge Kirov, an old friend and revolutionary companion of Stalin since 1909, recently elected a key member of the party secretariat, showed signs of leading the disaffected; in 1934 he was assassinated in his office, very probably by a police agent of Stalin's. Stalin used the assassination to strike out at his opponents, imagined or real, by a revival of terror, immediately executing over a hundred persons and launching the extraordinary "purges" of the 1930s.

A series of sensational trials took place. In 1936 sixteen Old Bolsheviks were brought to trial. Some, like Zinoviev and Kamenev, had been expelled from the party in 1927 for supporting Trotsky and subsequently, after the proper recantations, had been readmitted. Now they were charged with the murder of Kirov, with plotting the murder of Stalin, and with having organized, in 1932, under Trotsky's inspiration, a secret group to disorganize and terrorize the Central Committee. To the amazement of the world, all the accused made full confession to the charges in open court. All blamed themselves as unworthy and erring reprobates. All were put to death. In 1937, after similar trials, seventeen other Old Bolsheviks met the same fate or received long prison sentences; and in 1938 Bukharin and the rightists, charged with wanting to restore bourgeois capitalism and conspiring with Trotsky to revolutionize the U.S.S.R., were executed. The same confessions and self-accusations followed in almost every case, with no other verifiable evidence adduced. How these confessions were obtained in open court, from men apparently in full possession of their faculties and bearing no sign of physical harm, long remained one of the great mysteries of modern statecraft. Later revelations of psychological torture and physical mistreatment that broke their will and destroyed their reasoning powers gave some insight into the techniques used. In addition to these public trials there were thousands of arrests, private inquisitions, and executions. In 1937, in a secret court-martial, Marshal Tukhachevski and seven other ranking generals were accused of Trotskyism and of conspiring with the Germans and Japanese and were shot. The purges not only included men who had held the highest rank in party, government, and military circles but reached down into the lesser echelons of all these groups as well. Before the purges were over late in 1938, an unknown number of persons, but probably in the millions, were either executed or sent off into prison labor camps. Years later the innocence was established of many of the victims of Stalin's almost paranoid suspicion, and their reputations were posthumously restored.

By these famous "purge trials" Stalin's dictatorship and party discipline were reinforced. It may be that a real danger of renewed revolution was averted. Had the tsarist government dealt as summarily with Bolsheviks as Bolsheviks dealt with one another there could have been no November Revolution. Above all, Stalin rid himself by the trials of all possible rivals for his own position. He disposed of the embarrassment of having men about him who could remember the old days, who could quote Lenin as a former friend, or belittle the reality of 1937 by recalling the dreams of 1917. After 1938 there were virtually no Old Bolsheviks left. The aging but still explosive professional revolutionaries were now dead. A younger group, products of the new order, successful men of affairs, practical, constructive, impatient of "agitators," and acquiescing in Stalin's dictatorship, were operating what was now an established system.

95. THE INTERNATIONAL IMPACT OF COMMUNISM, 1919–1939

Socialism and the First World War

Marxism had always been international in its outlook. To Marx, and the early Marxists, existing states (like other institutions) owed their character to the class struggle. They were committees of the bourgeoisie to govern the proletariat. National states were regarded as frameworks, destined to be dismantled and pass away in the course of inevitable historic processes. After Marx's death, as Marxist parties grew in numbers, and as states of western Europe became more democratic, most people who called themselves Marxists actually accepted the national state, seeing in it a means by which the workers' lot could be gradually improved. This view was part of the movement of "revisionism," or what more rigorous Marxists called "opportunism."[35] In the First World War national loyalty proved its strength. The socialist parties in the Reichstag, the French Chamber, and other parliamentary bodies voted for war credits without hesitation. Socialist workers reported for mobilization like everyone else. In Germany socialists said that the reactionary Russian tsardom must be resisted; in France, that the Germans menaced all Frenchmen alike. In general, all political parties, including the socialists, declared a moratorium on party politics during the war.

Small minorities of socialists in every country, however, refused to accept the war. Marxian socialism had long taught that workingmen of all nations were bound by the supreme loyalty of class, that their real enemies were the capitalists of their own countries, that international wars were capitalist and "imperialist" quarrels, and that class struggle was the only kind of warfare that the proletarian should accept. These socialists denounced the action of the socialist majorities as a sellout to capitalism and imperialism. They met in international conferences with each other and with socialists from the neutral countries. Active among them were Lenin and other Russian Social Democrats then in Switzerland. "The only task for socialists," wrote Lenin in 1914, "is to convert the war of peoples into a civil war." The minority or antiwar socialists met at the small Swiss town of Zimmerwald in 1915, where they drew up a "Zimmerwald program," calling for

35 See pp. 488, 581–583.

immediate peace without annexations or indemnities. This had no effect on most socialists in the belligerent countries. The Zimmerwald group itself soon began to split. Most Zimmerwalders regarded peace, or the repudiation of the war, as their aim. But a "Zimmerwald Left" began to develop, inspired mainly by Lenin and the Russian émigrés. This faction made its aim not peace but revolution. It hoped that the war would go on until it caused social revolution in the belligerent countries.

Then in April 1917, with the German imperial government wishing them *bon voyage,* Lenin and the other Bolsheviks went back to Russia and accomplished the November Revolution. Lenin, until his death in 1924, believed that the Russian Revolution was only a local phase of a world revolution—of *the* revolution of strict Marxian doctrine. Russia, for him, was the theater of currently most active operations in the international class war. Because he expected proletarian upheaval in Germany, Poland, the Danube valley, and the Baltic regions, he accepted without compunction the treaty of Brest-Litovsk. He took no pride in Russia; he was no patriot or "social-chauvinist," to use his own term. In the founding of the U.S.S.R. in 1922 he saw a nucleus around which other and greater soviet republics of any nationality might coalesce. "Soviet republics in countries with a higher degree of civilization," he wrote, "whose proletariat has greater social weight and influence, have every prospect of outstripping Russia as soon as they start upon the road of proletarian dictatorship."

The First World War was in fact followed by attempted revolutions in Germany and eastern Europe. With the German and Austro-Hungarian empires wrecked, socialists and liberals of all descriptions strove to establish new regimes. Among socialists the old differences persisted, between Social Democrats favoring gradual, nonviolent, and parliamentary methods, and a more extreme (and smaller) group which saw in postwar disintegration a chance to realize the international proletarian revolution. The first group looked upon the Bolshevik Revolution with horror. The second looked upon it with admiration. The first group included not only trade union officials and practical socialist politicians, but such prewar giants of Marxian exegesis as Karl Kautsky and Eduard Bernstein. Even Kautsky, who had upheld pure Marxism against the revisionism of Bernstein, could not stomach the methods of Lenin. The mass of European socialists, with their fiercest leaders removed, were to remain characterized by relative moderation. Marxist in principle, they were in fact more than ever wedded to gradual, peaceable, and parliamentary methods.

In the second group, the sifted residue of uncompromising Leninist neo-Marxists, who accepted the Bolshevik Revolution, were Karl Liebknecht and Rosa Luxemburg. Organizing the Spartacist movement[36] in Germany, they attempted, in January 1919, to overthrow the majority socialist government in Germany, as Lenin had overthrown the Provisional Government in Russia in November 1917. In the second group also was Béla Kun, who had turned Bolshevik during a sojourn in Russia, and who set up and maintained a soviet regime in Hungary for several months in 1919.

Lenin and the Bolsheviks, though absorbed in their own revolution, gave all possible aid to the fringe of left socialists of Europe. They sent large sums of money to Germany, to Sweden, to Italy. When the Bolshevik Radek was arrested

[36] See pp. 741–742 and note.

in Berlin he was said to have a plan for proletarian revolution in all central Europe in his possession. The party considered sending Russian troops to Hungary to support Béla Kun. But the chief instrument of world revolution, created in March 1919, was the Third or Communist International.

The Founding of the Third International

The Second International, which since its foundation in 1889 had met every two or three years until 1914, held its first postwar meeting at Berne in 1919.[37] It represented socialist parties and labor organizations of all countries. The Berne meeting was stormy, for a small minority vehemently demanded "revolution as in Russia, socialization of property as in Russia, application of Marxism as in Russia." Overruled at Berne, they repaired to Moscow and there founded a new International in conjunction with the Russian Communist party, and with Lenin and the Russians dominating it completely. It was Lenin's hope, by founding a new International of his own, to discredit moderate socialism and to claim for the Communists the true line of succession from the First International of Karl Marx. The First International, he declared, had laid the foundations for proletarian struggle, the Second had broadened it, the Third "took over the work of the Second International, cut off its opportunistic, social-chauvinist, bourgeois and petty-bourgeois rubbish, and began to carry into effect the dictatorship of the proletariat."

The first congress of the Third International in 1919 was somewhat haphazard, but at the second, in 1920, the extreme left parties of thirty-seven countries were represented. The Russian party was supposedly only one component. Actually, it supplied most of the personnel and most of the funds; the Bolshevik Zinoviev was its first president, remaining in this office until his disgrace as a Trotskyist in 1927. The Third or Communist International—the Comintern—was in part a spontaneous rallying of Marxists from all countries who accepted the Bolshevik Revolution as the true fruition of Marxism and so were willing to follow the Russian lead; but, even more, it was the creation and weapon of the Bolsheviks themselves, by which to discredit and isolate the moderate socialists and effectuate world revolution. Of all enemies the Communists hated the socialists most, reserving for them even choicer epithets than they bestowed upon capitalists and imperialists, because Communists and socialists were competing for the same thing, the leadership of the world's working class.

Parties adhering to the Comintern were obliged to drop the old name "socialist" and call themselves Communist. They were obliged to accept strong international centralization. Where the Second International had been a loose federation, and its congresses hardly more than forums, the Third International put strong powers in the hands of its Executive Committee, whose orders the Communist parties of all countries had to obey. Since there was a kind of interlocking directorate by which members of the Central Committee of the party in Russia sat also as members of the Executive Committee of the Third International, the top Communists in Russia had, in the Comintern, an "apparatus" by which they could produce desired effects in many countries—the use of party members to penetrate labor unions, foment strikes, propagandize ideas, or interfere in elections.

[37] See pp. 581–583.

The second congress of the International, in 1920, endorsed a program of Twenty-One Points, written by Lenin. These included the requirements that each national party must call itself Communist, repudiate "reformist" socialism, propagandize labor unions and get Communists into the important union offices, infiltrate the army, impose an iron discipline upon members, require submission of each party worker to his national committee and to the orders of the international Executive, use both legal channels and secret underground methods, and expel promptly any member not hewing to the party line. Making no pretense of respect for parliamentary democracy, the second congress ruled that "the only question can be that of utilizing bourgeois state institutions for their own destruction." As for the labor movement, Lenin wrote that "the struggle against the Gomperses, the Jouhaux, the Hendersons[38] . . . who represent an *absolutely similar* social and political type as our Mensheviks . . . must be waged without mercy to the end." The Comintern was not an assemblage of humanitarians engaged in welfare work; it was a weapon for revolution, organized by revolutionaries who knew what revolution was.

For several years the U.S.S.R., using the Comintern or more conventional diplomatic channels, promoted world revolution as best it could. Communists from many countries went to Russia for indoctrination. Native-born or Russian agents proceeded to the Dutch Indies, to China, to Europe, to America. Until 1927 the Chinese revolutionists welcomed assistance from Moscow; the Russian Borodin became an adviser in their affairs. In 1924, in England, publication of the "Zinoviev letter," in which, at least allegedly, the Comintern urged British workers to provoke revolution, led to a great electoral victory for the Conservative party. The Bolshevik menace, real and imagined, produced everywhere a strong reaction. It was basic to the rise of fascism described in the following chapters.

In 1927, with the suppression of Trotskyism and world revolutionism in Russia, and with the concentration under Stalin on a program of building socialism in one country, the Comintern entered upon a period of inaction. About 1935, as fascist dictators became more noisily bellicose, the U.S.S.R. turned to a policy of international collective security, and the Comintern instructed all Communist parties, each in its own country, to enter into coalitions with socialists and advanced liberals, in what were called "popular fronts," to combat fascism and reaction. During the Second World War (in 1943), as a gesture of good will to Great Britain and the United States, the U.S.S.R. abolished the Comintern entirely, but it reappeared for a few years from 1947 to 1956 under a new name, the Communist Information Bureau or Cominform.[39]

It was not through the Comintern that the U.S.S.R. exerted its greatest influence on the world. It exerted its influence by the massive fact of its very existence. By 1939 it was clear that a new type of economic system had appeared. Before 1917 no one in Europe or Asia had thought that anything was to be learned from Russia. Twenty years later even critics of the U.S.S.R. feared that it might repre-

---

[38] Samuel Gompers (1850–1924), began as a cigar maker, president of the American Federation of Labor, 1886–1924; Léon Jouhaux (1879–1954), began as a factory worker, secretary general of the French General Confederation of Labor, 1909–1947, resigned in 1947 to found a new labor organization in opposition to communism; Arthur Henderson (1863–1935), began as an iron-molder's apprentice, chairman of the Parliamentary Labour Party, 1908–1910, 1914–1917, Member of Parliament, 1903–1931, Secretary of State for Foreign Affairs, 1929–1931.

[39] For the U.S.S.R. and for international communism after 1945, see pp. 849–865.

sent the wave of the future. Its sheer power was soon demonstrated in the Second World War. However one judged the U.S.S.R., no one could dismiss its socialism as visionary or impracticable. An alternative to free enterprise and capitalism had been brought into being. Marxism was not merely a theory; there was an actual society, embracing a sixth of the globe, which called itself Marxist.

In every country those who were most critical of capitalist institutions compared them unfavorably to those of the Soviet Union. Most of those who in the 1930s hoped to profit from the Soviet experience were not actually communist. Some believed that something like Soviet results might be obtained without the use of Soviet methods, which were dismissed as typically Russian, a deplorable heritage from the Byzantine Empire and the tsars. With the appearance of Communism and Communist parties, socialism and socialist ideas seemed in contrast to be middling and respectable. Everywhere in the 1930s the idea of "planning" began to find favor. Workers obtained more security against the fluctuations of capitalism. The so-called backward peoples, especially in Asia, were particularly impressed by the achievement of the U.S.S.R., which had shown how a traditional society could modernize itself without falling under the influence of foreign capital or foreign guidance.

For a long time, and long after the abolition of the Comintern, the Communist party in Russia tried to present itself as the leader of world revolution and to exert control over Communist parties in other countries. After the Second World War this became increasingly difficult. Fifty years after the November Revolution the U.S.S.R. no longer seemed very innovative, and in some ways not even efficient. European Communist parties sought to establish their independence from Moscow, and with the success of the Chinese Revolution, after 1950, new movements of the Left emerged by which even the Soviets were called bourgeois and Soviet society was denounced as state capitalism. But all Communist parties derived from the meeting of the Third International in 1920; they all professed adherence to Marxism; and for all of them the Russian Revolution stood as the first great victory over capitalism and imperialism.

XVIII.
The
Apparent
Victory of
Democracy

e have followed events in the Soviet Union to about the year 1939 but have left the story of Europe and the rest of the world at the signing of the peace treaties of 1919. We must deal now with the period of just twenty years that elapsed between the formal close of the First World War in 1919 and the outbreak of the Second World War in 1939. In these twenty years the world made a dizzy passage from confidence to disillusionment and from hope to fear. It went through a few years of superficial prosperity, abruptly followed by unparalleled economic disaster. For a time, in the 1920s, democracy seemed to be advancing almost everywhere; then, in the 1930s, the new phenomenon of totalitarianism began to spread. Let us first examine the apparent triumphs of democracy in the 1920s, turn next to the devastating world-wide effects of the great depression that began in 1929, and then, in the following chapter, trace the painful decade of the 1930s.

96. THE ADVANCE OF DEMOCRACY AFTER 1919

Gains of Democracy and Social Democracy

The first years following the war were troubled. Even the victors faced serious difficulties in reconversion from war to peace. Men demobilized from the huge armies found themselves unemployed and psychologically restless. Farms and

Chapter Emblem: A medal struck in honor of the Peace of Versailles, 1919.

735

factories geared to maximum production during the war faced a sudden disappearance of markets. They produced more than could now be sold, so that the war was followed by a sharp postwar depression, which, however, had run its course by 1922. Basically, the economic position even of the victors was seriously damaged, for the war had disjointed the world of 1914, in which industrial western Europe had lived by exchange with eastern Europe and with overseas countries.

The war, President Wilson had said, had been fought to make the world safe for democracy. Political democracy now made advances everywhere. The new states that emerged from the war all adopted written constitutions and universal suffrage. Democracy made advances even in countries that had long been in large measure democratic. The last significant steps toward universal male suffrage were taken in Great Britain in 1918. The most conspicuous innovation was the growing enfranchisement of women. In 1918 female suffrage with certain restrictions was adopted in Great Britain; in 1928 the restrictions were dropped and the vote was granted on an equal basis with men. In 1920, through an amendment to the constitution, female suffrage became general in the United States. Women voted also in Germany and in most of the new states of Europe. In the Soviet Union women received the vote on an equal basis with men after the Revolution in 1917.

In most European countries the successors of the old prewar socialists gained in strength. With the left of the old socialists generally seceding, calling themselves communists, and affiliated with each other and with Moscow in the Communist International, the European socialists or social democrats were preponderantly a party of peaceable or revisionist Marxism, entirely willing to carry on the class conflict by parliamentary and legislative methods. Labor unions, with new self-confidence gained from the role they had played in the war, grew in membership, prestige, and importance.

Social legislation which before the war would have seemed radical was now enacted in many places. An eight-hour legal working day became common, and government-sponsored insurance programs against sickness, accident, and old age were either adopted or extended; an act of 1930, in France, insured almost 10 million workers. An air of progressive democracy pervaded Europe and the Euro-

AUTOUR d'ELLE
by Marc Chagall (Russian, then French, 1887–   )

Where some painters departed from the Western tradition by cultivating pure abstraction or geometrized patterns (see pp. 590–593, 908–910), others did so by evoking unconscious or dreamlike mental phenomena. This picture was painted by Chagall in France in 1945 in memory of his wife. The houses in the center represent the Russian city of Smolensk, where they had been married thirty years before. The surrounding faces and figures are individually quite distinct, but they float disconnectedly like the vivid images in a dream, without location in space or time, or any rational relationship to each other. Past and present, memory and perception, fantastic and real objects flow together in a kind of free play of the unconscious mind. These qualities characterized surrealism, of which Chagall in his younger days had been a forerunner. Courtesy of the Musée d'Art Moderne, Paris (Service Photographique). Permission A.D.A.G.P. 1970 by French Reproduction Rights, Inc.

pean world. The social service, or welfare, state, already under way in the late nineteenth century, was becoming more firmly established.

Only in Italy in the early postwar years, of the states that might have been expected to continue their prewar democratic gains, did democracy receive a sharp setback. Italy had been a parliamentary state since 1861 and had introduced a democratic suffrage in the elections of 1913. In 1919 the Italians held their second elections under universal male suffrage. But Italian democracy was abruptly ended. In 1922 an agitator named Benito Mussolini, leading a movement which he called Fascism, killed off the Italian parliament.[1] Lenin had already founded the first single-party state; Mussolini became the first of the personal dictators of postwar Europe outside Russia. Fascist Italy, in the 1920s. was the chief exception in what seemed to be a rising tide of democracy.

The New States of Central and East-Central Europe

In central and east-central Europe—in Germany, in the territory of the former Austro-Hungarian empire, and in the western fringe of former tsarist Russia—entirely new states and new governments struggled to establish themselves. The new states included, besides republican Germany, the four successor states to the Habsburg empire—Austria, Hungary, Czechoslovakia, and Yugoslavia; and the five states that had broken away from the Russian empire—Poland, Finland, Estonia, Latvia, and Lithuania.[2] The other small states in eastern Europe, Rumania, Bulgaria, Greece, and Albania, had already been independent before 1914; their boundaries underwent some modification and their governments considerable reorganization after the war. The Turkish Republic is considered elsewhere.[3]

The new states were to a large extent accidents of the war. Nowhere, except possibly in Poland, did they represent a deeply felt, long-maturing, or widespread revolutionary sentiment. Only an infinitesimal number of Germans in 1914 would have voted for a republic. Even among the nationalities of Austria-Hungary in 1914 few persons would have chosen the complete breakup of the Habsburg empire. The republicans, moderate socialists, agrarians, or nationalists who now found themselves in power had to improvise governments for which there had been little preparation. They had to contend with reactionaries, monarchists, and members of the old aristocracy. They had also to deal with the real revolutionaries, who, inspired by Lenin's success, hoped to bring about the dictatorship of the proletariat. A communist revolt broke out in Germany in 1919 but was quickly suppressed; soviet regimes were actually set up but soon crushed in Hungary and in the German state of Bavaria; and as late as 1923 there was a communist uprising in the German state of Saxony.

The new states all embodied the principle of national self-determination, which held that each nationality should enjoy political sovereignty one nation, one government. But people in this region were and always had been locally intermixed.[4] Each of the new states therefore included minority nationalities; for, with

1 See pp. 510–511, 776–781.
2 See map, pp. 686–687.
3 See pp. 749–750.
4 See map, p. 433.

the exception of an exchange of populations between Greece and Turkey, arranged in 1923, there was no thought of the actual physical removal of "alien" groups. Poland and Czechoslovakia were the most composite of the new states. Each of these two possessed, in particular, among its several minorities, a considerable population of disaffected Germans.

Nevertheless, despite economic and nationalist troubles, the new states and governments attempted at the outset to make themselves democratic. Except for the German republic they were all relatively small. All the newly created states were republics except Yugoslavia, which was under the older Serbian dynasty. Hungary started out in 1918 as a republic, but the attempt of Béla Kun to found a Hungarian Soviet Republic in 1919 brought back the counterrevolutionaries who restored the Habsburg monarchy in principle, though they were prevented by foreign pressure from restoring the king in person. Hungary emerged in 1920 as a monarchy with a perennially vacant throne, under a kind of dictatorship exercised by Admiral Horthy. All smaller states of Europe, including Hungary, possessed at least the external apparatus of democracy until the 1930s; that is, they had constitutions, parliaments, elections, and a diversity of political parties. If civil liberty was sometimes violated, the right to civil liberty was not denied; and if the elections were sometimes rigged, they were at least in principle supposed to be free.

Economic Problems of Eastern Europe: Land Reform

Eastern Europe for centuries had been an agrarian region of large landed estates, which supported on the one hand a wealthy landowning aristocracy of almost feudal outlook, and on the other an impoverished mass of agricultural workers with little or no property of their own. The landed aristocracy had been the chief support of the Austro-Hungarian empire and an important pillar of the old order in the tsarist empire and in eastern Prussia. The mass of the rural population, through all this region, had been free from serfdom, or released from subjection to manorial landlords, only since the middle of the preceding century.[5] The middle class of business and professional men was small except in Austria and Bohemia, the western portion of Czechoslovakia. In general, the whole region was conscious of lagging behind western Europe, not only in industry, factories, railroads, and great cities, but also in literacy, schooling, reading habits, health, death rates, length of life, and material standard of living.[6]

The new states set out to modernize themselves, generally on the model of the West. They introduced democratic and constitutional ideas. They put up protective tariffs, behind which they tried to develop factories and industries of their own. But the new national boundaries created difficulties. Where Europe in 1913 had had 6,000 miles of frontiers, after the war it had almost 10,000, and all the increase was in eastern Europe. Goods circulated much less easily. Protected industries in the old agricultural regions produced inefficiently and at high cost. Old and established industries, in Austria, Czechoslovakia, and western Poland, cut off by the new frontiers and new tariffs from their former markets, fell upon hard times. The working class of Vienna lived in misery, because Vienna, a city of

5 See p. 481 and map, p. 202.
6 See pp. 544–545.

2 million persons, formerly the capital of an empire of 50 million, was now the capital of a republic of 6 million. In Czechoslovakia the German minority, the Sudetens, complained that in hard times the German businessmen and workers, because of government policies, always suffered more than their Czech counterparts. Economically, the carving up of eastern Europe into a dozen independent states was self-defeating.

The greatest of reforms undertaken by the new east-European states was the reform of landownership. Although it far from solved basic economic problems in the area, it did have substantial effect on the pattern of land distribution. The whole traditional agrarian base of society was overturned. The work of the revolutions of 1848, which, in the Habsburg lands, had liberated the peasants but left them landless, was now carried a step further. The example of the Russian Revolution gave a powerful stimulus, for in Russia in 1917 peasants had driven off landlords, and communists and communist sympathizers won a hearing among discontented and propertyless peasants from Finland to the Balkans. Not until 1929, it should be recalled, did the Soviet Union embark on the collectivization of agriculture; until then, communism appeared to favor the small individual farmer. But it may be said with equal truth that the model for agrarian reform lay in the West, especially in France, the historic land of the small peasant proprietor.

Land reform worked out differently in different countries. In the Baltic states the big properties belonged almost entirely to German families, the "Baltic barons," descendants or at least successors to the medieval Teutonic Knights.[7] In Estonia, Latvia, and Lithuania the nationalist dislike for Germans thus made it easier to liquidate landlords. Small farms here became the rule. In Czechoslovakia over half the arable land was transferred from large to small owners; here again, the fact that many great landowners had been German, in some cases since the days of the Thirty Years' War,[8] made the operation in a sense more palatable, though it inflamed the German minority in Bohemia. In Rumania and Yugoslavia the breakup of large estates, though considerable, was less thorough. In Finland, Bulgaria, and Greece the issue hardly arose, since small landownership was already common. Land reform had least success in Poland and Hungary, where the landed magnates were exceptionally strong and well rooted.

After the land reforms, political parties of peasants or small landholders became the chief democratic force within the various states on the western border of Russia. Often they inclined to socialism, especially since capitalism was associated in their minds with foreign investors and outsiders. On the other hand, the great landowners, the former aristocrats of the prewar empires, whether already expropriated or merely threatened with expropriation, were confirmed in a reactionary outlook. The land reforms did not solve basic economic problems. The new small farms were very small, frequently no more than ten acres. The peasant owners lacked capital, agricultural skill, and knowledge of the market. Farm productivity did not rise. In place of old differences between landlord and tenant there developed new differences between the more comfortable peasant and the proletarian hired man—between the kulak and the toiler, in communist parlance. The continuance of relative poverty, the obstinacy of reactionary upper classes,

---

[7] See p. 74 and map, p. 40.
[8] See pp. 136, 214–215.

the new stresses and strains among the peasants themselves, the economic distortions produced by numerous tariff walls, and the lack of any sustained tradition of self-government all helped to frustrate the democratic experiments launched in the 1920s.

97. THE GERMAN REPUBLIC AND THE SPIRIT OF LOCARNO

The keystone of Europe was Germany. Germany, too, had its revolution in 1918. But it was a revolution without revolutionaries, a negative revolution caused more by the disappearance of the old than by any vehement arrival of the new. The emperor and the High Command of the army, in the last weeks of the war, had bowed out of the picture, leaving it to others to face defeat and humiliation.[9] For a time, after November 1918, the men in charge of affairs were mainly Social Democrats. The Social Democrats were Marxists, but their Marxism was the tamed, toned down, and revisionist Marxism that had prevailed for twenty years before the advent of Lenin. They were trade union officials and party managers. They could look back, in 1918, on decades spent in developing labor organizations and building up the Social Democratic party, which in 1912 had become the largest single party in the Reichstag.[10] Now, in 1918, they were a cautious and prudent group, essentially conservative, more anxious to preserve what they had already achieved than to launch audacious new social experiments. Before 1917 the Social Democrats considered themselves well to the left. But the Bolshevik Revolution in Russia, and the emergence of a pro-Bolshevik or communist element in Germany, put the Social Democrats in the middle. The middle is an awkward spot, especially in disturbed times; the Communists regarded the Social Democrats as reactionaries, despicable traitors to the working-class movement; whereas the true reactionaries, recruited from old monarchists, army officers, Junker landowners, and big business groups, saw in social democracy, or professed to see in it, a dangerous flirtation with Bolshevism.

The middle group in Germany, the Social Democrats reinforced by the Catholic Center party and others, was more afraid of the left than of the right. They were appalled, in 1918 and 1919, by the stories brought out of Russia, not merely by fugitive bourgeois or tsarist aristocrats, but by refugee Social Democrats, Mensheviks, and anti-Leninist Bolsheviks, men whom all socialists had long known and trusted in the Second International. In January 1919 the Spartacists,[11] led by Karl Liebknecht and Rosa Luxemburg, attempted to bring about a proletarian revolution in Germany, like that in Russia. Lenin and the Russian Bolsheviks lent their aid. For a time, there seemed to be a possibility that Germany might go communist, that the Spartacists might succeed in imposing a dictatorship of the proletariat. But the Social Democratic Provisional Government crushed the Spartacist uprising, turning for that purpose to demobilized army officers and volunteer vigilantes recruited from the disbanding army. The Sparta-

9 See pp. 675–677.
10 See pp. 574–575, 580–582.
11 So named from Spartacus, a Roman slave who led a slave revolt in south Italy in 72 B.C.

cist leaders Liebknecht and Luxemburg were arrested and shot while in police custody. The events of "Spartacus Week" widened a chasm between Social Democrats and Communists which was not to be bridged even in Hitler's concentration camps.

Shortly after, elections were held for a National Constituent Assembly. No single party received a majority, but the Social Democrats were the leading party. A coalition of Social Democrats, Center party, and liberal democrats dominated the Assembly. After several months of deliberations at the city of Weimar, in July 1919, a constitution was adopted establishing a democratic republic. The Weimar Republic (as the regime in Germany from 1919 to the advent of Hitler in 1933 is called) was soon threatened ominously from the right. In 1920 a group of disaffected army officers staged a *Putsch,* or armed revolt, put the republican government to flight, and attempted to place a puppet of their own, one Dr. Kapp, at the head of the state. The Berlin workers, by turning off public utilities, stopped the Kapp *Putsch* and saved the republic. But the Weimar government never took sufficiently firm measures to put down private armed bands led by reactionary or outspokenly antidemocratic agitators. One of these was soon to be Adolf Hitler, who as early as 1923 staged an abortive revolt in Munich.[12] Nor, being democratic and liberal, did it ever deny the rights of election to the Reichstag, and of free speech in the Reichstag and in public, either to communists or to antidemocratic reactionaries.

The Weimar Republic was in principle highly democratic. The constitution embodied all the devices then favored by the most advanced democrats, not only universal suffrage including the vote for women, but proportional representation and the initiative, referendum, and recall. But except for the legal eight-hour day and a few other such safeguards to the workers' welfare (and traditional demands of organized labor) the republic of which the Social Democrats were the main architects in its formative years was remote from anything socialistic. No industries were nationalized. No property changed hands. No land laws or agrarian reforms were undertaken, as in the new states of eastern Europe; the East-Elbian Junkers remained untouched in their landed estates. There was almost no confiscation even of the property of the former kaiser and other ruling dynasties of Bismarck's federal empire. The very statues of emperors, kings, princes, and grand dukes were left standing in the streets and squares. Officials, civil servants, police agents, professors, schoolteachers of old imperial Germany remained at their respective duties. The army, though limited by the Versailles treaty to 100,000 men, remained the old army in miniature, with all its essential organs intact, and lacking only in mass. The soldiers were peasant youths enlisted for long terms and soon formed to German and Prussian military traditions. In the officer corps the old professional and aristocratic influences remained strong.

Never had there been a revolution so mild, so reasonable, so tolerant. There was no terror, no fanaticism, no stirring faith, no expropriation, no émigrés. There had in truth been no revolution at all, in the sense in which France, England, the United States, Russia, and other countries, either recently or in the more distant past, had experienced revolutions.

12 See pp. 781–782.

The German Democracy and Versailles

The supreme question, for Europe and the world, was how Germany would adjust itself to the postwar conditions. How would the Germans accept the new internal regime of democracy? How would they accept the new German frontiers and other provisions of the Treaty of Versailles? These two questions were unfortunately interconnected. The Weimar Republic and the Treaty of Versailles were both products of the defeat of Germany in the war. There were many in Germany who favored democracy, notably the numerous Social Democrats, and many more possibly could have been won over to it, given time and favorable conditions. But no one, not even the Social Democrats, accepted the Treaty of Versailles or the new German frontiers as either just or final. If "democracy" in Germany meant the perpetual acceptance of the treaty without amendment, or if it meant economic distress or hardship which could either reasonably or unreasonably be explained as consequences of the treaty, then "democracy" would lose such appeal as it had for the Germans.

The German republicans, we have seen, protested against the Versailles treaty before signing, and signed only under pressure.[13] The Allies continued the wartime naval blockade after the armistice; this confirmed, in German eyes, the argument that the Treaty of Versailles was a *Diktat,* a dictated peace, Carthaginian, ruthless, and vengeful. The "war guilt" clause, while it perhaps on the one hand satisfied a peculiar Anglo-American sense of morality, on the other hand offended a peculiar German sense of honor. Neither the reparations demanded of them, nor the new frontiers, were accepted by the Germans as settled. Reparations they regarded as a perpetual mortgage on their future. They generally expected, some day, to revise their eastern frontier, get back at least the Polish corridor, and incorporate Austria.

The French lived in terror of the day when Germany would recover. Their plans for their own security, and for the collective security of Europe against a German revival, had been disappointed. They had been unable to detach the Rhineland from Germany. The United States Senate had refused to ratify the treaty, signed at Paris by Wilson, by which the United States was to guarantee France against German invasion in the future.[14] Both Britain and the United States showed a tendency to isolation, to pull away from the Continent, to get back to "normalcy," to work mainly for a restored trade in which a strong Germany would be a large customer. The League of Nations, of which the United States was not a member, and in which every member nation had a veto, offered little assurance of safety to a people so placed as the French. The French began to form alliances, against a potentially resurgent Germany, with Poland, Czechoslovakia, and other east-European states. They insisted also on German payment of reparations. The amount of reparations, left unstated in the treaty, was fixed by a Reparations Commission in 1921 at 132 billion gold marks. This sum, the equivalent of $35 billion, was soon pronounced by various Western economists to be more than Germany could possibly contrive to pay.

The Weimar government in these circumstances looked to Russia, which had

13 See p. 684.
14 See pp. 682–683, 688–689.

been no party to the Versailles treaty and claimed no reparations. The Soviet government meanwhile, concluding from the failure of proletarian revolution in Germany and Hungary that the time was not ripe for the sovietizing of Europe, prepared to enter into normal diplomatic relations with established governments. Germany and Russia, despite ideological repugnance, thus signed the treaty of Rapallo in 1922. In the following years the Soviet Union obtained needed manufactures from Germany, and German factories and workers were kept busy by orders from Russia. The German army dispatched officers and technicians to give instruction to the Red Army. Obliged by the Treaty of Versailles to restrict its activities, the German army was in fact able, through its work in Russia, and through a number of subterfuges at home, to maintain a high standard of training, planning, technical knowledge, and familiarity with new weapons and equipment. The good understanding between Germany and Russia naturally caused apprehension in the West.

Reparations, the Great Inflation of 1923, Recovery

The French, blocked in the attempt to collect reparations, and assisted by the Belgians, in 1923 sent units of the French army to occupy the industrial sites of the Ruhr valley. The Germans responded by general strikes and passive resistance. To sustain the workers in this patriotic idleness the Weimar government paid them benefits, grinding paper money off the printing presses for this purpose. Germany, like other belligerent countries, had suffered from inflation, i.e., rising prices, during and after the war; neither the imperial government nor the Weimar statesmen had been willing to impose heavier taxes to offset inflation. But what now swept Germany was different from ordinary inflation. It was of catastrophic and utterly ruinous proportions. Paper money became literally worthless. By the end of 1923 it took over 4 trillion paper marks to equal a dollar.

This inflation brought far more of a social revolution than the fall of the Hohenzollern empire had ever done. Debtors paid off debts in worthless money. Creditors received baskets full of meaningless paper. Salaries even when raised lagged behind the soaring cost of living. Annuities, pensions, proceeds of insurance policies, savings accounts in the banks, income from bonds and mortgages—every form of revenue which had been arranged for at some time in the past, and which often represented the economy, foresight, and personal planning of many years—now turned to nothing. The middle class was pauperized and demoralized. Middle-class people were now materially in much the position of day workers and proletarians. Their whole view of life, however, made it impossible for them to identify themselves with the laboring class or to accept its Marxist or socialist ideologies. They had lost faith in society itself, in the future, in the old burgher codes of self-reliance and rational planning of their own lives in an understandable world. A kind of moral void was created, with nothing for them to believe in, hope for, or respect.

The inflation, however, by wiping out all outstanding indebtedness within the country, made it possible, once the losses were written off and accepted, to start up economic production afresh. The United States was persuaded to play a reluctant role. The United States, in these years, demanded payment of the huge war debts owed to it by the Allies.[15] The Allies—Britain, France, Belgium—insisted that they could not pay debts to the United States unless they collected reparations from Germany. In 1924 the Dawes Plan, named for the American Charles G. Dawes, was instituted in Germany to assure the flow of reparations. By the Dawes Plan the French evacuated the Ruhr, the reparations payments were cut down, and arrangements made for the German republic to borrow abroad. A good deal of American private capital was invested in Germany in the following years, both in German government bonds and in German industrial enterprises. Gradually, so at least it seemed, Germany was put on its feet. For four or five years the Weimar Republic even enjoyed a bustling prosperity, and there was a good deal of new construction in roads, housing, factories, and ocean liners. But the prosperity rested in good measure on foreign loans, and the great depression that began in 1929 reopened all the old questions.

The Spirit of Locarno

These years of economic prosperity were years also of relative international calm. No issue, in truth, was dealt with fundamentally. The universal German hatred for the Treaty of Versailles elicited no concessions from the Allies. Conceivably, had the Allies been willing at this time to amend the treaty by international agreement, they might have taken wind from the sails of nationalistic rabble-rousers in Germany and so spared themselves much later grief. It may be, however, that no possible concession would have sufficed. The great problem was to prevent a German overthrow of the treaty structure by violence, especially in eastern Europe where the Germans regarded the new frontiers as basically subject to reconsideration. After the Ruhr incident, and adoption of the Dawes Plan, a group of moderate and peace-loving men shaped the foreign policy of the principal countries—Gustav Stresemann in Germany, Édouard Herriot and Aristide Briand in France, Ramsay MacDonald in England.

The charter of the League of Nations provided for international sanctions against potential aggressors. Like the system of congresses after the Peace of Vienna, the League was supposed to assure peaceable compliance with the peace treaties, or their modification without resort to force.[16] No one expected the League, by any authority of its own, to prevent war between Great Powers, but the League achieved various minor pacifications in the 1920s, and in any case its headquarters at Geneva offered a convenient meeting place in which statesmen could talk.

As a further assurance against war, in 1925 at Locarno, the European powers signed a number of treaties. These marked the highest point in international good will reached between the two World Wars. Germany signed a treaty with France and Belgium guaranteeing their respective frontiers unconditionally. It signed arbitration treaties with Poland and Czechoslovakia—not guaranteeing these frontiers as they stood, but undertaking to attempt changes in them only by international discussion, agreement, or arbitration. France signed treaties with Poland and Czechoslovakia promising military aid if they were attacked by Germany. France thus fortified its policy of balancing German power in the East by

---

15 See pp. 678, 679–680, 684.
16 See pp. 441–447.

its own diplomatic alliances and by supporting the Little Entente, as the postwar alliance of Czechoslovakia, Yugoslavia, and Rumania was called. Great Britain "guaranteed"—i.e., promised military aid in the event of violation—the frontiers of Belgium and France against Germany. It did not give an equivalent guarantee with respect to Czechoslovakia or Poland. The British took the view that their own basic security would be threatened by German expansion westward, but not by German expansion to the east. It was on the borders of Czechoslovakia and Poland, fourteen years later, that the Second World War began. Had Britain gone along with France in 1925 in guaranteeing these two countries, then stuck to the guarantee, the Second World War might possibly have been prevented. On the other hand, no war ever depends on any single decision; it is the accumulation of many decisions that matters.

In 1925 people talked with relief of the "spirit of Locarno." In 1928 international harmony was again strengthened when the French foreign minister Briand and the United States Secretary of State Frank B. Kellogg arranged for the Pact of Paris. Ultimately signed by sixty-five nations, it condemned recourse to war for the solution of international controversies. Although no measures of enforcement were provided and a number of reservations were added before certain countries signed, the Pact solemnly affirmed the will of the nations to renounce war as an instrument of national policy.

In the mid-1920s the outlook was indeed full of hope. At Locarno, Germany had of its own volition (and not by the *Diktat* of Versailles) accepted its borders both east and west, to the extent of abjuring violence and unilateral action even in the east. In 1926 Germany joined the League of Nations. Germany was a going concern as a democratic republic. Democracy seemed to work, as well as could be expected, in most of the new states of eastern Europe—the *cordon sanitaire* against Communist Russia, which itself had halted its postwar revolutionary offensive. The world was again prosperous, or seemed to be so. World production was at or above the prewar level. In 1925 the world's production of raw materials, it was estimated, was 17 percent greater than in 1913. World trade, by 1929, measured in hard money—gold—had almost doubled since 1913. The war and the postwar troubles were remembered as a nightmare escaped from. It seemed that, after all, the world had been made safe for democracy.

But complacency was shattered by the great world depression, by the growth of a malignant nationalism in Germany, due in some part to the depression, and by the assertion of a new militancy in Japan, which also was not unrelated to the depression. But let us turn first to the postwar years in Asia.

98. THE REVOLT OF ASIA

Resentments in Asia

The peoples of Asia had never been satisfied with the position in which the great European expansion of the nineteenth century had placed them.[17] Increasingly they condemned everything associated with "imperialism." In this respect there

[17] See Chapter XV, pp. 601–653.

was little difference between countries actually governed by Europeans as parts of European empires, such as British India, the Netherlands Indies, French Indochina (or the American Philippines), and countries that remained nominally independent under their own government, such as China, Persia, and the Ottoman Empire. In the former, as political consciousness awakened, there was objection to the monopoly of Europeans in the important offices of government. In the latter, there was objection to the special rights and privileges enjoyed by Europeans, the widespread impounding of customs revenues to pay foreign debts, the capitulations in Turkey, the extraterritorial rights in China, the spheres of influence in Persia which divided the country between British and Russians.

By imperialism, in either case, aroused Asians meant a system whereby the affairs of their own country were conducted, its resources exploited, its people employed, for the benefit of foreigners, Europeans, or white men. They meant the system of absentee capitalism, by which the plantations, docks, or factories before their eyes, and on which they themselves labored, were the property of owners thousands of miles away whose main interest in them was a regular flow of profits. They meant the constant threat that an alien civilization would disintegrate and eat away their own ancient cultures. They meant the nuisance of having to speak a European language, or the calamity of having to fight in wars originated by Europeans. And they meant the airs of superiority assumed by white men, the race consciousness exhibited by all whites, though perhaps most of all the British and Americans, the color line that was everywhere drawn, the attitudes varying between contempt and condescension, the relation of native "boy" and European "sahib." Imperialism to them signified the gentlemen's clubs in Calcutta to which no Indian was ever admitted, the hotels in Shanghai from which Chinese were carefully kept out, the park benches in various cities on which no "native" could ever sit. In deeper psychology, as well as in economics and in politics, the revolt of self-conscious Asians was a rebellion against social inferiority and humiliation.

The revolt against the West was generally ambivalent or two-sided. It was a revolt against Western supremacy, but at the same time, in most cases, those who revolted meant to learn from and imitate the West, in order that, by taking over Western science, industry, organization, and other sources of Western power, they might preserve their own identity and emerge as the West's equals.

The crisis in Asia had broken out with the Russo-Japanese War, when an Asian people, in 1905, defeated a great European power for the first time.[18] In 1906 revolution began in Persia, leading to the assembly of the first majlis, or parliament. In 1908 the Young Turks staged a successful revolution in Constantinople and summoned a parliamentary assembly to represent all regions then in the Ottoman Empire. In 1911 the revolutionists in China, led by Sun Yat-sen, overthrew the Manchu dynasty and proclaimed the Chinese Republic. In each case the rebels charged their old monarchs—shah, sultan, emperor—with subservience to Western imperialists. In each case they summoned national assemblies on the prevailing democratic model of Europe, and they proposed to revive, modernize, and westernize their countries to the degree necessary to avoid domination by the West.

[18] See pp. 638–641.

First World War and Russian Revolution

In the First World War almost all the Asian peoples were somehow involved. The Ottoman Empire, allied with Germany, immediately repudiated all the capitulations, or special legal rights of Europeans. Persia attempted to remain neutral and to get rid of the partition made in 1907 between British and Russian spheres, but it became a battleground of British, Russian, and Turkish forces. China, which joined the Allies, attempted at the peace conference to have the extraterritorial rights in China abolished. We have seen how this request of the Chinese Republic was refused, and how the Allies, instead, transferred many of the prewar German concessions to the Japanese.[19] The dependent regions of Asia, the Dutch, French, and British possessions, were stimulated economically by the war.[20] The Netherlands Indies, though remaining neutral, increased its output of foodstuffs, oil, and raw materials. India developed its steel industry and textile manufactures and contributed over a million soldiers, combat and service troops, to the British cause. All the dependent regions were stirred by Woodrow Wilson's call to make the world safe for democracy.

The home governments made concessions. They were naturally afraid to go too far; they insisted that their subject peoples were not yet capable of self-government. They had huge investments at stake, and the whole world economy depended on the continuing production of tropical and subtropical countries. But they did compromise. In 1916 the Dutch created a legislative assembly to advise the governor general of the Indies; half its members were elected from native races. In 1917 the British agreed to a measure of self-government in India; an Indian legislative assembly was set up with 140 members, of whom 100 were elected, and in the provinces of British India the number of elected representatives and of native Indian officials was increased. The French in 1922 provided for a somewhat similar assembly in Indochina. Thus all three imperial powers, at about the same time, began to experiment with consultative bodies whose membership was partly elective, partly appointive, and partly native, partly European. The United States introduced an elected assembly in the Philippine Islands in 1916.

The Russian Revolution added a new stimulus to unrest in Asia. The Bolsheviks denounced not only capitalism but also imperialism. In Marxist-Leninist ideology imperialism was an aspect of capitalism.[21] Colonial peoples also tended to identify the two, not so much for Marxist reasons as because modern capitalism was a foreign or "imperialist" phenomenon in colonial countries, where the ownership and the management of large enterprises were both foreign. Nationalism in Asia, the movement for independence or for more equality with the West, thus easily shaded off into socialism and the denunciation of capitalistic exploitation. The Bolsheviks were quick to see the advantages for themselves in this situation. As it became clear that the world revolution, as expected by Lenin, would not soon come to pass in Europe, the Russian communists turned to Asia as the theater in which world capitalism might be attacked by a great flanking movement. In September 1920 a "congress of oppressed Eastern peoples" assem-

19 See p. 683.
20 See p. 680.
21 See pp. 697–698.

bled at Baku, on the coast of the Caspian Sea. Zinoviev, head of the Communist International, called for war upon "the wild beasts of British capitalism." Not much was accomplished at the conference. But a few extremists from Asian countries in the following years sojourned in Moscow, and a few communists dispatched from Moscow stirred up the discontents which existed, quite without Russian instigation, all over Asia.

The postwar situation in Asia was thus extremely fluid. Men who were not communists hailed communism as a liberating force. Anti-westerners declared that their countries must westernize. Nationalism overshadowed all other isms. In the Indian National Congress rich Indian capitalists consorted with socialist leaders, with whom they were held together in relative harmony so long as the common enemy was the British.

The Turkish Revolution: Kemal Atatürk

The most immediately successful of the revolutionary movements was the one in Turkey. The Young Turks at first, in 1908, had meant to prevent the further dissolution of the Ottoman Empire.[22] This proved to be impossible. In the Balkan wars of 1912–1913 the Ottoman power was almost totally excluded from the Balkan peninsula. In the World War, in which the Turks were on the losing side, the Arabs with a great deal of British assistance broke away. After the war the Greeks invaded the Anatolian peninsula. They dreamed of a Great Greece embracing both sides of the Aegean. Europeans still regarded Turkey as the sick man of Europe, the Ottoman state as doomed to extinction, and the Turkish people as barbarous and incompetent. The Allies had agreed in 1915 to partition Turkey; and after the war the Western powers favored the Greek invasion. Italian and French forces occupied parts of Anatolia, and Italians, French, and British undertook to take Constantinople from Turkish rule, though its disposition remained uncertain. (It had been promised to Russia in 1915, before the Bolshevik Revolution.[23]) In these circumstances a powerful army officer named Mustapha Kemal rallied Turkish national resistance. Gradually, and with aid from Soviet Russia, the Turks drove the Greeks and the Western Allies away. They affirmed their hold on the Anatolian peninsula, and on both shores of the Straits, including Constantinople, which was renamed Istanbul.[24]

The Nationalists, under the energetic drive of Mustapha Kemal, now put through a sweeping revolution. They abolished the sultanate and the caliphate, since the sultan had somewhat compromised himself with foreigners, and was also, as caliph or commander of the faithful, a religious functionary for all Islam and hence a conservative influence. The Turkish Republic was promulgated in 1923.

Where the Ottoman Empire had been a composite organization made up of diverse religious communities, among which the Muslims were the ruling group, the Turkish Republic was conceived as a national state in which the "people," i.e., the Turkish people, were sovereign. Universal suffrage was introduced, along with a parliament, a ministry, and a president with strong powers. Non-Turks in

22 See pp. 615–619, 659.
23 See p. 669.
24 See map, p. 618.

Asia Minor now became "foreign" in a way they had not been before. Chief among these were the Greeks. About 1.4 million Greeks either fled or were officially transported from Asia Minor to Greece, and, in exchange, some 400,000 Turks residing in northern Greece were transported to Turkey. The exchange of populations caused great hardship, it uprooted most of the Greek element that had lived in Asia Minor since 1000 B.C., and it overwhelmed the impoverished Greek kingdom by obliging it suddenly to absorb a mass of destitute refugees, who were a quarter as numerous as the population of Greece itself. But it enabled the Turkish Republic to acquire a relatively homogeneous population, ending minority disputes between Greece and Turkey until Cyprus posed new problems after the Second World War.

For the first time in any Muslim country the spheres of government and religion were sharply distinguished. The Turkish Republic affirmed the total separation of church and state. It declared religion to be a private belief, and it tolerated all religions. Government was reorganized on secular and nonreligious principles stemming from the French Revolution. The law of the Koran was thrust aside. The new law was modeled on the Swiss Code, the most recently codified European legislation, itself derived from the Code Napoleon.

Mustapha Kemal urged women to put aside the veil, to come out of the harem, to vote, and to occupy public office. He made polygamy a crime. Men he required by law to discard the fez. He fought against the fez as Peter the Great had fought against the beard, and for the same reason, seeing in it the symbol of conservative and backward habits. The hat, "headgear of civilization," correspondingly became the symbol of progress. The people shifted to Western dress. The Western alphabet became mandatory; literate Turks had to learn to read again, and illiteracy was reduced. The Western calendar and the metric system were adopted. Turks were required to assume hereditary family surnames, like Westerners; Kemal himself took the name Atatürk, or Great Turk. The capital was moved from Istanbul to Ankara. The republic put up a high tariff. In 1933 it adopted a five-year plan for economic development. The Turks, having shaken off foreign influence, were determined not to become again dependent on Western capital or capitalism. The five-year plan provided for mines, railroads, and factories, mainly under government ownership. At the same time, while willing to accept Russian aid against the Western powers, the republic had no patience with communism, which it suppressed. The Turks wanted a modern Turkey—by and for the Turks.

Persia experienced a similar revolution, somewhat less drastic. The old concessions, capitulations, and spheres were done away with, and the Persian government renegotiated its oil contracts, asserting more control over foreign corporations and receiving a larger return from them in taxes and royalties. In 1935, to emphasize its break with the past, Persia took the name of Iran.

The National Movement in India: Gandhi and Nehru

India at the close of the World War was on the verge of revolution against British rule.[25] Discontented Indians looked for leadership to Mohandas K. Gandhi, the Mahatma, or Holy One, who in the following decades, though hardly typical of modern Asia, attained a world-wide eminence as the spokesman of subjected

25 See pp. 628–631, 641.

peoples. Gandhi had been educated in England in the 1890s and had practiced law in South Africa, where he became aware of racial discrimination as a world-wide problem. In India, after 1919, he led a movement for self-government, for economic and spiritual independence from Great Britain, and for greater toler-ance within India itself both between Hindus and Muslims and between upper-caste Hindus and the depressed outcastes and untouchables. The weapons he favored were those of the spirit only; he preached nonviolence, passive resistance, civil disobedience, and the boycott. He took to self-imposed fasts and hunger strikes to break the firmness of British jailers, and later of Indians themselves. He and his most loyal followers, as the troubles mounted, refused to be elected or take part in the partially representative institutions that the British cautiously introduced and also boycotted the British economic position in India, by refusing to buy or use goods imported from England. The latter touched the British in a sensitive spot. Before the World War half of all exports of British cotton cloth had gone to India. By 1932 this proportion fell to a quarter. Gandhi turned against all industrialism, even the mechanized industry that was growing up in India itself. He put aside Western costume, took to using a spinning wheel and living on goat's milk, urged Indian peasants to revive their old handicrafts, and appeared on solemn occasions clad in no more than a homespun loincloth. By the high level of his principles Gandhi made himself an inspiration to many groups that differed on more mundane matters. Even in the West he was regarded as one of the great religious teachers of all time.

India was very much divided within, and the British maintained that because of these divisions the ending of British rule would precipitate anarchy. There were Hindus and Muslims, between whom clashes and terrorist outrages were chronic. (Gandhi was himself murdered in 1948 by an anti-Muslim Hindu fa-natic.) There were the hundreds of oriental potentates of the native states. There were Indian capitalists, like the Tata family, and growing masses of proletarians produced by Indian industrialization.[26] There were the higher castes and the outcastes, and there were hundreds of millions of peasants living in a poverty unimaginable in the West. In politics, there were those who demanded full inde-pendence, boycotted the British, and spent years in jail, as did Gandhi and his more practical-minded but devoted follower, Jawaharlal Nehru; and there were the moderates who believed that they might best advance the welfare of India by accepting government office, cooperating with the British, and working for do-minion status within the British Empire. Marxism exerted a strong appeal, not indeed on the spiritual and pacific Gandhi, but on Nehru and even many of the less radical leaders. In the 1920s the Soviet Union stood in their eyes for the overthrow of imperialism; in the 1930s it pointed the way by its adoption of five-year plans. For a people wishing to raise itself by its own bootstraps, to move from poverty to industrial strength and higher living standards without loss of time, and without dependence on foreign capital and capitalism, the Soviet Union with its economic planning seemed to offer a more appropriate model and more practical lessons than the rich democracies of the West, with their centuries of great progress behind them.

The twenty years between world wars were years of repeated disturbance, of rioting and repression of sporadic violence despite the exhortations of Gandhi, of

26 See p. 680.

conferences and round tables, reforms and promises of reform, with a drift in the 1930s toward more participation of Indians in the affairs of the Indian empire. Independence was not won until after the Second World War; with it took place a partition of the Indian subcontinent into two new nations, a predominantly Hindu India and a predominantly Muslim Pakistan.[27]

In the Netherlands Indies, where the nationalist movement was less developed than in India,[28] the interwar years were more quiet. A serious rebellion, in which communists took part broke out in 1922 but was suppressed by the Dutch. The peoples of the archipelago were almost as diverse as those of India. Only the Dutch empire had brought them politically together. Opposition to the Dutch gave them a common program. In 1937 the legislative council petitioned for the grant of dominion status. But not until after the Second World War and the failure of a military effort to repress the nationalists did the Dutch concede independence.[29]

The Chinese Revolution: The Three People's Principles

The Chinese Revolution had opened in 1911 with the overthrow of the Manchu dynasty, which itself had belatedly begun to introduce westernizing reforms. The Chinese Republic was proclaimed, but the first immediate result was the establishment in Peking of a military dictatorship exercised by General Yüan Shih-kai, who had been a close adviser to the Manchus and who, until his death in 1916, never ceased to cast covetous eyes on the now empty imperial throne itself. In the south the veteran revolutionary Dr. Sun Yat-sen reorganized the Kuomintang (National People's, or Nationalist party), successor to the pre-revolutionary network of underground societies of which he had been the chief architect. Sun, elected the first president of the republic by a revolutionary provisional assembly, resigned within a few months in favor of General Yüan, who he mistakenly believed would unite the country under a parliamentary regime. Subsequently, in the confusion that followed the struggle for power in Peking after Yüan's death in 1916, Sun was proclaimed president of a rival government in the south at Canton, which exercised a nominal power over the southern provinces. Not until 1928 could any government have any basis for claiming actual rule over China—and even then, there were important exceptions. For most of these years the country was virtually in the hands of contending war lords, each of whom pocketed the customary taxes in his own locality, maintained his own army, and recognized no superior authority.

It was Sun Yat-sen who best expressed the ideas of the Chinese Revolution. Born in 1867 and educated under American influence in the Hawaiian Islands, he had received a medical degree at Hong Kong, had traveled extensively about the world, studied Western ideas, lectured to Chinese audiences in America, collected money for his conspiracies against the Manchus, and had returned from Europe to take part in the revolution. Shortly before his death in 1925 Sun gathered the lectures which he had been expounding for years into a book, *The*

27 See pp. 865–867.
28 See pp. 628–629.
29 See pp. 867–868.

Three People's Principles. The book sheds much light on the revolt of China, and of all Asia, against the supremacy of the West.

The three people's principles, according to Sun Yat-sen, were democracy, nationalism, and livelihood. Livelihood meant social welfare and economic reform—a more equitable distribution of wealth and land, a gradual end to poverty and unjust economic exploitation. By nationalism Dr. Sun meant that the Chinese who had always lived mainly in the clan and family had now to learn the importance of the nation and the state. They were in fact a great nation, he thought, the world's most cultured, and had once prevailed from the mouth of the Amur to the East Indies. But they had never been cohesive. The Chinese had been "a sheet of loose sand"; they must now "break down individual liberty and become pressed together into an unyielding body like the firm rock which is formed by the addition of cement to sand."

By democracy Sun Yat-sen meant the sovereignty of the people. Like Rousseau, he gave little attention to voting, elections, or parliamentary processes. He believed that while the people were sovereign, the able should govern. Government should be conducted by experts, a principle he criticized the West for neglecting. Dr. Sun felt a warm sympathy for Lenin. Yet he was by no means a doctrinaire Marxist. Marxism he thought inapplicable to China, arguing that the Chinese must take Marxism as they took all other Western ideas, avoiding slavish imitation, using, adapting, amending, rejecting as they saw fit. China had no native capitalism in any Marxist or Western sense. The "capitalists" in China, he said, were owners of land, especially in the cities, such as Shanghai, where the coming of Westerners had raised land values to dizzy heights. Hence if China could get rid of imperialism it would take a long step toward getting rid of capitalism also; it could begin to equalize landowning and confiscate unearned rents. Since China, he observed, had no true capitalists the state itself must undertake capitalist and industrial development. This would require loans of foreign capital and the services of foreign managers and technicians, adding another reason why the Chinese state, to maintain control, must be strong.

With Sun Yat-sen, in short, democracy easily shaded off into a theory of benevolent and constructive dictatorship. Marxism, communism, socialism, "livelihood," the planned society, welfare economics, and antiforeign and anti-imperialist sentiment were all mixed together—in some ways as the ideas of the Chinese Communists would later be.

The first aim of Sun Yat-sen and of the revolutionists in China was to shake off the "treaty system" that had bound China to outside interests since 1842.[30] In this respect the Paris peace conference had been disappointing; the Chinese not only failed to obtain the abolition of Western privileges and extraterritorial rights but could not block the retention by Japan of many of the former German concessions that the Japanese had taken over during the war.[31] Widespread student and worker demonstrations directed against the Western powers took place on May 4, 1919. The May Fourth movement heightened the antiforeign consciousness.

As the Western powers proved obdurate, Sun and the Kuomintang turned to Russia. They declared the Russian and Chinese revolutions to be two aspects of

[30] See pp. 633–638.
[31] See p. 683.

the same world-wide movement of liberation. The Chinese Communist party, organized in 1921, became allied with the Kuomintang in 1923. The latter accepted Russian communist advisers, notably the veteran revolutionist Borodin, whom Sun Yat-sen had known years before in the United States.[32] The Soviet Union, following its strategy of outflanking world capitalism by penetrating Asia, sent military equipment, army instructors, and party organizers into China. It also surrendered the Russian concessions and extraterritorial rights acquired in China by the tsars. The Chinese policy of friendliness to Russia began to produce the hoped for effects; the British, to draw China from Russia, gave up a few of their lesser concessions at Hankow and other cities.

China: Nationalists and Communists

The Kuomintang, its armies reorganized and strengthened, now displayed a fresh vitality and after 1924 launched a military and political offensive, planned by the ever active Russian advisers, supported by the Chinese Communists, and headed by Chiang Kai-shek who succeeded to the leadership of the Kuomintang upon Sun's death in 1925. Chiang's main objectives were to compel the independent war lords and the regime still holding office in Peking to accept the authority of a single Nationalist government. By the end of 1928 Chiang's armies had swept northward, occupied Peking, and transferred the seat of government to Nanking. Chiang now exercised at least nominal control over most of China, although effective control was still limited by the recalcitrance of many provincial war lords. The outside powers, acknowledging the accomplishments of the Kuomintang, extended diplomatic recognition to the Nanking government and conceded its right to organize and run the country's tariff and customs affairs. They also partially surrendered their extraterritorial privileges and pledged to abolish them completely in the near future.

In 1927, while a measure of national unity was being forged in the country, an open break occurred between the Kuomintang and its left wing. In the course of the northern military campaign, and particularly in the seizure of Nanking, popular disturbance and excesses, including the killing of a number of foreigners, had taken place, allegedly fomented by the Communists. These radical disturbances frightened and alienated the wealthier and more conservative element in the Kuomintang and so jeopardized Chiang's chief source of financial assistance for his government and army. Chiang himself, also, had never apparently considered the alliance with either the Communists or the Russians as anything more than one of convenience. Now Chiang took decisive action. Communists, and Russian advisers, were forthwith purged from the Kuomintang; many were executed; Borodin and others fled to Moscow; and a Communist-led uprising in Canton was forcefully suppressed. A number of armed Communist groups fled to the safety of the mountain regions in the south and joined other guerrilla contingents. In that way the Chinese Red Army was formed; among its leaders were Mao Tse-tung, a former librarian, teacher, newspaper editor, and union organizer, who had been one of the founding members of the party, and Chu Teh, who had held high rank in the Kuomintang armies and who had traveled and studied in Germany and elsewhere in Europe.

[32] See p. 733.

Chiang, with the renewed financial and moral support of the Kuomintang bankers, resumed the northern offensive whose success by 1928 has been described. But the original revolutionary impulse of the Kuomintang was now very much dissipated. Made up of men who feared social upheaval and who often regarded their own maintenance in power as their chief problem, it exercised a kind of one-party dictatorship over most of China under Chiang's leadership. Chiang himself recognized mounting popular dissatisfaction with the reluctance or inability of the Kuomintang to initiate reforms, but he was still busy consolidating the regime and after 1931 he had to contend with Japanese aggression. During these years he conceived a deadly hatred for Communists and those who actively agitated for revolutionary reform.

The Communists, operating now in southeast China, fed on popular discontent and drew support from the poor peasantry by a systematic policy of expropriation and distribution of large landed estates as well as by intensive propaganda. They succeeded in fighting off Chiang's armies and even in winning over part of his troops. Organizing a network of local soviets, in 1931 they proclaimed a Chinese Soviet Republic in the southeast. When after many years the Nationalist armies succeeded in dislodging them, the Communists, under Mao's leadership, undertook in 1934–1935 an amazing 6,000-mile march over near-insuperable terrain in north-central Yenan, closer, it was said, to Soviet supply lines. About 90,000 began the Long March, of which only half survived. They entrenched themselves again, fought off the Nationalist armies, and built up a strong popular following among the rural masses. With the Japanese invasion of north China well under way they abandoned their revolutionary offensive and pressed Chiang to end the civil war and to create a united front against the Japanese aggressor. Chiang reluctantly consented, so that by 1937 an alliance was formed between the Kuomintang and the Communists; the Chinese Red Army was placed under Nationalist control and disposition; a united China would face the Japanese. But the uneasy alliance between Kuomintang and Communists was not to last even until the defeat of the common Japanese foe in the Second World War, and the Chinese Revolution was about to enter a new, dynamic, and vastly different phase.[33]

Japan: Militarism and Aggression

The Nationalist movement in China caused apprehension in Japan, whose rise as a modern power has already been traced.[34] The Japanese, at least since the Sino-Japanese War of 1895, had looked upon the huge disintegrating area of China as a field for expansion of their own interests, in this scarcely differing from Europeans, except that they were closer to the scene. During the World War they had presented their Twenty-One Demands on China, taken over the German concessions in Shantung, and sent troops into eastern Siberia.[35] During the war the industrialization of Japan proceeded apace; Japan captured many markets while the Europeans were locked in the struggle; and after the war the Japanese remained one of the chief suppliers of textiles for the rest of Asia. The Japanese

33 See pp. 858–865.
34 See pp. 536–541.
35 See pp. 669–670, 683, 710.

could produce at lower prices than the Europeans, prices at which the penniless masses of Asia were more able to buy. Densely packed in their mountainous islands, they sustained their standard of living by importing raw materials and selling manufactures. But the Chinese Nationalists hoped to erect a protective tariff; it was for this reason, among others, that they denounced the treaty system, which for almost a century had bound China to international free trade. The Chinese, like the Turks, hoped to industrialize and westernize their own country behind a high tariff wall, which would shut out Japanese manufactures as well as others.

During the 1920s the civilian, liberal, Western-oriented element in Japan remained in control of the government. In 1925 universal male suffrage was adopted. It was still the fashion in Europe and America to view the Japanese with sympathetic approval, as the most progressive of all non-Europeans, the one Asian people who had ably learned to play its part in the advancing world-wide civilization. But there was another facet to Japan. The constitution of 1889 and parliamentary operations were but a façade that concealed political realities. Only in Japan of all modern countries did a constitutional law prescribe that the war and navy ministers must be active generals or admirals. The diet itself had sharply restricted powers. Ministers governed in the name of the supreme and sacred authority of the emperor, to whom they were alone responsible. Economically, the government's sponsorship of industrial growth had resulted in a tremendous concentration of economic power in the hands of four family trusts known collectively as the Zaibatsu. The business interests and the civilian political leaders all looked to an expanding empire and growing markets, but the most restless group in Japan drew its strength from the nationalist revival which, even before the "opening" of Japan in 1854, had cultivated Shinto, emperor worship, and the way of the warrior as a new and modern way of life.[36] This element was recruited in large part from the old clansmen and samurai, whom the "abolition of feudalism" had uprooted from their accustomed ways, and who in many cases found no satisfying field of effort in the new regime. Many of these men now served as officers in the army. Often they regarded the West as decadent. They dreamed of the day when Japan would dominate all East Asia.

About 1927 this group began to hold ministries in the Japanese government and to turn Japanese policy into increasingly aggressive and militaristic attitudes toward China. In 1931 Japanese army units stationed in southern Manchuria (where the Japanese had been since defeat of the Russians in 1905), alleging the mysterious murder of a Japanese officer at Mukden, began to seize Chinese arsenals and spread northward over all Manchuria. In 1932, charging the Chinese with economic warfare against Japan (Chinese boycotts were in fact damaging the Japanese export trade materially), the Japanese landed 70,000 troops at Shanghai. They soon withdrew, preferring to concentrate at this stage on the occupation of the northern part of China. They declared Manchuria to be an independent state under an emperor picked by themselves, renaming it Manchukuo.

After the Manchurian invasion the Chinese appealed to the League of Nations. The League sent a commission of inquiry, which, under Lord Lytton, found Japan at fault for disturbing the peace. Japan defiantly withdrew from the League. The

36 See pp. 538, 540–541.

small powers in the League generally cried for military sanctions, but the Great Powers, knowing that they would be the ones to bear the burden of military intervention against Japan, and in any case inclined to see no threat to their own immediate security, refused to take any stronger measures, so that, in effect, the Japanese remained in occupation of Manchuria and northeast China. With the Japanese conquest of Manchuria one tributary of the coming torrent had begun to flow. But the world at this time was also stunned by economic depression. Each government was preoccupied with its own internal social problems.

99. THE GREAT DEPRESSION: COLLAPSE OF THE WORLD ECONOMY

The capitalist economic system was a delicate and interlocking mechanism, in which any disturbance was rapidly transmitted with accelerating impact through all the parts.[37] For many basic commodities prices were determined by the free play of supply and demand in a world-wide market. There was much regional division of labor; large areas lived by producing a few specialized articles for sale to the world as a whole. A great deal of production, both local and international, especially in the 1920s, was financed by credit, which is to say by promises of repayment in the future. The system rested upon mutual confidence and mutual exchange—on the belief of the lender, creditor, or investor that he would get his money back, on the belief of the borrower that he could pay his debts, on the ability of farms and factories to market their products at prices high enough to bring a net return, so that farmers and factory people might purchase the output of other factories and farms, and so on round and round in countless circles of mutual interdependence, and throughout the world as a whole.

The Prosperity of the 1920s and Its Weaknesses

The five years after 1924 were a period of prosperity, in that there was a good deal of international trade, building, and development of new industries. The automobile, for example, still an oddity in 1914, became an article of mass production after the war; and its widespread use increased the demand for oil, steel, rubber, and electrical equipment, caused the building or rebuilding of tens of thousands of miles of roads, and created whole new secondary occupations for thousands of men as truckdrivers, garage mechanics, or filling-station attendants. Similarly the mass popularity of radios and moving pictures had repercussions in all directions. The ensuing expansion was most phenomenal in the United States, but almost all countries enjoyed it in greater or lesser degree. "Prosperity" became a mystic term, and some thought that it would last indefinitely, that the secret of human plenty and of progress had been found, and that science and invention were at last realizing the hopes of ages.

But there were weaknesses in this prosperity, various imperfections in this or that gear or valve of the mechanism, flaws which, under stress, were to bring the whole intricate structure to a halt. The expansion was largely financed by credit,

[37] See pp. 556–562, 597, 677–680.

or borrowing. Laboring people received less than a balanced share; wages lagged behind profits and dividends, so that mass purchasing power, even when inflated by installment buying (another form of credit), could not absorb the vast output that it was technically possible to produce. And throughout the world the whole decade of the 1920s was a time of chronic agricultural depression, so that farmers could neither pay their debts nor purchase manufactures to the degree required for the smooth functioning of the system.

Military operations in the First World War had reduced wheat fields under cultivation in Europe by a fifth. The world price of wheat went up, and farmers in the United States, Canada, and elsewhere increased their acreage. Often, to acquire land at high prices, they gave mortgages which in later years they were unable to repay. After the war Europe restored its own wheat production, and eastern Europe reentered the world market. Agriculture was increasingly mechanized. Where, in the nineteenth century, one man could cut ten times as much grain with a single horse-drawn reaper as with a scythe, and where, before 1914, he could cut fifty times as much with a combined reaper and binder, he could again increase his output fivefold after the war, by using a tractor-drawn harvester-thresher combine. At the same time dry farming opened up new land, and agronomic science increased the yield per acre. The result of all these numerous developments was a superabundant output of wheat. But the demand for wheat was what economists call "inelastic." By and large, within the area of the Western world, people already ate as much bread as they wanted and would buy no more; and the undernourished masses of Asia, who in pure theory could have consumed the excess, could not pay even low costs of production or transportation. The world price of wheat fell incredibly. In 1930 a bushel of wheat, in terms of gold, sold for the lowest price in four hundred years.

Wheat growers in all continents were faced with ruin. Growers of many other crops faced the same dismal prospect. Cotton and corn, coffee and cocoa all collapsed. Brazilian and African planters were caught by overproduction and falling prices. In Java, where not only had the acreage in sugar been extended, but the unit yield of sugar from the cane had multiplied ten times under scientific cultivation over the past century, the bottom dropped out of prices in the world market. There were indeed other and more profitable forms of agricultural production—for example, in oranges and eggs, of which world consumption was steadily growing. But the coffee planter could not shift to eggs, nor the Iowa farmer to oranges. Not to mention the requirements of climate, the ordinary farmer or peasant lacked the capital, the special knowledge, or the access to refrigerated transportation that these newer branches of agriculture demanded. For the one thing that the average farmer or peasant knew how to do—grow wheat and other cereals—the new wonderful world of science and machinery had too little place.

The acute phase of the great depression, which began in 1929, was made worse by this chronic background of agricultural distress, since there was no reserve of purchasing power on the farms. The farmer's plight became even worse when the city people, struck by depression in industry, cut down their expenditures for food. Agricultural depression, rather than industrial depression, was at the bottom of widespread troubles in the interwar years throughout eastern Europe and the colonial world.

The Crash of 1929 and the Spread of Economic Crisis

The depression, in the strict sense, began as a stock market and financial crisis. Prices of stocks had been pushed upward by years of continuing expansion and high dividends. At the beginning of 1929 prices on the European stock exchanges began to weaken. But the real crisis, or turning point, came with the crash on the New York Stock Exchange in October 1929. Here values had been driven to fantastic heights by excessive speculation. Not only professional speculators, but quite ordinary people, in the United States, as an easy way to make a good deal of money, bought stock with borrowed funds. Sometimes, trading on "margin," they "owned" five or ten times as much stock as the amount of their own money put into it; the rest they borrowed from brokers, and the brokers borrowed from banks, the purchased stock in each case serving as collateral. With money so easy to obtain, people pushed up stock prices by bidding against each other and enjoyed huge fortunes on paper; but if prices fell, even a little, the hapless owners would be obliged to sell their stock to pay off the money they had borrowed. Hence the weakening of values on the New York Stock Exchange set off uncontrollable tidal waves of selling, which drove stock prices down irresistibly and disastrously. In a month stock values dropped by 40 percent, and in three years, from 1929 to 1932, the average value of fifty industrial stocks traded on the New York Stock Exchange dropped from 252 to 61. In these same three years 5,000 American banks closed their doors.

The crisis passed from finance to industry, and from the United States to the rest of the world. The export of American capital came to an end. Americans not only ceased to invest in Europe but sold the foreign securities that they had. This pulled the foundations from under the postwar revival of Germany and hence indirectly of much of Europe. Americans, their incomes falling, ceased to buy foreign goods; from Belgium to Borneo people saw their American markets slip away, and prices tumbled. In 1931 the failure of a leading Vienna bank, the *Creditanstalt*, sent a wave of shivers, bankruptcies, and business calamities over Europe. Everywhere business firms and private people could not collect what was owed them, or even draw on money that they thought they had in the bank. They could not buy, and so the factories could not sell. Factories slowed down or closed entirely. Between 1929 and 1932, the latter year representing the depth of the depression, world production is estimated to have declined by 38 percent, and the world's international trade fell by two-thirds. In the United States the national income fell from $85 billion to $37 billion.

Unemployment, a chronic disease ever since the war, now assumed the proportion of pestilence. In 1932 there were 30 million unemployed persons statistically reported in the world; and this figure did not include the further millions who could find work only for a few hours in the week, or the masses in Asia or Africa for whom no statistics were to be had. The worker's wages were gone, the farmer's income now touched bottom; and the decline of mass purchasing power forced more idleness of machinery and more unemployment. Men in the prime of life spent years out of work. Young people could not find jobs or establish themselves in an occupation. Skills and talents of older people grew rusty, young people found no opportunity to learn. Millions were reduced to living, and supporting their families, on the pittances of charity, doles, or relief. Great modern cities saw an outburst of sidewalk art, in which, at busy street corners, jobless able-bodied men drew pictures on the pavement with colored chalk, in the hope of attracting a few sixpences or dimes. People were crushed in spirit by a feeling of uselessness; months and years of fruitless job hunting left them demoralized, bored, discouraged, embittered, frustrated, and resentful. Never had there been such waste, not merely of machinery which now stood still, but of the trained and disciplined labor force on which all modern societies were built. And people chronically out of work naturally turned to new and disturbing political ideas.

Reactions to the Crisis

Optimists at the time, of whom President Herbert Hoover in the United States was one, declared that this depression, though a severe one, was basically only another periodic low point in the business cycle, or alternation of expansion and contraction, which had ebbed and flowed in the Western world for over a century. Prosperity, they plaintively said, was "just around the corner." Others felt that the crisis represented the breakdown of the whole system of capitalism and free private enterprise. These people, in many cases, looked for signs of the future in the planned economy then being introduced in the U.S.S.R. There was something in both views. After 1932, in part for purely cyclical reasons—because the depression cut down indebtedness and reduced the costs of doing business—it again became possible to produce and sell. World steel production, for example, which had stood at 121 million tons in 1929, and then collapsed to 50 million in 1932, by 1936 again reached 122 million. (To what degree revival was due to armament building is debated.) On the other hand, the Great Depression did put an end to the old economic system in the old sense. Even if such a stricken economy had internal powers of full recuperation after a few years, people would not stand for such terrifying insecurity in their personal lives. The horrors of mass unemployment were long remembered.

All governments took steps to provide work and incomes for their people. All, in one way or another, strove to free themselves from dependency on the uncertainties of the world market. The interlocking world economy collapsed both from the depression itself and from the measures adopted to cure it. The most marked economic consequence of the depression was a strong movement toward economic nationalism—toward greater self-sufficiency within the sphere which each government could hope to control.

The internationalism of money, the gold standard, and the free convertibility of currencies one into the other were gradually abandoned. Countries specializing in agricultural exports were among the first to be pinched. Agricultural prices were so low that even a large quantity of exports failed to produce enough foreign currency to pay for needed imports; hence the exporting country's currency fell in value. The currencies of Argentina, Uruguay, Chile, Australia, and New Zealand all depreciated in 1929 and 1930. Then came the turn of the industrial countries. England, as the depression went on, could not sell enough exports to pay for imports. It had to pay for imports in part by sending gold out of the country; thus the gold reserve supporting the pound sterling declined, and people who had pounds sterling began to convert their pounds into dollars or other currencies for which they thought the gold basis was more secure. This was known, in the poetic language of economics, as the "flight from the pound." In 1931 Great Britain went off the gold standard, which is to say that it devaluated the pound. But after Britain devaluated, some twenty-odd other countries, to protect their own exports and their own industries, did the same. Hence somewhat the same relative position reappeared. Even the United States, which possessed most of the world's gold supply, abjured the gold standard and devalued the dollar in 1934. The purpose was mainly to help American farmers, for with dollars cheaper in terms of foreign currencies, foreigners could afford to buy more American agricultural products. But it became harder for foreigners to sell to the United States.

Hence the depression, adding its effects to those of the World War and postwar inflation, led to chaos in the international monetary exchanges. Governments manipulated their currencies to uphold their sagging exports. Or they imposed definite exchange controls: they required that foreigners from whom their own people purchased, and to whom they thus gave their own currency, should use this currency to buy from them in return. Trade, which had been multilateral, became increasingly "bilateral." That is, where a Brazilian importer of steel, for example, had formerly bought steel wherever he wished, at such price or of such quality as he preferred, he now had to obtain steel, often regardless of price or precise quality, from a country to which Brazil had sold enough of its own products to make payment possible. Sometimes, notably in the relations between Germany and east-European countries in the 1930s, bilateralism degenerated into actual barter. The Germans would exchange a certain number of cameras with Yugoslavia in return for a certain number of pigs. In such cases the very conception of a market disappeared.

Currency control was one means of keeping one's own factories from idleness, by holding or capturing export markets in time of depression. Another way of keeping one's own factories going (or farms, or mines, or quarries) was to shut out competitive imports by the old device of protective tariffs. The United States, hit by depression in 1929, enacted the unprecedentedly high Hawley-Smoot tariff in 1930. Other countries, equally or more distressed, now could sell less to America and hence buy less American goods. Other countries likewise raised their own tariffs, in the desperate hope of reserving national markets for their own people. Even Great Britain, citadel of free trade in the nineteenth century, turned to protectionism. It also revived and adopted Joseph Chamberlain's old idea of an imperial tariff union, when in 1932, by the Ottawa agreements, Britain and the British dominions adopted a policy of having lower tariffs against one another than against the world outside.[38]

Even tariffs were not always enough. Quotas or quantitative restrictions were adopted in many states. By this system a government said in effect not merely that goods brought into the country must pay a high tariff duty, but that above a certain amount no goods could be brought in at all. Increasingly both importers and exporters worked under government licenses, in order that a country's entire foreign trade could be centrally planned and managed. Such methods approached those of the Soviet Union, which asserted a government monopoly of all foreign trade, exported only in order to finance imports, and determined, without the bother of tariffs, the exact quantity of imported commodities that it would take.

[38] See p. 607.

Thus the world economy disintegrated into fiercely competing national economic systems. In the oceanic wreckage of the great depression, each state tried to create an island of economic security for its own people. Some efforts were made to break down the rising barriers. An International Monetary and Economic Conference, meeting in London in 1933, attempted to open the clogged channels of world trade; it ended in failure, as did attempts to stabilize the exchange rates of various currencies. Soon thereafter, the wartime Allies defaulted on their debt payments to the United States.[39] Legislation in Congress then denied them the right to float bonds, or obtain new loans, in the American securities market. American actions thus reinforced economic nationalism. The era that had opened with Woodrow Wilson's dream of international economic cooperation was ending with an unprecedented intensification of economic rivalry and national self-centeredness; it was only one of the promises of the twentieth century to be blasted by the Great Depression.

[39] See pp. 678, 684, 734–744.

XIX.
Democracy
and
Dictatorship

I n the 1920s, people in a general way believed that the twentieth century was realizing all those goals summed up in the idea of progress; in the 1930s, they began to fear that "progress" was a phantom, to speak the word self-consciously with mental quotation marks, and to be content if only they could prevent a relapse into positive barbarization and a new world war.

The Great Depression ushered in the nightmare of the 1930s. Everywhere the demand was for security. Each nation tried to live economically, so far as possible, within itself. Each regulated, controlled, guided, planned, and tried to rescue its own economic system, attempting to be as little influenced as possible by the unpredictable behavior of other countries, or by the free rise and fall of prices in an uncontrolled world market. Within each country the same search for security encouraged the advancement of the welfare state and social democracy. Where democratic institutions were strong and resilient, governments took steps to protect individuals against the ravages of unemployment and destitution, and to help guard against future catastrophes. These governments remained democratically controlled but they assumed heavy new social responsibilities. On the other hand, where democratic governments were not well established or taken for granted, which was the case in many countries after the First World War, dictatorship spread alarmingly in the 1930s with the coming of the depression. Democracy was said to be suited only to wealthy or prosperous countries. Unemployed people generally cared far more for economic help, or for promises of economic help, than for any theory of how persons wielding public power should be selected. The cry was for a leader, someone who would act, make decisions,

Chapter Emblem: A postage stamp featuring Hitler and Mussolini, and reading "Two Peoples, One War," for use in Italian East Africa about 1940.

assume responsibilities, get results, inspire confidence, and restore national pride. The Great Depression opened the way for unscrupulous and ambitious political adventurers, for dictators like Adolf Hitler in Germany, whose solution to all problems, economic, political, and international, it turned out, was war.

100. THE UNITED STATES: DEPRESSION AND NEW DEAL

Profound changes took place in the United States, where the stock market crash of 1929 had precipitated the great economic collapse. In 1932 national income had dropped to less than half of what it had been in 1929; 12 million to 14 million were unemployed. The Republican President Herbert Hoover, elected in 1928 at the floodtide of prosperity, was identified in the public mind with the hard times. Hoover viewed with disfavor any large-scale government intervention, convinced that the business cycle that had brought the depression would in turn bring prosperity, and that once business confidence was restored recovery would begin. Eventually his administration did act, proposing for the world economy a one-year suspension of payments on all intergovernmental debts and at home giving financial assistance to banks and railroads, expanding credit facilities, and helping to save the mortgages of some farmers and small home owners. But Hoover would not go further; he opposed immediate direct federal relief to the jobless; veterans seeking payment of their wartime bonuses to tide them over the bad times were ejected from Washington; unemployment, business failures, and farm foreclosures continued. In the election of 1932 the millions of unemployed workers, disheartened urban lower middle classes, and distressed farmers swept the Republican administration from office and elected the first Democratic president since Woodrow Wilson. The new president was Franklin Delano Roosevelt. The combination of recovery, relief, and reform legislation that he inaugurated is known as the New Deal.

The new president embarked on a program of improvisation and experimentation, but with such dispatch and vigor as to generate at once an electric enthusiasm. Within a short time an impressive array of legislation was put through Congress. The program of assistance to farmers, small home owners, and industry

THE ASSEMBLY LINE
by Diego Rivera (Mexican, 1886–1957)

Not all twentieth-century artists have been attracted to pure abstraction or exploration of the unconscious. Among others, social activists and revolutionaries have continued to engage in narrative painting and realistic representation. Diego Rivera was one of the great painters of the Mexican Revolution. Regarded as the greatest living muralist and known also for his Marxist opinion, he was commissioned in 1931 by The Detroit Institute of Arts to decorate the walls of a large new hall. The fragment reproduced here shows part of the assembly line in an automobile plant, with workers of various races working speedily and as a team, while "bourgeois" visitors in the background somewhat stupidly watch and marvel. It was the machine age that Rivera meant to portray, rendering it with a mixture of realism and artistic heightening, and a sense of automatism, movement, and power. Courtesy of The Detroit Institute of Arts.

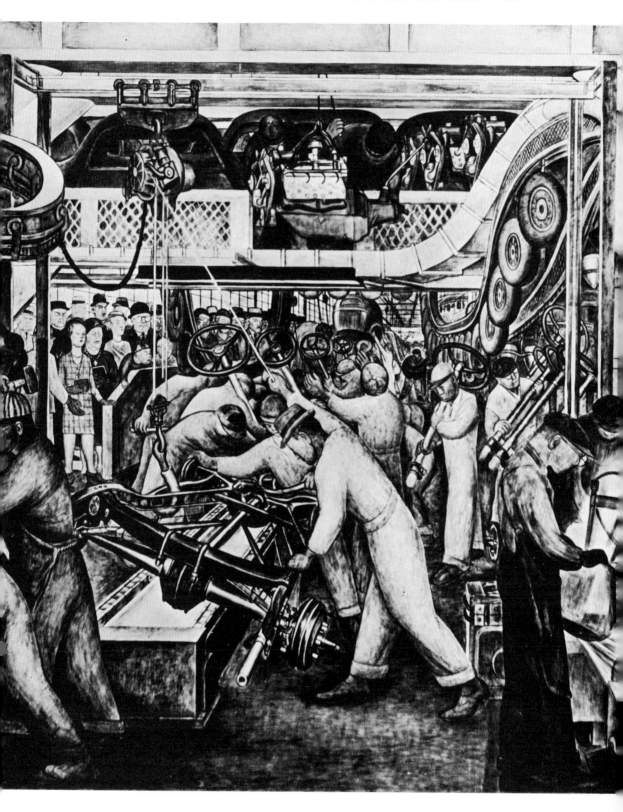

initiated under the Hoover administration was expanded so that it was no longer recognizable.

The government provided financial assistance for the relief of the unemployed and sponsored a broad public works program to absorb the jobless, first by loans to the states for the construction of housing, roads, bridges, and schools, later by a direct federal works program. To meet the financial crisis, the banks were temporarily closed and then reopened under stricter supervision. The dollar was taken off the gold standard and devalued, principally to help the farmers compete in foreign markets. In agriculture the government gave subsidies to farmers who agreed to curtail farm production, even subsidizing the destruction of crops and livestock, so that ruinous surpluses which had been one cause of the agricultural distress might be eliminated. It was a paradox, to be sure, for the government to reduce acreage and destroy agricultural products while city populations were in want. But the administration was endeavoring not only to cope with the immediate situation but also to meet the deep-seated agricultural crisis that antedated the depression. Subsequently, farmers received subsidies for devoting part of their land to soil-conserving crops. A Civilian Conservation Corps also promoted conservation and reforestation, and relieved unemployment by giving jobs to almost 3 million young people. For industry a National Recovery Administration (the NRA) for a time encouraged business firms to set up voluntary "codes of fair competition," which helped to regulate prices and production.

All these measures were designed to set the ailing capitalist system on its feet again by creating purchasing power and stimulating industrial activity. The major innovation was government spending, or "deficit financing." Although never following any consistent economic philosophy, the New Deal policies indirectly reflected the theories of the British economist John Maynard Keynes. In his earlier writings and in his most famous book, *The General Theory of Employment, Interest, and Money*, published in 1936, he argued that if private investment funds were idle, government funds must be employed to encourage economic activity and to increase purchasing power until such time as private funds flowed again. In order to get money into circulation and to "prime the pump" of industrial production, the government undertook a huge borrowing and spending program. Unorthodox as "deficit financing" was, it seemed then, and even later, the only direct and rapid method of preventing economic collapse in a capitalist system. In all these recovery and reform activities the federal government assumed a role that it had hitherto played only in wartime. Alphabetical agencies proliferated; the federal payroll grew; the government debt mounted—between 1932 and 1940 it more than doubled.

From the beginning, some longer-range reform measures were adopted in addition to the recovery measures. To prevent overspeculation and the recurrence of a crash such as that of 1929, a Securities and Exchange Commission was created to regulate the issuance of stock and to supervise the operations of the stock exchange. Bank deposits were guaranteed by federal insurance so that depositors would never again lose their lifetime savings. A Tennessee Valley Authority served as a pilot program in flood control, regional economic development, and cheap public power production—a yardstick, it was said, for the private utility companies.

After 1935 the focus shifted to regulation and reform. Sound economic recovery had not been achieved; there were still at least 5 million persons who could not find jobs in private industry. Businessmen who at first had been responsive to the government's leadership were now resisting the government's regulation of finance and industry. The Supreme Court declared the NRA and other New Deal measures unconstitutional.

Some of the major New Deal reforms after 1935 were laws to improve the condition of labor and to moderate the insecurity of the ordinary citizen. A broad national Social Security Act in 1935 provided for unemployment, old-age, and disability insurance. Here the United States was a latecomer. Germany, Britain, and other European countries had had such legislation since before the First World War. A Fair Labor Standards Act established forty hours as a maximum normal workweek and set a minimum hourly wage; child labor was abolished. With the passage of a third measure, the National Labor Relations (or Wagner) Act, the American industrial scene was virtually transformed. For the first time the unions found the federal government and the law solidly aligned on their side in the campaign to organize labor. Under the new act, which guaranteed the right of workers to set up and bargain through unions of their own choice, company unions were outlawed and employers were forbidden to interfere with union organization or discriminate against union members. Under its aegis the older American Federation of Labor (AFL) was revitalized and a new vigorous organization came into being, the Congress of Industrial Organizations (CIO), organizing workers on an industry-wide basis and reaching down to unskilled workers in such industries as automobile, steel, textile, maritime, and rubber. Millions never before organized, including women and black workers, became part of powerful labor unions with expanding treasuries. Total union membership rose from about 4 million in 1929 to 9 million by 1940; in the 1970s it was over 17 million. Militant and conscious of its new strength but hardly touched by revolutionary ideology, American labor chose not to create a third party but to operate within the traditional two-party system.

Other reforms included a tax revision bill, which arranged for steeply graduated income taxes, levies on corporate profits, and the plugging of various corporate tax-evasion loopholes. The New Deal later tried also to reverse the trend toward the concentration of economic power, which it had itself stimulated under the NRA, by an investigation into monopoly and monopoly practices, and a trust-busting campaign. A program of slum clearance and low-cost housing made a start toward providing adequate housing. Aid was given to the tenant farmer and the sharecropper. All this was undertaken to help those whom the president described in 1937 as "one-third of a nation ill-nourished, ill-clad, ill-housed." If the New Deal did not feed, clothe, and house them, or strike at the deeper roots of American poverty, urban decay, and racial discrimination, as many later argued, it at least demonstrated that the national community cared, and it showed the enormous potential for government action along all those fronts.

Government spending and renewed confidence in the soundness of the country's institutions created a slow, gradual, and partial recovery. In mid-1937, however, a recession occurred, i.e., business activity slid backward, when government spending slowed down; the recession did not end until 1938 when government spending was resumed. National income reached $71 billion by 1939, double what it had been at the depth of the depression but still short of 1929. Despite substantial progress, business activity did not regain the high-water mark of June 1929. Resistance from the business community itself may have played a part. The rising public debt, antibusiness pronouncements by the government, heavier corporate and income taxes, and the many concessions to labor undoubtedly frightened off business investments and led to what was called a "sit-down strike" of capital. Some claimed that wage rates had risen too sharply, adding to production costs and therefore discouraging business expansion. The New Deal did much to help economic recovery, but it did not end the depression. Complete recovery, the elimination of unemployment, the full use (and expansion) of the nation's productive capacity had to wait upon the huge war expenditures, by which depression spending was to be dwarfed. By 1938 or so the New Deal was over; the administration turned its attention from domestic reform to the gathering storm in Europe and the Far East.

The changes were substantial under what some called the "Roosevelt Revolution." Carrying forward a process that went back at least to the era of Theodore Roosevelt, but enlarging the role of the federal government as no previous administration had done, the New Deal transformed the noninterventionist state into a social service or welfare state. The government imposed controls on business, entered business itself (as in the TVA), used its powers to redistribute wealth, and established a broad social security system. Labor's power and political influence grew. The responsibility of public authority for the social and economic welfare of the people was clearly established. Here perhaps was the real essence of the New Deal. The Republican party, when it returned to power after the war, retained and even extended the New Deal reforms—a tacit admission, despite grumblings at the time, that the New Deal had not intended to destroy capitalism but to rehabilitate and strengthen it by regulation and reform.

The New Deal, however, engendered violent feelings, which lingered on. Roosevelt, himself of patrician and well-to-do background, denounced the "economic royalists"; in turn he was called a "traitor to his class." When the Supreme Court declared New Deal measures unconstitutional, he made plans to reorganize and enlarge the court, which aroused more political hostility. Despite vociferous opposition, in the election of 1936 Roosevelt won all but two states, and he was subsequently reelected in 1940 and 1944 (during the wartime emergency, to be sure, and with increasingly smaller majorities) for an unprecedented four terms. Such an occurrence was later barred for the future by a constitutional amendment of 1951.

No one could be neutral about Roosevelt. By some it was argued that he had created an enormous, regulatory, governmental bureaucracy, expensive and cumbersome, a positive threat to the freedom and self-reliance of the individual citizen. But despite its waste and inconsistencies, its costliness and unorthodox financial policies, its enlargement of the executive power and expansion of the governmental bureaucracy, the New Deal represented a bold and humanitarian way of meeting the greatest crisis the American republic had ever faced short of the challenge of arms; it preserved and reaffirmed American faith in its democratic system—and that at a time when democracy was succumbing elsewhere.

101. TRIALS AND ADJUSTMENTS OF DEMOCRACY IN BRITAIN AND FRANCE

British Politics: The 1920s and the Depression

Britain, like the United States, even in the troubles of the depression, remained firmly attached to representative institutions and democratic principles. The Great Depression aggravated and intensified Britain's older economic difficulties. More dependent on overseas markets than any other people, the British until 1914 had managed to hold their lead, exporting industrial products and capital, selling insurance and other services, and importing foodstuffs. But in the years before 1914 the British were increasingly losing their markets because of many circumstances: the emergence of other economically aggressive industrial nations, the growth of tariff barriers, the development of native textile and other industries in India and elsewhere in the East, the competition of new textile products with British cottons and woolens, and the substitution of new sources of fuel for British coal. The losses were accelerated by the economic disruption of the First World War, the disappearance of many investments, and the postwar disorganization and impoverishment of markets, though British trade for about a year enjoyed a short-lived boom caused by pent-up demands that could not be satisfied during the war. The general rise in tariffs after the war and the customs barriers raised in the new small states of Europe also hurt British exports. After 1918 Britain lived in a world no longer dependent on, or eager for, its manufactures. Britain's very historical primacy as the pioneer industrial country was also a handicap. Both labor and management had become adjusted to older conditions, and the more recently industrialized countries had less antiquated techniques and machinery.

The net result of all this was that in the interwar years, even in times of relative prosperity for the rest of the world, Britain was in depression and suffered severely from unemployment. The unemployment insurance adopted in 1911 was called heavily into play. By 1921 over 2 million unemployed were receiving benefit payments, contemptuously called the "dole" by those who disliked it. Unemployment insurance, an expanded old-age pension system, medical aid, government-subsidized housing, and other social welfare measures helped to relieve economic distress and to prevent any drastic decline in the living standards of British workers. The welfare state was well under way in Britain before the Labour party took office after the Second World War.

The labor unions made a strenuous effort to retain wage gains and other concessions won in wartime. Industry, hard-pressed itself, resisted. This situation reached a climax in 1926 in the coal-mining industry, which was in a particularly bad plight; government subsidies had not helped and even conservative investigators had recommended some form of amalgamation and public management. A strike by the coal miners led to a "general strike" supported by the other British unions; about half of the 6 million organized workers in Britain left their jobs as a token of their sympathy and solidarity. But the government declared a state of emergency and made use of army and navy personnel and middle-class volunteers to take over essential services. The strike ended in failure, and even in a setback for the trade unions, which were put under stricter control by the Trades Disputes Act of 1927, a measure that declared all general or sympathy strikes illegal and even forbade the unions from raising money for political purposes. The act remained in effect until repealed after the Second World War.

After the election of 1922, the Labour party displaced the Liberal party as the second of the two great parties of the country and faced the Conservatives as the official opposition.[1] The Labour party could more consistently and more actively champion both labor legislation and bolder measures to deal with Britain's troubled economic state. The Labour party, moreover, which had been no more than a loose federation of trade union and socialist organizations before the war, tightened its organizational structure and, bridging the gap between the trade unionists and the socialists, committed itself in 1918 to a program of socialism. But it was a program of gradualist, democratic socialism operating through customary British parliamentary procedures and hence able to gain the good will of large sections of the middle classes.

Twice, in 1924 and in 1929, Labour governed the country with Ramsay MacDonald as prime minister, in each case as a coalition government, with Labour dependent on the support of the Liberals for its majority. In 1924 the Labourites proved their moderation. Their administration went no further than an extension of unemployment relief and the inauguration of housing and public works projects; indeed the Labour government acted firmly in the face of a series of strikes that broke out. Its overthrow was precipitated by its diplomatic recognition of the Soviet Union and the pledge of a loan to the Soviets for the purchase of British goods. Defeat was ensured by the preelection publication of the so-called Red (or Zinoviev) letter purporting to be secret instructions to British labor groups from the head of the Communist International urging preparations for a Communist uprising in Britain.[2] The document's authenticity has never been established, but the Conservatives successfully exploited it and won the election of 1924.

In the election of May 1929, however, Labour's representation almost doubled, and the Conservative representation dropped proportionately. MacDonald again became prime minister of a Labour-dominated coalition government. Thus the Wall Street crash and the world-wide depression came while the Labour party government was in office. The effects of the depression were quickly felt. Unemployment, which had hovered about the 1 million mark in 1929, soon approached the 3 million figure. The government expended large sums to supplement the unemployment insurance payments. Gold flowed out of the country, tax receipts declined, the public debt grew. Alarmed at the mounting deficit, MacDonald took the advice of a committee of financial experts and made plans to introduce a severe retrenchment policy, even to the extent of reducing the "dole" payments. The Labour party was outraged; some of the Labour ministers in his cabinet refused to support him. He was read out of the party, along with those ministers who had gone along with him. MacDonald thereupon formed an all-party coalition cabinet known as the National government, which in an election of 1931 won an overwhelming victory, the Conservative members of the coalition alone winning a majority of the seats in Parliament.

The new government, though Conservative in essence, represented an effort to

[1] See pp. 571–572, 579–581, 599–600.
[2] See p. 733.

maintain national unity in the face of economic emergency, within the framework of the British parliamentary democracy. Not a single seat in Parliament in the depression election of 1931 went to either the Communists or to a British Fascist party organized by Sir Oswald Mosley; in 1935 the Communists won one seat.

The National government coped with the depression chiefly along retrenchment lines, under Ramsay MacDonald from 1931 to 1935, Stanley Baldwin to 1937, and Neville Chamberlain after 1937. In addition to retrenchment and budget balancing, the government encouraged industry to reorganize and rationalize production by providing low-interest loans. Mainly, the government concentrated on the kind of economic nationalist measures that have already been described.[3] As in the United States, despite some recovery from the depths of the depression, none of the steps taken brought full recovery or full employment. Unemployment persisted until military conscription and an expanded armament program absorbed the jobless. The Labour party, partially recovering its strength in the election of 1935, denounced the timid expedients of the Conservatives, whom it held responsible for the apathy and gloom gripping the country.

Britain and the Commonwealth: Imperial Relations

To the older British Empire—India, the crown colonies, protectorates, and spheres of influence—the postwar settlement added a number of League of Nations mandates. British rule in its various forms extended to almost 500 million people, a fourth of the earth's population and land surface. It was principally in Ireland, Egypt, India, and Palestine that the British faced complex imperial problems after the First World War. In Palestine, where the British exercised a League of Nations mandate, Arabs and Jews fought with each other and with Britain. In Egypt, in 1922, Britain, although retaining the right to station some troops there, formally ended the protectorate it had established forty years earlier; but many questions, especially the status of the Sudan, remained unresolved. In India the agitation for national independence, as we have seen, grew more intense. In these areas nothing resembling a solution was arrived at until after the Second World War. In Ireland the independence movement managed to establish a separate republic.

The Irish question had disoriented English politics for forty years.[4] Irish home rule, authorized by Parliament in 1914, had been deferred for the duration of the war. Irish nationalists, during the war, had accepted German support and had risen in rebellion in 1916. After the war, in 1919 and 1920, the Irish Nationalist or Sinn Fein party fought a small but savage war of independence against the British forces known as "Black and Tans." The British blocked independence, but in 1922 recognized the Irish Free State, granting it dominion status. The Protestant majority in Ulster, the northern counties where Presbyterians of Scottish origin had lived for three centuries, preferred to remain outside the Free State and continued to be joined in the United Kingdom of Great Britain and Northern Ireland, to the vehement dissatisfaction of the Irish republicans. In 1937 a new constitution for the Irish Free State affirmed the full sovereignty of Ireland (or Eire, as it was for a time called), the country remaining, however, in the British

3 See pp. 760–761.
4 See pp. 572, 856; for developments after 1945, see p. 891.

Commonwealth of Nations. Politics remained unsettled, for the Irish agitated for the annexation of Ulster, conducted tariff wars with a Britain from which they were now cut off, strove to revive Celtic in place of the English language, and fell into disputes in which Irish moderates were pitted against Irish extremists, the latter perpetrating an occasional assassination, or other outrage, to further their cause. The last formal ties with the British Commonwealth were severed in 1949, when the Republic of Ireland was proclaimed. The Irish continued to claim jurisdiction over Ulster and to support the cause of the Irish Catholic minority there.

As for the dominions, the political status of these areas of white settlement overseas was now more clearly defined than ever before. The dominions— Canada, Australia, New Zealand, and the Union of South Africa—had long pursued their own policies, even levying tariffs against British goods. They had all joined loyally with Great Britain in the First World War, but all were stirred by a nationalism of their own and desired their virtual independence to be regularized and promulgated to the world. An imperial conference of 1926 defined "dominion status," which was corroborated by the Statute of Westminster of 1931. The dominions became legally equal with each other and with Great Britain. No act passed by the British Parliament could apply to a dominion save by the dominion's own consent. Despite independent policies in economic matters and even in foreign affairs, the bonds between the dominions and Britain were firm; the support of the dominions in the Second World War was to be vital in Britain's survival. After the war the Commonwealth was to become a larger and even more flexible institution.

France: The 1920s and the Coming of the Depression

When the depression came to France, agitation of fascist type made more headway there than in Britain or the United States. Earlier, in the 1920s, France was preoccupied with recovery from the physical destruction of the war, the instability of public finances, and the fear of a resurgent Germany. Immediately after 1919, and for most of the 1920s, the government was run by coalitions of parties of the conservative right, i.e., parties supported by business and financial interests, well disposed toward the army and church, and interested in economy and stability in domestic affairs. For about two years, from 1924 to 1926, the Radical Socialists were in control; this party of the moderate left, whose leader was Edouard Herriot, served as spokesman for the lower middle classes, the small businessmen and farmers; it advocated progressive social legislation so long as increased taxes were not necessary. Despite its name, a carryover from an earlier era, it was firmly committed to private enterprise and private property; it was staunch in its defense of individual liberties and was fervently anticlerical; sometimes, it seemed, its anticlericalism was a substitute for any more positive program. Although the Radical Socialists could cooperate in elections with the Socialists, the other major party of the left, the two parties differed too profoundly on economic policies to preserve stable coalitions. In the 1920s the Socialists, led by Léon Blum, were still recovering from the secession of the more orthodox Marxists who had formed a French Communist party. Both left and right in France shaded off into antidemocratic groups that were hostile to the parliamentary republic as such. These included the Communists on the left, who sat in parliament and took part in elections; and on the extreme right, royalists of the *Action Française* and other antirepublican organizations, which operated principally outside the Chamber as militant and noisy pressure groups.

The outstanding figure of the moderate conservative right was Raymond Poincaré; it was he who sent troops into the Ruhr in 1923, when the Germans failed to pay reparations; and it was he who now "saved" the franc. The reparations question was extremely important for French finances. The country had undertaken a large-scale reconstruction program to repair the wartime devastation of northern and eastern France, and had counted upon the defeated enemy to pay. When German reparations were not paid as anticipated, the public debt mounted, a balanced budget became impossible, and the franc declined precipitously. The huge war expenditures, heavy wartime investment losses, notably in Russia, and an outmoded taxation program which invited widespread evasion added to French difficulties. After 1926, when the financial crisis reached a climax, a "national union" ministry under Poincaré inaugurated new taxes, tightened tax collection somewhat, cut down drastically on government expenditures in order to balance the budget, and eventually stabilized the franc—at about one-fifth of its prewar value. The internal debt was thus in effect largely repudiated, to the despair of many bondholders, but the threat of a runaway inflation, like that of the Weimar Republic, and of national bankruptcy was avoided. From 1926 to 1929 the country prospered. New factories, replacing those destroyed in the war, were modern and up to date. The index of industrial production rose; tourists flocked in. As in many other countries, workers did not share proportionately in the prosperity of the 1920s. The unions received a sharp setback when, immediately following the war, a series of strikes of major proportions ended in failure; the unions were also divided between a Communist and non-Communist national confederation; collective bargaining in the country was virtually unknown. The workers were not mollified by a social insurance program adopted by a reluctant parliament, which went into effect in 1930.

The Great Depression came later to France and was less severe than in the United States or Germany. Trade declined. Unemployment and part-time employment increased; at the worst period, in 1935, close to 1 million workers were unemployed; perhaps half of those employed worked part-time. Industrial production, which in 1930 was 40 percent above the prewar level, sank by 1932 back to the 1913 figure. The government displayed the usual pattern of unstable, shifting, short-lived ministries; in 1933 five ministries rapidly succeeded one another (there were some forty all told in the twenty interwar years). The cabinets formed after 1932 followed a policy of retrenchment and economy, and clung to the gold standard. Meanwhile, in Germany Adolf Hitler had become chancellor in 1933; France's domestic difficulties were intensified by mounting international tension.

Depression Ferment and the Popular Front

In the uneasy years of the depression, the latent hostility to the republic came to the surface. Fascist-type "leagues" appeared in open imitation of Italian and German fascist organizations, many obtaining funds from wealthy industrialists;

the older *Action Française* and right-wing veterans' associations like Colonel de la Rocque's *Croix de Feu* were also active. The same elements that had been antirepublican, antidemocratic, or monarchist since the French Revolution and which had rallied behind Boulanger and denounced Dreyfus[5] now grew more strident in their attacks on the parliamentary republic.

In 1934 it seemed for a moment that the opportunity awaited by the antirepublican elements had come. A political and financial scandal of the kind familiar in prewar French public life broke over the country. A financial manipulator and adventurer with excellent political connections, Stavisky by name, induced the municipal authorities at Bayonne to launch a flotation of worthless bonds. Faced with exposure, he fled and apparently committed suicide; the sensationalist press encouraged the rumor that he had been shot by the police to prevent the implication of high-ranking politicians. A clamor went up accusing the government of involvement in the financial scandal. Where elsewhere such an affair would have called only for turning the incumbents out of office, in France it supplied ammunition for those who demanded the end of the republic itself, which was equated with corruption and venality.

The agitation reached a climax in the riots of February 1934. A mob of fascist tendency assembled in the Place de la Concorde, threatened the Chamber, and battled with the police; several were killed and hundreds injured. French liberals and democrats, organized labor, and the Socialist party were outraged by the threat to the republic. The Communists, hostile to the fascist groups, were unfriendly to the government too, but soon, along with the Comintern, they sensed the danger to themselves and to the Soviet Union in the event of a French fascist triumph and joined with the antifascists. As elsewhere, in the 1930s the Communists emerged from their sectarian revolutionary isolation, became intensely patriotic, and widened their prestige, influence, and appeal. An impressive labor-sponsored general strike was held a week after the riots. Shortly thereafter, the Radical Socialists, Socialists, and Communists drew together in a political coalition that came to be known as the Popular Front, of the kind that was being organized, or advocated, in many countries in the 1930s. It campaigned on a pledge to defend the republic against fascism, to take measures against the depression, and to introduce labor reforms. In the spring of 1936 it won a decisive victory at the polls. The French Socialists for the first time in their history became the leading party in the Chamber; their chief, Léon Blum, long a spokesman for democratic and reformist socialism, became premier of a coalition cabinet of Socialists and Radical Socialists; the Communists, who had increased their representation in the Chamber from 10 to 72 seats, did not join the cabinet but pledged their support.

The Popular Front and After

Blum's Popular Front ministry, although it lasted little more than a year, put through a program of far-reaching legislation. In part, this was due to the Popular Front election program, in part to unforeseen events, for the tremendous enthusiasm generated by the victory led to a spontaneous nationwide wave of "sit-down

5 See pp. 566–568.

strikes," which did not subside until Blum pledged a number of immediate reforms.

Through Blum's mediation, industry at once awarded a blanket wage increase to all workers and promised to cooperate with social legislation passed by parliament. Parliament in short order passed laws providing for a forty-hour week, vacations with pay, and a collective bargaining law. As in the case of the Wagner Act in the United States, the encouragement given to collective bargaining led to the nationwide signing of collective contracts for the first time in the country's history and to an enormous growth in trade union membership, from about 1 million to 5 million in a year's time. Labor's strength was increased also by a reunification of the Communist and non-Communist labor confederations. Other legislation was important too. Steps were taken to nationalize the armaments and aviation industry; the fascist armed leagues were, at least in theory, dissolved; the Bank of France was reorganized and placed under government control to break the power of the "two hundred families." Machinery was established for the arbitration of labor disputes. Aid was given to farmers through price fixing and government purchases of wheat. As in the United States all these measures aimed at both recovery and reform; Blum spoke openly of his program as a "French New Deal." But French conservatives, and the quasi fascists to their right, cried revolution; they uttered dark predictions that a French Lenin would follow Blum. They did not conceal their sullen resentment at what had come to pass: the fate of Catholic France was in the hands of a leftist, a Socialist, and a Jew. Even salvation by a warrior from outside the country, one who had demonstrated his anti-Bolshevism, would be preferable. They envied the protection given to established interests by Mussolini, and there were those who even muttered "better Hitler than Léon Blum."

In all truth the Popular Front reforms, long overdue though they were, came to France at a time when the sands were rapidly running out. While France had a forty-hour week, German arms plants were operating at full capacity. In the shadow of Nazi remilitarization a rearmament program had to be undertaken at the very same time as reform; even moderates argued that the country could not afford both. Opposition from many quarters hindered success. French employers balked at cooperating in the new reforms and tried to pass on rising production costs to the consumer. Labor was disgruntled at the rise in prices that canceled out their wage gains. Both employers and labor applied the forty-hour week in such a manner that plants were shut down for two days a week instead of operating in shifts, as the law had intended. Nothing could check the flight of gold from the country. Industrial production hardly rose; even in 1938, when it had shown substantial recovery in other countries, it was only 5 percent higher in France than at the depth of the depression. The Communists attacked the Blum government for refusing aid to the hard-pressed Spanish Popular Front government across the Pyrenees; Blum, following the lead of Britain and fearing involvement, resisted. In 1937, after a year in office, the Blum government was overthrown by the Senate, which refused to grant it emergency financial powers. The Popular Front coalition rapidly disintegrated. By mid-1938 the Radical Socialists had abandoned their allies on the left, and under Édouard Daladier formed a conservative ministry, whose attention was increasingly occupied by the international crisis. Little remained of the Popular Front, or indeed of the strength of labor, which declined rapidly and exhausted itself further by an unsuccessful general strike in 1938 in protest against nullification of the forty-hour week. For the French worker, 1936 had gone the way of other "great years"; the comfortable classes had been thrown into panic by the social turmoil; internal division and class hatreds had grown sharper. Yet the French democracy, the Third Republic itself, had been successfully preserved and its domestic enemies repulsed, at least for a time.

Western Europe and the Depression

Britain and France, and indeed all western Europe, Europe's "inner zone," never fully recovered from the Great Depression before the Second World War came. When economic expansion later resumed after the war, the interwar years seemed like a deep trough in Europe's economic history. Western Europe barely maintained its old inherited equipment in the depression and was unable to utilize even its existing machinery to capacity. Moreover, as the events of 1929 had clearly shown, Europe's economic dependence on the United States was pronounced, and the U.S.S.R. was becoming an industrial giant. The economic destiny of Europeans in the 1930s was very much in doubt.

There were other signs of decline. The birth rate in western Europe in the 1930s declined to its lowest recorded levels as young people postponed marriage and married people limited the size of their families because of economic and psychological stresses. Birth rates did not run significantly higher than death rates, the population stagnating and growing older. There was a scarcity of men of vigorous middle age because of the casualties of the First World War. Politically neither British nor French democratic political leaders were able to cope successfully with the economic dilemmas of the depression era. Nor could the Socialists, who found neither Marxian economics nor class struggle ideas helpful but who failed to renew or reinvigorate their doctrines in any significant way.

102. ITALIAN FASCISM

Though they shade into each other imperceptibly, it is well to distinguish dictatorship from totalitarianism. Dictatorship, an old phenomenon in history, has commonly been regarded as a mere expedient, designed for emergencies and believed to be temporary; at most, it is a theory of government. Totalitarianism, as it arose after the World War, was not merely a theory of government but a theory of life and of human nature. It claimed to be no expedient but a permanent form of society and civilization, and so far as it appealed to emergency for justification, it regarded life itself as an everlasting emergency. Let us first review the pertinent events in Italy and Germany, return next to the general ideas of totalitarianism, and then, in the following chapter, trace the crises that in 1939 again led to a world war.

The belief widely held in the 1920s that democracy was generally advancing was not deeply disturbed by the failure of Russia or Turkey or China to develop effective parliaments or liberal institutions. These were backward countries, in the throes of revolution; some day, when conditions quieted down, it could be supposed, they would move forward to democracy as known in the West. The first jarring exception to the apparent victory of democracy was furnished by Italy, a country that was an integral part of civilized Europe, one that since 1861 had accepted parliamentary liberalism, but where, as early as 1922, Benito Mussolini seized control of the government and proclaimed *Fascismo*.

Mussolini, born in 1883, the son of a blacksmith, was a fiery and pugnacious character, who before the war had followed the career of professional revolutionary, left-wing socialist, and radical journalist. He had read and digested such works as Sorel's *Reflections on Violence* and Nietzsche's writings.[6] During the war he turned intensely nationalist, clamored for intervention on the side of the Allies, and demanded the conquest from Austria of *Italia irredenta*, the "unredeemed" Italian lands to the north and across the Adriatic. In the war he rose to the rank of corporal. In March 1919 he organized, mainly from demobilized and restless ex-soldiers, his first fighting band, or *fascio di combattimento*. *Fascio* meant a bunch or bundle, as of sticks; it called to mind the Latin *fasces*, or bundles of rods, carried by the lictors in ancient Rome as a symbol of state power—for Mussolini loved to conjure up ancient glories.

In 1919 Italian glories were dim. Italy had entered the war on the side of the Allies quite frankly for territorial and colonial spoils; the secret treaty of London in 1915 promised the Italians certain Austrian lands and a share in German and Turkish possessions. During the war Italian arms did not especially shine; Italian troops were routed at Caporetto in 1917. Yet Italy lost over 600,000 lives in the war, and the Italian delegates came to the peace conference confident that their sacrifices would be recognized and their territorial aspirations satisfied. They were rapidly disappointed. Wilson refused to honor the provisions of the London secret treaty and other demands of the Italians. Britain and France displayed no eagerness to side with Italy. The Italians received some of the Austrian territories promised to them, but they were given no part of the former German or Turkish possessions as mandates.

After the war Italy, like other countries, suffered from the burden of wartime debt and from acute postwar depression and unemployment. Social unrest spread. In the countryside land seizures took place, not in any significant proportions but enough to spread concern among landowners; tenant farmers refused to pay rents; peasants burned crops and destroyed livestock. In the cities great strikes broke out in heavy industry and in transportation. Some of the strikes turned into sit-down strikes, the workers refusing to leave the plants; demands were raised even for worker control of the factories. Moderate socialist and labor leaders disavowed all such extremism, but left-wing socialists who, as elsewhere, had turned communist and joined the Third International, fanned the existing discontents. Meanwhile, armed bands of young men, most prominent of whom were the Blackshirts or Fascists, brawled with Communists and ordinary workers in the streets. By the late summer of 1920 the strikes and the agrarian unrest had subsided, although violence in the streets persisted.

During the months of turmoil the government refrained from any bold action. The Italian parliamentary system in the prewar years had never functioned impressively nor commanded widespread esteem; now respect for parliament and

6 See pp. 589, 599.

the weak, shifting, coalition ministries sank even lower. In 1919 the first postwar election had been held, under a law that added proportional representation to the universal male suffrage introduced in 1913. The Socialists and a new Catholic Popular, or Christian Socialist, party made an impressive showing. In 1921, in the wake of the postwar disturbances, new elections were held. Liberals and democrats, moderate socialists, and the Catholic Popular party were all returned in large numbers. Mussolini's Fascist movement won 35 of the 500-odd seats. Despite this less than impressive showing (the best ever made by the Fascists in a totally free election), the Fascist ranks had been swelling, in the backwash, as it were, of the postwar unrest. Although the social agitation died down, burning itself out on its own, and there had never been any real threat of a Soviet-style revolution, the propertied classes went through a great fright; they found comfort in the Fascist movement and were willing to lend it financial support.

Mussolini and the Fascists had at first gone along with the radical tide; they had not disapproved the factory seizures; they had inveighed against plutocracy and war profiteers and called for a high levy on capital and profits. But Mussolini, never one to sacrifice opportunity for principles or doctrine, soon came forward with his Fascists as the upholders of national law and order, and hence property; he pledged battle "against the forces dissolving victory and nation." The propertied interests gave financial aid to the self-styled bulwark against Bolshevism; patriots and nationalists of all classes rallied to it; and the lower middle class, pinched by economic inflation and, as elsewhere, unable to find protection or solace in labor unions or socialist movements, joined too. The black-shirted upholders of national order meanwhile proceeded methodically to administer beatings (and doses of castor oil) to Communists and alleged Communists, to Socialists and Christian Socialists, and to ordinary persons who did not support them; nor did they refrain from arson and murder. Vigilante squadrons, the *squadristi*, broke up strikes, demolished labor union headquarters, and drove from office duly elected Socialist and Communist mayors and town officials. Mussolini reinforced his claim as paladin of law, authority, and order by declaring his loyalty to king and church; a few years earlier he had been a rabid republican and anticlerical.

In October 1922 the "March on Rome" took place. The Blackshirts mobilized for a threatened coup and began to converge from various directions on the capital; Mussolini remained at a safe distance in Milan. The liberal-democratic coalition cabinet had viewed the events of the past two years with disapproval but at the same time with the undeniable satisfaction that the Blackshirts were serving something of a useful national purpose by suppressing trouble-makers on the left. Now they made belated but ineffectual gestures to save the situation by an effort to have martial law declared; the king refused to approve. The cabinet resigned and Mussolini was named premier. It was all quite legal, or almost so. Indeed Italy was still in form a constitutional and parliamentary government. Mussolini headed only a coalition ministry and received from parliament no more than a year's grant of full emergency powers to restore order and introduce reforms.

But soon it was clear in whose hands power rested. Before the expiration of his emergency powers Mussolini forced through parliament a law providing that any party securing the largest number of votes in an election should automatically receive two-thirds of the seats in the legislature. This was Mussolini's solution to the instability of coalitions and blocs in parliamentary governments like those of Italy and France (and indeed of most other Continental democracies), where a single party hardly ever enjoyed a majority. The two-thirds law was not even necessary. In the 1924 elections, although seven opposition slates appeared, the Fascists received well over three-fifths of the total vote, aided by government control of the electoral machinery and use of the *squadristi*.

Within a few years after 1924 Mussolini reduced the Italian parliament to a nonentity, curtailed universal male suffrage, put the press under censorship, destroyed the labor unions, deprived labor of the right to strike, and abolished all other political parties. A secret police was established and special tribunals set up to try opponents of the regime; a new official Fascist militia replaced the *squadristi*—it continued to employ many of the old methods.

Fascism in the 1920s was an innovation which the rest of the world was slow to understand. In 1924 (when dissenters were still allowed in the parliament) the Socialist deputy Matteotti publicly exposed hundreds of cases of armed Fascist violence, and of fraud and chicanery in elections. He was soon murdered by Fascists. For a government in civilized Europe to dispose of its critics by assassination was something of a novelty. Mussolini strutted, stuck out his jaw, and glared ferociously; he jumped through flaming hoops to show his virility and had his chief subordinates do likewise; to the outside world this seemed an odd way of demonstrating fitness for public office. He denounced democracy as historically outmoded and declared that it accentuated class struggle, split people into countless minority parties, and led to selfishness, futility, evasion, and empty talk. In place of democracy he preached the need of vigorous action, under a strong leader; he himself took the title of Leader, or *Duce*. He denounced liberalism, free trade, laissez faire, and capitalism, along with Marxism, materialism, socialism, and class consciousness, which he said were the evil offspring of liberal and capitalistic society. In their place he preached national solidarity and state management of economic affairs, under the same Leader's farseeing and audacious vision. And in fact Mussolini seemed to bring a kind of efficiency to easygoing Italy; as the saying went, at least he made the trains run on time.

Mussolini introduced, at least in theory, the syndical, or corporative state. This had been discussed in both left- and right-wing circles for many years. Left-wing syndicalism, especially before the First World War, looked to revolutionary labor unions to expropriate the owners of industry and then to assume the direction of political and economic life. A more conservative syndicalism was endorsed and encouraged by the Catholic church, with which, as has been noted in a previous chapter, Mussolini made his peace with the signing of the Lateran accord in 1929.[7] The conservative type looked nostalgically toward a revival of the medieval guilds, or "corporations," in which master and journeymen, employer and employees, had labored side by side in a supposedly golden age of social peace. The Fascist corporative system really resembled neither, because in it the hand of the state was writ large, something that none of the older corporative doctrines had anticipated. It went through a number of complicated stages, but as it finally emerged in the 1930s, it provided for the division of all economic life into twenty-two major areas, for each of which a "corporation" was established. In each corporation representatives of the Fascist-organized labor groups, the employers,

[7] See p. 594.

and the government determined working conditions, wages, prices, and industrial policies; and in a national council these representatives were supposed jointly to devise plans for Italy's economic self-sufficiency. In each case the role of government was decisive and the whole structure was under the jurisdiction of the minister of corporations. As a final step, these corporative economic chambers were integrated into the government proper so that in 1938 the old Chamber of Deputies was superseded by a Chamber of Fasces and Corporations representing the corporations and the Fascist party, its members selected by the government and not subject to popular ratification.

None of this was democratic, but this was an improvement over democracy, the Fascists asserted. A legislature in an advanced economic society, they said, should be an economic parliament; it should represent not political parties and geographical constituencies but economic occupations. Organization along such lines would do away with the anarchy and class conflict engendered by free capitalism, which only sap the strength of the national state. Real authority in any event rested with the government—the Head of the Government, who settled most matters by decree. In point of fact, social unrest and class conflict were "ended," not by the corporative system as such, but by the prohibition of strikes and lockouts and the abolition of independent labor unions. The corporative system represented the most extreme form of state control over economic life within a framework of private enterprise and a relatively capitalistic economy, that is, one in which ownership continued to rest in private hands. It was the Fascist answer to Western-style democracy and to Soviet proletarian dictatorship. Fascism, said Mussolini, is the "dictatorship of the state over many classes cooperating."

When the depression struck, none of Italy's economic controls availed very much. Mussolini was eager to lay upon the world depression the blame for Italy's continuing economic ills. He turned to a vigorous program of public works and to increasing economic self-sufficiency. A "battle of wheat" was launched as a campaign to increase food production; progress was made in reclaiming swamp areas in central Italy and in developing hydroelectric power as a substitute for the coal that Italy lacked. Throughout the Fascist era no fundamental reform took place in the position of the peasants. The existing structure of society, which in Italy meant social extremes of wealth and poverty, remained unaltered. Fascism failed to provide either the economic security or the material well-being for which it had demanded the sacrifice of individual freedom. But it undeniably substituted a widespread psychological exhilaration, a feeling that Italy was undergoing a heroic national revival; and after 1935 to support that feeling Mussolini turned increasingly to military and imperialist adventures.

Fascism came to be regarded in other countries as a possible alternative to democratic or parliamentary government, as an actual corrective to troubles whose reality no one could deny. All communists hated it, and so did all socialists, labor leaders, moderate leftists, and idealistic liberals; wealthier or established people, because of fear of Bolshevism, made more allowances in its favor. In east-European countries, often highly nationalistic, or influenced by disgruntled landowners, or simply unused to settling questions by majority vote, Fascism made a considerable appeal. In the Latin countries, in Spain, Portugal, and France, Mussolini's corporative state found champions and admirers. Sometimes, in Europe and elsewhere, intellectuals spun refined, respectable theories about the new order of discipline and authority, forgetting how Mussolini himself with unusual candor had written, "Fascism was not the nursling of a doctrine worked out beforehand with detailed elaboration; it was born of the need for action."

103. TOTALITARIANISM: GERMANY'S THIRD REICH

The Rise of Adolf Hitler

It was in Germany that Mussolini found his aptest pupil. Born in Austria in 1889, Adolf Hitler was too young to have done much before the war. He was not an intellectual, like the prewar journalist Mussolini. He was never a socialist, but he fell into a restless and somewhat ignorant type of radicalism. Son of a government employee, orphaned at an early age, he came at nineteen to the great metropolis of Vienna, without friends, money, or means of making a living, a good example of uprooted humanity that the preceding half-century had thrown pell-mell into huge industrial cities. The young Hitler did not like what he saw in Vienna: neither the trappings of the Habsburg court, nor the noblemen of eastern Europe who rode by in their carriages, nor the mixed nationalities of the Danubian empire, nor the Vienna worker's attachment to international Marxism, nor above all the Jews, who thanks to a century of liberal influences had become assimilated to the German culture and now occupied many distinguished positions in business, law, medicine, and journalism in the city. He became exceedingly race conscious, like many others in many countries at the time;[8] the youthful Hitler took a special satisfaction in thinking of himself as a pure German of the good old German stock. He became violently anti-Semitic, and he also disliked aristocracy, capitalism, Marxism, cosmopolitanism, internationalism, and "hybridization."

His aversion for Austria led him to move to Munich, in the south German state of Bavaria, in 1913. Here he followed no particular trade but managed to sell a few watercolors. In the war he served in the German army. Like Mussolini, he rose no further than corporal. For Hitler, as for Mussolini, and for countless others, the war was a thrilling, noble, and liberating experience. The average man, in modern society, led a pretty dull existence. Peace, for many, was a drab routine from which war was an exciting emancipation. Human atoms, floating in an impersonal and unfriendly world, they were stirred by the nationalism that the war aroused into a sense of belonging to, believing in, fighting for something greater than themselves, but which was yet their own. When peace returned, they felt a moral letdown.

After the war the demobilized Hitler, with no future, and no place in society to which to return, drifted back to Munich. Bavaria in 1919 was a main focus of the Communist offensive in central Europe; a Bavarian Soviet Republic even existed for about three weeks until crushed by the predominantly Social Democratic German federal government. But the Communist threat made Bavaria a busy center of all kinds of counterrevolutionary agitation—anticommunist, antisocialist, antirepublican, and antidemocratic. A transposition in fact occurred after the World War, by which southern Germany, always in the past more liberal than the north, became the seat of a disgruntled illiberalism, while Prussia became the

---

[8] See pp. 586, 595–596, 609, 656, 747.

main pillar of German democracy because of the large working-class population in Berlin and the Ruhr. Bavaria in particular swarmed with secret societies led by discontented army officers or others who fitted with difficulty into the new regime. One tiny group pretentiously called itself the German Workers' party, and of this "party," in 1919, Adolf Hitler became one of the early members. In 1920 it renamed itself the National Socialist German Workers' party. Thus were born the Nazis, so called from the German way of pronouncing the first two syllables of *National.*

In earlier pages we have noted the beginnings of the Weimar Republic and the burdens it was compelled to bear from the start—the Versailles peace, reparations, the catastrophic inflation of 1923.[9] Something has been said also of the failure of the republicans to inaugurate the kind of deep social changes that might have democratized the political and social structure of German society and thereby strengthened republican forces. For five years after the war, violence remained sporadic in Germany. Communist agitation continued; but more dangerous, because they attracted more sympathy among the Germans, were the maneuvers of monarchist and antirepublican organizations, which maintained armed bands and threatened uprisings like the Kapp *Putsch* of 1920.[10] (One such private "army" was the Brownshirts or Storm Troopers maintained by the Nazis.) Such bands even resorted to assassination. Thus Walter Rathenau was murdered in 1922; he had organized German production during the war, and in 1922 he was foreign minister, but he had democratic and internationalist inclinations—and was a Jew. Another victim was Matthias Erzberger, a leading moderate politician of the Catholic Center party—he had helped "betray" the army by signing the armistice.

In 1923, when reparations payments were not forthcoming, the French army occupied the Ruhr. A clamor of national indignation swept over Germany. Hitler and the National Socialists, who since 1919 had obtained a considerable following, denounced the Weimar government for shameful submission to the French. They judged the moment opportune for seizing power, and at the end of 1923, in imitation of Mussolini's march on Rome the year before, the Brownshirts staged the "beer hall *Putsch*" in Munich. Hitler jumped on the platform, fired a revolver at the ceiling, and shouted that the "national revolution has broken out." But the police suppressed the disturbance, and Hitler was sentenced to five years in prison. He was released in less than a year; the Weimar democracy dealt mildly with its enemies. In prison he wrote his book, *Mein Kampf* (*My Struggle*), a turbid stream of personal recollection, racism, nationalism, collectivism, theories of history, Jew baiting, and political comment. The former corporal was not alone in his ideas; no less a person than General Ludendorff, who had distinguished himself in the war,[11] and after the war became one of the most grotesquely unbalanced of the old officer class, gave his warm support to Hitler and even took part in tho beer hall *Putsch.*

Beginning in 1924, with the French out of the Ruhr, reparations adjusted, a new and stable currency adopted, and loans from foreign countries, mainly America, Germany began to enjoy an amazing economic revival. National Socialism lost its appeal, the party lost members, Hitler was regarded as a charlatan

9 See pp. 744–745.
10 See p. 742.
11 See pp. 674–676.

and his followers as a lunatic fringe. All seemed quiet. Then came the Great Depression in 1929. Adolf Hitler, who might have faded out of history, was made by the circumstances attending the depression in Germany into a figure of Napoleonic proportions.

No country suffered more than Germany from the world-wide economic collapse. Foreign loans abruptly ceased or were recalled. Factories ground to a halt. There were 6 million unemployed. The middle class had not really recovered from the great inflation of 1923;[12] when struck again, after so brief a respite, they lost all faith in the economic system and in its future. The Communist vote steadily mounted; the great middling masses, who saw in communism their own death warrant, and who are extremely numerous in any highly developed society, looked about desperately for someone to save them from Bolshevism. The depression also stirred up the universal German loathing for the Treaty of Versailles. Many Germans explained the ruin of Germany by the postwar treatment it had received from the Allies—the constriction of its frontiers, the loss of its colonies, markets, shipping, and foreign investments, the colossal demand for reparations, the occupation of the Ruhr, the inflation, and much else.

Any people in such a trap would have been bewildered and resentful. But the way out chosen by the Germans was perhaps a product of deeper attitudes formed by German experience in the past centuries. Democracy—the agreement to obtain and accept majority verdicts, to discuss and compromise, to adjust conflicting interests without wholly satisfying or wholly crushing either side—was hard enough to maintain in any country in a true crisis. In Germany democracy was itself an innovation, which had yet to prove its value, which could easily be called un-German, an artificial and imported doctrine, or even a foreign system foisted upon Germany by the victors in the late war.

Hitler inflamed all such feelings by his propaganda. He denounced the Treaty of Versailles as a national humiliation. He denounced the Weimar democracy for producing class struggle, division, weakness, and wordy futility. He called for "true" democracy in a vast and vital stirring of the people, or *Volk*, behind a Leader who was a man of action. He declared that Germans, pure Germans, must rely only on themselves. He inveighed against Marxists, Bolsheviks, communists, and socialists, throwing them all together in a deliberate beclouding of the issues; but he claimed to favor the right kind of socialism for the little man, i.e., the doctrine of the National Socialist German Workers' party. He ranted against unearned incomes, war profits, the power of the great trusts and chain stores, land speculators, interest slavery, and unfair taxes. Above all, he denounced the Jews. Jews, like others, were found in all political camps. To the left, Jewish capitalists were anathema. To the right, Jewish revolutionaries were a horror. In anti-Semitism Hitler found a lowest common denominator upon which to appeal to all parties and classes. At the same time the Jews were a small minority (only 600,000 in all Germany), so that in an age of mass politics it was safe enough to attack them.

In the election of 1930 the Nazis won 107 seats in the Reichstag; in 1928 they had won only 12; their popular vote went up from 800,000 to 6.5 million. The Communist representation rose from 54 to 77. By July 1932 the Nazis more than doubled their popular vote, won 230 seats, and were now by far the largest single

---

[12] See pp. 744–745.

party though because of the multiplicity of parties they fell well short of a majority. In another election, in November 1932, the Nazis, though still well out in front, showed some loss of strength, losing 2 million votes, and dropping to 196 seats. The Communist vote had risen progressively to a peak of 100 in November 1932.

After the relative setback of November 1932 Hitler feared that his moment was passing. But certain conservative, nationalist, and antirepublican elements—old aristocrats, Junker landowners, army officers, Rhineland steel magnates, and other industrialists—had conceived the idea that Hitler could be useful to them. From such sources came a portion of Nazi funds. This group of big men, mainly of the small Nationalist party, imagined that they would be able to control Hitler and hence control the wave of mass discontent of which in such large measure he had made himself the leader; they were little disturbed by his anticapitalist program.

After Bruening's resignation in June 1932, Franz von Papen headed a Nationalist cabinet with the backing of the influential army leader, General Kurt von Schleicher. In December 1932 Schleicher forced Papen's downfall and succeeded him. When he, too, was compelled to resign a month later, both men, intriguing separately, prevailed upon President Hindenburg to name Hitler chancellor of a coalition cabinet. On January 30, 1933, by entirely legal means, Adolf Hitler became chancellor of the German Republic; other positions in the new cabinet were occupied by the Nationalists, with whom the Nazis were to share power. But to share power was not their aim. Hitler called for another election. A week before election day the Reichstag building caught fire. The Nazis, without any real evidence, blamed it on the Communists. They raised up a terrific Red scare, suspended freedom of speech and press, and set loose the Brownshirts to bully the voters. Even so, in the election, the Nazis won only 44 percent of the vote; with their Nationalist allies, they had 52 percent. Hitler, trumpeting a national emergency, was voted dictatorial powers by a pliant Reichstag from which the Communist deputies had been excluded. The Nazi revolution now began.

The Nazi State

Hitler called his new order the Third Reich. He declared that, following on the First Reich, or Holy Roman Empire, and the Second Reich, or empire founded by Bismarck, the Third Reich carried on the process of true German history, of which, he said, it was the organic outgrowth and natural culmination. The Third Reich, he prophesied, would last a thousand years.

Like Mussolini, Hitler took the title of Leader, or, in German, the *Führer*. He claimed to represent the absolute sovereignty of the German people. Jews were considered un-German. Democracy, parliamentarianism, and liberalism were stigmatized as "Western" and together with communism labeled as "Jewish." The new "racial science," whose high priest was Alfred Rosenberg, classified Jews as non-Aryan[13] and included as Jewish anyone who had one Jewish grandparent. The Nuremberg laws of 1935 deprived Jews of all citizenship rights and forbade intermarriage between Jews and non-Jews. Jews were beaten up, hounded, driven from public office, ruined in private business, fined as a community, put to death, or allowed to flee the country after being stripped of all their possessions.

[13] See note p. 5.

The anti-Semitism of some fanatics descended to positive bestiality; it fore-shadowed the wartime physical extermination of millions of German and east-European Jewry.

The new order was thought of as absolutely solid, or monolithic, like one huge single slab of rock in which no particle had any separate structure. Germany ceased to be federal; all the old states such as Prussia and Bavaria were abolished, so that the historic process of German unification was carried forward. All political parties except the National Socialists were destroyed. The Nazi party was itself violently purged on the night of June 30, 1934, when many of the old Brownshirt leaders, those who represented the more social revolutionary wing of the movement, were accused of plotting against Hitler and were summarily shot. A secret political police, the Gestapo (*Geheime Staatspolizei*), together with People's Courts, and a system of permanent concentration camps in which thousands were detained without trial or sentence, suppressed all ideas at variance with the Leader's. Law itself was defined as the will of the German people operating in the interests of the Nazi state. Churches, both Protestant and Catholic, were "coordinated" with the new regime; their clergy were forbidden to criticize its activities, international religious ties were discouraged, and efforts were made to keep children out of religious schools. The government encouraged anti-Christian pagan movements, in worship of the old Teutonic gods, but nothing was sponsored so much as worship of Nazism and its *Führer*. A Nazi Youth Movement, and schools and universities, indoctrinated the rising generation in the new concepts. The total, all-encompassing repression thwarted the efforts of a few dedicated men to develop a broad resistance movement.

Labor unions also were "coordinated"; they were replaced by a National Labor Front. Strikes were forbidden. Under the "leadership principle" employers were set up as small-scale *Führers* in their factories and industries and given extensive control, subject to close government supervision. An extensive public works program was launched, reforestation and swamp drainage projects were organized, housing and superhighways were built. A vast rearmament program absorbed the unemployed and within a short time unemployment had significantly declined. Even under Nazi statistics labor's share in the national income was reduced, but workers had jobs; and an organization called Strength Through Joy attended to the needs of people with small incomes, providing entertainment, vacations, and travel for many who could never otherwise afford them.

The government assumed increasing controls over industry, while leaving ownership in private hands. In 1936 it adopted a Four-Year Plan of economic development. All countries after the Great Depression tended to economic nationalism, but Nazi Germany set up the goal of autarchy and self-sufficiency—absolute independence from foreign trade. German chemists developed artificial rubber, plastics, synthetic textiles, and many other substitute products to enable the country to do without raw materials imported from overseas. Germany took advantage of its position as the chief market on which east Europeans were dependent. Mixing political threats with ordinary business, the Nazis bartered for Polish wheat, Hungarian lumber, or Rumanian oil, often giving in return such articles as it was convenient for Germany to dispose of, rather than those that the east Europeans wanted. For Europe as a whole one of the basic economic problems, especially after the World War, was that while the Continent was economically a unit dependent on exchange between diverse regions, politically it was cut to pieces by tariff restrictions, currency differences, and hothouse industries artificially nurtured by nationalist ambition. The Nazis claimed to have a solution for this problem in a network of bilateral trade agreements assuring all neighboring peoples an outlet for their products. But it was a solution in which Germans were to be the most industrial, most advanced, most powerful, and most wealthy, and other Europeans relegated to permanently inferior status. And what could not be accomplished under trade agreements and economic penetration could be accomplished by conquest and war. Within a few years after 1933, although the regime had its share of confusion and personal rivalries, the Nazi revolution had turned Germany into a huge disciplined war machine, its internal foes liquidated or silenced, its mesmerized masses roaring their approval in giant demonstrations, ready to follow the Führer in storming new Valkyrian heights. "Today Germany," went an ominous Nazi phrase, "tomorrow the whole world."

Totalitarianism: Some Origins and Consequences

Totalitarianism was a many-sided thing. It had appeared first with the Bolshevik Revolution, for in the denial of individual liberty the Soviet regime did not differ from the most extreme anti-Soviet or fascist totalitarianism as manifested in Germany. There were at first important differences in principle. Theoretically, the proletarian dictatorship was temporary; it did not glorify the individual Leader-Hero; and it was not nationalistic, for it rested on a principle of world-wide class struggle in all nations alike. It adopted a democratic-sounding constitution and paid at least lip service to the idea of a bill of rights. Its constitution officially condemned racism, and it did not deliberately and consciously cultivate an ethics of war and violence. But as time passed, Soviet totalitarianism became harder to distinguish from others. The Soviet dictatorship and one-party state seemed as permanent as any political system; the hollowness of the constitution and bill of rights became more apparent; a cult developed around the person of Stalin; and the emphasis became more nationalistic, falling less on the workers of the world and more on the glories of the Soviet Fatherland.

Totalitarianism, as distinct from mere dictatorship, though it appeared rather suddenly after the First World War, was no historic freak. It was an outgrowth of a good deal of development in the past. The state was an institution that had continuously acquired new powers ever since the Middle Ages; step by step, since feudal times, it had assumed jurisdiction over law courts and men at arms, imposed taxes, regulated churches, guided economic policy, operated school systems, and devised schemes of public welfare. The First World War had continued and advanced the process.[14] The twentieth-century totalitarian state, mammoth and monolithic, claiming an absolute domination over every department of life, now carried this old development of state sovereignty to a new extreme. For centuries, for example, the state had clashed with the church; from Philip the Fair of France in 1303, down through Henry VIII, the enlightened despots, the French Revolutionaries, Napoleon, Mazzini, Bismarck—the list was a long one of those who had come into conflict with the Christian churches. The twentieth-century dictators did the same. In addition, however, they were in most

14 See pp. 677–679.

cases not merely anticlerical but explicitly anti-Christian, offering, or rather imposing, a "total" philosophy of life.

This new philosophy drew heavily upon a historic nationalism which it greatly exaggerated. It derived in part from the organic theory of society, which held that society (or the nation or state) was a kind of living organism within which the individual person was but a single cell. The individual, in this theory, had no independent existence; he received life itself, and all his ideas, from the society, people, nation, or culture into which he was born and by which he was nurtured. In Marxism, the absolute subordination of the individual to his class came to much the same thing. The individual was a microscopic cell, meaningless outside the social body. He was but clay to be molded by the imprint of his group. It made little sense, given such theories, to speak of the individual's "reason" or "freedom," or to allow individuals to have their own opinions (which were formed for them by environment), or to count up individual opinions to obtain a merely numerical majority. Valid ideas were those of the group as a whole, of the people or nation (or, in Marxism, the class) as a solid block. Even science was a product of specific societies: there was a "Nazi science" which was bound to differ in its conclusions from democratic, bourgeois, Western, or "Jewish" science; and for the Soviets there was a Soviet science, consistent with dialectical materialism, and better equipped to see the truth than the decadent bourgeois, capitalistic, or "fascist" science of the non-Soviet world. All art, too—music, painting, poetry, fiction, architecture, sculpture—was good art insofar as it expressed the society or nationality in which it grew.

The avowed philosophy of totalitarian regimes (like much modern thought) was basically subjective. Whether an idea was held to be true depended on whose idea it was. Ideas of truth, or beauty, or right were not supposed to correspond to any outer or objective reality; they had only to correspond to the inner nature, interests, or point of view of the people, nation, society, or class that entertained such ideas. The older concepts of reason, natural law, natural right, and the ultimate alikeness of all mankind, or of a common path of all mankind in one course of progress, disappeared.[15]

The totalitarian regimes did not simply declare, as a dry finding of social science, that peoples' ideas were shaped by environment. They set about shaping them actively. Propaganda became a principal branch of government. Propaganda was hardly new, but in the past, and still in the democratic countries, it had been a piecemeal affair, urging the public to accept this or that political party, or to buy this or that brand of coffee. Now, like all else, it became "total." Propaganda was monopolized by the state, and it demanded faith in a whole view of life and in every detail of this coordinated whole. Formerly the control of books and newspapers had been mainly negative; under Napoleon or Metternich, for example, censors had forbidden statements on particular subjects, events, or persons. Now, in totalitarian countries, control of the press became frighteningly positive. The government manufactured thought. It manipulated opinion. It rewrote history. Writers were required to present whole ideologies, and books, newspapers, magazines, and the radio diffused an endless and overwhelming cloud of words. Loudspeakers blared in the streets, gigantic blown-up photographs of the Leader looked down in public places. The propaganda experts were

[15] See pp. 291, 294, 296, 303–306, 542–543, 596–597.

sometimes fanatics, but often they were cynics like Dr. Goebbels in Germany, too intelligent to be duped by the rubbish with which they duped their country.

The very idea of truth evaporated. No norm of human utterance remained except political expediency—the wishes and self-interest of the men in power. No one could learn anything except what the government wanted him to know. No one could escape the omnipresent official doctrine, the insidious penetration of the very recesses of his mind by ideas planted by outsiders for their own purposes. People came to accept, and even to believe, the most extravagant statements when they were endlessly repeated, year after year. Barred from all independent sources of information, having no means by which any official allegation could be tested, the peoples of totalitarian countries became increasingly in fact, and not merely in sociological theory, incapable of the use of reason.

Racism, more characteristic of Nazi Germany than of totalitarianism in general, was a further exaggeration, or degradation, of older ideas of nationalism and national solidarity. It defined the nation in a tribal sense, as a biological entity, a group of persons possessing the same physical ancestry and the same or similar physical characteristics. Anti-Semitism was the most venomous form of racism in Europe. While a latent hostility to Jews had always been present in the Christian world, modern anti-Semitism had little to do with Christianity. It arose in part from the fact that, in the nineteenth century, with the general removal of religious disabilities, the Jews entered into general society and many of them achieved positions of prominence, and nowhere more so than in Germany, so that from the point of view of any individual non-Jew they could be represented as dangerous competitors in business or the professions. But most of all, anti-Semitism was inflamed by propagandists who wished people to feel their supposed racial purity more keenly or to forget the deeper problems of society, including poverty, unemployment, and economic inequities.

For totalitarianism was an escape from the realities of class conflict. It was a way of pretending that differences between rich and poor were of minor importance. Typically, a totalitarian regime came into power by stirring up class fears, then remained in power, and represented itself as indispensable, by declaring that it had settled the class problem. Thus Mussolini, Hitler, and certain lesser dictators, before seizing office, pointed alarmingly to the dark menace of Bolshevism; and, once in power, declared that all classes stood shoulder to shoulder in slablike solidarity behind the Leader. Nor were events in Russia altogether different. The Bolsheviks in 1917, armed with the ideas of Karl Marx, aroused the workers against capitalists, landlords, middle-class people, and rich peasants; then, once in power, and after extensive liquidations, they declared that the classless society had arrived, that no true social classes any longer existed, and that all Soviet citizens stood solidly behind a regime from which, they said, all good citizens benefited equally. Only the democracies admitted that they suffered from internal class problems, from maladjustments between rich and poor or between favored and unfavored groups in society.

The dictatorships blamed their troubles on forces outside the country. They accused dissatisfied persons of conspiring with foreigners or refugees—with being the tools of Trotskyism, imperialism, or international Jewry. Or they talked of the struggle between rich nations and poor nations, the "have" and the "have-not" countries, and thus transformed the problem of poverty into an international struggle. In the distinction between "have" and "have-not" countries there was, of course, more than a grain of truth; in more old-fashioned language some countries (in fact the European democracies, as well as the United States and the British dominions of the 1930s) had "progressed" farther than others. It is probable that any propaganda is more effective if partly true. But when the totalitarians blamed their troubles on other countries and transformed the conflict between "have" and "have-not" into a struggle between nations, they gave the impression that war might be a solution for social ills.

Violence, the acceptance and even glorification of violence, was indeed the characteristic most clearly distinguishing the totalitarian from the democratic systems. We have seen how a cult of violence, or belief that struggle was beneficial, had arisen before the First World War.[16] The war itself habituated people to violence and direct action. Lenin and his followers showed how a small group could seize the helm of state under revolutionary or chaotic conditions. Mussolini in 1922 taught the same lesson, with further refinements; for the Italy in which he seized power was not at war, and it was merely the threat or possibility of revolution, not revolution itself, that provided him with his opportunity. In the 1920s, for the first time since the seventeenth century, some of the most civilized parts of Europe, in time of peace, saw private armies marching about the country, bands of uniformed and organized ruffians, Blackshirts or Brownshirts, who manhandled, abused, and even killed law-abiding citizens with impunity. Nor would anyone in the 1920s have believed that, by the 1930s, Europe would see the reintroduction of torture.

The very ethics of totalitarianism was violent and neopagan. It borrowed from Nietzsche and other prewar theoreticians, who, safe and civilized, had declared that men should live dangerously, avoid the flabby weakness of too much thought, throw themselves with red-blooded vigor into a life of action. The new regimes all instituted youth movements. They appealed to a kind of juvenile idealism, in which young people believed that by joining some kind of squad, donning some kind of uniform, and getting into the fresh air they contributed to a great moral resurgence of their country. Young men were taught to value their bodies but not their minds, to be tough and hard, and to regard mass gymnastics as patriotic demonstrations. Young women were taught to breed large families without complaint, to be content in the kitchen, and to look with awe upon their virile mates. The body cult flourished while the mind decayed. Especially in National Socialism the ideal was to turn the German people into a race of splendid animals, pink-cheeked, Nordic, and upstanding. Contrariwise, euthanasia was adopted for the insane and was proposed for the aged. Later, in the Second World War, when the Nazis overran eastern Europe, they committed Jews to the gas chambers, destroying some 6 million human beings by the most scientific methods. Animals were animals; one bred the kind one wanted and killed the kind one did not.

The Spread of Dictatorship

The trend of dictatorship spread over Europe in the 1930s. By 1939 only ten out of twenty-seven European countries remained democratic, in the sense that different political parties honestly competed for office and that citizens within generous limits thought and acted as they pleased. They were Great Britain and

16 See pp. 598–599.

France; Holland, Belgium, and Switzerland; Czechoslovakia and Finland; and the three Scandinavian countries. The Soviet Union still exemplified the dictatorship of the proletariat, and all other European countries possessed more or less dictatorial regimes somewhat vaguely called, with more or less accuracy, "fascist."

The promise of the early 1920s that constitutional and democratic government would flourish was thwarted. The weakness or absence of a parliamentary or democratic tradition, low education and literacy standards, the hostility of reactionary elements, the fear of Bolshevism, and the dissatisfaction of existing national minorities, all coupled with economic strains, many resulting from the Great Depression, contributed to the collapse of the new representative institutions. Apart from the avowedly totalitarian or fascist regimes of Germany and Italy, the new dictatorships and authoritarian systems generally rested on a combination of personal and military power. To name but a few, this was true of Poland under Marshal Pilsudski and his successor, General Smigly-Rydz; Hungary under General Julius Gömbös, successor to Count Bethlen; Greece under General Metaxas; Spain (after a bloody civil war to be described), under General Franco; and Yugoslavia, Bulgaria, and Rumania under their respective kings. In Portugal, Salazar began a clerical-corporative dictatorship in 1932 that lasted for over four decades. In Austria, Dollfuss fused various right-wing political and military elements into a clerical-fascist "Christian" dictatorship which violently suppressed the Socialists and sought in vain with this dictatorship to counter the German threat; assassinated in July 1934, he was succeeded by Kurt von Schuschnigg, who headed a similar regime until the German annexation of Austria in 1938. In many respects the dictatorships of Latin America under a diversity of caudillos and military juntas, in both origin and character, resembled the European dictatorships.

The authoritarian regimes were alike in repressing individual liberties, banning opposition parties, and abolishing or nullifying parliamentary institutions. Many borrowed features of the corporative state, outlawing independent labor organizations and forbidding strikes; many, like Hungary, Rumania, and Poland, instituted anti-Semitic legislation. None went so far in the total coordination of all political, economic, intellectual, and biological activities in a revolutionary mass-based dictatorship as did Hitler's Third Reich.

The acceptance and glorification of violence, it has been noted, was the feature most clearly distinguishing the totalitarian from the democratic systems. War in the Nazi and Fascist ethics was a noble thing, and the love of peace a sign of decadence. (The Soviet regime, while by its own theory it regarded war with non-Soviet powers as inevitable some day, did not preach it as a positive moral good.) The exaltation of war and struggle, the need for maintaining national solidarity, the habit of blaming foreign countries for social troubles, together with the considerable armaments program in which the dictatorships engaged, plus the personal ambition and egotistical mania of individual dictators, made the decade of the 1930s a time not only of domestic reaction but of recurrent international crises, of which the last one led to war.

XX.
The
Second
World War

Peace in the abstract, the peace that is the mere absence of war, does not exist in international relations. Peace is never found apart from certain conditions; it means peaceable acceptance of given conditions, or peaceable and orderly transformation of conditions by negotiation and agreement. The conditions, in the 1930s, were basically those laid down by the Paris peace conference of 1919—the states recognized, the frontiers drawn, the terms agreed to, at the close of the First World War. In the 1930s neither Germany, Italy, Japan, nor the U.S.S.R. was content with these conditions; they were "revisionist" or dissatisfied powers; and the first three were willing to undertake war itself to make a change. Great Britain, France, and the United States were satisfied powers, expecting no benefit from change in the conditions; but on the other hand they had lost faith in the conditions and were unwilling to risk war for the sake of upholding them. They had made a treaty in 1919 which a dozen years later they were unwilling to enforce. They stood idly by, as long as they could, while the dissatisfied powers tore to pieces the states recognized, the frontiers drawn, and the terms agreed to at the Peace of Paris. From the Japanese invasion of Manchuria in 1931 to the outbreak of European war in 1939, force was used by those who wished to upset international order, but never by those who wished to maintain it.

Chapter Emblem: A clock stopped when the atomic bomb was dropped on Hiroshima, Japan, in 1945.

104. THE WEAKNESS OF THE DEMOCRACIES: AGAIN TO WAR

The Pacifism and Disunity of the West

While dictators stormed, the Western democracies were swayed by a profound pacifism, which may be defined as a somewhat doctrinaire insistence on peace regardless of consequences. Many people now believed, especially in England and the United States, that the First World War had been a mistake, that little or nothing had been gained by it, that they had been deluded by wartime propaganda, that wars were really started by armaments manufacturers, that Germany had not really caused the war of 1914, that the Treaty of Versailles was too hard on the Germans, that vigorous peoples like the Germans or Italians needed room for expansion, that democracy was after all not suited to all nations, that it took two to make a quarrel, and that there need be no war if one side resolutely refused to be provoked—a whole system of pacific and tolerant ideas in which there was perhaps the usual mixture of truth and misunderstanding.

The pacifism of the West had other roots, most evident in France. About 1.4 million Frenchmen had died in World War I; half of all French males between the ages of 20 and 32 in 1914 had been killed. To the French it was inconceivable that such a holocaust should be repeated. French strategy was therefore defensive and sparing of manpower. If war came, the French expected to fight it mainly in the elaborate fortifications, called the Maginot Line, which they built on their eastern frontier facing Germany, from the Swiss to the Belgian border; to its north the Ardennes forest was to be a barrier to any invader. Moreover, as we have seen during the depression France was torn by internal class conflict and by fascist and quasi-fascist agitation.[1] Many Frenchmen of the right, historically unsympathetic to the republic and seeing, or claiming to see, in such movements as the Popular Front the threat of social revolution, did not conceal their admiration for Mussolini or even for Hitler. Abandoning their traditional role as ardent nationalists, they would do nothing to oppose the dictators. On the other hand, many on the left looked with sympathy upon the Soviet Union. France was ideologically too divided in the 1930s to possess any firm foreign policy, and all elements took false comfort from the supposed impregnability of the French Chinese Wall.

A similar situation, in lesser degree, prevailed in Great Britain and the United States. The loss and bloodshed of the First World War were remembered. It was well known that another world war would be even more horrible; there was an unspeakable dread of the bombing of cities. Typical of the time was a resolution adopted by students at Oxford in 1933 that they would never take up arms for their country under any conditions; peace movements appeared among American college students too. The pull between left and right was felt in England and America. In the 1930s, when any international action seemed to favor either the U.S.S.R. on the one hand, or Hitler and Mussolini on the other, it was hard to establish any foreign policy on a firm basis of national unity. In Britain some members of the upper classes were overtly sympathetic to the fascist dictators, or at least saw in them a bulwark against communism. The government itself tried

1 See pp. 773–776.

to be noncommittal; it believed that some means of satisfying or appeasing the more "legitimate" demands of the dictators might be found. Neville Chamberlain, prime minister after 1937, became the principal architect of the appeasement policy.

The United States government, despite President Roosevelt's repeated denunciation of the aggressors, followed in practice a policy of rigid isolation. Neutrality legislation, enacted by a strong isolationist bloc in Congress in the years 1935 to 1937, forbade loans, export of munitions, and use of American shipping facilities to any belligerent once the president had recognized a state of war in a given area. It was then believed, by many, that the United States had been drawn into the First World War by such economic involvement. From this American neutrality legislation the aggressors of the 1930s were to derive great benefit, but not the victims of aggression.

As for the men who ruled the U.S.S.R., they were revisionist and dissatisfied in that they did not accept the new frontiers of eastern Europe nor the territorial losses incurred by Russia in the First World War. They resented the *cordon sanitaire* created in 1919 against the spread of Bolshevism, the ring of small states on their borders from Finland to Rumania, which were almost without exception vehemently anti-Soviet. They had no fondness for the international status quo nor had they abandoned their long-range revolutionary objectives. But, as Communists and as Russians, they were obsessed by fear of attack and invasion. Their Marxist doctrine taught the inherent hostility of the entire capitalist world; the intervention of the Western Allies in the Revolution and civil wars confirmed their Marxist theory. And long before the Bolshevik Revolution, in the days of Napoleon and earlier, the fertile Russian plains had tempted ambitious conquerors. Resentful and suspicious of the outside world, in the 1930s the men in the Kremlin were alarmed primarily by the signs of aggressive intentions in Germany. Hitler, in *Mein Kampf* and elsewhere, had declared that he meant to obliterate Bolshevism and subordinate large stretches of eastern Europe to Germany.

The Soviets became interested in collective security, in international action against aggression. In 1934 they joined the League of Nations. They instructed Communist parties to work with socialists and liberals in popular fronts.[2] They offered assistance in checking fascist aggressors, signing mutual assistance pacts with France and Czechoslovakia in 1935. But many people fled from the Soviet embrace with a shudder. They distrusted Soviet motives, or they were convinced that the purges and trials of the 1930s had left the Soviets weak and undependable as allies, or they felt that the fascist dictators might be diverted eastward against the Soviets and so spare the Western democracies. Here again, though the Russians were ostensibly willing, no effective coalition against aggression could be formed.

The March of Nazi and Fascist Aggression

Adolf Hitler perceived these weaknesses with uncanny genius. Determined to wreck the whole treaty system, he employed tactics of gradual encroachment that played on the hopes and fears of the democratic peoples. He inspired in them

[2] See p. 733.

alternating tremors of apprehension and sighs of relief. He would rage and rant, arouse the fear of war, take just a little, declare that it was all he wanted, let the former Allies naïvely hope that he was now satisfied and that peace was secure; then rage again, take a little more, and proceed through the same cycle.

Each year he precipitated some kind of emergency, and each time the French and British saw no alternative except to let him have his way. In 1933, soon after seizing power, he took Germany out of the League and out of the Disarmament Conference then taking place. He successfully wooed Poland, long France's ally, and in 1934 the two countries signed a nonaggression treaty. That same year the Nazis of Austria attempted a *Putsch,* assassinated the Austrian chancellor, Doll-fuss, and demanded the union of Austria with Germany. The Western powers did nothing. It was Mussolini who acted. Not desiring to see Germany installed at the Brenner Pass, he mobilized large Italian forces on the frontier; he thus discouraged Hitler from intervening openly in Austria and so preserved the independence of Austria for four more years. In January 1935 a plebiscite was conducted in the Saar by the League of Nations as stipulated under the Versailles treaty. Amidst intense Nazi agitation, the Saar voted for reunion with the Reich. Two months later, in March 1935, Hitler dramatically repudiated those clauses in the Versailles treaty intended to keep Germany disarmed; he now openly built up the German armed forces. France, England, and Italy protested at such arbitrary and one-sided denunciation of an international treaty but did nothing specifically about it. Indeed, Great Britain entered into a naval agreement with Germany, to the consternation of the French.

On March 7, 1936, using as his justification the new Franco-Soviet pact, Hitler repudiated the Locarno agreements[3] and reoccupied the Rhineland; i.e., he sent German troops into the German territory west of the Rhine, which by the Treaty of Versailles was supposed to be a demilitarized zone. There was talk in the French government of action, and at this time Hitler might have been checked, for German military strength was still weak and the German army was prepared to withdraw, or at least consult, at signs of resistance. But the French government was divided and unwilling to act without Britain; and the British would not risk war to keep German troops from occupying German soil. The next year, 1937, was a quiet one, but Nazi agitation flared up in Danzig, which the Treaty of Versailles had set up as a free city. In March 1938 German forces moved into Austria, and the union of Austria and Germany, the *Anschluss,* was at last consummated. In September 1938 came the turn of Czechoslovakia and the Munich crisis. To understand it we must first pick up other threads in the story.

Mussolini, too, had his ambitions and required sensational foreign triumphs to magnetize the Italian people. Since 1919 the Italians had been dissatisfied with the peace arrangements. They had received nothing of the former Turkish territories and former German colonies that had been liberally parceled out, as mandates, to Great Britain, France, Belgium, and Japan, and even to South Africa, Australia, and New Zealand.[4] They had never forgotten the humiliating defeat of Italian forces by Abyssinia at Adowa in 1896.[5] Ethiopia, as Abyssinia was now

---

3 See pp. 745–746.
4 See pp. 682–683, 688, 777.
5 See p. 625.

called, remained the only part of black Africa (with the exception of Liberia) that was still independent.

In 1935 Italy went to war with Ethiopia. The League of Nations, of which Ethiopia was a member, pronounced the Italian action an unwarranted aggression and imposed sanctions on Italy, by which members of the League were to refrain from selling Italy either arms or raw materials—oil was excepted. The British even gathered large naval forces in the Mediterranean in a show of strength. In France, however, there was considerable sympathy for Mussolini in important quarters, and in England there was the fear that if sanctions became too effective, by refusal of oil or by closure of the Suez Canal, Italy might be irritated into a general war. Mussolini was thus able to defeat Ethiopia in 1936 and to combine it with Italian Somaliland and Eritrea in an Italian East African empire. The Ethiopian Emperor Haile Selassie made futile pleas for further action at Geneva. The League of Nations again failed, as in the case of the occupation of Manchuria by Japan, to provide machinery for disciplinary action against a wayward Great Power.[6]

The Spanish Civil War, 1936–1939

Hardly had the Ethiopian crisis been disposed of, to the entire satisfaction of the aggressor, when an even more serious crisis broke out in Spain. In 1931, after a decade of political disturbance, a rather mild revolution had driven out Alfonso XIII, of the Bourbon family, and brought about the establishment of a democratic Spanish Republic. Old hostilities within the country came to a head. The new republican government undertook a program of social and economic reform. To combat the ancient entrenched power of the church, anticlerical legislation was enacted; church and state were separated, the Jesuit order was dissolved and its property confiscated, and the schools were removed from clerical control. The old movement for Catalonian independence was somewhat mollified by the grant of considerable local autonomy. To placate the peasantry the government began to break up some of the larger landed estates and to redistribute the land. The government's program was never pushed vigorously enough to satisfy extremist elements, who manifested their dissatisfaction in strikes and uprisings, particularly in industrial Barcelona, the Catalonian capital, and the mining areas of the Asturias, but it was radical enough to antagonize the great property owners and the churchmen. After 1933 the government fell into the hands of rightist and conservative parties, who ruled through ineffective and unpopular ministries. An insurrection of the miners in the Asturias was put down with much brutality. Agitation for complete Catalonian independence was repressed.

In February 1936 new general elections were held. All elements of the left—republicans, socialists, syndicalists, anarchists, communists—joined in a Popular Front against monarchists, clericals, army officers, other adherents of the old regime, and Falangists, or Spanish fascists. The left won a victory at the polls. Thereupon, in July 1936, a group of military men led an insurrection against the republican government; General Francisco Franco emerged as leader. The parties of the left united in resistance and the whole country fell into civil war. It was the

[6] See pp. 756–757.

most devastating war in all Spanish history; over 600,000 human beings lost their lives, and was accompanied by extreme cruelties on both sides. For nearly three years the republican or loyalist forces held their own before finally succumbing to the insurgents led by Franco, who in March 1939 established an authoritarian, fascist-type rule over the exhausted country.

Spain provided a rehearsal for the greater struggle soon to come. The republican government could legitimately have looked forward to the purchase of arms abroad to suppress the rebellion, but Britain and France were resolved not to let the war expand into a general conflict. They forbade the shipment of war materials to the republican government; even the French Popular Front government put obstacles in the way of aid to the hard-pressed Spanish Popular Front. The United States extended its neutrality legislation to cover civil wars and placed an embargo on the export of arms to Spain despite much pressure in the country for support to the loyalists. At British and French instigation twenty-seven nations, including all the major European powers, agreed not to intervene or take sides. But the nonintervention policy proved a fiasco. Germany, Italy, and the Soviet Union intervened anyway. The former two supported Franco and denounced the republicans as the tools of Bolshevism, while the U.S.S.R. supported the republic and stigmatized the rebels under Franco as the agents of international fascism. Germans, Italians, and Russians sent military equipment to Spain, testing their tanks and planes in actual battle. The fascist bombings of Madrid and Barcelona horrified the democratic world. The Germans and Italians sent troops (the Italians over 50,000); the Soviets if only for geographical reasons could not do likewise but sent technicians and political advisers. Thousands of volunteers of leftist or liberal sympathy, from the United States and Europe, went to Spain as individuals to serve with the loyalist republican forces. Spain became the battlefield of contending ideologies. The Spanish Civil War split the world into fascist and antifascist camps.

Like Ethiopia, the war in Spain helped bring Germany and Italy together. Mussolini had at first, like others, feared the revival of a militant Germany. He had been the one who outfaced Hitler when the latter threatened to absorb Austria in 1934. The Ethiopian war, Italian ambitions in Africa, and a clamorous Italian demand for ascendancy in the Mediterranean, the *mare nostrum* of the ancient Romans, estranged Italy from France and Britain. In 1936, soon after the outbreak of the Spanish Civil War, Mussolini and Hitler came to an understanding, which they called the Rome-Berlin Axis—the diplomatic axis around which they hoped the world might turn. That year Japan signed with Germany an Anti-Comintern Pact, soon ratified by Italy too; ostensibly an agreement to oppose communism, it was actually the foundation for a diplomatic alliance. Each, thus furnished with allies, was able to push its demands with more success. In 1938 Mussolini accepted the German absorption of the very Austria which in 1934 he had denied to Hitler.

And in 1937 Japan, using as a pretext the firing upon Japanese troops at the Marco Polo Bridge near Peking, launched a new full-scale invasion of China. Within a short time, despite resistance from the Chinese forces, both Kuomintang and Communist, the invader controlled most of China. The Chinese fought on from the hinterland, obtaining equipment and supplies by difficult and devious routes. The League again ineffectually condemned the Japanese action. The

United States refrained from applying its neutrality legislation, since no war was officially declared. This made possible the extension of loans to the Chinese government, but it also made possible the purchase by the Japanese of vitally needed scrap iron, steel, oil, and machinery from American industrial firms. The Japanese profited from the tension in the Western world; and in 1938 the tension in Europe was rapidly mounting.

The Munich Crisis: The Climax of Appeasement

By annexing Austria in March 1938 Hitler added about 6 million Germans to the Reich. Another 3 million Germans lived in Czechoslovakia.[7] All those who were adults in 1938 had been born under the Habsburg empire. They had never, since 1918, been contented with their new position as a minority in a Slavic state, and they had long complained against various forms of subtle discrimination. There were Polish, Ruthenian, and Hungarian minorities also, and since even the Slovaks felt a basic separatism from the Czechs, there was in truth no preponderant national majority of any kind. The fact that Czechoslovakia had one of the most enlightened minorities policies in Europe, enjoyed the highest living standard east of Germany, and was the only country in central Europe in 1938 that was still democratic only demonstrated the difficulty of maintaining a multinational state under the most favorable of conditions.

Czechoslovakia was strategically the keystone of Europe. It had a firm alliance with France, which had repeatedly guaranteed to defend it against German attack, and an alliance with the Soviet Union; Soviet aid was made dependent on the functioning of the French alliance. With Rumania and Yugoslavia it formed the Little Entente, upon which France relied to maintain the existing boundaries in that part of Europe. It had a well-trained army, important munitions industries, and strong fortifications against Germany, which, however, were located in precisely the Sudeten border area where the population was almost all German. When Hitler annexed Austria—since Vienna is further east than Prague—he enclosed Czechoslovakia in a vise. From the German point of view it could now be said that Bohemia-Moravia, which was almost a third German anyway, formed a bulge protruding into the German Reich.

The Sudeten Germans of Czechoslovakia, whether Nazis or not, fell under the influence of agitators whose aim was less to relieve their grievances than to promote National Socialism. Hitler fomented their demands for union with Germany. In May 1938 rumors of an imminent German invasion caused the Czechs to mobilize; Russia, France, and England issued warnings. Hitler, not actually intending to invade at that time, was forced to issue assurances but was nevertheless determined to smash the Czechs in the autumn. France and England, instead of rejoicing in having prevented aggression, were appalled by their narrow escape from war. The French were nervous and acquiesced in the leadership of Britain, which in the following months strove to avoid any firm stand that might precipitate war. The Czechs, under pressure from Britain and France, accepted British mediation on the Sudeten issue and in the summer of 1938 offered wide concessions to the Sudeten Germans amounting to regional autonomy; but these were never enough to satisfy Hitler, who loudly proclaimed that the plight of the

[7] See pp. 683, 685–689, 859–861, and map, pp. 686–687.

Germans in Czechoslovakia was intolerable and must be corrected. The Soviets urged a firm stand, but the Western powers had little confidence in Soviet military strength and, given the Soviet geographical situation, their ability to render assistance to Czechoslovakia; moreover, they feared a firmness that might mean war. They could not be sure whether Hitler was bluffing. He might, if opposed, back down; but it seemed equally likely, or indeed more so, that he was entirely willing to fight. The Western powers discounted intelligence reports, which happened to be true, of a military-civilian plot to unseat Hitler if, in the event of Western firmness, a war broke out over Czechoslovakia.

As the tension mounted in September 1938, the British prime minister, Neville Chamberlain, who had never flown in his life before, flew to Germany twice to sound out Hitler on his terms; the second time Hitler raised his demands so that even the British and French could not accept them. Mobilization began; war seemed imminent. Suddenly, in the midst of the unbearable tension, Hitler invited Chamberlain and Édouard Daladier, the French premier, to a four-power conference at Munich, to be attended also by his ally, Mussolini. The Soviet Union, and Czechoslovakia itself, were excluded. At Munich Chamberlain and Daladier accepted Hitler's terms and then put enormous pressure on the Czech government to yield, to sign its own death warrant in cold blood. France, urged on by England in a pacific course that it was only too willing to follow, repudiated its treaty obligation to protect Czechoslovakia, ignored the Russians who had reaffirmed their willingness to aid the Czechs if the French acted, and abandoned its whole system of a Little Entente in the East. It was agreed at Munich that Germany should annex the adjoining fringe of Bohemia in which the majority of the people were Germans. This fringe contained the mountainous approaches and the fortifications, so that its loss left Czechoslovakia militarily defenseless. After promises to guarantee the integrity of what remained of Czechoslovakia, the conference disbanded. Chamberlain and Daladier were received with cheers at home. Chamberlain happily reported that he had brought "peace in our time." Again the democracies sighed with relief, hoped that Hitler had made his last demand, and told themselves that, with wise concessions, there need be no war.

The Munich crisis, with its death sentence to Czechoslovakia, revealed the helpless weakness into which the Western democracies had fallen by 1938. There was, in fact, little that the French and British could do, at Munich, to save Czechoslovakia. Their countries lagged behind Germany in military preparedness. They were impressed by the might of the German army and air force. Bolder men than Daladier and Chamberlain, knowing the state of their own armed forces, would have declined to risk a quarrel. They loved peace and would buy it at a high price, not daring to believe that they were dealing with a blackmailer whose price would always be raised. They suffered, too, from another moral uncertainty; by the very principle of national self-determination, accepted by the victors after the First World War, Germany had a right to all that it had hitherto demanded. Hitler, in sending German troops into the German Rhineland, in annexing Austria, stirring up Danzig, incorporating the Bohemian Germans, had only asserted the right of the German people to have a sovereign German state. Moreover, if Hitler could be diverted eastward, enmeshed in a war with Russia, then communism and fascism might destroy each other—so one might hope. Possibly it was one of Hitler's motives, in the Munich crisis, to isolate Russia from the West and the West from Russia. If so, he succeeded well enough.

In the weeks following Munich the international commission set up to arrange the new boundaries worked further injustices on Czechoslovakia, dispensing even with the plebiscites which had been agreed to for disputed areas. Meanwhile the Poles and Hungarians brought forth their demands on the hapless Czechs. The Poles seized the Teschen district; and Hungary, under a German and Italian award, took 7,500 square miles of Slovakia. France and Britain were not consulted and did not seriously protest.

The End of Appeasement

The final disillusionment came in March 1939. Hitler marched into Bohemia-Moravia, the really Czech part of Czechoslovakia, which he transformed into a German protectorate. Exploiting Slovak nationalism, he declared Slovakia "independent." Czechoslovakia, merely trimmed down at Munich, now disappeared from the map. Having promised to take only a bite, Hitler swallowed the whole. He then seized Memel from Lithuania and raised demands for Danzig and the Polish Corridor. A horrible realization now spread in France and Britain. It was clear that Hitler's most solemn guarantees were worthless, that his designs were not limited to Germans, but reached out to all eastern Europe and beyond, that he was essentially insatiable, that he could never be appeased. In April 1939 his partner in aggression, Mussolini, took over Albania.

The Western powers now began to make military preparations. Britain, changing its east-European policy at the eleventh hour, now gave a guarantee to Poland, and followed that with guarantees to Rumania and Greece. That spring and summer the British tried to form an anti-German alliance with the U.S.S.R. But Poland and the Baltic states were unwilling to allow Soviet armies within their borders, even for the purpose of defending them against the Germans. The Anglo-French negotiators refused to put pressure on them. Since the Poles, in 1920, had conquered more territory than the Allies had meant them to have,[8] pushing their eastern border well into White Russia, almost to Minsk, the Anglo-French scruples seemed to the Soviets unnecessarily delicate. The Russians did not wish the Germans to launch an attack on them from a point as far east as Minsk. They thought, too, with good reason, that what the French and British really wanted was for the Soviet Union to take the brunt of the Nazi attack. They considered it an affront that the British sent lesser officials as negotiators to Moscow when the prime minister himself had three times flown personally to deal with Hitler. Having quietly undertaken negotiations earlier that spring, the Soviets, on August 23, 1939, openly signed a treaty of nonaggression and friendship with Hitlerite Germany. In a protocol kept secret at the time, it was agreed that in any future territorial rearrangement the Soviet Union and Germany would divide Poland between them, that the Soviet Union would enjoy a preponderant influence in the Baltic states and have its claim to Bessarabia, lost to Rumania in 1918, recognized. In return the Soviets pledged to stay out of any war between Germany and Poland, or between Germany and the Western democracies.

The Nazi-Soviet Pact stupefied the world. Communism and Nazism, supposed

[8] See pp. 710, 711, and map, p. 319.

to be ideological opposites, had come together. A generation more versed in ideology than in power politics was dumbfounded. The pact was recognized as the signal for war; all last minute negotiations failed. The Germans invaded Poland on September 1. On September 3 Great Britain and France declared war on Germany. The second European war in a generation, soon to be a world war, had begun.

105. THE YEARS OF AXIS TRIUMPH

Nazi Europe, 1939–1940: Poland and the Fall of France

The Second World War opened with the assault on Poland. German forces totaling over 1 million men, spearheaded by armored divisions and supported by the massed air power of the *Luftwaffe*, rapidly overran western Poland and subdued the ill-equipped Polish armies. The outcome of the campaign, a spectacular, perfectly executed example of *Blitzkrieg*, or lightning warfare, was clear within the first few days; organized resistance ended within a month. The Germans undertook to integrate their Polish conquest into the Reich.

Simultaneously, the Soviet Union, acting under the secret clauses of the Nazi-Soviet Pact, moved into the eastern half of Poland two weeks after the German invasion; the territory occupied was roughly equivalent to that lost to Poland in 1920. The Soviets proceeded also to establish fortified bases in the Baltic states—Estonia, Latvia, and Lithuania. Finland alone resisted Soviet demands. The Finns refused to cede border territories sought by the Russians or to yield military rights within their country. The Soviets insisted; Leningrad, the second major city of the U.S.S.R., lay only twenty miles from the Finnish frontier. When negotiations foundered, the Soviets attacked in November 1939. Finnish resistance was valiant and at first effective, but the small country was no match for the U.S.S.R., even though the latter used only limited forces in the war. Western democratic sympathies were with the Finns; the British and French sent equipment and supplies and even planned an expeditionary force. The Soviet Union was expelled from the League of Nations for the act of aggression—the only power ever to be so expelled. By March 1940 the fighting was over. The Finns had to yield somewhat more territory to the U.S.S.R. than originally demanded but retained their independence.

Meanwhile all was deceptively quiet in the West. The pattern of 1914, when the Germans reached the Marne in the first month of hostilities, failed to repeat itself. Unlike 1914, the opening phase of the war was one of position at the outset. The French sat behind their Maginot Line; the British had few troops; the Germans did not stir from behind their Siegfried Line, or West Wall, in the Rhineland. Hardly any air action took place. It was called the "phony war." The two great Western democracies rejected Hitler's peace overtures after the conquest of Poland but still clung to their peacetime outlook. The mad hope still lingered that somehow a real clash might even yet be averted. During this same strange winter, a cold and bitter one, the Germans put their forces through special training, whose purpose became apparent in the spring.

On April 9, 1940, the Germans suddenly attacked and overran Norway, ostensibly because the British were laying mines in Norwegian waters in an endeavor to cut off German sources of Swedish iron ore. Denmark, too, was overrun, and an Allied expeditionary force with inadequate air strength had to withdraw. Then on May 10, the Germans delivered their main blow, striking at the Netherlands, Belgium, Luxembourg, and France itself. Nothing could stand against the German armored divisions and dive bombers. The Nazi use of massed tanks, though already demonstrated in Poland, took the French and British by surprise. Strategically, the Allies expected the main advance to be in central Belgium, as in 1914, and indeed as in the original German plan, which had been altered only a few months earlier. Hence the French and British sent into Belgium the best-equipped troops they had. But the Germans delivered their main armored thrust, seven divisions, through Luxembourg and the Ardennes forest, long considered by the French General Staff impassable to tanks. In France, skirting the northwestern end of the Maginot Line, which had never been extended to the sea, the German armored divisions crossed the Meuse, drove deep into northern France against confused and ineffective resistance and, racing westward toward the Channel ports, cut off the Allied armies in Belgium. The Dutch, fearful of further air attack on their crowded cities, capitulated. The Belgian king sued for an armistice, and a large part of the French armies surrendered. The British fell back upon Dunkirk and could hope only to salvage their broken forces before the trap closed completely. They were able to accomplish their rescue operation only because Hitler had some days earlier halted the advance of his armored divisions. In the week ending June 4 an epic evacuation of over 330,000 British and French troops was successfully executed from the beaches of Dunkirk, under air cover, with the help of all kinds of British vessels, manned in part by civilian volunteers, but the precious equipment of the shattered army was all but totally abandoned.

In June the German forces drove relentlessly southward. Paris itself was occupied on June 13, Verdun two days later; by June 22 France had sued for peace and an armistice had been signed. Hitler danced with glee.

France, obsessed by a defensive military psychology at the outset of the war, its armies unprepared for mechanized warfare, lacking armored divisions and an adequate air force, its government divided, its people split into hostile and suspicious factions, had fallen into the hands of a group of men who were openly defeatist. The fall of France left the world aghast. Everyone knew that France was no longer its former self, but it had still been considered a great power, and its collapse in one month seemed inconceivable. Some Frenchmen, fleeing to England, established a Free French movement under General Charles de Gaulle; others formed a Resistance movement in France. The British made the bitter decision to destroy a part of the French fleet anchored in the Algerian harbor of Oran to prevent its falling into enemy hands.

France itself under the terms of the armistice was occupied in its northern half by the Germans. The Third Republic, its capital now at Vichy in the unoccupied southern half, was transformed by vote of a confused and stunned parliament into an authoritarian regime headed by the eighty-four-year-old Marshal Pétain and the cynical and unscrupulous politician Pierre Laval. The republic was dead; the very slogan *Liberty, Equality, Fraternity* was banned from official use. Pétain, Laval, and others proceeded to collaborate with the Nazis and to integrate Vichy France into the Nazi "new order" in Europe.

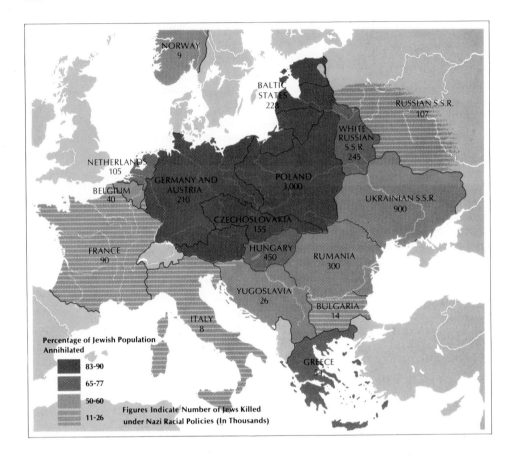

THE HOLOCAUST

The map shows what the Nazis called their Final Solution, that is, their program of exterminating the Jews and Judaism. Before the Second World War most European Jews lived in Poland and the adjoining parts of the Soviet Union which the Germans occupied during the war, so that most of the deaths occurred in these areas. In Germany itself, and in regions where German control was firmest or of longest duration, the proportion of Jews put to death rose as high as 90 percent. The map shows both the number killed in each country and the percentage of its Jewish population that were victims of this deliberate genocide. The numbers add up to 5,933,900 men, women, and children, or an estimated two-thirds of the Jewish population of Europe as a whole.

Mussolini attacked France in June 1940, as soon as it was clear that Hitler had defeated it. Shortly thereafter, he invaded Greece and moved against the British In Africa. The *Duce* tied his own destinies, for good or ill, to those of the *Führer*. Since the Germans were emphatically the senior partner in this combination, since they were on good terms with Franco in Spain, and since the U.S.S.R. was benevolently neutral, they now dominated the entire European continent. History seemed to repeat itself, in the distant and unreal way that is the only way in which it ever repeats. The Germans controlled almost exactly the same geographical area as Napoleon. Organizing a new "continental system," which they called the "new order," they made plans to govern, exploit, and coordinate the resources, industry, and labor of Europe. Not having made plans for a long war, and only belatedly mobilizing their own resources for a sustained military effort, they had to intensify the exploitation of their conquered subjects. They garrisoned virtually the whole of Europe with their soldiers, creating what they called *Festung Europa*, the Fortress of Europe. In every country they had their sympathizers, collaborators, or "quislings"—the prototype was Vidkun Quisling, who had organized a Norwegian Fascist party in 1933, and was premier of Norway from 1942 to 1945.

But Hitler never commanded the following of Napoleon. It is significant that he never remotely approached Napoleon in raising an international army to fight his battles. Instead, by what the West called slave labor, he impressed millions of Frenchmen, Poles, Czechs, and others, prisoners of war or civilians, to work under close control in his war industries. It became one of the largest forcible displacements of population in all history. No liberating reforms, political, social, or legal, like those of Napoleon and the French Revolution, followed in the wake of Hitler's armies. A generation reared to mistrust the fabricated atrocity tales of the First World War painfully became aware of the very real German horrors of the Second—hostages rounded up and shot in reprisal for resistance; a whole village like Lidice in Czechoslovakia razed to the ground and its inhabitants killed or deported; concentration camps converted into mass extermination centers, with gas chambers and crematory ovens, at Maidanek, Treblinka, Dachau, Buchenwald, Auschwitz, and elsewhere, where "inferior" peoples could be systematically liquidated. Before the six-year war was over, in the areas of Nazi domination, many millions of human beings were so destroyed; by far the largest proportion were almost 6 million European Jews, but Poles, Russians, and other peoples were killed as well. All this was done in the effort to "Germanize" Europe, to make it work and sacrifice for the greater glory of the *Herrenvolk*, the master race. Genocide, the attempted destruction of whole ethnic groups or peoples, was the greatest of the Nazi sins against mankind.

The Battle of Britain and American Aid

In 1940, as in 1807, only Great Britain remained at war with the conqueror of Europe. After Dunkirk the British awaited the worst, momentarily expecting invasion. Winston Churchill, who had replaced Chamberlain as prime minister in May 1940 during the military debacle, rose to the summit of leadership in adversity. To Parliament and the British people he promised nothing but "blood, toil, tears, and sweat." He pledged implacable war against "a monstrous tyranny, never surpassed in the dark, lamentable catalogue of human crime." To the American democracy across the Atlantic he appealed "Give us the tools, and we will finish the job." The United States began to respond.

Since 1939, and even before, the American government had been anything but neutral. Opinion was excitedly divided. One group, called isolationist, opposed any involvement in the European war, believing that Europe was hopeless, or that the United States could not save it, or that the Germans would win anyway before America could act, or that Hitler, even if victorious in Europe, constituted no danger to the United States. Another group, the interventionists, urged immediate aid to the Allies, believing that Hitler was an actual menace, that fascism must be destroyed, or that the Nazis, if they subjected all Europe, would soon begin to tamper with the American republics. President Roosevelt was an interventionist, convinced that American security was endangered; he tried to rally national opinion by declaring that the United States might openly assist the Allies without itself fighting, by using "measures short of war." His Republican opponent in 1940, Wendell Willkie, took an identical stand.

The neutrality legislation of the mid-1930s was amended in November 1939, when the ban on the sale of arms was repealed.[9] Britain and the British Empire the President described as "the spearhead of resistance to world conquest"; the United States was to be "the great arsenal of democracy." Both were fighting for a world, he said, in which the Four Freedoms were to be secure—freedom of speech, freedom of worship, freedom from want, and freedom from fear. In June 1940, immediately after Dunkirk, the United States sent a small initial shipment of arms to Britain. A few months later the United States gave the British fifty over-age destroyers in return for the right to maintain American bases in Newfoundland, the Bermudas, and the British Caribbean islands. In 1941 it adopted Lend-Lease, a policy of providing arms, raw materials, and food to powers at war with the Axis. At the same time, in 1940 and 1941, the United States introduced conscription, built up its army and air force, and projected a two-ocean navy. Plans for joint hemisphere defense were developed with the Latin American republics. To protect its shipping it secured bases in Greenland and Iceland and convoyed Allied shipping as far as Iceland. In October 1941 German submarines sank an American destroyer. It is likely that the Germans, as in 1917, would have eventually provoked war with the United States to stop the flow of aid to their enemies even had war not come from another quarter.

Meanwhile, after the fall of France, the Germans stood poised for the invasion of Britain. But they had not calculated on such rapid and easy successes in Europe, they had no immediately practical plan for an invasion, and they needed to win control of the air before a sea invasion could take place. Moreover, there was always the hope that the British might sue for peace, or even become an ally

9 See p. 793.

GERMANY SINCE 1919

The upper panel shows the boundaries established after the Treaty of Versailles. Note the free city of Danzig and the Polish Corridor; for these and other areas lost in the First World War see also the map on pp. 686–687. In the middle panel we see the borders at the height of the Second World War in 1942. The Reich proper had then annexed (1) Luxembourg, (2) Alsace and Lorraine from France, (3) Carniola from Yugoslavia, (4) Austria, (5) the Sudeten regions and a Bohemian-Moravian protectorate from Czechoslovakia, (6) the free city of Danzig, and (7) Poland, which was renamed the "General Government." Beyond the borders of the Reich, the Germans occupied France, Belgium, the Netherlands, Denmark, and Norway, and in Eastern Europe had set up controls over the former Baltic states, White Russia, and the Ukraine. The lower panel shows Germany after Hitler's defeat. All conquests have been lost, and Poland now reaches westward almost to Berlin. A communist East Germany and a democratic West Germany have grown out of the zones occupied respectively by the Soviet and Western armies in 1945.

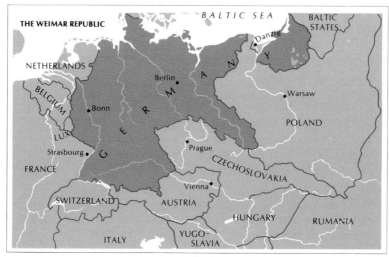

THE WEIMAR REPUBLIC

HITLER'S
GROSSDEUTSCHES REICH

GERMANY DIVIDED

of Germany—so Hitler's mind ran. The assault on Britain, which began that summer and reached its climax in the autumn of 1940, took the form of an air offensive. Never until then had any bombing been so severe. But the Germans were unable to win control over the air in the battle of Britain. Gradually the British Royal Air Force fought off the bombers with more success; new radar devices helped detect the approach of enemy planes. Although Coventry was wiped out, the life and industry of other cities badly disrupted, and thousands of people killed (20,000 in London alone), still the productive activity of the country carried on. Nor, contrary to the predictions of most theorists of air power, did the bombings break the morale of the civilian population.

In the winter of 1940–1941 the Germans began to shift their weight to the east. Hitler postponed indefinitely the planned invasion of Britain for which he seems never to have had much enthusiasm anyway. He had already decided, like Napoleon before him, that before committing his resources to an invasion of England he must dispose of Russia, a project much closer to his heart.

The Nazi Invasion of Russia: The Russian Front, 1941–1942

The Nazi-Soviet Pact of 1939 which had precipitated the war, like the alliance between Napoleon and Alexander I, was never a warm or harmonious understanding. Both parties, foreseeing war with each other, probably entered it mainly to gain time. The Soviets gained space as well, pushing their borders westward. The two soon began to dispute over eastern Europe. The Soviets, with their Nazi ally preoccupied by the war, hoped to win more influence in the Baltic, as promised them, and in the Balkans. They had already occupied eastern Poland and the three Baltic states and won territory from Finland. In June 1940, to the chagrin of the Germans, they had quietly sovietized and converted the three Baltic states into member republics of the U.S.S.R. The old German landowning class, the famous "Baltic barons," who had lived there for centuries, were uprooted and were returned to German soil. At the same time the Soviets seized from Rumania the Bessarabian province that they had lost in the First World War and incorporated it as a Soviet republic. The Russians were expanding toward the Balkans, another area of historic Russian interest, and seemed bent on winning control over eastern Europe.

This the Germans viewed with dismay. They wished to reserve eastern Europe for themselves as a counterpart to industrial Germany. Hitler moved to bring the Balkans under German control. By early 1941 he had blackmailed or, by territorial concessions, cajoled Rumania, Bulgaria, and Hungary into joining the Axis; they became Axis lesser partners and were occupied by German troops; Yugoslavia also was occupied despite resistance by the army and population. Greece too was subjugated, the Germans coming to the rescue of Mussolini's hard-pressed troops. Hitler thus barred Russian expansion in the Balkans and made them part of the Nazi new order. The Balkan campaigns delayed his plans, but now, to end the threat from the East, and to gain the wheat harvests of the Ukraine and the oil wells of the Caucasus, the core of the Eurasian "heartland," Hitler struck. After mutual deception that had continued since the pact of 1939, on June 22, 1941, he invaded Russia.

The German army, supplemented by Finnish, Rumanian, Hungarian, and

Italian contingents, threw 3 million men into Russia along a vast 2,000-mile front. One swift moving battle melted into another. The Russians resisted but gave way. By the autumn of 1941 the Germans had overrun White Russia and most of the Ukraine. In the north, Leningrad was in a state of siege; in the south, the Germans had entered the Crimean peninsula and were besieging Sebastopol. And toward the center of the vast front, the Germans stood, exhausted, but apparently victorious, within twenty-five miles of Moscow. But the overconfident German forces had not calculated on the stubbornness of Russian resistance, nor were they prepared to fight in the bitter Russian winter, which suddenly came upon them. A counteroffensive, launched by the Russians in the winter of 1941, saved Moscow. Hitler, disgusted and impatient with his subordinates, took over direct command of military operations; he shifted the main attack to the south and began a great offensive in the summer of 1942 directed toward the oil fields of the Caucasus. Sebastopol soon fell; the siege of Stalingrad began.

1942, The Year of Dismay: Russia, North Africa, the Pacific

A year after the invasion, in the fateful summer of 1942, the German line reached from beleaguered Leningrad in the north, past the western outskirts of Moscow, past Stalingrad on the Volga southward to the Caucasus Mountains; the Germans were within a hundred miles of the Caspian Sea. But the Russians had traded space for time. Though the industrial Don basin and the food-producing Ukraine were overrun, the deliveries of Caucasus oil rendered hazardous and uncertain, still the Russians continued to fight; industries were shifted to the new Ural and Siberian cities; and neither the Soviet economy nor the Soviet government was yet struck in a vital spot. A "scorched earth" policy, in which the retreating Russians destroyed crops and livestock and guerrilla units wrecked industrial and transportation facilities, guaranteed that Russian resources would not fall into the hands of the advancing conqueror.

Simultaneously, late in 1942 the Axis also was moving forward in North Africa. Here the desert campaigns had started in September 1940 with an Italian eastward offensive mounted from Libya, which succeeded in crossing over into Egypt. The stakes here too were high—control over Suez and the Mediterranean. At the height of the battle of Britain, Churchill had made the decision to send vitally needed supplies and men to North Africa. To the satisfaction of the British, a counteroffensive against vastly superior numbers swept the Italians out of Egypt and by early 1941 the British moved deep into Libya. Shortly thereafter the British overran Ethiopia and ended entirely Mussolini's short-lived East African empire; the Italian navy suffered reverses as well. But in North Africa for-

EUROPE, 1942

The map shows Europe at the height of Axis military successes during World War II, just before the Soviet victory at Stalingrad and the Western invasion of North Africa. Austria, the Sudetenland, Bohemia-Moravia, Poland, and Alsace-Lorraine were all joined to Hitler's Reich. The Atlantic Coast from southern France to northern Norway was under German military occupation, as was much of Russia almost to the Caspian Sea. Southern Europe from Vichy France to Rumania was also occupied or allied.

RTH CAPE

Murmansk

WHITE SEA

Archangel

Farthest Axis Penetration
—— December 1941
..... November 1942

INLAND

L. Onega

L. Ladoga

Leningrad
Helsinki

ESTONIA

Riga

VIA

S   O   V   I   E   T   U   N   I   O   N

Moscow

Kuibyshev

HUANIA

Smolensk

Tula

BYELO-RUSSIA

SUWALKI

Volga R.

saw

Donetz R.

Stalingrad

POLAND

Kiev

Kharkov

Don R.

Astrakhan

UKRAINE

Rostov

Dniester R.

BESSARABIA

Maikop

Grozny

CASPIAN SEA

Sevastopol   Yalta

RUMANIA

Bucharest

BLACK SEA

Batum

TRANSCAUCASIA

Baku

rade

Danube R.

Sofia

BULGARIA

Istanbul

Ankara

T   U   R   K   E   Y

Tabriz

IRAN

Athens

GREECE

AEGEAN SEA

SYRIA

Baghdad

CRETE

CYPRUS
(Britain)

LEBANON

IRAQ

A

PALESTINE

TRANS-
JORDAN

SAUDI ARABIA

tunes were fickle. A German elite force, the Afrika Korps under General Rommel, reorganized the Axis armies and in the spring of 1941 attacked in Libya. The British, their forces depleted by transfers that had been made to the Greek front, were driven back to the Egyptian frontier. Then, a few months later, in a second successful offensive, the British once more advanced into Libya. Again fortunes shifted. By mid-1942 Rommel had repulsed the British and penetrated Egypt. The British took up a stand at El Alamein, seventy miles from Alexandria, their backs to the Suez Canal. Here they held the Germans.

But it seemed in 1942 that the Axis armies, breaking through the Soviet Caucasus and across the isthmus of Suez in North Africa, might enclose the whole Mediterranean and Middle East in a gigantic vise, and even, moving farther east, somehow make contact with their allies the Japanese, who were at this time penetrating into the Indian Ocean. For the Pacific situation in the latter half of 1941 had also exploded. It was Japan that finally drew the United States into war.

The Japanese, in 1941, had conducted a war against China for ten years. In the second war in Europe, as in the first, Japanese expansionists saw a propitious moment to assert themselves throughout the Far East. In 1940 they had cemented their alliance with Germany and Italy in a new three-power pact; the following year they had concluded a neutrality treaty with Russia. From the Vichy French government the Japanese obtained a number of military bases and other concessions in Indochina and began the occupation of that area. The United States belatedly placed an embargo on the export of such materials as scrap iron and steel to Japan. Hesitating to precipitate any all-out drive of the Japanese toward the Dutch East Indies and elsewhere, the United States government still sought some definition of Japanese ambitions in southeast Asia. The new Japanese prime minister General Hideki Tojo, a staunch champion of the Axis, publicly proclaimed that the influence of Britain and the United States was to be totally eliminated from the Orient, but he agreed to send representatives to Washington for negotiations. At the very time that the Japanese representatives in Washington were carrying on conversations with the American Secretary of State Cordell Hull, on December 7, 1941, without warning, the Japanese launched a heavy air raid on the American naval base at Pearl Harbor in Hawaii and began to invade the Philippines. Simultaneously, they launched attacks on Guam, Midway, Hong Kong, and Malaya. The Americans were caught off guard at Pearl Harbor; close to 2,500 were killed; the fleet was crippled; and the temporary disablement of the American naval forces allowed the Japanese to roam at will in the western Pacific. The United States and Great Britain declared war on Japan on December 8. Three days later Germany and Italy declared war on the United States, as did the Axis puppet states.

The Japanese, working overland through Malaya, two months later captured Singapore, a British naval base long fabulous for its supposed impregnability, the veritable Gibraltar of the East. The sinking by air of the mighty British battleship *Prince of Wales*, a feat often pronounced by naval experts to be impossible, added to the general consternation. In 1942 the Japanese conquered the Philippines, Malaya, and the Netherlands Indies. They invaded New Guinea and threatened Australia; they moved into the Aleutians. They streamed into the

Indian Ocean, occupied Burma, and seemed about to invade India. Everywhere they found ready collaborators among enemies of European imperialism. They held up the idea of a Greater East Asia Co-Prosperity Sphere under Japanese leadership, in which the one clear element was that the European whites should be ejected. Meanwhile, as noted, the Germans stood at the Caucasus and almost at the Nile. And in the Atlantic, even to the shores of the United States and the American republics, German submarines were sinking Allied ships at an unprecedented and disastrous rate. The Mediterranean was unusable. For the Soviet-Western alliance, 1942 was the year of dismay. Despite Allied naval victories, the late summer and autumn of 1942 was the worst period of the war. Few realized, wrote the United States Chief of Staff General George C. Marshall some years later, how "close to complete domination of the world" were Germany and Japan and "how thin the thread of Allied survival had been stretched."

106. THE WESTERN-SOVIET VICTORY

Plans and Preparations, 1942–1943

But by January 1942 twenty-six nations, including the three Great Powers—Britain, the United States, and the U.S.S.R.—and representing Europe, Asia, and both Americas, were aligned against the Axis, a combination to which President Roosevelt gave the name the United Nations. Each pledged to use all its resources to defeat the Axis and never to make a separate peace. The Grand Alliance against the Axis aggressors, which could not be created in the 1930s, had at last been consummated.

The two Atlantic democracies, the United States and Great Britain, pooled their resources under an organization called the Combined Chiefs of Staff. Never had any two sovereign states formed so intimate a coalition. In contrast with the First World War an overall strategy was in effect from an early date. It was decided that Germany was the main enemy, against which it was necessary to concentrate first. For the time being the Pacific war was relegated to the background. Australia became the chief base for operations against the Japanese. The American General Douglas MacArthur, who had been ordered to abandon the doomed American garrison in the Philippines, assumed command in the southwest Pacific; Admiral Chester Nimitz was in command of the Pacific naval forces. A separate organization was established for the China-Burma-India theater. The American navy and air force soon brought Japanese southward expansion to a halt and frustrated Japanese efforts to cut off supply lines to Australia; impressive naval and air victories were won in the spring of 1942 in the battle of the Coral Sea and at Midway, the only relief to the overall gloom of that period. In the summer American forces landed at Guadalcanal in the Solomon Islands. A long ordeal of "island hopping" with inadequate forces began.

In Europe the first point of concentration was an air bombardment of Germany. The Russians, dissatisfied, called for a true "second front," an immediate invasion by ground forces that would relieve the pressure of the many German divisions that were devastating their country. Suspicious of the West as ever, doubly suspicious since the Munich conference of 1938, in which they saw a Western attempt to deflect the Germans into an attack on Russia, they regarded the failure to establish a second front as new evidence of anti-Soviet feeling.

But the United States, in 1942, was not ready to undertake land action by a direct assault on *Festung Europa*. Although in the Second World War, as in the First, more than two years elapsed between the outbreak of war in Europe and the intervention of the United States, and although in the second war American military preparations began much sooner, the United States in 1942 was still involved in the cumbersome processes of mobilization, converting industry to the production of war materials for itself and its Allies, imposing controls on its economy to prevent a runaway inflation, and giving military training to its profoundly civilian-minded people, of whom over 12 million eventually served in the armed forces—over three times as many as in the First World War. In any case, for a year after the United States entered the war, German submarines enjoyed enough control of the Atlantic to make large shipments of troops too risky. In effect, they blockaded the American army in the United States. The American and British navies gradually won the battle of the Atlantic; the submarine menace was reduced to tolerable proportions by the first part of 1943. The Americans and British decided to begin the assault upon Germany, from Great Britain as a base, with a massive and prolonged air bombardment of its factories and cities. Since not everything could be shipped across the Atlantic at the same time, and since the United States and Britain were engaged in war with Japan as well, land invasion had to be deferred until 1944. The embattled Russians questioned whether the Western Allies ever really meant to face the German army at all.

The Turning of the Tide, 1942–1943: Stalingrad, North Africa, Sicily

Meanwhile, at the end of 1942 the tide began to turn. In November an Anglo-American force effected a surprise invasion of Algeria and Morocco in an amphibious operation of hitherto unparalleled proportions. The Allies, failing to win the cooperation of the French in North Africa as they had hoped to do, turned to the Vichy French political leader Admiral Darlan in a calculated act of expediency that brought a loud outcry of protest in many quarters. Darlan assisted the Allies in assuming control but was assassinated in late December. In the competition that developed in the succeeding months for leadership of the French liberation committee, newly established in Algiers, General de Gaulle, though mistrusted and virtually ignored by President Roosevelt, easily bested all rivals.

On the Continent, after the North African landings, the Germans took over control of unoccupied France as well; they were frustrated, however, in the effort to obtain possession of the remainder of the French fleet by the action of French crews which scuttled the ships at Toulon. In North Africa the invading forces under the command of General Dwight D. Eisenhower fought their way eastward into Tunisia. Meanwhile the British forces under General Montgomery, having held the Germans at El Alamein in June 1942, had already launched their third (and final) counteroffensive in October, even before the invasion; they now pushed the Germans westward from Egypt until a large German force was crushed between the two Allied armies and destroyed in Tunisia. By May 1943

Africa was cleared of Axis forces. Mussolini's dream of an African empire had been thwarted; the Mediterranean was open; the threat to Egypt and the Suez Canal was ended.

At the same time it became clear, in the winter of 1942–1943, that the Germans had suffered a catastrophic reversal in the Soviet Union in the titanic battle of Stalingrad. In August 1942 massive German forces began an all-out assault on Stalingrad, the vital key to all transport on the lower Volga; by September they had penetrated the city itself. Stalin, who from the start of the war personally commanded military operations in Russia, ordered his namesake city held at all costs; Russian soldiery and the civilian population took a desperate stand. Hitler was as obstinate in ordering the city taken. After weeks of fighting the Germans had occupied most of the city when suddenly the Russians began a great counter-attack, led by General Zhukov; twenty-two German divisions were forced to capitulate; over 330,000 Germans were lost. The Russians followed up their victory with a new counteroffensive, a great westward drive that netted them wholesale advances and regained for them what they had initially lost in the first year of the war. After Stalingrad, despite some setbacks, the Russians were on the offensive for the remainder of the war. Stalingrad (or Volgograd as it was later renamed) was a turning point not only in the history of the war but in the history of central and eastern Europe as well.

American equipment meanwhile all through 1943 was arriving in Russia in prodigious quantities. The terms of Lend-Lease were liberally extended to the Soviets; a stream of American planes, guns, vehicles, clothing, and food made its way laboriously to Russia through the Arctic Ocean and through the Persian Gulf. Machinery and equipment were sent for the Soviet arms plants, which were themselves tremendously increasing their output. Anglo-American bombing was crippling the German aviation industry at home. The Allied contribution to the Soviet war effort was indispensable, but Russian human losses were tremendous. The Russians lost more men in the battle of Stalingrad than the United States lost in combat during the entire war, in all theaters combined.

With contemporary American successes in the Solomon Islands at the end of 1942 and the slow throttling of German submarines in the Atlantic, the beginning of the year 1943 brought new hope for the Allies in all quarters. In a spectacular campaign of July–August 1943, the British, Canadians, and Americans conquered the island of Sicily. Mussolini immediately fell; the twenty-one-year-old Fascist regime came to an end. Mussolini set up an "Italian Social Republic" in the north, but it was no more than a German puppet government. (Some months later, in April 1945, the Duce, as he attempted to flee the country, was seized, shot, and strung up like a slaughtered pig by anti-Fascist Italians.) The new Italian government under Marshal Badoglio, in August 1943, tried to make peace. The German army then occupied Italy. The Allies, having crossed to the Italian mainland, attacked from the south. In October the Badoglio government declared war on Germany, and Italy was recognized by the Allies as a "cobelligerent." But the Germans stubbornly blocked the advance of the Allies to Rome despite new Allied landings and beachheads. The Italian campaign turned into a long and disheartening stalemate because the Western Allies, concentrating troops in Great Britain for the approaching cross-Channel invasion, could never spare enough for the Italian front.

The Allied Offensive, 1944–1945: Europe and the Pacific

Festung Europa, especially along its western approaches, the coasts of Holland, Belgium, and France, bristled with every kind of fortification that German scientific and military ingenuity could devise. A seaborne attack upon Europe was an operation of wholly unprecedented kind. It differed from the earlier amphibious attacks on Algeria, Sicily, or the Pacific islands in that the defender in Europe, in the very part of Europe where the road and railway network was thickest, could immediately rush overwhelming reserves to the spot attacked—except insofar as feinting tactics kept him uncertain, air power destroyed his transport, or the Russians held the bulk of his forces in the East. Precise and elaborate plans had been worked out. Ten thousand aircraft were to provide aerial protection, scores of warships were to bombard the coast, 4,000 ships were to carry the invading troops and their supplies across the Channel, artificial harbors were to be created where none existed.

The invasion of Europe began before dawn on June 6, 1944. The spot selected was the coast of Normandy directly across the Channel from England. An unparalleled combination of forces, British, Canadian, and American, land, sea, and air, backed up by huge accumulations of supplies and reserves of men assembled in Great Britain, and the whole under the unified command of the American General Eisenhower, assaulted the French coast, established a beachhead, and maintained a front. The Allies poured in their strength, over 130,000 men the first day, 1 million within a month. The Germans were at first thrown back more easily than had been expected. By August Paris was liberated, by September the Allies crossed the frontier of Germany itself. In France, Italy, and Belgium the Resistance movements, which had grown up in secret during the later years of German occupation, now came into the open and drove out Germans and pro-German collaborators. In Germany itself no deep-rooted Resistance movement ever developed, but a small group of men, military and civilian, formed an underground group. On July 20, 1944, it attempted to assassinate Hitler by exploding a bomb at his military headquarters in East Prussia; Hitler was only injured and took a fearsome revenge.

In August, in another amphibious operation, the Allies landed on the French Mediterranean coast and swept up from southern France to join the Allied forces advancing against stiffening resistance. At one point, momentarily, the Allied offensive even suffered a serious reversal. A sudden German drive, launched under Hitler's direct personal orders in December 1944 against thinly held American lines on the Belgian sector in the Ardennes, created a "bulge" in the advancing armies and caused heavy losses and confusion. But the Allies rallied. Neither Hitler's Ardennes counteroffensive nor the use of new destructive weapons rained on Britain, jet-propelled flying bombs and rockets, availed the Germans. The Western Allies pushed on and smashed through the heavily fortified Siegfried Line. The last natural obstacle, the Rhine, was crossed when in March 1945 American forces by a stroke of luck discovered an undestroyed bridge at Remagen; they poured troops over it and established a bridgehead—the first troops to cross the Rhine in combat since the armies of Napoleon. The main crossing, under the British, subsequently took place farther to the north. Soon the Allies were accepting wholesale surrenders in the Ruhr valley.

Meanwhile in 1944 the Russian armies swept the Germans from the Ukraine, White Russia, the Baltic states, and eastern Poland. By August they reached the suburbs of Warsaw. The Polish underground rose against the Germans but the Russians, determined that Poland must not be liberated by noncommunist Polish leadership, refused to permit aid to the rising, and it was crushed. The Russians, their lines overextended, and checked for several months by German strength in Poland, pushed southward into Rumania and Bulgaria; both countries changed sides and declared war against Germany. Early in 1945 the Russians, reopening their offensive, forced their way into East Prussia and Silesia and by February they reached the Oder, forty miles from Berlin, where Zhukov paused to regroup his forces. In March and April Russian forces occupied Budapest and Vienna.

The final drive on Germany began. Hitler moved troops from the collapsing western front to reinforce the stand on the Oder and to protect his capital. The German population did little to impede Western advances, hopeful that the Western allies might reach Berlin and indeed occupy as much of their country as possible before the Russians. In April the Americans drew up on the Elbe, about sixty miles from Berlin, with hardly any obstacles before them; but here they halted, by decision of General Eisenhower who was without any firm political guidance from home. The Americans, whose supply lines were already overextended, wanted a clear line of demarcation from the Russians; they also believed it necessary to divert some forces southward against a possible German last stand in the Alps. But mainly the decision was a gesture of good will toward the Russians, who were to be permitted to take Berlin as compensation for the heavy sacrifice in the common cause. Similarly, the American troops that moved southward were held back from taking Prague and the Russians were permitted to take the Czech capital too. By some it was later said that the fate of central Europe was determined by the war in the Far East; the Americans sought Russian aid against Japan, which it turned out, could readily have been dispensed with. In any event, the Russians were in control of all the major capitals of central and eastern Europe; in the case of Berlin and Prague it need not have been that way.

The Western Allies and the Soviets offered no terms to Hitler, nor to any Germans. They demanded unconditional surrender, and the Germans fought on in the very streets of Berlin. On the last day of April Hitler perished by his own hand in the ruins of his capital after denouncing some of his closest party subordinates as traitors. Admiral Doenitz, designated by Hitler as his successor, went through the formalities of surrender on May 8, 1945. Since fighting had already ceased on the Italian front a few days earlier, the war in Europe was now over.

In the Pacific, against Japan, operations had dragged on for three years, hampered by the strategic decision to concentrate against Germany first. Slowly, from points in the Solomon Islands, the easternmost fringe of the Indonesian archipelago, American forces, at first very small, worked their way in a northwesterly direction toward faraway Japan. They had to fight in turn for Guadalcanal, for New Guinea, for the reconquest of the Philippines. They had to fight for the Japanese islands and atolls in the mid-Pacific (taken by Japan from the Germans after the First World War and converted into powerful naval bases), the Gilbert Islands, the Marshalls, the Carolines, the Marianas. In October 1944 they won a great naval victory at the battle of Leyte Gulf. Finally, in one of the war's greatest and final battles, they won the island of Okinawa, only 300 miles from Japan

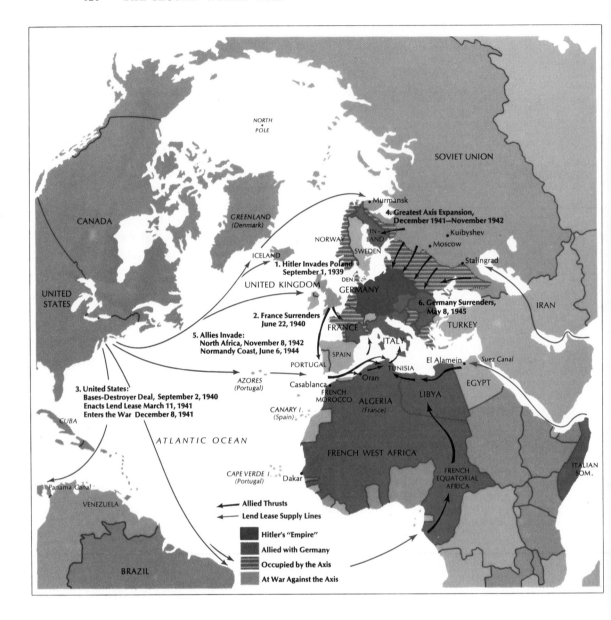

WORLD WAR II

These two maps show the global character of the war and the central position of the United States with respect to the European and Pacific theaters. The numbered legends summarize the successive stages of the war in both the Eastern and Western hemispheres. In 1942, with the Germans reaching as far east as Egypt and Stalingrad, and the Japanese as far west as Burma, the great danger to the Soviet-Western alliance was that these two might join forces, dominate southern Asia, control the oil resources of the Persian Gulf, and stop the flow of Western supplies to the Soviet Union from this direc-

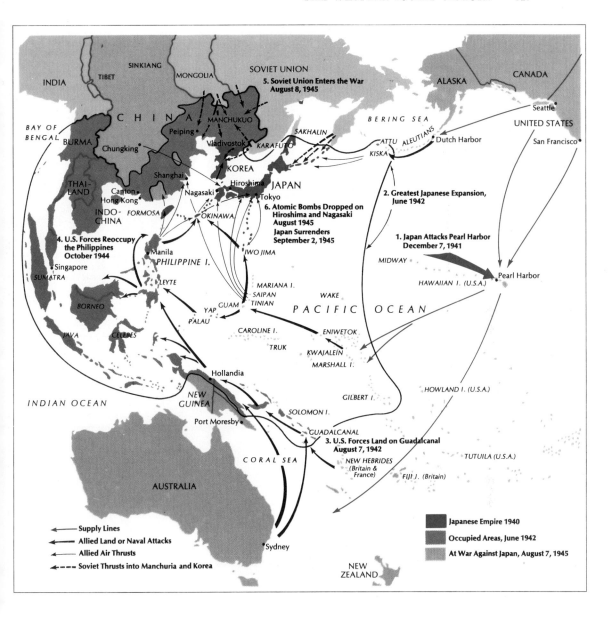

tion. The almost simultaneous Soviet-Western successes, late in 1942, at Stalingrad and El Alamein, and in the invasion of Morocco-Algeria and of Guadalcanal, proved to be the turning point of the war. In 1943 the German submarine campaign in the Atlantic was defeated, so that American troops and supplies could move more freely to Europe. The invasion of Normandy in June 1944, with continuing Soviet pressure from the east, brought about German surrender in May 1945. Meanwhile, in the Pacific, American occupation of the islands and reoccupation of the Philippines prepared the way for the surrender of Japan, consummated by two atomic bombs in August 1945.

THE SURVIVOR
by George Grosz (German, then American, 1893–1959)

George Grosz, born in Germany, came to the United States in 1932 to avoid the Nazis. He painted this powerful picture in 1945 at the close of the Second World War. It suggests what is meant by the collapse of civilization. The hideous figure crawling out of the wreckage, according to the artist's own explanation, is insane with fear. He is starving, filthy, abandoned, and alone. In his teeth he desperately clasps a knife, which he will use to fight another terrified survivor, should he meet one, or to hunt for and cut up food. Note the symbolism of a broken swastika in the arrangement of the man's body and the debris. The picture is of course meant to be repulsive, to show the depths to which humanity can be degraded, and so shock people into constructive action. The tormenting question is whether this picture may be an omen of the future. Courtesy of Mrs. Marc J. Sandler.

itself. Okinawa was captured just as the Germans collapsed in Europe. From the new Allied bases that had been won, from Saipan, from Iwo Jima, and from Okinawa, and from aircraft carriers a heavy bomber offensive was launched against Japan, such as had devastated Germany in the preceding two years, shattering Japanese industry, destroying the remnants of the Japanese navy, and compelling the Japanese government to give serious thought to suing for peace. The Allied leaders refused to believe that Japanese defenses were ready to crumble or that the Japanese were ready to negotiate. The American army prepared to shift combat troops from the European theater to the Far East. The stage was being set for a full-scale invasion of Japan itself.

Then, on August 6, 1945, an atomic bomb, prepared in utmost secrecy by American and European scientists, hit the city of Hiroshima, with a population of 200,000 people. The city was destroyed in this single explosion, and over 70,000 lives were lost. Two days later, the Soviet Union, which had pledged itself to enter the conflict in the East within three months after the surrender of Germany, declared war on Japan and invaded Manchuria. On August 9 an even more powerful atomic bomb struck Nagasaki and killed many more thousands. The Japanese made peace at once. On September 2, 1945, the formal surrender was signed. The emperor was permitted to remain as head of the state, but the Japanese islands were placed under the rule of a United States army of occupation.

The Second World War of the twentieth century was over. The same cold impersonal statistics that had recorded 10 million killed in the First World War now reported some 15 million military deaths and at least that many civilian fatalities. Russian military deaths were estimated at over 7 million, German at 3.5 million, Chinese at 2.2 million, Japanese at 1.3 million; British and Commonwealth losses were about 350,000, American about 300,000, French about 200,000. The death figures would have been greater except that one of every two soldiers seriously wounded was saved by new sulfa and penicillin drugs and by blood plasma transfusions. None of these military statistics could be more than approximate and no one could begin to estimate the complete toll of human lives lost in the war, directly or indirectly, from the bombings, the mass-extermination and deportation policies and the postwar famines and epidemics. Perhaps the losses came to 35 million or 40 million men, women, and children, but at such figures the human mind retreats and human senitivities are dulled. It is enough to say that peace had come.

107. THE FOUNDATIONS OF THE PEACE

Whereas the First World War had been concluded by a peace conference a few months after the close of hostilities, the Second World War ended in no such clear-cut settlement. Nothing like the Treaty of Versailles of 1919 followed the defeat of Germany in 1945. The terms of peace, as they gradually developed, left no such single symbol of humiliation as the Versailles treaty had represented. The peace terms emerged episodically, at first during a series of conferences among the victors during the war, and then in a series of de facto arrangements in the years after 1945.

The foundations of a peaceable postwar world had been laid, it was then thought, at a number of meetings where the war itself was being planned. In August 1941 Roosevelt and Churchill had met at sea off the coast of Newfoundland and had drawn up the Atlantic Charter. There were meetings in 1943 at Casablanca, at Cairo, and at Teheran (in the latter Stalin participated for the first time); and in the final phase of the war, in February 1945, at Yalta, and in July 1945, at Potsdam, in the environs of shattered Berlin.

The Atlantic Charter, issued jointly by Roosevelt and Churchill at their first meeting, resembled in spirit the Fourteen Points of Woodrow Wilson. It pledged that sovereign rights and self-government would be restored to all who had been forcibly deprived of them, that all nations would have equal access to world trade and world resources, that all peoples would work together to achieve improved living standards and economic security. The postwar peace, it promised, would assure for men in all lands freedom from fear and want and would end force and aggression in international affairs. Here, and in the Four Freedoms enunciated earlier by President Roosevelt, the ideological basis of the peace was proclaimed. At the 1943 conferences, and through other consultations, the Allies endeavored to concert their military plans. At Casablanca, in January 1943, they resolved to accept nothing less than the "unconditional surrender" of the Axis powers. This vague formula, adopted somewhat cavalierly at American initiative, and without much thought to possible political implications, was intended mainly to prevent a recurrence of anything like the ambiguity surrounding the armistice of 1918.[10] Though much criticized in later years (and not fully applied in the case of Japan), it is doubtful whether the decision had any true bearing on the outcome of events. German resistance was stubbornly prolonged because of Hitler's fierce obstinacy and his support by the military, not because responsible leaders would have been willing or able to sue for peace if the Allies had offered them appropriate terms. At Teheran, in December 1943, the Allies discussed the occupation and demilitarization of Germany and laid plans for the establishment of a postwar international organization.

As the Russian armies advanced against the Germans in 1944, the fate of central and eastern Europe became a very important question. Throughout the war Roosevelt and the Americans, unwilling to disturb the unity of the Western-Soviet coalition in the global struggle, followed a policy of postponing controversial territorial and political decisions until victory was assured. Churchill was more apprehensive. Steeped in traditional balance-of-power politics, he sensed that, without bargaining and prior political arrangements, the victory over the Nazis would leave Russia dominant over all eastern Europe. Acting on his own, he visited Stalin in October 1944 and sketched out a demarcation of spheres of influence for the Western powers and the Soviets in the Balkan states (a Russian preponderance in Rumania and Bulgaria, a Western preponderance in Greece, and an even division of influence in Hungary and Yugoslavia). Russian control over the Baltic states had virtually been conceded by the British earlier. But Roosevelt and the State Department would not ratify any such agreement, which they considered old-fashioned and a dangerous revival of the worst features of pre-1914 diplomacy. Soon, however, political decisions had to be made. The two

10 See p. 682.

conferences that arrived at the most important political decisions were the meetings at Yalta and at Potsdam in 1945.

The Yalta meeting in February 1945 took place when the Allies were close to final victory—closer, events disclosed, than anyone at the time realized. The three Allied statesmen met at an old tsarist Crimean summer resort on the Black Sea, toasted their common triumphs, and took the measure of each other. Roosevelt thought of himself in the role of a mediator between Churchill and Stalin where European issues were involved. He took pains to avoid giving Stalin the impression that he and Churchill were in any sense united against him; in point of fact, Roosevelt was suspicious of Churchill's devotion to empire and colonial ties, which he considered anachronistic for the postwar world. Despite differences, the Big Three reached agreements, at least formally, on Poland and eastern Europe, the future of Germany, the war in the Far East, and the projected postwar international organization, the United Nations.

The discussion of Poland and eastern Europe raised the most serious difficulties. Stalin's armies, having driven the Nazi forces to within forty miles of Berlin, were in control of Poland and almost all eastern and central Europe. The Russians remembered these areas as anti-Soviet, and Poland particularly as the perpetrator of aggression against Soviet territory in 1920, and as the ancient corridor of attack upon Russia. Stalin had already taken steps to establish a "friendly" government in Poland, i.e., a government subservient to the Soviets. Neither Roosevelt nor Churchill had fought the war against the Nazis to leave the Soviet Union the undisputed master of all eastern Europe and in a position to impose a totalitarian political system on all this vast area. At Yalta, Roosevelt and Churchill extracted from Stalin a number of promises for the areas he controlled. In accordance with the Atlantic Charter, the liberated states were to be permitted provisional governments "broadly representative of all democratic elements in the population," i.e., not consisting merely, as in the case of the provisional government of Poland already established, of authorities subservient to the Soviets. They pressed Stalin to pledge also the "earliest possible establishment through free elections of governments responsive to the will of the people." The pledge was a verbal concession that cost the Russian leader little; he rejected the suggestion of international supervision over the elections. The Declaration on Liberated Europe, promising sovereign rights of self-determination, provided a false sense of agreement.

A number of territorial changes were also accepted, pending final settlement at a postwar peace conference. It was agreed that the Russian-Polish, or eastern, boundary of Poland should be set roughly at the so-called Curzon line, the frontier contemplated by the Allies in 1919 before the Poles conquered territory to their east. The Poles were to be compensated, in the north and west, at the expense of Germany.[11] On this and on other matters relating to Germany there was a large area of accord; the three were united in their hatred of German Nazism and militarism. Germany was to be disarmed and divided into four occupation zones under the administration of the Big Three powers and France—the latter at the insistence of Churchill. There was vague talk, at Yalta and earlier, of dismembering Germany, of undoing the work of Bismarck, but the difficulties of such an

[11] See maps, p. 319 and front endpapers; and see p. 711.

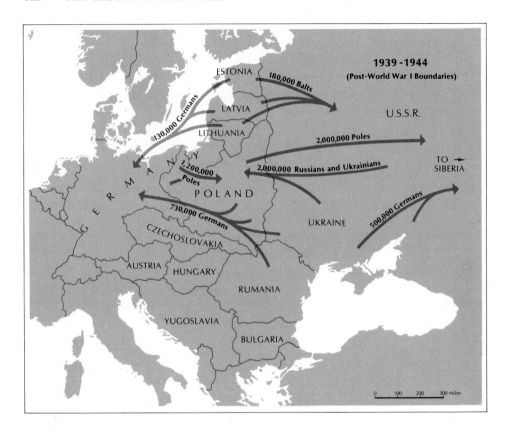

DEPORTATION AND RESETTLEMENT, 1939–1950

The age-old distribution of nationalities in Central and Eastern Europe was radically transformed between 1939 and 1950. Not only were about 6,000,000 Jews put to death, with over 300,000 of the survivors emigrating to Israel by 1950, but millions of Germans, Poles, and others were forcibly uprooted.

The first stage, shown in the left-hand panel, began with the Nazi-Soviet Pact of 1939, after which the Germans occupied western Poland, while the Russians annexed eastern Poland and the three Baltic republics. Western Poland received Poles expelled from Germany, while in eastern Poland about 2,000,000 Poles were deported to Siberia, being replaced by about the same number of Russians and Ukrainians. Many Estonians, Latvians, and Lithuanians were moved to other parts of the Soviet Union. Germans who had lived in Eastern Europe for centuries were displaced. Thousands "returned" to Germany from the Baltic republics and from places in Rumania and elsewhere where they had long formed German enclaves. The "Volga Germans" and others in south Russia were sent to Siberia.

undertaking were understood and the proposal was postponed, later to be discarded completely. Also discarded, as impracticable, was the Morgenthau plan, seriously considered as late as 1944, which was designed to transform industrial Germany back into an eighteenth-century pastoral and agricultural economy. The Americans and British rejected as excessive the demands for reparations raised by

A second stage (right-hand panel) came with the Soviet victory and the collapse of Hitler's Reich. The German-Polish frontier was now moved westward to the Oder River. Millions of Germans from east of the Oder, along with more millions from the Sudeten regions of Czechoslovakia and a continuing stream from Hungary and Rumania, were thrown back into what remained of Germany, most of them fleeing to the Western zone, but some to what was the Soviet zone in 1945. Poles streamed into what had been Germany east of the Oder; others came into Poland from the Ukraine. Russians moved into what had been eastern Poland and the Baltic states. Ukrainians and various non-Russian minorities were sent to Siberia. Some Balts escaped to the West (including the United States); others were redistributed to various places in the Soviet Union.

There was a considerable resettlement also of Hungarians, Slovaks, and Finns. The most conspicuous changes, however, in addition to the virtual disappearance of East European Jewry, were the expulsion of the Germans from Eastern Europe and a westward movement of Poles and Russians. (Source: *Westermanns Atlas zur Weltgeschichte.*)

the Soviets, a sum of $20 billion to be paid in kind, half to the Soviets. It was agreed, however, that reparations would go to those countries that had borne the main burdens of the war and suffered the heaviest losses. The Soviet Union was to receive half of whatever total sum was set.

To the satisfaction of everyone, the participants agreed on plans for a postwar international organization, to be called the United Nations. Roosevelt believed it essential to win the Soviets over to the idea of an international organization. He was convinced that the big powers, cooperating within the framework of the United Nations, and acting as international policemen, could alone preserve the future peace and security of the world. No less than Stalin or Churchill, he emphasized the importance of the big powers in the new organization, although he accepted a dignified role for the smaller nations as well. All agreed that each of the big powers, the permanent members of the new organization's Security Council, would have a veto power on important decisions. The Soviets pressed for more than one vote in the General Assembly of the new organization, arguing that their constitution gave sovereign rights to each of their constituent republics and that the British dominions would each have a seat. In the interests of harmony they were given three seats.

Critical agreements were reached on the Far East. Here political and military decisions were inextricably linked. In April 1941 the Soviets had concluded a nonaggression treaty with Japan and had remained neutral in the Pacific war despite their historic interests in the Far East. Given the magnitude of the war effort on the European front, no one pressed the Soviets to enter the Pacific war. It was agreed to wait at least until the Germans were on the verge of defeat. At Yalta, Stalin agreed to enter the war against Japan, but Soviet "public opinion," he averred, would demand compensation. It was stipulated that the U.S.S.R. would enter the war against Japan "two to three months" after Germany had surrendered. In return, the Soviets were to have restored to them territories and rights that tsarist Russia had lost to Japan forty years before in the Russo-Japanese war of 1904–1905—the southern half of Sakhalin Island, and in Manchuria special concessions at the warm-water port of Dairen and at the naval base of Port Arthur, as well as joint control with China over the Manchurian railroads leading to these ports; in addition, the Soviets were to receive the Kurile Islands, which had not been Russian before.[12] The Russian position in Outer Mongolia was also to remain unaltered. Meanwhile Stalin confirmed Chinese political sovereignty over Manchuria, despite the privileges granted to the Soviets, and pledged Soviet support for the Nationalist government of China, then on uneasy terms with the Chinese Communists.[13]

But China was not a party to any of these concessions, which for a time were kept secret. Roosevelt took it upon himself to secure the consent of Chiang Kai-shek, which he subsequently did. By the territorial concessions to the Soviets in the Far East, the Western powers seemed to be sanctioning the replacement of Japanese imperialism by Russian imperialism in the long contested area of northeast China, and without China having any voice in the matter at all. The concessions were the price to be paid for Soviet assistance against the Japanese, assistance then considered indispensable for the final defeat of Japan. What really exasperated so many in later years was that Russia's entry into the war, as pledged, was not of any military consequence; it came two days after the atomic bomb had been dropped and at a time when the Japanese were in a desperate state, near collapse and surrender, even without the dropping of the atomic

---

[12] See pp. 638–640 and map, p. 639.
[13] See pp. 754–755, 858–859.

bomb. The concessions in the Far East need not have been made. Even without the Yalta agreement, nothing perhaps except outright force could have deterred Stalin from moving into Manchuria after the Japanese collapse, or indeed from controlling eastern Europe as he wished. The Yalta agreement, however, lent an aura of respectability to Soviet expansion.

Roosevelt made concessions at Yalta not only because he appreciated the Soviet war effort against the Germans but because he believed that he needed their support in the last phase of the war against the Japanese; he wished to preserve the Western-Soviet coalition until final victory was guaranteed. Above all else, he believed that wartime harmony would produce postwar cordiality, especially if all the participating personalities remained alive to assure it. Churchill, less certain of the future and of "diplomacy by friendship," would have preferred a franker recognition and definition of spheres of influence. Such ideas were ruled out as the thinking of a bygone era. Yet the spirit of the Atlantic Charter, so closely identified with the American president, the pledge of sovereign self-determination for all peoples, was contravened at Yalta in many ways. Like the Versailles treaty of 1919, the decisions at Yalta would not have been so disappointing had the ideals not been set so high.

At Potsdam, in July 1945, after the German collapse, the Big Three met again. A new American president, Harry S. Truman, represented the United States; President Roosevelt had died in April, on the eve of final victory. Churchill, in the midst of the conference, was replaced by a new British prime minister, Clement Attlee, after the Labour party's victory at the polls. Stalin still represented Russia. By now, disagreements between the Western Allies and the Soviets had deepened, not only over Soviet control in Poland, eastern Europe, and the Balkans, but over German reparations and other matters. Yet the Western leaders were still prepared to make concessions in the hope of establishing harmonious relations. Agreements were announced on the postwar treatment of Germany, on German disarmament, demilitarization, "denazification," and the punishment of war criminals. It was agreed that each power might take reparations in kind from its occupation zone and that the Russians would get substantial additional deliveries from the Western zones so that the original $10 million Soviet demand was virtually met. Pending the final peace treaty, German territory east of the Oder-Neisse rivers was committed to Polish administration. The details of this decision had earlier been postponed; now the Polish-German boundary was set at the western Neisse, even further west than originally envisaged. Poland thus extended its territorial boundaries about a hundred miles westward as compensation for Russian westward expansion at Polish expense. German East Prussia was similarly divided between Russia in the north and Poland in the south. Königsberg, founded by the Teutonic Knights, for centuries the ducal seat of Prussian dukes and the coronation city of Prussian kings, became the Russian city of Kaliningrad. The ancient German cities of Stettin and Breslau became the Polish cities of Szczecin and Wroclaw. The de facto administration of these areas hardened into permanent rule. The transfer of the German population in these eastern areas was supposed to be effected in an orderly and humane fashion; but millions of Germans were driven from their homes or fled within a few months. For them (and for the Germans who were expelled from the Sudetenland) it was the final consummation of the war that Hitler had unleashed.

It was agreed at Potsdam that peace treaties would be signed as soon as possible with the former German satellite states; the task of preparing them was entrusted to a Council of Foreign Ministers representing the United States, Britain, France, the Soviet Union, and China. In the months that followed, the widening chasm between the Soviets and the West manifested itself in stormy meetings of the Foreign Ministers' Council in London, Paris, and New York, as well as in a peace conference held in Paris in 1946, at which were represented the twenty-one states that had contributed substantial military forces to the defeat of the Axis powers. Eighteen months after Potsdam, in February 1947, treaties were signed with Italy, Rumania, Hungary, Bulgaria, and Finland. All these states paid reparations and agreed to certain territorial adjustments. In 1951 a peace treaty was signed with Japan, but not by the Soviets, who made their own peace in 1956. The years went by but no final peace treaty was signed with Germany, a Germany divided into two. For the wartime Western-Soviet coalition had fallen apart, shattering the dreams and aspirations of those who had fought the Second World War to a resounding triumph over one kind of aggression and totalitarianism, and then found themselves confronted with a new age of crisis.

Paradoxes of Modernity

"Modernization" is an experience that peoples throughout the the world are undergoing in the later twentieth century. It takes many forms, but among its most obvious signs are airplanes and supermarkets, computer technology and urban congestion. That these can now be found in all continents is suggested in the following pages.

One consequence is a new global uniformity in certain aspects of civilization. It is no longer a matter of Westernization, as used to be said of what happened in Japan and Russia, nor of the Americanization of the world that has sometimes been pointed to with alarm. It is a process in which Americans and Europeans have been instrumental, but which arises from the effects of modern science, engineering, medicine, transportation, and electronic communications wherever they are introduced. It seems that human beings of all cultures and races may develop an aptitude to pursue these activities, and that they have wants which such activities can supply.

But as modern civilization becomes more widespread, paradoxical countercurrents are set up. Cultures interpenetrate one another. While Asia and Africa adopt new techniques from the West, Europeans and Americans seek out Eastern religions or find a new meaning in West African tribal art. Older cultures are eroded in Asia and Africa, and in the West itself, where practices that have characterized Europe at least since the Renaissance—in painting, sculpture, architecture, literature, religion, personal values, child rearing, and family life—have been increasingly called into question. Some peoples, on the other hand, feel a new attachment to their own background as a means of heightening their own identity. Accepting the interdependence of a world civilization, they strive not only for political but for cultural or spiritual independence.

To operate an airline, or any other appurtenance of modern civilization, requires a high degree of accuracy, division of labor, and the synchronization of the efforts of many persons who must perform certain actions at a given time. These in turn presuppose the objectivity of knowledge and rationality of behavior, and an acceptance of discipline, foresight, organization, and management. But these very qualities generate their opposites. It is a further paradox that new philosophies of subjectivity and irrationalism, revolts against form, and demands for free self-expression have been thought of as signs of modernity in the twentieth century. Organization restricts liberty, yet is necessary to modern life. It is not easy for man to adapt to the social environment that he has himself created to improve his condition. The paradox is as old as Rousseau, yet is felt increasingly every day.

The office of International Business Machines seems in strange company alongside the
mosque in Istanbul, Turkey, but it would seem no more so alongside a Gothic church
in Europe. Here there is the additional juxtaposition of East and West.

At the right, two youths work on a computer problem at Ibadan University in Nigeria.
Their costume reflects their own time and place, but the young man at the right shows
a concentration and perplexity that are universal. Ibadan University is a new institution,
dating from 1962, but the multiplication of universities, with their attendant problems,
is a sign of modernization in all countries.

The scene above is in Mongolia, where the modernizing slogan has been "Today a million horses, tomorrow a million machines." A rider sits on a small horse of the kind on which his ancestors have repeatedly swept across inner Asia, while his smiling companion on a motorcycle looks as if he might like to do the same.

At the right, three Yoruba women shop in a supermarket at Lagos, Nigeria. Urbanization has proceeded so rapidly in Africa that Lagos now has about a million people in its metropolitan area. Most of them were born in rural villages under very different conditions.

The assumptions underlying Western art since the Renaissance have perhaps been abandoned most fully in sculpture. The statue which celebrated a great man or an allegorical figure from the fifteenth century through the nineteenth has become even more rare than the realistic portrait painting; it might even be thought ludicrous today.

Henry Moore, at the left, born in England in 1898, is one of the leading sculptors of the twentieth century. He is shown in a room where he keeps his collection of plaster maquettes, the working models for the finished products over his long career. As early as 1920, breaking with European traditions of sculpture, he became interested in the art of pre-Columbian America, black Africa, and archaic or preclassical Greece. The models on these shelves reveal influences of this kind. In the quest for a new accent, for boldness of line or emphatic abstraction, the modern and the primitive come together.

At the right, workmen decorate the base of a new building in Lagos. The building itself, the 25-story Independence House, is a monument to modernization, but the façade shown here, with its bas-relief by the Nigerian sculptor Relix Idubor, represents three figures from traditional folklore or history.

Above: A group of women in India hear a social worker explain family planning and contraception, as part of a national and international program to control the explosive growth of population, which in India has been increasing by about ten millions a year.

834

At the left: Rush hour in Tokyo. Except for the three Japanese characters, and the Japanese faces, this could be a picture from many other cities in the world, where thousands of men and women must start for home over considerable distances at exactly the same time.

Above: American motor cars are unloaded at a dock in the Persian Gulf. They are destined for Kuwait, to which a hundred of them will be driven in a modern-style desert caravan. The dependence of industrial countries on the Middle East for oil is partly offset by its dependence on them for motorized vehicles.

Above: Five disciples consult a guru or religious teacher in an obscure retreat in the foothills of the Himalayas. The two in front are from Latin America and have come to India in the belief that the philosophies of Hinduism and the ancient Mayas may have much in common. They are in any case seeking for something that they do not find in modern civilization.

Left: A Japanese super-express passes Mt. Fuji between Tokyo and Osaka. If not a paradox, it is at least worthy of comment, that some forms of modernization have gone further in Japan than in Europe or North America.

XXI.
The Contemporary Age: Cold War, Communism, and Colonial Revolution

A cataclysm, according to Webster's dictionary, is "any violent change involving sudden and extensive alterations of the earth's surface; hence, any upheaval, especially a social or political one." A cataclysm in nature, as we may imagine it, is a time when volcanoes erupt, earthquakes rumble, old mountain systems are broken down, new peaks and ranges thrust themselves upward, the very coastlines assume new shapes, living creatures flee from destruction, old forms of life become extinct, and new forms of life, at first unnoticed, enter upon careers in which they are later to flourish. The human world has been in the grip of such a cataclysm since 1914. The two World Wars, the Russian and Chinese revolutions, the Great Depression, the Nazi and Fascist dictatorships, the development of nuclear energy, the end of the European colonial empires in Asia and Africa, and the emergence of dozens of new nations—all are part of the changes that have altered the coastlines of modern human society beyond recognition, and for which "cataclysm" is not too strong a word.

Many of the changes have taken place since 1945. It is difficult to do justice to the complexities of our own world and to keep abreast of the onrushing events of our day. The following two chapters attempt to sketch the most memorable developments of what we have called the contemporary age.

Chapter Emblem: The earth as seen from a satellite 22,300 miles away, transmitting a photograph to a station in North Carolina.

108. THE COLD WAR AND THE RECOVERY OF WESTERN EUROPE

People and Nations

Broadly speaking, the world in the second half of the twentieth century faced no wholly new problems, yet certain basic problems that had troubled mankind for over a century had become both more complex and more urgent. Three can be singled out—science, industrialism, and national sovereignty.

The problem of science was dramatized by the atomic bomb. The world shuddered at the instantaneous destruction of Hiroshima. The postwar contest to produce even more sophisticated atomic and hydrogen bombs spurred the realization that a third world war would be unimaginably more awful. The use of intercontinental guided missiles, radio controls, proximity fuses, and probably biological warfare could be foreseen. Human beings now possessed the means to annihilate not only their civilizations but almost their existence on the planet. This thought was especially shocking to a world that had set its highest values on social progress.

The problem of science was not new. Science, and its partner, invention, had for a long time transformed both industry and war. It had conquered many of the dreaded plagues and diseases of the world. Observant people had long known that science could be applied either constructively or destructively. It was the magnitude of destructive possibilities that made formerly indifferent persons now worry over the problem. The accumulation of scientific knowledge, instead of heightening the quality of human life, had taken on the ghastly distortions of a nightmare. Scientists themselves, after the first atomic explosion, affirmed the need for a moral regeneration. They insisted that science was neutral, free from blame for the horror of Hiroshima, that the trouble lay not with science but the uses to which scientific knowledge was put.

One answer was that there must be more social science. With better understanding of society and of human behavior, it seemed, people need not use physical science to kill each other. It was certainly true that the more fully society was understood, the better for all concerned. But here too lay a danger. From the scientific understanding of human behavior it could be a short step to the scientific control of human behavior. We have seen how, in totalitarian states, governments not only accepted the fact that people were shaped by environment but undertook to monopolize the environment and do the shaping themselves. A society in which science was pursued as one of many interests was one thing; a purely "scientific" society was another. In the latter, people might simply be manipulated by experts. George Orwell's 1984 and Aldous Huxley's Brave New World, among the best known of the "antiutopias," were fictional projections of such manipulation.

The problem of industrialism and of security in an industrial society also persisted. There were in theory two opposite social poles. At one, best represented by the U.S.S.R., all capital was owned by the state and supplied to workers as needed, and all interchange was carefully planned by public authorities in advance. At the other pole, best demonstrated by the United States, capital was owned by private persons who chose the channels of investment and hence determined the availability of jobs, and interchange took place through the mechanism of the market. Neither system was in practice logically pure, and in fact mixed economies became the rule in many countries, but the differences remained pronounced. The chief drawback in the Soviet system was its lack of freedom, in the American system its lack of stability and economic security. Americans spent a good deal more time trying to correct the lack of security than the Soviets did in trying to correct the lack of freedom.

The devastation of Western Europe in 1945, the problem of a ruined industrialism in one of the world's chief industrial areas, of a society unable to produce with efficiency yet obliged to produce enough to satisfy a civilized population, inevitably raised political questions. Nor was Europe the only center of trouble. In Asia and Africa the impact of Western ideas and technologies had helped create societies that sought Western technological proficiency but also at the same time sought independence from the West. The conditions of a world-wide industrialism, and advances in medicine, sanitation, and public health, helped to build up dense populations, which after the war grew at unprecedented rates. The new governments believed that only by industrializing could they raise their living standards. They needed machinery, loans, advisers; they looked in part to the Soviet Union and in part to the United States. Colonialism in Asia and Africa was dead, but the need of Asians and Africans for assistance was very much alive; in the furnishing of assistance there was bound to be competition.

Another question hinged on the unity and diversity of the modern world. Was the modern world really "one world," or was it not? It was one world in the sense that it required a good deal of mutual exchange and in the sense that political repercussions traveled over it rapidly and world cultures interacted as never before. But it was far from homogeneous; all admired the steam turbine, and stood in awe of atomic fission, but beyond the material level their schemes of values diverged widely. No people wished to be subordinated to another or to lose its way of life in a uniform world civilization. Here lay the root of the problem of national independence and of its corollary, world organization.

After the Second World War, as after the First, an international organization was set up to prevent war in the future.[1] A conference of all anti-Axis powers, held at San Francisco in 1945, established the United Nations and drew up its Charter. The new organization was designed to maintain international peace and security, encourage cooperation in solving international social, economic, and cultural problems, and work for equality and the expansion of human freedom. Of its numerous agencies, two were central. The General Assembly was a deliberative body in which all recognized sovereign states, however small, were considered equal. The Security Council, whose primary responsibility was the preservation of peace, consisted of fifteen members, the five states regarded as Great Powers as permanent members and ten additional rotating members to be chosen by the Assembly for two-year terms. Apart from the United States and the U.S.S.R., it was not easy to define the Great Powers in 1945 but the permanent seats were assigned to the United States, the Soviet Union, Great Britain, France, and China.

Each permanent member had a veto power. Thus the Security Council could act on important matters only if the Great Powers were unanimous. There was

[1] See pp. 682, 689, 823–824.

much criticism of the Great Power veto but it was considered necessary. In major crises the agreement of the Great Powers would be needed to maintain world peace. The U.S.S.R. demanded the veto most frankly (and used it most freely), but the United States, too, would not have joined without this safeguard. Many remembered that the old League was weak because the United States had never joined, and the Soviet Union had been admitted only belatedly. In the following years even small countries on occasion refused to abide by judgments of the United Nations. The fact was that no nation, large or small, was willing to forego its independence in a matter considered vital, or submerge itself in a world state with authority to put down violence anywhere—as the national state could do within its own borders.

The United Nations had fifty-one original members—the countries involved in some way in the war against the Axis. Its headquarters was located in New York. The Charter provided for the admission of new members, including the former Axis countries and their satellites, and also wartime neutrals, so that it could be truly international. From 1947 to 1955 a few additional states were admitted, in 1955 sixteen additional nations, and then in the following two decades the organization expanded to almost three times its original number. Not only in membership but in other ways the United Nations, and especially the General Assembly, evolved along lines unanticipated in 1945.[2] But for the most part, in the postwar period, the rivalry between the two superpowers, the United States and the Soviet Union, frustrated any international efforts to bring about disarmament and peace.

The Struggle for Europe

Although the United Nations Security Council provided permanent seats for five powers, the war, in effect, left only two Great Powers still standing in any strength, the United States and the Soviet Union. Since the seventeenth century the world has normally had about a half dozen Great Powers. That there were only two in 1945 made a great difference. Moreover, the two were superpowers, continental land giants, possessing enormous resources and military strength, overshadowing all other states, including the powers of Europe that had long dominated events in the modern centuries. The characteristic of a two-state system, not found in a multiple-state system, is that each superpower knows in advance who its only dangerous enemy can be. In such a situation diplomatic delicacy breaks down. Measures that either power takes for its own security seem to be provocations to the other. After the war the United States and the U.S.S.R. fell into this unpleasant dualistic relationship. From 1945 on, a diplomatic and ideological clash of interests and ideas set in that came to be known as the Cold War.

We have already noted the state of affairs at the close of hostilities.[3] Russian armies occupied eastern Europe as far west as the river Elbe; American, British, and French armies held the remainder of Germany, most of Austria, and all of Italy. The movement of ground armies during the fighting generally determined the spheres of influence after the peace, except that the four Allied powers effected the necessary transfer of troops in order to occupy the zones of Germany

2 See below, pp. 937, 941–942.
3 See pp. 815–819.

agreed upon at Potsdam. The Soviets at the last moment, in August 1945, had declared war on Japan and moved into Manchuria and Korea. After the war, from 1945 to 1947, they lent aid to separatists in northern Iran; pressed the Turks for joint control of the Turkish Straits; favored the Communists in a civil war in Greece; forced Communist governments upon the countries of eastern Europe; installed a Communist regime in East Germany; refused to cooperate in economic policies toward occupied Germany; and rejected atomic disarmament proposals. In Asia, they supported Communist-led independence movements in Indochina and elsewhere, and helped to establish a pro-Communist regime in North Korea.

It was not possible for anyone (even in the U.S.S.R.) to know what Stalin and his associates in the Kremlin really believed or intended in 1945. Probably, as confirmed Marxist-Leninists, they considered a clash between the U.S.S.R. and the Western powers to be inevitable at some indefinite future date. Probably they were disturbed by the American monopoly of the atomic bomb, and possibly by the economic strength of American capitalism, which might seek to recapture markets in eastern Europe and elsewhere. Probably they felt that the fluid postwar situation gave them a chance to establish an outer buffer zone favorable to the U.S.S.R., a program on which they had already embarked in their alliance with Germany in 1939, which had allowed them to absorb eastern Poland and the Baltic states (or to reabsorb them, since these regions had been Russian for over a century before 1918). Probably they saw in the aftermath of the Second World War, as in the First, an opportunity to advance the international Marxist revolution in Europe and Asia. Whether the Russians were acting defensively to protect their own national security or aggressively to promote communism on a world scale, President Truman and his advisers became convinced that the Soviets were embarked on a universal Communist offensive which it was their responsibility to halt.

One of the early casualties of the rift was a plan advanced by the United States to put the manufacture of atomic weapons under international supervision. The United States proposed an international control body to prevent the manufacture of atomic bombs by national governments; that body would have the right to send inspectors at will into all countries and to enforce sanctions, regardless of the veto, against any country found guilty of unauthorized uses of atomic power. To the Soviets the idea of having foreigners freely examine their society had always been repugnant. They declared that inspection would violate national sovereignty, and they questioned the good faith of the American proposal. Rejecting the proposal, they proceeded with their own atomic research, as did the United States. By 1949 the U.S.S.R. was equipped to conduct atomic warfare. The atomic armaments race, universally dreaded, began.

The Soviet Union, to protect its interests in an international body where the overwhelming majority was consistently against it, made frequent use of its veto in the United Nations. From 1945 to 1955 the Soviets used the veto seventy-five times, the United States three. The United States still found the United Nations inadequate as an instrument to check Communist expansion. With Britain unable to help in any meaningful way because of economic weakness, the United States formulated a positive national policy of its own to "contain" communism, committing the United States to new global responsibilities. In 1947, by the "Truman Doctrine," it supplied military equipment and professional military advisers to

Greece and Turkey, and announced a policy of assisting all peoples to prevent forcible capture of their governments by minority parties. At the same time, Secretary of State George Marshall announced in 1947 an American program of broad economic aid to all European countries—including the Soviet satellites if they would accept it. The hope was that the economic reconstruction of Europe would prevent Communist gains from hunger and distress.

The Soviets for their part denounced the American capitalist and imperialist "warmongers." With the United States arming Greece and Turkey, with American carriers able to sail the length of the Mediterranean or lie off the coast of Murmansk, with American air bases established or easy to establish in the Middle East, with the Americans in occupation of southern Korea and Japan and virtually annexing Okinawa, and with the bulk of the United States lying across the North Pole from the vital centers of the Soviet Union, and the American capacity for long-range bombardment already sufficiently demonstrated, the Soviets not unnaturally felt encircled. Soviet suspicions—dating from Western intervention in the Russian civil wars of 1918–1919, the Munich Pact of 1938, the second-front controversy in the Second World War, the abrupt cessation of Lend-Lease at the end of the war, and other sources of friction—became inflamed.

The great object of rivalry in the early postwar years was Europe. Europe, the main protagonist of this long history, was in ruins in 1945. The Second World War left it in a worse state of shock and disorder than the First. Physical destruction was incomparably greater. In the First World War trench warfare had thoroughly destroyed limited regions. In the Second the ground fighting had made a ruin of western Russia, and the air bombing had reduced whole cities, especially in Germany, to piles of debris. The so-called strategic bombing of the Allies had blighted the productive industry and the transport facilities of the Continent. Goods, even if produced, could not be moved; millions of refugees from bombed-out cities or from hostile political regimes sought desperately for an asylum. The war had ruined one of the world's chief industrial areas and brought its economic system to collapse.

In a year or two the worst local devastation was repaired, but the problems of transportation and exchange remained. Industrial Europe was unable to trade with agricultural eastern Europe or with the world. The Continent was in the position in which the First World War had left Vienna. Europe was a world metropolis, a kind of huge continental city, cut off from the areas with which it had carried on its trade. It had long lived by imports for which it could no longer afford to pay. It could not pay because in the Second World War, as in the First, Europeans had lost their overseas investments, and overseas countries had built up their own industries and needed those of Europe less. At the same time, Europe had a politically awakened population that would not accept starvation or suffer in mute resignation.

Europe was not to be written off; its combined population exceeded that of either of the superpowers, and even in ruins it possessed one of the world's leading industrial plants. One of the chief postwar questions was therefore the rescue of Europe, or, in practical politics, who Europe's "rescuer" would be. There were only two candidates, the U.S.S.R. and the United States. Europeans did not relish the prospect of being rescued by either. Most Europeans regarded communism as slavery. In France and Italy, to be sure, almost a quarter of the people voted Communist, and Communists held important positions in labor unions; but the number of those actually desirous of a Communist society was not large, and much of the Communist vote represented mainly opposition to traditional and routine ways of handling social and economic problems. Social cleavages existed between the classes, but short of catastrophe, Europe would not go Communist. Nor was the number large of those who wished to be remodeled according to the economy or culture of the United States. Dependency even on the benefactions of the United States they feared as a gamble; remembering the depression of 1929, and how all Europe had gone down after the cessation of American loans, they had no desire to be dependent upon American capitalism. Europe, like the world's other great aggregates, wanted to preserve its identity and its spiritual independence. But between the programs of the two superpowers there was the difference that the Soviets had more to gain by chaos in Europe, and the United States more to gain by its rebuilding. Immediately after the war the United States sent billions of dollars' worth of goods to relieve the distress of Europe and then embarked on the Marshall Plan. The motives behind the Marshall Plan were much discussed and even impugned. In effect, the Americans satisfied their humanitarian impulse, found markets for their own industries (at the American taxpayers' expense), reduced the drift of working-class Europeans into the Communist camp, and soon made possible an amazing and rapid revival of industrial Europe.

The key to the rebuilding of Europe was Germany. The Ruhr was still Europe's industrial heartland. The former Allies had agreed to have common policies and joint control for Germany even though each occupied a separate zone. They agreed that Germany should pay reparations, especially to the Soviet Union, which had suffered most from German military power. Gradually the American government, to make Europe self-supporting and less dependent on American aid, came to favor the economic reconstruction of Germany. The Russians became apprehensive. They wished to use Germany to rebuild the Soviet Union. The Americans wished to use it to rebuild Europe; they did not wish to pour aid into Germany to have it drained off as reparations to the U.S.S.R. By 1946 joint administration of Germany broke down. The Russians reaffirmed their hold on eastern Germany; the Americans, British, and French went their own way in the western zones. Each side competed for the good will of the late enemy. Each accused the other of partitioning the country in violation of their agreements.

In 1947 relations between the two superpowers deteriorated further. In France and Italy the Communists, who had earlier cooperated in postwar reconstruction, now encouraged quasi-insurrectionary strikes, and Communist ministers were dropped from the cabinet. Early in 1948 the Czech Communist party seized power in Prague, ending a democratic coalition experiment and turning Czechoslovakia into a Communist-dominated regime. The Soviets forbade their satellites to participate in the Marshall Plan. In the summer of 1948, retaliating for the American, British, and French unification of western Germany and the introduction of currency reform there, the Soviets blockaded Berlin and cut off all rail and road routes through East Germany to the western sectors of the city. The Western powers, notably the United States, responded with a massive "air lift," daily flying in thousands of tons of supplies to prevent starvation among the Berlin populace. After almost a year, the blockade was lifted; but it was only the first of several crises over Berlin. Meanwhile, the United States and the western European powers proceeded with plans for the economic reconstruction and defense of Europe, and the U.S.S.R. drew it satellites closer together.

The Recovery of Western Europe

Under the Marshall Plan, which went into effect in 1948, the huge grants to western Germany and to Europe continued, but the grants no longer were regarded as stopgap relief. American aid was henceforth to be so apportioned among the various countries, and so coordinated with each country's policies and with joint policies of the European countries acting together, as to enable Europe to stand on its own feet and play its own part in international trade. American officials pressed the Europeans to reduce tariff barriers and currency controls against each other. Only by creating a free and Europe-wide internal market could Europeans obtain the advantage of mass production and lower costs such as prevailed in the United States.

The results of the Marshall Plan exceeded the boldest anticipations of its sponsors. The trend after the First World War toward high tariffs and economic rigidity, the United States taking the lead, had culminated in the Great Depression and with it had come an intensification of economic nationalism. Under the Marshall Plan the trend was reversed. There were now freer trade conditions among the participating Western European countries and freer world trade as well. In Western Europe industrial production rose dramatically. By 1950, within only two years of the inauguration of the plan, industrial production in West Germany reached and exceeded prewar levels, and continued to rise; by the early 1950s the boom spread to France and Italy and, though to a lesser degree, to Britain. Western Europeans began to enjoy a remarkable prosperity; their economies grew at unprecedented rates, and living standards and consumption levels rose strikingly, even if not rapidly enough to satisfy all the expectations aroused. For about twenty years this economic growth and prosperity continued without serious interruption.

The Marshall Plan was in a sense revolutionary; it had proposed nothing less than that a wealthy country like the United States should use its economic resources to revive its competitors. It was a mixture of creative generosity and shrewd statesmanship. It recognized the mutual interdependence of all members of the world-wide economy, and it served American interests by guaranteeing a revived world market, of which the United States would be one of the chief beneficiaries. For Asia, Africa, and Latin America, where the problem was not to revive a sick industrial economy but to create industry, other programs of long-range capital investment were launched. There, too, communism would be combatted by removing its breeding grounds of poverty and want.

The countries of Western Europe, having received their initial impulse from the Marshall Plan, then acted boldly and imaginatively. They took additional steps on their own toward economic integration. In 1952, under a French plan developed by Robert Schuman and Jean Monnet, the six Continental industrial countries—France, Italy, West Germany, Belgium, the Netherlands, and Luxembourg—set up a European Coal and Steel Community to pool their coal and steel resources. Not only were the production results significant but the supranational agencies established in Luxembourg became the groundwork for later economic and political cooperation. In 1957, under treaties signed at Rome, an even more ambitious step by the same six countries created the European Economic Community, or Common Market, which aimed at the elimination of all internal tariff barriers, the development of a common tariff system with respect to the outside world, and the free movement of labor and capital within the Common Market itself. Moreover, the six signatories pronounced European economic integration the avenue to political unity. Under the same treaties, to pool their atomic resources and research, the six also set up a European Atomic Community.

The Common Market, in operation by 1958, became one the thriving economic aggregates of the world. By 1968 the last internal tariff was dropped; over 175 million people were joined in a large free trade area. Britain, undecided whether its Commonwealth ties and dependence on low-priced agricultural imports made it feasible to link up with Continental Europe, at first refrained from seeking membership. Subsequently, in 1963 and 1967, the British bid for membership was twice blocked by France, then under the leadership of General de Gaulle, who regarded Britain as a bridgehead for excessive American influence on the Continent and believed that Continental unity would be weakened by British affiliation. In 1960 Britain and six other small nations formed a European Free Trade Association, which also contributed to the liberalization of trade, but lacked the dynamism of the Common Market and disappeared after a decade. In 1973 Britain finally became a member of the European Economic Community, as did Denmark and Ireland, and the original six nations became nine.

The countries of Western Europe also moved slowly and with less dramatic results toward political unity, the creation of a European Community. The legislative machinery set up for budgetary and supervisory authority over the various supranational agencies became a European Parliament, which met in Brussels: many hoped that one day the delegates would be elected by a European-wide electorate, rather than appointed by their respective governments. Western Europe might move from customs union to political unity, as individual nations once had done. The supranational economic and political machinery of the European Economic Community, the day-to-day labors of a European bureaucracy in Brussels and in Luxembourg, the close consultation on common interests, were favorable signs of European unification. The purely political Council of Europe, established earlier at Strasbourg in 1949, continued to meet and to champion the federation of Europe by political cooperation, but was less effective. The likelihood of any real European unity was still remote. The European governments showed no haste to surrender their national sovereignty and independence. France, which had been a pioneer in building postwar European internationalism, showed signs under de Gaulle's influence of a stubborn and persistent older nationalism.

The nations of Western Europe also cooperated closely in making military arrangements with each other and with the United States, at first to ensure against any military revival of Germany but soon directed only against Soviet expansion. Under the Brussels treaty of 1948, Britain, France, Belgium, the Netherlands, and Luxembourg agreed to consult on mutual defense matters. In 1949 the United States took the lead in creating the North Atlantic Treaty Organization (NATO). The treaty, originally signed by twelve nations, but soon joined by West Germany (after 1949, the Federal Republic of Germany), Greece, and Turkey, called for the United States to supply equipment for European rearmament and to guarantee Western Europe against invasion, the unspecified but only enemy being the U.S.S.R. In 1950 the United States pressed to rearm West Germany. When a plan for a European Defense Community (with a common "European army," in which the German military would serve as "European" soldiers) failed to pass the French National Assembly in 1954, the Western European Union came into existence instead. It joined together the five Brussels powers, and the United States, Canada, Italy, and West Germany, and authorized the Federal Republic of Germany to create a national army under the overall command of NATO. The United States, Britain, and Canada were now firmly committed to the defense of the Continent. With American and British commitments, and with European anxiety directed at Soviet expansion, alarm at the possibility of a resurgent German militarism was laid to rest; there remained only a common agreement that Germany would be prohibited from manufacturing atomic weapons. In atomic warfare, all of Western Europe had to depend for protection on an American nuclear umbrella.

In less than a decade after the most devastating war in its history, Western Europe had recovered economically, regained its identity, and was advancing toward economic and political unity. The U.S.S.R. could not be expected to view with equanimity the creation of a new superpower on its western border, for it was as a superpower that a restored and unified Western Europe was taking shape. Any power, not merely the Soviet Union, might object to such consolidation among its neighbors. American encouragement of the unification of Europe thus seemed to the U.S.S.R. another hostile act. The Soviets drew their own satellites closer together. Emulating the European Economic Community, they formalized ties among the East-European satellites by creating a Council for Mutual Economic Aid in 1949, and consummated a network of military alliances in the Warsaw Pact of 1955. But these were only a small part of the vast changes taking place in the Communist worlds that had come into being after 1945.

109. THE COMMUNIST WORLDS: EASTERN EUROPE AND THE SOVIET UNION

Eastern Europe, 1945–1953

If after the Second World War there was nothing so epochal as the Russian Revolution of 1917, the triumph of communism in Eastern Europe in the years after 1945 and in China by 1949 was equally momentous. Whereas communism in 1918 had been chaos, in 1945 it was the way of life of an organized Great Power. The Communist flare-ups in Eastern and Central Europe in 1919 had flickered out, but in 1945 communism materialized in these areas, not through spontaneous popular revolution but through Soviet military strength and the backing the Soviets gave to local Communist leaders.

The Soviets came to control Eastern Europe in the sweep of military operations against the Germans in the last months of the Second World War. The states that fell into the orbit of Soviet influence included Poland, Hungary, Rumania, Bulgaria, and Czechoslovakia; East Germany was also shaped into a Soviet satellite. In all these states Communist-dominated coalition governments were established, closely bound to the Soviet Union. Yugoslavia and Albania, liberated by their own partisan leaders and not by the Red Army, were under single-party Communist regimes but not tied to the Soviet Union. Since the three Baltic states had been incorporated into the Soviet Union in 1940, an additional 100 million Europeans and eleven European states were under Communist-style governments after the Second World War. The areas considered in 1919 a protective buffer against Bolshevism were now under Russian domination. An "iron curtain" was said to have descended, roughly along the old Elbe-Trieste line, sharpening and deepening the centuries-old divergencies in the development of Western and Eastern Europe.[4] Finland, Austria, and Greece escaped Communist domination, Greece only after a fierce civil war that dragged on to 1949, in which anti-Communist forces, aided by a British occupation army, defeated the Communists and restored the Greek monarchy. Elsewhere after 1945, as after the First World War, monarchies fell—in Italy, and in Yugoslavia, Bulgaria, Rumania, and Albania, where the new revolutionary regimes could not be expected to retain their royalty. The Greek monarchy was replaced by a republic in 1974.

The consolidation of Communist control in Eastern Europe took place in stages. During the war it had been understood that the power or powers emancipating an area from the enemy would temporarily exercise political control until the peace treaties were signed. In that way the Western powers controlled political events in Italy without consultation with the Soviets. In Poland, Bulgaria, Rumania, and Hungary, Soviet military occupation made it possible for local Communist leaders, many trained in Moscow and returning from exile, to dominate united front coalition governments. In a state like Bulgaria, Communist domination was complete from the beginning. In the case of Poland, pressure at Yalta and Potsdam forced the Soviets to give representation to the Western-sponsored government-in-exile then in London; the leader of the agrarian party returned to Poland as deputy premier. In all postwar coalitions in Eastern Europe, the Communists shared power, but they held the key ministries of interior, propaganda, and justice, and controlled the police, the army, and the courts. Elements alleged to have been "fascist" or to have collaborated with the Nazis were barred from public life and even from voting. Although many of the nationalist and rightist political elements so excluded were undoubtedly guilty of collaboration and even of fascist sympathies, the loose definition of "fascist" and "reactionary" made it possible to bar many who were only anti-Communist. In the first elections, in Poland and elsewhere, purges and disfranchisement of political "undesirables" made a mockery of Stalin's pledge at Yalta to hold free and unfettered elections in Eastern Europe. This the United States and Great Britain pointed out in strong but ineffectual protests.

All the new regimes introduced important reforms. Continuing the land distribution programs begun after the First World War under non-Communist regimes, they confiscated and redistributed numerous large estates and put uncultivated land to use so that 3 million peasant families acquired about 6 million acres of land; the agrarian reforms were the final blow to the landed aristocracy that had once ruled in the east. Relatively inefficient small farms probably would not raise

[4] See pp. 200–237, 546, and map, p. 202.

productivity, but the reforms, pressed by the agrarian and small landowners' parties, were popular. The new regimes, taking advantage of the fact that industry had been in foreign hands or run by collaborators, also nationalized much of the economy. Struggling with the burden of postwar reconstruction, they even lent a sympathetic ear to the American invitation to them in the summer of 1947 to accept Marshall Plan aid. But Stalin was not disposed to permit these countries to drift into the Western economic orbit, nor did he view favorably the growing strength of the small landowners, or the movement toward free elections in which the Communists could lose their hold. After the summer of 1947, wherever non-Communist elements were still strong, the Communists ousted their political rivals, banned or reduced to impotence all other political parties, and set up single-party Communist regimes, which were styled "people's democracies." In Czechoslovakia, where liberal leaders like Eduard Beneš and Jan Masaryk hoped for a time that their country would serve as a bridge between the Soviets and the West, the coalition government lasted longer than elsewhere but ended with a Communist coup in February 1948 and with the young Masaryk a suicide or victim of political murder.

With the Communists in control, the leaders of the opposition political parties, especially the agrarian leaders, were forced into flight, imprisoned, or in other ways silenced. The people's democracies clashed also with the Catholic church; high-ranking prelates in Hungary, Yugoslavia, and elsewhere were denounced, brought to public trial and imprisoned, and church property confiscated. As in the Russian Revolution, the leaders themselves became victims. From 1949 to 1953, reflecting the tightening repression within the Soviet Union in Stalin's last years, there occurred in the highest ranks of the party the familiar Soviet pattern of purges, arrests, trials, confessions, and executions. Party leaders were accused of nationalist deviations, of which they were undoubtedly guilty, and of conspiring with Tito, the independent-minded Communist leader of Yugoslavia. Later, after Stalin's death, many received the somewhat dubious vindication of posthumous rehabilitation.

The tempo of change quickened under the new regimes. As in the Soviet Union it was decided to collectivize the land as a prelude to industrialization; collectivization and mechanization would enable fewer farms to produce more crops, release surplus workers for industrial production, and even provide capital from agricultural surpluses for industrial investment. Though never applied as brutally as in the Soviet Union in 1929, the collectivization program was accompanied by pressure and coercion. The results varied. In Bulgaria, the most docile of the satellites, over half the arable land was collectivized by the end of 1952, but in Hungary by 1953 only about a third. In Poland, where resistance was strongest, collectivization was halted, and 85 percent of the land remained in private possession. Collectivization postponed the postwar recovery of Eastern Europe; and agriculture in that region, no less than in the Soviet Union, remained the weakest part of the socialist economies. Peasants diligently cultivated the acre or so permitted them on an individual basis and worked reluctantly on the large collectives. On the other hand, industry made striking gains. The Eastern European countries all launched Soviet-type five-year plans. But because of the emphasis on heavy industry and the pressures to contribute to the economic needs of the Soviet Union, industrialization brought little improvement in living standards. In the last years of Stalin's life, economic and national discontent mounted in the Soviet Union's Eastern European satellites.

For a time the policies of the new regimes were coordinated through a new international organization created in 1947 and given the innocuous name of the Cominform, or Communist Information Bureau. Although more loosely organized than the Comintern, which had been dissolved by Stalin in 1943 as a gesture of wartime harmony, it became the chief center of the propaganda war against the West until its dissolution in 1956.[5] The relationship of the people's democracies to the Soviets was formalized also, as we have seen, by a network of military alliances under the Warsaw Pact and by trade agreements and economic cooperation projects under the Council for Mutual Economic Aid, which, to the chagrin of the satellite states, principally benefited the Soviet Union.

In the early postwar years, Yugoslavia, freed from the Nazis largely by its own partisan armies, made a remarkable and successful show of resistance to the Soviets. The Yugoslav Communist leader, Marshal Tito, demonstrated the centrifugal power of nationalism even in the Communist international order and openly defied Moscow. The Soviet leadership first excommunicated and anathematized the heretic in 1948, and then after Stalin's death sought to woo him back to the fold. The first major Communist figure to declare his independence of Moscow, Tito established a model that other Communist leaders and parties would later follow.

The Soviet Union: The Post-Stalin Era

In March 1953 Russia's twentieth-century Peter the Great died. Stalin's accomplishments had been massive—the industrialization of Russia, the rallying of the country in the Fatherland War, postwar reconstruction, and the expansion of communism.[6] At the same time it was Stalin's mistrust of the West and his inflexibility that aggravated the tensions of the postwar international atmosphere and the Cold War. Inside his own country his dictatorial ruthlessness and paranoid suspicions, growing sharper with the passage of years, filled even his closest associates with dismay. Economic reconstruction after the war was accompanied by tightened ideological restrictions. Controls over all phases of intellectual life multiplied and grew more repressive. The emphasis was vehemently nationalistic and xenophobic; deviations in economics, music, genetics, linguistics were condemned on grounds of "cosmopolitanism." An officially inspired anti-Semitism made an appearance, thinly disguised as anti-Zionism, and became a continuing feature of Soviet life. Plots were fabricated to create an atmosphere of terror, as in the revelation of an alleged "doctors' plot" in 1952, most of the doctors being Jewish, to poison Stalin and other Kremlin leaders. Forced labor camps were again filled with suspected dissidents. The Soviets claimed a leadership in technological inventiveness, denying even that the Russia of Peter the Great had ever been "Europeanized" by borrowings from the West.[7]

Three years after Stalin's death, Nikita S. Khrushchev, his successor as party secretary, in a speech to the party on the "crimes of the Stalin era," made startling

5 See pp. 732–733.
6 See pp. 720–730, 806–824, 843–844.
7 See pp. 224–235, 524–525.

disclosures of Stalin's dictatorial rule that confirmed the worst speculations of Western critics over the years. Stalin had been personally responsible for the purges and executions of the 1930s, had built up a cult of personality around himself, and had created an atmosphere of terror so that his most intimate colleagues lived in fear for their own lives. His initial loss of nerve and ineptitude at the time of the German invasion in 1941 were also clearly revealed for the first time.

After Stalin's death in 1953 a struggle for power ensued. At first Georgi Malenkov served as premier but others exercised collective control behind the scenes. All agreed that no one should dominate the regime as Stalin had. To prevent a seizure of power by Lavrenti Beria, head of the dreaded secret police and one of Stalin's principal lieutenants, the new leaders arrested and executed him. Malenkov, who tried to ease the austerity of postwar reconstruction by providing greater quantities of consumer goods at the expense of heavy industry and military needs, was ousted after two years. Marshal Nikolai Bulganin, who succeeded him for the next three years, was only a figurehead. Gradually, authority shifted to Khrushchev, rotund, jovial, and ebullient but in actuality a shrewd, tough, pragmatic realist who had governed the Ukraine for Stalin in the years from 1939 to 1950.

Khrushchev, secretary of the party after 1954, systematically built up support in the Central Committee. His strength was apparent when he made his speech in February 1956 on the crimes of the Stalin era. Within a few years, his competitors were ousted from office, discredited, or relegated to obscure posts; on the other hand, after the Beria episode, rivals were no longer executed. By March 1958 Khrushchev had emerged as the unchallenged leader, serving both as premier and first secretary of the party, his ascent as much a personal victory as a triumph of the party over other competing institutions in Soviet society—the army, the bureaucracy, and the secret police. In 1964 he too fell from command, the victim of rebellion in the party at his accumulation of power, and of discontent over his economic failures, especially in agriculture; ousted, he lived quietly in Moscow until his death in 1971. In replacing him, the party apparatus separated the top governmental and party posts, and again stressed collective leadership. Leonid I. Brezhnev became party secretary and Aleksei N. Kosygin premier. Within a few years, however, Brezhnev eclipsed all others and dominated the political scene into the 1970s, presiding over the introduction of a new constitution in 1977 that altered the structure of the regime very little. That same year the Supreme Soviet elected him president.

After Stalin, the Soviet leaders softened many aspects of the older tyrant's reign of almost thirty years and even rehabilitated the reputations of many of Stalin's victims. They permitted something of a "thaw," a greater freedom in literary and intellectual activity and even in political criticism, but nonetheless continued to maintain vigilant supervision. Controls were alternately relaxed and tightened. In 1958 Boris Pasternak was forbidden to accept the Nobel Prize in literature because his writings, notably *Dr. Zhivago*, which had been published abroad, implicitly condemned Soviet society by stressing individual freedom. Other intellectuals were similarly repressed and some imprisoned. The writer Alexander Solzhenitsyn, who himself spent years as a prisoner in forced labor camps after the war, devoted his prodigious literary talents to describing the human suffering in the world of the Soviet concentration camps. Most of his writings circulated in the Soviet Union in underground privately printed editions before being published abroad. In 1970 he was forbidden to go to Stockholm to accept a Nobel Prize, and in 1974 was arrested, accused of treason, and forcibly deported. The physicist Andrei Sakharov, another outspoken critic of the regime, was also refused permission to leave the country to accept a Nobel Prize.

The finest minds and talents in the Soviet Union found the atmosphere repressive. Although the arbitrary, capricious, and extreme repression of the Stalin era diminished, the essential features of Soviet totalitarianism persisted. The control of the party pervaded all aspects of Soviet life, and many ugly features of repression, including the psychiatric confinement of dissident intellectuals and anti-Semitic persecution, were rampant. Soviet Jews, seeking permission to leave for Israel, were subjected to many restrictions until under Western, mainly American, pressure the restrictions were loosened in the 1970s and over 150,000 Jews emigrated.

The system of centralized economic planning inaugurated under the five-year plans of the 1930s[8] was resumed after the war. The Soviet economy continued to expand. Between the Fourth Five-Year Plan (1946–1950) and the Tenth (1976–1980), once wartime devastation was repaired, economic growth, especially in heavy industry, was steady. By the 1970s the Soviet Union was the world's leading producer of steel, pig iron, coal, cotton, and oil. Whereas in 1950 the Soviet gross national product was only 30 percent of the American, in 1975 it was close to 60 percent. The attempt to strike a better balance between heavy industry and consumer goods, however, was less successful; consumer goods amounted to little more than a fourth of the total economic output. At one point, in the late 1960s under the Eighth Plan, the government for the first time projected a higher growth rate for consumer goods than for heavy industry, but this was reversed halfway through the plan and subsequent planning reverted to the older emphasis on heavy industry. The Tenth Five-Year Plan (1976–1980) stressed quality in industrial production more explicitly than ever before, a tacit admission of the previous emphasis on quantity alone and the inferiority of much that had been produced. Under the later postwar plans, the government permitted a greater degree of decentralization in economic decisions and delegated more authority to regional planning agencies and even to management at the factory level.

Agriculture persisted as the weakest part of the economy. Despite massive investments in collectivized mechanized farms, agricultural production did not keep pace with industrial and urban growth. The system of collective farms failed to provide adequate incentives for increased production, and there was some evidence of the poor use, or even abuse, of farm machinery. Production on the small, privately owned, half-acre plots, which the collectivized peasants were permitted to cultivate, often showed larger yields in proportion to the size of the holdings—as in the case of the farms in Eastern Europe. Serious harvest failures in 1972 and 1975 required the Soviet Union to make huge grain purchases from the United States and Canada. The difference in productivity as compared to American agriculture remained striking. Whereas one Soviet agricultural worker

[8] See pp. 720–728.

fed seven persons in the U.S.S.R., one agricultural worker fed forty-six in the United States; one-fourth of the labor force in the Soviet Union was employed in agriculture as against a comparable one twenty-fifth in the United States.

Expenditures on heavy industry and on armaments, as well as agricultural weakness—all features of the Soviet economy since the 1930s—made it difficult for living standards to rise significantly; urban housing remained an especially chronic problem. After sixty years of the socialist regime, despite industrial growth that made the country one of the world's two superpowers, the Soviet citizen could still purchase only half the consumer goods and services that the average American could. The U.S.S.R. also found itself lagging in newer industrial technology and in the late 1960s, in a significant economic shift, it welcomed capital investment and advanced technology from the Western countries. In other ways the future of the Soviet economy continued to depend heavily on resources in its eastern regions. For cities like Kazakhstan, Samarkand, and Tashkent, the pace of modernization proceeded rapidly. The Asian parts of the U.S.S.R. furnished over half the country's iron and steel, cement, and hydroelectric power, and almost all of its magnesium and aluminum; rich new mineral resources were constantly being discovered, like copper, found in eastern Siberia in 1975.

Soviet industrial advances were crowned by remarkable achievements in nuclear power and space technology. In 1949 the Soviets successfully tested their first atomic bomb, in 1953 their first hydrogen bomb, and they continued to experiment with record-breaking blasts. In 1957 the U.S.S.R. successfully launched *Sputnik*, the world's first artificial earth satellite, alerting even the most skeptical to the advanced state of Soviet technology and science. In 1961 they orbited the first man around the earth and in the 1960s launched manned space flights of an extent and duration that for a time overshadowed American accomplishments.[9]

The People's Democracies after 1953

The changes in the Soviet Union after Stalin's death in 1953 directly affected the Soviet satellites. Riots in East Berlin that year served notice that the brutal exploitation of Eastern Europe for the benefit of the U.S.S.R. could not continue. Discontent mounted over forced industrialization and land collectivization, and at repression by Stalinist-type leaders who continued to rule even after Stalin's death. The Eastern Europeans sought a relaxation of controls, economic concessions, and some relief in their austere living standards. The ferment rose to the surface after Khrushchev himself denounced the brutal character of the Stalin dictatorship and, in an attempt to win back Yugoslavia, made the official concession that "different roads to socialism" were possible. The "de-Stalinization" program opened a Pandora's box; destroying Stalin's infallibility destroyed Soviet infallibility as well. In October 1956 open revolt broke out in Poland and Hungary.

In Poland the demand for greater independence emerged within the Polish party itself. The Polish Communist leader Wladyslaw Gomulka, once discredited

9 See p. 926.

and imprisoned for his nationalist deviationism, returned to power and pressed for greater Polish independence. Khrushchev blustered and threatened military action, but backed down, convinced that at least in foreign affairs Poland could be counted an ally. Gomulka soon received wide backing in Poland, even from the church, most of the population viewing him as a desirable alternative to the return of Moscow control. He halted collectivization of the farms, curbed police terror, and for a time created a freer political and intellectual atmosphere.

In Hungary events in 1956 took a different course. Only a few days after the news of the Polish success, rioting broke out in the streets of Budapest and other cities. The moderate-minded Communist leader Imre Nagy, whose earlier efforts to liberalize the Hungarian regime had failed, returned to power. He undertook a policy of liberal concessions, even freeing political prisoners, but those concessions only increased revolutionary pressures from workers and students. Rioting again erupted, the rioters threatening to end the Communist regime, restore parliamentary government, and cut ties with Moscow. Khrushchev thereupon dispatched an army of tanks and artillery, suppressed the revolt, and forcefully reestablished Communist rule. The tougher János Kadár, subservient to Moscow, replaced Nagy, who later was executed. The Hungarian revolt of 1956 was crushed by Russian troops just as the revolution of 1848–1849 a century before had been.[10] The United States, preoccupied with events in the Middle East at the moment, showed no signs of intervening. The open show of force by Moscow in Budapest destroyed illusions about the benevolence and liberalism of Stalin's successors and shook the Communist faithful in Western Europe and elsewhere.

Despite the Hungarian episode and the limits placed by the Soviets on independence in the satellites, liberalizing changes did take place after 1956. The Soviets allowed more flexible economic policies adapted to the needs of each country; the pace of collectivization slowed down. A freer atmosphere, even in Hungary, came to prevail. The government in Rumania, repressive at home, showed signs of independence in foreign affairs and resisted Soviet pressures for closer economic integration. Of all the regimes, Czechoslovakia democratized its government more than any other in the late 1960s, permitting freedom of the press and allowing non-Communist political organizations to flourish.

The Soviet leaders grew nervous as they saw their grip on Eastern Europe threatened, especially in Czechoslovakia. They viewed the liberalization of the Czech regime both as a threat to socialism and as a subversion of the Warsaw Pact military network, threatening the Soviet hegemony in Eastern Europe. In August 1968 they dispatched 250,000 troops, including token Polish, Hungarian, Bulgarian, and East German contingents, into the hapless country to crush the incipient revolution. The Czechs, stunned and infuriated, were forced to accept Soviet political demands for a restoration of censorship and governmental changes designed to thwart democratization. The "Brezhnev doctrine" served notice that the Soviets reserved the right to intervene in the affairs of any member of the socialist commonwealth if communism seemed threatened, and that the satellites were to enjoy only a qualified sovereignty. It served notice also of the strictly circumscribed limits within which freedom and independence would be tolerated in Eastern Europe. Yet it was obvious that the Soviet Union could turn

10 See p. 474.

back the tides of internal liberal change and of national self-assertiveness in Eastern Europe only by its continued military presence.

Meanwhile, by the mid-1960s, the years of forced industrialization were yielding important social and economic results. Eastern Europe was being transformed from a rural and agrarian society into an urban and industrial one. Consumer goods were in greater supply, often, as in the case of Hungary or East Germany, more abundantly available than in the Soviet Union itself. The German Democratic Republic, as East Germany became known, emerged as one of the world's leading industrial powers. After 1968, as in the Soviet Union, the relaxation of internal political controls in Eastern Europe fluctuated. In Poland Gomulka, who ruled for fourteen years after 1956, reintroduced repressive measures, persecuted the church, and even embarked on an anti-Semitic campaign against the small number of Jews still remaining in Poland after the Nazi wartime extermination. In 1970, because of growing economic dissatisfaction, he was driven out and replaced by Edmund Gierek, who made cultural life freer, curbed the anti-Semitic campaign, and encouraged economic growth that transformed Poland into a major industrial power. Like the U.S.S.R. itself, Poland and the other Eastern European countries now sought capital and advanced technology from the West. All traded with countries outside the Soviet sphere and encouraged foreign tourists. The value of trade between the Soviet bloc and the outside world increased fourfold in the 1970s. The countries of Eastern Europe, within limits, were loosening their bonds to the Soviet Union.

Even more than the intervention in Hungary in 1956, the intervention in Czechoslovakia in 1968 shattered Soviet leadership of the world Communist movement. Tito and the Chinese leaders had earlier rejected Soviet leadership, and there had been protests by the Western Communist parties over the intervention in Hungary in 1956. In 1968 only seven of the world's Communist parties, in addition to the five participating countries, supported the intervention in Czechoslovakia. The large Communist parties of France and Italy openly protested. In the 1970s they and other important parties made explicit their determination to pursue an independent role in advancing communism. No longer was the U.S.S.R. an unquestioned model for political, social, and economic emulation. Quite the contrary, loyal Communists questioned the bureaucratic inertia, cultural repression, and social inequities in the U.S.S.R. The once monolithic Communist world of the 1930s was becoming increasingly fragmented. In a sense a Protestant Reformation had taken place in Marxism; the authority of Moscow to speak for world communism had succumbed to national and doctrinal challenges. The French and Italian Communist parties even repudiated the concept of the dictatorship of the proletariat as a universally valid goal, or necessary revolutionary stage, for all national parties. In the mid-1970s the Soviet Union, accepting the changed situation, openly acquiesced in the theory that each party was free to find its own path to socialism, and that Moscow was not to be the sole interpreter of Marxist ideology. It was clear, however, that in Eastern Europe where Soviet troops had once intervened, the "Brezhnev doctrine" might still apply, but it would be more difficult to use ideological grounds for such an intervention. Meanwhile the most formidable challenge to Soviet leadership issued from the new Communist power that had emerged in the East since 1949.

110. THE RISE OF COMMUNIST CHINA

The Civil War

The emergence of Communist China by the end of 1949 was among the most momentous of postwar events. The Communist triumph was the final episode in the long civil war between the Kuomintang, or Nationalists, and the Communists that began in 1927.[11] An uneasy alliance, formed between the two groups in 1937 to fight the Japanese, barely held together through the war years. The Communists had placed their armies under the nominal command of Chiang Kai-shek and the Kuomintang. But retaining actual control and waging successful guerrilla warfare against the Japanese, they moved deep into the Japanese zones, organized villages and local governments along Communist lines, and mobilized support among the peasants through popular land reforms. Toward the end of the war a Nationalist China, a Communist China, and a Japanese-occupied China confronted each other. The Nationalists deteriorated in morale and efficiency and lost popular support. Expelled by the Japanese from their industrial and financial bases in eastern China, they suffered from chaotic economic conditions, inflation, heavy taxation, and outright corruption. To the growing strength of the Communists, the Nationalist government responded with repression that transformed it into an increasingly authoritarian regime.

In the last stage of the Pacific war, Chiang Kai-shek offered the Communists representation in his government if they agreed to scale down the Chinese Red Army and incorporate it fully into his Kuomintang forces. The Communists refused. They demanded instead a constitutional convention to decide on the form of the postwar government and insisted on an equitable allotment of military supplies to their own army, which in many areas had been fighting more effectively against the Japanese than the Nationalists. The victory over Japan set the stage for renewed civil war. Nationalist troops, with United States aid, took over the big cities in eastern and northern China but the Communist forces, moving out from their guerrilla bases, poured into the hinterland of the northern Chinese provinces and also moved into Manchuria, where they made contact with the Russians. The Soviets at this juncture, however, were maintaining scrupulously correct relations with the Kuomintang and refused direct encouragement to the Communists. Mao Tse-tung, the indomitable Communist leader, declined to surrender the northern provinces, disband his army, and accept Kuomintang political control over the country as a whole; in the autumn of 1945 fighting broke out. A truce mediated by General George Marshall temporarily halted hostilities, but with the withdrawal of the U.S.S.R. from Manchuria in the spring of 1946, many months after it had pledged to do so and after it had removed Manchurian industrial assets as reparations, Nationalists and Communists again clashed over control of the important border province. As Marshall noted, the Communists were quite willing to plunge the country into civil war to achieve their ends; but, as he also noted, political power in the Kuomintang remained concentrated in the hands of an inner group bent on repressing all opposition, even non-Communist. One of the tragedies of the postwar era was that the anti-Communist forces in China, and in many other parts of Asia, were themselves undemocratic.

[11] See pp. 754–755.

In the fighting, which lasted from the spring of 1946 to September 1949, the Nationalists lost ground steadily. The United States gave large sums of money to bolster the Kuomintang but to no avail; the Nationalists seemed to lack the ability and will to resist. On the other hand, the Red Army, equipped with captured Japanese arms, now receiving aid from the Soviets, and indirectly obtaining American supplies through mass surrenders and sales by corrupt Kuomintang functionaries, moderated their propaganda so as to attract wide sections of the population and pressed forward victoriously, routing the Kuomintang armies in the north and then, moving south, occupying the Nationalist capital at Nanking. By the autumn of 1949 Nationalist resistance had ended on the Chinese mainland. Chiang withdrew his shattered forces to the island of Taiwan. There, and on a few small offshore islands, Chiang in subsequent years regrouped and revitalized his armies with American aid, and governed in considerably more enlightened fashion until his death in 1975, when his son succeeded him.

The New Regime

The Chinese Communist leader, Mao Tse-tung, and his lieutenants proceeded to shape the new Chinese People's Republic that they proclaimed in October 1949. For the next twenty-seven years Mao guided the destinies of the new state. The new regime reestablished the national capital in the ancient northern city of Peking.

For the first time since the Revolution of 1911, and indeed for generations, a unified central government controlled all China, able to direct and mobilize the most populous nation in the world. The Chinese Communists might be a small hardened group of successful Marxist-Leninist revolutionaries exercising supreme power over the submissive Chinese masses, but they were not as alien to the Chinese cultural tradition as most Westerners believed. They continued a long familiar pattern of bureaucratic government that stretched back for centuries; they were articulate spokesmen for a universal hostility to Western imperialism that had all but carved their country to pieces in the nineteenth century;[12] and they were the legatees of an ancient tradition of Chinese political and cultural preeminence in the east Asian world. With traditional social and religious patterns already disrupted in the twentieth century by revolutions, civil struggle, and the war against Japan, the Communists accelerated the disintegration of older Confucian values but provided a stability unknown to the country for years and launched one of the most extraordinary political experiments of the twentieth century.

The Chinese Communists leaned on Russian experience but added innovations of their own. They promulgated a Soviet-type constitution, providing a parallel structure of party and government, with party officials controlling each level of governmental organization.[13] The apparatus of totalitarianism appeared. The party manipulated all organs of information for indoctrination purposes. Political education was accompanied by mass arrests and executions, forced labor, the liquidation of anti-Communist opponents, and internal party purges, styled "rectification" drives. In 1957 Mao, echoing the "de-Stalinization" program in the

[12] See pp. 632–638, 747, and maps, pp. 634–635, and 639.
[13] See pp. 716–718.

U.S.S.R., conceded that in the first five years of the Revolution excesses had been committed and that some 800,000 opponents had been executed, a figure that was undeniably understated. As the years passed, repression continued, but the external forms of coercion were often less important in China than the mobilization of mass peer pressures for conformity to the new social order. Political opponents were rehabilitated rather than liquidated and sometimes even permitted to return to positions of responsibility.

As the Soviet Union had earlier, the leaders of the new Communist regime mobilized the nation in a vast program of economic development designed to transform China from an agricultural country into an industrial power. As a first step, from 1949 to 1952, the regime restored and rehabilitated the war-devastated economy that it had inherited. At the same time it inaugurated a vast land redistribution program, establishing cooperatives as a preliminary to collectivization and eliminating the old landlord class. The country's initial Five-Year Plan, postponed because of the outbreak of the Korean War in 1950, was launched in 1953. Concentrating on heavy industry, the plan, with some Soviet economic and technical assistance, had considerable success; substantial advances were recorded in the output of coal, electric power, iron ore, and steel. Not all targets were reached, especially not in agriculture, where the same floods and droughts that had troubled China for centuries refused to obey government decrees. Yet the First Five-Year Plan, running from 1953 to 1957, inaugurated a period of industrial expansion and economic growth.

In 1958 a second plan, more ambitious and heralded as the "great leap forward," was launched. Faced with a serious lack of balance between the growth of industry and the lag in agriculture, the planners were determined to continue industrial expansion and simultaneously to revolutionize agricultural production by a mass mobilization of the countryside. Mao, who in his writings always stressed the importance of the peasantry, was resolved to avoid the Soviet experience and not permit industrialization to take place at the expense of the peasants. On the premise that Soviet-style agricultural cooperatives and collectives were inadequate for Chinese purposes, the government began to amalgamate the existing cooperatives into far larger and more comprehensive units, "people's communes," which would be responsible not only for agricultural mechanization and improvement but for local industrialization and many other social and economic functions as well. Intended to be a self-sufficient rural city, tightly organized in military fashion with a hierarchy of production brigades and battalions, the commune was to use the reservoir of local labor and resources to raise agricultural and industrial production. Communal kitchens, nurseries, and boarding schools were established to free women from household chores and child care so that they too could work on an equal basis in the fields and factories.

All kinds of obstacles thwarted the communal experiment. In 1960 the government, acknowledging the stubborn resistance it was encountering from a recalcitrant peasantry that had learned over the centuries to reject external compulsion, backed down. By 1961 the "great leap forward" was in retreat. With successive years of crop failures and deficiencies, some of which were caused by natural disasters, the government abandoned the communal program. Agriculture continued to be organized along collective lines, but peasants were permitted to sell or barter surplus products as an added incentive to production. Handicrafts and manufactures were still encouraged. In that way the regime industrialized the countryside itself, utilizing the labor power always available in rural areas. The government stressed the fundamental importance of agriculture as the necessary prerequisite for future economic development, but it did not abandon its ambitious plans for industrial growth. By the 1960s the Chinese economy had made significant progress toward industrialization. In the years before the Communist regime, annual steel production had never reached 1 million tons; by 1960 the official figures set it at over 18 million tons. Although per capita output was understandably low, given its huge population, China by 1960 already ranked among the top ten powers in the world in total industrial output. An industrial base for further expansion had been built even if only modest annual growth rates were achieved under successive five-year plans. Nor was the country's scientific prowess to be minimized; it successfully tested an atomic bomb in 1964 and a hydrogen bomb in 1967, and orbited unmanned satellites in the 1970s.

The most serious problem, as in other developing countries, was the pressure of the expanding population on the economy. The population, conservatively estimated at 800 million in 1975, was certain to reach 1 billion before the end of the century. Of all the developing countries, China was the most successful in coping with population growth. Through a unique system involving central directives and local controls, massive education programs, social pressures stopping just short of compulsion, the extensive employment of women in industry and agriculture, and the ready availability of a wide variety of birth control devices, a slowdown in the birth rate was achieved, which in China's case significantly affected global statistics as well.[14] Moreover, the regime was feeding its enormous population. Through intensive irrigation schemes, the use of fertilizers, and the harnessing of the vast peasant labor power, the land was more efficiently cultivated than ever before. Nor were the cities permitted to swell with urban consumers; 80 percent of the population remained rural and worked the land. All programs in China were carried out in a concerted way. The very garbage collected in the cities was systematically processed into agricultural fertilizer, and industrial waste carefully recycled.

The regime transformed life in many ways. Road, rail, and air transport physically unified the country. Impressive strides were made in public sanitation and in public health, which was highly organized and given a top national priority. Labor gangs systematically drained and filled in infested canals. The government made progress in overcoming illiteracy, reforming and simplifying the written Chinese language, and moving toward a single spoken tongue. Women were given full equality with men and played a large role in political and economic life, sharing in the sacrifices imposed and the progress achieved in the new regime. Old abuses like child marriage and concubinage were outlawed. More profoundly than the Russian, the Chinese Revolution was refashioning the habits and ethos of a gigantic population, reaching remote villages and hamlets untouched for centuries. Within a generation an agrarian, semifeudal country had moved toward becoming a modern industrial society; the full transformation was promised before the end of the century.

In the two and a half years from 1966 to 1969, when the country went through

14 See p. 935.

a period of turbulence known as the Great Cultural Revolution, the stability of the regime received its severest test. Yet the turbulence was unleashed by Mao himself. The aging leader, fearful that he would lose his grip after the failure of the country's economic experiments, or that the social revolution would not survive him, or that the purity of the Revolution would be tarnished by material success and a new elitism, called for a purge of the highest ranks of government and party, directed against all who lacked the zeal to push on with the Revolution, or who had succumbed to bureaucratic routine and indifference to the masses. A principal target of abuse was Liu Shao-ch'i, president of the republic since 1959, a leading party theoretician, and once Mao's heir apparent. Even then the purge, as begun by party leaders, was judged too moderate. Mao and his closest followers, including his wife, Chiang Ching, mobilized hundreds of thousands of young people and galvanized them into action as Red Guards or shock troops to take up the Maoist revolutionary cause. Converging on Peking in the spring of 1966, they denounced the old ways, attacked the vestiges of Western imperialist culture, and harassed and humiliated their opponents. Rival factions emerged among the revolutionaries, and bloody clashes took place in the south. When the uncontrolled mobs threatened to tear the country apart, committees of party functionaries, army leaders, and government officials gradually restored order in the capital and in the provinces.

By the time the disturbances were over in 1969, thousands of lives were lost, the economy disrupted, and more than two-thirds of the party's central committee had been replaced. Mao's control was assured and his revolutionary legacy reinforced. In the aftermath of the Cultural Revolution, Mao reasserted the virtues of the land. White-collar workers from the cities, even party officials, spent time in special party schools in the countryside, where they learned to till the soil and labor in the fields. Before entering universities students worked the land and learned firsthand something of the hard life of the peasants. To combat elitism, education, especially in the universities, became more politically oriented than before.

When Mao died in 1976, long ailing and in his eighties, he was widely mourned as the towering father of the Revolution and as one of the great figures in the centuries-old history of China, a true Son of Heaven, though a Marxist one. In dedicated service of over half a century he had forged a revolutionary party and a revolutionary army, led the Long March, defeated the Nationalists, and presided over a revolution that unified, transformed, and strengthened the country. His theoretical teachings on the struggle against imperialism and his practical successes in guerrilla warfare influenced revolutionaries in other parts of Asia and elsewhere. His homilies, published in a little red book called *The Living Thoughts of Chairman Mao*, were widely quoted and assiduously studied in the new schools. Mao's revolution had brought equality for the peasants, emancipation for women, a sense of dignity for labor, technological progress, unity, and pride. He had broken with the old elitist Confucian principles of inequality and respect for hierarchical authority, and had even in his own way tried to prevent a new revolutionary elite from canceling the gains of the social revolution. Mao believed in power and authority, the notion that the masses had to be led to emancipation, and he believed in economic progress; but he also glimpsed a moral quality in the social revolution that required further nurturing, and he was concerned that material progress and technical expertise alone might choke human initiative and creativity.

Of all his associates, Chou En-lai served Mao most closely in later years in the councils of government and party; for many years he was premier and foreign minister. While Mao and Chou both lived, a balance between the moral and the material aspects of the Revolution was maintained. Chou died a few months before Mao. Other once-designated successors to Mao, such as Liu Shao-ch'i and Lin Piao, had earlier fallen out of favor, the latter dying in a plane crash while allegedly fleeing an attempted coup. After Mao's death, a division appeared in the party leadership between a small group of ideologically oriented leaders, including Mao's widow, Chiang Ching, and a more pragmatic group that viewed modernization and economic progress as crucial for continuing the great social experiment. A relatively unknown provincial party official, Hua Kuo-feng, succeeded Chou as premier and a few months later also became Mao's successor as chairman of the party. Hua promptly took steps to purge the leaders of the opposition. His emergence seemed to be a compromise solution, but on balance it was a triumph for the party bureaucracy and army, both of which had been temporarily eclipsed in the unrest of the Cultural Revolution; it was also in part a signal that modernization and economic development would receive the highest priority.

Foreign Affairs

Although proclaiming peace, the new regime from the beginning displayed an aggressive foreign policy. In 1951, pressing old claims of Chinese suzerainty, the Communist People's Republic occupied Tibet and in 1959 forcibly suppressed a revolution there. Relations with India became strained; border disputes along India's northeastern frontier led to an open clash and an undeclared war in 1962. The Chinese invaded the border areas, easily overran Indian defenses, then suddenly called off the fighting. The episode destroyed the Indian leaders' illusion that Chinese military power had been built only for defense against Western encroachments in Asia. The Chinese entered the Korean War in the 1950s and took pride in the fact that they successfully thwarted the alien American intruders in the neighboring buffer state.[15]

The existence of a second major Communist power, with the world's largest population and the world's largest Communist party (close to 30 million members in the late 1970s), with a militant program and ambitions for world revolutionary leadership, and self-appointed as champion of the nonwhite peoples of the world, undermined the ideological leadership of the Soviet Union in the Communist world. The Soviets had not wholeheartedly supported the Chinese Communists in their civil war with the Kuomintang at the end of the Second World War. Once the Communist victory was an established fact, the U.S.S.R. accepted it and in 1950 surrendered the rights and concessions in Manchuria acquired by the Yalta agreement in 1945. Relations between Mao and Stalin always remained cool but correct. The Korean War made the Chinese dependent on the Soviets for military aid, capital loans, and technical assistance. Hostility to the United States also caused the Chinese Communists for a time to draw closer to the Soviets. The

[15] See pp. 917–918.

Chinese Communists resented the United States' refusal to grant them diplomatic recognition, its efforts to block them from representation in the United Nations, and its continued support for the Nationalists on Taiwan.

In the first critical years of the new regime Mao relied on Soviet assistance and grudgingly submitted to Stalin's guidance, but he never considered himself subordinate to Stalin, and certainly not to his successors. Indeed Mao projected himself as a new prophet of Marxism-Leninism, adapting the "revolution" to Asian conditions, where the peasant masses and not the proletariat represented the engine for social change. After Stalin's death the Chinese Communists openly asserted their independence of Soviet control. Mao echoed Khrushchev's pronouncement in 1956 that there were "different roads to socialism" with: "Let a hundred flowers bloom, let a hundred schools of thought contend." Neither, of course, believed in toleration of differences or in mere ideological debate. Ironically, as if to flout Stalin's successors, Mao never publicly condemned Stalin after the Russian dictator's death, nor ousted him from the shrine of Marxist heroes; it was one of the many paradoxes in Chinese communism.

In international communism Mao became the spokesman for a more orthodox hard-shell Marxism-Leninism.[16] He vehemently denounced Stalin's successors as archrevisionists who were abandoning the class struggle, developing new bureaucratic elites, capitulating to capitalism and imperialism, and formulating appeasement-like theories of coexistence with the Western powers out of a cowardly and un-Marxist fear of nuclear war. The Chinese Communists also openly pressed their claim to leadership of the emergent nations in the former colonial world. The Soviets, who were viewed as "half-Asian" by many in the West, were repudiated as Westerners by the Chinese Communists and denounced as "social imperialists." The friction between the two major Communist states reflected not only ideological rivalry but also territorial differences over the lands of inner Asia into which Russia had expanded in the age of the tsars. In 1960 the Chinese Communists and the Soviets were hurling polemics at each other; in 1968 they clashed in armed conflict over disputed border territory that divided Manchuria and Russia's maritime provinces.

In Europe the only Chinese Communist outpost was tiny Albania, which thus protected itself from falling into either the Soviet or Yugoslav orbit. For a time the Chinese made headway in expanding their influence in various countries in Africa and Asia, and, in the Western Hemisphere, in Cuba. Patient and geared to their own timetable, the Chinese Communists used diplomatic as well as revolutionary channels for their purposes, and offered economic aid as well. With the United States, diplomatic channels of communication were finally opened in the 1970s, following a visit to China by President Nixon. Before full diplomatic relations could be established, the unresolved question of American treaty ties to Taiwan had to be resolved; but the Chinese were confident that they would one day regain their *irredenta* What they most resented in the 1970s was the American rapprochement with the Soviet Union. In 1971 the Chinese People's Republic replaced the Nationalist Republic of China in the United Nations, and occupied a seat as one of the Great Powers on the Security Council. With the emergence of China as a vast new center of Communist power, with Yugoslavia maintaining its

16 See pp. 697–699.

own independent form of communism, and the satellite states of Eastern Europe openly reasserting their national identities, with the Communist parties of Western Europe pronouncing their freedom of decision, and with all these elements profiting from the growing Soviet-Chinese tension, Moscow's ideological monopoly was ended. A new "polycentrism" replaced it, unheard of in Stalin's day. And in the Chinese People's Republic, in the new Marxist amalgam that had emerged, hundreds of millions of men and women added the teachings of Mao to the Marxist scriptures.

111. EMPIRES INTO NATIONS: ASIA AND AFRICA

The colonial revolt in Asia and Africa, having built up pressure in the years after the First World War, reached a veritable flood tide in the years after the Second.[17] The British, French, Dutch, and Belgian empires in Asia and Africa all but disappeared in an amazingly short span of about fifteen years, from 1947 to 1962, as did the Portuguese in 1975. In some instances the liquidation of these empires occurred peacefully, with the imperial power resigned to the end of colonial rule, as in the British withdrawal from the Indian subcontinent; in other instances the Western powers withdrew only after long and protracted bloody wars, as in the case of the Dutch in Indonesia, the French in Indochina and Algeria, and the Portuguese in Angola and Mozambique. Everywhere the end of empire came as a result of rising nationalist agitation inspired by principles of self-determination, anti-imperialism, and the wartime Atlantic Charter. Western political ideas of sovereignty, independence, and freedom were compounded with hatred of European whites and denunciation of imperialism and capitalism. After the war Europeans could rule in their Asian and African empires only at prohibitive military cost, if at all, and in blatant contradiction to their own professed ideas of self-government.

Asia: End of the British and Dutch Empires

The peaceful end in 1947 of British rule in India, the largest and most populous of all colonial areas directly ruled by Europeans, was epoch making. The drive for self-government and independence gathered momentum in the 1930s and resulted in the grant of a constitution, a legislature, and other concessions to self-government. The British had also trained an Indian civil service to carry on the functions of a modern state. In the Second World War, even more than in the First, India rendered substantial aid to the British. To rally Indian support and to counter Japanese propaganda demanding the expulsion of all Europeans from Asia, the British promised dominion status—to take effect at the war's end, a pledge that did not satisfy the Indian Congress party leaders who agitated for immediate independence. Meanwhile the Muslim League, which claimed to speak for 100 million Muslims unwilling to live in an India dominated by the Hindus and the Congress party, insisted on a state of their own. After the war the British decided on partition.

[17] See pp. 746–755.

In 1947 the Indian empire was dissolved and the subcontinent was divided into two dominions, both of which shortly thereafter became republics—India, predominantly Hindu, with 350 million people at the time of independence, and Pakistan, mainly Muslim, with a population of 75 million. Because of the Muslim distribution in the old Indian empire, Pakistan (the made-up name means "land of the pure" in Urdu) had to be established in two disconnected parts separated by 1,000 miles of Indian territory; even so, almost 40 million Muslims were left in India, which helped keep India a multireligious and secular state. As the British had warned, independence resulted in bloody riots between the religious communities, forcible mass expulsions and migrations involving millions, and the deaths of over 1 million people. The uglier features of the communal rivalry then subsided, although religious tension remained high and later flared up on several occasions. Relations between the two nations were also strained because of a quarrel that dragged on for years over the status of the disputed border state of Kashmir, a dispute finally settled with the accession of the state to India in 1975.

Politically, the republic of India under Jawaharlal Nehru and the Congress party offered to Asia an example of parliamentary democracy, humanitarian leadership, and slow evolutionary progress in meeting enormous problems of poverty, overpopulation, and linguistic and cultural diversity. After Nehru's death in 1964 his successors continued his policies, but there was growing restlessness. By 1966 Nehru's daughter, Indira Gandhi (her married patronym only coincidentally the same as that of the founder of Indian nationalism), came forward as prime minister and as leader of the Congress party. Economic progress continued to be slow despite numerous development plans that led to significant growth in some areas such as steel production. The huge increase in the population, which nearly doubled to reach 600 million in the first twenty-five years after independence, outstripped economic gains. In 1975 when Indira Gandhi's political hold on the country and even her political career were threatened because the courts found her guilty of electoral improprieties, she peremptorily set aside constitutional government, proclaimed emergency rule, and silenced thousands of opponents by arrest and imprisonment. When she relented and permitted parliamentary elections in the spring of 1977, the opposition parties united to win control of the legislature and to drive her from office. India's experience demonstrated the problems of democracy in cultures and climates where governments had to cope with overwhelming social and economic difficulties.

Pakistan, after an initial decade of turmoil, came to be governed under a paternalistic military dictatorship. Despite a written constitution and parliamentary forms, there were few illusions about parliamentary democracy. As in India, population growth outpaced economic advance. The most critical problem, not unexpectedly, was the division between West Pakistan, where the federal government was located, and East Pakistan, the eastern part of the old Indian state of Bengal, 1,000 miles away. Friction between the two eventually exploded into secession and civil war. Although both provinces were Muslim in religion, they differed in language, culture, historical tradition, and even in their basic food crops. The eastern rice-producing state, with more than half the nation's population crowded into an area one-sixth that of the western, protested, among other grievances, that it did not receive a proportionate share of the country's development funds. The Bengali political leaders of East Pakistan, who eventually won a majority for their party in the National Assembly at Karachi, pressed for full autonomy. When their demand was rejected, they proclaimed independence in 1971 as the new state of Bangladesh (or "Bengali nation"). The government in Karachi dispatched an army to the east to suppress the rebellion; hundreds of thousands were killed in the unequal civil war and over 10 million refugees, mostly Hindu, crossed the border to West Bengal in India. India soon intervened, quickly defeated the Pakistani army, and forced the recognition of the new state.

The remaining parts of the British empire in Asia also became independent in 1948, or shortly thereafter, including Ceylon (later renamed Sri Lanka), Burma, and Malaya. Malaya suffered from a decade of internal strife that delayed its independence until 1957; it joined in 1963 with other former British dependencies to form the Federation of Malaysia. Most of the new states in Asia (and in Africa), even after their progression from self-governing dominions to independent republics, retained a voluntary association with the Commonwealth of Nations, as the British Commonwealth was now called. The adherence of the newly independent states made the Commonwealth an even more flexible institution than it had been earlier.[18] In the decades after 1947 it grew into an association of over thirty independent communities, most of them republics, which accepted the British sovereign as symbolic head of the Commonwealth and agreed to consult, though not necessarily to act in concert, on matters of common concern. Although the new members of the Commonwealth lacked the tie of sentiment that bound Australians, New Zealanders, and Canadians of European descent to Great Britain, the Commonwealth remained one of the world's significant political groupings, a transmission belt for the communication of Western technology, political institutions, and economic aid, and for the interaction of Western and non-Western ideas and values in parts of the world as far flung as the British empire had once been. Not all the former members of the British empire joined or stayed in the Commonwealth, however. Burma from the beginning chose to remain outside, and as the years went by, the Commonwealth lost Ireland in 1949, South Africa in 1961, and Pakistan in 1975.

Another great empire in the East, the Netherlands Indies, which the Dutch had been consolidating since the early modern centuries, also came to an end.[19] In 1942 the Dutch abandoned the Indonesian archipelago to the Japanese under humiliating circumstances. At the war's end the Japanese proclaimed Indonesian independence, and the Indonesian nationalist leader, Sukarno, who had been agitating for independence since the 1920s, took control. The Dutch tried to return and reconquer the country, and open warfare followed for four years. In 1949 the Dutch recognized Indonesia with its 75 million people (129 million twenty-five years later) as an independent republic joined in a tenuous union with the Dutch crown; in 1954 even these ties were dissolved.

In Indonesia, as elsewhere in the former colonial world, independence was won but constitutional democracy and economic welfare were not assured. Sukarno, elected president in 1949, governed dictatorially under a policy variously called "guided democracy" and "Indonesian socialism," setting aside the constitution, suspending the elected parliament, and exercising unrestricted powers as "presi-

18 See pp. 536, 771–772.
19 See pp. 157, 628–629, 752.

dent for life." Here and elsewhere, the leadership upon which the former colonial countries relied in the struggle for national independence turned into personal dictatorship once independence was won. After much bloodshed Sukarno was overthrown in 1966. His successor, General Suharto, restored political stability and resumed some of the country's unfulfilled social and economic programs.

End of the French Empire in Indochina

European domination ended in 1954 in the former French colonial union of French Indochina but not until after seven and a half years of fighting between French armies and Communist-led nationalist forces. The leader of the nationalist forces in Vietnam was the Paris-educated, Moscow-trained Communist, Ho Chi Minh, who, after waging guerrilla warfare against the Japanese during the war, proclaimed an independent republic at the war's end. The Japanese, as they withdrew, also proclaimed Indochinese independence under an emperor. The French in Paris were willing to concede a large measure of self-rule to the peoples of Indochina, but not independence. Negotiations broke down and fighting began at the end of 1946. Because the leadership of the independence movement fell into the hands of Ho Chi Minh and the Communists, the French could claim that they were bent not on preserving nineteenth-century colonial privileges but on stemming the tide of world communism. Yet the advance of communism in Asia, as distinct from its advance in Eastern Europe, was closely linked to nationalism and to genuine popular discontent.

The United States, anticolonialist but ready to champion anti-Communist movements, gave considerable financial aid to the French but refrained from open intervention. The war severely drained French morale and resources. After a disastrous French defeat at the battle of Dien Bien Phu in 1954, a truce was negotiated, and at an international conference in Geneva the independence of Vietnam, Laos, and Cambodia was recognized. Vietnam, the state most seriously contested, was partitioned at the seventeenth parallel into a Communist-governed North Vietnam and a non-Communist South Vietnam. The partition was to be temporary, to last only until elections could be held. The armistice of 1954 proved to be an uneasy one. Vietnam remained in turmoil and hostilities soon reopened, as will be explained in the next chapter.[20]

The Arab States, Pan-Arabism, Israel

In the Muslim states communism made little headway, but nationalism grew in intensity as did the self-consciousness of the Islamic world as a political entity. The Muslim world included Arabs and non-Arabs and stretched from Morocco on the Atlantic Ocean to Pakistan and Indonesia in Asia; it embraced the Arab states of the Middle East and stretched north to include the non-Arab states of Afghanistan and Iran on the borders of the Soviet Union. Within the Muslim world the Arab states made efforts to create a united bloc. Syria, Lebanon, and Jordan, which had emerged from the old Turkish empire in 1919 as European-mandated areas, emerged from the Second World War as independent countries; Iraq had

[20] See pp. 919–925.

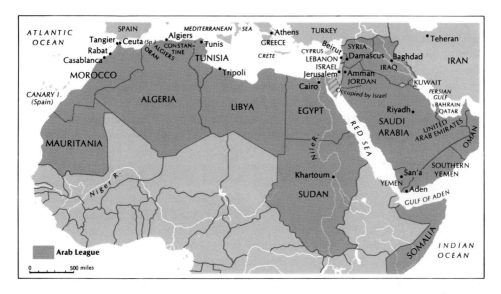

THE ARAB WORLD

The Arabic language zone is one of the most extensive in the world, reaching from the Atlantic Ocean to the Persian Gulf. In 1945 the Arab states formed a League, whose members are shown on the map as of 1976. The League has proved to be rather loose, with much disagreement among its members, but it has been opposed to the establishment of an Israeli state in the midst of an otherwise predominantly Arab world.

been independent since 1937. Egypt, where the British for a time retained treaty rights, was in other respects independent.[21] In 1945 the chief Arab states, Egypt, Iraq, Syria, Jordan, Lebanon, Saudi Arabia, and Yemen formed an Arab League to act jointly in international affairs and to advance Arab interests. In the following two decades Morocco, Tunisia, and Algeria, whose independence movements the Arab League had supported, joined, as did Libya, Sudan, and the smaller Arab states; by the 1970s the League came to include eighteen members. Within this Middle Eastern area, Arab and non-Arab, lay two-thirds of the world's petroleum reserves, on which much of the economic activity of the industrial West and of Japan depended.

The Arab countries were aroused most by the emergence of a Jewish state in Israel. After the war the homeless survivors of the Nazi barbarism in Europe sought out Palestine as a place of refuge that they considered pledged to them as a Jewish homeland in the First World War.[22] The Arabs objected to making territorial sacrifices because of Europe's persecution of the Jews. Britain, which held a mandate over Palestine, sought to placate the Arabs by limiting Jewish immigration. In 1948, after unsuccessful negotiations, the British announced the end of their mandate and the partition of Palestine. The Zionist leaders thereupon proclaimed the republic of Israel and took up arms against sizable invading Arab armies, which they succeeded in defeating quickly. In setting up the Israeli state

21 See pp. 619–620, 685, 771.
22 See pp. 595–596, 669, 803.

over half a million Arabs were dispossessed and remained disgruntled; Israeli offers to relocate the refugees were spurned. To the Arabs, the state of Israel seemed like a new form of Western invasion of the Middle East. The Israelis saw themselves as a bridgehead for Western scientific, technological, and democratic advances in an economically underdeveloped, semifeudal area. They succeeded in developing modern industry and in reclaiming vast stretches of the Negev desert, where they grew citrus fruits and other crops. They succeeded also in creating a democratic society out of widely disparate elements and in developing powerful modern military forces. The Arab countries refused even to recognize the state and worked for its destruction. Three more wars were fought after 1948—in 1956, 1967, and 1973. All had international ramifications because the United States supported Israel and the U.S.S.R. gave aid to the Arab states.

Egypt at first took the lead in the holy war against Israel. After a military revolution in 1952 that drove out the Egyptian monarch and inaugurated a military-dominated republic, Egypt emerged for a time as the chief Arab state. An army colonel, Gamal Abdel Nasser, concentrated power in his own hands. To build the country's economic and military strength, Nasser, though vehemently anti-Communist, sought and obtained arms and economic aid from the Soviet Union as well as from the United States. He was incensed when the United States, in retaliation for his friendship with the Soviets, cut off funds he needed to construct the Aswan Dam.

Matters came to a head in 1956. The British, as they had promised earlier, evacuated the Suez Canal zone and surrendered their remaining military rights in Egypt. To a startled world Nasser announced that the Suez Canal would be nationalized and placed under Egyptian control. The British prime minister, Anthony Eden, haunted by the appeasement of the European dictators in the 1930s, retaliated with military intervention. Joining with him were the French, who were irritated at the flow of Egyptian aid to Algerian nationalists, and the Israelis, who saw their security imperiled by permanent Egyptian control over the canal. The United States, however, refused to support intervention. The Soviet Union backed Nasser, as did many of the states of Asia and Africa which saw the Egyptian leader resisting an old-fashioned imperialist invasion. Britain, France, and Israel were compelled to withdraw their forces. Although the Egyptians agreed to operate the canal on an impartial basis, they continued to bar Israeli shipping.

In 1967 the Egyptians moved to close the Gulf of Aqaba. This action, combined with the continued barring of the Suez Canal to Israeli shipping, threatened to strangle the Israeli economy. In a quick six-day war the Israelis destroyed the Egyptian air forces, shattered the Egyptian, Syrian, and Jordanian armies, captured vast amounts of equipment, mostly of Soviet origin, and occupied extensive territories belonging to the three Arab states, including the Jordanian sector of the city of Jerusalem. Over 1 million additional Arabs came under Israeli rule. The Arab states, smarting under the humiliating defeat, refused to sign a peace treaty or recognize Israel, and received new arms, equipment, and advisers from the Soviet Union.

The Palestinian refugees added a highly volatile element to the situation. Concentrated in camps in neighboring Arab states, they became increasingly militant, conducting guerrilla warfare and carrying on terrorist activities. In 1964 they organized themselves as a government-in-exile, the Palestinian Liberation Organization, which received official recognition from many quarters, including eventually the United Nations. Refusing to recognize the existence of Israel, they professed to speak for 2.5 million Palestinians and demanded the establishment of a Palestinian state on territory, to be taken from Israel, on the west bank of the Jordan River. Border raids, Israeli reprisals, and the involvement of the Great Powers unsettled the entire Middle East.

Other changes took place in the Arab leadership. Nasser's Pan-Arab ambitions did not prosper. Many Arab states remained cool to Nasser, whom they suspected of using Pan-Arab aspirations for personal ambitions. But always the hostility to Israel remained paramount. After 1967 Egypt received massive military and economic aid from the Soviet Union. The primary objective was to oust Israel from the territories it occupied after 1967, including the Sinai peninsula and the east bank of the Suez Canal.

After Nasser died in 1970 his successor, Anwar-al-Sadat, continued the tough line against Israel but also showed concern over Soviet penetration of Egypt. Reversing almost two decades of close ties to the U.S.S.R., Sadat ousted Soviet military personnel and took direct charge of Soviet bases and equipment in the country. Though less flamboyant than Nasser, Sadat also tried to project himself as leader of the Arab crusade against Israel. In October 1973 Egyptian forces, surprising the Israelis by attacking on the Jewish holy day Yom Kippur, moved eastward across the Suez Canal and established a bridgehead on the Sinai peninsula; Syria simultaneously attacked in the north on the Golan Heights. Israel, after recovering from the surprise attack, mounted extensive ground and air operations. Having stabilized the Syrian front, the Israelis crossed the Suez Canal and trapped the Egyptian forces that had invaded the east bank.

With the Israelis again near victory and in control of still more Arab territory, the oil-producing Arab countries supporting Egypt and Syria dramatically resorted to a new strategic weapon, an embargo on the shipment of oil. They hoped to pressure the United States and Western Europe into demanding Israeli withdrawal from all Arab territories occupied since 1967, including the newly conquered ones. Although the embargo was lifted a few months later in the winter of 1974, the oil-producing nations had meanwhile quadrupled the price of oil. The embargo and the rise in world oil prices opened a new era in international economic and political relations and had implications far beyond the conflict in the Middle East, as we shall subsequently see.

The United States and the Soviet Union both supported a United Nations resolution calling for an immediate cease-fire. The fourth Arab-Israeli War ended with a settlement mediated by the American secretary of state, Henry Kissinger. By March 1974 the United States had persuaded Israel to withdraw from the occupied west bank of the canal to the east bank, behind an Egyptian zone and a UN-patrolled buffer area, in which an American civilian patrol also participated. Israel gave up some but not all territories on the Syrian border.

The hitherto united Arab front against Israel was disrupted by Egyptian willingness to negotiate and by new Egyptian efforts to resume friendlier relations with the United States and the Western countries. The other Arab states rejected the settlement with Israel and opposed further negotiations. They lobbied extensively for Israeli withdrawal from occupied Arab territories and even persuaded the General Assembly of the United Nations in 1975 to adopt a resolution condemning Zionism as "a form of racism and racial discrimination"; it was an ironic resolution in that Zionism had come into being as a defense against anti-Semitism, and Israel as a result of the Nazi persecution of the Jews. Yet passion and rhetoric aside, the conviction grew that unless a comprehensive settlement was negotiated in the Middle East, new and even more deadly conflicts would explode. To be settled was the demand of the Palestinian refugees for an independent national state and the recognition and guarantee of Israel's legitimacy and security. Always in the background was the awareness that with the proliferation of nuclear

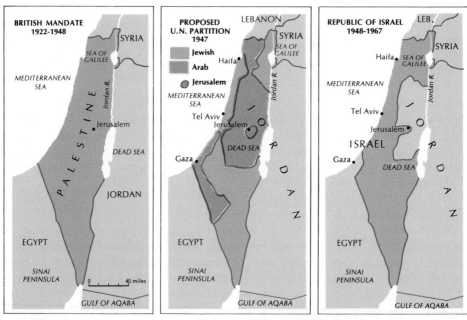

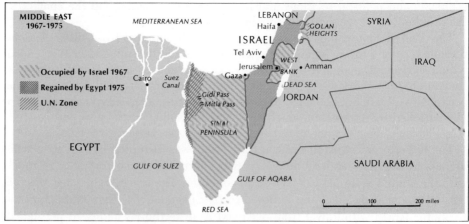

arms the Arabs and Israelis might have available even deadlier weapons in any new conflict.

The uneasy relationships and rifts in the Arab bloc came into sharp focus during the lengthy and confused civil war in Lebanon, which broke out in the spring of 1975 and resulted in the loss of thousands of lives and the physical uprooting of thousands of others before it ended a year and a half later. Beginning as a rebellion of leftist Muslims against the Arab Christians who, though a minority, dominated the government, the war was rapidly transformed into a battleground of conflicting ambitions. The Palestinian Liberation Organization intervened, stirring up Arab guerrilla extremists and threatening established authority in all the Arab countries. To restore order Syria sent in troops on the side of the Christian government, and the Arab League, to counter the unilateral Syrian intervention, also dispatched a peacekeeping mission. It was the Syrian army that brought an end to the brutalizing civil war, and Syria remained in control of large areas of the troubled country.

In all the Muslim world, Arab and non-Arab in Asia and in Africa, the older age of imperialism had ended. A powerful new sense of identity swept the Islamic world. Pride in its great cultural heritage was reinforced by the huge wealth pouring in from its oil resources. It sought to redress its industrial backwardness by rapid modernization, but it was determined to share in Western material advances on its own terms, not in a client role, and to bargain for its own military effectiveness in arms and nuclear power. Arab states such as Kuwait, Saudi Arabia, and Libya, as well as non-Arab states such as Iran, were so rich in oil resources that the question was raised of their helping the less favored Islamic nations. Within all these countries, however, still mainly elitist in social organization, wealth remained in the hands of the privileged classes and only slowly trickled down to alleviate the lot of the impoverished, often illiterate lower classes. In many of the Muslim countries numerous obstacles to modernization

ISRAEL AND THE MIDDLE EAST

"Palestine" is the term by which Europeans long designated a small region of mixed population, but predominantly Arab, which belonged to the Ottoman Empire until the First World War. European Jews, with the Zionist movement, began to migrate to it in the nineteenth century. In 1922 the League of Nations "mandated" it to the British, who tried to restrict Jewish immigration in an attempt to satisfy the Arabs. After the death of millions of Jews during the Second World War the Zionist idea of an independent Jewish state won increasing numbers of adherents. In 1947 the United Nations proposed a partition between Jewish and Arab states, with Jerusalem as a separate zone. The Arabs rejected the plan, and in the Arab-Israeli War of 1948 the Israelis won recognition of wider boundaries than those first proposed. The Arab states still refused recognition of Israel. Three more wars were fought in the following decades—in 1956, 1967, and 1973. After the Six-Day War of 1967 and after the war launched by Egypt and Syria against Israel in 1973, the Israelis occupied additional territory. Among the uprooted Palestinian Arabs a terroristic movement developed against Israel, threatening even some of the Arab governments themselves. The war of 1973 ended in a truce under United Nations auspices, but the rival interests of the United States and the Soviet Union in the Middle East made the situation dangerously explosive.

remained, including traditional religious and cultural barriers to the full absorption of women into society. The pace of change in the Muslim world was uneven, but older life styles were visibly being undermined by the new wealth, industry, urbanization, and the spread of education.

The French in North Africa: The Algerian War

The postwar history of Morocco, Tunisia, and Algeria (the Maghreb, as these Arab states of North Africa along with Libya are sometimes called) belongs at once to the history of the Muslim world, of emergent Africa, and of France. Morocco and Tunisia, never outright colonial dependencies, were French protectorates under their traditional native rulers, the Moroccan sultan and the Tunisian bey. North African nationalists, who had been educated in France and had discussed ideas of freedom and independence in Paris cafés after the First World War, were now bent on achieving these goals.[23] The decision by the wartime Allies to grant independence to the former Italian colony of Libya in 1951, and agitation for the British to end the vestiges of their control in Egypt, galvanized all North Africa in the 1950s. To mollify the rising nationalist agitation, the French offered various political concessions but in 1956 felt compelled to grant complete independence to Morocco and Tunisia.

The course of events was different in Algeria. The French considered Algeria not a colony but an integral part of France; it had representation in the French National Assembly like any constituency in metropolitan France except that the vote for representatives was heavily weighted in favor of the European settlers and to the disadvantage of the Arab majority. Of the 9 million inhabitants, at least 1 million were European settlers, or *colons*, mostly French who, like the family of the great French writer Albert Camus, had lived there for generations. Since the European settlers controlled the economy and owned most of the land and industry, they feared for their political and economic privileges if Algeria were cut loose from France and governed by an Arab majority smarting from years of unequal treatment. They were adamant on keeping Algeria French. At a moment when France and the French army had barely recovered from the disastrous rout in Indochina, large-scale revolt broke out in Algeria in the autumn of 1954.

The French-Algerian War lasted seven and a half years, involving 500,000 French troops at its peak, and costing the lives of at least 100,000 Arab and 10,000 French soldiers, and of additional thousands of civilians. The Algerian Liberation Front received aid and support from Egypt and other sympathetic Arab states. Torture and cruelty were common on both sides; the violence spread to Paris as extremist Algerians attacked moderates. The French were confronted with a choice of losing Algeria or of continuing to bear the military, financial, and moral strain of the colonial war. The army, the settlers in Algeria, and rightists in France sought to press on relentlessly and subdue the rebels. In the spring of 1958, in the midst of a prolonged cabinet crisis in Paris, an insurrection on May 13, 1958, led by die-hard settlers and army leaders in Algiers, brought General Charles de Gaulle to power.[24]

23 See pp. 619, 746–749.
24 See pp. 893–894.

Although no one knew how de Gaulle would meet the Algerian crisis, and many looked upon him and his entourage as ardent nationalists who would not abandon Algeria, he moved to solve the crisis at his own tempo and in his own style. At first continuing the war, he spoke of autonomy for the Algerians once the rebellion had ended. Soon he spoke of self-determination and promised a referendum when a truce had been arranged. In 1961 he won the backing of the French electorate for his proposal to grant independence. Army leaders rebelled, and some of his closest former political associates helped form a secret army of terrorists that bombed and killed, and even attempted his assassination, all to no avail. In July 1962 French rule dating back to the 1830s ended. After independence there was a mass exodus of Europeans from Algeria, but most of the French and Algerians were grateful that de Gaulle had ended the ordeal. The new regime in Algeria narrowly escaped civil war; for the first three years the country was under the authoritarian rule of an army-backed leftist regime, which nationalized much of the economy. After 1965 it was governed by a military dictatorship that emphasized rapid industrial development, in part based on the country's oil resources. The French accepted the loss of Algeria and, with a prospering economy, turned their attention to other matters.

Sub-Saharan Africa: End of British, French, Belgian, and Portuguese Rule

In Asia and in North Africa nationalist agitation for independence and the end of colonial empires might have been expected. But in black Africa south of the Sahara the movement for liberation was nothing short of breath-taking. In 1945, and even in 1950, the political complexion of Africa was scarcely different from what it had been in 1914: with the exception of Ethiopia, Liberia, and Egypt, it was all European governed or controlled. By the early 1960s the exact opposite was true; most of Africa was independent or close to achieving independence. In 1976 there were fifty independent sovereign states in Africa, comprising a third of the membership of the United Nations, and the number was still growing.[25] In many ways the new states were different from the older European states. Almost without exception they included diverse tribal, ethnic, and linguistic groups, some antagonistic to each other. Because African geographical boundaries had been drawn by the European colonial powers in the nineteenth century, peoples and tribes were often distributed over several countries. The new states also enjoyed less of a unified national heritage than did nations in Europe and elsewhere. But once the African states obtained independence against Western rule, they rapidly assumed the complete panoply of national sovereignty and tried to weld their disparate peoples into nationhood.

The liberation movement was stimulated by the events in Arab North Africa in the 1950s, when Libya received independence in 1951 by international agreement, and the British, under pressure, renounced their treaty privileges in Egypt in 1954. Sudan, breaking away from Egypt, established itself as an independent state in 1956, and that same year the French granted independence to Morocco and Tunisia even though they fought to retain Algeria for several more years. These events spurred nationalist movements in sub-Saharan Africa, where black populations lived in colonial empires carved out by the British, French, Belgians,

25 See pp. 626–627.

and Portuguese either in the early modern centuries or in the decade and a half of imperialist scramble after 1885.[26] The British led the way in granting independence. After dissolving their Indian empire and cutting their other imperial commitments for economic reasons, they prepared for African self-rule through a gradual transfer of authority to local officials and through economic development programs.

In 1957 Ghana, then the Gold Coast, in West Africa, became the first British African colony to achieve independence. Here the independence movement was uncomplicated by the presence of any sizable white settler minority, as would be the case elsewhere; moreover the inhabitants enjoyed a degree of economic stability and by 1948 had a legislative council with an African majority. Nonetheless, the nationalists, led by the American-educated Kwame Nkrumah, demanded immediate independent status as a dominion. The British, after first jailing Nkrumah, released him and in 1951 appointed him prime minister. After a transitional period of a few years before independence, in 1957 the Gold Coast became an independent dominion, the first of the new African members of the Commonwealth. It immediately shed a name identified with imperialist exploitation and took for itself the name of Ghana, recalling an African kingdom that had flourished on the Niger River from the fourth to the eleventh centuries A.D. In 1960 Ghana became a republic, retaining its voluntary association with the Commonwealth. After independence Nkrumah gathered extensive powers into his own hands. He became president for life, banned opposition parties, and governed as a dictator. After a decade, his arbitrary government, unbridled extravagances, and cult of personality led to his overthrow in 1966 by army leaders and the establishment of a military dictatorship.

In 1960 Nigeria also moved from colonial status to independence, first as a dominion and then, three years later, as a republic voluntarily linked to the Commonwealth. Nigeria, with by far the largest population of any country in Africa (close to 80 million in 1976), had numerous ethnic groups, of which the principal ones were the Hausa and the Fulani in the north and the Yoruba and the Ibo in the south. For a few years ethnic and regional antagonisms remained quiescent while parliamentary self-government was launched, but in the mid-1960s these antagonisms flared into open violence. Ibo army officers, apprehensive about the declining position of their people, who were mainly Christian and more economically advanced than most others in the country, overthrew the government and set up a military regime in 1966. They in turn were overthrown by other army officers, and bloody reprisals began. In 1967 the Ibos made an unsuccessful bid for independence. They proclaimed the secession of their eastern region as the state of Biafra (named for the eastern bay of the Gulf of Guinea). The civil war that broke out lasted two and a half years, and in it as many as 1 million people may have died. After initial Biafran successes, the federal forces crushed the outnumbered rebels. In the age of African independence Africans, tragically, were destroying Africans. After the war the new military government embarked on a policy of reconstruction and reconciliation, attempting to reintegrate the Ibos into national life and pledging a return eventually to civilian rule. But the leading general was deposed in 1975 by a group of army officers, his successor was

[26] See pp. 620–627; for earlier years, see pp. 101–103, 157, 241–243, 262–267, 412.

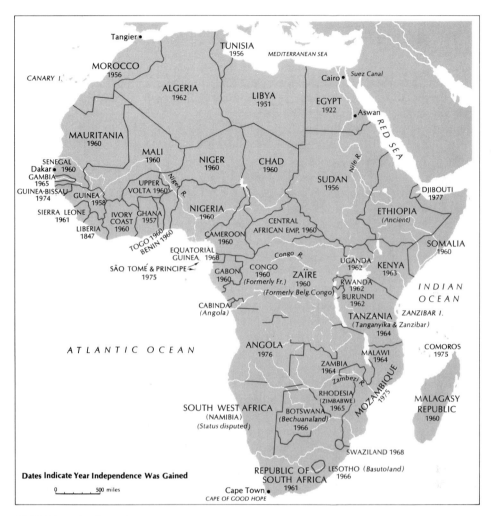

Tangier •

TUNISIA
1956   *MEDITERRANEAN SEA*

MOROCCO
1956

CANARY I.

Cairo •   Suez Canal

ALGERIA
1962

LIBYA
1951

EGYPT
1922

• Aswan

RED SEA

MAURITANIA
1960

MALI
1960

SENEGAL
Dakar • 1960
GAMBIA
1965

NIGER
1960

CHAD
1960

GUINEA-BISSAU
1974   GUINEA
1958

UPPER
VOLTA 1960

Niger R.

SUDAN
1956

DJIBOUTI
1977

SIERRA LEONE
1961
LIBERIA
1847

IVORY
COAST
1960

GHANA
1957

NIGERIA
1960

CENTRAL
AFRICAN EMP. 1960

ETHIOPIA
(Ancient)

TOGO 1960
BENIN 1960

CAMEROON
1960

SOMALIA
1960

EQUATORIAL
GUINEA 1968

Congo R.

SÃO TOMÉ & PRINCIPE
1975

GABON
1960

CONGO
1960
(Formerly Fr.)

ZAIRE
1960
(Formerly Belg.Congo)

UGANDA
1962

KENYA
1963

RWANDA
1962
BURUNDI
1962

*INDIAN
OCEAN*

CABINDA
(Angola)

TANZANIA
(Tanganyika & Zanzibar)
1964

ZANZIBAR I.

ATLANTIC OCEAN

ANGOLA
1976

ZAMBIA
1964

MALAWI
1964

COMOROS
1975

Zambezi R.

RHODESIA
(ZIMBABWE)
1965

MOZAMBIQUE
1975

MALAGASY
REPUBLIC
1960

SOUTH WEST AFRICA
(NAMIBIA)
(Status disputed)

BOTSWANA
(Bechuanaland)
1966

SWAZILAND 1968

Dates Indicate Year Independence Was Gained

0   500 miles

REPUBLIC OF
SOUTH AFRICA

LESOTHO *(Basutoland)*
1966

Cape Town •   1961
CAPE OF GOOD HOPE

CONTEMPORARY AFRICA

This map should be compared with those for Pre-Colonial Africa (p. 622) and for Africa in 1914 at the height of European colonialism (p. 626). The first of the new states was Ghana, the former British Gold Coast, which became independent in 1957 and took its name from a medieval African kingdom that had been located further north. The following decades saw the independence of Algeria and other Arab countries in North Africa and of numerous republics in black Africa in place of the French, British, Belgian, and Portuguese colonial empires. In southern Africa the long settled white population broke its British connection, proclaimed the Republic of South Africa, and enforced a regime of white supremacy over the far more numerous blacks. Whites in the former Southern Rhodesia set up an independent republic, Rhodesia, never internationally recognized, and followed the same course.

assassinated the following year, and a collective military dictatorship took over. Nigeria was a booming, bustling country with busy and congested cities like Lagos and Ibadan, each with populations of over 1 million, enjoying the benefits of vast petroleum wealth, but suffering from corruption, inflation, and a rapidly growing population. By the 1970s Nigeria's gross national product was equal to that of all other black African countries combined.

In East Africa the independence movements of the 1950s encountered obstacles. In Kenya (as in southern Africa), an economically privileged minority of white settlers at first set themselves against a government of nonwhite Africans. The nationalist movement responded with violence and terrorism, reaching a climax in the early 1950s with the activities of the secret Mau Mau society. The British imprisoned Jomo Kenyatta and other nationalist leaders and forcibly suppressed the extremists, but after a decade of unrest, they granted independence to Kenya in 1963. For many years Kenyatta presided over the country, governing firmly but with parliamentary institutions.

Of the other important colonial areas of East Africa, Uganda became independent in 1962 and for a time was under a constitutional regime. A struggle ensued in 1966, however, between the central government and the centuries-old kingdom of Buganda, which had been promised autonomy in the new state. The central government triumphed, but itself fell under a presidential dictatorship. In 1971 General Idi Amin took power and earned a reputation as a capricious and brutal dictator. In Uganda (and in Kenya) the process of "Africanization" was directed against Asians as well as against Europeans, so that thousands of Indians who had come to East Africa in the days of British rule and had long been the country's merchants, shopkeepers, and bankers were expelled, and their property expropriated.

In other parts of East Africa, Tanganyika (once German East Africa) became independent in the early 1960s, as did Zanzibar, the former British protectorate; the two merged in 1964 adopting the name Tanzania. For a time Tanzania served as a bridgehead for Chinese Communist influence on the continent. In 1975 an important rail link from the Tanzanian port capital of Dar es Salaam to Zambia was completed with the help of the Chinese People's Republic. Zambia, another new nation, once known as Northern Rhodesia, became independent in 1964; Kenneth Kaunda, a former schoolteacher and independence leader, was its first president. Unlike the leaders in so many of the new nations who established open dictatorships, Kenneth Kaunda in Zambia, Jomo Kenyatta in Kenya, and Julius Nyerere in Tanzania all emerged from their role as independence leaders to govern their respective countries as presidents for many years, generally respecting parliamentary and constitutional forms, although not encouraging genuine political ferment or an active opposition. They provided enlightened stability, but stability in all three countries depended on the concentration of power in the hands of respected elder statesmen who did not groom successors.

Of the former British empire in Africa it was in southern Africa that the white settlers held out longest against granting majority rule to the black population. In South Africa about 4 million whites held firm political control over 15 million blacks and an additional 3 million mixed peoples treated as nonwhites. The dominant political leaders, the Afrikaner descendants of the old Boer settlers, upheld a policy of apartheid, or racial segregation, and planned, at best, independent homelands for the various black peoples. Blacks were required to carry passbooks for identification, were restricted in their places of employment and residence, and were barred from many public facilities; opponents of the policy, black and white, were jailed. The regime found itself increasingly isolated. In 1961 it withdrew from the Commonwealth, whose members were critical of its racial policies, and proclaimed itself a republic. When Portuguese rule ended in Angola and Mozambique in 1975, as we shall see, and black governments were formed there, South Africa was even more isolated. In the late 1970s, while still adhering rigidly to its ideological position of apartheid, it began to abandon some of the more blatant forms of discrimination. Another issue, apart from segregation, remained a point of contention. After the Second World War South Africa refused to give up the mandate it had held since 1919 over what had once been German Southwest Africa. In 1966 the United Nations declared South African rule at an end there and recognized an independent Namibia, but the South African government refused to leave and faced the threat of increasing guerrilla warfare.

Rhodesia also resisted surrendering white minority rule. A white minority of 270,000 governed 6 million blacks and denied political rights to the blacks, who here too suffered the humiliation of passbooks and legal ghettos. In 1953 a Federation of Rhodesia and Nyasaland was organized as a first step toward independence from Britain. Black majority governments were established in Northern Rhodesia, which became independent as Zambia in 1964, and in Nyasaland, which gained independence as Malawi that same year. In Southern Rhodesia the white leaders insisted on independence, but the British sought in vain to negotiate political rights for blacks before granting it. In 1965 Ian Smith, the Rhodesian prime minister, unilaterally proclaimed independence, and in 1970 a new constitution made Rhodesia a republic. Pressure continued on the Rhodesian government from the British, from the United Nations, which voted economic sanctions against the country, and even from South Africa, which was attempting to cooperate with the other black states of Africa; and the United States also attempted to mediate. Black nationalist leaders continued to press for an African majority government in a new Rhodesian state to be called Zimbabwe.

The French, like the British, also dissolved their colonial empire in West and Equatorial Africa, reacting very differently here than in Algeria. In the 1950s these French colonies were quiet. For years the French had hoped that a French-educated African elite would maintain strong political and cultural ties to France. Under the French Union of the Fourth Republic the overseas territories had representation in the French assemblies even though effective control remained centralized in Paris. The French republican leaders announced plans to extend the suffrage and to provide self-governing institutions in Africa, but by the mid-1950s the sub-Saharan African colonies, inspired by the example of events elsewhere in Africa, sought full independence.

In 1958 de Gaulle, though still fighting the war in Algeria, offered the African colonies the right of self-determination and voluntary association with France, which they all accepted. Guinea alone insisted on secession. The French African states moved in two or three years from autonomy to complete independence and sovereignty, some choosing to remain associated with France and with each other in a loosely organized association known as the French Community; even those who withdrew retained economic and cultural ties with France. It was a tribute to the older empires, French and British, that many of the new states voluntarily retained associations with the former imperial powers. Indeed, French and English remained the only common tongues for the continent of Africa, and English for the Indian subcontinent. But some Asians and Africans, alarmed by the continuing cultural and economic relationships with the West, believed themselves threatened with a revival of imperialism, or "neocolonialism."

By the early 1960s over a dozen new sovereign and independent states that had once been under French sovereignty had become independent, and a few others gained independence in the 1970s.[27] The poet-president of Senegal, Léopold Senghor, spoke not only of independence but also of *négritude,* a powerful and far-reaching black self-consciousness and self-assertiveness, a pride in ancient cultural roots and modern independence, which struck responsive chords in Americans of African descent whose ancestors had been brought in chains from some of the very lands now emerging as nations.

European withdrawal in the 1950s was accompanied by tragedy in Zaïre, long called the Belgian Congo. The Belgian Congo had once been a byword for imperialist exploitation.[28] The most abusive features were remedied before the First World War and progressive reforms instituted, but political control remained concentrated in Brussels and no provision was made for self-administration or for training a native civil service. When nationalist agitation for independence burst forth in 1959, the Belgian government in panic decided against gradualism and, without preparation, precipitously announced withdrawal in six months' time. The nationalist leadership was itself divided. Some favored a unitary state, others a federal state; some immediately arranged for the secession of Katanga, the wealthiest province. There were ethnic and regional antagonisms, and hardly anyone was prepared to take over the functions of government. The Belgian withdrawal and the proclamation of the Congo Republic in June 1960 led to anarchy, riots, looting, and atrocities. Katanga (now Shaba) province seceded; Europeans fled; Belgian troops were flown back in American planes to restore order; and the Soviet Union threatened to intervene to defend the Congo against the Western imperialists. In the midst of the crisis the United Nations organized an international police force, composed chiefly of Africans, and averted what might have been a civil war of potentially grave danger because of Soviet-Western complications. The secession of Katanga ended after two and a half years, and the Congo Republic began to govern itself. By 1965 an army leader, Colonel Mobutu, had established a strong personal dictatorship that provided political stability and made it possible to reorganize the economy. In 1971 under a program of "national authenticity," he Africanized the names of all geographical places; the country was renamed Zaïre, as was the famous river. Cities like Leopoldville, the capital, and Stanleyville, with names reminiscent of the imperialist era, were renamed Kinshasa and Kisangani. All Christian or first names were dropped and the people addressed each other as "citizen." Zaïre, the largest country in Africa, its cities widely separated and without adequate connecting facilities, had vast copper and other mineral resources. Important economic projects were under way in the 1970s, but the nation's great potential riches were still

27 See map, p. 877.
28 See pp. 620–623.

undeveloped. The hope for economic progress received a setback when a new attempt at the secession of Shaba province was made in 1977.

Of all the older colonial powers, Portugal, itself under an authoritarian dictatorship for decades, resisted the tide of colonial liberation and clung longest to its colonies, symbols of Portuguese grandeur in the early age of European expansion. To retain Angola and Mozambique, two large colonies on the western and eastern coasts of Africa respectively, which had once flourished on the slave trade, António Salazar, the Portuguese dictator, fought a prolonged and fierce war. In the course of the struggle, as we shall see, Portuguese officers and soldiers, disaffected by the fighting in the colonial war, turned against the regime and in 1974 successfully overthrew it.[29] In 1975 the new revolutionary regime granted independence to all of its African colonies—Angola, Mozambique, São Tomé e Príncipe, and the Cape Verde islands. Almost 500 years of Portuguese rule ended. Angola at once became a battleground for three competing nationalist groups, each backed by different outside powers, including the Soviet Union, which arranged for the dispatch of Soviet-armed Cuban soldiers, as well as the United States, South Africa, China, and Zaïre. Angola threatened to repeat the pattern of the Belgian Congo of the 1960s and to become an extension of the Cold War, but the fighting ended in the spring of 1976, in a victory for the group supported by the Soviet Union and Cuba.

Africa remained an arena of rivalry for the superpowers. Although many of the African governments were professedly Marxist oriented or vaguely socialist, few wished to be client states of the Soviet Union; they had not ousted their earlier European rulers to replace them with new ones. But many African leaders were perhaps more resentful of the United States for its wealth and power, for its alleged neglect of African affairs, and for what Africans considered neocolonial economic and cultural intrusions. Meanwhile the two superpowers continued to supply arms of all kinds to the African countries, and resources sorely needed for economic development were used for military purposes.

The End of Empire

The European empires in Africa were gone. In the late 1970s on the entire continent only a few tiny territories were still held by a European power. The unfinished agenda for the African revolution included the extension of political rights to the black majority in South Africa and Rhodesia, the recognition of independence for Southwest Africa (Namibia), and the long struggle ahead to make independence a prelude to the improvement of human lives.

Of all the great political changes in the history of the modern world, affecting hundreds of millions of people, nothing was more revolutionary, more dramatic, or more sudden than the end of the European overseas colonial empires. The German and Turkish empires had disappeared with military defeat in the First World War, the Italian and the Japanese in the Second. But in 1945 the British, the French, the Dutch, the Belgians, and the Portuguese still governed more than a quarter of the world's population. Within two decades after 1945, however, all but the Portuguese empire had disappeared, and that, too, ended

[29] See pp. 903–904.

abruptly in 1975. The United States in the postwar years also participated in these changes; it withdrew from the Philippines, granted Puerto Rico commonwealth status, and took in Alaska and Hawaii as equal members of the federal union.

The age of imperialism dated to the fifteenth century when the Europeans first set sail on their voyages of discovery; it reached a climax from 1885 to 1900 when Europeans penetrated the interior of Africa and expanded their holdings and spheres of influence in Asia, and Americans took the Philippines and asserted their power in the Caribbean and in Latin America. The age of imperialism was ended. A new chapter in world history opened, of which the Europeans and their American descendants were only a part. But it was European technology and European civilization that had brought the contemporary world into one great stream and made all contemporary history world history.

The age of imperialism had its share of exploitation, brutality, and degradation that left a permanent scar, yet it was also the instrument whereby the scientific, material, intellectual, and humanitarian advances of western Europe had been spread to the rest of the world. The West no longer dominated these areas politically, but Western civilization, technology, and institutions were still important everywhere. In that sense it was truer to speak of the rise of the West than of its decline. Modernization, generally speaking, meant westernization. Industry, science, secularization, social mobility, individual freedoms had long been characteristic as actual accomplishments, or as goals, of the West; now they were reaching remote parts of the world. The impact of the new values and institutions brought dislocations and tensions, and transformed the landscape of the non-Western world. At the same time the Western world deepened its appreciation of non-Western thought, literature, music, religion, and art forms. The merging of Western and non-Western culture in the contemporary age meant cultural interaction, not the domination of the one by the other.

No one at the beginning of the twentieth century, or even in 1945, could have predicted the nature or extent of the colonial revolution. The colonial empires seemed enduring, or at least susceptible only to slow evolution toward independence. To be sure, the Marxists stressed the relationship of imperialism to capitalism and predicted the decline of both, but they, too, failed to foresee the rapidity or completeness with which the end of the colonial empires would take place. The two World Wars, by weakening the European powers and by encouraging nationalism, played a vital part; it was difficult to fight wars in the name of self-government and democracy, often with the colonial countries as allies, without reinforcing such ideas among subject peoples. The end of the colonial empires and the emergence of the new nations would have to be counted among the most far-reaching consequences of the two wars, and especially of the Second.

But the end of colonialism did not bring freedom or democratic government to most of the newly independent peoples. As we have seen, although most of the new nations began their political careers with constitutions or constituent assemblies, provisions for elected parliaments, an independent judiciary, and a concern for civil freedom, much of the machinery of constitutional government quickly disappeared. Many of the new nations fell under one-party rule and often under military regimes; in some, serious civil wars were also fought. Ethnic loyalties often transcended loyalties to states whose boundaries had been artificially drawn for their own purposes by Europeans in the course of their earlier conquests. The end of colonialism brought national independence and freedom in the sense that the former colonies were free from foreign rule, but it did not bring genuine self-government or political liberties for the peoples of the new nations. Perhaps the social and economic problems they faced and their relative inexperience with democratic self-government were too great; or perhaps it was an error to have believed that European-style democratic self-government could flourish in all soils. More will be said in the following chapter of the role of the newly independent states in world affairs and of the overwhelming problems all confronted in the era of independence.

XXII.
The Contemporary Age: Crises and Coexistence

For about twenty years, from the postwar recovery in Western Europe in the early 1950s, which we have already traced, to the early 1970s, the United States and Western Europe experienced greater prosperity and economic growth than anyone could have anticipated and were able to enjoy democratic government without the strain of serious economic tensions. The nations of Western Europe absorbed with a minimum of shock the momentous loss of their colonial empires. But, in the early 1970s, simultaneous recession and inflation sharply slowed economic growth and in some cases threatened even to undermine political stability. A new world pattern, far different from the bipolarity of the early postwar period, was also emerging. Having examined in the previous chapter the Communist worlds in the U.S.S.R., Eastern Europe, and China, we must touch here upon the domestic experience of the Western nations and Japan, as well as the social and intellectual ferment of the age. Then we return to the wars and tensions of the troubled international scene and the sharp new global challenges that burst upon the contemporary world.

112. THE DEMOCRACIES SINCE 1945

In the domestic affairs of the Western countries there were again, as after the First World War, decisive democratic advances in the early postwar years. To have rid the world of the aggressive dictatorships and military regimes in Germany, Italy, and Japan and to have restored constitutional government where it

Chapter Emblem: The official symbol for the World Population Year, 1974.

had been crushed for many years was a triumph for democracy. Another advance was the widening of the suffrage. Women were given the vote in France, Italy, and Japan immediately after the war, and in Switzerland in 1971, and the franchise became even broader when at various times in the early 1970s the legal voting age for men and women was reduced to eighteen in the United States, Britain, France, the German Federal Republic, and elsewhere. The prewar trend toward the welfare state also was accelerated. The memories of the Great Depression and the sacrifices demanded in the war, the ambitions and hopes raised in the Resistance movements, and the desire for protection against economic insecurity imposed new responsibilities on democratic governments everywhere.

The United States

For the United States, and indeed for much of the world, the most important single fact in the early postwar years was the productivity of the American economic system. The American economy, after recovering partially from the Great Depression during the New Deal years and expanding enormously to meet military needs during the Second World War, continued to grow after 1945. War damage in such industrial countries as the U.S.S.R., Germany, Britain, and Japan made United States economic superiority for a time greater than ever. Income per capita in the United States in 1938 had been only a little higher than in Great Britain, Sweden, or Switzerland, the next wealthiest countries. In 1948 it was about twice as high. A few years later, in the early 1950s, Western Europe, the U.S.S.R., and Japan had recovered from the war and embarked on a period of rapid industrial expansion. Even so, the United States retained a substantial lead in per capita output, wealth, and consumption levels. Per capita output in the United States in the 1970s was still twice as high as that of Western Europe, its closest competitor. With 5 percent of the world's population, the United States in the 1970s owned and produced half the world's wealth.

The great wealth and vast resources of the United States provoked in other countries a suspicious and hostile view of American policies, but it was American wealth that made possible a program of financial aid to the European countries, without which the Europeans could not have overcome the ravages of the war and then proceeded to modernize their economies and expand their productive output in so sensational a way. At the same time the economic ascendancy of the United States produced problems. Exporting profusely yet not importing in the same proportion, it tended to unbalance world exchanges by its very productivity. Until 1957 there was a chronic "dollar shortage," in that other countries could not earn dollars with which to buy American goods. The United States at that time, as it had for two decades, held almost half the non-Communist world's gold and foreign exchange, and in 1945, by an international monetary agreement reached at Bretton Woods, the dollar had been accepted as the equivalent of gold itself.

By the early 1960s, because of the economic recovery of Western Europe, and because of large American military expenditures abroad, the American balance of payments shifted unfavorably and the dollar weakened. The Europeans meanwhile had accumulated large dollar reserves (or "Eurodollars"), for which they had the right to demand gold—as France did in 1965. American gold and foreign currency reserves declined dramatically. In 1971 the United States unilaterally suspended gold convertibility and had to devalue the dollar. Later, in the mid-1970s, because of more expensive oil imports the American deficit increased still further. The image of the American dollar as an unassailable citadel of strength in the early postwar years no longer held, and the international monetary system set up at Bretton Woods broke down. The American economy, despite the recession that began in the early 1970s, was still strong, but its vulnerability to international price and monetary fluctuations, and its dependence on foreign natural resources, were strikingly clear. Large-scale American industry and banking were also more concentrated and their operations conducted on more of a world-wide scale than ever before; fewer than 1,000 "multinational corporations," as the giant conglomerates doing business in dozens of countries at home and abroad were called, accounted for 70 percent of all international corporate transactions.

In the 1950s the rapid rate of industrial growth in continental Western Europe as well as in the Soviet Union aroused the fear that the American economy might be failing to keep pace with other industrial countries. For two decades after the war, production in the United States rose at a rate of less than 3 percent annually, more slowly than in the Soviet Union or in Western Europe, but the American economy had a larger base on which to build than did those countries. Economic growth also had to keep up with the nation's expanding population, which grew from 132 million in 1940 to 216 million in 1976—as compared with fewer than 3 million Americans at the time of the country's independence 200 years earlier. Although the population increase slowed about 1957 and declined noticeably in the 1970s, the United States was still growing by over 2 million each year, an annual increase of just under 1 percent. In matters of general well-being, despite by some criteria the highest living standards in the world, the country was plagued by much poverty and many unresolved problems, especially in the decaying cities and economically depressed regions. Throughout the postwar decades huge military expenditures diverted funds from domestic needs and also contributed to inflation. The very efficiency of American technology threatened to displace workers. All these continuing concerns were intensified by the industrial slowdown, unemployment, and inflation that afflicted the economy through much of the 1970s.

In the early postwar years domestic developments in the United States were closely affected by the country's new world-wide international commitments, anxiety over the intentions and actions of the U.S.S.R., and an obsessive concern with internal subversion and disloyalty. A "Red scare," fanned by the Wisconsin Senator Joseph McCarthy, flared in the early 1950s amidst the country's chagrin and humiliation at the Communist triumph in China and American setbacks in the Korean War. By many it was argued that the toleration of dissent, long the hallmark of American freedom, was threatened by repression aimed ostensibly at Communist activities; others argued that the foundations of American security were menaced by internal sedition and world conspiracy. The most abusive features of the McCarthy era faded after 1953.

President Harry S. Truman, taking office at Franklin Roosevelt's death in 1945, and then elected in 1948, attempted in his Fair Deal to continue the New Deal of his predecessor.[1] The labor unions remained a powerful force in American life although measures were taken under Republican auspices to curtail what were

1 See pp. 764–768.

alleged to be unfair industrial practices of the unions. When the Republican party took over the presidency for eight years after 1952 under the wartime hero, General Dwight D. Eisenhower, the government became more business-oriented, but the New Deal was not dismantled; in fact social security coverage was extended, legal minimum wages raised, and public housing built. In 1960 a Democratic administration was returned to office with the election of John F. Kennedy. Tragically assassinated toward the end of his third year in office, he was succeeded by his vice-president, Lyndon B. Johnson, who in the presidential election of 1964 won a sweeping victory. Both Kennedy and Johnson favored strong executive leadership and government action to combat lagging economic growth, persistent pockets of poverty, and racial discrimination. Under Johnson federal aid to education was increased, and medical and health services, especially for the aged, were expanded. His intense commitment to the war in Vietnam cost him his large popular following, however, and he did not run for reelection. In 1968 Richard M. Nixon defeated the Democratic candidate by a narrow margin of the popular vote.

Although President Nixon had built much of his earlier reputation on a strong anti-Communist stance in the 1950s, he and his energetic secretary of state, Henry Kissinger, moved to soften the ideological tensions of the Cold War in a widely heralded effort at détente, holding that great-power relationships should be based less on ideology than on the mutual recognition of national interests. Nixon's efforts in foreign affairs were nullified by scandals that shook his administration. His vice-president, under charges of accepting bribes and income tax evasion, resigned. Then the president himself, reelected by a landslide victory in 1972, was implicated in an attempt to cover up a politically motivated burglary of Democratic party headquarters during the election campaign. In August 1974 under threat of impeachment he resigned, and Gerald Ford, whom he had earlier appointed vice-president, succeeded him as president. Ford was not elected on his own in 1976, and Jimmy Carter, a relatively unknown former governor of Georgia, benefiting from a coalition of trade union, black, and urban middle-class support, became the first president to be elected from the Deep South since before the Civil War.

In the 1970s the United States, like the industrial world generally, suffered from a combination of economic recession and inflation. Some of the inflation originated in the expenditures on the Vietnam War and in other military and nonmilitary spending. Sales of grain to the Soviet Union in 1972 to reinforce the policy of détente increased domestic food prices. The quadrupling of oil prices in 1973–1974 by the oil-producing countries accelerated the price rise. To curb inflation the government tried to reduce expenditures and to hold wages and prices in line, but the budgetary cuts only reinforced the economic slowdown. The recession of the 1970s was the most severe economic setback in forty years; in 1975 unemployment reached over 8 million, or 9 percent of the work force. There was "double-digit" inflation for a time (i.e., prices rising at 10 percent or more a year), and gross industrial output showed the sharpest decline since the 1930s. After 1975 there were signs of recovery but it was slow and incomplete. With a large share of world trade depending on the United States, the world's economy was closely linked to economic recovery in the United States.

In addition to economic and political problems, the United States continued to grapple with its special "American dilemma," the crucial question of whether the American democracy could effectively absorb its black citizens into American society. For the black population, over 25 million in the mid-1970s, or 12 percent of the total population, the myth of the American melting pot had never fully applied; blacks had never shared equally in the political, social, and economic gains made by the rest of the citizenry. The new American role in world affairs made equality even more urgent. Afro-Americans, the young especially, took pride in the new African states and developed a strong sense of black identity. Civil rights demonstrations and pressures to end discrimination mounted. In May 1954 a Supreme Court decision prescribed equal access to the nation's public schools, and Presidents Eisenhower and Kennedy used federal troops to enforce the ruling. In 1964, at President Johnson's instigation, Congress adopted legislation to halt discrimination in employment, housing, and public accommodations. But there were many setbacks. In 1968 the assassination of the American black leader, Martin Luther King, Jr., shocked the country and led to widespread rioting and demonstrations. The economic slowdown in the 1970s meant even higher unemployment figures for blacks. Expanded educational opportunities, the Supreme Court rulings, federal action, and the determination of the great majority of the American people to work toward a peaceful remedy to the most glaring defect in the American democracy brought some results, but much remained to be done.

Beginning in the late 1960s women, too, pressed for full equality and demanded affirmative steps to rectify past discrimination and guarantee equal opportunities in the future. As a result of such pressure professions and occupations once considered traditionally male started opening to them. The number of women workers more than doubled in the thirty years from 1947 to 1977, and many of these were married women. The sobering experience of American involvement in the Vietnam War in the 1960s, which provoked unprecedented militancy in young people, will be recounted shortly.

Great Britain

In Great Britain, even before the Second World War had ended, an election in July 1945, the first in ten years, unseated Winston Churchill and voted in a Labour government under Clement Attlee. Once the center of high capitalism, Britain for a time became the world's chief exemplar of parliamentary socialism. The Labour party, governing from 1945 to 1951 for the first time in history with a majority of its own, put through a broad social program that left permanent changes in British society.[2] Insisting that in an ailing economy the country's basic industries, the "commanding heights" of the economy, could not be left to the unplanned anarchy of capitalism and free competition, the Labour government brought under public ownership an important segment of the British economy, including the Bank of England, the coal mines, such public utilities as electricity and gas, communications and transportation, and iron and steel production. Since four-fifths of the economy remained in private hands, what emerged was not socialism but a mixed economy. Even in the private branches of the economy, however, steps were taken to influence the direction and amount of private in-

2 See pp. 579, 581, 770–771.

vestment on the theory that it was in the national interest to supplement the self-interest of private enterprise and the profit motive. At the same time the Labour government greatly expanded and revamped the program of social insurance inherited from the Liberal reforms of 1906–1914.[3] All parties had committed themselves during the war to an extension of these welfare services as the just due of a population that had accepted wartime rigors and sacrifices. The Beveridge Report in 1942 had sketched a program designed to guarantee "full employment in a free society" and to provide social security for all from cradle to grave. The Labour government now extended insurance coverage for unemployment, old age, and other contingencies, and inaugurated a comprehensive free medical and health service for the entire population. Income and inheritance taxes were also sharply increased.

All of this program—the public ownership of an important sector of the economy, governmental controls over the economy as a whole, the extensive social security system, and the use of taxation to redistribute wealth—furthered the idea of the welfare state, described by some as an oppressive, regimented, bureaucratic apparatus, and the road to a "new serfdom," and by others as a demonstration that political democracies could protect the social and economic welfare of their citizens and thereby ensure an even greater devotion to democratic processes. The only constitutional change under the Labour government was an act of 1949 to reduce the power of the House of Lords to delay legislation from three years to one; it was not invoked until a quarter of a century later, by another Labour government. Restrictions on labor activities dating from the general strike of 1926 were repealed.[4]

The electorate, growing restive at the continuation of wartime austerity controls, gave Labour a smaller majority in 1950, and in 1951 returned the Conservatives to office. The Conservative majority grew substantially in succeeding elections, so that the Conservatives governed uninterruptedly from 1951 to 1964. After 1964 the two parties alternated: Labour, under Harold Wilson, governed from 1964 to 1970; the Conservatives, under Edward Heath, from 1970 to 1974. Labour was returned in 1974 by a narrow margin.

During their years in office, the Conservatives halted the nationalization program, restored iron and steel and truck transportation to private control, introduced fees into the national health insurance program, and encouraged private construction over public housing. Although critical in principle of the welfare state, they did not alter the basic structure of the social security and health insurance program, and they grudgingly accepted the mixed economy and welfare democracy established by Labour in the early postwar years. When Labour returned to office from 1964 to 1970, the party encouraged public housing and slum clearance, reorganized the educational system along more democratic lines, restored free medical services, and increased social security pensions. (Later, in 1974, they moved to renationalize steel.) Ironically, the first election under a Labour reform that dropped the voting age to eighteen in 1970 was won by the Conservatives.

Both major parties had to cope with Britain's serious economic problems, which grew even more acute in the 1970s. Britain was in a much worse state after the Second World War than after the First because most of its foreign holdings,

3 See pp. 571–572.
4 See p. 770.

amounting to almost $40 billion before the war, had to be liquidated in the course of the fighting; in addition, a large part of the British merchant marine had been lost. As always Britain was dependent on imports for its food and raw materials; the loss of interest on its investments and the reduced income from its shipping services adversely affected its balance of payments.[5] With American financial aid, postwar European economic cooperation, an intensified export drive, and a curtailment of military and imperial commitments, the British economy and trade position improved in the 1950s. For a time the country experienced a modest prosperity that, despite some dark spots, exceeded anything it had known since before the First World War. In the 1960s wages increased more rapidly than prices, and working men and women had medical care, enlarged educational opportunities, and subsidized housing. Throughout the postwar years Britain showed continued intellectual and cultural vitality; it had its share of restless intellectuals and angry young rebels who took satisfaction in assaulting the vested interests and the status quo, socialist or conservative, all of which was vaguely identified as the Establishment.

But the country could pay for its large imports of food and raw materials, sustain its level of prosperity, and support the heavy burden of public services only with a modern, expanding economy. British industry was being outstripped in the contest for export markets by other Western Europeans and the Japanese, and was unable to compete even in its home market. The British economy grew more slowly than that of the rest of Western Europe and Japan, and was less productive and efficient. When out of power, the Labour party argued that the Conservatives lacked economic dynamism and were responsible for the lagging economy. But when Labour returned to office in 1964, it, too, faced economic troubles and in 1967 was forced to devalue the pound and extend austerity measures. Inflationary pressures mounted and the militant trade unions sought wage increases to match soaring prices. In 1972, when the Conservatives were in office and tried to keep wages in line, the coal miners called a nationwide strike, and a prolonged work stoppage followed. The Arab oil embargo and the dramatic rise in oil prices in the winter of 1973–1974 aggravated the inflationary spiral.

Britain was even harder hit by the combination of industrial stagnation and inflation in the 1970s than other countries. Of all the industrial nations, it suffered the highest rate of inflation—a staggering 27 percent in 1975. Unemployment passed the 1 million mark; under new international arrangements for a "floating" exchange, the pound, equivalent to $4 in American currency in 1945 and already twice devalued in the postwar years, dropped from its 1967 value of $2.40 to the lowest point in its history, around $1.60 in the autumn of 1976. To avert collapse the country was dependent upon heavy foreign loans and an austerity program for which it desperately needed trade union support.

No one proposed to discard entirely the national health insurance system, low income housing, the nationalized industries, or other benefits of the welfare state that had accrued in the immediate postwar years. Yet even Labour and the trade unions were reexamining priorities. The Labour party, shortly after its return to office in 1974, sought to curb public expenditures, make funds available for private investment, and limit wage increases. The highest priority was assigned to industrial expansion and to support for key industries that gave promise of real

[5] See pp. 556–561, 760–762, 769.

economic growth. Success would depend on whether the trade unions would accept the sacrifices involved. Under the new strategy the Labour party was abandoning expansionist full-employment policies and for the first time in thirty years was favoring the private sector.

Britain suffered also from troubles in Northern Ireland. The settlement of 1922 had left a large number of Catholics in Northern Ireland, which after the partition of Ireland became a self-governing part of the United Kingdom.[6] Of the 1.5 million inhabitants, two-thirds were Protestant and one-third Catholic. The Catholic minority militantly protested that they were victims of discrimination and pressed for the annexation of Northern Ireland to the Republic of Ireland. The Irish Republican Army, though disavowed by the Dublin government, inflamed matters, and Protestant extremists responded in kind. Open violence broke out in 1969 and over 1,500 persons were killed in the next several years. For Britain the bloody troubles in Northern Ireland were a torment, like Algeria for France in the 1950s and Vietnam for the United States in the 1960s.

On a less violent scale, other separatist pressures were at work in the United Kingdom. The Scots and the Welsh pressed for economic and cultural autonomy, and the Scottish nationalist party in particular grew in strength. In 1976 the British government moved to establish Scottish and Welsh regional assemblies with jurisdiction over health, education, housing, and other areas of local concern. Although matters such as the budget remained under the control of Westminster, to many it seemed like the first step toward a devolution of power and a restructuring of the Act of Union of 1707.[7] The Scots had a special reason to press for autonomy: oil fields discovered in the North Sea lay mainly in Scottish waters. Scottish separatism was similar to that found in France, Belgium, the Netherlands, Spain, Canada, and other countries with long national histories, where separatist movements were emerging as the manifestation of a new kind of ethnic search for identity.

The French Republic: Fourth and Fifth

France's Fourth Republic, which lasted from 1946 to 1958, inherited most of the weaknesses of the Third. Whereas the Third Republic lasted seventy years, the Fourth survived barely twelve before it fell victim to its constitutional defects and the burden of colonial wars.[8] For two and a half years after liberation, from 1944 to 1946, a provisional government was in office while a constitution was being drawn up. In January 1946 General Charles de Gaulle resigned as head of the provisional government to protest the emergent parliamentary regime and contest of political parties. Later that year a constitution was adopted in a referendum, unenthusiastically and by a narrow margin. The constitution of the Fourth Republic differed only in a few details from that of the Third. One innovation adopted without debate at the time of liberation was the extension of suffrage to women. The president of the republic was again a ceremonial figure, and the premier and his cabinet were responsible to the whims of the legislature, with only a few technical but ineffective safeguards against cabinet instability. The

6 See pp. 771–772.
7 See p. 171.
8 For the Third Republic, see pp. 564–568, 772–776, 801.

new political system came to be dominated, as the Third Republic had been, by an all-powerful National Assembly, as the Chamber of Deputies was now called, jealous of its prerogatives and deeply suspicious of a strong executive.

As head of the provisional government, de Gaulle had governed in cooperation with three major parties of the left—the Communist party, the Socialist party, and the Popular Republican Movement (or MRP), the latter a new phenomenon in republican history, a Catholic progressive party devoted to the republic. All three had emerged from the Resistance movement enhanced in strength and prestige, but the Communists emerged as the leading party, largely on their well-advertised but undeniably heroic record in the wartime Resistance movement after the German invasion of the Soviet Union in 1941. Almost a fourth of the electorate voted for candidates of the Communist party in France, as in Italy, the maximum that communism in Western Europe was able to attain in the early postwar years. De Gaulle and his successors refused the Communists the key ministries in the cabinet that they had sought but gave them several posts vital to the rehabilitation of the national economy. After de Gaulle resigned, the three parties continued to cooperate in governing; but in May 1947 the Communists, reflecting the heightening tension between the Soviet and Western camps, fomented a series of strikes directed against the government and were expelled from the cabinet.

After 1947 parliamentary and ministerial instability grew worse; the Socialists and MRP formed unstable coalitions with the once moribund but now reviving Radicals, and with other center parties. Periodically de Gaulle returned to the political scene, heading a movement called the "Rally of the French People," which he described as "above parties." Inveighing with good cause against the instability of the regime, he nonetheless alarmed the democratic parties of the non-Communist left who saw the republic threatened by communism on the left and dictatorship on the right. By 1953 the Rally of the French People faded, and de Gaulle returned to retirement. The immediate threat to the constitutional regime subsided. In the next few years parliamentary instability and ineffectiveness filled the public with cynicism, hostility, and indifference; the spirit of enthusiasm and regeneration carried forward from the Resistance movement flickered, except for a brief revival under the eight-month ministry of the reforming Radical, Pierre Mendès-France, in 1954–1955.

Yet despite its uninspiring political record, the economic and social accomplishments of the Fourth Republic were substantial. The provisional governments under de Gaulle and the tripartite combination of left parties laid the foundation for a modern industrial democracy. The government had nationalized a number of key industries, including the coal mines, gas and electricity, and the major banking, credit, and insurance facilities. As in Britain, a mixed economy emerged. The government expanded the existing body of social security legislation and added the innovation of family allowances as a supplement to the wages of heads of family. In 1946 a farsighted economic plan, drawn up by Jean Monnet, channeled investments into six key sectors of the economy, enlarging and modernizing the economic base and creating the potential for industrial expansion. The Monnet plan, along with American financial aid under the Marshall Plan, helped to modernize the French economy and to make possible a spectacular economic growth. By 1952 production levels were one and a half times those of 1938, and industrial output began to grow at an annual rate of at least 5 percent. Frenchmen like Monnet and Robert Schuman took the lead in many of the imaginative proposals for European economic integration launched in the 1950s such as the European Coal and Steel Community. The country also showed a demographic vitality that confounded earlier pessimists.[9] The population decline in the years before the war gave way to regular annual increases so that the prewar French nation of less than 40 million reached 52.5 million in the census of 1975; even so, there was concern in the 1970s over slower growth rates. There were many weak spots in the economy; public finances and tax evasion remained serious problems; and labor unrest persisted, in part provoked by the Communists, in part motivated by genuine grievances, including inflation. But the economic record and the rise in living standards were impressive.

What rendered the Fourth Republic's political problems insoluble was the strain of trying to preserve the old French empire. The regime was unable to cope with the exhausting colonial wars that it waged first in Indochina from 1946 to 1954 and then in Algeria from 1954 to 1962.[10] France alone, of all the major powers, was almost continuously at war for almost fifteen years in the postwar era. It could envy the lot of the losers in the Second World War, Germany, Italy, and Japan, which had no restless colonies to subdue.

As promised during the war, the constitution of 1946 democratized the government of the French Union but, as we have seen, the limited reforms did not satisfy national revolutionaries pressing for independence in Tunisia, Morocco, Madagascar, Indochina, or Algeria. From December 1946 to June 1954, the French army fought the nationalists in Indochina until finally, after the disastrous defeat at Dien Bien Phu, it had to withdraw. Then, only a few months after the rout in Indochina, the Algerian war broke out, the main outlines of which have been described. As the fighting dragged on, savagery and brutality mounted on both sides. With over 400,000 troops in Algeria, three-fourths of whom were young conscripts, with the Algerian nationalists waging elusive guerrilla operations in the hills, with the war spilling over into the very streets of Paris, the police raiding the homes of Algerian sympathizers, and Algerian extremists striking at moderates, the war drained the financial resources, morale, and self-esteem of the French. To check the flow of aid from Egypt to the Algerian nationalists the French also participated in the ill-fated Suez expedition in 1956, but nothing availed. The settlers in Algeria and the army leaders smarting under their earlier defeat in Indochina adamantly opposed French withdrawal. Taking matters into their own hands, in May 1958, they staged an insurrectionary coup in Algiers. A new cabinet, hastily formed in Paris, proved impotent against the junta in control in Algeria, feared a paratroop invasion of the capital, and welcomed the one man who could save the situation, de Gaulle. The vast majority of the French people hailed his return. The army leaders, the settlers in Algeria, and the parties of the right were convinced that with his solicitude for the army and for French national greatness he would keep Algeria French. He also mollified the left, except for the Communists and a tiny group of stubborn, inflexible republicans, by recalling the democratic way in which he had governed after liberation and by insisting that he would return to power only in a legal way. In June 1958 the National Assembly

9 See pp. 548–549.
10 See pp. 868, 874–875.

invested de Gaulle as premier with emergency powers for six months and with the authority to prepare a new constitution.

In that way the Fifth Republic was born. In quick succession in the autumn of 1958 the new constitution was prepared and accepted overwhelmingly by a popular referendum, and elections were held; a new Gaullist party (the Union for the New Republic) emerged, and de Gaulle was elected president. The presidency was the key office and focus of power in the Fifth Republic, which was governed by a mixed presidential and parliamentary system. The president was empowered to dissolve the Assembly and call for new elections, submit important questions to popular referendums, and assume emergency powers, all of which de Gaulle did in his eleven years in office. Political instability disappeared; in the first ten years of the Fifth Republic there were only three premiers; in the fourteen years from 1944 to 1958 under the Fourth Republic there had been twenty-five.

We have already noted how de Gaulle settled the Algerian crisis, how an independent Algeria came into existence in July 1962, and how even earlier, de Gaulle granted self-determination and independence to the former French colonies in sub-Saharan Africa. With French self-confidence restored because of the stability of the new regime, with economic prosperity continuing, and with France playing an active and independent role in world affairs, the French reconciled themselves to the loss of empire and took pride in their heightened importance on the world scene. In 1960 France became the fourth nation to develop a nuclear capacity, following in the steps of the United States, the U.S.S.R., and Britain. Rejecting the rigid patterns of the Cold War and viewing postwar international affairs as a struggle between Great Powers rather than a clash of ideologies, de Gaulle declined to follow the American or British lead in Europe or Asia and aspired to a large diplomatic role for France on the European continent, in Asia, and elsewhere.

After the settlement of the Algerian crisis de Gaulle made himself an even stronger master of the French domestic scene. He continued to build a kind of plebiscitary democracy by frequent direct appeals to the people and by ignoring parliament. In one major instance, bypassing parliament, he secured a constitutional amendment providing for the direct popular election of future presidents. In the elections of 1962 his party won an absolute majority in the Assembly, the first time any party had done so in republican history. Although civil liberties were for the most part preserved, and free speech and free elections maintained, the old democratic ferment seemed to be disappearing; the political parties, including the Communist, seemed paralyzed or impotent. Despite sporadic street demonstrations, sterility and torpor for a time settled over French political life. Skilled technicians ran the affairs of state, and de Gaulle, an uncrowned republican monarch, presided as arbiter over the nation's destinies.

But the nation grew restless. In 1965 de Gaulle was reelected president, but with a runoff necessary because he failed to secure a majority on the first ballot. The labor unions chafed at inflation and inadequate attention to housing; students objected to government expenditures on nuclear arms instead of on educational facilities; opposition political leaders criticized the government's control over the mass information media. The parties of the left grew closer together. The country as a whole became impatient with de Gaulle's extravagant posturing in world affairs, as when he called for Quebec to free itself from Canada, or allied himself with the Arab cause against Israel, or upheld doctrinaire anti-British and anti-American attitudes. Suddenly in May 1968 grievances in the universities sparked a revolt that led to demonstrations by hundreds of thousands of students and then brought 10 million workers out on strike, paralyzing the economy and threatening the regime itself. De Gaulle survived the revolt but only after assuring himself of army support and promising wage increases and broad educational and labor reforms.

New elections in June 1968, in which de Gaulle held out the threat of communism and chaos, resulted in an overwhelming majority for his party. The country seemed to forget the outburst. Educational reforms were inaugurated, and de Gaulle weathered an assault on the franc despite the economic disruption of the spring. But in April 1969 he chose to make a referendum on a complicated series of constitutional reforms a vote of confidence in himself. When it was defeated at the polls by a small margin, he resigned in pique and retired to his country estate, where he died a year later, an august, heroic, and austere figure whose exploits in war and peace had even during his own lifetime assured him a place in history.

The Fifth Republic continued without de Gaulle. His successors as president, Georges Pompidou from 1969 to 1974, and Valéry Giscard D'Estaing (a conservative but not a Gaullist) after 1975, gave firm presidential leadership and followed de Gaulle's independent foreign policy but avoided his more extreme positions in international affairs. The opposition on the left meanwhile grew in strength, and the Socialist party under François Mitterand developed a working alliance with the Communists, to the alarm of the Gaullists who took steps to reorganize themselves in order to protect the Gaullist heritage. Like other industrial countries in the 1970s, France had to cope with high inflation, industrial slowdown, and unemployment. Although the institutions of the Fifth Republic afforded stability, France faced growing political, social, and economic tensions, partly built up within a system that did not permit much latitude for constructive political opposition, and partly occasioned by the world-wide recession.

Germany: Divided but Restored

In 1945 Germany was in ruins, its cities gutted, three-fourths of the homes in its great cities destroyed, its industrial plants burned and bombed, its land divided into four zones and occupied by United States, British, French, and Soviet troops. Economic chaos, a worthless currency, food and housing scarcities, an active black market, and shattered morale combined to create a grim picture. Moreover, under the arrangements at Potsdam, Germany surrendered control to Poland and the U.S.S.R. of an area along its eastern borders roughly equivalent to a fourth of the German territory as defined at Versailles.[11] Some 12 million refugees, expelled or in flight from these eastern areas, as well as from former German population centers such as the Sudetenland, had to find homes in the bombed-out German cities.

The four powers cooperated in 1946 in holding an international trial at Nuremberg of twenty-two major Nazi leaders charged with crimes against humanity and world peace, and executed all but a few of the defendants. The evidence of evil deeds, massive and incontrovertible, was set down for posterity in many volumes

11 See pp. 821–825, maps, pp. 805, 822–823.

of testimony but misgivings of many kinds arose, including the precedent of punishing the leaders of a defeated enemy and even the propriety of one totalitarian power, the Soviet Union, sitting in judgment over another. A "denazification" program, carried out by the occupation authorities, each in its own way, and by German courts under Allied supervision, had mixed results; sometimes lesser offenders were punished because their cases were less complicated, whereas more serious offenders benefited from postponements and delays. Since so many technically trained and professional Germans had in some way been identified with Nazi organizations, it became impossible to exclude all of them from public life. In general, the Allied countries rejected the notion of collective or mass German guilt for Nazi misdeeds. Individuals guilty of the more heinous crimes associated with the Third Reich were still being apprehended and tried two and three decades after the war's end—in German courts and, in the spectacular case of Adolf Eichmann, who played a leading role in the Jewish liquidation program, in Israel. In 1947 the Allied authorities formally dissolved the historic state of Prussia; the spirit of Prussian militarism and authoritarianism was thus to be exorcised from the German body politic; on this, Western and Soviet authorities were in agreement.[12]

Late in 1946 the Americans and British fused their occupation zones; the French followed in 1948. The Soviets went their separate way in their zone in East Germany. They encouraged the East German Communists to swallow up the Social Democrats and in 1949 oversaw the establishment of a German Democratic Republic. Under the stern rule of Communist party leader Walter Ulbricht, who dominated East German political affairs for over twenty years, East Germany followed the pattern of the Soviet satellites, building a disciplined one-party state and industrializing the economy. Even under Stalin's successors there was less liberalization here than in any of the other satellites. Riots in East Berlin in June 1953 and continued mass flight to West Germany were symptoms of unrest and dissatisfaction with the regime.

In West Germany, after the establishment of state governments, a constitutional convention representing the state diets met in 1948–1949, with the encouragement of the Western occupying powers, and established the Federal Republic of Germany, its capital in the Rhineland city of Bonn. The political leaders in Bonn were resolved to create an enduring German democracy, which their predecessors at Frankfurt in 1848–1849 and at Weimar in 1919 had failed to do.[13] The political fortunes of the new republic from the beginning rested largely in the hands of the Christian Democrats, heir to the old Catholic Center party. The dominating figure in postwar Germany was Konrad Adenauer, a patriarchal, strong-willed, powerful personality recalling Bismarck. Adenauer took office as chancellor at the age of seventy-three and governed with skill and shrewdness for fourteen years from 1949 to 1963, resigning reluctantly at the age of eighty-seven. For twenty years from 1949 to 1969, the elections held every four years confirmed the Christian Democrats in office, although a reinvigorated and modernized Social Democratic party supported by one-third of the voters provided a strong and energetic opposition. Adenauer, relegating to an indefinite future the question of German unification and the lost eastern territories, strengthened ties of friendship

12 See pp. 217–224, 404–405, 512–519.
13 See pp. 477–480.

with France, cooperated in the movement of European political and economic integration, won the support and confidence of the Western powers, and provided the domestic stability and continuity that made possible a phenomenal German economic recovery.

The most spectacular achievement of West Germany was its industrial recovery and subsequent expansion, justifiably styled the "German miracle." After the chaos of the first two postwar years, from 1945 to 1947, conditions began to improve. The damage to German industry, whose capacity had been greatly expanded during the war, proved less extensive than appeared on the surface; many of the German plants were usable after repairs, to which the population set itself with diligence and ingenuity. The influx of deportees and refugees from Eastern Europe turned into an asset, adding to the labor force. Reparations, over which the Western powers and the Soviets wrangled, were soon halted in the Western zone. In 1948 the Western powers effected a much needed currency reform in their zone. Then, with large sums of money provided by the United States under the Marshall Plan, West Germany embarked on an unprecedented industrial expansion, carefully allocating resources and planning capital investments and cooperating closely with other European countries in lowering trade barriers. The economic system remained capitalist, although the government shaped economic policies, guiding and channeling investments into the vital sectors of the economy and conscientiously overseeing social needs as well. Ludwig Erhard served as Adenauer's economics minister and from 1963 to 1968 as his successor, restoring the sense of partnership with cabinet and legislature that Adenauer had ignored. In 1968 Kurt Georg Kiesinger became chancellor, continuing the Christian Democratic ascendancy.

With the population accepting a relatively modest scale of living and thereby making imports less necessary, the industrial scene undisturbed by labor strife, the country free from the burden of military expenditures and profiting from the increased demand created by the Korean War in 1950–1953, a substantial proportion of the national product was reinvested year after year and made possible continuous industrial growth and full employment. By 1950 industrial production had already surpassed prewar German levels; by 1958 Germany had all but doubled its output of 1938 and was the leading industrial country of Western Europe. By the 1960s it was producing well over twice as much as before the war, even though its industrial rate of growth showed signs of slowing down, largely because of a labor shortage. At the same time the West German population grew in the three decades after 1945 from 48 million to 62 million, whereas the population of East Germany, despite important economic progress there too, declined from 19 million to 17 million. Even by the early 1950s, only a few years after the disastrous military defeat, the German Federal Republic had become an impressive industrial and political power, a coveted ally of the Western camp, an equal member after 1955 of Western military structures, including the North Atlantic Treaty Organization. With the passage of time a new generation appeared that felt little responsibility for the crimes of the Nazis; Chancellor Kiesinger had even once been a member of the party. Political issues of an inflammatory nature faded; material progress seemed triumphant over ideology, at least as far as older and middle-aged people were concerned. A small National Democratic party tried to agitate the burned-out ashes of Nazism but with limited success. The real sources of discontent appeared among students and young people, who rebelled against West German society for its materialism and embraced a vaguely defined anarchism.

In 1969 the more than twenty-year tenure of the Christian Democrats ended. Since 1961 the Christian Democrats had been able to govern only as part of a coalition, with the Free Democrats. In 1965 the Social Democrats also joined the coalition, and Willy Brandt, long the popular Social Democratic mayor of West Berlin, became foreign minister. But the coalition did not last. The Free Democrats, though conservative in other ways, wished to see Brandt's *Ostpolitik,* his policy of flexibility toward Eastern Europe, given a trial. They shifted their support to the Social Democrats, who had broadened their appeal, even renouncing their original Marxist platform some years earlier. In 1969 Willy Brandt became the first Social Democratic chancellor since 1930. To improve political and economic relations with Eastern Europe, he negotiated important agreements with the Soviet Union and with Poland, conceding the frontiers established at the end of the war and renouncing the former German territories in the east. In Warsaw and in Israel he paid homage to the Jewish victims of the Nazis. Despite restlessness at Brandt's personal style and complaints that he was neglecting domestic affairs, his party won additional seats in the election of 1972, the first in which the voting age in Germany was reduced to eighteen. The startling discovery that a member of Brandt's staff was spying for East Germany cut short his chancellorship in 1974; the less sentimental Social Democratic leader, Helmut Schmidt, succeeded him

Thirty years after the fall of Hitler the German Federal Republic in 1975 was the strongest economic power in Western Europe, producing more goods and services than any other nation except the two superpowers and Japan. Its industrial output was a third that of all the members of the Common Market combined; it held twice as much gold as the United States. With a population less than one quarter the American, Germany's gross national product was one-third that of the United States, and its volume of foreign trade was nearly equal. In industrial relations it pioneered in bringing labor and capital together; a policy of "codetermination" allowed half the boards of directors of many leading enterprises to be labor representatives. In the recession of the 1970s Germany coped more successfully than any other industrial country, including the United States, with inflation, industrial slowdown, and unemployment. Because the self-disciplined labor movement accepted minimal wage increases, the government succeeded in keeping its inflationary rate well below 10 percent. All the political parties and labor and industrialists were haunted by the memory of what the inflation of the 1920s and the swollen unemployment ranks of the 1930s had once done to their country.

Just as Germany remained divided, so did Berlin, which lay 100 miles deep within East Germany, partitioned into a Western and a Soviet sector, the scene of international friction for many years. In 1961 the Soviet and East German authorities erected a physical wall to check the exodus of East Berliners; thousands had already fled in pursuit of the more democratic atmosphere and material plenty of the West. With the building of the Berlin Wall the East German government halted an exodus that had already cost it 3 million people. It then began to make remarkable economic progress under its system of centralized economic planning.

By the late 1960s, despite its relatively small population the German Democratic Republic was one of the world's ten leading industrial powers, the wealthiest country in all Eastern Europe, with standards of living higher than those in the U.S.S.R. In 1971 the more flexible Erich Honecker succeeded Ulbricht as party leader.

In the early postwar years Christian Democrats and Social Democrats in West Germany, and Communists in East Germany, had been at one in their determination some day to reunite their divided nation. Under Brandt's conciliatory foreign policy, communications were improved and family visits across the border of East Germany permitted, but reunification remained remote. In 1973 the two German states recognized each other diplomatically. The two social systems were evolving along very different lines, and each in its way, by material and other standards, was enormously successful. If the leading industrial power of Western Europe and the leading industrial power of Eastern Europe outside the U.S.S.R. were one day to unite, the implications for European and world affairs would be far-reaching. But reunification was less in German hands than in the larger framework of international relationships. As the years passed, the two Germanies were fast developing a separate sense of national destiny and identity, and each population was coming to view the "other" Germans as foreigners. They spoke more frequently than in earlier years of two nations and of coexistence; many remembered that Germany in modern times had been united only for the seventy-five years from 1871 to 1945, and that in the early modern centuries it had long been common to speak of the Germanies.

The Japanese Revival

In Japan, as in Germany, the Americans used military occupation in 1945 to foster democratic institutions. A new constitution promulgated in 1946 ended the divine right rule of the emperor and transformed him into a constitutional sovereign. Under the firm hand of General Douglas MacArthur the political machinery of democratic government was established; women voted; local self-government was encouraged. Labor unions grew in size and militancy. The large industrial and banking combinations were ordered dissolved, although new forms of economic concentration took their place. A sweeping program of land redistribution was inaugurated. Unfortunately, many peasants lacked the means to purchase the holdings offered them, and larger landowners resisted the reforms. Although the moderate socialists, the Social Democrats, emerged as an important party, political control remained largely in the hands of conservative groups drawn from the upper social classes who had long ruled Japan.

Japan, like Germany, profited from the tension between the Soviets and the Western world. In the peace treaty signed in 1951, to which the Soviets were not a party, no reparations were exacted nor were any drastic limitations on armaments imposed. Japanese sovereignty was reestablished, although the United States, by treaty, retained some military rights in Japan and occupied the Ryukyu Islands, including Okinawa, until 1972. The Soviets made no move to return the Kurile Islands, which they had occupied at the end of the Second World War. Japan early recognized, and had close relations with, the People's Republic of China. A militant peace movement, stirring up memories of Hiroshima, tried to steer Japan on a neutralist course and opposed mutual defense arrangements with the United States; anti-American demonstrations and riots, led by dissatisfied university students, recurred.

In 1968 Japan celebrated the centennial of the Meiji Restoration,[14] which had launched the country into the mainstream of world history; in 1975 Hirohito became the first Japanese emperor to visit the United States. Despite its disastrous defeat in the Second World War, with a population surpassing 100 million but having successfully stabilized its rate of population growth, Japan was the third leading industrial power of the world, surpassed only by the United States and the U.S.S.R. As in other industrial countries, the process of continuing economic expansion was interrupted in the 1970s, and Japan suffered severely from industrial slowdown and inflation. The country was also rocked by scandals revealing the improper involvement of its political leaders with international business corporations. Intent upon making its democratic machinery work, Japan remained, despite social ferment, a bastion of conservative stability in the troubled Orient of the postwar years.

The Italian Republic

In Italy, after more than two decades of fascism, democratic processes were resumed after the war.[15] The country adopted a new constitution, voted the Savoy monarchy out of existence in favor of an Italian Republic, and extended the suffrage to women. In the first postwar elections, held in June 1945, three left parties, the Christian Democratic, the Communist, and the Socialist, came forward. Communism was a powerful force in Italian political life, emerging, as in France, with great prestige from the partisan movement of the Resistance and successfully exploiting existing economic and social grievances, of which there were many in Italy; until 1947 the Communists held seats in the cabinet. In the divided Socialist party a Left majority insisted on close ties with the Communists while a minority insisted on an independent democratic socialism. The Christian Democrats, as in the case of West Germany, dominated the political scene. A revival of the Catholic Popular party of the prefascist 1920s, the party was sparked initially by a high sense of Christian idealism and social justice yet was moderate enough in its social and economic outlook to attract conservatives, who saw their own parties disappear in the wake of the democratic reaction to fascism.

The dominating figure in postfascist Italy was the Christian Democratic leader, Alcide de Gasperi, who survived the Mussolini years as a librarian in the Vatican. He provided strength and stability in the first chaotic period after the war, and for seven formative years in the life of the republic, from 1946 to 1953, presided over a strong government that advanced political freedom and introduced moderate reforms. In 1947, in the context of the Cold War, de Gasperi dismissed the Communists from his cabinet. The general elections of 1948 followed shortly thereafter. In Italy, as in France, the Communists wished to win back their seats in the government. Adopting a revolutionary militancy, and winning the support of the Left Socialists, they made a concerted bid for power. De Gasperi triumphed, backed by the conservative parties, the Vatican, and the United States,

14 See pp. 540–541.
15 See pp. 776–781, 813.

which for the first time in its history openly intervened to influence the outcome of a European election; the Communists and their Left Socialist allies received only one-third the vote.

The Christian Democrats continued to govern the country, but without the majority they had won in 1948. They governed in coalition with the smaller parties of the left and left center, and by the late 1960s, often with the support of the right. Moving cautiously in their reform program, they took care not to alienate propertied interests. Although they attempted to break up the larger landed estates, and to raise living standards in the south, the tempo of change was slow. After de Gasperi's resignation in 1953, a succession of prime ministers followed one another with scarcely a year in office for each. The party was divided by factionalism and dominated by economically and socially conservative interests, in which the church hierarchy played a significant role. The government came to be marked by cabinet instability, inertia, and an inability to initiate needed social and economic changes. Even when joined briefly by the Socialists in the early 1960s, in "an opening to the left," the Christian Democrats showed little enthusiasm for reform; the Socialists, meanwhile, lost working-class support and soon withdrew. The Communists, manifesting increasing independence from Moscow after 1956, remained a powerful latent force, gaining substantial strength in each election after 1958. Supported by over a fourth of the electorate, they profited from popular restlessness with the perennial Christian Democratic coalitions. The fact that in 1963 Pope John XXIII spoke openly for a rapprochement with the Soviet world in the interests of preserving peace also made it easier for many Italians to vote Communist. In the meantime the economic boom that reached a peak in Italy about 1963 began to show trouble signs.

In the two decades after the war, for reasons that baffled economists, Italy enjoyed an unprecedented economic expansion. By 1949, with Marshall Plan aid, industrial production had reached prewar levels. From 1953 on, Italian industrial growth rivaled that of West Germany and France. Benefiting from the Common Market, and with foreign capital streaming in, the economy flourished; by the 1960s economic output was more than double the level of the prewar years. Italy became a leading industrial power. Italian automobiles and motor scooters, shoes and other leather goods, typewriters, calculating machines, sewing machines, as well as Italian films, enjoyed popular esteem in the United States and elsewhere. The south remained an economic problem. Although the region made more economic progress in the decade from 1955 to 1965 than ever before, the gap between the industrial north and the largely agricultural south widened rather than narrowed. There was a steady migration of southern workers to the more advanced northern industrial areas, so that a city like Milan had to absorb a stream of untrained, often illiterate immigrants who seemed to be coming from a foreign country; others from the south, close to 3 million, found jobs in the booming economies of France, Germany, and Switzerland.

In the 1960s Italy, despite its many unresolved problems, was a constitutional democracy with a thriving capitalist economy, a quiet revolution elevating living standards for all classes. Most Italians hoped that the continuing growth of a prosperous middle class, the gradual economic improvement in the south, and close political and economic ties with the other countries of democratic Western Europe would allay social and labor unrest, extinguish the flickering ambitions of any revived neofascism, and frustrate the advance of a powerful and growing Communist party. But the economic boom had affected Italian society very unevenly. The margin between the highest and lowest incomes remained larger than in other industrial countries. Nor did the Christian Democratic governments adequately direct public and private investment into such neglected areas as education, the cities, and the still impoverished south. After 1963 economic conditions took a turn for the worse. Prosperity itself was partly responsible. As consumer demand arose, increased imports hurt the balance of payments, weakened the currency, and encouraged inflation; wages were increased to keep up with rising prices, and the inflationary spiral mounted. Italian products became less competitive, profits declined as costs rose, and investment shrank. Austerity measures undertaken in 1964 helped to curb inflation and the trade deficit, but they also postponed government spending on social needs and contributed to the economic slowdown.

Worsening economic conditions accentuated political problems. The conservatism of the Christian Democrats increased. The Socialists, who lost heavily in the 1968 elections, split once again and disappeared as a major political force. The Communists advanced in strength. In the "hot autumn" of 1969 labor discontent burst out in a great wave of strikes that subsided only after substantial wage increases. These increases further accelerated inflation and undermined the country's ability to compete in world markets. More dependent on oil imports than any other industrial country, Italy suffered intensely from the oil embargo and the sudden steep oil price increases in 1973–1974. By mid-1974 it faced an economic crisis unlike anything it had known in the twenty years since postwar recovery. Inflation and unemployment were worse than in other countries in the Common Market; in 1975 inflation reached 25 percent annually, over 1 million were unemployed, and the value of the lira dropped precipitously.

Only a few years earlier Italy had looked forward to rising living standards and a resolution of its social and economic difficulties. Now the very existence of parliamentary and constitutional democracy was at stake. The Christian Democrats had previously muddled through because of widespread political apathy and a relatively quiescent labor movement, but the labor unions and the Communist party were now actively mobilizing mass support. The Communists, long the second largest party and increasing their share of the popular vote over the years, emerged as a major element. In 1974 they proposed a reconciliation between themselves and all other parties and groups in the interests of the troubled nation. The strongest Communist party in the Western world and one of those most independent of the Soviet Union, it had condemned Soviet intervention in Czechoslovakia in 1968, renounced such tenets of Marxist orthodoxy as the dictatorship of the proletariat, and insisted that each country, in keeping with its political traditions, should be free to follow its own road to socialism. Communist mayors and municipal councils were already governing a number of major cities. Many Italians turned to the Communists to break the thirty-year tenure of the Christian Democrats, whose hold seemed to be weakening. In the elections of 1976, although the Communists did not surpass the Christian Democrats in popular vote, the margin narrowed. It was clear that the Communists would play an important role in the Italian political future. Meanwhile, neofascists and rightist extremists were mobilizing Italians against the growing strength of the left. With an unbalanced economy and a precarious currency, declining political authority, governmental instability, provocative acts by the extreme right, widespread dissatisfaction with the Christian Democrats, division over such social issues as divorce and abortion, and an increasingly strong Communist party bidding for power, the Italian Republic, until recently buoyant and self-confident, was in deep trouble. Able to cope only minimally with its urgent problems, it seemed in the late 1970s to be moving toward a constitutional crisis.

The Iberian Peninsula

Spain and Portugal have long been absent from these pages, but nowhere in Europe in the 1970s did political changes take place so dramatically as in the Iberian peninsula. In 1975 the thirty-six-year-old authoritarian rule of General Francisco Franco in Spain ended with the death of the dictator. In his last two decades Franco held power with a minimum of overt force, never popular but grudgingly accepted because the Spanish wished to wipe out memories of the bloody civil war that had torn the country apart in the previous generation.[16] Despite the political backwardness of the regime, remarkable economic progress occurred, comparable to that in Western Europe. Within a decade, in the 1960s, a predominantly agricultural country became an industrial power. During Franco's last year, while the dictator suffered from a lingering illness, and immediately after his death, a limited program of political reform was put into effect. The tempo of reform proved too slow to satisfy democratic-minded Spaniards, the working class, and the unexpectedly robust political parties of the left that had emerged from their clandestine existence. During his lifetime Franco had pledged the restoration of the house of Bourbon, and upon his death Juan Carlos I took the throne, the first Spanish monarch since the abdication of Alfonso XIII, his grandfather, in 1931. With the house of Bourbon restored, Spain was in the hands of a loose coalition of conservative interests that hoped to contain the new and aggressive opposition forces even as the country moved toward representative government and democracy. In 1977 the first parliamentary elections in forty-one years resulted in a victory for a moderate coalition.

In Portugal, as in Spain, an authoritarian regime survived the Second World War.[17] The dictatorship's narrow fiscal policies had stifled economic expansion, and unlike Spain, Portugal remained in a state of economic backwardness and poverty. In 1961, not long after the inauguration of economic development plans that might have opened the way to modernization, revolt broke out in the Portuguese colonies in Africa. The regime diverted its attention to subduing the colonial rebellions in Angola and elsewhere, and a long, dreary, and unsuccessful military effort began. In the midst of the struggle, António Salazar, who had ruled Portugal for forty years, became incapacitated in 1968 and died two years later. In the next few years the regime loosened the dictatorial controls slightly but continued the costly and hopeless effort to subdue the colonies.

The colonial struggle precipitated the "Flower Revolution." An army officer, General António de Spínola, published a sensational book that reflected the frustration of many in the military who had become increasingly radicalized by the

16 See pp. 795–796.
17 See pp. 780, 790.

struggle in Africa. He proclaimed as hopeless the thirteen-year effort to crush the independence movement and warned that it could only destroy progress in Portugal itself. In April 1974 a group of captains and majors led troops, brandishing red carnations, in a bloodless seizure of power, and the regime fell without resistance. The officers, calling themselves the Armed Forces Movement, declared themselves custodians of the revolution but pledged democratic civilian rule in the near future. There followed, however, in the next two years a complicated succession of coups and countercoups. After a half-century of political inertia, compromise was difficult among the many contending groups, but no one could have anticipated the deep-seated revolutionary ferment that boiled up, or the unlikely instrument of this fervor, the activist elements of the army, who received the support of the Communists as well. Six provisional governments followed one another, the military dissolving each at various times. Eventually, at the end of 1975 the chief of staff, General António Eanes, purged the extreme leftist military commanders and took control. A constitution was adopted providing for a strong executive to share power with a parliament.

In the spring of 1976, two years after the revolution began, parliamentary elections were held and the Socialists emerged as the leading party; General Eames was elected president. By that time the economy, strained by the costly African wars even before the revolution, was in chaos. The provisional governments had introduced sweeping structural changes but neglected pressing immediate problems. They had nationalized the banks, industry, mining, and transportation, expropriated large landholdings, and awarded substantial wage increases. Economic disruption, the fall in productivity during the revolutionary turbulence, and the return of close to 1 million embittered former colonials brought the country to the edge of bankruptcy.

On the other hand, the colonial issue that had precipitated the tumultuous events had been resolved by the end of 1974. The revolution ended almost five centuries of Portuguese rule over its colonial empire in Africa. Mozambique, at first under a transitional regime, gained full independence in the summer of 1975. As we have seen, the pledge of independence in November 1975 to Angola, where three separate groups with outside support competed for leadership, caused grave international tensions that were not resolved until after many months of open warfare.[18] Just as the insoluble Algerian conflict had brought about a revolution in France in 1958, although a controlled one because of the presence of de Gaulle, so the agonizing struggle over the Portuguese colonies in Africa unleashed a revolution that overthrew a long-established dictatorial regime and ushered in a period of tempestuous change. The advances toward parliamentary government in Spain and Portugal in the 1970s were exceptions to the eclipse of democracy in many parts of the globe.

113. INTELLECTUAL AND SOCIAL CURRENTS

Along with the sweeping political and economic changes that engulfed nations and continents in the contemporary age, many new cultural and intellectual currents could be discerned. Much of contemporary twentieth-century culture had

[18] See p. 881.

its origins in the years from 1871 to 1914.[19] But since that time science, philosophy, the arts, and religion have opened new frontiers or have taken new directions.

The Advance of Science: Nuclear Physics

In science the preponderant characteristic of the years since 1914 was the acceleration of scientific discovery and its technological application. Although science and technology expanded rapidly in the half-century before the First World War, more scientific activity could be said to have taken place in the years since 1919, and at a more rapid rate, than in all previous human history. More scientists are at work in the contemporary era than ever before. About 15,000 trained scientists, it is estimated, were exploring scientific problems at the opening of the twentieth century; in the latter part of the century, over 500,000 scientists were engaged in research, more than the total of all previous centuries.

The average person experienced the triumphs of science most dramatically in medicine and public health. Sulfa drugs, penicillin, cortisone, and antibiotics were used to combat infections and ailments that were formerly crippling or deadly; vitamins, hormones, adrenalin, and insulin were available to promote health or relieve suffering. Vaccines were invented to combat a number of dread diseases, including, after 1955, poliomyelitis; by 1975 smallpox had been eradicated world-wide. The advances in medicine were accompanied by remarkable accomplishments in surgery, including the transplantation of vital organs. Apart from the advances in medical science, citizens in an industrial society benefited from modern technology in ways too familiar to need recounting. For entertainment radio and the motion picture were available and, after the Second World War, television; it was hinted that the revolution in electronics would spell an end to the age of Gutenberg. After 1947 airplanes could fly faster than the speed of sound; giant airships could traverse huge distances in a few hours; tourist travel to distant parts of the earth became commonplace. A new world of computers, rocketry, and space technology also opened, and the world seemed to be on the threshold of a new industrial age based on atomic power.

We have already noted the profound transformation in physics in the opening years of the twentieth century, comparable to the scientific revolution that began in the sixteenth century and the impact of Darwinian evolution in the nineteenth.[20] After 1919 a new series of discoveries led to a deeper understanding of the structure of the atom and its nucleus. The cyclotron, developed in 1932, made it possible to penetrate or "bombard" the nucleus of the atom with high-speed particles and explore it further. The atom, it appeared, was not simply a nucleus of protons surrounded by electrons. In 1932 the British physicist Sir James Chadwick discovered that the atomic nucleus, or nucleon, consisted not only of protons but of neutrons as well. Earlier, at the turn of the century, scientists had discovered the natural radioactivity of certain elements, and Einstein had propounded his formula for the equivalence of energy and mass.

Now it was discovered that the atomic nucleus of elements like uranium, when

[19] See pp. 583–600.
[20] See pp. 269–282, 584–587.

bombarded by neutrons, could release unprecedented energy. Scientists explained that when a certain form, or isotope, of the uranium atom absorbs a neutron it becomes violently unstable and splits into two parts, releasing not only energy but neutrons of its own that then trigger the splitting of other atoms in a giant chain reaction, resulting in the emission of energy in prodigious amounts. In 1938 German scientists for the first time succeeded in accomplishing the fission, or splitting, of the uranium atom in the laboratory. By then the advance of atomic science, though the achievement of scientists of many different nationalities, was geared to war. Learning of the German developments, some scientists, including Albert Einstein who had fled the Nazis in 1934, prevailed upon the United States government to explore the use of atomic energy for military purposes before the Germans succeeded in doing so. In 1942 American and British scientists, aided by European refugee scientists including the Italian Enrico Fermi, brought about the first sustained nuclear chain reaction; this, in turn, led to the secret preparation of the atomic bomb and, as has been related, its use in August 1945.[21]

The destructive power of the bomb dropped at Hiroshima heralded the atomic age. The first use of atomic energy was for military purposes, but it could be used for constructive peacetime purposes as well; a tiny gram of uranium could produce power equal to almost three tons of coal. Even more staggering technical developments followed, involving nuclear fusion or the joining together of lighter atoms to form heavier ones, at great heat, with accompanying thermonuclear chain reactions. This was the basis of the hydrogen bomb developed in the 1950s in which atomic fission bombs were used as detonators. Such thermonuclear fusion was believed to be responsible for the energy of the sun itself. Twentieth-century nuclear physics had discovered the cosmic secret that the production of all energy in the universe depended on nuclear transformation.

The Implications of Science

As in the case of nuclear physics, science in the contemporary age was more closely allied with technology than ever before. There was a conscious organized effort to exploit new scientific findings. It became necessary for government or industry to subsidize most scientific research. Laboratory equipment was expensive, and complex investigation required large-scale collaborative efforts; the solitary scientific investigator or even inventor was disappearing. A new danger appeared. As scientific research came to be subsidized for national purposes, anxiety grew that scientific discoveries would serve political and not human goals.

Science had always affected the way people thought about themselves and their universe. The Copernican revolution had removed the earth from its position of centrality in the scheme of things; Darwinian evolution had demonstrated that *Homo sapiens* was biologically no more than a species that had survived. The philosophical implications of twentieth-century physics were only vaguely understood, yet they reinforced theories of relativism in all spheres. Ironically, at the very time that the average person was awed by the capabilities of science, scientists themselves recognized that they had no magic key to the nature of things. Generally they claimed no more than to determine, or guess at, relationships.

21 See p. 892.

Some of these within the world of the atom were mysterious and uncertain indeed.

Among some observers, there was a growing tendency to question the value of scientific and technological advance as such, and to ask whether modern technology, like some Frankenstein monster, had not grown beyond human control. Ecologists pointed to the wastage and spoliation of natural resources and to the pollution of the atmosphere by smoke, soot, and smog. They spoke of the threat to the human environment and the menace even to continued biological existence on the planet. The very life-preserving features of modern medicine and public health threatened to result in overpopulation and in unmanageable pressure upon the limited resources of the globe for sustaining life. The techniques developed to save or prolong human life also raised ethical and legal questions including definitions of life and death, and the rights of patients, families, and physicians. Some critics condemned modern technology and extolled the virtues of a pre-scientific and preindustrial age; others called for sharper awareness of the dangers involved and for increased controls by society. No longer was the idea of progress equated with the advance of science and technology.

Meanwhile, in the quest to understand nature the old divisions between the sciences were breaking down and new sciences were appearing. Biochemistry, biophysics, astrophysics, geophysics, and other subdisciplines arose, and all made intensive use of mathematics. The study of genetics made great advances. While physicists explored the atom, biochemists isolated the organic substance found in the genes and chromosomes of all living cells, the chemical carriers of all hereditary characteristics. When they discovered the genetic "code," and when they synthesized the basic substance of heredity, the implications of genetic engineering for the future evolution of the race were staggering. Here, too, the destiny of all human beings was more than ever linked to science.

The other life sciences and social sciences also grew in importance. Psychological exploration of human behavior, as well as the the applied medical sciences of psychiatry and psychoanalysis, expanded rapidly. Freud, who had first developed his theories of psychoanalysis before 1914, became widely known in the 1920s. His emphasis on the human sex drive and sexual repression was much modified by disciples like Alfred Adler, Carl Jung, and many others, but the original creative concepts persisted. On the other hand, many students of human behavior rejected Freud and argued that his contributions were not universally or scientifically valid but reflected the values of pre-1914, middle-class, male-dominated Viennese society. New schools emerged with different interpretations and techniques, but the search continued in modern psychology for the unconscious, nonrational sources of individual and collective human conduct.

As in the late nineteenth century, sociology and anthropology increasingly stressed the relativism of all culture. They denied notions of cultural superiority or hierarchies of cultural values, or even that there were objective criteria of historical progress. If Western society, they argued, made notable progress in science and technology, other cultures accomplished more in self-discipline, individual integrity, and human happiness. The very adjective "primitive," as opposed to "civilized," tended to disappear, and a new cultural humanism emerged that recognized and emphasized values distinct from the Western tradition.

The Creative Arts

The revolution against older traditions in the creative arts continued. Ever since the Renaissance, artists had followed certain norms of representation and space perspective. But much of modern, or contemporary, art prided itself on being nonobjective; it rejected the idea of imitating or reconstructing nature, or mirroring it with realism or photographic fidelity. The fundamental innovations of the artistic revolution began in the decade before 1914. At the turn of the century the French postimpressionist painters such as Paul Gauguin and Vincent Van Gogh made color the prime element in their art; cubists such as Braque rejected representational art even more thoroughly and placed the primary emphasis on abstract form. After 1919 the revolution in painting picked up in intensity; it seemed to mirror the political turbulence of the times and the disillusionment with rationalism and optimism. It reflected the influence of psychoanalysis and the emphasis on the unconscious and irrational elements in human beings, as well as the relativity of the new physics and the uncertainties raised about the nature of matter, space, and time. Surrealists such as Dali openly derided rationality and reality, focusing on the artist's subconscious in an orgy of uncontrolled subjectivism.

Matisse, Braque, Picasso, and others continued the pre-1914 experimentation in color and in form. Picasso systematically distorted and deformed his objects, as in the famous painting memorializing the German bombing of Guernica in 1937 during the Spanish Civil War, in which he strove for effects of anguish and intensity by distortions. Chagall deliberately painted the exaggerations of a dream world. At the same time the possibilities inspired earlier by the cubists led to a stricter sense of geometry and a focus on form alone. The results were sometimes pleasing, as in the case of Mondrian, but often strange; but here, too, science taught that solid everyday objects have a different kind of reality in space and in movement. After the Second World War, especially in the United States, Jackson Pollock and other artists developed a new school of abstract art; it included techniques of artistic improvisation and automation in which the artist's unconscious was said to dictate his or her work. Other, even broader, experimentation followed.

For the first time, beginning with the 1950s, the United States took the leadership from France in the new artistic developments. Contemporary art resulted in

TWINNED COLUMN
by Antoine Pevsner (Russian, then French, 1886–1962)

Antoine Pevsner, like Kandinsky and Chagall (see pp. 591 and 737), left his native Russia after the Soviet regime began to disapprove of "modern" art. The picture here shows one of his sculptures, a bronze piece about forty inches high, constructed in 1947. The symmetry and the column recall the classical tradition, but the work also conveys the scientific and technological interests of the twentieth century. Pevsner's sculptural space is not the familiar medium in which human beings live and move, but a more abstract space, known to mathematics, quite apart from man's peculiarities of size and physical senses. Courtesy of the Solomon R. Guggenheim Museum.

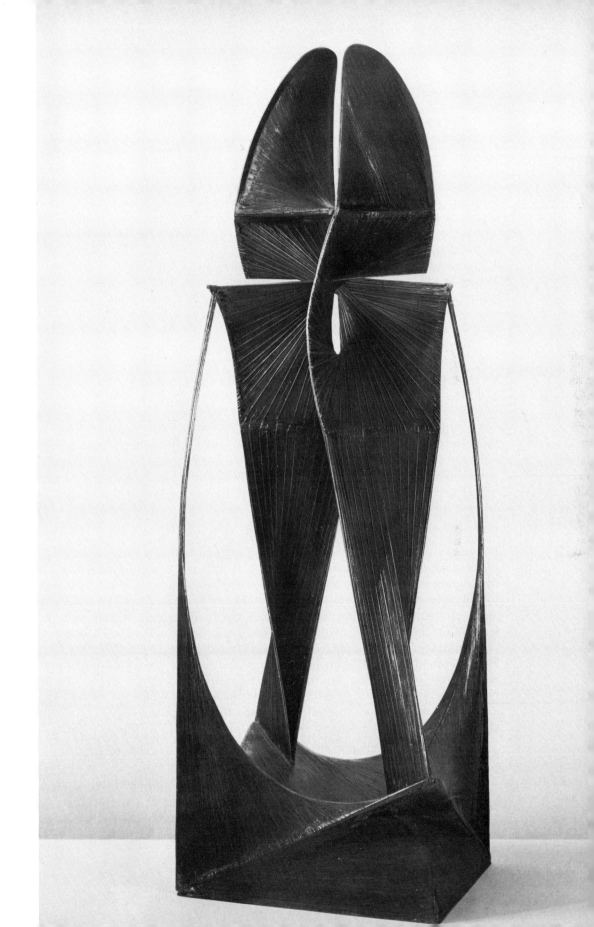

bold and original expressions of form and color, but the conscious subjectivism widened still further the gap between artist and public. The artist, painter, and sculptor (and the poet, musician, and novelist who were also rejecting the older conventions) were conveying their own vision of the world, not an objective reality shared by others. Perhaps the greatest innovation was that the public, baffled as it was by much of contemporary art, came to recognize the avant-garde as normal. Or at least this was so in freer societies; in totalitarian societies—Nazi Germany in the 1930s or the Soviet Union—such experimentation or innovation was frowned upon and banned as degenerate or socially dangerous. Realism, of course, never completely disappeared anywhere, but it was overshadowed by the newer schools of experimentation.

The focus on subjectivism and on the unconscious and the stress on the transformation and turbulence of Western society were reflected in literature too. The artistic reconstruction of lost time and the unfolding of the individual's innermost experience through a stream of consciousness and a flood of memories appeared first in the work of Marcel Proust and James Joyce. Perhaps T. S. Eliot reflected best the spiritual malaise of the contemporary age in the tone of his long poem, *The Waste Land*, written in 1922 but just as relevant over fifty years later. After the Second World War advanced writers, particularly in France, experimented with the "antinovel," a novel without heroes or plots in a conventional sense, often reconstructing little closed worlds shut off from the realities of the present. Here, too, the writers' subjectivism deliberately reflected a world of crumbling certainties. Film makers and directors experimented with the cinema along similar lines. All of this was in sharp contrast to the literature and entertainment provided through the mass communications media, especially popular movies and television, and hardly touched the average citizen.

Philosophy: Science, Logic, and Language

Philosophy in the twentieth century seemed to contribute less to an understanding of contemporary problems than in the past. Whereas it had formerly focused on metaphysics and ethics, and shared common concerns with theology, it now sought, at least for a time, to adopt the precision of mathematics and the methodology of science. The effort to understand the fundamentals of philosophy in terms of empirical science, mathematics, and symbolic logic was known as logical positivism (or logical empiricism). It was developed in England by Bertrand Russell and Alfred North Whitehead, who published their *Principia Mathematica* on the eve of the First World War, and simultaneously by the Viennese philosopher Ludwig Wittgenstein, who later moved to Cambridge. Opposed to all that was metaphysical, it rejected as invalid the traditional questions of philosophy and theology, and insisted that philosophers could not speak, in Wittgenstein's phrase, of "God, death, what is higher." Another major development favored linguistic analysis. Rejecting the mathematical formulations of logical positivism, some philosophers, including Wittgenstein himself in his later work, argued that philosophical questions and statements could not be similar to those of science; philosophers had to explore language and the ambiguities of language. A. J. Ayer, a British philosopher, summed up the argument in his *Language, Truth, and Logic,* published in 1936. Contemporary philosophy, especially in

Great Britain and the United States, devoted itself to language, semantics, and linguistic analysis. All this was somewhat remote for the average person. When they asked philosophers for help in exploring the meaning of human freedom, the philosophers replied that the question was unfruitful and that the inquirer might more profitably inquire in how many and in what ways human beings used the word "free." Such philosophy offered no reassurance amidst the perplexities of the modern age. But many philosophers were becoming increasingly responsive to new concerns and were grappling with many unresolved human and social dilemmas, not the least of which were the ethical implications raised by modern advances in scientific technology and medicine.

Religion: Protestantism, Catholicism, Judaism

Christianity was in great flux. With the continued advance of secularism, the end of the European colonial empires in Asia and Africa, and the triumphs of communism in Eastern Europe and other parts of the world, Christianity suffered a number of setbacks. The Christian churches continued to grapple also with the pressures of adjustment to modern civilization and with the challenges inherited from the nineteenth century of reconciling religious insights or traditional teachings with the conclusions of natural science, biblical scholarship, and comparative religion.[22]

In Protestantism in the years before the First World War liberal, or modernist, thought had tended to dominate. The churches absorbed the new scientific findings, minimized the supernatural and dogmatic aspects of their faith, and tried to adapt the religious teachings of the gospel to the social needs of the contemporary world. But the First World War and the disillusionment that followed dealt a blow to the ideal of the social gospel and its inherent optimism. Sometime in the 1920s, as a reaction, a revived emphasis on revealed religion, the supernatural, and the mystical set in. The Swiss theologian Karl Barth, whose writings from 1919 to the 1960s exerted great influence, sought to lead Protestantism back to the root principles of the Reformation. After the Second World War, as a result of the work of Barth, Paul Tillich, and others, a powerful movement in Protestantism reasserted its dependence on revealed truth and denied that human reason with its fallibility and corruption could ever properly judge divine revelation. Some theologians turned also to Søren Kierkegaard, a nineteenth-century Danish theologian, who, like Luther, had resolved his own deep anguish by a commitment to religious experience. Despite these developments the liberal, or modernist, trend remained strong. The World Council of Churches, established in 1948 to further the ecumenical movement, an effort to unite all branches of Protestantism and even to work out a rapprochement with the Roman Catholic church, continued its endeavors.

The Roman Catholic church in the second half of the twentieth century seemed to be in one of its great historic phases. Like Protestantism, it suffered from the advances of secularism in the twentieth century. It lost followers, and church attendance and recruitment for the clergy declined. With the vast increase in global population, mainly in the non-Western areas, the world proportion of Catholics was significantly reduced.

[22] See pp. 590–596.

The papacy became the center of ferment. After the Second World War many criticized Pius XII (1939–1958) for having failed to protest, as "God's deputy," against the Nazi destruction of European Jewry; his defenders insisted on the need to keep the church from temporal quarrels in order to preserve its eternal mission. To cope with the advance of communism in the postwar years the church prohibited Catholics in 1949 from reading the Communist press; and in the 1950s it suppressed the "worker-priest" movement in which a number of priests, especially in France, had lived and worked among ordinary workers and studied Marxism. Although the church no longer sought to stamp out modernism—the reconciliation of religion with science and scholarship—it continued to emphasize dogmatic training in the seminaries. In 1950 the newly pronounced dogma of the Assumption (i.e., the bodily assumption of Mary to heaven) was a blow to liberal Catholics and to ecumenical-minded Protestants. But both Catholics and Protestants absorbed without great shock the Dead Sea Scrolls, the first manuscripts of which were discovered in 1947, and which cast new light on the origins of Christianity.

When Pius XII died in 1958, he was succeeded by John XXIII. Although elected at the age of seventy-seven, and reigning for only four and a half years, John was one of the most remarkable popes of modern times. He enlarged the College of Cardinals and increased its non-Italian majority. He took important steps to renew the Catholic church in its organization and doctrine by convening in 1962 a Second Vatican Council, the first since 1870.[23] John, along with a reforming majority in the council, consciously sought to modernize, to bring the church into harmony with the political and social changes of contemporary times. He issued a series of powerful encyclicals, one reaffirming the social reform doctrine of the church, *Mater et Magistra* (1961), and another appealing for international peace and the protection of human rights through world organization, *Pacem in Terris* (1963). He sought to forward the ecumenical movement by encouraging a dialogue with non-Catholics and to establish fraternal ties with all faiths. Non-Catholics, Protestants, and Orthodox Christians were present as observer-delegates at the council.

In 1963 John was succeeded by the more conservative Paul VI. The Second Vatican Council continued its labors until 1965. In a series of decrees it redefined the church's position on many matters, including its relationship to non-Christian religions, and revised a number of practices. The Mass, for example, could henceforth be said in the vernacular. Above all, it affirmed the principle of collegiality, that is, that the pope must share authority with the bishops of the church. Paul was unhappy about some of these innovations. Although he reaffirmed the Catholic commitment to social progressivism and applied it to the world's underprivileged peoples in the encyclical *Progressio Populorum* (1967), he opposed attempts to impugn or repudiate either orthodox theology or papal supremacy. A synod of bishops convened in 1967 found its agenda severely restricted. On the critical question of birth control, a vital matter in Latin America and in all Catholic countries, Paul rejected the recommendations of a commission he had himself appointed and in a much discussed encyclical, *Humanae Vitae* (1968), condemned the use of scientific birth control methods. A modernist catechism,

23 See p. 594.

prepared by Dutch bishops, was also condemned. The result was a great deal of restlessness in the church and impatience with the failure to pursue the modernization of ancient rules and practices. Many Catholics advocated abandoning the injunction of celibacy for the clergy; some monks, nuns, and priests set aside their vows and married. Theologians continued to reaffirm the principle of shared authority. Paul's insistence on papal obedience went unheeded, and his strictures against birth control were openly criticized and often ignored.

Judaism, the third important faith of the Western world, was haunted in the years after 1945 by the great traumatic experience of the 1930s and 1940s, the Nazi attempt at genocide, the "Holocaust," as it was called.[24] Although the older trend of assimilation to a secular society persisted, there was a revived adherence to religion, both orthodox and reform. There was also unprecedented support by Jews everywhere, and especially in the United States, for the state of Israel, and not only among Jews who were Zionists. Support for Israel was reinforced by the harassment and persecution of Jews in the Soviet Union and Eastern Europe and in the Arab countries; in turn these countries used Jewish allegiance to Israel as justification for their attacks.

Like the Western religions, Islam, Hinduism, Buddhism, and the other great non-Western faiths, of which little can be said in these pages, all faced serious challenges to their doctrinal principles and were making efforts to adjust millennial old doctrines to the secularism of the contemporary age. At the same time some of these Eastern religions touched new groups in the West. Buddhist teachings gained many adherents and there was a revived interest in the West in the mystical, the transcendental, and the occult.

Existentialism

Outside organized religion, and generally outside professional philosophy too, a loosely organized body of ideas called "existentialism" made an effort to grapple with the human predicament. The existentialists formed no one school of thought and held no coherent body of principles; there were Christian, agnostic, and atheist existentialists. Yet all held some beliefs and attitudes in common. All reflected a troubled civilization, a world disturbed by war, totalitarianism, and oppression, a world of material progress and moral uncertainty in which the individual could be crushed by the very triumphs of science and technology. The existentialists questioned the idea of progress or dismissed it as an illusion. Emphasizing the fact of "existence" in the present, they sometimes doubted whether a living generation could learn from the past or contribute to the future. Accepting what they liked to call the "absurdity" of the human situation, they sought to reconcile the discrepancy between human ideals and a universe considered devoid of purpose.

Existentialist thought owed a debt to thinkers such as Blaise Pascal in the seventeenth century and Friedrich Nietzsche in the nineteenth, and to many others who throughout Western history had underscored the tragic element in human existence and the limitations on the power of human reason. More directly it owed a debt to Kierkegaard, the Danish religious philosopher whose writings became better known when translated into German in 1909. Existentialism was

24 See map on p. 802, and p. 803.

further explored in Germany after the First World War. But it was French writers, after the emergence of their country from defeat, occupation, and resistance in the Second World War, who developed it in literature and philosophy in a form that gave it a wide intellectual following. The novelist, dramatist, and essayist Jean-Paul Sartre was an outstanding exemplar, as was Albert Camus. These writers drew directly upon the Resistance experience. In a hostile world, they contended, man had to reassert his freedom. Human beings were "condemned to be free," said Sartre, totally free and entirely responsible for the choices they made. The authentic existentialist, moreover, was not merely contemplative but *engagé*, committed to action, even though aware that such action could not change the world. Camus drew upon the myth of Sisyphus to communicate his message. Sisyphus was condemned to roll his stone uphill even though it rolled back down again, his very humanity growing out of courage and perseverance at a hopeless and absurd task. Most existentialists rejected the notion of human perfectibility and the utopian (and Marxian) idea that perfect social systems could somehow be established to suit future unborn generations.

Some of these beliefs were shared by Christian existentialists who adopted Nietzsche's nineteenth-century assertion that "God is dead." The universe, they asserted, was no longer ruled by a deity who decreed and revealed the rules individuals must live by; human beings had to make their own choices and commitments. The existentialists spoke even of a post-Christian era. But mainly their ideas were part of an atheistic humanism, like that of Sartre. In their emphasis on the anguish of human existence, the frailty of human reason, the fragility of human institutions, and the need to reassert and redefine human freedom, the existentialists repeated an old theme but gave it new meaning, emphasizing both the tragic element of human destiny and the irrepressible struggle to combat despair.

The New Activism: The Youth Rebellion and the Woman's Movement

In the 1960s a new activism, not unrelated to existentialism, emerged, especially among younger people. A generation came to maturity that knew nothing firsthand of the Great Depression or of the Second World War. Young people grew up in an age of rapid political and social change, amid revolutionary advances in science and technology, and on a globe that was shrinking dramatically; and they were made aware of these changes by the new mass communications media. They tended to take for granted the scientific, technological, and other accomplishments of their society and pointed instead to its deficiencies—the flagrant contradictions of wealth and poverty within nations and among nations, racial injustices, the impersonal quality of mechanized society and large institutions, the violence that destroyed human beings in continuing wars, and always the threat of universal nuclear destruction.

The rebelliousness of the young developed into more than the traditional manifestation of a generation gap. It burst forth in the late 1960s in widely separate parts of the world. Students demonstrated and rioted in Paris, Berlin, San Francisco, New York, Mexico City, Tokyo, and many other places. They made heroes of the sworn foes of the established order: Fidel Castro and his martyred lieutenant, Ernesto Che Guevara, Ho Chi Minh, Mao Tse-tung, American black leaders such as the assassinated Malcolm X, the heralds of the colonial revolution such as Franz Fanon, and others. They read the neo-Marxist philosopher Herbert Marcuse, who warned that the very tolerance of bourgeois society was a trap to prevent true protest against injustice. As part of a New Left, they dismissed the older revolutionaries in the Soviet Union as timid bureaucrats who were unaware that the revolution had entered a post-Marxist phase and that the genuine ferment was to be found in the underdeveloped Third World. They attacked material comfort, affluence, and conformity. Sometimes they turned to violence themselves; more often, they sang its praise. Championing a new anarchism and nihilism, and a commitment to the present, they called on each other to destroy in order to purify and to restore creative freedom by releasing society from the "burdens" of the past. The youth rebellion in its dramatic phase of the 1960s subsided after a short interval. Older people shuddered at the assault on established institutions and rational processes but found it less easy to be complacent about social inequities of all kinds. The youth rebellion was part of the changes and upheavals that all modern civilization seemed to be experiencing in the second half of the twentieth century, and whose meaning could only be vaguely grasped.

The feminist, or woman's liberation, movement was another manifestation of contemporary social ferment. From the time of the French Revolution a few thinkers in France and in England had raised the question of equal rights for women. The modern movement had its origin in the United States in the mid–nineteenth century, and the beginnings of its contemporary phase there as well. In 1848 Elizabeth Cady Stanton and a small group of associates had proclaimed a declaration of independence for women, demanding the right to vote, equal compensation for work, legal equality, and expanded educational opportunities. The movement also spread abroad and was taken up in Britain by the suffragists. The right to vote was won in Britain and in the United States after the First World War, but progress in other respects was slow. The militant contemporary phase began in the United States in the mid-1960s, sparked in part by the civil rights movement in behalf of the American black population, and took form as the woman's liberation movement. Its leaders stressed the fact that women, who comprised half the human race (and over half the population in many regions of the globe) were still the objects of discrimination and did not enjoy positions of authority, leadership, and power proportionate to their numbers. Although some of the more blatant forms of legal discrimination had been removed, feminist leaders now demanded an end to all legal and social barriers to equality, admission to occupations formerly barred to them, and an equitable share in political and economic power. Some discrimination in contemporary society, they noted, was subtle and indirect. Sometimes it involved acculturation patterns by which children at an early age absorbed stereotyped notions of their future lives and narrowly limited career horizons. Language itself, the conventional use of the male gender in many instances, as in school textbooks, was seen as reinforcing the pattern. The process was self-perpetuating, because with few women in visible positions of leadership there were few models to emulate.

Many of the arguments for equal rights had most meaning in the advanced industrial countries. Elsewhere, in the poorer, less developed nations women had to overcome centuries-old neglect, oppression, abuse, and disregard of the most elementary human rights. The United Nations, from the time of its founding in 1945, had committed itself to equal political, economic, and educational rights for women. But in Africa, Asia, and Latin America adult illiteracy rates a generation later were still significantly higher for women than for men and were declining more slowly. Opportunities for higher education were also more circumscribed for women. In the developing areas, where a majority of the world's women lived, women faced problems of sheer survival and were burdened with large families and backbreaking chores. In those countries equal rights for women probably hinged upon the massive development of resources and social advances for the entire population.

Discrimination was not a problem confined to capitalist societies. In a Communist country like the Soviet Union women, at least constitutionally, were guaranteed equal rights with men. They made up over 30 percent of the elected representatives to the Supreme Soviet, whereas in the United States the corresponding figure for the American Congress was less than 3 percent. Yet there were few women represented in the organs of the Communist party with real power, such as the Politburo. In professional opportunities, the Soviet Union had many more women than men in medicine and dentistry but these professions did not enjoy the high economic and social standing that they did in the United States and Western Europe, nor did women occupy many important research or administrative positions in Soviet hospitals or universities. Women were encouraged to work, and in fact had to work out of economic necessity and social pressure, but not necessarily to develop their potentiality or to achieve positions of responsibility. Not much more attention was paid in the Soviet Union than elsewhere to overcoming the patterns of a male-dominated society. In the People's Republic of China, women were afforded wide opportunities within the limits of a controlled society, and equality between the sexes was proclaimed as a social goal. At the same time women in China, as in the Soviet Union, worked along with men at heavier and more arduous work than in Western industrial countries. Everywhere there was much to be done. An equal rights amendment to the Constitution, although adopted by the United States Congress in 1972, was still not ratified several years later by the necessary number of states. Some women, as in the past, held positions of the highest authority in their countries, among them in recent times Indira Gandhi in India, Golda Meir in Israel, and Sirimavo Bandaranaike in Sri Lanka (Ceylon); in Britain, Margaret Thatcher headed the Conservative party, and could one day be prime minister.

The development of contraceptive devices, including the birth control pill in the early 1960s, provided a new biological freedom for women. Changing social patterns that tolerated greater sexual freedom and new forms of marital relationships also contributed to their social liberation. There remained a contradiction between the demand for equal rights and the special protection in the form of labor legislation that democratic societies had long adopted for women. Although disagreement persisted on the methods and tempo of change, wide agreement existed on the need to open up opportunities for women and to utilize all of society's human resources, male and female, in every part of the globe to confront the challenges of the contemporary world. If that could be accomplished, it would count among the most memorable of the revolutionary changes of the contemporary era.

114. CRISES, CLASHES, AND COEXISTENCE

The War in Korea

We have already noted the origins and course of the Cold War in Europe to about 1950.[25] In June 1950 the Korean War broke out. To the consternation of the Western world, the Soviet-sponsored regime of North Korea crossed the border along the thirty-eighth parallel and launched an invasion of the Western-supported republic in the south. During the Second World War it had been agreed that Korea, once a source of imperialist contention between Japan and Russia, and after 1910 under Japanese rule, would again become free and independent. At the war's end Soviet troops by arrangement occupied the northern part of the country to the thirty-eighth parallel, and United States troops the southern part. The U.S.S.R. established a satellite government under a Moscow-trained Communist leader, Kim Il Sung, and supported a large North Korean army. The Soviets rejected an American proposal to hold elections in a unified Korea under international supervision.

Elections held in South Korea alone in 1948 resulted in the presidency of Syngman Rhee, who despite democratic forms governed the republic dictatorially for the next twelve years. After the election the United States withdrew its occupation forces but continued to give military and economic support to South Korea. The Soviet Union similarly withdrew from North Korea but continued to provide arms and economic aid to its client state. The American government did not at that time include Korea, as it did Japan and the Philippines, in the perimeter explicitly defined as vital to the defense of American interests in Asia. Yet when the North Koreans crossed the thirty-eighth parallel in their attack in June 1950, President Truman was outraged. He was convinced that the act was incited by the Soviet Union, with the acquiescence of the new Chinese Communist regime. He viewed it as part of the Soviet Union's world-wide ideological offensive, a further stage in the Cold War in which communism had now passed from subversion to armed aggression.

The North Korean attackers expected a quick victory because of the boldness of their initiative and their superior forces. They gambled that the United States would not intervene and that the outside world would lodge no more than a moral protest. The precise inspiration for the invasion cannot be known for certain. The U.S.S.R., concerned over American entrenchment in occupied Japan, may have encouraged it, or the North Koreans may have decided on their own to unify the country, confident that they would win Stalin's approval. In any event the Russians seemed to be caught by surprise too; they were absent from the Security Council, boycotting the United Nations for its failure to recognize the Chinese People's Republic, when the American government brought the matter before the Council. That the North Koreans were capable of independent action was difficult for Americans to believe. The attack challenged the entire collective security system built since 1945 to stem the tide of Soviet communism. Truman, remembering how weakness and appeasement in the 1930s had brought disaster, prevailed on the Security Council to condemn North Korea as an aggressor and to

25 See pp. 843–849.

take military action against it; because of their absence, the Soviets could not exercise their veto. At the same time Truman committed American troops.

In the fighting that summer the American-led United Nations forces under General Douglas MacArthur were compelled to retreat at first, but a brilliant amphibious landing at Inchon reversed the situation. The American forces hurled the Communist armies northward, and then, in a momentous decision, crossed the thirty-eighth parallel, pushing rapidly toward the Yalu River, the boundary line between Korea and the Manchurian province of Communist China. In November 1950 the Chinese People's Republic entered the war; hundreds of thousands of Chinese Communist troops, supported by Russian-made jet planes, drove the American-led forces southward in what looked like a repetition of the early phase of the conflict.

Although President Truman and the majority of nations in the United Nations were determined to check the North Koreans, they were also resolved to prevent a third world war, which was a possibility if Manchuria or other parts of China were bombed as General MacArthur demanded. When MacArthur insisted on drastic action against China, President Truman relieved him of his command. The American people were stunned by the worst military reverses in their history; many wanted to punish Communist China, but most saw the wisdom, or feasibility, of restricting the fighting. In the following months the United Nations forces fought their way back to the thirty-eighth parallel, and even slightly to its north. In July 1951 a cease-fire agreement ended large-scale fighting, but not until 1953 was an armistice signed, negotiations being snarled for two full years principally over the exchange and repatriation of prisoners of war. Fifteen nations participated in the Korean War, mostly with token contingents fighting alongside the United States. The Americans suffered over 54,000 battle and battle-related deaths, almost half as many as in the First World War; the American wounded were estimated at 100,000.[26] As for the Koreans, losses were roughly equal for North and South; over 2 million Koreans were dead, wounded, or missing, of which 1 million were battle deaths.

Politically, conditions reverted to what they had been before 1950. Korea was again divided roughly at the thirty-eighth parallel. The North Korean government, the Chinese People's Republic, and the U.S.S.R. continued to reject elections for the entire country under international supervision. It was an uneasy armistice, punctuated by numerous border and other incidents. In Western eyes a flagrant act of aggression had been checked; to the Communist world, and to many non-Communists in Asia, the great capitalist power, the United States, had been prevented from reasserting Western imperialist supremacy in the East. In practical terms the United States, both in the Korean War and in its efforts to create regional security pacts in the East, found little enthusiasm for its policies among the larger non-Communist Asian powers such as India, Indonesia, or Burma. Most of them disliked communism but also distrusted the West. Although the United States had been the least involved of all the Great Powers in nineteenth-century Asian colonialism, its new leadership in the Western world, and the suspicion that it was seeking world markets for American capitalism, made it the symbol of Western oppression and exploitation, a picture assiduously cultivated

26 See statistics in table, p. 925.

by the Soviets and even more belligerently, for a time, by the Chinese Communists. On the other hand, success in deterring the North Koreans reinforced the American belief that military strength and decisiveness could check Communist expansion everywhere. The Korean War inaugurated an era of deep American entanglement in eastern Asia; it was a prelude to a larger and more serious conflict, the war in Vietnam in the following decade.

Soviet-American Relations after Stalin

In the early 1950s Soviet-American relations and the Cold War entered a new phase. The political leaders of the U.S.S.R. who took over after Stalin's death in 1953 seemed more conciliatory or at least were willing to pursue their ends in less ruthless ways.[27] Although they kept the Western powers and the world oscillating between tension, relaxation, and renewed tension, the alternative of a peaceful coexistence of competing world systems seemed possible. There were signs, too, that in the United States not all compromise was to be shunned as appeasement. At Geneva in 1955 President Eisenhower, along with British and French leaders, met face to face with the heads of the Soviet state in a friendlier atmosphere than any since the Second World War.

But the Geneva spirit did not last. Crises reopened over Western access to Berlin. In 1960 a summit conference at Paris broke up when Khrushchev brought forth evidence of American reconnaissance flights over Russian territory, which the Americans did not deny. The tension shifted to the Western hemisphere. In Cuba Fidel Castro had ousted a rightist dictatorship in 1959 and established a pro-Communist regime to which both Soviet and Chinese Communists lent support. In 1961 Cuban anti-Communist exiles, encouraged by the United States, invaded the island but met with disaster. The following year President Kennedy, charging that Soviet missile bases installed in Cuba represented a menace to American security, placed a naval quarantine on the further shipment of military equipment to Cuba and issued stern warnings to the Soviets. The world held its breath but Khrushchev backed down and agreed to dismantle the bases (for which he was berated as a capitulationist by the then more belligerent Chinese Communists). Berlin, where a huge concrete and barbed wire "wall" was thrown up in 1961 to prevent East Germans from traveling to West Berlin, remained a recurrent source of friction. In Korea border incidents and the seizure in 1968 of an American ship, avowedly on an intelligence-gathering mission, disturbed the armistice. The Middle East, as we have seen, broke out in open warfare in 1956, in 1967, and again in 1973, the Soviets wooing and arming the Arab states. Most of all, Southeast Asia, after the withdrawal of the French in 1954, remained a troubled area.

The Vietnam War

In Vietnam a complex and serious war developed in the early 1960s. In the course of the fighting against the French, the former French colony had become divided into a Communist-dominated regime in the north and a non-Communist regime in the south, much as in the case of Korea. After the French defeat and withdrawal, an international conference at Geneva in 1954 partitioned the country at

[27] See pp. 852–854.

VIETNAM AND ITS NEIGHBORS

French Indochina, for about sixty years before World War II, comprised the old Asian territories of Cambodia, Laos, and Vietnam, though the French called northern Vietnam Tonkin and southern Vietnam Annam. Shaken by Japanese invasion in World War II, the French proved unable after a long struggle to resist the Vietnamese movement for independence that drew strength also from Communist affiliations. When the French withdrew in 1954, an international agreement (the Geneva Accords) provided for partition of Vietnam until unity could be restored. Since the north was now Communist, the United States undertook to strengthen South Vietnam by favoring reforms and by measures of economic and military assistance. This involvement grew in the 1960s into a large-scale though undeclared war, in which the United States intervened with over half a million troops. Hostilities ended in 1975 with Communist regimes established in Vietnam, Laos, and Cambodia.

the seventeenth parallel until elections could be held and the country unified. North Vietnam, or the Democratic Republic of Vietnam, with its capital at Hanoi, was presided over by Ho Chi Minh, the Communist leader who had successfully led the independence movement against the French. Below the seventeenth parallel an anti-Communist, Western-backed South Vietnam was established, with Saigon as its capital. The partition left the population divided into roughly equal halves of 20 million people each, but without relationship to any historic or ethnic differences. South Vietnam, concerned that the Communists had acquired a large popular following in the struggle against the French, and even earlier against the Japanese, refused to participate in the elections for the entire country scheduled for 1956 on the ground that it had not been a signatory to the Geneva agreement. When the elections were not held, events took a different turn. The Viet Cong, Communist guerrilla soldiers left behind in the south when the northern armies withdrew under the Geneva agreement, began to harass the authorities in South Vietnam. Skilled in insurgent warfare, the Viet Cong often terrorized and coerced the peasantry, but they also won support by redistributing land and by denouncing the Western-backed government of South Vietnam. They were soon reinforced by North Vietnam regular troops, who infiltrated the south and received economic and military aid from the Chinese People's Republic. In 1960 a National Liberation Front projected itself as a revolutionary government for the south. South Vietnam, despite technical advice and assistance from the United States, found itself unable to cope with the guerrilla activities and appealed for greater American aid.

The United States, from Eisenhower on, took the position that it was necessary to fill the vacuum created by the French withdrawal and to check Communist expansion in South Vietnam in order to prevent the other states in Asia from toppling one by one—like a set of dominoes, the theory went. Accordingly, in the 1960s the United States bolstered the Saigon regime with military advisers, financial backing, and arms. At the same time it sought to democratize the regime, whose authoritarian practices and widespread corruption were becoming increasingly embarrassing.

American involvement then deepened. Under President Eisenhower a few hun-

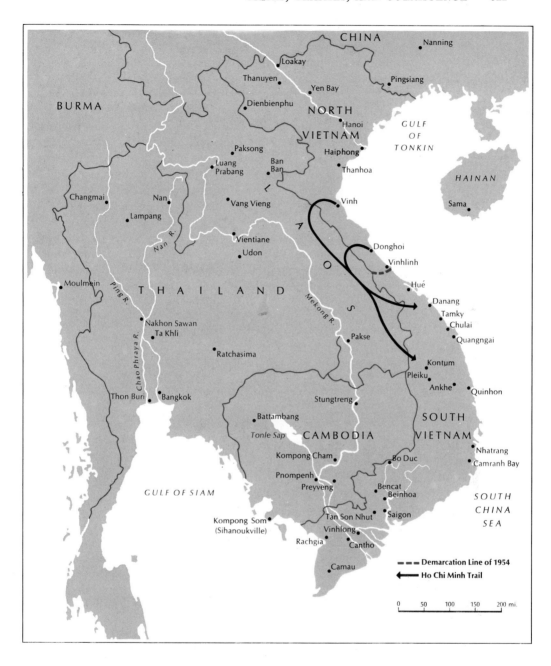

dred military advisers were present, and military and economic aid began; as early as 1959 two military advisers were killed in an attack north of Saigon. In 1961 under President Kennedy an agreement promising military and economic aid led to the arrival of the first American support troops and the formation in 1962 of the United States Military Assistance Command; by that year 4,000 supply troops were on hand and the first battle deaths were reported. The United States under Kennedy also involved itself actively in South Vietnam politics, first propping up and then in 1963 actively helping to overthrow the repressive government of President Ngo Dinh Diem.

Under President Johnson American intervention reached a climax. In August 1964, on the alleged ground that North Vietnamese torpedo boats in the Gulf of Tonkin had attacked United States destroyers, Johnson ordered immediate air strikes against North Vietnam. The next day he secured support for a joint congressional resolution empowering him to take "all necessary measures" to defend the United States and its ally. The Gulf of Tonkin resolution was the only explicit congressional sanction for American involvement in the years that followed, and it was later revoked, in 1970, by a disenchanted Congress. That summer and in 1965 Johnson ordered heavy air raids on supply bases in the north and on Communist-controlled areas in the south. After 1965 the air raids became an almost daily occurrence. American bombers destroyed highways, bridges, and rail lines, and attacked as far north as Hanoi. In searching out the elusive Viet Cong in the south, an incendiary material, napalm, was dropped from the air, burning and destroying entire villages, defoliating hundreds of thousands of acres of land, and turning the survivors into homeless refugees. The bombing raids, the commitment of American ground troops, and the number of casualties mounted. In 1966 there were close to 200,000 American troops in South Vietnam. By 1969 at the maximum there were close to 550,000 troops. (About 50,000 South Korean and Thai troops also participated.) In the massive bombings from 1965 to 1968 more tons of explosives were dropped on Vietnam than against all the Axis powers in the Second World War.

Despite the flow of United States military aid, and the temporary stabilization of the South Vietnamese government with the election in 1967 of President Nguyen Van Thieu, the regime was unable to cope with the growing popular and material strength of North Vietnam. With aid from the Soviet Union and from the People's Republic of China the northerners rebuilt their destroyed factories and kept the supplies flowing south, principally over the Ho Chi Minh Trail through neighboring Laos. Optimistic reports to Washington by United States military authorities on the pacification of the countryside and on the number of enemy casualties inflicted were confounded by a successful Communist offensive at the opening of 1968. It became clear that a negotiated settlement had to be sought.

From the beginning America's allies in Western Europe showed their lack of enthusiasm and gave little support. In the United States the war became a root cause of riots and disorders on college campuses and in the cities; protest demonstrations took place in Washington and elsewhere. Many young people fled to Canada or to Europe to avoid military service in what they considered an unjust or hopeless war; a disproportionate share of those drafted or who voluntarily accepted military service were black or from the poorer economic classes.

Widely debated were the questions of whether the United States, despite its enormous strength, should assume the responsibility, or even had the capability, to police the world against Communist aggression, whether the American presence in Vietnam was an unwanted foreign presence reminiscent of Western intrusion in the age of imperialism, whether bombing raids that reached to within ten miles of the Chinese border might lead to direct Chinese intervention and provoke a third world war, whether the South Vietnamese regime could be stabilized and democratized to make the sacrifices worthwhile, and whether the air raids and continued hostilities might end in the utter destruction of the entire hapless country. Critics with a knowledge of Asian history argued that the Vietnamese had a long record of protecting themselves from their Chinese neighbors and that even a Vietnam united under the Communists would not necessarily mean subjugation by the Chinese.

The need to win the war became an obsession with President Johnson. He regarded withdrawal or even a diminishing of the military effort as a form of weakness that would only encourage future Communist aggression elsewhere. But with victory remote, and with popular and congressional resentment against the war rising, he decided not to seek reelection in 1968 and in the spring of that year announced a halt to the bombing in the north so that negotiations for peace could go forward. By November 1968 all bombing had ceased—for a time. The Hanoi government and the National Liberation Front in the south opened preliminary peace talks in Paris with the United States and the Saigon government in the spring of 1968, but the fighting went on.

In 1969 under President Nixon and his versatile and energetic secretary of state, Henry Kissinger, peace negotiations seemed to gain a new momentum. Nixon pledged an early end to the war and promised to shift to the South Vietnamese the major responsibility for their own defense. The United States began to withdraw troops, turning over bases and equipment to the South Vietnamese. Yet involvement in the next three years in some ways became even more intense. In response to stalemated talks in Paris and continuing Communist advances, Nixon ordered the resumption of air attacks against military installations in the south and widened the war by an "incursion" into Cambodia to cut off Communist supply lines. In 1972 North Vietnam's ports were mined and that year at Christmas time North Vietnam was subjected to the heaviest saturation bombing of the entire war. Meanwhile Secretary of State Kissinger made intermittent progress in direct secret talks with the North Vietnamese representatives and finally reached a peace agreement in January 1973. The agreement ended direct involvement for the United States, concluding the longest war—though an undeclared one—the country had ever fought. Over eight years had elapsed from the arrival of the first Marine contingent in 1965 to the withdrawal of the last troops at the end of March 1973, or twelve, if the involvement is dated from 1961.

Even though American troops were withdrawn, hostilities between North Vietnam and South Vietnam continued as each sought additional territory before any final settlement was reached. Both sides violated the cease-fire, and the fighting resumed on a major scale in 1973. Although the United States remained committed to the defense of South Vietnam, Congress refused the additional expenditures for military aid that the administration sought, and weapons and equipment lost by the South Vietnamese were not replaced. North Vietnam continued to receive support from the Communist powers, the Soviet Union and the Chinese People's Republic, and dominated the fighting. Corruption and demoralization in South Vietnam grew worse; army desertions mounted. Nevertheless, the end came as a surprise. At the close of 1974, the North Vietnamese captured key cities in the southern provinces. Even before they could launch their main attack in the spring of 1975, the government of South Vietnam lost heart, abandoned the central highlands, and without even informing the American government (now under President Gerald Ford), ordered withdrawal to the coast. The precipitous order and the planned retreat degenerated into rout. General Vo Nguyen Giap, long the commander of Communist forces, deciding that after years of fighting complete victory was in his grasp, and gambling correctly that the United States would not return even in the face of a full-scale offensive, poured thousands of troops south across the demilitarized zone. Swarms of refugees fleeing south added to the confusion. By April North Vietnam's armies controlled three-fourths of South Vietnam. Saigon fell at the end of the month.

When on April 30, 1975, North Vietnamese troops entered Saigon, they renamed the capital Ho Chi Minh City in honor of the Communist leader who had died in 1969 and who thirty years earlier, in 1946, had first proclaimed Vietnamese independence from the French. After thirty years of almost uninterrupted fighting, first between the French and the Vietnamese, and then in the civil war between North and South in which the United States had massively intervened, peace had finally come, and with it total Communist victory. Reunification and reorganization of the country along Communist lines proceeded quickly, with the takeover less brutal than anticipated. Nonetheless, a "political reeducation" campaign was launched and property was nationalized. Cities, crowded with refugees, were emptied by a concerted campaign to move the urban populations into the countryside where land, seed, and tools were distributed. Within a year, by the spring of 1976, the first national elections for a National Assembly were held, with only Communist-approved candidates permitted. Reunification of the country as the People's Democratic Republic of Vietnam was formally pronounced in July 1976. In foreign relations there was reason to believe that the new regime would maintain correct relations with Peking and yet resist domination by its giant northern neighbor. It had often been said during Ho Chi Minh's lifetime that he, like Tito and Mao, would insist on his own road to communism, and that communism in Europe and in Asia was less monolithic than many believed.

In the wake of North Vietnam's victory Cambodia and Laos also fell under Communist control. Thirty years after the end of the Second World War, all that had once been French Indochina was in Communist hands, and a reunified Vietnam had emerged as an important military power in Southeast Asia. American influence was sharply diminished even though the United States remained committed to the defense of South Korea and had treaty obligations to the Nationalist Chinese in Taiwan.

The Vietnam War was costly; about one and a quarter million Vietnamese were estimated to have died as a result of the fighting, over two-thirds of them North Vietnamese and Viet Cong soldiers. For the United States the undeclared war was a searing experience. Battle and battle-related deaths were estimated at over 56,500, with 300,000 wounded and 900 missing. The number of battle deaths exceeded those of the Korean War and approached the number of Americans killed in the First World War.[28] From 1960 to 1975 the hostilities cost the United

---

28 Department of Defense figures showed:

	Battle Deaths	Other Deaths	Wounded	Total Deaths
World War I (1914–1918)	53,402	63,114	204,002	116,516
World War II (1941–1945)	291,357	113,842	607,846	405,199
Korean War (1950–1952)	33,629	20,617	103,284	54,246
Vietnam War (1965?–1973)	46,229	10,326	303,654	56,555

States over $140 billion. The impact of these expenditures on the American economy was heightened by the failure to place taxes on a wartime basis, contributing to the inflation that set in during the late 1960s. The political and moral costs were enormous. The war alienated young people more sharply than any previous American war. It created also a mistrust of presidential power, of the military, and of the intelligence services. The deadly bombings, the reports of enemy casualties, the gruesome war scenes visible on home screens in the first war reported in detail by television were deeply disturbing. The revelation of atrocities and war crimes committed by American troops, as at My Lai in 1968, first covered up and then made the subject of a public inquiry and trial, also had a troubling emotional impact. For Americans it was a tragic and chastening experience. America's giant industrial and military power had failed to bring victory. Unlike the war in Korea, where regular troops fought each other along recognized frontiers, in Vietnam, quite apart from the political and moral issues involved, technological superiority in armaments and air power was inadequate against an enemy skilled in insurgent warfare and imbued with a revolutionary zeal.

Changing Balances of Power

No nuclear weapons were used in Vietnam, but over every crisis, large or small, hung the threat that armed conflict might escalate into nuclear catastrophe. The early atomic disarmament negotiations had been broken off in 1948. In 1949 the Soviets exploded their first atomic bomb, in 1952 the British. The United States, despite the misgivings of some scientists, had proceeded with the manufacture of the hydrogen bomb and successfully tested it in 1952; through its chain reaction and thermonuclear effect, it had vastly more destructive capacity than the atomic bomb. A year later the Soviets also exploded a hydrogen bomb. In 1958 the atomic powers agreed to a temporary moratorium on the testing of nuclear weapons, but in 1961 the Soviets tested a fifty-megaton bomb, that is, one with the explosive power of 50 million tons of TNT, dwarfing the mere 20,000 tons of TNT of the Hiroshima bomb. No one doubted that the United States could do the same. The threat existed that testing alone would poison the atmosphere and damage the genetic endowment of unborn generations; at stake was the biological as well as the cultural heritage of humanity.

In 1963 the United States, the Soviet Union, and Britain signed a treaty to ban nuclear testing in the atmosphere. But the French, who in 1960 had become a fourth atomic power, refused to subscribe. In 1964 the People's Republic of China became a fifth atomic power and three years later successfully tested a hydrogen bomb. The enormous nuclear capacity of the superpowers and the threatened proliferation of nuclear arms loomed menacingly over a world split by deep rivalries. On this the United States and the Soviet Union could agree, and their negotiations led in 1970 to a nonproliferation treaty, to which many but by no means all nations subscribed.

The danger also existed that atomic weapons would spread in indirect ways. An international commission helped make available the peaceful use of atomic energy. A nation able to purchase nuclear power plants and equipment from any of the industrial powers could reprocess the plutonium from the spent fuel and build atomic bombs. India did precisely that in 1974 and became a sixth atomic power. It was common knowledge that many other countries had the same capabilities. The search for alternative sources of energy when the oil supply was threatened in the 1970s stimulated many nations to build nuclear power plants that could easily be diverted from peaceful to nonpeaceful purposes. The terrorist and guerrilla organizations that had multiplied by the 1970s might also divert explosive atomic materials for their purposes.

The United States and the Soviet Union possessed not only the most destructive weapons but the delivery systems, including nuclear-armed submarines, that could make mutual, and even global, annihilation possible. Thermonuclear strategists calculated the potential casualties of even a limited atomic clash in millions of deaths, or "megadeaths," and evaluated the effects of deterrents and counter-deterrents, of "first strikes" and "second strikes," on a nation's ability to wage atomic war and survive. The balance of power was spoken of as a "balance of terror"; military experts referred to doctrines of "mutual superiority," cynics of "mutually assured destruction." So delicately suspended over the human race was the nuclear sword of Damocles that in 1963 a direct communication link, or "hot line," was installed between the Kremlin and the White House to prevent the accidental outbreak of a nuclear war because of some human error or mechanical failure; direct communication between the tribal chieftains was necessary now that the safety of the planet was at stake.

Expenditures on conventional arms, and international trade in all kinds of advanced weapons, with the United States and the Soviet Union the chief merchants and suppliers, also expanded rapidly. From 1960 to 1975 the world's annual military expenditures nearly doubled. The United States and the Soviet Union together accounted for 60 percent of the total, but such expenditures were also rising rapidly in the developing countries, though they could afford them least because their nonmilitary needs were so urgent.

There were some encouraging signs, however. In 1976, in a period of relaxed tensions, the two superpowers agreed to a maximum limit on the atomic explosions used in underground testing, which still permitted tests equivalent to eight times the power of the Hiroshima bomb. Moreover, for the first time the Soviets agreed in principle to on-site international inspection of their tests.

Less dangerous was the competition in space exploration that developed between the Russians and the Americans, who each orbited spaceships and for the first time in history explored lunar and planetary frontiers. As noted previously, the Soviets pioneered with the orbiting of the first unmanned satellite in 1957 and the first manned spaceship in 1961. The Americans soon did the same. Although the Soviets successfully launched rocket probes of the moon, it was American astronauts who in 1969 made the quarter-million mile journey to the moon and, while millions over the globe watched on television, walked on its surface. Both countries proceeded in the 1960s with the deployment of experimental space stations, unmanned probes of distant planets, and additional accomplishments. A number of countries joined in the building and operation of artificial satellites. In 1975, Soviet and American astronauts orbited the earth simultaneously and linked, or "docked," their spaceships in a spectacular rendezvous before proceeding their separate ways. While the Soviets made remarkable space probes in the vicinity of Venus and Mars, in 1976 American technologists succeeded in guiding a spaceship that landed instruments on the surface of Mars, 220 million miles from the earth, and sent back photographs and scientific information. The earth's inhabitants were acquiring more knowledge in these years about the planets in their own solar system than ever before in history. Because space exploration could be undertaken only at enormous cost, some complained when acute social needs remained unfulfilled, but others saw such activities as the newest phase of the continuing human effort to expand horizons and probe the unknown.

By the end of the 1960s the world was no longer polarized into two camps, each led by one of the superpowers, as it appeared to be at the beginning of the Cold War. In the Communist world, we have noted, the ideological and diplomatic rift that opened up after 1963 between the Soviet Union and the Chinese People's Republic set the two countries on increasingly hostile courses. Moreover, the Soviet Union faced growing restlessness among its satellites in Eastern Europe and, as the invasion of Czechoslovakia in 1968 made clear, could control its empire only by military force. The major Communist parties outside the Soviet Union were demonstrating their independence from Moscow. In the Western camp the United States had to take into account the independence and pride of a revived Western Europe. The Europeans insisted on more of an equal partnership with the United States if the Atlantic alliance was to survive.

De Gaulle, while president of France from 1958 to 1969, made himself the spokesman for European self-assertiveness and called for Europe to act as a counterpoise to the "dual hegemony" of the superpowers. He vetoed British entry into the Common Market because it would mean transatlantic, or American, influences at work on the Continent. He ended French participation in the North Atlantic Treaty Organization's military command and caused the removal of its headquarters from Paris to Belgium, viewing the Atlantic alliance as an instrument for American domination of the Continent. He adopted an independent, generally anti-American, stance in Asia, Africa, and the Middle East. He sought to bridge the gap between Western Europe and Eastern Europe, to end the Cold War at French initiative, and to reunite Europe "from the Atlantic to the Urals." At the same time he set obstacles in the path of integration, so hopefully inaugurated in the 1950s. The economic cooperation of the Common Market remained on a solid base, but de Gaulle made sure that no steps toward political integration or supranational control took place. The result of his policies in the 1960s was to revive an older European nationalism but at the same time to restore an older balance of power politics based on national self-interest.

Although de Gaulle's anti-American and anti-British views failed to persuade France's continental partners, and even alarmed them by what at times seemed a bid for French hegemony, his assertion of independence from the United States struck a sympathetic chord. Many new factors disturbed them. The Americans, it was acknowledged, were committed to the defense of Western Europe, but since 1960 the Soviet Union had achieved the capability of launching direct nuclear attacks on the United States and, in the event that the United States defended Western Europe, could incinerate American cities and their inhabitants. In such an emergency the Americans would undoubtedly have to consult their interests. Nor did the Europeans have a voice, they complained, in American nuclear strategies and policies; as much as they could, the French and the British developed nuclear deterrents of their own. Moreover, the United States had acted unilaterally in the Cuban missile crisis, and had fought in Asia, in Korea and

Vietnam, with what was considered a reckless disregard at times for the risks involved. Supported by its economy and enormous military strength, with an exaggerated notion of its omnicompetence and with its excessive anti-Communist zeal, the United States might continue to act without consulting its European partners. Europeans, long accustomed to a central role in world affairs, had to adjust to a world balance of power in which the Americans and the Russians were preponderant, and had to reckon also on the possibility that under the new conditions of warfare the superpowers might agree to localize or avoid conflicts to prevent their own mutual destruction. They were even suspicious that the relaxation of tensions between the United States and the Soviet Union could mean a joint hegemony of the two superpowers, at their expense.

Détente

The relaxation of tensions between the two superpowers, interrupted by the Cuban missile confrontation of 1962, became a more formal policy of "détente" after 1969 under the leadership of President Nixon and Secretary of State Kissinger. Despite the continuing war in Vietnam, in which the Soviet Union and the United States backed opposing sides, a policy of coexistence was shaped. American and Soviet leaders exchanged visits. Talks on limiting strategic arms, begun in 1969, culminated in preliminary agreements signed in Moscow in 1972. That year the Soviet Union, faced with a serious grain failure, negotiated an enormous grain purchase from the United States. In 1975 thirty-five nations met at Helsinki and pledged themselves to work for peaceful cooperation and permanent peace in Europe. They agreed to accept the European territorial boundaries set up after the Second World War, including the Oder-Neisse boundary established at Potsdam in 1945 between West Germany and Poland, but never ratified in an international peace treaty. All countries, including the Soviet Union, pledged also the freer movement of persons and ideas, permission for separated families to reunite, freedom of marriage outside national frontiers, and other human rights. Whether these were only verbal concessions remained to be seen. The policy of détente between the U.S.S.R. and the United States, although reducing the direct threat of war between the two superpowers, did not end the ideological contests or rivalries in numerous disputed areas. The Soviet Union and the United States supported opposing sides in the Arab-Israeli conflicts. The United States tried to counter the strength of Communist parties in Western Europe, especially in Italy, and in parts of Latin America. The Soviet Union continued to press for advantageous positions in Africa. Both countries actively intervened in the civil war that broke out in Angola in 1976. One factor altering the strategic balance, wholly new since Stalin's era, was the creation of a powerful Soviet navy capable of utilizing conventional and nonconventional arms in all parts of the globe from Asian waters to the Caribbean.

In February 1972 President Nixon made a dramatic official visit to the People's Republic of China, opening the way for friendlier relations with the Communist regime. Cultural and scientific exchanges and visits followed, and the complete normalization of relations was promised. Full diplomatic and friendly relations were difficult to achieve while the United States maintained its alliance with the Nationalist government in Taiwan. The Chinese were also disturbed by the

American policy of détente with the Soviet Union, with whom Chinese relations were steadily deteriorating. The resumption of relations with China, as well as the policy of détente with the Soviet Union, were all the more remarkable because they occurred during the years when the United States was not yet disengaged from the Vietnam War.

Crises, rivalries, and tests of strength would not disappear, but coexistence between the superpowers seemed possible as the world entered the fourth quarter of the twentieth century. Not only China but other emerging nations were creating new alignments, shifting the balance of power, raising bold new challenges, and altering the bipolarity of the years after 1945.

115. CHALLENGES AND DILEMMAS

Trying to reconstruct the international pattern taking shape in the contemporary age, we have examined the Communist worlds in Eastern Europe and the People's Republic of China; the new nations of Africa, Asia, and the Middle East; the United States and the industrial countries of Western Europe. We have explored the tensions and relaxation of tensions between the two superpowers, and the limited wars and uneasy peace in the decades after 1945. In this age Western Europe after its postwar economic recovery returned to play a role of its own. Its independence in foreign affairs in the 1960s was in part traceable to its economic success, which also made it possible to absorb the loss of its colonial empires with relative ease. Prosperity, economic cooperation, and a growing sense of unity characterized Western Europe—until the setbacks of the 1970s.

Economic Problems

In the 1960s the European Economic Community or Common Market was thriving, providing a mobility of labor, machinery, and capital that made possible trade over a wide market, high productivity, and economic advantages for business, labor, and consumers alike. The Europeans, as in the past, played a central international role in the world's global economy, accounting for a fourth of the world's productive output, surpassed in per capita output only by the North Americans, and even that gap seemed to be narrowing. The steel production of Western Europe was surpassing that of the United States. Among national economies the Federal Republic of Germany followed the United States and Japan in gross national product. The countries of Western Europe were again at the center of world trade, accounting for a fourth of all world exports and a third of all imports; they held half the world's gold and had the power to influence the world's money market in many ways.

The European economy, to be sure, did not maintain its pace in all areas. The world itself had entered a new phase of the Industrial Revolution. Progress was no longer measured in coal and steel or in ships and textiles but in atomic energy, electronics, and computer and space technology. Here the Europeans found themselves outdistanced by the United States, and in some ways by the U.S.S.R. They observed with anxiety the economic penetration of Europe by giant American industrial firms which, among other things, controlled the computer market. The Western Europeans chose to meet the American challenge by emulating American techniques.

When Britain, Denmark, and Ireland were admitted in 1973 to the Common Market, the European Economic Community totaled nine members and counted some 255 million citizens.[29] Europeans of member states could travel across each other's borders without passports but were still far from having common citizenship or a common currency. Political unification was not forgotten. There was still hope that direct elections could be instituted for the European Parliament, which helped to supervise the Common Market and which might at some future time assume wider jurisdiction. By 1970, twenty-five years after the end of the Second World War, Western Europe seemed to have submerged the fierce national antagonisms and economic rivalries that had contributed to two great World Wars in the twentieth century, almost destroyed Europe itself, and led to the ascendancy of the two superpowers outside Europe. Although in the late 1960s individual nations like Britain and Italy were having economic problems, and although inflation and signs of a general economic slowdown were on the horizon, none of this changed the general picture of economic prosperity and cooperation for the Common Market nations. A quarter of a century of progress toward a stable, democratic, and peaceful Western Europe had followed postwar recovery, a more stable and more prosperous quarter of a century than anyone might have predicted. With prosperity and continuing cooperation the European Community could hope to compete even with the superpowers in all but military ways.

Sometime in the early 1970s this optimistic outlook received some rude shocks. The Arab-Israeli War in the autumn of 1973 had sweeping consequences for world affairs, and for the political and economic fortunes of Western Europe. In the course of the war the Arab oil-producing nations proclaimed an oil embargo against states accused of supporting Israel, notably the United States, and among the countries of Western Europe, the Netherlands. In addition, oil supplies were reduced for everyone because of a cutback in production. That winter the oil-exporting countries quadrupled the price of oil. The embargo, the decline in oil supplies, and the price increases threw Europe into panic. With 70 percent of its oil imports dependent on Middle Eastern sources, the price rises threatened to

[29] See pp. 848, 927.

WHEEL MAN
by Ernest Trova (American, 1927–)

Shown here is a somewhat dehumanized, life-size bronze figure of a human being of no particular sex, age, race, culture, or environment. Compressed between the two wheels, it seems to present humanity as the victim of its own complicated inventions. The wheels also symbolize the blind ups and downs of fortune. The date 1965 is inscribed on the base, and the whole sad assemblage seems to say that human history and civilization have not exactly turned out as was once more hopefully expected. Ernest Trova, though widely exhibited internationally, is an American sculptor living in St. Louis. Courtesy of the Solomon R. Guggenheim Museum, John V. Powers Fund.

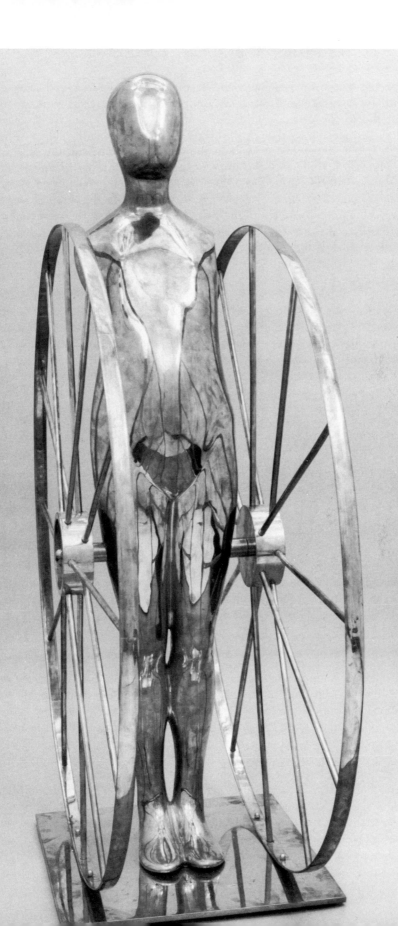

wreck the European economy—and the world economy as well. Never had an essential industrial commodity risen in price so rapidly; never was the vulnerability of the whole Western industrial complex (and of Japan too) so clearly revealed. It appeared as though the Arab states could also develop a stranglehold on the world's monetary system. In the long run, some said, the oil crisis could have the salutary effect of encouraging the search for other forms of energy; the industrial countries had enjoyed cheap oil for too long. But in the short run the price rise and the balance of payments deficits had the devastating effect of boosting the inflationary spiral that was already troubling the industrial countries before 1973. The inflation and the political uncertainties made it even more difficult to cope with the world economic recession that had already begun.

The growth of Western European economies, developing at such spectacular rates over the past two decades, was abruptly interrupted. But the oil crisis also revealed the precarious foundation on which European unity and even the Atlantic alliance, was built. The Europeans resented the fact that the United States, obligated by treaty to help Israel, did not consult the Europeans in the crisis. Many, apprehensive over Arab oil supplies, took a neutralist stand. Disputes arose among the partners of the Atlantic alliance over the appropriate way to meet the Arab challenge. Within the Common Market several of the member countries acquiesced in the Arab boycott of the Netherlands. The French, indicating that the Arabs should be free to sell to whom they wished, negotiated their own arrangements, as did the British. European solidarity, tested for the first time since the 1950s, broke down; the crisis was a watershed in the postwar history of Western Europe. Europeans in the mid-1970s were less self-confident and more apprehensive about the future than at any time since postwar recovery.

The economic recession that struck the Western industrial countries and Japan in the mid-1970s was the severest in over forty years. The Communist countries, with their controlled economies and with more adequate oil resources of their own, were less affected. Not since the Great Depression of the 1930s had the Western industrial countries known such an economic setback. Bankruptcies and threatened bankruptcies of giant corporations shook several countries; steel production declined by a third; in the twenty-four non-Communist industrial countries the number of jobless totaled 15 million in 1975. The recession partly reflected the business cycle, which seemed to have reached the end of a boom period in the early 1970s. The economic boom itself had engendered mounting inflationary pressures; higher costs and a concern over sustained consumer demand had led to a decline in business confidence and to a cutback in production, investment, and employment. The traumatic impact on the world economy of the rise in oil prices in the winter of 1973–1974 made it even more difficult to control inflation and stimulate recovery.

Simultaneous industrial stagnation and sharp inflation, which for many countries raced on for several years at double digit annual figures, was unprecedented. The higher cost of oil imports affected the balance of payments, weakened currencies, and required vast borrowing. Governments were in a quandary. Efforts to restrict domestic borrowing in order to curb inflation aggravated the business slowdown and led to unemployment. Government expenditures to encourage business, if not carefully controlled, fed the inflationary spiral. The combination of stagnation and inflation ("stagflation," the journalists called it) and unemployment—each of which varied in severity in different countries—produced a frustrating economic situation. The nonindustrial countries were also hurt by reduced demand and lower prices for their commodities and by the higher cost of industrial imports and of oil. In the new economic crisis, opinion even among the experts was divided about the most effective way to revive the economy, that is, how to increase production, employment, and investment without at the same time stimulating inflation. For the first time since 1945 the precepts of John Maynard Keynes, which had gained wide following after the Second World War, were questioned; Keynes, writing for the 1930s, had not visualized a combination of recession and inflation.[30] Some argued that if governments pumped money into the sluggish economy, it would feed inflation; others insisted that the economy was not self-adjusting and that government spending and tax relief were needed. Inflation was not inevitable, they said, if flexible fiscal policies were maintained and a close watch kept on wages and prices.

The economic troubles of the 1970s were cushioned for working people in almost all industrial countries. Labor unions were stronger and welfare benefits more advanced than they had been in the 1930s. Unemployed automobile workers in Essen, Turin, or Detroit could count on severance pay, trade union benefits, and unemployment compensation far beyond the welfare payments and dole of earlier generations; this not only reduced human suffering but prevented an even greater decline in consumer purchasing power. Yet unemployment, especially for older people and for the young, was still a baneful experience. In countries like Italy there was apprehension also that inflation and unemployment could undermine social stability and threaten democratic government. Although there were some indications of improvement after the spring of 1976, when and how the recession and inflation would level off were not known. It was widely agreed that economic growth rates in the industrial countries would slow down and fall short of their earlier performance.

While most observers lamented the failure of economic expansion to continue at the pace established since the early 1950s, some social critics questioned the whole idea of economic growth. They rejected the notion that human progress was synonymous with economic advance, arguing that industrialization meant spoliation of the environment, pollution of the atmosphere, and attrition of the earth's limited resources. They called for new life styles and new ideas and institutions, rejecting the bigness and ugliness of industrial society. Progress, they insisted, must not be equated with industrial success or the exploitation of nature. All these arguments ran counter to the push for modernization in the less developed parts of the world.

Population Problems

The nonindustrial countries of the world, in various stages of economic development, though affected by the recession too, were grappling with deeper social and economic problems to which solutions seemed distant. The most acute was the growth of population. With improved health and sanitation measures and with

[30] See p. 766.

more efficient food production and distribution, a decline in death rates without a counterbalancing reduction in births led to vast population increases in less developed areas, and hence in the world as a whole. The population of the world was growing so rapidly during the second half of the twentieth century that demographers spoke of a population explosion. At some point in 1976 the world's population passed 4 billion. It has been estimated that from the first century A.D. to the sixteenth century the number of human beings increased from about a quarter billion to a half billion; by the mid–nineteenth century the half billion grew to 1 billion. Put another way, it required almost 2 million years, from the beginnings of human life on the planet to about 1850, for the world's population to reach its first billion. Only seventy-five years later, about 1925, the population reached 2 billion; thirty-five years after that, in 1960, it reached 3 billion, and sixteen years later, in 1976, 4 billion. If the annual global growth rate of 1.9 percent were maintained, it would require only thirteen more years, to 1989, to add a fifth billion, and by the year 2010 the population figure of 1976 could double and reach 8 billion. It is easy to see that uncontrolled population growth develops a dynamic of its own as a larger population base moves into the reproductive age. There were many examples of the fall in death rates all over the globe, with nothing comparable in all previous history; for example, in India the death rate in 1976 was half what it had been in 1950. With a population of 630 million in 1976, and a growth rate of 2.4 percent, India was adding 15 million people annually and could reach 1 billion by the end of the century. In the industrial countries, as noted earlier,[31] population was growing at considerably slower rates because birth rates had stabilized. Developed economies, industrialization, urban life, social pressures for smaller families, and easier access to contraception had slowed the birth rate since the late nineteenth century in much of Europe and North America. In Asia, Africa, and Latin America such a decline had not yet occurred.

Although the problems in limiting population growth were immense, there were some favorable signs. More than two-thirds of the world's population now lived in countries with some form of government-sponsored population program. From the 1960s the birth control movement grew in scope. The development of the oral contraceptive for women and of other contraceptive technology, as well as the legalization of abortion in many countries, made the planning of family size and a leveling off of growth rates possible. Japan, an industrial country to be sure, led the way for areas outside the West in dramatically lowering the birth rate. A carefully concerted government program in the People's Republic of China lowered the growth rate in the 1970s to below the world growth rate; even so, as noted earlier, China's population would probably exceed 1 billion by the year 2000. Striking advances in curbing population growth were also made in South Korea, Taiwan, Hong Kong, and Singapore, and progress was visible in Indonesia and the Philippines, and even in parts of India. By contrast, in Mexico, Brazil, and other parts of Latin America, annual growth rates were as high as 3 percent.

For population programs to be effective, it would be necessary to change deeply rooted attitudes, many of them based on cultural or religious outlook, or

[31] See pp. 548–549.

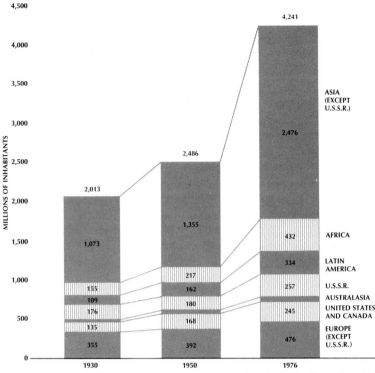

Source: *United Nations Demographic Yearbook.*

THE POPULATION EXPLOSION

As the twentieth century entered its fourth quarter the world's population passed the 4 billion mark. It had doubled in less than half a century, and more than doubled in Asia, Africa, and Latin America. Growth was most rapid in the poorer countries, where it contributed to chronic social unrest and political instability. The wealthier or "developed" part of the world, including Japan, parts of Latin America, and South Africa, had a slower growth rate, but in the 1970s they comprised only about 28 percent of the world's population.

Comparison may be made with the table on page 547, where the categories are somewhat different, being designed to show the rise and decline in the proportion of "Europeans" in the global total. But the table shows no doubling of world population in any half-century from 1650 to 1950, so that the recent increase is truly an "explosion." Such a rate of increase cannot continue indefinitely; the question is whether it can be slowed down without disaster.

deriving from economic dependence on a large family for support in hard times or in old age or infirmity. The assertion of women's voices in such matters was proving important. On the other hand, some political leaders, opposed to population control, argued that pressure to lower growth rates in the less developed parts of the world represented a deliberate effort by the West to check the growth of the emergent nations. Ironically, Communist China, successfully coping with population control at home, pressed these claims at international conferences.

Although there was no reason to accept uncritically the most extreme projections for the doubling rate of the world's population, or even of individual countries, the problem remained acute. The dissemination and popularization of birth control techniques was a partial answer, but it required reaching into remote villages, overcoming popular resistance, and an adjustment of attitude on the part of some of the world's major religions. One day, with growing standards of comfort and security, the size of families might be deliberately controlled everywhere, as had happened earlier in Western Europe, the United States, Japan, the Soviet Union, and Eastern Europe, and was under way in China, but that day was distant. It was distant because growing standards of comfort and security were not in sight for two-thirds of the world's peoples who, in the hundreds of millions, still lived on inadequate and unrelieved rations of grain or rice. Experts estimated that 10 percent of the world's population suffered from malnutrition. Economic development programs designed to increase industrial and agricultural output, feed swelling populations, and raise living standards were under way everywhere, but the question remained whether economic advances could keep pace with population growth. Since its independence in 1947, India increased its food production by 60 percent but its population grew by 70 percent, so that even with good harvests India could not feed its people. The gloomy prognostications of Malthus at the end of the eighteenth century that population growth, if unchecked, would outstrip food supply,[32] a proposition that most other social thinkers had since rejected, were again much discussed. But technical improvements in agriculture had made possible enormous increases in food production since Malthus' day, and world food production continued to rise; there was thus no reason why his predictions must necessarily prevail. Yet distribution remained unequal and there were striking differences in productivity. A key need was to raise productivity in the less developed parts of the world by allowing everyone to benefit from modern agricultural science, but that was part of a larger issue—the sharing of knowledge, technology, and resources among the wealthier and poorer nations.

Despite the economic progress that was observable in the years after 1945, the gap between the economies of the advanced industrial countries and those of the less developed countries widened rather than narrowed. Even when their economies were growing in the decades after 1945, the less developed countries did not advance as rapidly as the highly productive countries, certainly not at the same rate as Western Europe, Japan, the Soviet Union, Eastern Europe, or the United States.

Under the aegis of various international agencies, development programs had been projected. The aim of the economic planners was to help the less developed countries achieve an annual growth rate of 5 percent in the 1960s and 6 percent by the end of the 1970s. Given the rates of population growth and the low initial economic levels in these countries, the goals were modest though still difficult to achieve. Even if per capita income could be doubled before the end of the century, only a limited improvement in economic standards could be expected because for three-fifths of the world annual per capita income was barely $300. But for a time these goals inspired hope. To help achieve these economic targets

[32] See p. 425.

the industrial nations promised a share of their own gross national product in economic and technical aid. If most of the world's population lived on a bare subsistence level, they at least looked forward to a better day and could count on the assistance of the more favored, then prospering, nations to help them. A revolution of rising expectations was under way.

In the 1970s the less developed countries, more impatient, conscious of their growing political strength, alert to the vulnerability of the Western economy, and irritated by the reduction in aid from the Western countries, became more aggressively militant in their demands for a new international economic order in which the Third World nations would share more equitably.

The Third World

The term "Third World" came to be used in the postwar years to describe the less economically advanced nations of Asia, Africa, and Latin America, most of whom had once been dominated by the West in the age of imperialism. The Third World countries were distinguished from the "Western," or non-Communist, bloc of industrial nations in which the United States predominated, and the Communist bloc of industrial or industrializing nations, dominated for the most part by the Soviet Union. In the tensions of the Cold War between the Western and Soviet camps, the Third World nations often refused to align themselves directly with either camp and drew together in the United Nations and elsewhere for mutual reinforcement. Toward the end of the 1970s the Third World included over 100 independent sovereign states, almost all formerly part of the old Western colonial empires and comprising a total of 2 billion persons, or half the world's population. They lived in the southern continents or parts of continents—in South Asia, Africa, and Latin America. The growing confrontation with the industrial nations, Western, Japanese, and Soviet, therefore became also a form of north-south contest.

From an economic point of view the Third World countries, dependent on agriculture, had the lowest per capita income, the highest illiteracy rates, and the highest rates of population growth. Within the Third World itself there were divisions. Some countries, such as Saudi Arabia and other Arab states, Iran, and Nigeria, although underdeveloped, had important natural resources; these nations, with time, capital, and technological assistance, could hope to build modern economies, and indeed were already making significant progress. A second group, a kind of "Fourth World," including such states as Pakistan, Egypt, and Peru, were without adequate resources or were so beset with growing populations that they could not feed their people or expect much economic improvement in the near future. In this group of thirty-six poor countries, two-thirds of them in Africa, states such as Mali, Chad, Niger, Ethiopia, Somalia, and Bangladesh formed a kind of "Fifth World"—an impoverished group of about 175 million people at the very bottom of the economic scale; they possessed few resources and were unable even to grow enough food for their peoples.

Despite economic development programs, the gap between the Third World countries, viewed as a whole, and the wealthier industrial nations, non-Communist and Communist, grew so wide that there were really only two worlds, one

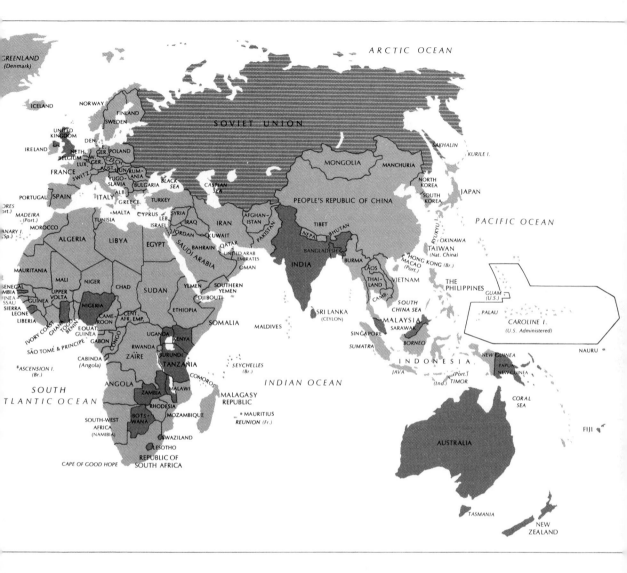

THE CONTEMPORARY WORLD

On a small political map of the contemporary world the most readily visible changes, as compared to a map of the world before the Second World War, are the breakup of the European colonial empires in Asia and Africa, the emergence of several new states in Asia, and of some fifty independent republics in Africa, the enlargement of the Commonwealth of Nations to include such new Asian and African members as India, Bangladesh, Nigeria, the peripheral expansion of the Soviet Union to include the Baltic states, and the rise of a Communist China.

relatively rich and one poor. The poorer countries, with half the world's population, had access to only a small share of the world's income. At the top of the scale the wealthiest nations—the United States, the countries of Western Europe, and Japan—controlled two-thirds or more of the world's production, trade, and monetary resources. The poverty of the Third World countries had profound social and human implications. In parts of West Africa, of every 1,000 children born, over 170 died before they were one year old; in Sweden, the figure was 10. Life expectancy for a child born in Nigeria or Afghanistan in the 1970s was about forty, in India about fifty-three—a higher life expectancy, to be sure, than for the European or American upper classes only a century ago, but no match for the comparable life expectancy figure of close to eighty in most modern European countries. In the twenty-four wealthiest industrial nations the gross national product on a per capita basis was $4,550 in the mid-1970s; for the twenty-five poorest countries it was $116. The distribution of wealth within all countries remained an unresolved problem, but it was particularly acute in the poorer countries where there were fewer goods and services to distribute, and where they were often distributed with gross inequity between an elite cultivating Western standards of luxury and the impoverished masses.

In the 1970s the Third World states pressed for a more complete eradication of the colonial past and for a reshaping of the international economy to give them a more equitable share in the world's resources and wealth. They noted vehemently that they had shared only minimally in the remarkable economic advances made elsewhere since the 1950s. A number of related developments pushed them into a more activist political position. They discovered, for example, that the primary resources on which the economies of the industrial nations depended—particularly oil—could be used as a bargaining weapon, and the petroleum-producing states used oil as such a weapon in 1973–1974. To be sure, no other product was so critical as oil, and few other essential resources were as concentrated outside the West. Yet if other of the less developed states were to create cartels for their commodities, the consequences could be far-reaching for world trade. The industrial recession of the 1970s also revealed the dependence of the less developed states on the prosperity of the advanced countries. As demand dropped for raw materials, the prices of commodities declined. The less developed countries had less money with which to purchase capital equipment, which was now more expensive and yet vitally needed for their economic development plans. The Third World countries saw with dismay that the resumption of their economic growth depended on the return of prosperity to the West.

The Third World countries, in calling for a new international economic order, raised demands for freer access to the investment funds, capital goods, and technology of the West, and an end to dependence on the wealthier, economically developed nations. They rejected the notion that their progress should be only a footnote to the prosperity of the industrial world. Stirring up memories of the imperialist era in which as colonies they had not been permitted to develop industrially or diversify their economies, they repudiated talk of interdependence, which, they said, could mean only exploitation given their condition of inequality. They called for a doubling or tripling of foreign aid—even some form of mandatory capital investment—as well as a shift of international financing away from agencies that they considered dominated by the West. Western spokesmen, in the midst of their own economic troubles, were reluctant to make important concessions on these demands, nor would they agree to any major economic restructuring of the globe. The debate went on. The West had lost its political dominance; its economic preeminence was being challenged.

The debate sharpened differences between the West and the Third World. The revolution of rising expectations of the years after 1945 appeared to be turning into a revolution of rising frustrations in the last quarter of the twentieth century. The Soviet Union and the People's Republic of China, each in its own way, watched the debate closely. The Soviets gave far less in economic aid to the Third World than did the Western countries, but less was expected of them. It was certain that Moscow would not abandon an important role in Third World economic development, even though it had been less active after building the Aswan Dam in Egypt in the 1950s. Peking, too, sought to extend its influence in the less developed countries; by its own experiences, it hoped to serve as a model for others.

Despite the rebellious protests all economic problems were interdependent and international. There was reason to hope that the world as a whole could sustain continuous economic growth, and with proper management could do so without depleting its natural resources or polluting and destroying the environment. But only if the industrial world and the less developed world worked together could they both advance, or the gap in production and productivity between them be reduced. The Third World countries, for their part, would have to overcome many political, institutional, and cultural barriers if they were to develop economically and raise living standards for their people. They needed to bring large new tracts under agricultural cultivation, double or triple productivity, and develop manufactures to reduce imports. Regional cooperation—Common Markets in Africa and in Latin America—was necessary. The developed countries, on the other hand, would have to give economic and financial aid and encourage capital investment, reduce tariffs, and help stabilize commodity prices. It might mean a sacrifice of their own economic growth rates. But if the industrial countries and the Third World countries worked together, and reasonable economic plans were followed, many believed that the existing gap in per capita income could be significantly narrowed by the end of the century. For millions, that could mean the difference between malnutrition, or even starvation, and a new dawn.

One World: The Fate of Humanity

All the problems of the contemporary age—the awesome implications of science, the challenge of technology, the population explosion, the dangerous rivalry between nations, the quest within nations for freedom, security, and even food— were really aspects of one overriding problem, the fate of humanity. How could human beings, men and women, regardless of color or creed—beings said by some to be made in the image of God, by others to have a natural right to liberty and happiness, by still others to have the freedom to create meaning in a meaningless universe—live out and fulfill their humanity in the contemporary world?

The worst of all eventualities would be another world war. In 1945 the victors in the Second World War had founded the United Nations as an instrument for preserving peace. The UN managed, indeed, to play a significant peacekeeping role in Cyprus, the Sinai peninsula, and the buffer area between North and South Korea, but in the major hostilities described in the preceding pages it proved to be helpless. Of the 51 original members of the United Nations, in 1945, a majority were democracies, inclined to be sympathetic to the United States at that time, and willingly proclaiming the United Nations Universal Declaration of Human Rights. By 1977 there were 149 members, most of them under various degrees of dictatorial government, in which respect for individual human rights was heavily at a discount. The enlargement of the membership reflected political realities, with the eventual admission of Japan, the two Germanies, and the People's Republic of China in 1971 after the United States ceased to oppose its inclusion. But the tripling of numbers also meant a proliferation of very small states as the former colonial empires disintegrated. Countries such as the Comoro Islands, Bahrain, and Equatorial Guinea had no more inhabitants than a small city. The seventy-five smallest members of the United Nations, in Africa, Asia, Latin America, and certain oceanic islands, when added together, represented less than 10 percent of the earth's population. Yet each member had an equal vote in the UN Assembly, so that any seventy-five members might form a majority. An organization with such a disparity between voting power and actual importance could hardly be more than a forum for the expression of opinion.

As early as the 1960s the African and Asian members held over half the Assembly seats. The United States lost the majority that it had been able to muster in earlier years against the Soviet Union. The Third World countries, despite their nonalignment policy, were vehemently critical of the United States; most of them systematically voted against the United States on all issues. The United States found it to its interest to keep major issues confined to the Security Council, and both the United States and the Soviet Union tended to deal with each other outside the framework of the UN. It was only a matter of time before the Great-Power veto in the Security Council would be openly challenged. Other channels would have to be found for the development of international confidence, cooperation, and order. In the end, international organization was only a mechanism. The world needed some kind of international organization, but above all its peoples needed mutual respect for, and confidence in, one another.

We began these two concluding chapters with the image of a cataclysm. The analogy is still pertinent. But even a cataclysm, as already made clear, is not a time of downfall only. Mountains crumble, but others are thrust up. Lands vanish, but others rise from the sea. So it is with the political and social cataclysm of our times. Old landmarks are worn down. The colonial empires and the gold standard pass away. The ascendancy of Europe, of the West, and of the white races draws to a close; all these have learned to negotiate with others, not to rule them. Upper- and middle-class people lose their former ease of life, but times are better for farmers and industrial workers. Young people everywhere question traditional life styles and values. Women press for full equality. Everywhere there is a new crudeness in language, a fluidity in social relations, a disregard for conventional amenities, but people grapple boldly with real problems. Never has war been so potentially destructive, and it is certain that another world war would blight much of civilization; but it would be wrong to suppose that no part of civilization would survive. Individual lives are fragile; but the human species is tough, and there are billions of human beings on earth. To close this book on a note of placidity would indeed be foolish, but so would it be to close it on a note of doom. It is highly probable that if everybody in the world could express an opinion, and if literally everybody were included, as many or more would say that the land is rising as that it sinks.

APPENDIXES, BIBLIOGRAPHY, and INDEX

Appendix I:
Chronological Tables

TABLE FIVE: 1815–1871

WORLD AS A WHOLE	EUROPE AS A WHOLE	BRITISH ISLES
		1760–1820 George III
1806–1825 Latin American countries win independence		1760–1830 Beginnings of modern industry
	1814–1815 Congress of Vienna	1807 British slave trade ended
		1815 Corn Laws: higher taxes on grain imports
	1818 Congress of Aix-la-Chapelle	
		1819 Peterloo
	1820 Congress of Troppau	
	1822 Congress of Verona	
1823 Monroe Doctrine		
	1830 Revolutions	
	1833 Lyell's *Principles of Geology*	1832 First Reform Bill
1839–1842 First Anglo-Chinese (Opium) War		1833 Abolition Act: abolished slavery
		1837–1901 Victoria
		1838–1848 Chartism
		1842 Mines Act
1842–1858 "Treaty System" established in China		1846 Repeal of Corn Laws
		1847 Ten Hours Act
	1848 Revolutions; Marx and Engels' *Communist Manifesto*	
1850 World population estimate: 1.2 billion		1850–1873 Golden age of British capitalism: free trade
1850–1864 Taiping Rebellion in China		
1854–1868 Westernizing of Japan	1854–1856 Crimean War	
1857 Indian Rebellion		
	1859 Austro-Italian War	
	1859 Darwin's *Origin of Species*	
1860 Russians found Vladivostok		
1861–1865 American Civil War		

WESTERN EUROPE	CENTRAL EUROPE	EASTERN EUROPE
		1801–1825 Alexander I of Russia
1814–1830 Restoration: Bourbons in France 1814–1824 Louis XVIII of France	1814–1848 Influence of Metternich	
	1819 Carlsbad Decrees	
1824–1830 Charles X of France		
1830 Revolution in France and Belgium 1830–1848 July Monarchy in France: Louis Philippe	1830 Revolutionary flurries	1825 Decembrists in Russia 1825–1855 Nicholas I of Russia 1828–1829 Russo-Turkish War 1829 Independence of Greece 1830 Revolution in Poland
1848 Revolution: Second French Republic	1848 Revolution: Frankfurt Assembly 1848–1916 Francis Joseph of Austria	
1852 Napoleon III: Second French Empire	1852–1890 Bismarck active	1853 Russo-Turkish War 1854–1856 Crimean War
	1859–1870 Unification of Italy	1855–1881 Alexander II of Russia 1858 Formation of Rumania
1860 Free trade with England 1860–1870 Liberal empire		1861 Emancipation of Russian serfs

WORLD AS A WHOLE	EUROPE AS A WHOLE	BRITISH ISLES
1863–1867 French in Mexico	1864–1876 First International 1866 Austro-Prussian War	
1867 Dominion of Canada 1870 Vatican Council I	1867 Marx's *Capital* 1870 Franco-Prussian War 1871–1918 German Empire	1867 Extension of suffrage 1870–1874 Gladstone's first ministry

TABLE SIX: 1871–1919

WORLD AS A WHOLE	EUROPE AS A WHOLE	BRITISH ISLES
	1871 Darwin's *Descent of Man*	

1880–1914 Height of
  imperialism
	1878 Congress of Berlin, Austro-
	  German Alliance
	1880s Socialist parties founded:
	  revisionism
		1874–1880 Disraeli's ministry

1883–1893 French in Indochina	1882 Triple Alliance	
1885 Berlin Conference on Africa 1885–1898 Partition of Africa		1884 Extension of suffrage

1893 New Zealand: vote to
  women
1895–1898 Far Eastern crisis
1898 Fashoda crisis; Spanish-
  American War
1899–1902 Boer War
1900 World population estimate:
  1.6 billion
1902 Anglo-Japanese Alliance
1902 Australia: vote to women
1904 Russo-Japanese War
	1889 Second International
	1894 Franco-Russian Alliance
	
	1900 Freud's *Interpretation of
	Dreams*
	
	1904 Anglo-French Entente
	1905 Einstein's relativity theory
	1905 Morocco crisis
		1899–1902 Boer War

1907 Anglo-Russian division of
  Persia
 	
1911 Chinese Revolution
	1907 Triple Entente
	1908 Bosnian crisis
	
	1911 Agadir crisis
	1912–1913 Balkan crisis
		1906–1911 Social insurance and
		  parliamentary reform

1914–1918 First World War 1917 United States enters War 1917 Russian Revolution 1919 Peace of Paris	1914–1918 First World War 1919 Peace of Paris	1914 Ulster crisis 1916 Battle of Jutland 1916–1922 Irish troubles

WESTERN EUROPE	CENTRAL EUROPE	EASTERN EUROPE
1870–1940 Third Republic in France	1866–1871 Unification of Germany 1867 Dual Monarchy in Austria-Hungary	1870s Populism and Nihilism in Russia

WESTERN EUROPE	CENTRAL EUROPE	EASTERN EUROPE
1870–1940 Third Republic in France 1871 Paris Commune	1871–1918 German Empire 1871–1883 *Kulturkampf* 1878–1890 Bismarck's Anti-Socialist laws 1883–1889 Bismarck's social insurance laws 1888–1918 William II of Germany	1877 Russo-Turkish War 1878 Autonomy of Bulgaria; independence of Serbia 1881 Assassination of Alexander II
1889 Boulanger in France 1894–1906 Dreyfus affair in France		
	1898–1914 German naval race with England	
1901–1905 Laic laws separate church and state in France 1900ff. Growth of democracy: male suffrage in Netherlands 1896, etc.	1900ff. Growth of democracy: male suffrage in Austria 1907, etc.	1903 Bolshevik-Menshevik split 1904 Russo-Japanese War 1905 Revolution in Russia 1906 Finland: vote to women 1908 Bosnian crisis 1908 Young Turk Revolution 1912–1913 Balkan Wars 1913 Norway: vote to women
1914 Battle of Marne 1916 Verdun and the Somme 1918 Armistice	1914 Assassination of Francis Ferdinand 1918 Fall of German and Austro-Hungarian empires	1914 Battle of Tannenberg 1917 Fall of Tsardom; Bolshevik Revolution

TABLE SEVEN: 1919–1945

WORLD AS A WHOLE	EUROPE AS A WHOLE	BRITISH ISLES
		1918 Limited suffrage for women
1919 Peace of Paris	1919 Peace of Paris 1919 Spread of democracy	
1920 U.S.: vote to women		
1922–1929 "Prosperity Decade" 1923 Turkish Republic	1922–1943 Fascism in Italy 1923 Ruhr crisis	1922 Irish Free State
		1924 First Labour coalition government
1925 World population estimate: 2 billion	1925 Locarno Pacts	1926 General Strike 1926 Definition of Dominion status
		1928 Full suffrage for women
1929 Great Depression begins		1929–1931 Second Labour Government
	1930s Depression 1930s Decline of democracy; rise of dictators	1931–1940 National Government
1931–1932 Manchurian crisis 1931–1945 Japanese in China		1931 Britain leaves gold standard 1932 Britain adopts Empire tariff protection
1933–1945 F. D. Roosevelt's presidency 1933 Failure of World Economic Conference	1933–1945 Hitler in Germany 1933 Germany leaves League of Nations and rearms	
1935–1936 Ethiopian crisis 1936–1939 Spanish Civil War	1936–1939 Popular fronts	
	1937 Rome-Berlin-Tokyo Axis	1936 Edward VIII abdicates; George VI
1938 Munich crisis 1939–1945 Second World War	1939 Nazi-Soviet Pact	1939–1945 Britain at war
1940–1945 Japan aims at "Greater East Asia" 1941 U.S.S.R., U.S.A. enter war	1940–1945 German domination of Europe: racist policies, extermination of Jews, etc.	1940 Churchill replaces Chamberlain 1940 Battle of Britain
1944 Allies invade Europe 1945 Yalta and Potsdam conferences 1945 First atomic bomb 1945 United Nations established	1945 Death of Hitler and Mussolini	1945 Labour election victory

WESTERN EUROPE	CENTRAL EUROPE	EASTERN EUROPE
1919 Paris Peace Conference	1919 Treaty of Versailles, etc.	1918–1920 Russian Civil War
		1919–1923 Greek-Turkish War
	1919–1933 Weimar Republic	
		1920–1943 Third International
		1920–1921 Russo-Polish War
		1921–1928 NEP in Russia
	1922–1943 Mussolini in power in Italy	1922 Founding of U.S.S.R.
	1923 French occupy Ruhr	1922 Russo-German treaty of Rapallo
	1923 Inflation in Germany	
	1924 Dawes Plan	
		1924 Death of Lenin; emergence of Stalin
		1927 Expulsion of Trotsky
1928–1974 Dictatorship in Portugal: Salazar		1928–1933 First Five-Year Plan
1930s Depression	1930s Depression	
1931 Spanish revolution		
1934 Stavisky riots in Paris	1933–1945 Third Reich: Hitler in power	
1936–1939 Spanish Civil War	1934 First Austrian crisis	
1936–1937 Popular Front in France	1936 Germany re-militarizes Rhineland	
	1938 Germany annexes Austria	1934 U.S.S.R. joins League of Nations
	1938–1939 Germany annexes Czechoslovakia	1936–1937 New Soviet constitution; purge trials
1937–1975 Spain: Franco dictatorship		1939 Nazi-Soviet Pact
1940 Fall of France		1939–1940 Russo-Finnish War; Soviets absorb Baltic states
1940–1944 German occupation of Western Europe	1941–1944 Allies bomb Germany	1941 Germans invade Russia
		1942 Battle of Stalingrad
	1943 Allies invade Italy; fall of Mussolini	1943–1945 Russian offensives
1944–1945 Allies liberate Western Europe	1944–1945 Allied and Russian offensives	

TABLE EIGHT: 1945–1959

EUROPE AS A WHOLE	ASIA	AFRICA
1945 United Nations established: 51 members	1945 Arab League formed: 7 states	1945 Colonial empires continue; only four independent African states
1945–1947 Peacemaking breaks down: Cold War begins		
1945–1953 U.S.: Truman presidency; Marshall Plan, Truman Doctrine		
	1946–1954 French war in Indochina	
1947 British leave India	1947 India and Pakistan independent	
1947–1949 End of British and Dutch empires in Asia	1948 Assassination of Gandhi	
1948 UN: Declaration of Human Rights	1948 Burma an independent republic	
	1948 Israel established	
	1948 First Arab-Israeli war	
1949 Communist triumph in China: Chinese People's Republic	1949 Chinese People's Republic established	
1949 North Atlantic Treaty Organization	1949 Dutch leave Indonesia	
1950 World population estimate: 2.5 billion	1950 India a republic	
1950–1953 Korean War	1950–1953 Korean War	
	1950s Japan: regains sovereignty; economic expansion	
1951 Japanese peace treaty	1951 China occupies Tibet	1951 Libya independent
		1952 Egypt a republic; monarchy ousted
1953–1961 U.S.: Eisenhower presidency		
1954 U.S. hydrogen bomb tested	1954 French leave Indochina; Vietnam partitioned: North and South Vietnam	1954–1962 French-Algerian War
		1954 British surrender Suez Canal treaty rights
	1955 Bandung Afro-Asian conference	
1956 Suez Canal crisis	1956 Suez crisis: Second Arab-Israeli war	1956 Suez crisis: Britain, France, Israel vs. Egypt
	1956 Islamic Republic of Pakistan	1956 Morocco, Tunisia, Sudan independent
1957 U.S.S.R. launches space satellites		1957 Gold Coast (Ghana): first British African colony to gain independence

WESTERN EUROPE	CENTRAL EUROPE	EASTERN EUROPE
1945–1946 De facto split of Europe: east and west	1945 Allied occupation of Germany	1945–1948 Communist satellites established
1945–1946 Woman suffrage in France, Italy, Belgium, etc.	1945 Italian elections: Christian Democratic coalitions begin	1946–1950 Soviet Fourth Five-Year Plan
1945–1946 Britain: Labour Government		
1945–1958 Fourth French Republic	1946 Italian Republic	
	1946 Nuremberg trials	
	1946–1953 Italy: De Gasperi premier	
1947 Marshall Plan	1947 Peace treaties with Italy, Hungary, etc.	1947–1956 Cominform
	1948–1949 Berlin blockade and airlift	1948 Communist takeover in Czechoslovakia
	1948 Italian elections: Communist setback	1948–1955 Yugoslavia splits with U.S.S.R.
1949 Council of Europe	1949 German Federal Republic (West Germany); German Democratic Republic (East Germany)	1949 Council of Mutual Economic Assistance
1949 North Atlantic Treaty Organization		
	1949–1963 West Germany: Adenauer chancellor; economic expansion	1949 U.S.S.R. tests atomic bomb
1951 European Coal and Steel Community		1951–1955 Soviet Fifth Five-Year Plan
1951–1964 British Conservatives in office		
1952 Britain: Elizabeth II succeeds George VI	1952 Allied occupation of West Germany ends	
1953 West European economic recovery begins	1953 East Berlin uprising	1953 Death of Stalin
		1953 Russian hydrogen bomb
1954 Western European Union; West German rearmament		1953–1955 Malenkov premier; emergence of Khrushchev
1954 French defeat in Indochina; war in Algeria begins	1955 Austrian peace treaty	1955 Warsaw Pact
		1956 20th party congress: Khrushchev denounces Stalin regime
		1956 Polish, Hungarian risings crushed
		1956 U.S.S.R.–Japan peace treaty
1957 Rome treaties: Common Market; European Atomic Energy Community		1957 U.S.S.R. launches Sputnik I and II

EUROPE AS A WHOLE	ASIA	AFRICA
1957–1962 End of British, French, Belgian colonial empires in Africa		1957–1962 African states gain independence: Ghana, Nigeria, Kenya, Algeria, etc.
1958–1963 Pope John XXIII: reforms in Catholic Church	1958–1961 Syria part of United Arab Republic	1958 French colonies vote independence; French Community formed
		1958–1961 Egypt and Syria form short-lived United Arab Republic
1959 Cuban revolution: Castro in power		

TABLE NINE: 1960–

WORLD AS A WHOLE	ASIA	AFRICA
1960 World population estimate: 3 billion		
1960–1962 Congo civil war		1960–1962 Republic of Congo established: civil war
1960s U.S.: Civil rights movements, feminism	1960s North-South Vietnam war continues	
1961 U.S.S.R. and U.S. space flights begin; Soviets launch first man in space		1961 South Africa a republic: white minority government
1962 U.S.-Russian crisis over Cuba	1962 Chinese-Soviet rift	1962 Algeria independent
1962 Chinese-Soviet rift	1962 Chinese-Indian border war	
1962–1965 Vatican Council II: reforms in Catholic church		
1963– Pope Paul VI		1963 Organization of African Unity formed: 31 states
1963 Partial nuclear test ban agreement		
1963 President John F. Kennedy assassinated		
1963–1969 Lyndon B. Johnson's presidency		
1964 Cyprus crisis	1964 Death of Nehru	
1964 Vietnam war: U.S. involvement deepens	1964 Vietnam war: U.S. commits large-scale air and ground forces	
	1964 China tests atomic bomb	
1965 United Nations: 110 members		1965 Rhodesia: white minority government proclaims independence from British crown
	1966 Indonesia: Sukarno ousted	1966 UN recognizes Namibia (formerly South African trust territory)
	1966–1969 Chinese Cultural Revolution	1966 Nkrumah overthrown in Ghana
	1966–1977 Indira Gandhi in power	

WESTERN EUROPE	CENTRAL EUROPE	EASTERN EUROPE
1957 Britain tests hydrogen bomb		
1958 Fifth French Republic established		1958–1964 Khrushchev in power
1958–1969 De Gaulle president		
1959 British back European Free Trade Association		

WESTERN EUROPE	CENTRAL EUROPE	EASTERN EUROPE
1960 Belgium withdraws from Congo		
1960 France a nuclear power		
		1960s Liberalization in Soviet satellites
		1960s Industrialization in German Democratic Republic, Poland, etc.
	1961– Berlin Wall	1961 U.S.S.R. launches first man in space
1962 French leave Algeria		1962–1963 Chinese Communists split with U.S.S.R.
1963 Common Market: French veto British entry	1963–1968 Erhard succeeds Adenauer	
1964–1970 Britain: Labour in office		1964 Khrushchev ousted; replaced by Brezhnev, Kosygin
		1964– Brezhnev in power
1965 De Gaulle reelected president		

WORLD AS A WHOLE	ASIA	AFRICA
1967–1968 China and France join U.S., U.S.S.R., and Britain as thermonuclear powers	1967 Third Arab-Israeli war (Six-Day War)	1967–1970 Nigeria suppresses Biafra secession
1968 Student riots: U.S., France, Japan, etc.	1967 China tests hydrogen bomb	
1968 Vienam peace talks in Paris; war continues		
1968 Treaty to prevent spread of nuclear weapons: 61 nations sign		
1969 U.S.: Richard M. Nixon presidency	1969 Death of Ho Chi Minh	
1969 3 Americans in successful lunar flight	1969 Chinese-Soviet border clashes in Manchuria	
		1970s Agitation for black majority rule in Rhodesia and South Africa
1971 Chinese People's Republic admitted to UN		1971 Republic of Congo renamed Zaïre
1973–1974 Arab oil embargo	1973 Fourth Arab-Israeli war (Yom Kippur War)	
1973– Recession and inflation		
1974 India becomes sixth atomic power	1974 Turkey invades Cyprus	
1974 Resignation of President Nixon		
1975 End of Portuguese empire in Africa	1975 Bangladesh established	1975 End of Portuguese rule in Angola, Mozambique, etc.
1975 Helsinki agreements	1975 Communist victories in South Vietnam, Laos, Cambodia	1975–1976 Civil war in Angola
	1975–1976 Civil war in Lebanon	
1976 World population estimate: 4 billion	1976 Unification of Vietnam: Socialist Republic of Vietnam	1976 Organization of African Unity: 46 states
	1976 Death of Mao Tse-tung; successor: Hua Kuo-feng	
1977 United Nations: 149 members	1977 Arab League: 20 members	

WESTERN EUROPE	CENTRAL EUROPE	EASTERN EUROPE
		1967–1974 Military dictatorship in Greece
1968 France: student and labor demonstrations 1968 France tests hydrogen bomb		1968 Soviets invade Czechoslovakia; end liberal Czech regime
1969 De Gaulle resigns 1969– Northern Ireland: Catholic-Protestant clashes 1970 British voting age lowered to 18 1970–1974 Britain: Conservatives in office	1969 End of Christian Democratic rule 1969–1975 Willy Brandt heads Socialist coalition government 1970s Italy: economic difficulties and inflation	
1973 Britain, Denmark, Ireland join Common Market: 9 members 1973– Recession and inflation 1974– Britain: Labour in office 1974 Portugal: revolution and end of dictatorship 1975 Spain: death of Franco; constitutional monarchy	1972 West Germany: voting age lowered to 18 1973 German Federal Republic and German Democratic Republic admitted to UN 1975– Helmut Schmidt chancellor	1974 Greece: end of dictatorship; republic replaces monarchy 1975 Helsinki agreements
	1976 Italian elections: Communist strength increases	1976–1980 Soviet Tenth Five-Year Plan 1977 U.S.S.R.: new constitution adopted

Appendix II:
Rulers and Regimes
In Principal European Countries since 1500

HOLY ROMAN EMPIRE

Habsburg Line

Maximilian I	1493–1519
Charles V	1519–1556
Ferdinand I	1556–1564
Maximilian II	1564–1576
Rudolph II	1576–1612
Matthias	1612–1619
Ferdinand II	1619–1637
Ferdinand III	1637–1657
Leopold I	1658–1705
Joseph I	1705–1711
Charles VI	1711–1740

Charles VI was succeeded by a daughter, Maria Theresa, who as a woman could not be elected Holy Roman Emperor. French influence in 1742 secured the election of

Bavarian Line

Charles VII	1742–1745

On Charles VII's death the Habsburg control of the Emperorship was resumed.

Lorraine Line

Francis I   1745–1765
(husband of Maria Theresa)

Habsburg-Lorraine Line

Joseph II	1765–1790

(son of Francis I and Maria Theresa)

Leopold II	1790–1792
Francis II	1792–1806

The Holy Roman Empire became extinct in 1806.

AUSTRIAN DOMINIONS

The rulers of Austria from 1438 to 1740, and at least titular kings of Hungary from 1526 to 1740, were the same as the Holy Roman Emperors. After 1740:

Habsburg Line (through female heir)

Maria Theresa	1740–1780
Joseph II	1780–1790
Leopold II	1790–1792
Francis II	1792–1835

In 1804 Francis II took the title of Emperor, as Francis I of the Austrian Empire. Austria was declared an "empire" because Napoleon proclaimed France an empire in that year, and because the demise of the Holy Roman Empire could be foreseen.

Ferdinand I	1835–1848
Francis Joseph	1848–1916
Charles I	1916–1918

The Austrian Empire became extinct in 1918.

BRITISH ISLES

Tudor Line

Kings of England and Ireland

Henry VII	1485–1509
Henry VIII	1509–1547
Edward VI	1547–1553
Mary I	1553–1558
Elizabeth I	1558–1603

In 1603 James VI of Scotland, a great-great-grandson of Henry VII, succeeded to the English throne.

Stuart Line

Kings of England and Ireland, and of Scotland
JAMES I   1603–1625
CHARLES I   1625–1649

Republican Interregnum

The Commonwealth   1649–1653
The Protectorate
OLIVER CROMWELL   1653–1658
Lord Protector
RICHARD CROMWELL   1658–1660

Restored Stuart Line

CHARLES II   1660–1685
JAMES II   1685–1688

In 1688 James II was forced out of the country, but Parliament kept the crown in a female branch of the Stuart family, calling in Mary, the daughter of James II, and her husband William III of the Netherlands.

WILLIAM III   1689–1702,
AND MARY II   1689–1694
ANNE   1702–1714

In 1707, through the Union of England and Scotland, the royal title became King (or Queen) of Great Britain and Ireland. The Stuart family having no direct Protestant heirs, the throne passed in 1714 to the German George I, Elector of Hanover, a great-grandson of James I.

Hanoverian Line

Kings of Great Britain and Ireland
GEORGE I   1714–1727
GEORGE II   1727–1760
GEORGE III   1760–1820
GEORGE IV   1820–1830
WILLIAM IV   1830–1837

William IV having no heirs, the British throne passed in 1837 to Victoria, a granddaughter of George III. Though the British family has continued in direct descent from George I, it has dropped the Hanoverian designation and is now known as the House of Windsor. From 1877 to 1947 the British rulers bore the additional title of Emperor (or Empress) of India.

VICTORIA   1837–1901
EDWARD VII   1901–1910
GEORGE V   1910–1936
EDWARD VIII   1936
GEORGE VI   1936–1952
ELIZABETH II   1952–

FRANCE

Valois Line

LOUIS XI   1461–1483
CHARLES VIII   1483–1498
LOUIS XII   1498–1515
FRANCIS I   1515–1547
HENRY II   1547–1559
FRANCIS II   1559–1560
CHARLES IX   1560–1574
HENRY III   1574–1589

In 1589 the Valois line became extinct, and the throne passed to Henry of Bourbon, a remote descendant of French kings of the fourteenth century.

Bourbon Line

HENRY IV   1589–1610
LOUIS XIII   1610–1643
LOUIS XIV   1643–1715
LOUIS XV   1715–1774
LOUIS XVI   1774–1792

The Republic

Convention   1792–1795
Directory   1795–1799
Consulate   1799–1804

The Empire

NAPOLEON I   1804–1814
Emperor of the French
and King of Italy

Restored Bourbon Line

LOUIS XVIII   1814–1824

(Royalists count a Louis XVII, 1793–1795, and date the reign of Louis XVIII from 1795.)

CHARLES X   1824–1830

The Revolution of 1830 gave the throne to the Duke of Orleans, descendant of Louis XIII.

Orleans Line

LOUIS-PHILIPPE   1830–1848

The Second Republic

1848–1852

The Second Empire

NAPOLEON III   1852–1870
Emperor of the French

The Third Republic

1870–1940

Vichy Regime

1940–1944

Provisional Government

1944–1946

The Fourth Republic

1946–1958

The Fifth Republic

1958–

PRUSSIA (AND GERMANY)

A continuous Hohenzollern line ruled until 1918.

Electors of Brandenburg and Dukes of Prussia

GEORGE WILLIAM	1619–1640
FREDERICK WILLIAM	1640–1688
the "Great Elector"	
FREDERICK III	1688–1713

In 1701 Frederick III was permitted by the Holy Roman Emperor to entitle himself King in Prussia, as Frederick I.

Kings of Prussia

FREDERICK I	1701–1713
FREDERICK WILLIAM I	1713–1740
FREDERICK II, the "Great"	1740–1786
FREDERICK WILLIAM II	1786–1797
FREDERICK WILLIAM III	1797–1840
FREDERICK WILLIAM IV	1840–1861
WILLIAM I	1861–1888

In 1871 William I took the title of German Emperor.

German Emperors

WILLIAM I	1871–1888
FREDERICK III	1888
WILLIAM II	1888–1918

The German Empire became extinct in 1918. It was succeeded by the

Weimar Republic

1919–1933

(an unofficial title for what was still called the Deutsches Reich, a phrase not easy to translate accurately)

The Third Reich

1933–1945

(an unofficial title for the Deutsches Reich under Adolf Hitler)
Allied Military Government in 1945 was followed by

German Federal Republic (West Germany)

1949–

German Democratic Republic (East Germany)

1949–

SARDINIA (AND ITALY)

In 1720 Victor Amadeus II, Duke of Savoy, took the title of King of Sardinia, having acquired the island of that name.

Kings of Sardinia

VICTOR AMADEUS II	1720–1730
CHARLES EMMANUEL III	1730–1773
VICTOR AMADEUS III	1773–1796
CHARLES EMMANUEL IV	1796–1802
VICTOR EMMANUEL I	1802–1821
CHARLES FELIX	1821–1831
CHARLES ALBERT	1831–1849
VICTOR EMMANUEL II	1849–1878

In 1861 Victor Emmanuel II took the title of King of Italy.

Kings of Italy

VICTOR EMMANUEL II	1861–1878
HUMBERT I	1878–1900
VICTOR EMMANUEL III	1900–1946
HUMBERT II	1946

In 1936 Victor Emmanuel III took the title of Emperor of Ethiopia, which became meaningless with British occupation of Ethiopia in 1941.
In 1946 the Kingdom of Italy became extinct and was succeeded by the

Italian Republic

1946–

SPAIN

FERDINAND AND ISABELLA	1479–1504/1516

Isabella died in 1504, but Ferdinand lived until 1516, whereupon the Spanish thrones were inherited by their grandson Charles, who became Charles V of the Holy Roman Empire, but was known in Spain as Charles I.

Habsburg Line

CHARLES I	1516–1556
PHILIP II	1556–1598
PHILIP III	1598–1621
PHILIP IV	1621–1665
CHARLES II	1665–1700

With Charles II the Spanish Habsburg line became extinct, and the throne passed to the French Bourbon grandson of Louis XIV of France and great-grandson of Philip IV of Spain.

Bourbon Line

PHILIP V	1700–1746
FERDINAND VI	1746–1759

CHARLES III	1759–1788
CHARLES IV	1788–1808

Bonaparte Line

JOSEPH	1808–1813

(brother of Napoleon)

Restored Bourbon Line

FERDINAND VII	1813–1833
ISABELLA II	1833–1868

In 1868 Isabella abdicated; after a regency, and a brief reign by Amadeus I (Savoy), 1871–1873, there was a short-lived First Republic, 1873–1874, succeeded by

ALFONSO XII	1874–1885
ALFONSO XIII	1885–1931

In 1931 a republican revolution unseated Alfonso XIII.

Second Spanish Republic

1931–1936

Spanish Civil War

1936–1939

Regime of General Francisco Franco

1939–1975

Upon the death of Franco the Bourbon family was restored.

JUAN CARLOS I	1975–

RUSSIA (AND U.S.S.R.)

Grand Dukes of Moscow

IVAN III, the "Great"	1462–1505
BASIL III	1505–1533
IVAN IV, the "Terrible"	1533–1584

In 1547 Ivan IV took the title of Tsar of Russia.

Tsars of Russia

IVAN IV, the "Terrible"	1547–1584
THEODORE I	1584–1598
BORIS GODUNOV	1598–1605

Time of Troubles

1604–1613

Romanov Line

MICHAEL	1613–1645
ALEXIS	1645–1676
THEODORE II	1676–1682
IVAN V AND PETER I	1682–1689
PETER I, the "Great"	1689–1725
CATHERINE I	1725–1727
PETER II	1727–1730
ANNA	1730–1740
IVAN VI	1740–1741
ELIZABETH	1741–1762
PETER III	1762
CATHERINE II, the "Great"	1762–1796
PAUL	1796–1801
ALEXANDER I	1801–1825

NICHOLAS I	1825–1855
ALEXANDER II	1855–1881
ALEXANDER III	1881–1894
NICHOLAS II	1894–1917

In 1917 the tsardom became extinct.

Provisional Government

1917

Communist Revolution

1917

Union of Soviet Socialist Republics

1922–

Appendix III:
Historical Populations
of Various Countries
and Cities

Figures for dates before the nineteenth century arise from estimates, in some cases subject to a wide margin of error. Those for the nineteenth and twentieth centuries generally reflect census returns, at dates within two or three years before or after the round date indicated. For cities, the figures for 1950 and 1970 refer to "urban agglomerations" as defined in the *United Nations Demographic Yearbook*. Estimates for cities for earlier dates are conveniently assembled in Tertius Chandler and Gerald Fox, *3000 Years of Urban Growth* (New York, 1974).

For countries, the use of the table is mainly for rough comparisons. It shows, for example, that France was about five times as populous as England in the Middle Ages, and was still more populous than all the German states at the time of the French Revolution, or that Spain declined under the Habsburgs in the seventeenth century, and that Ireland lost population after the famine and ensuing emigration. All countries except Ireland grew rapidly in population in the nineteenth century. For Russia, the figures from 1750 to 1950 reflect territorial expansion as well as internal growth. All figures for China are very uncertain, though unquestionably very large.

For 1950 and 1970 the figures for Ireland include both the Republic of Ireland and Northern Ireland, and "Germany" includes both East and West Germany. In 1970 the Irish Republic was about twice as populous as its northern neighbor, and West Germany was over three times as populous as East Germany.

CITIES in thousands

	LONDON	MANCHESTER	PARIS	MARSEILLES
14th Century	50	3–	200	
15th Century				
16th Century	100			
17th Century	500	15–	450	50 +
18th Century	750		500	90
1800	959	77	600	111
1850	2681	303	1422	195
1900	6581	544	3670	491
1950	8346	2421	4823	655
1970	7281	2389	8196	964

	FLORENCE	BERLIN	VIENNA	PRAGUE
14th Century	50 +			
15th Century	60	10 –	20	25 +
16th Century	65	12	40 +	40 +
17th Century	75	20	100	40 +
18th Century	75	100	220	75
1800	84	172	247	75
1850	114	500	444	206
1900	206	2712	1675	382
1950	374	3337	1766	922
1970	461	3136	1614	1095

AMSTERDAM	ANTWERP	LISBON	MADRID	ROME
	5	20 +	5 –	30 –
20 –	35			50
35	100	100	60	100
100 +	50	73	80	130
150	50	120	120	150
201	62	180	160	153
224	88	240	281	175
511	277	356	540	463
838	584	790	1618	1652
1023	672	1612	3146	2800

WARSAW	BUDAPEST	STOCKHOLM	ST. PETERSBURG LENINGRAD	MOSCOW
70		60	100	
100	54 +	76	220	250
150	178	93	485	365
700	732	301	1150	1000
804	1571	928	3182	4847
1377	2044	1350	4243	7528

COUNTRIES in millions

	ENGLAND AND WALES	SCOTLAND	IRELAND	FRANCE
1300	3.5			15.0
1500	2.8			16.0
1700	5.5	1.2		19.0
1800	8.9	1.6	5.2	27.0
1850	17.9	2.9	6.5	34.2
1900	32.5	4.5	4.5	38.5
1950	43.0	5.0	4.3	41.8
1970	48.7	5.2	4.5	49.8

	SWEDEN	POLAND	RUSSIA U.S.S.R.	CHINA
1300		1.3		
1500		2.0		
1700	1.6		12	200
1800	2.3		30	
1850	3.5		62	400
1900	5.1	28.3	104	
1950	7.0	24.8	180	547
1970	8.1	32.6	242	750

BELGIUM	NETHERLANDS	GERMANY	SPAIN	ITALY	
.7	.4	7.0		8.0	
		7.0	8.3	6.0	
1.6	1.8	15.0	6.0	11.0	
3.0	2.0	25.0	10.5	17.2	
4.3	3.1	33.8		24.3	
6.7	5.1	56.3	19.1	33.6	
8.6	10.1	68.3	27.9	46.8	
9.7	13.0	77.7	34.0	53.7	

JAPAN	EGYPT	MEXICO	BRAZIL	U.S.A.	
				.3	
	2.5	6.0		5.3	
30.0	5.0			23.2	
45.0	10.0	13.6	20.0	76.0	
83.2	20.0	25.7	52.6	152.0	
104.6	33.3	48.4	93.2	200.3	

Bibliography

The following reading lists are intended for the convenience of general readers, students, and teachers. Although professional students of history also may find them useful, no attempt has been made to provide comprehensive coverage of any areas or topics. The aim throughout has been to call attention to the leading and most reliable works, to which the reader may also turn for specialized bibliographies and for information on source materials. Classification follows the plan of chapters in the present book. Few titles are intentionally repeated; to find books on some topics, it will sometimes be necessary to look in several places. For reasons of space, works in foreign languages have been excluded, as are (with few exceptions) general textbooks, articles in periodicals, and primary source materials.

Many of the titles listed below are now or will be available in paperback; up-to-date lists of such paperbacks may be found in the *Paperback book guide for colleges*, published and distributed by the R. R. Bowker Company. An asterisk in the reading lists below indicates availability in a paperback edition.

WORKS OF GENERAL COVERAGE

Bibliographical Guides

There are literally hundreds of thousands of books on historical subjects, and it is difficult to find the titles and authors of those one wants on a particular topic. One bibliographical tool is the American Historical Association's *Guide to historical literature* (1961), the successor to a similar volume published thirty years earlier. It makes no effort at exhaustive coverage and has quickly fallen out of date, but it contains some 20,000 items, mostly annotated, in all fields and periods of history. It also lists the most useful reference sources for the study of history, specialized bibliographies, and professional periodicals. Of such periodicals, the *American historical review* and the *Journal of modern history* are valuable sources for lists and reviews of current historical literature;

the annual *International bibliography of historical sciences* also provides comprehensive lists. Some of the most discerning appraisals of new history books are to be found in the *Times literary supplement* (London).

Brief Reference Works

W. L. Langer, *An encyclopedia of world history: ancient, medieval, and modern, chronologically arranged* (rev., 1972), is a vast table of dates and important events. A similar service is performed by S. H. Steinberg, *Historical tables, 58* B.C.–A.D. *1972* (1974), and G. S. P. Freeman-Grenville, *Chronology of world history* (1076). A convenient one-volume reference tool is the *New Columbia encyclopedia* (4th ed., 1975).

Among many historical atlases, there are W. R. Shepherd, *Historical atlas* (rev., 1964); *Muir's historical atlas—medieval and modern* (rev., 1964); E. W. Fox, *Atlas of European history* (1957); *Chambers historical atlas of the world*° (1971); the *Penguin atlas of modern history: to 1815*° (1973); M. Gilbert, *Recent historical atlas* (1969); and R. R. Palmer and others, *Atlas of world history* (1957), which is also available in shorter form as *Abridged historical atlas*° (1958). H. C. Darby and H. Fullard, *Atlas*° (1975), is the final volume (vol. 14) of the *New Cambridge modern history*. Geographical information also may be readily located through *Webster's geographical dictionary* (rev., 1972).

Geographical influences on history are discussed in D. S. Whittlesey, *Environmental foundations of European history* (1949); C. T. Smith, *An historical geography of western Europe before 1800* (1967); and E. A. Freeman and J. B. Bury, *The historical geography of Europe* (1974).

Multivolumed Encyclopedias

Among the most useful are the *Encyclopedia Britannica* [now in its ambitious but controversial fifteenth edition (1975)], the *Encyclopedia Americana, Collier's encyclopedia*, and the *New international encyclopedia*. Each annually publishes a yearbook covering developments of the previous year. The *International encyclopedia of the social sciences* (17 vols., 1968) may be consulted for many topics. The *Dictionary of national biography* (1885–1949) is informative for British men and women; a shorter version is the *Concise dictionary of national biography* (2 vols., 1961). The *Dictionary of the history of ideas* (4 vols., 1973) has substantial articles on such important historical concepts as liberalism, militarism, and so forth, while the *Dictionary of scientific biography* (14 vols., 1970–1976) covers scientists of all nationalities since the Greeks.

Multivolumed Collaborative Works and Series on Modern European History

The *Cambridge modern history* (14 vols., 1902–1912), long a standard work, authoritative but usually dry, with contributors to each volume writing on their specialties, has been replaced by the *New Cambridge modern history* (14 vols., 1957–1975). The volumes in this series, many of which are described in the appropriate sections below, contain valuable chapters by specialists from all over the world but often fail to provide a synthesis for the period covered. An *Oxford history of modern Europe* also is appearing. A valuable series by American scholars on Europe since 1250 is the *Rise of modern Europe* (20 vols. projected, 1936 ff., now almost complete), also known as the "Langer series" for its editor, W. L. Langer; each volume contains a rich bibliography for the years covered; the individual volumes are referred to in the appropriate chapters. The *University of Michigan history of the modern world* (15 vols. projected, 1958 ff.) is a series of histories of individual nations, of which several have appeared to date. B. C. Shafer is editing *Europe and the world in the age of expansion* (10 vols. projected, 1975 ff.), which is to cover the thirteenth to the twentieth centuries. British scholars are preparing a *History of civilisation* to consist of thirty-five volumes, edited by R. Syme (1963 ff.), and J. H. Plumb is editing the *History of human society* series. The multivolumed collaborative *UNESCO history of mankind*, now in preparation (1963 ff.), suffers from the need to arrive at a political consensus on subjects covered. There are informative volumes for the general reader, with illustrations, in the Time-Life *Great ages of man* series (20 vols., 1965–1968) and in the British *Hamlyn history of the world in colour* (1969 ff.), which is derived from the French illustrated series, *Connaissance de l'histoire*.

Interpretive and Large-Scale Histories

Histories recounting and analyzing the human story in order to show that it follows a certain pattern or system, or that it obeys certain laws, are generally regarded with distrust by historians, who are not convinced by the evidence offered. In recent years, the most important such grand-scale interpretive account has been A. J. Toynbee's monumental *A study of history*° (12 vols., 1934–1961, of which vol. 12 consists of *Reconsiderations*) (abridgment edited by D. C. Somervell, 2 vols., 1947–1957); Toynbee's *Mankind and mother earth* (1976) was published posthumously. Some objections to Toynbee are discussed in M. F. Ashley-Montagu (ed.), *Toynbee and history: critical essays and reviews* (1956); E. T. Gargan and others, *The intent of Toynbee's history* (1961); and P. Geyl, *Debates with historians* (1956) and *Encounters in history* (1961). The attempt to find patterns or laws in historical evolution is to be distinguished from efforts to recount the scope of human history in a more purely narrative way. Here two works stand out: H. A. L. Fisher, *A history of Europe* (3 vols., 1935–1936; 2 vols., 1949), an older notable effort by a single author to tell the whole Western story from the Greeks to the twentieth century, and W. H. McNeill, *The rise of the West: a history of the human community* (1963), a brilliant presentation of Western history in its world setting stressing the interrelationships of human civilization at all stages; McNeill also has written *The shape of European history*° (1974), a briefer study of Europe from antiquity to the present stressing cultural and technological changes. Not always abreast of modern scholarship but colorful and readable are the volumes of W. Durant and A. Durant, *The story of civilization* (10 vols., 1935–1967), from early times to the late eighteenth century; their conclusions appear in *The lessons of history* (1968).

General Histories in Special Areas

[A number of books are relevant to many or all of the chapters of the present work and provide additional specialized bibliographies as well.] For European economic history, a valuable collaborative work is C. M. Cipolla (ed.), *The Fontana economic history of Europe* (6 vols., 1971–1974), with chapters contributed by an international roster of experts. Also useful are H. Heaton, *Economic history of Europe* (1936, 1948), and S. B. Clough and R. T. Rapp, *European economic history* (rev., 1975). On economic thought: E. Roll, *A history of economic thought* (rev., 1946); C. Gide and C. Rist, *A history of economic doctrines* (2nd ed., 1948); R. L. Heilbroner, *The worldly philosophers*° (1953); E. Heimann, *History of economic doctrines* (1964); and H. T. Overton, *Social ideals and economic theories from Quesnay to Keynes* (1962).

On rural and agrarian history consult: N. S. B. Gras, *A history of agriculture in Europe and America* (rev., 1940); B. H. S. van Bath, *The agrarian history of western Europe, 500–1850 A.D.* (trans. from Dutch, 1963); and D. B. Grigg, *The agricultural systems of the world: an evolutionary approach*° (1974), the best introduction.

On general intellectual and cultural history and related subjects: B. Russell, *A history of Western philosophy* (1945); J. H. Randall, *Making of the modern mind* (1926, 1976); the same author's *The career of philosophy* (2 vols., 1962–1965), from the Middle Ages to the age of Darwin; C. Brinton, *Ideas and men: the story of Western thought* (1950, 1963), which for the postmedieval period has been published as *The shaping of the modern mind*° (1953); and the same author's *A history of Western morals* (1959). Recommended also: J. Bronowski and B. Mazlish, *The Western intellectual tradition: from Leonardo to Hegel* (1960); E. N. Johnson, *An introduction to the history of the Western tradition* (2 vols., 1961); R. N. Stromberg, *An intellectual history of modern Europe* (rev., 1975); W. H. Coates, H. V. White, and J. S. Schapiro, *The emergence of liberal humanism* (1966); and the sequel volume by Coates and White, *The ordeal of liberal humanism* (1969). A comprehensive survey is F. C. Copleston, *A history of philosophy* (8 vols., 1950–1967).

On political thought: G. H. Sabine, *A history of political theory* (1937, 1973); F. Watkins, *The political tradition of the West: a study in the development of modern liberalism* (1948); and J. H. Hallowell, *Main currents in modern political thought* (1950); and E. S. Bogardus, *The development of social thought* (rev., 1960).

On the arts A. Hauser, *Social history of art* (4 vols., 1963); D. J. Groat, *A history of western music* (1960); and N. Persner, *An outline of European architecture* (rev., 1963).

On military history and related themes: T. Ropp, *War in the modern world*° (1959, 1962); A. Vagts, *A history of militarism; romance and realities of a profession*° (1937); J. U. Nef, *War and human progress* (1950); R. A. Preston and S. Wise, *Men in arms* (rev., 1970); and Q. Wright, *A study of war* (2 vols., 1942; 1

vol. abr., 1965). More specifically on strategy, there are E. M. Earle (ed.), *Makers of modern strategy: military thought from Machiavelli to Hitler** (1944); B. H. Liddell Hart, *Strategy: the indirect approach* (3rd ed., 1954); J. F. C. Fuller, *Decisive battles: their influence upon history and civilization* (2 vols., 1940) and *A military history of the Western world* (1954 ff.). D. Eggenberger, *A dictionary of battles* (1969), is a useful reference book, and F. L. Israel has edited *Major peace treaties of modern history, 1648–1967* (4 vols., 1967). Other books treating war as a social and human phenomenon include: M. Howard, *War in European history* (1976); J. Keegan, *The face of battle* (1976); J. Ellis, *Armies in revolution* (1974); and F. Fornari, *The psychoanalysis of war** (1966, trans. 1974).

Demographic, Statistical, Social, and Miscellaneous

On demography, a pioneer study still valuable is A. M. Carr-Saunders, *World population: past growth and future trends* (1936); more recent treatments include D. V. Glass and D. E. C. Eversley, *Population in history: essays in historical demography* (1965); E. A. Wrigley, *Population and history** (1969); C. M. Cipolla, *Economic history of world population** (1974); and T. McKeown, *The modern rise of population* (1977). E. Leroy Ladurie, *Times of feast, times of famine: a history of climate since the year 1000* (trans. 1971), examines the effects of climatic changes on history, and W. H. McNeill, *Plagues and peoples* (1976), of disease and epidemics. On famine and food, one may also read E. P. Prentice, *Hunger and history: the influence of hunger on human history* (1939); R. N. Salaman, *The history and social influence of the potato* (1949); and E. Forster and R. Forster (eds.), *European diet from preindustrial to modern times* (1975). T. Chandler and G. Fox provide statistical and other information on the historical growth of the world's cities in *3000 years of urban growth* (1974), and B. R. Mitchell, *European historical statistics, 1750–1970* (1975), is a valuable compendium of figures on population, trade, and other social and economic topics.

In recent years, historians have interested themselves increasingly in various aspects of social history quite apart from their older interests in the history of social classes and of labor and laboring conditions, and they have been examining such important questions as the history of the family, the role of women in history, and similar topics. Many such works, where they are now available, are listed below in the appropriate chapters. Two pioneer studies have been P. Ariès, *Centuries of childhood: a social history of family life** (trans. 1962), and P. Laslett, *The world we have lost: England before the industrial age* (1965). Some general introductions are A. Mitchell and I. Deak (eds.), *Everyman in Europe: essays in social history** (2 vols., 1974); V. J. Knapp, *Europe in the era of social transformation, 1700 to the present* (1976); R. Z. Bezucha (ed.), *Modern European social history** (1972); and P. Stearns, *European society in upheaval: social history since 1800* (1967). E. Shorter, *The making of the modern family* (1975), has been criticized for lacking an empirical base for some of his theoretical formulations. Other useful studies are J. R. Gillis, *Youth and history: tradition and change in European age relations, 1770 to the present* (1974); D. Hunt, *Parents and children in history** (1972); T. K. Rabb and R. I. Rothberg (eds.), *The family in history** (1971); L. de Mausa (ed.), *The history of childhood** (1975); P. Laslett and R. Wall (eds.), *Household and family in past time* (1972); and C. E. Rosenberg (ed.), *The family in history* (1975). I. Pinchbeck and M. Hewett, *Children in English society* (2 vols., 1969–1973), comprehensive and wide ranging, covers from the fifteenth to the mid-twentieth centuries. A. Esler (ed.), *The youth revolution: the conflict of generations in modern history** (1974), is an interesting anthology.

On the role of women in history, an early contribution was M. R. Beard, *Women as a force in history: a study in traditions and realities* (1946); newer emphases can be explored in M. Hartman and L. W. Banner (eds.), *Clio's consciousness raised: new perspectives on the history of women** (1974), and in R. Bridenthal and C. Koonz (eds.), *Becoming visible: women in European history** (1977), with chapters running from ancient times to the present; a useful anthology is A. S. Rossi (ed.), *The feminist papers: from (Abigail) Adams to (Simone) de Beauvoir** (1973). S. Rowbotham, *Women resistence, and revolution** (1974), is a stimulating series of historical essays ranging from the English civil wars of the seventeenth century to the twentieth century. Many other titles are included in the appropriate sections.

On the subject of literacy, one may read C. M. Cipolla, *Literacy and development in the West** (1969); and on the origins of higher education, L. Stone (ed.), *The university in society* (2 vols., 1974), from the fourteenth to the twentieth centuries. On the media, whereby ideas were transmitted in modern history, there is K. E. Olson, *The history makers: the press of Europe from its beginnings through 1965* (1966), and on a related subject, D. Kunzle, *History of the comic strip . . . narrative strips and picture stories in the European broadsheet from c. 1450 to 1825* (1973).

Two other subjects difficult to classify are covered in P. Ariès, *Western attitudes toward death: from the Middle Ages to the present* (trans. 1976), and M. Foucault, *Madness and civilization* (trans. 1965).

Historical Manuals and Historiography

Among manuals on methods of research and on the writing of history, a spirited introduction is J. Barzun and H. F. Graff, *The modern researcher** (rev., 1977); Barzun, *Simple and direct* (1976), is an excellent guide for all writers. Other introductions include A. Nevins, *The gateway to history** (rev., 1962); S. Kent, *Writing history* (rev., 1967); and L. Gottschalk, *Understanding history** (rev., 1969). There is practical information in W. Gray and others, *Historian's handbook** (1959); N. F. Cantor and R. I. Schneider, *How to study history** (1967); and in K. L. Turabian, *A manual for writers of term papers, theses, and dissertations** (many eds.), an adaptation of a standard guide, the University of Chicago, *A manual of style* (12th ed., 1969). Examples of books affording insight into the study and writing of history are C. Gustavson, *A preface to history** (1955), and *The mansion of history** (1975), the latter on modes of historical thinking; M. Bloch, *The historian's*

*craft** (1953); A. L. Rowse, *The use of history** (1946); G. R. Elton, *The practice of history* (1967); H. S. Hughes, *History as art and science: twin vistas on the past** (1967); and A. N. Gilbert (ed.), *In search of a meaningful past** (1972). For examples of historians practicing their craft, see R. W. Winks (ed.), *The historian as detective* (1969); L. P. Curtis, Jr. (ed.), *The historian's workshop** (1971); and P. Gay and V. G. Wexler (eds.), *Historians at work* (4 vols., 1972–1975).

The great historians of the past and the evolution of history are discussed in the encyclopedic M. A. Fitzsimons, A. G. Pundt, and C. E. Nowell (eds.), *The development of historiography* (1954), and in H. Butterfield, *Man on his past: the study of the history of historical scholarship* (1955). An older basic study is J. W. Thompson and B. H. Holm, *A history of historical writing* (2 vols., 1942). A good introductory anthology is F. Stern (ed.), *The varieties of history: from Voltaire to the present** (1956). Special studies of the historical craft and its practitioners include G. P. Gooch, *History and historians in the nineteenth century* (1913); E. E. Neff, *The poetry of history* (1947); B. E. Schmitt (ed.), *Some historians of modern Europe* (1942); S. W. Halperin (ed.), *Some twentieth-century historians* (1961); J. R. Hale (ed.), *The evolution of British historiography: from Bacon to Namier* (1967); V. Mehta, *The fly and the fly bottle* (1962), an intriguing journalistic account of some contemporary British historians; P. Gay, *Style in history* (1974); and the same author's *Art and act: on causes in history* (1976).

Theories of History

The historical manuals listed above all provide some introduction to the philosophy and theory of history, and generally have useful bibliographies. Two convenient introductions are the anthologies edited by H. Meyerhoff, *The philosophy of history in our time** (1959), and P. Gardiner (ed.), *Theories of History* (1950). There are valuable contributions and extensive bibliographies on the role and nature of historical studies in various publications sponsored by the Social Science Research Council: *Theory and practice in historical study* (1946); *Social sciences in historical* *study* (1954); L. Gottschalk (ed.), *The use of personal documents in history, anthropology, and sociology* (1945), and *Generalization in the writing of history* (1963).

Of the many volumes on the subject, mostly for the advanced student, there may be mentioned: M. Mandelbaum, *The problem of historical knowledge* (1938); R. Aron, *Introduction to the philosophy of history* (1948, trans. 1961); R. G. Collingwood, *The idea of history** (1946); E. H. Carr, *What is history?** (1962); and F. E. Manuel, *Shapes of philosophical history* (1964). Other studies include B. Mazlish, *The riddle of history: the great speculators from Vico to Freud* (1966); N. O. Brown, *Life against death: the psychoanalytical meaning of history** (1959); J. Lukacs, *Historical consciousness: or the remembered past* (1968); and J. T. Marcus, *Heaven, hell, and history: a survey of man's faith in history from antiquity to the present* (1967).

Among thoughtful reflections by practicing historians, the following sampling of titles may be suggested: H. S. Commager, *The search for a usable past and other essays in historiography* (1967); P. Smith, *The historian and history** (1964); G. Kitson Clark, *The critical historian* (1967); C. V. Wedgwood, *The sense of the past: thirteen studies in the theory and practice of history* (1960); D. H. Fischer, *Historians' fallacies: toward a logic of historical thought** (1970); G. Jackson, *Historian's quest* (1969); M. Duberman, *The uncompleted past* (1970); H. Zinn, *The politics of history** (1970); J. H. Plumb, *The death of the past* (1970); F. E. Manuel, *Freedom from history** (1971); B. Lewis, *History remembered, recovered, invented* (1975); and F. Gilbert, *History: choice and commitment* (1977).

The current state of historical studies and newer approaches may be explored in J. Higham and others, *History* (1965), a volume in a series examining humanistic scholarship in America; B. C. Shafer and others, *Historical study in the West: France, Western Germany, Great Britain, and the United States* (1968); W. Laqueur and G. L. Mosse (eds.), *The new history: trends in historical research and writing since World War II** (1968); M. Ballard (ed.), *New movements in the study and teaching of history* (1970); F. Gilbert and S. R. Graubard (eds.), *Historical studies today** (1972); P. Conkin and R. N. Stromberg, *The heritage and challenge of history* (1971); J. H. Hexter, *The history primer* (1971); G. G. Iggers, *New directions in European historiography* (1975); and T. Stoianovich, *French historical method: the Annales paradigm* (1976).

For relationships to the social sciences, see S. R. Lipset and R. Hofstadter (eds.), *Sociology and history* (1968); D. Landes and C. Tilly (eds.), *History as a social science* (1971); M. Harris, *The rise of anthropological theory* (1968); and two books by R. A. Nisbet, *The sociological tradition* (1967) and *Social change and history: aspects of the Western theory of development* (1969). Examples of quantitative, psychological, and behavioral approaches are to be found in W. O. Aydelotte and others, *The dimensions of quantitative research in history* (1972); V. Lorwin and J. Price (eds.), *Dimensions of the past* (1972); R. J. Lifton (ed.), *Explorations in psychohistory** (1974); B. Mazlish (ed.), *Psychoanalysis and history* (1963); and R. F. Berkhofer, Jr., *A behavioral approach to historical analysis* (1969). A provocative book lamenting the impact of the newer history is J. Barzun, *Clio and the doctors: psycho-history, quanto-history, and history* (1974).

Anthologies of Readings, Source Materials, and Historical Problems

The number of anthologies for classroom use has multiplied. New titles are publicized through publishers' releases and advertisements. The following titles are intended to give only a sampling of those available: Columbia University, *Introduction to contemporary civilization in the West* (2 vols., rev., 1960), a collection of fairly lengthy source selections; J. H. Hexter and others, *The traditions of the Western world** (1967); R. P. Stearns, *Pageant of Europe: sources and selections from the Renaissance to the present day** (rev., 1961); F. L. Baumer, *Main currents of Western thought: readings in Western European intellectual history from the Middle Ages to the present** (rev., 1964); E. Weber, *The Western tradition from the ancient world to the atomic age** (1959); L. S. Stavrianos, *The epic of modern man:*

a collection of readings° (1966), globally oriented; and G. L. Mosse and others, *Europe in review*° (rev., 1964). There are also numerous multivolumed series reproducing sources, documents, and extracts of historical writings.

Among the many anthologies that focus on source problems or on conflicting interpretations of historical issues, there are S. B. Clough, P. Gay, C. K. Warner, and J. M. Cammett, *The European past: reappraisals in history*° (2 vols., rev., 1970); B. D. Gooch (ed.), *Interpreting European history*° (2 vols., 1967); O. Ranum, *Searching for modern times*° (2 vols., 1969); L. W. Spitz and R. W. Lyman (gen. eds.), *Major crises in Western civilization*° (2 vols., 1965); and B. Tierney, D. Kagan, and L. P. Williams (eds.), *Great issues in Western civilization*° (2 vols., 1976), available also in separate pamphlets. The Great Lives Observed series° (1968 ff.) consists of sources, contemporary judgments, and latter-day interpretations relating to leading historical personalities.

A useful series maintaining a high level of quality is the Heath Problems in European Civilization (1958 ff.); the volumes often contain bibliographical essays and sometimes offer materials not otherwise available in English. A similar series is being published as European Problem Studies (Holt, Rinehart and Winston, 1963 ff.). By reprinting longer excerpts, the Modern Scholarship on European History series° (*New Viewpoints: Franklin Watts*, 1971 ff.) provides an extended sampling of recent scholarship on selected topics.

Anthologies of more specialized coverage include N. F. Cantor and M. S. Werthman (eds.), *The history of popular culture* (2 vols., 1968); by the same editors, *The English tradition: modern studies in English history* (2 vols., 1967); J. Friguglietti and E. Kennedy, *The shaping of modern France: writings on French history since 1715* (1969); and M. Kranzberg and C. W. Pursell, Jr. (eds.), *Technology in Western civilization* (2 vols., 1967).

Historical Series for Supplementary Reading in College Courses

Brief volumes on selected topics, especially suitable for undergraduate reading, are to be found in the following series: the Berkshire Studies in European History° (Holt, Rinehart and Winston, 1927 ff., revisions in progress); the Cornell University Narrative Essays in the History of Our Tradition° (1950 ff.); Teach Yourself History (Macmillan, 1948 ff.), a British series, edited by A. L. Rowse, successfully using a biographical approach to lure the general reader to historical topics; the Rand McNally European History series° (1968 ff.); and Europe Since 1500° (Crowell, 1967 ff.). The American Historical Association Pamphlets series (1971 ff.), replacing an older series of bibliographical essays (1957 ff.), is publishing brief critical and narrative accounts of selected subjects with bibliographies, some on the teaching of history. The Anvil series° (Van Nostrand, 1955 ff.), edited by L. L. Snyder, consists of introductory essays on given topics and selected readings and documents. Three recommended series, written and edited by British authorities but also published in this country, with each volume covering a segment of European history, are: G. Barraclough (gen. ed.), History of European Civilization Library° (Harcourt, Brace and World, 1965 ff.); D. Hay (gen. ed.), A General History of Europe° (Holt, Rinehart and Winston, 1966 ff.); and J. H. Plumb (gen. ed.), History of Europe° (Harper & Row, 1967 ff.). B. Mazlish (gen. ed.), Main Themes in European History° (Macmillan, 1964 ff.), brings together reprints of articles by leading authorities on selected "themes" of European history since 1500; booklets have appeared on religion, technology, labor, the modern state, science, agriculture, population, and imperialism. The New Dimensions in History series° (Wiley, 1966 ff.) focuses on selected cities in various historical eras. The Forum series° (Forum Press, 1970 ff.) provides useful brief essays on selected subjects. For an introduction to the use of film in the classroom, see J. E. O'Connor and M. E. Jackson, *Teaching history with film*° (1974), in the American Historical Association Pamphlets series.

XI: REACTION VERSUS PROGRESS, 1815–1848

The resettling of European institutions after the great French outburst in many ways marked the opening of a new historical era. There are numerous general, national, and topical histories, accordingly, that take their starting point in 1815; some that begin in 1789 are also included here. Accounts focusing on selected aspects include E. N. Anderson and P. R. Anderson, *Political institutions and social change in continental Europe in the nineteenth century* (1967); G. L. Mosse, *The culture of western Europe: the nineteenth and twentieth centuries* (1961); and R. N. Stromberg, *European intellectual history since 1789*° (1968). Two anthologies useful for the nineteenth and twentieth centuries are E. C. Black, *The posture of Europe, 1815–1940: readings in European intellectual history*° (1964); and E. C. Weber (ed.), *Paths to the present: . . . European thought from romanticism to existentialism*° (1960). P. N. Stearns (ed.), *A century for debate: problems in the interpretation of European history, 1789–1914*° (1969), and G. Rudé, *Debate on Europe*° (1972), summarize the historiographical debate on selected issues. A number of general works and books on social history are listed in the introductory section of this bibliography. For comparative social and economic data for the European countries, B. R. Mitchell, *European historical statistics, 1750–1970,* cited earlier, is invaluable. C. Tilly, L. Tilly, and R. Tilly, *The rebellious century, 1830–1930* (1975), is a sociological and statistical analysis of collective action during these years. There are informative chapters in C. Morazé (ed.), *The nineteenth century, 1775 to 1905* (1977), vol. V of the UNESCO History of Mankind.

The most useful general guides to the era of reconstruction and reorientation after 1815 are two volumes in the Langer series, F. B. Artz, *Reaction and revolution, 1814–1832*° (1934), and W. L. Langer, *Political and social upheaval, 1832–1852*° (1969). Also recommended is G. de Bertier de Sauvigny, *Metternich and his times* (1959, trans. 1967). Brief treatments in various historical series include J. Droz, *Europe between revolutions, 1815–1848*° (1967); C. Breunig, *The age of revolution and reaction, 1789–1850*° (1970); J. Roberts, *Revolution and improvement: the Western world, 1775–1847* (1976); J. L. Talmon, *Romanticism and revolution in Europe, 1815–1848*° (1967); A. J. May,

The age of Metternich, 1815–1848° (rev., 1963); H. Hearder, *Europe in the nineteenth century, 1830–1880*° (1966); and B. D. Gooch, *Europe in the nineteenth century* (1970). E. J. Hobsbawm has written a provocative Marxist survey, *The age of revolution: Europe, 1789–1848*° (1962). For this and the following two chapters, there are valuable sections in vols. IX and X of the New Cambridge Modern History: C. W. Crawley (ed.), *War and peace in an age of upheaval, 1793–1830* (1965), and J. P. T. Bury (ed.), *The zenith of European power 1830–70* (1960), with survey chapters by the editor. An important theme is developed in C. Morazé, *The triumph of the middle classes*° (trans. 1966).

National Histories: Britain

For Britain, the following one-volume accounts focus on the nineteenth century: G. M. Trevelyan, *British history in the nineteenth century and after* [1782–1919] (1922, 1937); A. Wood, *Nineteenth century Britain, 1815–1914* (1960); D. Thomson, *England in the nineteenth century*° (Pelican series, 1950, 1964); and R. W. Seton-Watson, *Britain in Europe, 1789–1914; a survey of foreign policy* (1937). P. Gregg, *Modern Britain: a social and economic history since 1760*° (1967), is especially useful, as is R. K. Webb, *Modern England: from the eighteenth century to the present*° (1968). E. Halévy's classic, *History of the English people in the nineteenth century* (6 vols., 1912 ff.), is a work of breadth and imagination by a French scholar. Many other books on British economic and social history are listed below. A valuable bibliographical guide for the first half of the century is L. M. Brown and I. R. Christie (eds.), *Bibliography of British history, 1789–1851* (1977).

France

The following general histories, some of which have been cited earlier, will be useful: A. Cobban, *A history of modern France*° (3 vols., 1957–1965); P. A. Gagnon, *France since the Revolution*° (1968); D. J. Harvey, *France since the Revolution*° (1968); and G. Wright, *France in modern times: 1760 to the present* (rev., 1974), with excellent bibliographical chapters. Two books that take the post-Napoleonic years as their starting points are J. P. T. Bury, *France, 1814–1940: a history* (rev., 1969), a balanced survey, and D. W. Brogan, *The French nation, 1814–1940; from Napoleon to Pétain*° (1957), brilliant but often too allusive for the general reader. On French society and social developments, there is the somewhat schematic G. Dupeux, *French society, 1789–1970* (trans. 1976). On economic development and policies, in addition to earlier works by A. L. Dunham, *The Industrial Revolution in France, 1815–48* (1955); S. B. Clough, *France, a history of national economics, 1789–1939* (1939); and J. H. Clapham, *The economic development of France and Germany, 1815–1914* (1921, 1936). There are two more recent studies: R. E. Cameron, *France and the economic development of Europe, 1800–1914* (1961, 1968), which stresses the French role in the European economy, and R. Price, *The economic modernization of France* (1975), which deemphasizes political change as a factor in French economic development. For a statistical and sociological examination of labor unrest in this and later periods, see E. Shorter and C. Tilly, *Strikes in France, 1830–1968* (1974).

For France in the years immediately after Napoleon, the best introductions are F. B. Artz, *France under the Bourbon Restoration, 1814–1830* (1931), and G. de Bertier de Sauvigny, *The Bourbon Restoration* (1955, trans. 1966). The somewhat anecdotal J. Lucas-Dubreton, *The Restoration and the July Monarchy* (1929), may be compared with M. R. D. Leys, *Between two Empires* (1955), on the same subject. An informative monograph is D. P. Resnick, *The white terror and the political reaction after Waterloo* (1966). Rising discontents are studied in A. B. Spitzer, *Old hatreds and young hopes: the French Carbonari against the Bourbon Restoration* (1971), and in D. L. Rader, *The journalists and the July Revolution in France* (1973); and for the events of 1830, an outstanding account is D. H. Pinkney, *The French revolution of 1830* (1972). J. M. Merriman has edited *1830 in France*° (1975). Subsequent labor stirrings are ably studied in R. J. Bezucha, *The Lyon uprising of 1834: social and political conflict in the early July Monarchy*

(1974). Focusing on population growth and other pressures in Paris, there is L. Chevalier, *Laboring classes and dangerous classes in Paris during the first half of the nineteenth century* (trans. 1973).

Of J. M. S. Allison's various studies of nineteenth-century France, the widest in scope is his *Monsieur Thiers* (1932). Centering around Guizot, another historian-statesman, there is an admirable study, D. Johnson, *Guizot: aspects of French history, 1787–1874* (1963); and on Guizot and others, S. Mellon, *The political uses of history: a study of historians in the French Restoration* (1958). For a biography of Charles X, one may read V. D. Beach, *Charles X of France: his life and times* (1971), and for Louis Philippe, one may turn to T. Howarth, *Citizen-King* (1961). Studies of conservative ideas and activities are C. T. Muret, *French royalist doctrines since the Revolution* (1933); N. E. Hudson, *Ultra-royalism and the French Restoration* (1936); P. Spencer, *Politics of belief in nineteenth-century France* (1954); P. N. Stearns, *Priest and revolutionary: Lamennais and the dilemma of French Catholicism* (1967); and D. Porch, *Army and revolution: France, 1815–1848* (1974). R. Rémond, *The right wing in France: from 1815 to de Gaulle* (1954, trans. 1966), is useful for this period on into the twentieth century. Special subjects are examined in I. Collins, *The government and the newspaper press in France, 1814–1881* (1959), and in T. D. Beck, *French legislators, 1800–1834: a study in quantitative history* (1974), analyzing the French lawmakers.

Germany

In addition to the histories by R. Flenley, *Modern German history* (rev., 1964); H. Holborn, *History of modern Germany* (3 vols., 1959–1968); and V. Valentin, *The German people* (1946), the following general accounts may be recommended for this and the chapters that follow: E. J. Passant and others, *A short history of Germany, 1815–1945*° (1959); K. S. Pinson, *Modern Germany: its history and civilization* (1954; rev., 1966); A. J. P. Taylor, *The course of German history . . . since 1815*° (1946), shrewd but sometimes antagonistic: M. Dill, Jr., *Germany: a modern history* (1961), in the University of Michigan series; A. Ramm, *Germany, 1789–1914: a political history* (1967), with considerable attention to political thought; W. Carr, *A history of Germany, 1815–1945* (1969); and the impressionistic G. Mann, *History of Germany since 1789* (1959, trans. 1968). E. Vermeil, *Germany's three Reichs: their history and culture* (1945), is a French interpretation. G. A. Craig, *The politics of the Prussian army, 1640–1945** (1955), deals in good part with the nineteenth and twentieth centuries. Political and economic issues are examined in T. Hamerow, *Restoration, revolution, and reaction: economics and politics in Germany, 1815–1871** (1958), and in R. H. Thomas, *Liberalism, nationalism and the German intellectuals, 1822–1847* (1952). Political manipulation over a century and a half is explored in G. L. Mosse, *The nationalization of the masses: political symbolism and mass movements in Germany from the Napoleonic wars through the Third Reich* (1975).

Austria, Poland, Greece, Spain, and Italy

On the Habsburg monarchy after 1815, the best study is C. A. Macartney, *The Habsburg empire, 1790–1918* (1969), a masterful survey. Recommended also are A. Wandruszka, *The house of Habsburg* (1956, trans. 1964); A. J. P. Taylor, *The Habsburg monarchy, 1809–1918** (1943, 1948 revision changes some conclusions), less paradoxical than his history of Germany; and R. Kann, *The multinational empire: nationalism and national reform in the Habsburg monarchy, 1840–1918* (2 vols., 1950–1964), and his shorter *A history of the Habsburg empire, 1526–1918* (1974). An informative brief introduction is B. Jelavich, *The Habsburg empire in European affairs, 1814–1918** (1969). Additional titles are cited in Chapter XIV.

Other European countries in the years 1815 to 1848 are treated in numerous books. For Poland, see in addition to the books cited earlier [O. Halecki, *A history of Poland* (rev., 1956); R. Dyboski, *Poland in world civilization* (1950); and the collaborative *Cambridge history of Poland* (2 vols., 1941–1950]: W. J. Rose, *The rise of Polish democracy* (1944), and R. F. Leslie, *Polish politics and the revolution of November 1830* (1956). For Greece,

the best introductions are C. M. Woodhouse, *A short history of modern Greece* (1968); J. Campbell and P. Sherrard, *Modern Greece* (1968); E. S. Forster, *A short history of modern Greece, 1821–1945* (1941, 1946); the portions on Greece in L. Stavrianos, *The Balkans since 1453* (1958), R. L. Wolff, *The Balkans in our time** (1956); and R. Ristelhueber, *A history of the Balkan peoples* (1950, rev. and trans. 1971). Stavrianos also has written the briefer *The Balkans since 1815** (Berkshire series, 1965). Valuable also for European attitudes toward the Balkans and the Ottoman Empire is M. S. Anderson, *The Eastern question, 1774–1923* (1966).

For Spain, see especially R. Carr, *Spain, 1808–1939* (1966), a volume in the Oxford History of Modern Europe, and S. G. Payne, *Politics and the military in modern Spain* (1967). For Italy, one may turn to A. J. B. Whyte, *The evolution of modern Italy, 1715–1920** (1944, 1950); H. Hearder and P. Waley (eds.), *A short history of Italy** (1963); R. Albrecht-Carrié, *Italy from Napoleon to Mussolini* (1950); S. B. Clough, *The economic history of modern Italy* (1964); and S. B. Clough and S. Saladino, *A history of modern Italy: documents, readings, and commentary* (1968). [Additional books on nineteenth-century developments in these countries are cited in connection with international politics at the end of this chapter and in the next three chapters.]

Industrial Revolution

An authoritative treatment is found in the collaborative Cambridge Economic History of Europe, vol. VI, *The industrial revolutions and after* (2 parts, 1965), to which D. S. Landes' important contribution has been published separately, in expanded form, as *The unbound Prometheus: technological change and industrial development in western Europe from 1750 to the present** (1969). Other illuminating accounts are C. M. Cipolla (ed.), *The emergence of industrial societies* (2 parts, 1973), vols. III and IV of the Fontana Economic History of Europe; and A. S. Milward and S. B. Saul, *The economic development of continental Europe, 1780–1870* (1973). The social and political implications behind the growth of an industrial civilization are examined with much insight in J. McManners, *European history: men, machines, and freedom*° (1967). The complexities of the Industrial Revolution also may be approached through four brief, informative books: T. S. Ashton, *The Industrial Revolution, 1760–1830*° (1948, 1962); W. O. Henderson, *The industrialization of Europe, 1780–1914*° (1969); P. Deane, *The first Industrial Revolution*° (1965); and G. N. Clark, *The idea of the Industrial Revolution* (1953). Advanced technical studies investigating rates of industrial growth in Britain include: W. G. Hoffmann, *British industry, 1700–1950* (trans. 1955); W. W. Rostow, *British economy of the nineteenth century* (1948); and P. Deane and W. A. Cole, *British economic growth, 1688–1959: trends and structure* (1962). Deane and B. R. Mitchell also have edited *Abstract of British historical statistics* (1962). Rostow has utilized the British experience as a model for other areas in *The process of economic growth* (1952) and *The stages of economic growth: a non-communist manifesto*° (1960).

There are many older studies of the rise of industrialism in Britain that have been superseded, including the classic P. Mantoux, *The Industrial Revolution in the eighteenth century*° (1906, 1937). British economic history in these years is studied in detail by T. S. Ashton, *The economic history of England: the eighteenth century* (1955); W. H. B. Court, *A concise economic history of Britain*° (1954); and J. H. Clapham, *An economic history of modern Britain* (3 vols., 1926–1938), which also is available as *A concise economic history of Britain*° (1949). One also may turn to J. D. Chambers, *The workshop of the world: British economic history from 1820 to 1880*° (rev., 1969); S. G. Checkland, *The rise of industrial society in England, 1815–1885* (1964); W. O. Henderson, *Britain and industrial Europe, 1750–1870* (1954); and P. Mathias, *The first industrial nation: an economic history of Britain, 1700–1914* (1969). S. Pollard and C. Holmes have edited a volume of documents, *The process of industrialization, 1750–1870* (1968).

Changes in British agriculture are analyzed in R. E. Prothero [Lord Ernle], *English farming, past and present* (5th ed., 1936); M. E. Seebohm, *The evolution of the English farm* (rev., 1952); R. Trow-Smith, *English husbandry, from the earliest times to the present day* (1951); C. S. Orwin and E. H. Whetham, *History of English agriculture, 1846–1914* (rev., 1964); and the relevant chapters in D. B. Grigg, *The agricultural systems of the world: an evolutionary approach*° (1974). On the changes in the countryside, see also E. C. Wingfield-Stratford, *The squire and his relations* (1956); G. E. Fussell and K. R. Fussell, *The English countryman: his life and work*, A.D. *1500–1900* (1955); and F. M. L. Thompson, *The English landed gentry in the nineteenth century* (1963).

Social and Political Changes in Britain

There is a large and controversial literature on the effects of industrial change on the well-being of the British working classes. J. L. Hammond and B. Hammond in several vehement books such as *The Town labourer, 1760–1832: the new civilization*° (1919) and *The age of the Chartists*° (1930) demonstrated indignantly that the common people were exploited. E. P. Thompson, *The making of the English working class*° (1964), a remarkable study that has had wide influence, marshals evidence to reinforce the picture of exploitation and working-class militancy, as does E. J. Hobsbawm in *Industry and empire: 1750 to the present day* (1968). Hobsbawm also has written *Labouring men: studies in the history of labour*° (1964) and other related books. The books by Ashton, Clark, Deane, and others cited above provide a less bleak view, as do J. T. Ward, *The factory system, 1830–1855* (1962), and M. I. Thomis, *The Industrial Revolution and the town laborer* (1975), but the debate continues. An extremist viewpoint minimizing the evil effects of early industrialism is set forth in a collection of essays edited by F. A. von Hayek, *Capitalism and the historians*° (1954).

For the social and political impact on Britain, the reader may turn to N. Smelser, *Social change in the Industrial Revolution* (1959); P. Laslett, *The world we have lost: England before the industrial age* (1965), cited earlier; D. Marshall, *Industrial England, 1776–1851* (1973); H. Perkin, *The origins of modern English society,*

1780–1880 (1969); and W. R. Ward, *Religion and society in England, 1790–1850* (1972). I. Pinchbeck, *Women workers and the Industrial Revolution, 1750–1850* (1930, reissued 1975), remains valuable.

Also available are volumes by G. D. H. Cole and R. Postgate, *The British people, 1746–1946°* (1957), and Cole, *British working class politics, 1832–1914* (1941), written from a Labour point of view. A. Briggs, *The age of improvement* (1959), is recommended, as are E. L. Woodward, *The age of reform, 1815–1870* (1938), a solid volume in the Oxford History of England; N. Gash, *Politics in the age of Peel, 1830–1850* (1953); and G. S. R. Kitson Clark, *An expanding society: Britain, 1830–1900* (1968). On the Chartists, the many older studies have been superseded by J. T. Ward, *Chartism* (1973), and D. Jones, *Chartism and the Chartists* (1975), although G. D. H. Cole, *Chartist portraits°* (1941), and A. Briggs (ed.), *Chartist studies* (1959), are still useful. R. J. Cruikshank, *Charles Dickens and early Victorian England* (1949), is a colorful study of the novelist and the people he wrote about. Some protest movements of the era are conveyed in R. J. White, *Waterloo to Peterloo* (1957); D. Rend, *Peterloo: the massacre and its background* (1958); E. J. Hobsbawm and G. Rudé, *Captain Swing* (1969), a study of the rural poor and agrarian unrest in the years 1815 to 1830; M. I. Thomis, *The Luddites: machine-breaking in Regency England* (1970); and W. J. Shelton, *English hunger and industrial disorders* (1973), on the riots of the 1760s. E. Gauldie, *Cruel habitations: a history of working class housing, 1790–1918* (1974), covers more than the title implies.

The widening functions of government are analyzed in E. W. Cohen, *The growth of the British civil service, 1780–1939* (1941); M. P. Hall, *The social services of modern England* (rev., 1955); K. B. Smellie, *History of local government* (1946); the monumental S. Webb and B. Webb, *English local government* (9 vols., 1906–1929); and D. Owen, *English philanthropy, 1660–1960* (1964). Social policy in general is sketched in D. Fraser, *The evolution of the British welfare state: a history of social policy since the Industrial Revolution* (1973). Reform legislation

is discussed in M. W. Thomas, *The early factory legislation* (1948), and in J. T. Ward, *The factory system, 1830–1855,* cited above. Other reform movements are examined in D. G. Barnes, *A history of the English Corn Laws, from 1660 to 1846* (1930); N. McCord, *The Anti-Corn-Law League, 1838–1846* (1958); and L. Radzinowicz, *A history of English criminal law: the movement for reform, 1750–1833* (1948). The antislavery movement is treated in M. M. Law, *British slavery and its abolition, 1823–38* (1926); F. J. Klingberg, *The anti-slavery movement in England* (1926); and in two books cited earlier, D. B. Davis, *The problem of slavery in the age of revolution 1770–1823,* and R. Anstey, *The Atlantic slave trade and British abolition, 1760–1810.* Schools and schooling are examined in E. G. West, *Education and the Industrial Revolution* (1975), and the plight of children, especially of the poorer classes, in the provocative wide-ranging I. Pinchbeck and M. Hewitt, *Children in English society,* cited earlier, covering from the fifteenth to the mid-twentieth centuries. A different subject is explored in R. W. Malcolmson, *Popular recreations in English society, 1700–1850* (1973). Books on socialism and trade unionism are cited elsewhere in this chapter and in Chapter XIV.

On the Reform Bill of 1832, the outstanding study is M. Brock, *The Great Reform Act°* (1973). For thinkers and reformers of the age, there are available E. Halévy, *The growth of philosophic radicalism* (3 vols., 1901–1904; 1 vol., 1949); L. Stephen, *The English utilitarians* (3 vols., 1900); S. Maccoby, *English radicalism* (5 vols., 1935–1955); J. Bowle, *Politics and opinion in the nineteenth century°* (1954); D. C. Somervell, *English thought in the nineteenth century°* (1929, 1962); and C. Brinton, *English political thought in the nineteenth century°* (1933, 1950). An interesting study is S. R. Letwin, *The pursuit of certainty: David Hume, Jeremy Bentham, John Stuart Mill, Beatrice Webb* (1965). [Other books on Mill are listed below.] Among biographies, there are M. Mack on Jeremy Bentham (1963); G. D. H. Cole on William Cobbett (1924) and on Robert Owen (1930); studies of Owen by F. Podmore (1924) and M. Cole (1953); G. M. Trevelyan,

Lord Grey of the Reform Bill (1920, 1929); N. Gash, *Peel* (1976), a condensation of his outstanding larger work (2 vols., 1968–1972); C. R. Fay, *Huskisson and his age* (1951); G. Wallas, *The life of Francis Place, 1771–1854* (1898, 1925); C. Driver, *Tory radical: the life of Richard Oastler* (1946); and G. F. A. Best, *Shaftsbury* (1964). On the pioneer feminist of the age, there are biographies of Mary Wollstonecraft by R. M. Wardle (1951), M. George (1970), C. Tomalin (1974), and especially E. Flexner° (1972). A notable historian is ably portrayed in J. Clive, *Macaulay: the shaping of the historian* (1973).

Among important studies of the Victorian Age, some going beyond the scope of this chapter, are G. M. Young, *Victorian England: portrait of an age°* (2 vols., 1934); A. Briggs, *Victorian cities* (1965) and *Victorian people°* (1955); O. Chadwick, *The Victorian Church, 1829–1860* (1966); E. R. Norman, *Church and society in England, 1770–1970* (1976); W. E. Houghton, *The Victorian frame of mind, 1830–1870* (1957); S. Marcus, *The other Victorians°* (1966); and E. Trudgill, *Madonnas and Magdalens: the origins and development of Victorian sexual attitudes* (1976).

The "Isms" and Social Thought— General

Among a number of works stressing nineteenth-century social thought are C. Brinton, *Political ideas of the English romanticists* (1926); J. Barzun, *Romanticism and the modern ego* (1943) and *Berlioz and the romantic century* (2 vols., 1950); D. O. Evans, *Social romanticism in France, 1830–1848* (1951); and B. Croce, *European literature in the nineteenth century* (1924). G. Brandes, *Main currents in nineteenth century thought* (6 vols., 1872–1890, trans. from Danish, 1901–1906), is still useful. Political and other meanings of romanticism are analyzed in R. F. Cleckner and G. E. Ensco (eds.), *Romanticism* (1962). Other notable studies of the interplay of ideas and politics include H. Marcuse, *Reason and revolution: Hegel and the rise of social theory* (1941); F. Wiedemann, *Hegel* (1968); B. T. Wilkins, *Hegel's philosophy of history* (1974); G. O. Griffith, *Interpreters of man: a review of secular and religious thought from Hegel to Barth* (1943); T. Whittaker, *Reason: a philosophical essay with historical illustrations: Comte, Mill, Schopenhauer, Vico, Spinoza* (1943); P. Roubiczek, *The misrepresentation of man: studies in European thought in the nineteenth century* (1947); M. Peckham, *Beyond the tragic vision: the quest for identity in the nineteenth century°* (1962); and J. L. Talmon, *Political messianism: the romantic phase* (1960).

On conservative and nationalist implications of "scientific" history, see T. H. Von Laue, *Leopold von Ranke: the formative years* (1950), and G. G. Iggers, *The German conception of history . . . from Herder to the present* (1968). A bold, somewhat complex book is H. White, *Metahistory: the historical imagination in nineteenth century Europe* (1973). D. Thomson, *Equality* (1949), and A. Rosenberg, *Democracy and socialism: a contribution to the political history of the past 150 years* (1939), both explore some of the problems posed by the French Revolution for the nineteenth and twentieth centuries. F. E. Manuel, *The prophets of Paris°* (1962), cited earlier, stresses the link between Enlightenment ideas and nineteenth-century social thought. P. Viereck, *Metapolitics: the roots of the Nazi mind°* (1941, 1961), and R. D. O. Butler, *The roots of national socialism* (1942), are two attempts to explain Nazism in historical terms—a procedure that can, of course, be quite unfair to the nineteenth century. E. Golob, *The "isms": a history and evaluation* (1954), is useful but less comprehensive than the title implies. On political alignments, D. Caute, *The left in Europe since 1789°* (1966), may be supplemented by H. Rogger and E. Weber (eds.), *The European right: a historical profile°* (1965).

Nationalism

The vast literature on this subject may be approached through the following: C. J. H. Hayes, *The historical evolution of modern nationalism* (1931, 1948); H. Kohn, *The idea of nationalism: a study in its origin and background* (1944), from Hebraic and Hellenic times: L. L. Snyder, *Varieties of nationalism: a comparative study* (1976), a convenient introduction; and B. C. Shafer, *Faces of nationalism:*

new realities and old myths (1972). Also useful are E. Kedourie, *Nationalism** (1966); K. W. Deutsch, *Nationalism and social communication** (1953, 1966); K. Deutsch and W. J. Folz (eds.), *Nation-building** (1963); and K. R. Minogue, *Nationalism* (1967). E. Kamenka (ed.), *Nationalism: the nature and evolution of an idea* (1976), is a collection of provocative essays. F. M. Barnard, *Herder's social and political thought: from Enlightenment to nationalism* (1965), focuses on cultural nationalism, and R. Schlesinger, *Federalism in central and eastern Europe* (1945), examines the interrelationship of various nationalities living close together. On language, the following may be consulted: J. Vendryes, *Language: a linguistic introduction to history* (1925, 1949); K. Vossler, *The spirit of language in civilization* (1932); and F. Bodmer, *The loom of language* (1944). C. Lévi-Strauss, *Structural anthropology** (trans. 1963), and other writings also are of prime importance. On a sometimes neglected element in nationalism, C. Rearick has written *Beyond the Enlightenment: historians and folklore in nineteenth-century France* (1974). B. C. Shafer has contributed to the American Historical Association Pamphlets series *Nationalism: interpretations and interpreters** (1976).

Liberalism

G. de Ruggiero, *The history of European liberalism* (1927), a comparative analysis of English, French, German, and Italian liberalism, has long been a fundamental work on this subject. L. T. Hobhouse, *Liberalism* (1911), is a valuable little companion to the sections on England, and J. H. Hallowell, *The decline of liberalism as an ideology* (1943), argues on the basis of German experience that liberalism is lost if separated from ideas of absolute truth and value. B. Croce, *History of Europe in the nineteenth century* (1933), a philosophical and historical treatment of the idea of liberty, may be compared with H. J. Muller, *Freedom in the modern world** (1966), the final volume of a three-volume study (1952–1966). On German political ideas, one may profitably compare L. Krieger, *The German idea of freedom* (1957); H. Kohn, *The mind of Germany: the education of a nation* (1960);

and K. Epstein, *The genesis of German conservatism* (1966). There are studies of de Tocqueville by J. P. Mayer (1939), R. Herr (1960), and D. S. Goldstein (1976). J. S. Schapiro, *Liberalism and the challenge of fascism: social forces in England and France, 1815–1870* (1949), deals with the concurrent growth of liberal and antiliberal ideas; and B. Russell, *Freedom vs. organization, 1814–1914** (1934, 1947), shows the dilemma of liberalism in a period of rapid economic change. The most provocative book of all on liberalism remains H. J. Laski, *The rise of European liberalism** (1936, 1947), which sees it as the gradual taming of a revolutionary doctrine. Among many books on John Stuart Mill, there are the interesting and controversial G. Himmelfarb, *On liberty and liberalism: the case of John Stuart Mill* (1974); M. Packe, *John Stuart Mill* (1954); A. Ryan, *J. S. Mill** (1975); F. L. Van Holthoon, *The road to utopia: . . . John Stuart Mill's social thought* (1971); and B. Mazlish, *James and John Stuart Mill: father and son in the nineteenth century* (1975), an interesting effort at psychohistory. A. Rossi has edited John Stuart and Harriet Taylor Mill, *Essays on sex equality* (1970). Two useful anthologies are A. Bullock and M. Shock (eds.), *The liberal tradition** (1957), and D. Sidorsky (ed.), *The liberal tradition in European thought** (1970).

Socialism

Among general surveys are H. W. Laidler, *History of socialism* (rev., 1968); P. Taft, *Movements for economic reform* (1950); and N. I. Mackenzie, *Socialism: a short history* (1949). A. Gray, *The socialist tradition: Moses to Lenin** (1946), is a witty, unsympathetic account. G. Lichtheim, *A short history of socialism** (1970), and other writings by the same author are highly recommended.

A large-scale comprehensive study, stressing the interaction of men, movements, and ideas is G. D. H. Cole, *A history of socialist thought* (4 vols., 1953–1956), covering the years 1789–1939. C. Landauer, *European socialism: a history of ideas and movements from the Industrial Revolution to Hitler's seizure of power* (2 vols., 1959), is also useful, as is L. Derfler, *Socialism since Marx: a century of* the European left* (1973), which is brief and informative. A valuable bibliography as well as thoughtful essays are available in D. D. Egbert, S. Persons, and T. Bassett (eds.), Socialism and American life (2 vols., 1952), part of which is concerned with the European setting; vol. II is entirely devoted to a descriptive and critical bibliography of socialism. Egbert also has written Social radicalism and the arts (1970), on cultural changes affected by political developments since 1789. E. H. Carr, Studies in revolution (1950), is a series of incisive essays on earlier and later socialists. Some useful studies of pre-Marxian anticapitalism are G. G. Iggers, The cult of authority: the political cult of the Saint-Simonians (1958); F. E. Manuel, The new world of Henri Saint-Simon (1956); D. W. Brogan, Proudhon (1934); and H. de Lubac, The un-Marxian socialist: a study of Proudhon (1948). [Additional literature on socialism and Marxism appears in Chapters XII and XIV.] A. Fried and R. Sanders, Socialist thought: a documentary history* (1964), is a useful anthology.

Economic Thought

For the development of economic ideas, one may turn to C. Gide and C. Rist, History of economic doctrines, E. Roll, A history of economic thought, and E. Heimann, History of economic doctrines, all mentioned in the introductory section. E. Whittaker, Schools and streams of economic thought (1960), contains an illuminating section on Adam Smith's moral and economic ideas, which may be read along with J. Rae's older biography (1895), but D. A. Riesman, Adam Smith's sociological economics (1976), best communicates the economic philosopher's unified thought. R. Heilbroner, The worldly philosophers,* cited earlier, also is useful on the economic liberals. A sprightly series of essays on economic thinkers from Adam Smith to the present is J. K. Galbraith, The age of uncertainty (1977).

International Politics after the Congress of Vienna

In addition to the books cited at the end of Chapter X and at the beginning of this chapter, the reader may turn to W. A. Phillips, The confederation of Europe: a study of the European alliance 1813–1823 (1914, 1920); E. L. Woodward, War and peace in Europe, 1815–1870, and other essays (1931); and H. G. Schenk, The aftermath of the Napoleonic wars: the concert of Europe—an experiment (1947). H. Kissinger, A world restored: Metternich, Castlereagh and the problems of peace, 1812–1822, already cited, discusses the balancing of power politics and ideology before the author became a practitioner of the art. I. C. Nichols, Jr., analyzes the congress system in action in The European pentarchy and the Congress of Verona, 1822 (1971). P. Viereck, Conservatism revisited: the revolt against revolt, 1815–1949* (1949, 1965), attempts to rehabilitate the reputations of the post-1815 conservatives, especially Metternich. On the latter, there are sympathetic biographies by A. Herman (1932) and H. du Coudray (1935), and a valuable study by P. W. Schroeder, Metternich's diplomacy at its zenith, 1820–1823 (1962).

British foreign affairs may be followed through these books and through C. K. Webster, The foreign policy of Castlereagh, 1815–1822 (1925); C. J. Bartlett, Castlereagh (1967); J. Derry, Castlereagh (1976); H. Temperley, The foreign policy of Canning, 1822–1827 (1925); W. Hinde, George Canning (1973); P. Dixon, Canning: politician and statesman (1976); H. C. F. Bell, Lord Palmerston (2 vols., 1936); P. Guedalla, Palmerston, 1784–1865 (1927, 1942); and D. Southgate, 'The most English minister' . . . the policies and politics of Palmerston (1966). C. Howard, Britain and the casus belli, 1822–1902 (1974), is a series of interpretive essays focusing on the foreign ministers.

The situation arising from the interest of the European powers in Latin America is presented in D. Perkins, A history of the Monroe Doctrine (1941, 1963); C. K. Webster, Britain and the independence of Latin America, 1812–1830 (1944); A. P. Whitaker, The United States and the independence of Latin America, 1800–1830 (1941); D. C. M. Platt, Latin America and British trade, 1806–1914 (1973); and the detailed study of Anglo-American relations in the years 1775–1823 by B. Perkins, cited earlier (3 vols., 1955–1964). Two biographical introductions to the subject are J. B. Trend, Bolivar and the independence of Spanish America* (Teach Yourself History series, 1948), and J. Kinsbrunner, *Bernardo O'Higgins*° (1968). Accounts of the independence movements are J. Lynch, *The Spanish American revolutions, 1808–1821* (1973), and R. Graham, *Independence in Latin America*° (1972). M. Savelle, *Empires to nations* (1974), examines the birth of nations in the late eighteenth and early nineteenth centuries in the Western Hemisphere.

Other important stirrings in the same period are described in C. M. Woodhouse, *The Greek war of independence* (1952); D. Howarth, *The Greek adventure* (1976), a narrative account; two volumes (one of essays, the other of documents) edited by R. Clogg: *The struggle for Greek independence: essays to mark the 150th anniversary . . .* (1973) and *The movement for Greek independence, 1770–1821* (1976); J. H. Brady, *Rome and the Neapolitan revolution of 1820–21* (1937); and G. T. Romani, *The Neapolitan revolution of 1820–1821* (1950). For developments in Russia, one may consult A. G. Mazour, *The first Russian revolution, 1825: the Decembrist movement*° (1937); M. Zetlin, *The Decembrists* (1958); and M. Raeff, *The Decembrist movement* (1966), a narrative with documents.

Two stimulating books on international affairs transcending this chapter are L. C. B. Seaman, *From Vienna to Versailles*° (1956), and W. N. Medlicott (ed.), *From Metternich to Hitler: aspects of British and foreign history, 1814–1939*° (1963). A useful reference tool is G. A. Kertesz (ed.), *Documents in the political history of the European continent, 1815–1939* (1969).

Problems and Readings°

Relevant pamphlets include G. A. Cahill (ed.), *The great Reform Bill of 1832: liberal or conservative?* (1969); J. M. Merriman (ed.), *1830 in France* (1975); J. B. Halsted (ed.), *Romanticism: definition, explanation, and evaluation* (1965); H. F. Schwarz (ed.), *Metternich: the "coachman of Europe": statesman or evil genius?* (1962); and M. Walker (ed.), *Metternich's Europe, 1815–1848* (1968). Social and economic themes are explored in P. A. M. Taylor (ed.), *The Industrial Revolution in Britain: triumph or disaster?* (1958); M. L. McDougall (ed.), *The*

working class in modern Europe (1975); A. Lees and L. Lees (eds.), *The urbanization of European society in the nineteenth century* (1976); and A. Esler (ed.), *The youth revolution: conflict of generations in modern history* (1974). Many pamphlets of essays and readings in the Anvil series are useful: H. Kohn, *Nationalism: its meaning and history* (1955); P. Viereck, *Conservatism: from John Adams to Churchill* (1956); J. S. Schapiro, *Liberalism: its meaning and history* (1958); the same author's *Movements of social dissent in modern Europe* (1962); J. H. Stewart, *The Restoration era in France, 1814–1830* (1968); and P. Beik, *Louis Philippe and the July Monarchy* (1965). On Latin American subjects, two titles are useful: R. A. Humphreys and J. Lynch, *The origins of the Latin American revolutions, 1808–1826* (1967), and J. J. Johnson, *Simon Bolivar and Spanish-American independence, 1783–1830* (1968).

XII: REVOLUTION AND THE REIMPOSITION OF ORDER, 1848–1870

The best introduction to the immediate background, the events of 1848, and their aftermath is W. L. Langer, *Political and social upheaval, 1832–1852*° (1969), in the series edited by the author. Other useful general studies include P. S. Robertson, *Revolutions of 1848: a social history*° (1952); P. N. Stearns, *1848: the revolutionary tide in Europe*° (1974); J. Sigman, *1848: the romantic and democratic revolutions in Europe* (trans. 1973); and the brief G. Fasel, *Europe in upheaval: the revolutions of 1848*° (1970). Also recommended are F. Fejtö, *The opening of an era: 1848, an historical symposium* (1948); A. Whitridge, *Men in crisis: the revolutions of 1848* (1949), studies of leading personalities in various countries; and J. Eastwood and P. Tabori, *'48, the year of revolutions* (1948), a journalistic survey garnished with *Punch* cartoons. Two studies opening with this period are G. Woodcock, *A hundred years of revolution: 1848 and after* (1948), and R. J. Cruikshank, *Roaring century, 1846–1946* (1946), colorful sketches from the files of the London *Daily Mail*. A special subject is well treated in C. B. Woodham-Smith, *The great hunger: Ireland 1845–1849* (1962).

Revolutions in Various Countries

In addition to the general accounts described above and in the previous chapter, the following are useful on the ferment of 1815–1850 and on the revolutions of 1848–1849 in the various European countries:

FRANCE.   R. Arnaud, *The Second Republic and Napoleon III* (1930), an older narrative account; G. Duveau, *The making of a revolution*° (trans. 1968); R. Price, *The French Second Republic: a social history* (1972); F. A. De Luna, *The French Republic under Cavaignac* (1969); D. C. McKay, *The national workshops: a study in the French Revolution of 1848* (1933); P. H. Amann, *Revolutions and mass democracy: the Paris club movement in 1848* (1976); and L. Loubère, *Louis Blanc: . . . the rise of French Jacobin socialism* (1961). R. Price has edited *Revolution and reaction: 1848 and the Second French Republic* (1976).

ITALY.   G. F. H. Berkeley and J. Berkeley, *Italy in the making* (3 vols., 1932–1940); G. M. Trevelyan, *Garibaldi's defense of the Roman republic, 1848–1849* (1907, 1949); and the same author's *Manin and the Venetian revolution of 1848* (1923). Also recommended: M. C. Wicks, *The Italian exiles in London, 1816–1848* (1937); R. J. Rath, *The provisional Austrian regime in Lombardy-Venetia, 1814–1815* (1968); K. R. Greenfield, *Economics and liberalism in the Risorgimento: . . . nationalism in Lombardy, 1814–1848* (1934); R. Grew, *A sterner plan for Italian unity: the Italian National Society and the Risorgimento* (1963); A. J. P. Taylor, *The Italian problem in European diplomacy, 1847–1849* (1934); and three books by E. E. Y. Hales: *Pio Nono* [Pius IX], *a study in European politics and religion in the nineteenth century* (1954), *Revolution and papacy, 1769–1846* (1960), and *Mazzini and the secret societies* (1956).

HABSBURG LANDS.   J. Redlich, *Emperor Francis Joseph of Austria* (1929), an absorbing biography; J. Blum, *Noble landowners and agriculture in Austria, 1815–1848: . . . the origins of the peasant emancipation of 1848* (1948); A. Schwarzenberg, *Prince Felix zu Schwarzenberg, prime minister of Austria, 1848–1852*

(1947); B. K. Király, *Ferenc Deák* (1975), a balanced account of the humanitarian liberal; R. J. Rath, *The Viennese revolution of 1848* (1957); and S. Z. Pech, *The Czech revolution of 1848* (1969). Metternich's career and fall are recounted in books listed earlier.

GERMANY AND THE FRANKFURT ASSEMBLY. V. Valentin, *1848: chapters of German history* (1940), an abridgment of the author's larger study in German; L. B. Namier, *1848: the revolution of the intellectuals*° (1946), sharply critical of the Frankfurt Assembly; and F. Eyck, *The Frankfurt Parliament, 1848–1849* (1968), a detailed account of the assembly itself. The impact of the failure of 1848 on German society is explored in E. Kohn-Bramstedt, *Aristocracy and the middle-classes in Germany: social types in German literature, 1830–1900* (1937). Many works relevant to the revolution of 1848 in various countries are also listed in the following chapter in connection with the successful unification movements.

Marx and Marxism

The best recent biography of Marx is D. McLellan, *Karl Marx: his life and thought* (1973). There are numerous others, including studies by M. Beer (1921, 1935), E. H. Carr (1938), F. Mehring (1918, 1948), R. Payne (1968), O. Rühle (1929, 1943), L. Schwarzchild (1947), C. J. Sprigge° (1949), and I. Berlin (rev., 1963). J. H. Jackson, *Marx, Proudhon, and European socialism*° (Teach Yourself History series, 1958), helps to provide the European setting. G. Mayer, *Friedrich Engels: a biography* (1920, 1936), and S. Marcus, *Engels, Manchester, and the working class* (1974), help to show that Engels played a greater role than previously realized; and D. Footman, *Ferdinand Lassalle: romantic revolutionary* (1946), is a colorful picture of the reformist socialist that by no means supersedes earlier biographies by E. Bernstein (1893), W. H. Dawson (1899), and G. Brandes (1925). The story of Marx's daughter is skillfully told in C. Tsuzuki, *The life of Eleanor Marx* (1967).

On the theoretical foundations and concrete manifestations of socialism, there is, of course, an enormous and highly controversial literature, to which the books cited under socialism for Chapter XI and those cited for Chapter XIV offer a certain amount of guidance; much current discussion stresses the relationship between Marx's mature thought and his early writings. Of efforts to rehabilitate the humanistic elements in the younger Marx on the basis of manuscripts now available, one of the most successful is R. N. Hunt, *The political ideas of Marx and Engels*, vol. I, *Marxism and totalitarian democracy, 1818–1850* (1976), the first of two projected volumes. Informative, interpretive accounts include R. Tucker, *The Marxian revolutionary idea** (1969) and *Philosophy and myth in Karl Marx* (rev., 1972); A. G. Meyer, *Marxism: unity of theory and practice** (1957); G. Lichtheim, *Marxism: an historical and critical study** (1961) and *A short history of socialism*,* already cited; S. Avineri, *The social and political thought of Karl Marx* (1969); B. D. Wolfe, *Marxism: one hundred years in the life of a doctrine* (1965); and G. D. H. Cole, *The meaning of Marxism** (1948). D. Childs, *Marx and the Marxists: an outline of practice and theory* (1973), is a brief introduction for the general reader. H. J. Laski wrote widely and incisively on socialism, and some of his keenest observations appear in his centennial edition of the Manifesto, *The Communist Manifesto: socialist landmark* (1948), which also contains the original text and prefaces by Marx and Engels. E. Wilson, *To the Finland station: a study in the writing and acting of history** (1940), is an imaginative discussion of the way in which early and later socialists, and nonsocialists, interpreted the past to influence the present. M. M. Bober, *Karl Marx's interpretation of history** (1927, 1948), is a technical study, as is H. Lefebvre, *The sociology of Marx* (1966, trans. 1968).

For Comte and positivism, W. M. Simon, *European positivism in the nineteenth century* (1963), may be supplemented by D. G. Charlton, *Positivist thought in France during the Second Empire* (1959). G. Lenzer has edited *Auguste Comte and positivism: the essential writings** (1975).

Napoleon III and Bonapartism

Readable and informative works are J. M. Thompson, *Louis Napoleon and the Second Empire** (1954); three books by R. L. Williams: *The world of Napoleon III** (1957, 1965), *The mortal Napoleon III* (1971), and *Manners and murders in the world of Louis Napoleon* (1975); T. A. B. Corley, *Democratic despot: a life of Napoleon III* (1961); B. D. Gooch, *The Second Empire: the reign of Napoleon III** (1969); and D. Kulstein, *Napoleon III and the working class* (1969). Other studies include T. Zeldin, *The political system of Napoleon III* (1958); G. P. Gooch, *The Second Empire* (1960), a series of judicious essays; and H. C. Payne, *The police state of Louis Napoleon Bonaparte, 1851–1860* (1966), although the title is misleading. Interesting interpretations appear in H. A. L. Fisher, *Bonapartism* (1908, 1914); A. Guérard's two books, *Reflections on the Napoleonic legend* (1924) and *Napoleon III: an interpretation* (1943); W. H. C. Smith, *Napoleon III* (1973), with a portrait similar to that of Guérard; and J. S. Schapiro, *Liberalism and the challenge of fascism*, already cited. Economic aspects are studied in A. L. Dunham, *The Anglo-French treaty of commerce of 1860* (1930), and the same author's *The Industrial Revolution in France*, already cited. A special subject is ably treated in R. D. Anderson, *Education in France, 1848–1870* (1975). On the rebuilding of Paris, one may turn to D. Pinkney, *Napoleon III and the rebuilding of Paris** (1958), and J. M. Chapman and B. Chapman, *The life and times of Baron Haussmann* (1957). A scholarly effort to rehabilitate the empress is H. Kurtz, *The Empress Eugénie, 1826–1920* (1964), which may be supplemented by N. N. Barker, *Distaff diplomacy: the Empress Eugénie and the foreign policy of the Second Empire* (1967).

Problems and Readings*

Three booklets are useful: M. Kranzberg (ed.), *1848: a turning point?* (1959); S. M. Osgood (ed.), *Napoleon III and the Second Empire* (1973); and B. D. Gooch (ed.), *Napoleon III, man of destiny: enlightened statesman or proto-fascist?* (1963). In the Anvil series, there are G. Bruun, *Revolution and reaction, 1848–1852: a midcentury watershed* (1958), and S. Hook, *Marx and the Marxists: the ambiguous legacy* (1955).

XIII: THE CONSOLIDATION OF LARGE NATION-STATES, 1859–1871

R. C. Binkley, *Realism and nationalism, 1852–1871*° (1935), in the Langer series, is a valiant effort to clarify the segment of European history that followed the revolutions of 1848; a good synthesis of the era is also provided in N. Rich, *The age of nationalism and reform, 1850–1890*° (1970). J. P. T. Bury (ed.), *The zenith of European power, 1830–1871*, already cited, in the New Cambridge Modern History, has many informative chapters. An outstanding attempt to view the period 1848–1918 as a whole, from the point of view of international affairs, is A. J. P. Taylor, *The struggle for mastery in Europe, 1848–1918* (1954). As a sequel to his earlier volume for the years 1789 to 1848, E. J. Hobsbawm has continued his provocative Marxist analysis in *The age of capital, 1848–1875* (1976), adding a global dimension to his account, and useful for this and the following two chapters. [Books on nationalism and on the earlier phases of national unification have been cited in Chapters XI and XII.]

The Crimean War

Some salient features of the Eastern question and of the Crimean War are treated in detail in M. S. Anderson, *The Eastern question, 1774–1923*, cited earlier; H. Temperley, *England and the Near East: the Crimea* (1936); V. J. Puryear, *England, Russia, and the Straits question, 1844–1856* (1931); and G. B. Henderson, *Crimean War diplomacy, and other historical essays* (1947). An impressive, detailed account rehabilitating Austrian policy is P. W. Schroeder, *Austria, Great Britain, and the Crimean War: the destruction of the European concert* (1972). A dramatic episode of the war is skillfully recounted in C. B. Woodham-Smith, *The reason why*° (1953), and the same author has written a biography of Florence Nightingale (1957). The impact on England is discussed in O. Anderson, *A liberal state at war: English politics and economics during the Crimean War* (1967). The military aspects are treated in L. F. V. Blake, *The Crimean War* (1972), and in P. Warner, *The Crimean War: a reappraisal* (1973). On the changing nature of warfare emerging in this era, see C. B. Falls, *A hundred years of war*° (1954).

Unification of Italy

A useful introduction is C. Beales, *The Risorgimento and the unification of Italy* (1971). In addition to the works cited on Italy for the two foregoing chapters, the following older accounts are still rewarding: W. R. Thayer, *The life and times of Cavour* (2 vols., 1911); A. J. Whyte, *The political life and letters of Cavour, 1848–1861* (1930); and two lively studies by G. M. Trevelyan: *Garibaldi and the Thousand* (1909, 1920) and *Garibaldi and the making of Italy* (1911, 1920). C. Hibbert, *Garibaldi and his enemies: the clash of arms and personalities in the making of Italy* (1966), is a sound, popular account. Highly recommended are three volumes by D. Mack Smith: *Cavour and Garibaldi in 1860* (1954), *Garibaldi: a great life in brief* (1956), and *Victor Emmanuel, Cavour, and the Risorgimento* (1971). G. O. Griffith, *Mazzini: prophet of modern Europe* (1932), is the best biography of Mazzini, but S. Barr, *Mazzini: portrait of an exile* (1935), is stimulating, and G. Salvemini, *Mazzini*° (1910, 1957), is still useful. J. Ridley, *Garibaldi* (1975), is a detailed biography. An informative special study is L. M. Case, *Franco-Italian relations, 1860–1865* (1932).

Bismarck and the Founding of the Second Reich

The outstanding study of the economic basis for unification is W. O. Henderson, *The Zollverein* (1939), supplemented by his larger work, *The rise of German industrial power, 1834–1914*° (1976), but see also A. H. Price, *The evolution of the Zollverein* (1949). H. Friedjung, *The struggle for supremacy in Germany, 1859–1866* (1897, trans. 1935), is a detailed diplomatic and military account by an Austrian historian; and on the key campaign of 1866, G. A. Craig has written *The battle of Königgrätz* (1964). On the events of 1870, recommended studies include L. D. Steefel, *Bismarck, the Hohenzollern candidacy, and the origins of the Franco-German War of 1870* (1962); H. Oncken, *Napoleon III and the Rhine: the origin of* the war of 1870–71 (1928); W. E. Mosse, *The European powers and the German question* (1958); and R. Millman, *British foreign policy and the coming of the Franco-Prussian War* (1965). The relevant documents on the origins of the war of 1870 are available in G. Bonnin (ed.), *Bismarck and the Hohenzollern candidature for the Spanish throne* (1957).

E. Eyck's extensive biography of Bismarck (3 vols., 1941–1944) is not translated, but a summary of Eyck's conclusions, *Bismarck and the German empire*° (1950), is available. W. N. Medlicott, *Bismarck and modern Germany*° (Teach Yourself History series, 1965), is an excellent brief introduction. Other studies of Bismarck include C. G. Robertson, *Bismarck* (1919); A. J. P. Taylor, *Bismarck: the man and the statesman*° (1955); F. Darmstaedter, *Bismarck and the creation of the Second Reich* (1949); L. L. Snyder, *The blood and iron chancellor: a documentary biography of Otto von Bismarck* (1967); and W. Richter, *Bismarck* (trans. 1965). The Prussian phase is studied in E. N. Anderson, *The social and political conflict in Prussia, 1858–1864* (1954). Two important works on the entire period are O. Pflanze, *Bismarck and the development of Germany: the period of unification, 1815–71* (vol. I, 1963), with a second volume projected on the period of consolidation, 1871–1890; and T. S. Hamerow, *The social foundations of German unification, 1858–1871* (2 vols., 1969–1972). An important study of Bismarck's Jewish financial advisor, illuminating much of German history during these years, is F. Stern, *Gold and iron: Bismarck, Bleichröder and the building of the German empire* (1977). An admirable study of military and other phases of the Franco-Prussian War is M. Howard, *The Franco-Prussian War: the German invasion of France, 1870–1871*° (1961).

For Austria-Hungary, the volumes by C. A. Macartney and others, cited in Chapter XI, should be consulted, as well as O. Jászi, *The dissolution of the Habsburg monarchy* (1929); A. J. May, *The Habsburg monarchy, 1867–1914*° (1951); and F. R. Bridge, *From Sadowa to Sarajevo: the foreign policy of Austria-Hungary, 1866–1914* (1972). A special subject is ably explored in G. E. Rothenberg, *The army of Francis Joseph* (1976).

The Russia of Alexander II

An authoritative treatment of nineteenth-century Russia is provided in H. Seton-Watson, *The Russian empire, 1801–1917* (1967), in the Oxford History of Modern Europe; in his *Decline of imperial Russia, 1855–1914*° (1952); and in R. Pipes, *Russia under the old regime* (1975). On the reign of the five emperors from Alexander I to Nicholas II, S. Harcave has written *Years of the golden cockerel: the last Romanov tsars, 1814–1917* (1968). On the reforms of Alexander II, one may turn to W. E. Mosse, *Alexander II and the modernization of Russia*° (1958), and to S. Graham, *Tsar of freedom: the life and reign of Alexander II* (1935), a sympathetic biography. The place of the peasant emancipation in Russian history may be studied in J. Blum, *Lord and peasant in Russia from the ninth to the nineteenth century,*° already cited, which carries the story to emancipation; G. Pavlovsky, *Agricultural Russia on the eve of the Revolution* (1930); G. T. Robinson, *Rural Russia under the old regime*° (1930, 1949); T. Emmons, *The Russian landed gentry and the peasant emancipation of 1861* (1968); and W. S. Vucinich (ed.), *The peasant in nineteenth-century Russia*° (1968).

The following are also useful for these years: M. B. Petrovich, *The emergence of Russian Pan-Slavism, 1856–1870* (1956); W. L. Blackwell, *The beginnings of Russian industrialization, 1800–1860* (1968); and J. S. Curtiss, *The Russian army under Nicholas I, 1825–1855* (1965). A special subject is explored in R. F. Leslie, *Reform and insurrection in Russian Poland, 1856–1865* (1963). The intellectual world is studied in D. Hecht, *Russian radicals look to America, 1825–1894* (1947); E. H. Carr's books, *The romantic exiles: a nineteenth century portrait gallery*° (1933, 1949) and *Michael Bakunin* (1937); and N. V. Riasanovsky, *Russia and the West in the teaching of the Slavophiles* (1952). An interesting interpretive account is J. Westwood, *Endurance and endeavor: Russian history, 1812–1971*° (1973). Other books on prerevolutionary Russia are described in Chapter XVII.

The United States, Canada

A rich literature has developed on the slave experience in America, of which the following is a sample of recent writings: E. D. Genovese, *Roll, Jordan, roll: the world the slaves made* (1974); H. G. Gutman, *The black family in slavery and freedom, 1750–1925* (1976); and the controversial R. W. Fogel and S. L. Engerman, *Time on the cross*° (2 vols., 1974), on the economic profitability of slavery. The best overall treatment of its subject is J. H. Franklin, *From slavery to freedom: a history of Negro Americans* (rev., 1974). A brief survey of the great mid-century conflict is P. J. Parish, *The American Civil War*° (1975), while the Reconstruction period may be approached through K. M. Stampp, *The era of Reconstruction, 1865–1877* (1965). Standard works on the European implications of the American struggle include E. D. Adams, *Great Britain and the American Civil War* (2 vols., 1925), and D. Jordan and E. J. Pratt, *Europe and the American Civil War* (1931).

A useful introduction to all subjects relating to Canada is G. M. Craig, *The United States and Canada* (1968), in the American Foreign Policy Library series. The growth of Canadian self-government within an imperial framework is discussed in D. G. Creighton, *Dominion of the North, a history of Canada* (1944), and external affairs in J. B. Brebner, *North Atlantic triangle: the interplay of Canada, the United States and Great Britain* (1945). The Australian story is ably recounted in the collaborative F. K. Crowley (ed.), *A new history of Australia* (1975).

Japan and the West

G. B. Sansom's two books, *Japan: a short cultural history* (rev., 1962) and *The Western world and Japan* (1950), describe Japanese civilization before and during the nineteenth century, respectively. His detailed multivolumed history carries the narrative to 1867 (3 vols., 1958–1964). Two excellent accounts by E. O. Reischauer, *Japan: the story of a nation*° (rev., 1977) and *The United States and Japan*° (rev., 1065), are highly recommended. Also recommended are H. Borton, *Japan's modern century* (rev., 1970); R. Storry, *A history of modern Japan*° (1960); W. L. Neumann, *America encounters Japan: from Perry to MacArthur*° (1963); I. Nish, *The story of Japan* (1968); and W. G. Beasley, *The modern

history of Japan*° (1963). The best account of the Meiji era is Beasley's *The Meiji restoration* (1972).

Problems and Readings°

A number of booklets will be useful for subjects touched on in this chapter. On the Crimean War: B. D. Gooch (ed.), *The origins of the Crimean War* (1969). On Italy: C. F. Delzell (ed.), *The unification of Italy, 1859–1861* (1965); M. Walker (ed.), *Plombières: secret diplomacy and the rebirth of Italy* (1968); D. Mack Smith (ed.), *The making of Italy, 1796–1870* (1968) and *Garibaldi* (Great Lives Observed series, 1969); and M. Salvadori, *Cavour and the unification of Italy* (Anvil series, 1961). On Germany: T. S. Hamerow (ed.), *Otto von Bismarck: a historical assessment* (rev., 1972); O. Pflanze (ed.), *The unification of Germany, 1848–1871* (1968); and F. B. M. Hollyday, *Bismarck* (Great Lives Observed series, 1970). On Austria-Hungary: H. J. Gordon and N. M. Gordon, *The Austrian empire: abortive federation?* (1975). On Japan: A. Tiedemann, *Modern Japan: a brief history* (Anvil series, rev., 1962).

XIV: EUROPEAN CIVILIZATION: 1871–1914

An indictment of the late nineteenth century (and by implication the age that followed) is C. J. H. Hayes, *A generation of materialism, 1871–1900*° (1941), in the Langer series; O. J. Hale, *The great illusion, 1900–1914*° (1971), the volume that follows in the same series, judiciously treats many subjects, domestic and international. The final two volumes in the New Cambridge Modern History cover these years, the titles indicating their emphases: F. H. Hinsley (ed.), *Material progress and world-wide problems, 1870–1898* (1962), and R. L. Mowat (ed.), *The shifting balance of world forces, 1898–1945* [1968, a revision of the original vol. XIII edited by D. Thomson under the title *The era of violence, 1898–1945* (1960)]. B. W. Tuchman, *The proud tower: a portrait of the world before the war, 1890–1914*° (1966), provides selected vignettes, while E. R. Tannenbaum, *1900: the generation before the Great War* (1976), offers an overall social history. Other thoughtful syntheses for these years are J. K. Munholland, *Origins of contemporary Europe, 1890–1914*° (1970); J. Joll, *Europe since 1870*° (1973); F. Gilbert, *The end of the European era, 1890 to the present*° (1970); and J. M. Roberts, *Europe, 1880–1945*° (1967), useful on economic and demographic subjects. G. Barraclough, *An introduction to contemporary history*° (1964), is a provocative essay, calling for a global approach to contemporary history. C. F. Ware, K. M. Pannikar, and J. Romein, *The twentieth century* (1966), vol. VI of the UNESCO History of Mankind, stresses cultural subjects but lacks coherent treatment. Special attention is given to intellectual matters in G. Lichtheim, *Europe in the twentieth century*° (1972).

Basic Demography

An introduction to historical demography is provided in C. M. Cipolla, *The economic history of world populations* (1962), and the sources for demographic studies are described in T. H. Hollingsworth, *Historical demography* (1969). Several other important books are listed in the introductory section of the present Bibliography. H. Moller (ed.), *Population movements in modern European history*° (1964), is a useful anthology of articles. The subject is also discussed in D. V. Glass and D. E. C. Eversley (eds.), *Population in history* (1965); D. V. Glass and R. Revelle (eds.), *Population and social change* (1972); E. A. Wrigley, *Industrial growth and population change* (1961); and the brief but provocative T. McKeown, *The modern rise of population* (1977), already cited.

Population movements are interpreted in the massive volumes by W. F. Willcox and others, *International migrations* (2 vols., 1929, 1931); J. Isaac, *Economics of migration* (1947); D. R. Taft and R. Robbins, *International migrations: the immigrant in the modern world* (1955); M. L. Hansen, *The Atlantic migration, 1607–1860: a history of the continuing settlement of the United States*° (1940); W. D. Forsyth, *The myth of open spaces: Australian, British, and world trends of population and migration* (1942); and P. Taylor, *The distant magnet: European migration to the United States* (1971).

Population statistics for the contempo-

rary era of spectacular growth must be brought up to date by consulting the United Nations, *Statistical yearbook* (1948 ff.), and *Demographic yearbook* (1948 ff).

The World Economy

In addition to the economic histories listed in the introductory section and in Chapter XI, one may consult W. Ashworth, *A short history of the international economy since 1850* (rev., 1963); the same author's *An economic history of England, 1870–1939* (1960); and on European agriculture since the 1800s, M. Tracy, *Agriculture in western Europe* (1963). Two important institutional studies are C. Wright and C. E. Fayle, *A history of Lloyd's* (1928), on the great English marine insurance center, and J. H. Clapham, *The Bank of England*, already cited.

Economic studies stressing the role of European capital include L. H. Jenks, *The migration of British capital to 1875* (1927, 1938); H. Feis, *Europe, the world's banker, 1870–1914*° (1930); D. C. M. Platt, *Finance, trade, and politics in British foreign policy, 1815–1914* (1968); and R. E. Cameron, *France and the economic development of Europe, 1800–1914*, cited earlier. Economic growth in the major European countries is studied in C. P. Kindleberger, *Economic growth in France and Britain, 1851–1950* (1963), which may be compared with W. W. Rostow, *The stages of economic growth*, cited earlier; and A. L. Levine, *Industrial retardation in Britain, 1880–1914* (1967). For Germany, one may read G. Stolper and others, *The German economy, 1870 to the present* (1940, trans. 1967), and W. O. Henderson, *The rise of German industrial power, 1834–1914*,° already cited. American developments in these years may be studied in T. C. Cochran and W. Miller, *The age of enterprise*° (1949); Cochran's *American business in the twentieth century* (1972); R. H. Wiebe, *The search for order, 1877–1920* (1967); and J. A. Garraty, *The new commonwealth* (1968).

France, 1870–1914

The general histories of modern France described in Chapter XI should be consulted as well as the bibliographical chapters in G. Wright, *France in modern times* (rev., 1974). On the years since 1870, one may turn to D. W. Brogan, *France under the republic, 1870–1939* (1940), and to his *The French nation, 1814–1940,* cited earlier, although both are difficult for the general reader. A. Sedgwick, *The Third French Republic, 1870–1914* (1968), is a useful brief introduction. D. Thomson's *Democracy in France since 1870* (rev., 1969), is a penetrating analytical study, and G. Chapman, *The Third Republic of France: the first phase, 1871–1849* (1962), is a detailed narrative. An important study demonstrating that French national unity was accomplished only belatedly by means of the schools and modern technology is E. Weber, *Peasants into Frenchmen: the modernization of rural France, 1870–1914* (1976). An unorthodox social history is T. Zeldin, *France, 1848–1945: ambition, love and politics* and . . . : *intellect, taste and anxiety* (2 vols., 1973, 1977).

French political thought may be examined in J. P. Mayer, *Political thought in France from the Revolution to the Fourth Republic* (1943, 1949), and in A. Scott, *Republican ideas and the liberal tradition in France, 1870–1914* (1951). Other recommended studies on France not strictly confined to the years before 1914 are G. Wright, *Rural revolution in France: the peasantry in the twentieth century* (1964); R. Challener, *The French theory of the nation in arms, 1866–1939* (1952); P. M. de la Gorce, *The French army: a military-political history* (1963); D. G. Ralston, *The army of the republic: the place of the military in the political evolution of France, 1871–1914* (1967); J. Rothney, *Bonapartism after Sedan* (1969); B. Reardon, *Liberalism and tradition: aspects of Catholic thought in nineteenth century France* (1975); and R. Shattuck, *The banquet years: the arts in France, 1885–1918* (1958). Religious questions since 1870 are treated comprehensively in A. Dansette's *Religious history of modern France*, vol. II: *Under the Third Republic* (trans. 1961), and in J. Mc-Manners, *Church and state in France, 1870–1914* (1972).

The tumultuous beginnings of the Third Republic are discussed from various points of view in A. Horne, *The fall of Paris: the siege and the Commune, 1870–1871* (1968); R. L. Williams, *The French Revolution of 1870–1871* (1969); M. Kranzberg, *The siege of Paris, 1870–1871* (1950); E. Thomas, *The women incendiaries* (trans. 1966), on the women active in the Commune; and S. Edwards, *The Paris Commune, 1871* (1971). Other studies before and beyond the Commune include J. P. T. Bury, *Gambetta and the national defence: a republican dictatorship in France* (1936) and its sequel, *Gambetta and the making of the Third Republic* (1973); J. T. Joughin, *The Paris Commune in French politics, 1871–1880* (2 vols., 1955); and F. H. Seager, *The Boulanger affair* (1969). S. Elwitt, *The making of the Third Republic: class and politics in France, 1868–1884* (1975), is a Marxist analysis of the early years.

On the Dreyfus affair, there are detailed and detached accounts by D. Johnson, *France and the Dreyfus affair* (1967), the best now available, and by G. Chapman, *The Dreyfus case: a reassessment* (1955). R. F. Byrnes presents part of the background in *Antisemitism in modern France: prologue to the Dreyfus affair* (1950).

On political men and movements of the right, there are valuable studies, many reaching beyond 1914, among them: M. Curtis, *Three against the Third Republic: Sorel, Barrès and Maurras* (1959); R. Soucy, *Fascism in France: the case of Maurice Barrès* (1972); C. S. Doty, *From cultural rebellion to counterrevolution: the politics of Maurice Barrès* (1976); W. C. Buthman, *The rise of integral nationalism in France* (1939), focusing on Charles Maurras; E. Weber, *Action Française: royalism and reaction in twentieth-century France* (1963), a remarkably full account; the same author's *The nationalist revival in France, 1905–1914* (1959); E. R. Tannenbaum, *The Action Française* (1962); and M. L. Brown, Jr., *The comte de Chambord: the Third Republic's uncompromising king* (1967). R. Rémond, *The right wing in France: 1815 to de Gaulle*, has already been cited; and it may be supplemented by D. Shapiro (ed.), *The right in France, 1890–1914* (St. Antony's Papers, 1962).

Other recommended biographical studies include R. Binion, *Defeated leaders: the political fate of Caillaux, Jouvenel and Tardieu* (1960); three biographies of Clemenceau: J. H. Jackson, *Clemenceau and the Third Republic* (Teach Yourself

History series, 1948), G. Bruun, *Clemenceau* (1943), and D. R. Watson, *Georges Clemenceau: a political biography* (1974); and H. A. Schmitt, *Charles Péguy: the decline of an idealist* (1967). As a sequel to his study of Louis Blanc, cited earlier, L. A. Loubère has written *Radicalism in Mediterranean France: its rise and decline, 1848–1914* (1974). [Additional studies of the left are described below under Socialist Movement and Socialist Parties.]

Italy

The best narrative account of Italy since unification is D. Mack Smith, *Italy: a modern history* (rev., 1969), in the University of Michigan series; economic developments are ably presented in S. B. Clough, *The economic history of modern Italy* (1964), cited in Chapter XI. For the years after unification, the best-balanced account is C. Seton-Watson, *Italy from liberalism to fascism, 1870–1925* (1967), which may be supplemented by J. A. Thayer, *Italy and the Great War: politics and culture, 1870–1915* (1964); S. Saladino, *Italy from unification to 1919: growth and decay of a liberal regime** (1970), a brief, readable introduction; and E. R. Tannenbaum and E. P. Noether (eds.), *Modern Italy: a topical history since 1861* (1974). The background chapters of H. S. Hughes, *The United States and Italy* (rev., 1965), are illuminating. Some specialized studies are A. W. Salomone, *Italian democracy in the making: the political scene in the Giolittian era, 1900–1914* (1949, 1960); F. J. Coppa, *Planning, protectionism and politics in liberal Italy* (1971), more sympathetic to Giolitti; and A. C. Jemolo, *Church and state in Italy, 1850–1950* (1960). An important monograph is R. A. Webster, *Industrial imperialism in Italy, 1908–1915* (1976), which argues that Italian foreign policy changed directions because of Italian economic needs.

Germany, 1870–1914

The general histories of Germany cited in Chapter XI and the studies on Bismarck in the preceding chapter also may be consulted, as well as the volumes by G. Stolper and by W. O. Henderson, cited earlier in this chapter. W. H. Dawson, *The German empire, 1867–1914, and the unity*

movement (2 vols., 1919), is still valuable. Another substantial study is W. F. Bruck, *Social and economic history of Germany, 1888–1938* (1938), and a well-organized synthesis is A. J. Ryder, *Twentieth-century Germany: from Bismarck to Brandt* (1973). Special insights are provided in R. H. Lowie, *The German people: a social portrait to 1914* (1945); H. Kohn, *The mind of Germany: the education of a nation,** cited earlier; and W. M. Simon (ed.), *Germany in the age of Bismarck* (1968). Other studies include J. A. Nichols, *Germany after Bismarck** (1959), on the Caprivi era; J. C. G. Röhl, *Germany without Bismarck: the crisis of government in the Second Reich, 1890–1900* (1968); N. Rich, *Friedrich von Holstein: politics and diplomacy in the era of Bismarck and Wilhelm II* (2 vols., 1965); L. Cecil, *Albert Ballin: business and politics in imperial Germany, 1888–1918* (1967); the same author's *The German diplomatic service, 1871–1914* (1976); F. B. M. Hollyday, *Bismarck's rival: General and Admiral Albrecht von Stosch* (1960); A. Gerschenkron, *Bread and democracy in Germany* (1943); and J. L. Snell and H. A. Schmitt, *The democratic movement in Germany, 1789–1914* (1976). M. Kitchen, *The German officer corps, 1890–1914* (1968), may be supplemented by H. H. Herwig, *The German naval officer corps, 1890–1918* (1973); and F. Lilge, *The abuse of learning: the failure of the German university* (1948), may be compared with F. W. Ringer, *The decline of the German mandarins: the German academic community, 1890–1933* (1969.) Two biographies of William II are V. Cowles, *The Kaiser* (1963), and M. Balfour, *The Kaiser and his times* (1963). Additional books providing background to later developments in Germany include R. Gellately, *The politics of economic despair: shopkeepers and German politics, 1890–1914* (1974); W. Struve, *Elites against democracy: leadership ideals in bourgeois political thought in Germany, 1890–1933* (1973); and U. Tal, *Christians and Jews in Germany: religion, politics, and ideology in the Second Reich, 1870–1914* (trans. 1975).

To the books on Austria cited in Chapter XIII may be added three books by W. A. Jenks: *The Austrian electoral reform of 1907* (1950), *Austria under the iron ring,*

1879–1893 (1965), and *Vienna and the young Hitler* (1960); and one by A. G. Whiteside, *The socialism of fools: Georg Ritter von Schönerer and Austrian pan-Germanism* (1975).

Great Britain, 1870–1914

A comprehensive bibliographical guide is H. J. Hanham, *Bibliography of British history, 1851–1914* (1977). R. C. K. Ensor, *England, 1870–1914* (1936, 1949), provides the best general account of the period, although stronger on domestic than foreign affairs. Important too is the epilogue to E. Halévy's *History of the English people,* cited earlier, covering the years 1895 to 1914. G. Dangerfield, *The strange death of liberal England*° (1935), is a searching study of tensions in English society between 1910 and 1914; it may be supplemented by S. Hynes, *The Edwardian turn of mind* (1968), and P. Thompson, *The Edwardians: the remaking of British society* (1975). A. P. Thornton, *The habit of authority: paternalism in British history* (1966), is a provocative essay. Syntheses moving on into the twentieth century are D. C. Somervell, *British politics since 1900* (1950); K. Hutcheson, *Decline and fall of British capitalism* (1950); D. Roberts, *Victorian origins of the British welfare state* (1960); and T. Lloyd, *Empire to welfare state: English history, 1906–1967*° (1970). Recommended also are the following, of which some have been cited in Chapter XI: R. J. Evans, *The Victorian age, 1815–1914* (1950); G. M. Young, *Victorian England: portrait of an age* (2 vols., 1934); G. Kitson Clark, *The making of Victorian England* (1962); W. E. Houghton, *The Victorian frame of mind* (1957); W. L. Burn, *The age of equipoise*° (1964); and H. McLeod, *Class and religion in the late Victorian city* (1974). P. Stansky has edited *The Victorian revolution: government and society in Victoria's Britain*° (1973), in the Modern Scholarship on European History series.

Almost every major figure in British life in this period has been the subject of at least one biography. Among biographical accounts are L. Strachey, *Queen Victoria*° (1921), and *Eminent Victorians*° (1918, 1933); A. Cecil, *Queen Victoria and her prime ministers* (1952); biographies of

Victoria by E. F. Benson (1935), R. Fulford (1951), and E. Longford° (1965); and P. Magnus, *King Edward the Seventh* (1964). On Gladstone: the older work of J. Morley (3 vols., 1903); W. P. Hall, *Mr. Gladstone* (1931); J. L. Hammond and M. R. D. Foot, *Gladstone and liberalism*° (Teach Yourself History series, 1953); P. Magnus, *Gladstone: a biography*° (1955); and E. J. Feuchtwanger, *Gladstone* (1975). On Disraeli: the older work by W. F. Monypenny and G. E. Buckle (6 vols., 1913–1920), now superseded by R. Blake, *Disraeli*° (1967), a distinguished biography. The same author also has written *The unknown prime minister: the life and times of Andrew Bonar Law* (1955). Joseph Chamberlain is the subject of an exhaustive multivolumed biography, *The life of Joseph Chamberlain,* the first four volumes by J. L. Garvin (1932–1951) and the latter two by J. Amery (1968–1969). An introduction to the lives of Austin and Neville Chamberlain is provided in the somewhat adulatory D. H. Elletson, *The Chamberlains* (1966). S. Koss has written an outstanding biography, *Asquith* (1976). Recommended also are W. Irvine, *The universe of G. B. S.* (1949), on George Bernard Shaw; M. Cole (ed.), *The Webbs and their work* (1949); K. Muggeridge and R. Adam, *Beatrice Webb: a life, 1858–1943* (1968); H. Ausubel, *In hard times: reformers among the late Victorians* (1960); and the same author's *John Bright: Victorian reformer*° (1966). R. Kelley, *The transatlantic persuasion: the liberal-democratic mind in the age of Gladstone* (1969), is of special interest.

Political and party issues are examined in depth in M. Cowling, *1867: Disraeli, Gladstone and revolution: the passing of the Second Reform Bill* (1967); F. B. Smith, *The making of the Second Reform Bill* (1966); and P. Smith, *Disraelian conservatism and social reform* (1967). The vicissitudes of the Liberals in the era after Gladstone and their accomplishments are studied in P. Stansky, *Ambitions and strategies: the struggle for the leadership of the Liberal party in the 1890's* (1964); M. Richter, *The politics of conscience* (1964); C. Cross, *The Liberals in power, 1905–1914* (1963); B. D. Gilbert, *The evolution of national insurance in Great Britain* (1966); and M. Bruce, *The coming of the welfare state* (1961, 1966). A pioneer work in electoral sociology is H. Pelling, *Social geography of British elections, 1885–1910* (1967). There are useful histories of the Liberal party by J. Vincent (1966, 1976), R. Douglas (1971), and C. Cook* (1976).

On the women's rights movement in this era, see J. Kamm, *Rapiers and battleaxes: the women's movement and its aftermath* (1966); C. Rover, *Women's suffrage and party politics in Britain, 1866–1914* (1967); D. Mitchell's somewhat popular account, *The fighting Pankhursts: a study in tenacity* (1967); M. Vicinus, *Suffer and be still: women in the Victorian age* (1973); D. Morgan, *Suffragists and liberals: the politics of woman suffrage in England* (1975); and A. Rosen, *Rise up, women!: . . . the women's Social and Political Union, 1903–1914* (1974).

The Irish question is discussed in J. E. Pomfret, *The struggle for land in Ireland, 1800–1923* (1930); J. C. Beckett, *The making of modern Ireland*, cited earlier; L. J. McCaffrey, *The Irish question, 1800–1922** (1968); and in a remarkable study focusing on the years 1912 to 1921, G. Dangerfield, *The damnable question: a study of Anglo-Irish relations* (1976).

Socialist Movement and Socialist Parties

[General histories of socialism are listed for Chapter XI, and works on Marx and Marxism for Chapter XII.] On the modern translation of Marxist ideas into institutional form, the books by G. D. H. Cole, *A history of socialist thought*, and by C. Landauer, *European socialism*, both already cited, are indispensable. To them may be added H. Mitchell and P. N. Stearns, *Workers and protest: the European labor movement, the working classes, and the origins of social democracy, 1890–1914** (1971). In addition, there are many specific studies of socialist parties and leaders in each country. For France: A. Noland, *The founding of the French socialist party, 1893–1905* (1956); S. Bernstein, *The beginnings of Marxian socialism in France* (1933); J. H. Jackson, *Jean Jaurès: his life and work* (1943); and an outstanding biography by H. Goldberg, *A life of Jean Jaurès* (1962). For Germany: C. E. Schorske, *German social democracy, 1905–1917** (1955), a master-

ful study; A. J. Berlau, *The German Social Democratic party, 1914–1921* (1949); P. Gay, *The dilemma of democratic socialism: Eduard Bernstein's challenge to Marx** (1952), a perceptive examination of Bernstein's revisionism; G. Roth, *The Social Democrats in imperial Germany* (1963); and V. L. Lidtke, *The outlawed party: social democracy in Germany, 1878–1890* (1966). An important biographical work is J. P. Nettl, *Rosa Luxemburg** (2 vols., 1966; abr. 1 vol., 1969), for whom there is also available N. Geras, *The legacy of Rosa Luxemburg* (1976).

On Britain: M. Beer, *History of British socialism* (1912, 1948); H. Pelling, *The origins of the Labour party, 1880–1900* (1954, 1965); other studies of early labor history by J. H. S. Reid (1955) and P. Poirier (1958); A. H. McBriar, *Fabian socialism and English politics, 1884–1918** (1926); W. Wolfe, *From radicalism to socialism: . . . the formation of Fabian socialist doctrines, 1881–1889* (1975); and N. MacKenzie and J. MacKenzie, *The Fabians* (1977), successfully combining biography and social and intellectual history. Christian socialism is explored in P. d'A. Jones, *The Christian Socialist revival, 1877–1914* (1968); and for Marx's somewhat negligible impact on the British labor scene, see H. Collins and C. Abramsky, *Karl Marx and the British Labour movement* (1965). On the Internationals, there are L. L. Lorwin, *Labor and internationalism* (1929); J. Joll, *The Second International, 1889–1914* (1955, 1974); and J. Braunthal, *History of the International* (1961; trans. 2 vols., 1966). The breakup of the International is ably described in G. Haupt, *Socialism and the Great War: The collapse of the Second International* (1972). The most comprehensive introduction to anarchism is G. Woodcock, *Anarchism: a history of libertarian ideas and movements* (1962), but also useful is J. Joll, *The anarchists** (1964).

Labor Movement and Labor Unions

An indispensable classic treatment is S. Perlman, *Theory of the Labor movement* (1928, 1949). Useful surveys are W. Galenson (ed.), *Comparative labor movements* (1952), and W. A. McConagha, *The development of the labor movement* in *Great Britain, France, and Germany* (1942). H. Pelling, *A history of British trade unionism* (1963), and D. Kynaston, *King labour: the British working class, 1850–1914* (1977), are valuable syntheses, although recent research tends to stress more the role of the rank and file—and the inarticulate. H. A. Clegg, A. Fox, and A. F. Thompson, *A history of British trade unions since 1889,* vol. I, *1889–1910* (1964), is the first volume of a detailed history. For French trade union development, the background chapters of V. R. Lorwin, *The French labor movement* (1954), are recommended. A fine study is J. W. Scott, *The glass-workers of Carmaux: French craftsmen and political action in a nineteenth-century city* (1974), portraying the militant stand of the artisans in the face of mechanization; it may be compared with B. H. Moss, *The origins of the French labor movement: the socialism of skilled workers, 1830–1914* (1977). For Germany, one may turn to W. H. Dawson's old but still useful *Social insurance in Germany, 1883–1911* (1912), and E. Anderson, *Hammer or anvil: the story of the German working-class movement* (1945), mostly on the period after 1914. On Italy, an important study, despite its extravagant title, is M. F. Neufeld, *Italy, school for awakening countries: the Italian labor movement in its political, social, and economic setting from 1860 to 1960* (1961). Finally, J. Kuczynski, *A short history of labour conditions under industrial capitalism* (4 vols., 1942–1946), is a comprehensive treatment, written from a Marxian viewpoint, and arguing with statistical detail that labor conditions deteriorated markedly.

The New Movement in Science

The best general history of science in the nineteenth century is W. P. D. Wightman, *The growth of scientific ideas* (1951). On biology, evolution, and Darwinism, one may turn to P. Fothergill, *Historical aspects of organic evolution* (1952); J C. Greene, *The death of Adam: evolution and its impact on Western thought* (1959); P. B. Sears, *Charles Darwin: the naturalist as a cultural force* (1950); G. Himmelfarb, *Darwin and the Darwinian revolution°* (1959); L. Eiseley, *Darwin's century* (1961); and G. R. deBeers, *Charles Darwin* (1958). C. C. Gillispie, *The edge of objectivity,* cited earlier, is important for Darwinism and other subjects. On the impact of the scientific developments on religion, the classic account is A. D. White, *A history of the warfare of science and theology°* (1896, many eds.); more recent studies include J. A. O'Brien, *Evolution and religion* (1932); C. C. Gillispie, *Genesis and geology* (1951); and W. Irvine, *Apes, angels, and Victorians* (1955). The impact on social thought is studied in J. W. Burrow, *Evolution and society: a study in Victorian social theory* (1966).

On the rise of twentieth-century physics, one may read I. B. Cohen, *The birth of the new physics* (1960); and A. Einstein and L. Infeld, *The evolution of physics* (1938). Einstein may best be approached through Infeld, *Albert Einstein: his work and its influence on our world°* (1950); L. Barnett, *The universe and Dr. Einstein* (1952); the brief H. Cuny, *Albert Einstein°* (1962); and R. W. Clark, *Einstein: the life and times°* (1971). F. Wittels, *Freud and his time* (1931, 1948), and P. Rieff, *Freud: the mind of the moralist* (1959), are two of the best interpretive studies of Sigmund Freud; they may be compared with the masterful biography by E. Jones (3 vols., 1953–1957; I vol. abr., 1961). A useful symposium is J. Miller (ed.), *Freud* (1972). B. P. Babkin has written *Pavlov: a biography* (1949).

Social Thought

The relations between science and social thought and other subjects are elucidated in considerable detail in J. T. Merz, *A history of European thought in the nineteenth century* (4 vols., 1897–1914), and in H. Höffding, *A history of modern philosophy* (1900, 1924); but two outstanding modern contributions on the latter part of the century are H. S. Hughes, *Consciousness and society: the reorientation of European social thought, 1890–1930°* (1958), and G. Masur, *Prophets of yesterday: studies in European culture, 1890–1914°* (1961). Virtually a history of thought from Herbert Spencer to the present is W. W. Wagar, *Good tidings: the belief in progress from Darwin to Marcuse* (1972). Other works on the period include E. Barker, *Political thought in*

England (1915, 1947); J. Bowle, *Politics and opinion in the nineteenth century,** already cited; E. Wilson, *Axel's castle: a study in the imaginative literature of 1870–1930* (1931); and J. Higham and others, *The origins of modern consciousness* (1965). More specialized studies are W. Irvine, *Walter Bagehot* (1939); H. Alpert, *Emile Durkheim and his sociology* (1939), on a leading French systematizer; J. P. Mayer, *Max Weber and German politics* (1944); J. Freund, *The sociology of Max Weber* (1966, trans. 1968); and R. Humphrey, *Georges Sorel: prophet without honor* (1951). The best study of Nietzsche is by W. A. Kaufmann, *Nietzsche: philosopher, psychologist, antichrist** (1950); and on one of Nietzsche's intimates, Lou Andreas Salomé, R. Binion has written a psychoanalytical biography, *Frau Lou: Nietzsche's wayward disciple** (1968). A useful anthology for these years is R. N. Stromberg (ed.), *Realism, naturalism, and symbolism: modes of thought and expression in Europe, 1848–1914* (1968).

Racism, Integral Nationalism, and the Cult of Violence

The later development of totalitarianism is dealt with in Chapter XIX. Books examining the revolt against rationalism in politics beginning with the late nineteenth century are H. Kohn, *The twentieth century* (1957); H. Arendt, *The origins of totalitarianism** (1951, 1958), a somewhat abstruse work that finds the roots of totalitarianism in late nineteenth-century imperialism, nationalism, and anti-Semitism; J. Barzun, *Darwin, Marx, Wagner: critique of a heritage** (1941), which points out resemblances in the assumptions and conclusions of the three men; E. Heller, *The disinherited mind* (1957); and K. Löwith, *From Hegel to Nietzsche: the revolution in nineteenth century thought* (1941, trans. 1964). Similar studies include A. Dorpalen, *Heinrich von Treitschke* (1957); P. W. Massing, *Rehearsal for destruction: a study of political anti-Semitism in imperial Germany* (1949); P. G. J. Pulzer, *The rise of political anti-Semitism in Germany and Austria* (1964); and K. von Klemperer, *Germany's new conservatism: its history and dilemma in the twentieth century** (1968). An important study portraying racism at the core of European cultural history is L. Poliakov, *The Aryan myth: a history of racist and nationalist ideas in Europe* (trans. 1974).

Religion since 1870

The continuing relationship between secularized European civilization and its Christian origins is ably treated in O. Chadwick, *The secularization of the European mind in the nineteenth century* (1976). Two scholarly surveys with considerable attention to contemporary Protestantism are J. H. Nichols, *History of Christianity, 1650–1950* (1956), and E. E. Cairns, *Christianity through the centuries* (1954). The theological contributions of David Friedrich Strauss are examined in books by H. Harris (1976) and R. S. Cromwell (1974).

More specifically on the Catholic church are C. C. Eckhardt, *The papacy and world affairs, as reflected in the secularization of politics* (1937); E. E. Y. Hales's sympathetic study of Pius IX, *Pio Nono,* cited earlier; L. P. Wallace, *The papacy and European diplomacy, 1869–1878* (1948); C. Butler, *The Vatican Council: the story told from inside in Bishop Ullathorne's letters* (2 vols., 1930); and R. Fülöp-Miller, *Leo XIII and our times* (1937).

Several valuable books on aspects of Jewish affairs, including Zionism, by J. W. Parkes are *The emergence of the Jewish problem, 1878–1939* (1946), *The Jewish problem in the modern world* (1946), *Anti-Semitism** (1963), and *A history of the Jewish people* (1952). The syntheses of Jewish history by H. M. Sachar, *The course of modern Jewish history** (1958) and *A history of Israel: from the rise of Zionism to our time* (1976), give attention to nineteenth-century ideological developments, as do B. Halpern, *The idea of the Jewish state* (1961), and W. Laqueur, *A history of Zionism* (1976). An intriguing if not entirely convincing study is J. M. Cuddihy, *The ordeal of civility: Freud, Marx, Lévi-Strauss and the Jewish struggle with modernity** (1975).

Problems and Readings*

Pamphlets relating to this chapter are R. L. Williams (ed.), *The Commune of Paris, 1871* (1969); S. Edwards (ed.), The Communards of Paris (1973); L.

Derfler (ed.), *The Dreyfus affair: tragedy of errors?* (1964); H. R. Kedward (ed.), *The Dreyfus affair: catalyst for tensions in French society* (1965); E. C. Helmreich (ed.), *A free church in a free state: the Catholic church, Italy, Germany, France, 1864–1914* (1964); T. S. Hamerow (ed.), *The age of Bismarck: documents and interpretations* (1974); J. J. Sheehan (ed.), *Imperial Germany* (1976); H. Shultz (ed.), *English liberalism and the state: individualism or collectivism* (1974); and E. C. Black (ed.), *Victorian culture and society* (1974). Also useful are H. Vanderpool (ed.), *Darwin and Darwinism* (1974), and N. G. Levin (ed.), *The Zionist movement in Palestine and world politics, 1880–1918* (1973). In the Anvil series, there are H. Ausubel, *The late Victorians: a short history* (1955); R. L. Schuyler and C. Weston, *British constitutional history since 1832* (1957); L. L. Snyder, *The idea of racialism: its meaning and history* (1962); and J. S. Schapiro, *Anticlericalism: conflict between church and state in France, Italy, and Spain* (1967).

XV: EUROPE'S WORLD SUPREMACY

Imperialism in General

An important book that stresses national power, prestige, and security over economic factors in European expansion is D. K. Fieldhouse, *Economics and empire, 1830–1914* (1973); his earlier book *The colonial empires,* * going back to the eighteenth century, has been cited earlier. W. L. Langer, *The diplomacy of imperialism, 1890–1902* (2 vols., 1935), contains a full, balanced discussion of imperialism in all aspects. Other valuable surveys include H. Gollwitzer, *Europe in the age of imperialism, 1880–1914** (1969); R. F. Betts, *Europe overseas: phases of imperialism** (1968); and M. Cunliffe, *The age of expansion, 1848–1917* (1974). The earlier phase of expansion, as background, is ably examined in B. Semmel, *The rise of free trade imperialism . . . 1750–1850* (1970). Motives and justifications for imperialist activities are analyzed in E. M. Winslow, *The pattern of imperialism: a study in the theories of power* (1948); R. Koebner and H. D. Schmidt, *Imperialism: the story and significance of a political*

word, *1840–1960* (1964); A. P. Thornton, *Doctrines of imperialism* (1965); T. Kemp, *Theories of imperialism* (1968); J. A. Schumpeter, *Imperialism and social classes* (trans. 1951); W. Woodruff, *Impact of Western man* (1967); and T. Geiger, *The conflicted relationship: the West and the transformation of Asia, Africa, and Latin America* (1967). Other important discussions and studies include R. Maunier, *The sociology of colonies: an introduction to the study of race contact* (2 vols., 1949), and D. Mannoni, *Prospero and Caliban: the psychology of colonization** (1956), stressing the psychological impact of colonial rule on both rulers and governed. Two key books that later stimulated much inquiry into the nature of imperialism are J. A. Hobson's *Imperialism: a study** (1902), an incisive critique by an English self-styled "economic heretic," and V. I. Lenin's *Imperialism, the highest stage of capitalism** (1916). A lucid exposition of the Marxist-Leninist interpretation is V. G. Kiernan, *Marxism and imperialism* (1975).

British imperialism is analyzed in R. Robinson and J. Gallagher, *Africa and the Victorians: the official mind of imperialism** (1961), which stresses British economic preeminence rather than deliberate policy as the explanation for unprecedented expansion. Two good surveys that also downplay directives from London are B. Porter, *The lion's share: a short history of British imperialism, 1850–1970** (1976), an especially lively account, and R. Hyam, *Britain's imperial century, 1815–1914: a study of empire and expansion* (1976). Other important books include R. Faber, *The vision and the need: late Victorian imperialist aims* (1966); B. Semmel, *Imperialism and social reform: English social imperial thought, 1895–1914** (1960); B. Porter, *Critics of empire: British radical attitudes to colonialism in Africa, 1895–1914* (1968); A. P. Thornton, *The imperial idea and its enemies: a study in British power** (1959); M. Beloff, *Imperial sunset:* vol. I, *Britain's liberal empire, 1807–1921* (1970); D. C. Gordon, *The moment of power: Britain's imperial epoch* (1970); C. C. Eldridge, *England's mission: the imperial idea in the age of Gladstone and Disraeli, 1868–1880* (1973); D. A. Low, *Lion rampant: essays in the study of British imperialism* (1973); and J. W. Cell, *British colonial administration* in the mid-nineteenth century: the policy-making process (1970). Biographical accounts include J. L. Garvin's multivolumed *The life of Joseph Chamberlain,* cited in the previous chapter; W. L. Strauss, *Joseph Chamberlain and the theory of imperialism* (1942); V. Halperin, *Lord Milner and the empire: the evolution of British imperialism* (1952); and G. H. Uzoigwe, *Britain and the conquest of Africa: the age of Salisbury* (1974), focusing on the Conservative statesman.

The imperial activities of the other leading European powers [except Russia—discussed at the end of this chapter and under Chapter XVII] are described in M. E. Townsend, *The rise and fall of Germany's colonial empire, 1884–1918* (1930); W. O. Henderson, *Studies in German colonial history* (1963); H. Brunschwig, *French colonialism, 1871–1914: myths and realities* (1960, trans. 1966); W. B. Cohen, *Rulers of empire: the French colonial service in Africa* (1971); A. W. Heggoy, *The African policies of Gabriel Hanotaux, 1894–1898* (1972); T. F. Power, Jr., *Jules Ferry and the Renaissance of French imperialism* (1944); H. I. Priestley, *France overseas: a study of modern imperialism* (1938); S. H. Roberts, *History of French colonial policy, 1870–1925* (2 vols., 1929); and C. Hollis, *Italy in Africa* (1941).

The Americas

On the expansion of the United States: A. K. Weinberg, *Manifest destiny** (1935), is a standard general work. E. R. May, *Imperial democracy* (1961) and *American imperialism: a speculative essay* (1968), are indispensable on American motivations. Other phases of American foreign policy are treated in U.S. diplomatic histories and in J. W. Pratt, *Expansionists of 1898** (1936) and *America's colonial experiment* (1950); W. Millis, *The martial spirit** (1931), an ironic discussion of the Spanish-American War; M. Tate, *The United States and the Hawaiian kingdom* (1965); and H. Sprout and M. Sprout, *The rise of American naval power, 1776–1918* (1939). D. Dawson, *The Mexican adventure* (1935), is a careful account of Napoleon III's fiasco during the 1860s; and F. Tannenbaum's *Mexico: the struggle for peace and bread* (1950), provides a running narrative of Mexican history.

The Ottoman Empire and the Balkans

General accounts, some of which have been cited earlier, are G. E. Kirk, *A short history of the Middle East* (rev., 1957); S. N. Fisher, *The Middle East: a history* (rev., 1968); P. K. Hitti, *The history of the Arabs** (rev., 1970); and P. Balfour [Lord Kinross], *The Ottoman centuries: the rise and fall of the Turkish empire* (1977). B. Lewis, *The emergence of modern Turkey* (1961; rev., 1969), an outstanding work, treats nineteenth-century developments as background. Other valuable studies are J. Haslip, *The Sultan: the life of Abdul Hamid II* (1958), a vivid scholarly account with insight into the empire; S. Mardin, *The genesis of Young Ottoman thought* (1963), on the decade 1867–1878; W. W. White, *The process of change in the Ottoman Empire* (1937); R. H. Davison, *Reform in the Ottoman Empire, 1856–1876* (1963); H. Dodwell, *The founder of modern Egypt: a study of Muhammad Ali* [Mehemet Ali] (1931); D. C. Blaisdell, *European financial control in the Ottoman Empire* (1929); D. S. Landes, *Bankers and pashas: international finance and economic imperialism in Egypt** (1958); and R. L. Tignor, *Modernization and British colonial rule in Egypt, 1882–1914* (1966). The diplomacy surrounding the construction of the Suez Canal may be studied in J. Marlowe, *World ditch: the making of the Suez Canal* (1964); J. Pudney, *Suez: de Lesseps' canal* (1969); and P. Balfour [Lord Kinross], *Between two seas* (1969). The Italian experience in Libya is studied in C. G. Segré, *Fourth shore: the Italian colonization of Libya* (1975).

The best introduction to the diplomatic status of Turkey in modern times is M. S. Anderson, *The Eastern question, 1774–1923,* already cited; other studies include F. E. Bailey, *British policy and Turkish reform: a study in Anglo-Turkish relations, 1826–1853* (1942); R. W. Seton-Watson, *Disraeli, Gladstone, and the Eastern question* (1935); W. N. Medlicott, *The Congress of Berlin and after: a diplomatic history of the Near Eastern settlement, 1878–1880* (1938, 1963); E. M. Earle, *Turkey, the Great Powers, and the Bagdad railway* (1923); and M. K. Chapman, *Great Britain and the Bagdad railway* (1948).

On the Balkans: L. Stavrianos, *The*

Balkans since 1453, and R. J. Wolff, *The Balkans in our times,*° already cited; in addition, one may turn to B. H. Sumner, *Russia and the Balkans, 1870–1880* (1937); C. Sforza, *Fifty years of war and diplomacy in the Balkans* (1941); J. A. Levandis, *The Greek foreign debt and the Great Powers, 1821–1898* (1944); T. W. Riker, *The making of Roumania: a study of an international problem, 1856–1866* (1931); W. C. Vucinich, *Serbia between East and West: the events of 1903–1908* (1954); C. Jelavich, *Tsarist Russia and Balkan nationalism* (1958); and C. E. Black, *The establishment of constitutional government in Bulgaria* (1943).

Africa

The best one-volume introduction is R. W. July, *A history of the African people*° (rev., 1964); the same author has also written *Precolonial Africa: an economic and social history*° (1975). A vivid account on a grand scale is R. Hallett, *Africa to 1875* (1970) and *Africa since 1875* (1974); here, and in *The penetration of Africa: European exploration in North and West Africa to 1815* (1965), the author seeks to examine the inner workings of African society as well as the European impact. Good also for the presentation of indigenous culture and thought are the essays in P. D. Curtin (ed.), *Africa and the West: intellectual responses to European culture* (1972). Other useful introductions and surveys are N. R. Bennett, *Africa and Europe from Roman times to the present*° (1975), a somewhat brief treatment for its scope; B. Davidson, *Africa in history: themes and outlines*° (rev., 1974); R. Oliver and J. D. Fage, *A short history of Africa*° (rev., 1976); R. I. Rotberg, *A political history of tropical Africa* (1965); and G. P. Murdock, *Africa: its peoples and their culture history* (1959). The use of "oral tradition" in the reconstruction of early African history is brilliantly demonstrated in J. Vansina, *Kingdoms of the savanna*° (1966). P. Curtin, *The image of Africa: British ideas and action, 1780–1850* (1964), is an important study in political and cultural interaction. W. E. B. Du Bois, *The world and Africa* (1947), presents ideas and historical materials not readily accessible elsewhere. The most interesting survey of African art is F. Willett, *African art: an introduction*° (1971). P. Duignan and L. H. Gann's *Burden of empire: an appraisal of Western colonialism south of the Sahara* (1967) attempts to demonstrate that the benefits of European expansion outweighed the debits. The same writers are coeditors of a five-volume collaborative history, *Colonialism in Africa, 1870–1960* (1969–1973), which examines the subject in competent but somewhat uneven fashion, although the bibliographical volume is especially valuable.

A monumental history of missionary activity in Africa since 1840 is C. P. Groves, *The planting of Christianity in Africa* (4 vols., 1948–1959). Biographical studies include J. Simmons, *Livingstone and Africa* (1955); G. Seaver, *David Livingstone, his life and letters* (1957); F. Debenham, *The way to Ilala: David Livingstone's pilgrimage* (1955); R. Hall, *Stanley* (1976); R. Oliver, *Sir Harry Johnston and the scramble for Africa* (1957); G. Elton, *Gordon of Khartoum* (1954); J. Marlowe, *Mission to Khartum* (1969); and M. F. Perham, *Lugard: the years of adventure, 1858–1898* (1936). The best biography of Cecil Rhodes, and a brief one, is by J. Flint (1976), although there are others by B. Williams (1921), A. Maurois (1953), and S. G. Millin (1933). B. Williams has written *Botha, Smuts, and South Africa* (Teach Yourself History series, 1948). The emergence of South Africa is recounted in L. Thompson, *The unification of South Africa, 1902–1910* (1960), which may be supplemented by B. Farwell, *The great Anglo-Boer War* (1976). The best study of the Congo to 1908 is R. Slade, *King Leopold's Congo* (1962), on which subject there also is N. Ascherson, *The king incorporated* (1963). R. Anstey has written *Britain and the Congo in the nineteenth century* (1962). Other important monographs are R. Coupland, *East Africa and its invaders* (1938), covering to 1856, and *The exploitation of East Africa, 1856–1890: the slave trade and the scramble* (1939); R. D. Wolff, *The economics of colonialism: Britain and Kenya, 1870–1930* (1974); M. M. Knight, *Morocco as a French economic venture: a study of open door imperialism* (1937); H. Rudin, *Germans in the Cameroons, 1884–1914; a case study in modern imperialism* (1938); J. Suret-Canale, *French colonialism in tropical Africa, 1900–1945* (trans. 1971);

and S. E. Crowe, *The Berlin West African conference, 1884–1885* (1942). On the slave trade and its abolition, one may read B. Davidson, *Black mother: the years of the African slave trade* (1961), and on the Brussels conference of 1889, S. Miers, *Britain and the ending of the slave trade* (1975).

Asia

[Japan is discussed mainly in Chapter XIII, and Asian problems in general after 1918 are treated in Chapters XVIII and XXI.] Among informative general surveys of the European impact on the Far East are J. Pratt, *The expansion of Europe in the Far East* (1947); K. M. Pannikar, *Asia and Western dominance: . . . the Vasco da Gama epoch of Asian history, 1498–1945** (rev., 1959); and P. H. Clyde and B. F. Beers, *The Far East: a history of Western impacts and Eastern responses, 1830–1974* (rev., 1975). Excellent introductions to Chinese history include J. K. Fairbank, *The United States and China** (rev., 1971), in the American Foreign Policy Library series; C. P. Fitzgerald, *China: a short cultural history* (rev., 1961); C. O. Hucker, *China's imperial past: an introduction to Chinese history and culture** (1975); and F. W. Mote, *Intellectual foundations of China** (1971). The best introduction to East Asia for all phases is J. K. Fairbank, E. O. Reischauer, and A. M. Craig, *East Asia: tradition and transformation* (1973).

European relations with China are taken up in G. F. Hudson, *Europe and China* (1930); J. Pratt, *China and Britain* (1944); J. K. Fairbank, *Trade and diplomacy on the China coast: the opening of the treaty ports, 1842–1854** (2 vols., 1953); Ssu-yu Teng and J. K. Fairbank, *China's response to the West: a documentary survey, 1839–1923** (1954, 1963); J. Spence, *To change China: Western advisers in China, 1620–1960** (1969); and V. Purcell, *The Boxer uprising* (1963). The best studies of the Opium Wars are J. Beeching, *The Chinese Opium Wars* (1976); P. W. Fay, *The Opium War, 1840–42* (1975); and B. Ingles, *The Opium War* (1976). A massive, authoritative study of the Taiping upheaval is Jen Yu-wen *The Taiping revolutionary movement* (1973). On the Open Door policy, there is M. H. Hunt, *Frontier defense and the open door: Manchuria in* *Chinese-American relations, 1895–1911* (1973).

For nineteenth-century developments in India, in addition to books already described in Chapter VI, see P. J. Griffiths, *The British impact on India* (1952); P. Moon, *Strangers in India* (1942); S. Sen, *Eighteen fifty-seven* (1957); and T. R. Metcalf, *The aftermath of revolt: India, 1857–1870* (1964). Especially useful are M. Edwardes, *British India, 1772–1947* (1968); W. Golant, *The long afternoon: British India, 1601–1947* (1975); and M. E. Chamberlain, *Britain and India: the interaction of the peoples* (1974), which shows how little control the British had over forces shaping Indian society. On Indochina: C. Robequain, *The economic development of French Indo-China* (1944), and J. F. Cady, *The roots of French imperialism in eastern Asia* (1954, 1967), may be consulted.

In addition to the works on Russian foreign policy cited in the chapters that follow, there should be added B. H. Sumner, *Tsardom and imperialism in the Far East and the Middle East, 1880–1914* (1942). For the story of the Russian fleet that was defeated at Tsushima by the Japanese, one may read A. Nobikov-Privoy, *Tsushima* (trans. 1944); F. Thiess, *The voyage of forgotten men* (1947); and R. Hough, *The fleet that had to die* (1958). The diplomatic history of the war is recounted in J. A. White, *The diplomacy of the Russo-Japanese War* (1964), and an admirable general narrative is D. Walder, *The short victorious war: the Russo-Japanese conflict, 1904–05* (1975).

Problems and Readings*

Relevant titles include H. M. Wright (ed.), *The "new imperialism": analysis of the late nineteenth century expansion* (rev., 1975); R. W. Winks (ed.), *British imperialism: gold, God, glory* (1963); W. R. Louis (ed.), *Imperialism: the Robinson and Gallagher controversy* (1976); R. F. Betts (ed.), *The scramble for Africa: causes and dimensions of empire* (1966); R. I. Rotberg (ed.), *Africa and its explorers* (1970); T. C. Caldwell (ed.), *The Anglo-Boer War* (1965); and R. A. Austen (ed.), *Modern imperialism: Western overseas expansion in the age of industrialism* (1969). On India, there are M. D. Lewis (ed.), *The British in India* (1962); P. J. Marshall (ed.), *Problems of empire: Britain and India, 1757–1813* (1968); and A. T. Embree (ed.), *1857 in India: mutiny or war of independence?* (1963). In the Anvil series, D. N. Rowe has written *Modern China: a brief history* (1959). Studies in the American Historical Association Pamphlets series include P. D. Curtin, *Precolonial African history* (1974); J. C. Miller, *Equatorial Africa* (1976); C. O. Hucker, *Some approaches to China's past* (1973); and R. I. Crane, *A history of South Asia* (1973).

XVI: THE FIRST WORLD WAR

Diplomatic Background

For the diplomatic history of the years 1870–1914, A. J. P. Taylor, *The struggle for mastery in Europe, 1848–1918,* cited earlier, is invaluable. On diplomacy in the two decades after 1870, there is the masterful study by W. L. Langer, *European alliances and alignments, 1871–1890** (1931, 1950); the same author's *The Franco-Russian alliance, 1880–1894* (1929) and *The diplomacy of imperialism, 1890–1902,* already cited. Two books by W. N. Medlicott, *The Congress of Berlin and after,* already cited, and *Bismarck, Gladstone, and the concert of Europe* (1956), and Medlicott and D. K. Coveney, *Bismarck and Europe* (1971), are more critical of Bismarck than is Langer. G. A. Craig, *From Bismarck to Adenauer* (1958), is informative on Bismarck's direction of foreign policy.

Some thoughtful analyses for the student and general reader incorporating the latest scholarship on the background to the First World War are L. C. F. Turner, *Origins of the First World War** (1970), the best brief introduction to the debate and to the historiography; L. Lafore, *The long fuse: an interpretation of the origins of World War I** (1965); and J. Remak, *The origins of World War I, 1871–1914** (Berkshire series, 1967). Of special value as an up-to-date synthesis is D. E. Lee, *Europe's crucial years: the diplomatic background of World War I, 1902–1914* (1974), rejecting the thesis of a German preventive war and reaffirming the argument that each state acted out of desperation in defense of its own presumed interests. Among older comprehensive treatments are S. B. Fay, *The origins of the World War** (1928, 1930); B. E. Schmitt, *The coming of the war, 1914* (2 vols., 1930); P. Renouvin, *The immediate origins of the war* (1928); N. Mansergh, *The coming of the First World War: a study in the European balance, 1878–1914* (1949); and L. Albertini, *The origins of the War of 1914* (3 vols., 1942–1943; trans. 1952–1957).

The war-guilt controversy was reopened by the West German scholar Fritz Fischer, who on the basis of new archival materials reaffirmed German culpability in *Germany's aims in the First World War** (1961, trans. 1967), the title somewhat modified in translation from the original German *Griff nach der Weltmacht.* Fischer also presents his interpretations in *War of illusions* (1969, trans. 1973) and in the briefer *World power or decline: the controversy over Germany's aims in the First World War* (1965, trans. 1974). His argument that Germany had to grasp for "world power" or decline is reinforced by I. Geiss, *German foreign policy, 1871–1914* (1976). The reopened controversy receives critical examination in J. A. Moses, *The politics of illusion: the Fischer revolution in German historiography* (1975). The question of German insecurity or German ambition also is debated among other topics in W. Laqueur and G. L. Mosse (eds.), *1914: The coming of the First World War** (1969), published originally as a volume of the *Journal of contemporary history.*

The books cited above will serve as guides to the many specialized accounts, of which the following represent a sampling: A. F. Pribram, *England and the international policy of the European Great Powers, 1871–1914* (1929, 1941); G. Monger, *The end of isolation: British foreign policy, 1900–1907* (1963); C. Andrew, *Théophile Delcassé and the making of the entente cordiale: a reappraisal of French foreign policy, 1898–1905* (1968); and S. R. Williamson, *The politics of grand strategy: Britain and France prepare for war, 1904–1914* (1969). The Balkan antecedents of the war are examined in R. W. Seton-Watson, *Sarajevo* (1926); E. C. Helmreich, *The diplomacy of the Balkan wars, 1912–1913* (1938); and V. Dedijer,

The road to Sarajevo (1966), while the British decision to go to war in 1914 is explored in C. Hazlehurst, *Politicians at war* (1971). A useful survey of French foreign policy for this and the chapters that follow is J. Néré, *The foreign policy of France from 1914 to 1945* (trans. 1975), in the Foreign Policy of the Great Powers series.

Anglo-German relations are discussed in H. Kantorowicz, *The spirit of British policy and the myth of the encirclement of Germany* (1931); R. J. Sontag, *Germany and England: background of conflict, 1848–1894*° (1938); P. R. Anderson, *The background of anti-English feeling in Germany, 1890–1902* (1939); and R. J. S. Hoffman, *Great Britain and the German trade rivalry, 1875–1914* (1933). The naval race is discussed in the memoirs of Tirpitz, Grey, Fisher, Haldane, and other participants; in J. Steinberg, *Yesterday's deterrent: Tirpitz and the birth of the German battleship* (1965); A. J. Marder, *The anatomy of British sea power . . . 1880–1905* (1940), on the predreadnought era, and *From the dreadnought to Scapa Flow: the Royal Navy in the Fisher era, 1904–1919* (5 vols., 1961–1970); and E. L. Woodward, *Great Britain and the German navy* (1935). The Italian role is ably discussed in C. J. Lowe and F. Marzari, *Italian foreign policy, 1870–1940* (1975), in the same series as the Néré volume.

Two books seeking to capture the mood of the summer of 1914 are J. Remak, *Sarajevo: the story of a political murder* (1959), and J. Cameron, *1914* (1959). W. S. Churchill, *The world crisis* (5 vols., 1923–1929), remains of interest even though it must be read with caution when it deals with events in which the author participated. N. Angell, *The great illusion* (1911), was a widely read book whose antiwar message went unheeded.

On the involvement of the United States in the war, one may consult the various general diplomatic histories of the United States, for example, those by S. F. Bemis, T. A. Bailey, R. Ferrell, A. DeConde, and R. Leopold, and the numerous works they cite. Of interest also is B. Perkins, *The great rapprochement: England and the United States, 1895–1914* (1968). An outstanding study is E. F. May, *The World War and American isolation, 1914–1917*° (1959), which may be supplemented by A. Link, *Woodrow Wilson and the progressive era, 1910–1917* (1954); and on a special subject, there is B. W. Tuchman, *The Zimmerman telegram*° (1958). T. A. Bailey and P. B. Ryan, *The Lusitania disaster: an episode in modern warfare and diplomacy* (1975), makes a scholarly case for the German legal position.

Military: Strategic and Operational

Here again the available material is staggering. The biographical notes in T. Ropp, *War in the modern world* (1962), should be consulted. There are general narratives by B. H. Liddell Hart (1934), C. R. M. Cruttwell (1934), H. Baldwin° (1962), C. B. Falls° (1959), A. J. P. Taylor° (1964), and M. Ferro° (1973). Recommended also is the *American Heritage history of World War I* (1964), superbly illustrated, with the narrative by S. L. A. Marshall. Decisions on strategy are studied in F. Maurice, *Lessons of Allied co-operation: naval, military and air, 1914–1918* (1942), and the same author's *The Supreme Command, 1914–1918* (2 vols., 1961). On plans and preparations, see J. Gooch, *The plans of war: the general staff and British military strategy, 1900–1916* (1974). The most complete history in English is the official *British history of the Great War based on official documents by the historical section of the Committee of Imperial Defence* (32 vols., 1920 ff.).

On the opening phase of the war: B. W. Tuchman, *The guns of August* (1962), has been justly praised for its colorful writing and mastery of materials. G. Ritter, *The Schlieffen plan* (trans. 1958), is a valuable analysis, but L. L. Farrar, *The short-war illusion*° (1973), also should be consulted. A sampling of literature on episodes of the war would include A. M. Moorehead, *Gallipoli* (1958); J. E. T. Harper, *The truth about Jutland* (1927); A. Horne, *The price of glory: Verdun, 1916*° (1963); and R. M. Watt, *Dare call it treason* (1963), on the French army mutinies of 1917. The war in eastern Europe is graphically described in N. Stone, *The eastern front, 1914–1917* (1976). One of the less-known tragedies of the war is recounted in D. H. Boyajian, *Armenia: the case for a forgotten genocide* (1972), on the slaughter directed against the Armenian population by Ottoman Turkey.

Economic and Social Impact of the War

[The Russian Revolution is discussed in Chapter XVII, and additional books on the German revolution and on the long-range effects of the war are described in Chapter XIX.] On the economic and social aspects of the war, one may turn to the multivolumed Carnegie Endowment series, Economic and Social History of the World War (1921 ff.), under the general editorship of J. T. Shotwell. Representative titles include J. A. Salter, *Allied shipping control: an experiment in international administration* (1921); W. Beveridge, *British food control* (1928); F. W. Hirst, *Consequences of the war to Great Britain* (1934); A. Fontaine, *French industry during the war* (1926); A. Mendelssohn-Bartholdy, *The war and German society: the testament of a liberal* (1938); J. Redlich, *Austrian war government* (1929); and D. Mitrany, *The effect of the war in southeastern Europe* (1936). The best one-volume account of the home front in the various countries is F. P. Chambers, *The war behind the war, 1914–1918* (1939); it can be supplemented by J. Williams, *The other battleground: the home fronts: Britain, France, and Germany, 1914–1918* (1972).

Wartime internal developments also are treated in E. L. Woodward, *Great Britain and the War of 1914–1918* (1967); P. Guinn, *British strategy and politics, 1914–1918* (1965); J. C. King, *Generals and politicians: conflict between France's high command, parliament and government, 1914–1918* (1951); G. D. Feldman, *Army, industry, and labor in Germany, 1914–1918* (1966); and R. B. Armeson, *Total warfare and compulsory labor* (1964), also on Germany. Two studies focusing on the end of the Habsburg empire are A. J. May, *The passing of the Hapsburg monarchy, 1914–1918* (2 vols., 1966), and Z. A. B. Zeman, *The breakup of the Habsburg empire, 1914–1918* (1961). The final volume of G. Ritter, *The sword and the scepter: the problem of militarism in Germany:* Vol. IV, *The reign of German militarism and the disaster of 1918* (trans. 1973), describes the misuse of the power that the generals had preempted as well as their political ineptitude. An illuminating study is J. M. Read, *Atrocity propaganda* (1941); and on the human costs of the war, see T. J. Mitchell and G. M. Smith, *Medical services: casualties and medical statistics of the Great War* (1931). A thoughtful comparative study is A. Marwick, *War and social change in the twentieth century: a comparative study of Britain, France, Germany, Russia and the United States* (1975).

Wartime Diplomacy, Armistice, and Peace

A good introduction to wartime diplomatic maneuvers is Z. A. B. Zeman, *The gentlemen negotiators: a diplomatic history of the First World War* (1971). Among specialized accounts are H. W. Gatzke, *Germany's drive to the West: a study of Germany's Western war aims during the First World War*° (1950); J. W. Wheeler-Bennett, *The forgotten peace: Brest-Litovsk, March 1918* (1939); H. C. Meyer, *Mitteleuropa in German thought and action* (1955); U. Trumpener, *Germany and the Ottoman Empire, 1914–1918* (1968); and V. H. Rothwell, *British war aims and peace diplomacy, 1914–1918* (1971). Two provocative studies focusing on the diplomatic duel between the United States and Russia are V. S. Mamatey, *The United States and east central Europe, 1914–1918* (1957), and A. J. Mayer, *Political origins of the new diplomacy, 1917–1918* (1959). The British policy toward the independence movements is explored in K. J. Calder, *Britain and the origins of the new Europe, 1914–1918* (1976). T. E. Lawrence, *Seven pillars of wisdom: a triumph*° (1926, 1935), on the revolt of the Arabs against the Turks, is a fascinating account that must be used with caution. Other studies focusing on the Middle East and on developing Arab-Zionist rivalries are E. Kedourie, *England and the Middle East* (1956), on the years 1914–1921; H. M. Sachar, *The struggle for the Middle East, 1914–1924* (1969); P. C. Helmreich, *From Paris to Sèvres: the partition of the Ottoman Empire at the Peace Conference of 1919–1920* (1974); L. Stein, *The Balfour declaration* (1961); and I. Friedman, *The question of Palestine, 1914–1918: British, Jewish, Arab relations* (1973).

For the armistice, one may turn to H. R. Rudin, *Armistice, 1918* (1944), and F. Maurice, *The Armistice of 1918* (1943).

On the conference, the best brief account is P. Birdsall, *Versailles twenty years after* (1941), sympathetic to Wilson. H. Nicolson, *Peacemaking, 1919* (1933, 1939), and G. B. Noble, *Policies and opinions at Paris, 1919* (1935), describe the intellectual climate in which the momentous decisions were reached. H. W. V. Temperley, *A history of the peace conference of Paris* (6 vols., 1920–1924), is a massive technical study, whereas F. S. Marston, *The peace conference of 1919* (1944), is a brief readable guide dealing mainly with organizational aspects.

For a brilliant although not entirely convincing study arguing with massive detail that the unconscious preoccupation underlying decisions at Versailles was the threat of Bolshevism and domestic radicalism, see A. J. Mayer, *Politics and diplomacy of peacemaking: containment and counter-revolution at Versailles, 1918–1919* (1967); it may be compared with J. M. Thompson, *Russia, Bolshevism, and the Versailles peace* (1966), which views the revolutionary threat as important but not dominating. Other studies examining aspects of the peace conference include S. P. Tillman, *Anglo-American relations at the Paris peace conference of 1919* (1961); A. Luckau, *The German delegation at the Paris peace conference* (1941); S. Bonsal, *Suitors and suppliants: the little nations at Versailles* (1946); R. Albrecht-Carrié, *Italy at the Paris peace conference* (1938); I. Morrow, *The peace settlement in the German-Polish borderlands* (1936); and A. Cobban, *National self-determination* (1944). There are monographs on many of the smaller countries at the conference: F. Deak on Hungary (1942), D. Perman on Czechoslovakia (1962), D. Spector on Rumania (1962), T. Komarnicki on Poland (1957), and I. J. Lederer on Yugoslavia (1963). J. C. King explores a special subject in *Foch versus Clemenceau: France and German dismemberment, 1918–1919* (1960).

One of the most hotly disputed issues was reparations, and on this, J. M. Keynes's *The economic consequences of the peace* (1920) has been the most influential single book. Etienne Mantoux, *The Carthaginian peace—or the economic consequences of Mr. Keynes* (1946), is a vigorous reply to Keynes. C. Bergmann, *The history of reparations* (1927), is a scholarly presentation of a German point of view, and in *The end of reparations* (1931), H. Schacht attempts to vindicate his own policy. A wider point of view is found in A. L. Bowley, *Some economic consequences of the Great War* (1930). On the colonial question, see W. R. Louis, *Great Britain and Germany's lost colonies, 1914–1919* (1967); and a special subject is explored in H. R. Winkler, *The League of Nations movement in Great Britain, 1914–1919* (1952).

The revolutionary mood of the early postwar era is described in G. Schulz, *Revolution and peace treaties, 1917–1920* (trans. 1972); F. L. Carsten, *Revolution in central Europe, 1918–1919* (1972); D. Mitchell, *1919: Red mirage* (1970); I. Völgyes (ed.), *Hungary in revolution, 1918–1919: new essays* (1971); and R. Tökés, *Bela Kun* (1967).

Biographies

There are innumerable biographies, which vary widely in quality, of the civil and military figures of the period. Some of the better biographical studies are G. Wright, *Poincaré and the French presidency* (1943); L. B. Namier, *In the margin of history* (1939); K. Jarausch, *The enigmatic chancellor* (1973), a major study of Bethmann Hollweg; K. Tschuppik, *Ludendorff: the tragedy of a military mind* (1932); W. K. Hancock, *Smuts* (2 vols., 1962–1968); R. S. Baker, *Woodrow Wilson: life and letters* (8 vols., 1927–1939); and A. Link's multivolumed biography of Wilson (5 vols. to date, 1947 ff.) and his other books on Wilson. The attempt to apply techniques of psychoanalysis in S. Freud and W. Bullitt, *Thomas Woodrow Wilson* (1967), has led to strange and unconvincing results; a more successful psychological approach is achieved in A. L. George and J. L. George, *President Wilson and Colonel House: a personality study°* (1956). On David Lloyd George, the best biographical account is T. Jones, *Lloyd George* (1951), which can be supplemented by J. Grigg, *The Young Lloyd George* (1973); M. Gilbert has edited *Lloyd George* (1968), in the Great Lives Observed series. The best study of Clemenceau is D. R. Watson, *Georges Clemenceau: a political biography*, cited earlier.

Problems and Readings*

Pamphlets relating to the war and the peace settlement include D. E. Lee (ed.), *The outbreak of the First World War* (rev., 1976), J. Remak (ed.), *The First World War: causes, conduct, consequences* (1971); H. W. Koch (ed.), *The origins of the First World War* (1972); I. Geiss (ed.), *July 1914* (1969); I. J. Lederer (ed.), *The Versailles settlement: was it foredoomed to failure?* (1960); and T. P. Greene (ed.), *Wilson at Versailles* (1957). Useful also are J. J. Roth (ed.), *World War I: a turning point in modern history* (1967), a brief anthology of essays, and G. Feldman, *German imperialism, 1914–1918* (1972). In the Anvil series, L. L. Snyder has edited *Historic documents of World War I* (1958).

XVII: THE RUSSIAN REVOLUTION AND THE SOVIET UNION

Russia before 1917

[Many books on tsarist Russia, Russian imperialism, and the First World War are listed for Chapters XIII, XV, and XVI.] R. V. Daniels, *Russia** (1964), is an excellent brief introduction to twentieth-century events, and J. H. Billington, *The icon and the axe: an interpretive history of Russian culture*, cited earlier, is rewarding and stimulating for cultural developments. New books are listed in the quarterly *Russian review* and in other professional publications.

The political situation in late tsarist Russia is best approached through H. Seton-Watson, *The Russian empire, 1801–1917* and *The decline of imperial Russia, 1855–1914*, both cited earlier; R. Pipes, *Russia under the old regime*, also cited earlier; B. H. Sumner, *Russia and the Balkans, 1870–1880* (1947), an analysis offering much more than the title suggests; and M. T. Florinsky, *The end of the Russian empire* (1931), one of several Russian studies in the Carnegie series described in Chapter XVI. R. F. Byrnes, *Pobedonostsev: his life and thought* (1968), describes in detail an outstanding exemplar of tsarist obscurantism.

In addition to books on late nineteenth-century Russia listed for Chapter XIII, economic and institutional topics are discussed in P. I. Liashchenko, *History of the Russian national economy to the 1917 revolution* (1949); L. A. Owen, *The Russian peasant movement, 1906–1917* (1937); J. S. Curtis, *Church and state in Russia: . . . 1900–1917* (1940); and T. H. Von Laue, *Sergei Witte and the industrialization of Russia** (1963). The intellectual ferment may be studied in T. G. Masaryk, *The spirit of Russia* (2 vols., 1919; 3rd posthumous vol., 1968), a profound and difficult work of extraordinary value; G. Fedotov, *The Russian religious mind* (1946); E. H. Carr, *Dostoevsky, 1821–1881* (1931); E. J. Simmons, *Leo Tolstoy* (1946); and W. H. Bruford, *Chekhov and his Russia: a sociological study* (1948). Other intellectuals are studied in R. Hare, *Pioneers of Russian social thought** (1951), and A. Vucinich, *Social thought in tsarist Russia: the quest for a general science of society, 1861–1917* (1976). H. Kohn has edited selections from the most important Russian writers in the years 1815 to 1917 in *The mind of modern Russia** (1954).

On the political side, books include G. Fischer, *Russian liberalism: from gentry to intelligentsia* (1958); S. H. Baron, *Plekhanov: the father of Russian Marxism** (1963); D. W. Treadgold, *Lenin and his rivals: the struggle for Russia's future, 1898–1906* (1950); L. Haimson, *The Russian Marxists and the origins of Bolshevism* (1955); F. Venturi, *Roots of revolution* (1960); A. P. Mendel, *Dilemmas of progress in tsarist Russia* (1961); M. Malia, *Alexander Herzen and the birth of Russian socialism** (1961, 1965); and A. Ascher, *Pavel Axelrod and the development of Menshevism* (1972). On the anarchists, there is P. Avrich, *The Russian anarchists* (1967), and on a leading exemplar, G. Woodcock and I. Avukamović, *The anarchist prince* (1950), and M. A. Miller, *Kropotkin* (1976).

The events of 1905 are described in W. Sablinsky, *The road to Bloody Sunday: Father Gapon and the St. Petersburg massacre of 1905* (1975), S. Harcave, *First blood: the Russian Revolution of 1905* (1964), and in H. D. Mehlinger and J. M. Thompson, *Count Witte and the tsarist government in the 1905 Revolution* (1972). Other explorations of the ill-fated effort to establish a constitutional monarchy include A. E. Healy, *The Russian autocracy in crisis, 1905–1907* (1976); A. Levin's two studies, *The Second Duma* (1940, 1966) and its sequel, *The Third Duma: election and profile* (1973); and G. A. Hosking, *The Russian constitutional experiment: government and duma, 1907–1914* (1973).

The Revolution of 1917 and the Establishment of the U.S.S.R.

Biographical introductions for the general reader are B. D. Wolfe, *Three who made a revolution: a biographical history* [Lenin, Trotsky, Stalin]* (1948, 1964); C. Hill, *Lenin and the Russian Revolution* (Teach Yourself History series, 1947); and the well-balanced lives of Lenin by D. Shub* (1948), L. F. Fischer* (1964); M. C. Morgan (1971), and R. H. W. Theen (1973). The biographies by R. Payne* (1964) and by R. Conquest (1972) are unsympathetic accounts. Lenin's wife and her fate in the Stalin years are ably studied in R. H. McNeal, *Bride of the revolution: Krupskaya and Lenin* (1972). An intriguing effort to apply Freudian techniques to an important subject is E. V. Wolfenstein, *The revolutionary personality: Lenin, Trotsky, Gandhi* (1967). An outstanding study focusing on Lenin is A. B. Ulam, *The Bolsheviks: the intellectual and political history of the triumph of communism in Russia* (1965), also available as *Lenin and the Bolsheviks* (1969). I. Deutscher has written two outstanding biographies: *Stalin: a political biography* (1949, 1967), and a remarkably vivid, although perhaps overly sympathetic, three-volume life of Trotsky (1954–1963). The best detailed and balanced biography of Stalin is A. B. Ulam, *Stalin: the man and his era* (1973), while an illuminating effort in psychohistory is R. C. Tucker, *Stalin as revolutionary, 1879–1929: a study in history and personality* (1973). E. E. Smith has put together the fragmentary evidence on Stalin's early life in *The young Stalin* (1967); and T. H. Rigby has edited *Stalin* (1966), in the Great Lives Observed series. R. Hingley, *Joseph Stalin: man and legend* (1974), contrasts the image of benevolence and the actuality of the dictatorship.

On the Revolution, W. H. Chamberlin, *The Russian Revolution, 1917–1921* (2 vols., 1935), is still valuable; other important studies are G. Vernadsky, *The Russian Revolution, 1917–1921* (1932); B. Pares, *The fall of the Russian monarchy* (1939); G. Katkov, *Russia 1917: the February Revolution* (1967); M. Ferro, *The Russian Revolution of February 1917* (1971); and R. V. Daniels, *Red October* (1967). Emphasizing personal relations at the court is the scholarly and well-written R. K. Massie, *Nicholas and Alexandra* (1967). A. Moorehead, *The Russian Revolution* (1958), is popularly written, although not completely dependable. The most comprehensive account in any language, written from the sources, is E. H. Carr's multivolumed *A history of Soviet Russia* (1950–1977), carrying the detailed, narrative from the Revolution to 1929. Two informative studies are A. Rabinowitch, *The Bolsheviks come to power: the Revolution of 1917 in Petrograd* (1977), and J. L. H. Keep, *The Russian Revolution: a study in mass mobilization* (1977).

On the early years, monographs include: O. H. Radkey, *The elections to the Russian constituent assembly of 1917* (1950); L. Schapiro, *The origins of the communist autocracy: political opposition in the Soviet state, 1917–1922* (1955); W. G. Rosenberg, *Liberals in the Russian Revolution: the Constitutional Democratic party, 1917–1921* (1974); R. E. Pipes, *The formation of the Soviet Union: communism and nationalism, 1917–1923* (1954); and P. Avrich, *Kronstadt, 1921* (1970), on the leftist uprising and its suppression. A key institution is studied in O. Anweiler, *The Soviets: the Russian workers, peasants, and soldiers councils, 1905–1921* (trans. 1975).

Foreign relations in the crucial early years are discussed in the following: J. W. Wheeler-Bennett, *The forgotten peace: Brest-Litovsk*, already cited; L. I. Strakhovsky, *Intervention at Archangel* (1944); J. A. White, *The Siberian intervention* (1950); R. Luckett, *The White generals: . . . the White movement and the Russian civil war* (1971); G. A. Brinkley, *The volunteer army and Allied intervention in south Russia, 1917–1921* (1966); P. S. Wandycz, *Soviet-Polish relations, 1917–1921* (1969); and R. H. Ullman, *Anglo-Soviet relations, 1917–1921* (2 vols., 1961,

1968), a remarkably detailed account. The ties with Germany are described in G. Freund, *Unholy alliance* (1957); K. Rosenbaum, *Community of fate: German-Soviet diplomatic relations, 1922–1928* (1965); and H. L. Dyck, *Weimar Germany and Soviet Russia, 1926–1933* (1966). Important documents and other source materials are printed in *Intervention, civil war, and communism in Russia, April-December 1918,* edited by J. Bunyan (1936). The most comprehensive study focusing on American relations to these events are G. F. Kennan's volumes: *Russia leaves the war*° (1956) and *The decision to intervene*° (1958).

Soviet Foreign Relations

For general guidance, see the *Foreign affairs bibliographies,* described at the beginning of the next chapter. Three important and provocative books extending to the end of the Second World War are E. H. Carr, *The Soviet impact on the Western world*° (1947); G. F. Kennan, *Russia and the West under Lenin and Stalin* (1961); and F. L. Schuman's sympathetic narrative and analysis, *Soviet politics at home and abroad* (1946), which manages to put about as good a construction on Russian policy as possible. The best surveys are M. Beloff, *The foreign policy of Soviet Russia, 1929–1941* (2 vols., 1947–1949), a solid and dispassionate narrative; the same author's *Soviet policy in the Far East, 1944–1951* (1953); two books by L. F. Fischer: *The Soviets in world affairs . . . 1917–29* (2 vols., 1930; 1 vol., 1960) and *Russia's road from peace to war: Soviet foreign relations, 1917–1941* (1969); and R. D. Warth, *Soviet Russia in world politics* (1963). An important volume focusing on the historical background to post-1945 events is A. B. Ulam, *Expansion and coexistence: the history of Soviet foreign policy, 1917–1973*° (rev., 1974). An attempt to see common elements in prerevolutionary foreign policy is B. Jelavich, *St. Petersburg and Moscow: tsarist and soviet foreign policy, 1814–1974*° (1974), while another general study in continuity is J. Westwood, *Endurance and endeavor: Russian history, 1812–1971*° (1973). [Other books, emphasizing the years since 1939, are cited in the chapters that follow.]

U.S.S.R.—Political and Economic Developments

A valuable introduction is P. Sorlin, *The Soviet people and their society: from 1917 to the present* (1969). On the structure and functioning of the Soviet government at various stages, the most useful books are S. N. Harper and R. Thompson, *The government of the Soviet Union* (1938, 1949); J. Towster, *Political power in the U.S.S.R., 1917–1947* (1948); M. Fainsod and J. F. Hough, *How Russia is ruled* (1953; rev., 1977); B. Moore, Jr., *Soviet politics: the dilemma of power*° (1950) and *Terror and progress in the U.S.S.R.*° (1954); J. N. Hazard, *The Soviet system of government* (1957; rev., 1960); Z. B. Brzezinski, *The permanent purge: politics in Soviet totalitarianism* (1956); and J. R. Azrael, *The Soviet political system* (1977). An important monograph is M. Fainsod, *Smolensk under Soviet rule*° (1958). On the party itself, there are J. S. Reshetar, *A concise history of the Communist party of the Soviet Union* (1960); L. Schapiro, *The Communist party of the Soviet Union*° (1960); J. A. Armstrong, *The politics of totalitarianism: the Communist party of the Soviet Union* (1961); and R. V. Daniels, *The conscience of the Revolution*° (1960), on the opposition within the party from 1917 to 1969. A stimulating essay is T. H. Von Laue, *Why Lenin? Why Stalin?: a reappraisal of the Russian Revolution, 1900–1930*° (1964); and a comprehensive analysis of the purges, stressing the enormity of the blood bath, is R. Conquest, *The great terror: Stalin's purges of the thirties* (1968), which may be supplemented by J. Carmichael, *Stalin's masterpiece: the show trials and purges of the thirties* (1976). The life of one Old Bolshevik is recounted in S. F. Cohen, *Bukharin and the Bolshevik Revolution, 1888–1938* (1973), in which Bukharin is presented as a one-time alternative to Stalin, and of another in W. Lerner, *Karl Radek: the last internationalist* (1970). The conditions that led to Stalinism are discussed in R. Pethybridge, *The social prelude to Stalinism* (1974). For insight into the party and regime, one also may profitably sample, and compare, the 1938 and later versions of the official *History of the Communist party of the Soviet Union.*

The most successful effort to assess economic progress (and the methods used to achieve it) is A. Nove, *An economic history of the U.S.S.R.* (rev., 1975). Two other thoughtful books assessing the accomplishments of the regime are J. P. Nettl, *The Soviet achievement* (1967), and I. Grey, *The first fifty years: Soviet Russia 1917–1967* (1967). Agriculture may be studied in N. Jasny, *The socialized agriculture of the U.S.S.R.* (1949); L. Volin, *A century of Russian agriculture: from Alexander II to Khrushchev* (1970); and M. Lewin, *Russian peasants and Soviet power: a study of collectivization* (1968, trans. 1975). A. C. Sutton examines the role of Western technology during the years 1917 to 1965 in *Western technology and Soviet economic development* (3 vols., 1968–1973).

Various important matters are taken up in J. Erickson, *The Soviet high command . . . 1918–1941* (1962); R. Kolkowicz, *The Soviet military and the Communist party* (1967); J. S. Curtiss, *The Russian church and the Soviet state, 1917–1950* (1953); R. Schlesinger, *Soviet legal theory: its social background and development* (1946); J. N. Hazard, *Law and social change in the U.S.S.R.* (1953); I. Deutscher, *Soviet trade unions: their place in Soviet labor policy* (1950); and S. Wolin and R. M. Slusser (eds.), *The Soviet secret police* (1957). The following works also may be suggested: R. Schlesinger, *The spirit of post-war Russia: Soviet ideology, 1917–1946* (1947); J. Somerville, *Soviet philosophy: a study of theory and practice* (1946); C. V. James, *Soviet socialist realism* (1973), on the official government philosophy for literature and the arts; and H. T. Dodge, *Women in the Soviet economy* (1966). The Jewish question is explored in S. W. Baron, *The Russian Jew under tsars and Soviets* (1964); J. Rothenberg, *The Jewish religion in the Soviet Union* (1971); and L. Kochan (ed.), *The Jews in Soviet Russia since 1917* (1970). There are, in addition, on all subjects relating to the Soviet Union many journalistic accounts and numerous polemical works of uneven quality.

World Communism

On the transformation of earlier socialism and Marxism into communism, a number of studies have been described at the beginning of this chapter and in Chapters XI, XII, and XIV. In addition, there are A. Rosenberg, *A history of Bolshevism from Marx to the first Five Year Plan* (1934); R. N. C. Hunt, *Theory and practice of communism*° (1950) and *Marxism: past and present* (1954); J. Plamenatz, *German Marxism and Russian communism*° (1954); R. Schlesinger, *Marx: his time and ours* (1950), written from a Marxian viewpoint; A. B. Ulam, *The unfinished revolution: an essay on the sources of Marxism and communism*° (1960); and A. G. Meyer, *Leninism* (1957) and *Communism*° (1960). R. T. deGeorge, *Patterns of Soviet thought: the origins and development of dialectical and historical materialism* (1966), is a technical but valuable study. E. H. Carr's *Studies in revolution*, cited earlier, presents thoughtful essays ranging from Saint-Simon to Stalin.

Personal testimonies about the impact of communism may be found in A. Balabanoff, *My life as a rebel* (1938), and in R. H. Crossman (ed.), *The God that failed*° (1950). On the Comintern, one may turn to H. Seton-Watson, *From Lenin to Khrushchev: the history of world communism*° (1953, 1960); F. Borkenau, *The Communist International* (1938), still not superseded, and *World communism*° (1953); and L. L. Lorwin, *The international labor movement* (1953). Special studies include J. W. Hulse, *The forming of the Communist International* (1964); R. Fischer, *Stalin and German communism* (1948); K. E. McKenzie, *Comintern and world revolution, 1928–1943* (1964); and B. Lazitch and M. M. Drachkovitch, *Lenin and the Comintern: Vol. I* (1972), a detailed account, to 1921, with a second volume projected to Lenin's death in 1924. The impact of Bolshevism on French, Italian, and German socialism is ably explored in A. S. Lindemann, *The "red years": European socialism vs. Bolshevism* (1974), while R. Wohl examines the French experience in depth in *French communism in the making, 1919–1924* (1966).

Problems and Readings°
Pamphlets in various problems series include R. H. McNeal (ed.), *Russia in transition, 1905–1914: evolution or revolu-*

tion? (1969); A. E. Adams (ed.), *Imperial Russia after 1861: peaceful modernization or revolution?* (1965); the same author's *The Russian Revolution and Bolshevik victory* (rev., 1973); B. M. Unterberger (ed.), *American intervention in the Russian civil war* (1969); S. W. Page (ed.), *Lenin: dedicated Marxist or pragmatic revolutionary?* (1969); R. V. Daniels (ed.), *The Stalin revolution* (rev., 1973); and R. C. Tucker and S. F. Cohen (eds.), *The great purge trials* (1965). Two booklets in the Anvil series are J. S. Curtiss (ed.), *The Russian Revolutions of 1917* (1957), and A. G. Mazour (ed.), *Soviet economic development: operation outstrip, 1921–1965* (1967). G. B. Carr has contributed to the American Historical Association Pamphlets series, *Russia since 1917: the once and future utopia* (1972), and W. L. Blackwell has edited *Russian economic development from Peter the Great to Stalin*, cited earlier.

XVIII: THE APPARENT VICTORY OF DEMOCRACY

The World since 1919: General

[Books on internal developments in the major countries outside Asia and on international relations between the two wars are listed in Chapters XIX and XX respectively.] As a tool for serious study of the forces and events of the twentieth century, one must turn to *Foreign affairs bibliography* (1933 ff.); these volumes are carefully compiled and annotated lists of books on international affairs and domestic affairs, for which space is utterly lacking in the present Bibliography. New publications are listed as they appear in the current issues of the quarterly *Foreign affairs* and provide the basis for future cumulative volumes. Equally useful is the bibliographical volume published as *Foreign affairs fifty year bibliography* (1972), a selection of important books published between 1920 and 1970.

Among several general surveys of twentieth-century history focusing on Europe, there may be mentioned H. S. Hughes, *Contemporary Europe: a history* (rev., 1976), and R. O. Paxton, *Europe in the twentieth century* (1975), both giving attention to social and cultural as well as

political developments. An interesting overview is provided in A. J. P. Taylor, *From Sarajevo to Potsdam*° (1960), and C. Horne is editing a series of brief volumes by British writers, The Making of the Twentieth Century° (Macmillan, 1967 ff.). G. Barraclough, *Introduction to contemporary history,*° cited earlier, focuses on the twentieth century and on the need to place European events in world perspective. Volume XII (rev., 1968) of the New Cambridge Modern History, *The shifting balance of world forces, 1898–1945,* has already been cited.

Of various anthologies of readings and source problems on twentieth-century history, there are useful ones by G. Wright and A. Mejia° (1963), A. Baltzly and W. Salamone (1950), and A. L. Funk° (1953; rev., 1968).

Problems of the 1920s

An outstanding synthesis of the interwar years, useful for this and the following two chapters, is R. J. Sontag, *A broken world, 1919–1939*° (1971), in the Langer series. Two informative monographs on the 1920s are C. S. Maier, *Recasting bourgeois Europe; stabilization in France, Germany, and Italy in the decade after World War I*° (1975), and S. Schuker, *The end of French predominance in Europe: the financial crisis of 1924 and . . . the Dawes plan* (1976). For a study of the human resources of Europe in the interwar years, one can turn to D. Kirk, *Europe's population in the inter-war years,* cited in Chapter XIV. The general economic problems facing the world after 1919 are discussed in W. S. Culbertson, *International economic policies* (1925); a League of Nations study, *Commercial policy in the inter-war period: international proposals and national policies* (1924); I. Svennilson, *Growth and stagnation in the European economy* (1954); and J. S. Davies, *The world between the wars, 1919–1939: an economist's view* (1975), a personal and impressionistic account.

On the League of Nations, there are innumerable studies published by the League itself; the following general accounts also may be mentioned: F. P. Walters, *A history of the League of Nations* (2 vols., 1952); J. T. Shotwell and M. Salvin, *Lessons on security and dis-*

armament from the history of the League of Nations (1949); W. E. Rappard, The quest for peace since the World War (1940); and B. Dexter, The years of opportunity: the League of Nations, 1920–1926 (1967). Books on disarmament include J. M. Wheeler-Bennett, Disarmament and security since Locarno, 1925–1931 (1932) and The pipe dream of peace: the collapse of disarmament (1935), and R. H. Ferrell, Peace in their time: the origins of the Kellogg-Briand pact° (1952). S. R. Smith, The Manchurian crisis, 1931–1932: a tragedy in international relations (1948), is a discriminating study of the League's most disastrous defeat, and W. W. Willoughby, The Sino-Japanese controversy and the League of Nations (1935), is a comprehensive treatment.

The Revolt of Asia: The Middle East

[For various peoples of the world in the age of imperialism, see Chapter XV, and in the age of independence, Chapter XXI.] An introduction to the ferment in Asia is provided in J. Romein and J. E. Romein, The Asian century: a history of modern nationalism in Asia (1956, trans. 1962).

Various historical surveys of the Middle East with attention to modern developments have been mentioned in Chapter XV. On the modernization of Turkey: B. Lewis, The emergence of modern Turkey, cited earlier, is invaluable. Other studies include H. N. Howard, The partition of Turkey, 1913–1923 (1931); A. J. Toynbee, The Western question in Greece and Turkey: a study in the contact of civilizations (1922); and P. Balfour (Lord Kinross), Ataturk: A biography of Mustafa Kemal (1965). Lord Kinross' The Ottoman centuries: the rise and fall of the Turkish empire, has already been cited. Stirrings in the Middle East also are discussed in G. Antonius, The Arab awakening° (1965); Z. B. Zeine, Struggle for Arab independence (1960); H. A. R. Gibb, Modern trends in Islam (1947); A. Williams, Britain and France in the Middle East and North Africa, 1914–1967 (1969); R. O. Collins and R. L. Tignor, Egypt and the Sudan° (1967); and T. Little, Modern Egypt° (1964).

For the Indian subcontinent, a number of books have been listed in Chapter XV. The best introductions to twentieth-century developments are W. N. Brown, The United States and India, Pakistan, and Bangladesh, already cited, and P. Spear, India, Pakistan, and the West° (rev., 1967). Other useful books are P. Spear, India: a modern history (rev., 1972); T. W. Wallbank, India (1948), in the Berkshire series, and India in the new era (1951); H. Tinker, India and Pakistan: a political analysis° (1962, 1968); A. Seal, The emergence of Indian nationalism (1968); R. J. Moore, The crisis of Indian unity, 1917–1940 (1974); A. T. Embree, India's search for national identity° (1972); and D. J. Mandelbaum, Society in India (2 vols., 1970), focusing on continuity and change. Nehru's autobiography, Toward freedom° (1941), his Glimpses of world history (1942), and his other writings make absorbing reading, as does Gandhi's Autobiography: the story of my experiments with truth (1948). There is a large literature on Gandhi. To the standard biography by L. Fischer° (1951), one may add G. Ashe, Gandhi: a study in revolution° (1968); V. Mehta, Gandhi and his disciples (1976); and E. H. Erikson, Gandhi's truth: on the origins of militant nonviolence° (1969), the latter a successful account that fruitfully draws upon psychoanalytical insights. Three recommended biographies of Nehru are by F. Moraes (1957), M. Brecher° (1959), and E. N. Pandey (1976), while S. Gopal has published the first volume of a detailed biography (1976).

The Revolt of Asia: The Far East

The social problems of East and Southeast Asia in general are discussed in E. H. Jacoby, Agrarian unrest in Southeast Asia (1949), and in B. Lasker, Asia on the move: population pressure, migration, and resettlement in eastern Asia under the influence of want and war (1945) and Peoples of Southeast Asia (1944). [Books on the historical background have been cited in Chapter XV.]

For China in the earlier part of the twentieth century, the best introductions are J. K. Fairbank, The United States and China,° already cited; O. E. Clubb, Twentieth century China° (1964); C. Hibbert, The dragon wakes: China and the West, 1793–1911 (1970); F. Wakeman, The fall of imperial China (1975); and M.

Gasster, *China's struggle to modernize* (1972). D. W. Treadgold's comparative study, *The West in Russia and China*° (2 vols., 1973), can be read with profit here; the second volume focuses on China in the years 1582 to 1949. On the 1920s, one may read H. F. McNair, *China in revolution: an analysis of politics and militarism under the republic* (1931), and H. R. Isaacs, *The tragedy of the Chinese revolution*° (3rd ed., 1961). Biographical studies include Leng Shao-chuan and N. D. Palmer, *Sun Yat-sen and communism* (1961); C. M. Wilbur, *Sun Yat-sen: frustrated patriot* (1976); and H. Z. Schiffrin, *Sun Yat-sen and the origins of the 1911 revolution* (1969). [Books on Communist China are listed in Chapter XXI.]

On the rise of militarism in Japan in the 1930s, the best account is J. B. Crowley, *Japan's quest for autonomy: national security and foreign policy, 1930–1938* (1966); also available are R. Benedict, *The chrysanthemum and the sword*° (1946); D. M. Brown, *Nationalism in Japan* (1955); and R. Storry, *The double patriots* (1957). [Other books on Japan have been listed in Chapter XIII.]

The Depression: Collapse of the World Economy

A useful background study for twentieth-century economic developments is A. Harrison, *The framework of economic activity*° (1967), while D. Landes, *Prometheus unbound,*° cited earlier, should be read for the 1930s. On the coming of the depression, J. K. Galbraith has written a vivid history in *The great crash: 1929*° (1955). G. Rees, *The great slump: capitalism in crisis, 1929–1933* (1972), is lively and informative, but anecdotal, while C. P. Kindelberger, *The world in depression, 1929–1933*° (1973), ably describes economic developments but without giving much political or social detail. C. Bird, *The invisible scar*° (1966), is a moving social history of the depression's impact on the United States. Useful economic surveys covering the world economy are H. V. Hodson, *Slump and recovery, 1929–1937* (1938), and W. A. Lewis, *Economic survey, 1919–1939* (1948); and there are valuable contributions in W. Laqueur and G. L. Mosse (eds.), *The Great Depression*° (1970), originally a volume of the

Journal of contemporary history. Other studies include M. Palyi, *The twilight of gold, 1914–1936: myths and realities* (1972); H. W. Arndt, *The economic lessons of the nineteen thirties* (1944); G. Haberler, *Prosperity and depression* (3rd ed., 1941); L. C. Robbins, *The Great Depression* (1934); E. Bennett, *The diplomacy of the financial crisis, 1931* (1962); and M. Friedman and A. J. Schwartz, *The great contraction, 1929–1933* (1965), an abstraction from the conservative economist's larger *A monetary history of the United States, 1867–1960* (1963). [For the impact of the depression on politics and society in various countries, see the following chapter.]

Problems and Readings°

In the Anvil series, L. L. Snyder has edited *The world in the twentieth century* (rev., 1964) and *Fifty major documents of the twentieth century* (1955); and on economic developments, S. B. Clough, T. Moodie, and C. Moodie have edited *Economic history of Europe: twentieth century* (1968). In the Heath Problems series, there are M. D. Lewis (ed.), *Gandhi: maker of modern India?* (1965), and R. F. Himmelberg (ed.), *The Great Depression and American capitalism* (1968).

XIX: DEMOCRACY AND DICTATORSHIP

[Books on international relations in the interwar years are listed in the following chapter, and books on the general economic problems of the 1920s and 1930s, including the Great Depression, have been listed in Chapter XVIII. The national histories of Britain, France, Germany, and Italy described in Chapters XI and XIV should also be consulted.]

On the general concept of the welfare state, these books may be recommended: J. M. Keynes, *The end of laissez-faire* (1927); J. A. Schumpeter, *Capitalism, socialism, and democracy*° (1942); G. Soule, *A planned society* (1934); B. Wooton, *Freedom under planning* (1945); and M. Bruce, *The coming of the welfare state* (rev., 1966). F. A. von Hayek, in *The road to serfdom*° (1944) and other writings, which subject the welfare state to an unsympathetic appraisal, may be contrasted with R. Titmuss, *Essays on the welfare state°* (rev., 1966), by an advocate. The best introduction to the welfare democracies in the north is F. D. Scott, *Scandinavia* (rev., 1976). A. Sturmthal, *The tragedy of European labor, 1918–1939* (1943, 1951), criticizes labor in the interwar period as too narrow in vision to be politically effective; it may be supplemented for other leaders of the left by the essays in W. Laqueur and G. L. Mosse (eds.), *The left-wing intellectuals between the wars, 1919–1939°* (1966), originally a volume of the *Journal of contemporary history.*

The American New Deal

The background and nature of the New Deal can best be approached through two volumes by W. E. Leuchtenburg: *The perils of prosperity°* (1958) and *Franklin D. Roosevelt and the New Deal°* (1964); other useful introductions are D. W. Brogan, *The era of Franklin D. Roosevelt* (1959), by an acute British writer; B. Rauch, *History of the New Deal, 1933–1938°* (1944); B. Mitchell, *Depression decade: from New Era through New Deal, 1929–1941°* (1947); D. Wecter, *The age of the Great Depression, 1929–1941* (1948); and the multivolumed study by A. M. Schlesinger, Jr., *The age of Roosevelt°* (1957 ff.), of which three lively volumes have appeared to date. Many biographical accounts and memoirs have appeared as well. Two outstanding studies of Roosevelt are J. M. Burns, *Roosevelt: the lion and the fox°* (1956), and F. Freidel's multivolumed *Franklin D. Roosevelt* (4 vols. to date, 1952–1973). R. J. Simon has edited *As we saw the thirties* (1967).

Britain between the Wars

Several thorough and balanced accounts are available: W. N. Medlicott, *Contemporary England, 1914–1964* (1967); C. L. Mowat, *Britain between the wars, 1918–1940* (1955); A. J. P. Taylor, *English history, 1914–1945* (1965); and S. Glynn and J. Oxborrow, *Interwar Britain: a social and economic history* (1976). Briefer surveys are D. Thomson, *England in the twentieth century, 1914–1963°* (1964), and B. B.

Gilbert, *Britain since 1918* (1967). These books may be supplemented by the impressionistic R. Graves and A. Hodge, *The long week-end: a social history of Great Britain, 1918–1939°* (1940); R. Blythe, *The age of illusion* (1963); J. Symons, *The thirties: a dream revolved* (1960); M. Muggeridge, *The thirties: 1930–40 in Great Britain* (1940, 1967); W. McElwee, *Britain's locust years, 1918–1940* (1962); and S. Hynes, *The Auden generation: literature and politics in England in the 1930s* (1977). The impact of the war and other aspects of British economic and social change are revealed in A. C. Pigou, *Aspects of British economic history, 1918–1925* (1947); F. W. Hirst, *Consequences of the war to Great Britain* (1934), in the Carnegie series; P. B. Johnson, *Land fit for heroes: the planning of British reconstruction, 1916–1919* (1968); B. B. Gilbert, *British social policy, 1914–1939* (1970); and A. Marwick's two informative books: *The deluge: British society and the First World War* (1965) and *Britain in the century of total war: war, peace, and social change, 1900–1967* (1968).

On some specific interwar developments and episodes, one may consult T. Wilson, *The downfall of the Liberal party, 1914–1935* (1966); R. McKibbin, *The evolution of the Labour party, 1910–1924* (1974); M. Cowling, *The impact of Labour, 1920–1924: the beginning of modern British politics* (1971); D. E. Moggridge, *The return to gold°* (1969); S. Graubard, *British labour and the Russian Revolution, 1919–1924* (1941); R. W. Lyman, *The first Labour government, 1924* (1957); L. Chester, S. Fay, and H. Young, *The Zinoviev letter* (1967); P. Renshaw, *Nine days that shook Britain: the 1926 general strike°* (1976), the best study of the episode; and M. Bowley, *Housing and the state, 1919–1944* (1945). The depression years are explored in R. S. Bassett, *1931: political crisis* (1958); R. Skidelsky, *Politicians and the slump: the Labour government of 1929–1931* (1967); and N. Branson and M. Heinemann, *Britain in the nineteen thirties* (1971).

There are many biographical studies: the biographies of Ramsay McDonald by D. Marquand (1977), a detailed and judicious account; of Stanley Baldwin by K. Middlemas and J. Barnes (1969); of Neville Chamberlain by K. Feiling (1946),

I. Macleod (1961), and W. R. Rock (1969); of Anthony Eden by L. Broad (1955); and of Halifax by Lord Birkenhead (1965). The multivolumed biography of Winston Churchill by his son R. S. Churchill [to 1914] (2 vols., 1966) and continued for subsequent volumes by M. Gilbert [the fifth volume (1976) covering the years 1922–1939] has been criticized as excessively detailed; there are briefer accounts, among others, by L. Broad (1956) and by H. Pelling (1974). H. Nicolson has written a biography of George V (1953), and J. W. Wheeler-Bennett one of George VI° (1958). A. Bullock, *The life and times of Ernest Bevin* (2 vols., 1960, 1967), is a work of distinction. The best introduction to Keynes is R. F. Harrod, *The life of John Maynard Keynes*° (1951); R. Lekachman, *The age of Keynes*° (1966), is mostly on post-1945 Keynesian influence in the United States. T. Jones, *Diary with letters, 1931–1950* (1954), is valuable on many subjects; and there are other memoirs by H. Dalton (1953), C. Attlee (1954), A. Eden (3 vols., 1960–1965), A. Duff-Cooper (1953), L. S. Amery (3 vols., 1952–1955), S. Hoare (1954), H. Macmillan (2 vols., 1966–1967), and others. R. Skidelsky, *Oswald Mosley* (1976), studies Britain's leading fascist of the era. An interesting collection of essays is H. R. Winkler (ed.), *Twentieth-century Britain: national power and social welfare*° (1976). On personalities in the Labour movement, F. Williams, *Fifty years' march: the rise of the Labour party* (1949), is colorful.

Among many useful studies of the Commonwealth of Nations, one may turn to D. Hall, *Commonwealth: history of the British Commonwealth of Nations* (1971), a detailed account, and N. Mansergh, *The Commonwealth experience* (1969).

France between the Wars

Histories of the Third Republic as a whole appear under Chapter XIV, and to these may be added two brief syntheses for the interwar years: N. Greene, *From Versailles to Vichy: the Third Republic, 1919–1940*° (1970), and E. J. Knapton, *France since Versailles*° (1952). The bibliographical chapters in G. Wright, *France in modern times*° (1974), also should be consulted. S. Hoffman and others, *In search of France: the economy, society and political system in the twentieth century*° (1963), has several incisive essays. The best introduction to French labor is through V. R. Lorwin, *The French labor movement,* already cited, and H. W. Ehrmann, *French labor: from Popular Front to liberation* (1947). A brief informative inquiry into French economic growth is T. Kemp, *The French economy, 1913–1939* (1972).

Invaluable for the stormy events of the 1930s, the Popular Front years, and the background to the fall of France is A. Werth, *The twilight of France, 1933–1940* (1942), a condensation of his earlier volumes, all of which may be read with profit. There are some interesting essays in J. Joll (ed.), *The decline of the Third Republic* (St. Antony's papers, 1959). On some specific subjects, there are C. A. Micaud, *The French right and Nazi Germany, 1933–1939* (1943); P. J. Larmour, *The French Radical party in the 1930's* (1964); J. T. Marcus, *French socialism in the crisis years, 1933–36* (1958); N. Greene, *Crisis and decline: the French Socialist party in the Popular Front era* (1969); D. R. Brower, *The new Jacobins: the French Communist party and the Popular Front* (1968); J. Colton, *Compulsory labor arbitration in France, 1936–39* (1951); and M. Wolfe, *The French franc between the wars, 1919–39* (1961). Léon Blum, *For all mankind* (trans. 1946), is a moving testimony and analysis of France's weaknesses in the 1930s as the Socialist leader saw them. On Blum himself, in addition to various journalistic books, there is a study by L. Dalby (1963); a chapter in J. Joll, *Intellectuals in politics: three biographical essays* [Blum, Rathenau, Marinetti] (1960); and a political biography, J. Colton, *Léon Blum: humanist in politics*° (1966), which attempts to illuminate the Popular Front era as well as the man. On an interesting political figure of the right, J. M. Sherwood has written *Georges Mandel and the Third Republic* (1970), and aspects of foreign policy are examined in J. E. Dreifort, *Yvon Delbos at the Quai d'Orsay: French foreign policy during the Popular Front, 1936–1938* (1974).

Germany, 1919–1945

Three well-balanced narrative accounts of the Weimar Republic and its fall are S. W.

Halperin, *Germany tried democracy: a political history of the Reich from 1918 to 1933** (1946); R. Grunberger, *Germany, 1918–1945** (1964); and A. J. Nicholls, *Weimar and the rise of Hitler** (1968). An interesting effort at reassessment is D. Childs, *Germany since 1918* (1976). E. Eyck, *A history of the Weimar Republic** (2 vols., trans. 1963), is a detailed narrative account by a distinguished liberal German historian. A. Rosenberg, *Imperial Germany: the birth of the German republic, 1871–1918** (1931), provides the background for the same author's *A history of the German republic* (1936). Works on the uneasy early years, many of them raising the question whether a genuine revolution took place, include R. Watts, *The kings depart* (1968); A. J. Ryder, *The German revolution of 1918: a study of German socialism in war and revolt* (1967); S. Haffner, *Failure of a revolution: Germany 1918–1919* (trans. 1973); W. T. Angress, *Stillborn revolution: the communist bid for power in Germany, 1921–1923** (1963); A. Mitchell, *Revolution in Bavaria* (1965); and R. G. L. Waite, *Vanguard of Nazism: the Free Corps movement in postwar Germany, 1918–1923** (1952). G. Freund, *Unholy alliance*, already mentioned, covers German-Soviet relations in the early years of the republic. Cultural developments are sympathetically treated in P. Gay, *Weimar culture: the outsider as insider* (1968), and many valuable insights are provided in R. Dahrendorf, *Society and democracy in Germany* (1967). Recommended also is O. Friedrich, *Before the deluge: a portrait of Berlin in the 1920s* (1972).

The personalities of the Weimar Republic are discussed in a number of books, among which are J. W. Wheeler-Bennett, *Wooden Titan: Hindenburg in twenty years of German history, 1914–1934* (1936); A. Dorpalen, *Hindenburg and the Weimar Republic* (1964); H. Kessler, *Walter Rathenau* (1929); K. Epstein, *Matthias Erzberger and the dilemma of German democracy* (1959); H. W. Gatzke, *Stresemann and the rearmament of Germany** (1954); and H. A. Turner, *Stresemann and the politics of the Weimar Republic** (1963). The much-debated question of army loyalties is studied in G. A. Craig, *The politics of the Prussian army, 1640–1945,** already cited; J. W.

Wheeler-Bennett, *The nemesis of power: the German army in politics, 1918–1945** (1954, 1964); H. J. Gordon, *The Reichswehr and the German republic, 1919–1926* (1957); R. J. O'Neill, *The German army and the Nazi party, 1933–1939* (1968); F. L. Carsten, *The Reichswehr and politics, 1918 to 1933** (1966); and G. Post, Jr., *The civil-military fabric and Weimar foreign policy* (1973). The liberal press is examined in M. Eksteins, *The limits of reason: the German democratic press and the collapse of Weimar democracy* (1975), and an aspect of the German Social Democratic party in D. L. Niewyk, *Socialist, anti-Semite, and Jew: German social democracy confronts the problem of anti-Semitism, 1918–1933* (1971).

D. Orlow, *The history of the Nazi party* (2 vols., 1969, 1973), is a comprehensive account; the first volume covers the years 1919 to 1933; the second to 1945. On the coming to power of the Nazis, one may profit from T. Eschenburg and others, *The path to dictatorship, 1919–1933* (1966); and an intriguing special study, W. S. Allen, *The Nazi seizure of power: the experience of a single German town, 1930–1935** (1965). R. Heberle, *From democracy to Nazism: a regional case study** (trans. 1945), deserves mention as a pioneer study in electoral sociology. On the events of 1932–1933, one may read R. Manvell and H. Fraenkel, *The hundred days to Hitler* (1974). On the Nazi era [aspects of Nazism also are discussed below under totalitarianism], there are many studies, but the outstanding comprehensive analysis is K. D. Bracher, *The German dictatorship: the origins, structure, and effects of national socialism** (1969, trans. 1970); also useful is M. Broszet, *National socialism* (1960, trans. 1967). There are good surveys in H. Mau and H. Krausnick, *German history, 1933–1945* (trans. 1958); in H. Vogt, *The burden of guilt: a short history of Germany, 1914–1945** (trans. 1964); and in the popular account by the journalist W. L. Shirer, *The rise and fall of the Third Reich** (1960), a vivid narrative that uses the available sources but makes no pretense of objectivity. A similar vigorous but oversimplified account is R. Goldston, *The life and death of Nazi Germany** (1969). Two older analytical and interpretive accounts are F. L. Neumann, *Behemoth: the structure and practice of national socialism*° (1942), and K. Heiden, *A history of national socialism* (1935). An indispensable newer treatment is D. Schoenbaum, *Hitler's social revolution: class and status in Nazi Germany, 1933–1939*° (1966). H. Krausnick and others, *Anatomy of the SS state* (trans. 1965), is the best account of the German police state, while E. N. Peterson corrects some misconceptions in *The limits of Hitler's power* (1969). P. H. Merkl, *Political violence under the swastika* (1975), reexamines the life histories of a number of Germans who became Nazis and who were originally studied in T. Abel, *Why Hitler came to power* (1938); it may be compared also with M. Mayer, *They thought they were free* (1955).

There has been an avalanche of books on Hitler and the Nazi era, but two biographical accounts stand out and also provide the most informative general introductions to the history of the era: A. Bullock, *Hitler: a study in tyranny*° (1952; rev., 1964), and J. C. Fest, *Hitler* (1973, trans. 1975), the latter a superb study utilizing the most recent research [the translation and documentation are somewhat condensed from the German original]. J. Toland, *Adolf Hitler* (1976), is a readable account geared to a general audience. R. Binion, *Hitler among the Germans* (1976), uses some strained psychoanalytical methods to explain the inner wellsprings of the man, while R. L. Waite, *The psychopathic god: Adolf Hitler* (1977), combines both psychoanalytical and more conventional techniques to provide some keen insights. Although W. Maser, *Hitler: legend, myth, and reality* (1971, trans. 1973), corrects some minor legends, it does not present a synthesis. Hitler's early years are reconstructed in F. Jetzinger, *Hitler's youth* (1956, trans. 1958), and in B. F. Smith, *Adolf Hitler: his family, childhood, and youth*° (1967); the same author also has written on the early years of another Nazi, *Heinrich Himmler: a Nazi in the making, 1900–1926* (1971). An important episode is explored in H. J. Gordon, *Hitler and the Beer Hall Putsch*° (1972), and the end of the leader and his regime is vividly recounted in H. R. Trevor-Roper, *The last days of Hitler*° (1947; rev., 1966).

The proceedings of the Nuremberg trials have been published as International Military Tribunal, *Trial of the major war criminals before the International Military Tribunal, 1945–1946* (42 vols., 1947–1949), and as *Nazi conspiracy and aggression* (8 vols., 2 supplements, 1946–1958). Discussions of the trial are found in P. de Mendelssohn, *Design for aggression* (1946); W. R. Harris, *Tyranny on trial: the evidence of Nuremberg* (1954); J. L. Stipp (ed.), *Devil's diary: the record of Nazi conspiracy and aggression* (1955); P. Calvacoressi, *Nuremberg: the facts, the law, and the consequences* (1948); and E. Davidson, *The trial of the Germans: Nuremberg, 1945–1946* (1966).

Other phases and institutions of the Nazi era are discussed in numerous books, among them, E. Crankshaw, *Gestapo: instrument of tyranny*° (1956); T. Taylor, *Sword and swastika: generals and Nazis in the Third Reich*° (1952); P. Seabury, *The Wilhelmstrasse: a study of German diplomats under the Nazi regime* (1955); G. A. Ziemer, *Education for death: the making of the Nazi* (1942); O. J. Hale, *The captive press in the Third Reich* (1964); Z. A. B. Zeman, *Nazi propaganda* (1964); J. Stephenson, *Women in Nazi society* (1976); A. Schweitzer, *Big business in the Third Reich* (1964); and G. Reitlinger, *SS: alibi of a nation, 1922–1945*° (1956). Books on the concentration camps are cited later. Aspects of religion and related matters are examined in J. S. Conway, *The Nazi persecution of the churches, 1933–1945* (1968); G. Lewy, *The Catholic church and Nazi Germany* (1964); and S. Friedlaender, *Pius XII and the Third Reich: a documentation* (1966). A popular overdrawn history of a special subject is W. Manchester, *The arms of Krupp, 1587–1968* (1968). G. L. Mosse (ed.) illustrates facets of the Nazi era in *Nazi culture* (1966), and on a special subject, there is B. M. Lane, *Architecture and politics in Germany, 1918–1945* (1968).

On the still incomplete story of the opposition to Hitler, the most comprehensive account is P. Hoffmann, *The history of the German resistance, 1933–1945* (trans. 1977). Among other accounts, the following may be mentioned: H. Rothfels, *The German opposition to Hitler* (1949); C. FitzGibbon, *20 July* [published in England as *The shirt of Nessus*] (1956); G. Ritter,

The German resistance: Carl Goerdeler's struggle against tyranny (1954, trans. 1959); T. Prittie, Germans against Hitler (1964); R. Manvell and H. Fraenkel, The July plot (1964); the same authors' The Canaris conspiracy (1969); and E. Zeller, The flame of freedom (trans. 1968). H. C. Deutsch has written two authoritative accounts focusing on the military, The German conspiracy against Hitler in the twilight war [1939–1940] (1968) and Hitler and his generals: the hidden crisis, January–June 1938 (1974), while R. Manvell and H. A. Jacobsen have edited a useful collection of essays, July 20, 1944: Germans against Hitler (1969). A comprehensive handbook of information on the Nazi regime is L. L. Snyder (ed.), Encyclopedia of the Third Reich (1977). [Other books on wartime Germany and German-dominated Europe are listed in the next chapter.]

Totalitarianism, Particularly Nazism

[Communism is discussed mainly in Chapter XVII, and Italian fascism is discussed separately below.]

Various attempts to explore the ideological roots of the German experience, some of which are less than fair to the earlier Germans, have been listed for earlier chapters. P. Viereck, Metapolitics: the roots of the Nazi mind,* has already been cited; other thoughtful accounts include F. Stern, The politics of cultural despair: a study in the use of the Germanic ideology* (1961); the same author's The failure of illiberalism: essays on the political culture of Germany (1972); and G. L. Mosse, The crisis of German ideology: intellectual origins of the Third Reich* (1964) and his other writings.

Among efforts to examine totalitarian attitudes and institutions on a comparative basis and to establish definitions are F. L. Carsten, The rise of fascism* (1967); H. R. Kedward, Fascism in western Europe, 1900–1945 (1969); E. Nolte, Three faces of fascism: Action Française, Italian fascism, national socialism* (1963, trans. 1966), a difficult book for most readers; J. Weiss, The fascist tradition: radical right-wing extremism in modern Europe* (1967); A. Cassels, Fascism* (1975); J. Gregor, The ideology of fascism: the rationale of totalitarianism (1969); H. Rogger and E. Weber (eds.), The European right: a historical profile,* cited earlier: W. Laqueur and G. L. Mosse (eds.), International fascism, 1920–1945* (1966), originally a volume of the Journal of contemporary history; and S. J. Woolf and others, European fascism (1968) and The nature of fascism (1968). To these may be added: C. J. Friedrich and Z. K. Brzezinski, Totalitarian dictatorship and autocracy* (rev., 1965); K. R. Popper, The open society and its enemies (2 vols., rev., 1963); E. Fromm, Escape from freedom* (1941), a psychological inquiry into the reasons for submission to tyranny; H. Arendt, The origins of totalitarianism,* already cited: G. W. F. Hallgarten, Why dictators? (1954); J. L. Talmon, The origins of totalitarian democracy,* cited earlier; E. Halévy, The era of tyrannies* (1938, trans. 1965); and H. Buchheim, Totalitarian rule: its nature and characteristics (trans. 1968). A special subject is explored in A. Hamilton, The appeal of fascism: . . . the intellectuals and fascism (1968), and some interesting correlations emerge from A. L. Unger, The totalitarian party: party and people in Nazi Germany and Soviet Russia (1974).

Italy, 1919–1945

The relevant chapters in C. Seton-Watson, Italy from liberalism to fascism, 1870–1925 (1967), are valuable, as are those in D. Mack Smith, Italy: a modern history (rev., 1969); the same author also has written Mussolini's Roman empire (1976), the first of two projected volumes on Italian fascism. Useful introductions to the Italian experience include A. Cassels, Fascist Italy* (1968); E. Wiskemann, Fascism in Italy: its development and influence* (1969); and F. Chabod, A history of Italian fascism (1963). An impressive book on the early years is A. Lyttelton, The seizure of power: fascism in Italy, 1919–1929 (1973), which for foreign affairs may be supplemented by A. Cassels, Mussolini's early diplomacy (1970). On the nature of the fascist state, four important books superseding earlier studies are E. R. Tannenbaum, The fascist experience: Italian society and culture, 1922–1945 (1972); M. Gallo, Mussolini's Italy: twenty years of the fascist era (1973); D. Germino, The Italian fascist party in power (1959); and R. Sarti, Fascism and the in-

dustrial leadership in Italy, 1919–1940 (1971). Foreign policy is examined in G. Barclay, *The rise and fall of the new Roman Empire: Italy's bid for world power, 1890–1943* (1973), giving credit to prefascist dynamism.

On *Il Duce* himself, there is a detailed biography by I. Kirkpatrick, *Mussolini: study of a demagogue*° (1964); the older G. Megaro, *Mussolini in the making* (1938), remains useful. There are also accounts by L. Fermi° (1961); C. Hibbert (1962), mostly on the latter phases of the dictator's career; and R. MacGregor-Hastie, *The day of the lion: the life and death of fascist Italy, 1922–1945* (1963), the latter not entirely reliable. The multivolumed biography of Mussolini in progress (1965 ff.) by the Italian historian R. de Felice is not available in translation. An outstanding account of the underground struggle from 1924 to 1943 is C. F. Delzell, *Mussolini's enemies: the Italian anti-fascist resistance* (1961). F. W. Deakin, *The brutal friendship: Mussolini, Hitler, and the fall of Italian fascism*° (1962; rev., 1966), is a detailed account of the last phase of Mussolini's career from his overthrow to his death.

Other European Developments

[Spain and the Spanish Civil War are discussed in the following chapter.] The most useful volume on eastern Europe after 1918 is J. Rothschild, *East Central Europe between the two World Wars*° (1975), virtually superseding earlier studies by H. Seton-Watson, *Eastern Europe between the wars, 1918–1941* (1946; rev., 1967), and C. A. Macartney and A. W. Palmer, *Independent eastern Europe* (1962). The relevant portions of R. L. Wolff, *The Balkans in our time,*° already cited, and C. Jelavich and B. Jelavich, *The Balkans*° (1965), are also helpful. The best treatment of the economic disruption following the end of the Austro-Hungarian empire is L. Pasvolsky, *Economic nationalism of the Danubian states* (1928), and aspects of the new democracies may be examined in P. F. Sugar (ed.), *Native fascism in the successor states, 1918–1945*° (1971), and in K. J. Neuman, *European democracy between the wars* (trans. 1971). Specialized accounts of various countries and selected topics include: For Austria:

C. A. Gulick, *Austria from Habsburg to Hitler* (2 vols., 1948), sympathetic to the Austrian socialists; and M. MacDonald, *The Republic of Austria, 1918–1934: a study in the failure of democratic government* (1946). For Hungary: C. A. Macartney, *October fifteenth: a history of modern Hungary, 1929–1945* (2 vols., 1957) and *Hungary: a short history* (1962); R. L. Tönés, *Bela Kun and the Hungarian Soviet Republic* (1967), on the short-lived Communist regime of 1919; and E. Pambenji (ed.), *A history of Hungary* (1975), a collaborative Marxist work, useful but to be read with caution for the more recent period. For Czechoslovakia: S. H. Thomson, *Czechoslovakia in European history* (1943, 1953); R. W. Seton-Watson, *A history of the Czechs and Slovaks* (1943, 1965); A. H. Hermann, *A history of the Czechs* (1976); E. Wiskemann, *Czechs and Germans* (1938, 1967); Z. Zeman, *The Mazaryks: the making of Czechoslovakia* (1976); V. Olivová, *The doomed democracy: Czechoslovakia in a disrupted Europe, 1918–1938* (1972); F. G. Campbell, *Confrontation in Central Europe: Weimar Germany and Czechoslovakia* (1975); and V. S. Mamatey and R. Luza (eds.), *A history of the Czechoslovakian Republic, 1918–1948* (1973), with excellent chapters on important turning points. For Yugoslavia: P. Auty (1965) and S. K. Pavlovitch (1971) have each written useful histories, and H. L. Roberts has written *Rumania: political problems of an agrarian state* (1951). For Poland: a good brief survey is H. Roos, *A history of modern Poland* (1966). For Finland and the Scandinavian countries: J. H. Wuorinen, *A history of Finland* (1965); F. D. Scott, *Scandinavia*, cited earlier; I. Andersson, *A history of Sweden* (rev., 1970); M. W. Childs, *Sweden: the middle way* (rev., 1947); T. K. Derry, *A history of modern Norway, 1914–1972* (1973); and W. G. Jones, *Denmark* (1970).

Problems and Readings°

On the American New Deal, a selection of conflicting interpretations is conveniently presented in E. C. Rozwenc (ed.), *The New Deal: revolution or evolution?* (rev., 1959), and in M. Keller (ed.), *The New Deal* (1963). For Britain: J. A. Thompson (ed.), *The collapse of the Brit-*

ish *Liberal party: fate or self-destruction?*
(1969). For Italy: S. W. Halperin, *Mussolini and Italian fascism* (1964), in the Anvil series, and R. Sarti (ed.), *The ax
within: Italian fascism in action* (1974).
For Weimar Germany: R. N. Hunt (ed.),
*The creation of the Weimar Republic: still-
born democracy?* (1969), and F. K. Ringer
(ed.), *The German inflation of 1923* (1969).
For the Nazi era: F. Stern (ed.), *The path
to dictatorship* (1967); H. A. Turner (ed.),
Nazism and the Third Reich (1972); J. L.
Snell and A. Mitchell (eds.), *Hitler's dictatorship and the German nation* (1973);
R. G. L. Waite (ed.), *Hitler and Nazi
Germany* (rev., 1969); and J. Noakes and
G. Pridham (eds.), *Documents of Nazism,
1919–1945* (1975). G. H. Stein has edited
Hitler in the Great Lives Observed series,
and J. Remak, *The Nazi years* (1969). On
totalitarianism, there are available P. T.
Mason, *Totalitarianism: temporary madness or permanent danger?* (1967); E.
Weber, *Varieties of fascism: doctrines of
revolution in the twentieth century* (Anvil,
1964); N. Greene (ed.), *Fascism: an anthology* (1968); C. F. Delzell (ed.), *Mediterranean fascism* (1970); W. Laqueur
(ed.), *Fascism: a reader's guide* (1974);
and H. A. Turner, Jr. (ed.), *Reappraisals
of fascism* (1975).

XX: THE SECOND WORLD WAR

There is no one comprehensive treatment
taking into account the sources now available for the diplomacy of the interwar
years and the background to the Second
World War. A scholarly survey is P. Renouvin, *World War II and its origins: international relations 1929–1945* (1969),
while R. J. Sontag, *A broken world, 1919–
1939,* cited earlier, in the Langer series,
also is a valuable guide. Useful general
accounts include E. Wiskemann, *Europe
of the dictators, 1919–1945** (1966); E.
Eubank, *The origins of World War II**
(1969); L. Lafore, *The end of glory: an
interpretation of the origins of World War
II** (1970); and J. Remak, *The origins of
the Second World War** (1975).

The war is placed in historical perspective in L. Dehio, *The precarious balance:
four centuries of the European power
struggle** (1948, trans. 1952), and in H.
Holborn, *The political collapse of Europe*

(1951), a provocative essay. For the impact of the war itself, G. Wright, *The ordeal of total war, 1939–1945** (1968), in
the Langer series, is indispensable for the
European phases. An excellent survey is
H. Michel, *Second World War* (trans.
1975). Of special value are the annual
volumes for the interwar years edited for
the Royal Institute of International Affairs
by A. Toynbee and others, *Survey of international affairs* (1920 ff.), and the accompanying *Documents on international affairs*; a *Survey* has been published to cover
the years 1939–1946 (1954), and the annual volumes have been resumed for the
years since 1946.

Spain and the Spanish Civil War

An outstanding work is G. Jackson, *The
Spanish republic and the Civil War, 1931–
1939** (1965); also valuable are P. Broué
and E. Témime, *The Revolution and the
Civil War in Spain* (1961, trans. 1972),
and H. Thomas, *The Spanish Civil War**
(1961, rev. 1977). Two informative books
stressing the Communist role are B. Bol-
loten, *The grand camouflage: the Spanish
Civil War and Revolution, 1936–1939*
(1961, 1968), and R. A. H. Robinson,
*The origins of Franco Spain: the right, the
Republic, and the Revolution, 1931–1936*
(1971). The turbulent background is ably
conveyed in G. Brenan, *The Spanish labyrinth** (1943); the relevant chapters of R.
Carr, *Spain, 1808–1939*, already cited;
E. E. Malefakis, *Agrarian reform and
peasant revolution in Spain: origins of the
Civil War* (1970); C. Meaker, *The revolutionary left in Spain, 1914–1923* (1974);
and S. G. Payne, *Politics and the military
in modern Spain*, also cited earlier. Payne
has, in addition, written an informative
monograph, *Falange: a history of Spanish
fascism** (1961), a brief account of the
Civil War in *The Spanish Revolution**
(1969), and has edited *Politics and society
in twentieth-century Spain** (1976). There
are valuable chapters in R. Carr (ed.), *The
Republic and the Civil War in Spain*
(1971). On the international aspects of
the war, there are P. van der Esch, *Prelude to war: the international repercussions of the Spanish Civil War, 1936–1939*
(1951); H. Feis, *The Spanish story: Franco
and the nations at war** (1948); N. J.
Padelford, *International law and diplo-*

macy in the Spanish civil strife (1939); D. A. Puzzo, *Spain and the Great Powers, 1936–1941* (1962); and D. T. Cattell's two volumes, *Communism and the Spanish Civil War* (1955) and *Soviet diplomacy and the Spanish Civil War* (1957). Three studies of the American response to the war are F. J. Taylor, *The United States and the Spanish Civil War* (1956); A. Guttmann, *The wound in the heart: America and the Spanish Civil War* (1962); and R. P. Traina, *American diplomacy and the Spanish Civil War* (1968). Other memorable aspects are touched upon in P. Stansky and W. Abrahams, *Journey to the frontier: Julian Bell and John Cornford: their lives and the 1930's*° (1966); G. Orwell, *Homage to Catalonia*° (1938), by one who fought and became disillusioned; V. Brome, *The international brigades* (1966); V. B. Johnston, *Legions of Babel* (1967); and S. Weintraub, *The last great cause: the intellectuals and the Spanish Civil War* (1968). The most balanced study of Franco is J. W. D. Trythall, *El Caudillo* (1970).

Background to the Second World War

The opening of the British and French archives and the availability of the German archives for these years has made many earlier works obsolete or at least incomplete, but the following older accounts remain useful: A. Wolfers, *Britain and France between two wars: conflicting strategies of peace since Versailles*° (1940); W. M. Jordan, *Great Britain, France, and the German problem, 1918–1939* (1943); E. H. Carr, *Britain: a study of foreign policy from Versailles to the outbreak of the war* (1939) and *The twenty years' crisis, 1919–1939*° (2nd ed., 1946); and W. N. Medlicott, *British foreign policy since Versailles* (1940). To these must be added F. S. Northedge, *The troubled giant: Britain among the Great Powers, 1916–1939* (1966); S. Marks, *The illusion of peace: international relations, 1918–1933* (1976); J. Jacobson, *Locarno diplomacy* (1972); and M. Cowling, *The impact of Hitler: British politics and British policy, 1933–1940* (1975). Focusing on France are R. Albrecht-Carrié, *France, Europe, and the two World Wars* (1961); E. R. Cameron, *Prologue to appeasement: a study in French foreign policy* (1942); W. E. Scott,

Alliance against Hitler: the origins of the Franco-Soviet pact (1962); and A. H. Furnia, *The diplomacy of appeasement* (1966). Two valuable books of essays by L. B. Namier review the documents and memoirs as they appeared in the postwar period: *Diplomatic prelude, 1938–1939* (1948) and *Europe in decay: a study in disintegration, 1936–1940* (1950). Four provocative books, highly critical of the appeasement policy, are F. L. Schuman, *Europe on the eve: the crisis of diplomacy, 1933–1939* (1939); A. L. Rowse, *Appeasement: a study in political decline, 1933–1939*° (1961); M. Gilbert and R. Gott, *The appeasers* (1963); and M. George, *The warped vision: British foreign policy, 1933–1939* (1965). W. R. Rock, *Appeasement on trial: British foreign policy and its critics, 1938–1939* (1966), and N. Thompson, *The anti-appeasers* (1971), analyze the opposition to the policy at the time, of which the most effective account is W. S. Churchill, *The gathering storm*° (1948), the first volume of his *The Second World War*° (6 vols., 1948–1953), which covers his years in the opposition.

On specific episodes and subjects, one may turn to E. Wiskemann, *The Rome-Berlin Axis: a history of the relations between Hitler and Mussolini* (1949) and *Undeclared war* (1939). The Ethiopian conquest is studied in G. W. Baer, *The coming of the Italo-Ethiopian war* (1967); F. Hardie, *The Abyssinian crisis* (1974); and A. del Boca, *The Ethiopian war, 1935–1941* (1969). On the annexation of Austria, one may read G. Brook-Shepherd, *Anschluss: the rape of Austria* (1963) and *Dollfuss* (1961); J. Gehl, *Austria, Germany and the Anschluss, 1931–1938* (1963); and D. Wagner and G. Tomkowitz, *Anschluss: the week Hitler seized Vienna* (1971). J. W. Wheeler-Bennett, *Munich: prologue to tragedy*° (1948, reissued 1963), is one of the best books on the entire era, but also useful are K. Eubank, *Munich* (1963); H. Noguères, *Munich: "peace for our time"* (trans. 1963); K. Robbins, *Munich 1938* (1963); and J. W. Bruegel, *Czechoslovakia before Munich: the German minority problem and British appeasement policy* (trans. 1973). F. Gilbert and G. A. Craig (eds.), *The diplomats, 1919–1939*° (1953), includes many valuable chapters on the men who made foreign policy in the era.

Books dealing with eastern Europe, in addition to those listed for Soviet foreign policy in Chapter XVII, include J. A. Lukacs, *The Great Powers and eastern Europe* (1952); P. Wandycz, *France and her Eastern allies, 1919–1925* (1962); L. Kochan, *The struggle for Germany, 1914–1945* (1963), on the rivalry between the West and Russia; G. Hilger and A. G. Meyer, *The incompatible allies: a memoir history of German-Soviet relations, 1918–1941* (1953); J. Korbel, *Poland between East and West: Soviet German diplomacy towards Poland, 1919–1933* (1963); and A. Cienciala, *Poland and the Western powers, 1938–1939* (1968). The first volume of a longer study focusing on eastern Europe is J. E. McSherry, *Stalin, Hitler, and Europe: the origins of World War II, 1933–1939* (vol. I, 1968). Important studies of German foreign policy include G. L. Weinberg, *The foreign policy of Hitler's Germany* (1970); N. Rich, *Hitler's war aims* (2 vols., 1973), explaining ideology and policy and their execution; and K. Hildebrand, *The foreign policy of the Third Reich*° (1973). The German-Soviet pact (and its subsequent history) may be studied in A. Rossi [pseud. A. Tasca], *The Russo-German alliance, August 1939–June 1941* (1950), and in G. L. Weinberg, *Germany and the Soviet Union, 1939–1941* (1954). On the events immediately preceding the outbreak of the war, a Swiss historian, W. Hofer, has written *War premeditated, 1939* (1955); C. Horne, the brief, informative *The approach of war, 1938–9*° (1967); and S. Aster, *1939: the making of the Second World War* (1973), with new material from archives opened in 1970. A provocative book based on a wide reading of the sources is D. C. Watt, *Too serious a business: European armed forces and the approach to the Second World War* (1975).

The opening gun in a campaign to "revise" the general picture of Nazi war responsibility was launched with A. J. P. Taylor's dazzling but unconvincing performance, *The origins of the Second World War*° (1961, 1963), in which he depicts Hitler as one who did not desire war but merely took advantage of the uncertainty of his opponents. A second book in the same category is D. L. Hoggan, *When peaceful revision failed: the origins of World War II* (1964), an English version of a book by an American scholar that appeared first in German translation (1961) and that goes even further in blaming the British.

The role of the United States in these years is traced in two comprehensive volumes by W. L. Langer and S. E. Gleason, *The challenge to isolation, 1937–1940* (1952) and *The undeclared war, 1940–1941* (1953); R. Ferrell, *American diplomacy in the Great Depression* (1957); and S. Friedlaender, *Prelude to downfall: Hitler and the United States, 1939–1941* (trans. 1967). The events in the Far East may be studied through David J. Lu, *From the Marco Polo Bridge to Pearl Harbor: Japan's entry into World War II* (1961); R. Butow, *Tojo and the coming of the war* (1961); J. B. Crowley, *Japan's quest for autonomy: national security and foreign policy, 1930–1938* (1966); and P. A. Varg, *The closing of the door: Sino-American relations, 1936–1949* (1973). On American involvement, one may turn to H. Feis, *The road to Pearl Harbor* (1950); P. W. Schroeder, *The Axis alliance and Japanese-American relations, 1941* (1963); and R. Wohlstetter, *Pearl Harbor: warning and decision*° (1962).

An invaluable source for diplomatic history of the interwar years is the German Foreign Office archives captured during the Second World War and edited by an international group of distinguished historians; many volumes on the years since 1933 have already appeared in English translation under the auspices of the U.S. Department of State as *Documents on German foreign policy, 1918–1945* (1949 ff.); other portions will remain available on microfilm for scholars. Guides have been edited by G. L. Weinberg (1952) and by G. O. Kent (3 vols., 1962–1965).

The War: Military and Domestic Developments

G. Wright, *The ordeal of total war,*° has already been cited. W. S. Churchill, *The Second World War*° (6 vols., 1948–1953; authorized 1-vol. condensation, 1959), is a full-dress treatment by a historian with unrivaled opportunities; in some ways, however, the work is as much autobiographical as historical and should be used with caution. For a thoughtful evaluation of Churchill as wartime leader, one may read with profit the essays in A. J. P. Taylor and others, *Churchill revised: a critical assessment* (1969).

Attempts to cover the events of the war in brief compass are L. L. Snyder, *A concise history: the war, 1939–1945*° (1960); P. Young, *World war, 1939–1945* (1966); B. Collier, *A short history of the Second World War* (1967); and B. H. Liddell Hart, *The history of the Second World War*° (1971). Military and diplomatic aspects are ably treated in P. Calvacoressi and G. Wint, *Total war*° (1972). H. Baldwin discusses with verve eleven major battles in *Battles lost and won: great campaigns of World War II* (1966) and also has written a history of the war to 1941 (1977). There are numerous other narrative histories. Many volumes of the detailed official histories of the United Kingdom, Canada, and the United States have appeared. Of special note is the official U.S. Navy history in fifteen volumes prepared by S. E. Morison (1947 ff.) and published in a one-volume abridgment as *The two-ocean war: a short history of the United States navy in the Second World War* (1963). On naval warfare, there also are available S. W. Roskill, *The war at sea, 1939–1945* (1954), and J. Creswell, *Sea warfare, 1939–1945* (1967).

On overall strategy, a valuable discussion of high-level decisions, Allied and Axis, by the Office of the U.S. Chief of Military History is K. R. Greenfield (ed.), *Command decisions* (1959). Also useful on strategy are the following: J. R. M. Butler's volume in the U.K. official history, *Grand strategy* (1957); the succeeding volume on strategy in the same series by J. M. A. Gwyer and J. R. M. Butler (1964), covering the 1941–1942 period; S. E. Morison, *American contributions to the strategy of World War II* (1958); F. H. Hinsley, *Hitler's strategy* (1951); E. Robertson, *Hitler's pre-war policy and military plans* (1963); M. L. Van Creveld, *Hitler's strategy, 1940–1941: the Balkan clue* (1973); and G. H. Liddell Hart, *The other side of the hill*° (1951; rev. ed. of *The German generals talk*, 1948), which may be supplemented by H. A. Jacobsen and J. Rohwer (eds.), *Decisive battles of World War II: the German view* (1965).

For studies of the wartime scene, there are some excellent volumes in the U.K. official history: W. C. Hancock and M. M. Gowing, *British war economy* (1949); R. M. Titmuss, *Problems of social policy* (1950); and M. M. Postan, *British war production* (1950). A graphic documentary and photographic account is A. Marwick, *The home front: the British and the Second World War* (1977). Various phases of the American domestic scene are treated in many books, of which one attempt at a synthesis is A. R. Buchanan, *The United States and World War II*° (2 vols., 1964). B. H. Klein, *Germany's economic preparations for war* (1959), stresses inefficiency and the belatedness of full-scale mobilization, as do A. S. Milward, *The German economy at war* (1965), and B. E. Carroll, *Design for total war: arms and economics in the Third Reich* (1968). The German front also is discussed in C. K. Webster and N. N. Frankland, *Strategic air offensive against Germany, 1939–1945* (1961), and in H. R. Trevor-Roper (ed.), *From Blitzkrieg to defeat* (1965). The German military may be examined in L. H. Addington, *The Blitzkrieg era and the German general staff, 1865–1941* (1971); H. Rosinski, *The German army* (1940, 1966); and a special aspect in G. H. Stein, *The Waffen SS: Hitler's élite guard at war, 1939–1945* (1966). A rewarding special study is J. W. Baird, *The mythical world of Nazi war propaganda, 1939–1945* (1975). For events in Italy, one may read F. W. Deakin, *The brutal friendship*, cited earlier, and A. N. Garland and H. M. Smyth, *Sicily and the surrender of Italy* (1965).

For the Russian front, there are some outstanding books. One may read A. Werth, *The year of Stalingrad* (1947) and *Russia at war, 1941–1945*° (1964); A. Clark, *Barbarossa: the Russian-German conflict, 1941–1945* (1965); T. Higgins, *Hitler and Russia: the Third Reich in a two-front war, 1937–1943* (1966); A. Seaton, *The Russo-German war* (1971); H. Salisbury, *The 900 days: the siege of Leningrad*° (1969); the remarkable J. Erickson, *The road to Stalingrad: Stalin's war with Germany* (1975), the first volume of a projected larger study; and the same author's valuable *The Soviet High Command . . . , 1918–1941*, already cited. The Russo-Finnish episode is well treated in R. W. Condon, *The winter war* (1972), and in F. Chew, *The white death* (1971). A. Seaton, *Stalin as military commander*

(1976), is a careful study. The war in the Pacific is ably sketched in C. Bateson, *The war with Japan* (1968). A challenging personalized interpretation of events to 1941 is provided in J. Lukacs, *The last European war, September 1939–December 1941* (1971). D. Irving, *Hitler's war* (1977), is a detailed account, defensive of Hitler, that should be read with caution. P. E. Schramm, *Hitler: the man and the military leader*° (1971), is rewarding, and the operation that broke the highest German secret code is recounted in the intriguing F. W. Winterbotham, *The ultra-secret* (1975).

The Fall of France and the Vichy Regime

[The books dealing with France in the 1930s listed in Chapter XIX and earlier in this chapter also should be consulted.] The political and military background to the fall of France may be approached through A. Horne, *To lose a battle: France, 1940* (1969); G. Chapman, *Why France fell: the defeat of the French army in 1940* (1969); the massive, popularly written W. L. Shirer, *The collapse of the Third Republic: an inquiry into the fall of France in 1940*° (1969); and P. H. M. Bell, *A certain eventuality: Britain and the fall of France* (1975). They may be supplemented by A. Goutard, *The fall of France* (trans. 1940); A. Beaufre, *1940: the fall of France* (trans. 1968); and L. Thompson, *1940* (1966). A moving memoir is M. Bloch, *Strange defeat*° (1940), by the eminent medievalist who was executed as a member of the Resistance. An outstanding study relating to these years is P. C. F. Bankwitz, *Maxime Weygand and civil-military relations in modern France* (1967); and part of the background is ably studied in J. M. Hughes, *To the Maginot Line: the politics of French military preparation in the 1920s* (1971). Paul Reynaud has written many volumes of self-vindicating memoirs, of which one has been translated as *In the thick of the fight, 1940–45* (trans. 1955).

For Vichy the best study is R. O. Paxton, *Vichy France: old guard and new order, 1940–1944* (1972); the same author also has written *Parades and politics at Vichy* (1966); and there are older books on Vichy by R. Aron (1958), P. Farmer

(1955), D. Pickles (1946), and A. Hytier (1959). Economic aspects are covered in A. S. Milward, *The new order and the French economy* (1970). Defensive on the controversial question of American relations with Vichy is W. L. Langer, *Our Vichy gamble*° (1947). There is a biography of Laval by H. Cole (1963), and a detailed biographical study focusing on diplomatic events by G. Warner, *Pierre Laval and the eclipse of France, 1931–1945* (1968). The Resistance movement in France [books on the European-wide Resistance are cited below] may be studied in the relevant chapters of A. Werth, *France, 1940–1955* (1957); in M. R. D. Foot, *SOE in France* (1966); in J. F. Sweets, *The politics of resistance in France, 1940–1944* (1976); and for a special aspect, P. Novick, *The resistance versus Vichy: the purge of collaborators in liberated France* (1969). The liberation is dramatically described in R. Aron, *France reborn . . . the liberation* (trans. 1964). For the years from the 1930s to liberation, the volumes of C. de Gaulle, *War memoirs*° (3 vols., 1954–1956; trans. 1958–1960), are incomparable; specifically on de Gaulle's unsatisfactory wartime relations with London and Washington, there are two able studies: A. L. Funk, *Charles de Gaulle: the crucial years, 1943–1944* (1959), and M. Viorst, *Hostile allies: FDR and Charles de Gaulle* (1965).

Hitler's New Order

[See also the many books on the Third Reich listed in Chapter XIX.] The volume of the *Survey of international affairs* covering the years 1939–1946, *Hitler's Europe* (1954), is valuable on all aspects of the German domination. Selected aspects are studied in W. Warmbrunn, *The Dutch under German occupation, 1940–1945* (1963), and A. S. Milward, *The fascist economy in Norway* (1972). A special subject is well treated in A. Dallin, *German rule in Russia, 1941–1945: a study of occupation policies* (1957), demonstrating the ineptitude of the Germans in exploiting discontent; it may be supplemented by J. A. Armstrong, *Ukrainian nationalism, 1939–1945* (1955). On the Jewish question, three books serve as a comprehensive introduction to the grim subject of the Holocaust: L. S. Dawidowicz, *The war*

against the Jews, 1933–1945° (1976); R.
Hilberg, *The destruction of the European
Jews*° (1961, 1967); and G. Reitlinger,
*The final solution: the attempt to exter-
minate the Jews of Europe, 1939–1945*
(1953, 1968). They may be supplemented
by K. A. Schleunes, *The twisted road to
Auschwitz* (1970); E. Kogon, *The theory
and practice of hell*° (1950); and H.
Arendt, *Eichmann in Jerusalem: a report
on the banality of evil*° (1963). On other
ethnic policies and refugee movements,
there are R. L. Koehl, *RKFDV: German
resettlement and population policy, 1939–
1945* (1957); J. B. Schechtman, *European
population transfers, 1939–1945* (1946);
E. M. Kulischer, *Europeans on the move:
war and population changes, 1917–1947*
(1948); and M. J. Proudfoot, *European
refugees, 1939–1952* (1957). For the European-wide Resistance, there is the judicious study by H. Michel, *The shadow
war: the European resistance, 1939–1945*
(trans. 1972), and the useful though somewhat anecdotal M. R. D. Foot, *Resistance:
European resistance to Nazism, 1940–
1945* (1977), while a special episode is
well covered in J. M. Ciechanowski, *The
Warsaw rising of 1944* (1971, trans. 1974).

Wartime Diplomacy and Origins of the Cold War

A growing literature has emerged stressing
the origins of the Cold War in Soviet-
American relations during the Second
World War. These books, many critical of
the United States, are for the most part
discussed in the following chapter. Wartime diplomacy and the successes and failures of the Soviet-Western coalition may
be approached through the latter volumes
of Churchill's history; J. L. Snell, *Illusion
and necessity: the diplomacy of global war,
1939–1945*° (1963); W. H. McNeill,
*America, Britain, and Russia: their coop-
eration and conflict, 1941–1946* (1953);
G. Smith, *American diplomacy during the
Second World War*° (1965); and J. W.
Wheeler-Bennett and A. Nicholls, *The
semblance of peace: the political settlement after the Second World War*°
(1972). Invaluable are the volumes of
H. Feis, sympathetic to the Western leaders: *Churchill, Roosevelt, Stalin: the war
they waged and the peace they sought*°
(1957), covering the years from 1941 to

the collapse of Germany and Yalta, *Between war and peace: the Potsdam Conference*° (1960), and on the last phase,
*The atomic bomb and the end of the war
in the Pacific*° (1961, 1966). A final volume follows, *From trust to terror: the onset of the Cold War, 1945–1950*° (1970).
On the last phase in the Pacific, see also
R. Butow, *Japan's decision to surrender*°
(1954), and W. Craig, *The fall of Japan*
(1968). On the significance of the atomic
bomb for relations with the Soviet Union,
see M. J. Sherwin, *A world destroyed: the
atomic bomb and the Grand Alliance*
(1975), an impressive and balanced study,
and the more vehemently critical G. Al-
perowitz, *Atomic diplomacy: Hiroshima
and Potsdam*° (1965), which may be supplemented by B. J. Bernstein, *The atomic
bomb: the critical issues*° (1975). An indispensable collaborative study is A. C.
Brown and C. B. MacDonald (eds.), *The
secret history of the atomic bomb*° (1977).
Hitler's relations with his two major allies
are discussed in F. W. Deakin's detailed
The brutal friendship,° already cited, and
in J. Menzel, *Hitler and Japan: the hollow
alliance* (1966). E. L. Woodward, *British
foreign policy in the Second World War*
(5 vols., 1962–1977), is based on the Foreign Office archives to which the author
was given early access. F. L. Loewenheim
and others have edited *Roosevelt and
Churchill: their wartime correspondence*
(1976), while J. P. Lash, *Roosevelt and
Churchill, 1939–1941* (1976), is interesting but anecdotal.

Problems and Readings°

In the various series there are available:
L. F. Schaefer (ed.), *The Ethiopian crisis:
touchstone of appeasement?* (1961); G.
Jackson (ed.), *The Spanish Civil War:
domestic crisis or international conspiracy?*
(1967); A. Guttman (ed.), *American neutrality and the Spanish Civil War* (1963);
F. L. Loewenheim (ed.), *Peace or appeasement: Hitler, Chamberlain, and the
Munich crisis* (1965), an especially full
selection of source materials; D. E. Lee
(ed.), *Munich: blunder, plot, or tragic
necessity?* (1969); S. M. Osgood (ed.),
The fall of France, 1940 (rev., 1972); I.
Morris (ed.), *Japan, 1931–1945: militarism, fascism, Japanism?* (1963); and G. O.
Totten (ed.), *Democracy and prewar*

Japan: groundwork or façade? (1965). W. C. Langsam has edited *Historic documents of World War II* (Anvil, 1958), and M. Gilbert, *Churchill* (1967), in the Great Lives Observed series. Four useful collections of essays on the origins of the war are H. Gatzke (ed.), *European diplomacy between the wars, 1919–1939* (1972); E. M. Robertson (ed.), *Origins of the Second World War* (1971); W. K. Eubank (ed.), *World War II: roots and causes* (1975); and W. R. Louis, *The origins of the Second World War: A. J. P. Taylor and his critics* (1972).

XXI–XXII: THE CONTEMPORARY AGE

It is difficult to assess the durable value of literature dealing with the events and developments of the recent era. The listings for these chapters therefore have been kept brief. Useful in keeping up with current developments, in addition to obvious periodical and newspaper sources, are the *Survey of international affairs*, published annually by the Royal Institute of International Affairs; the yearbooks published by the leading encyclopedias; the *Annual register*; and *Keesing's contemporary archives: weekly diary of important world events* (1931 ff.). The bibliographies published quarterly in *Foreign affairs* and in the professional journals should be used for new books on all contemporary subjects.

The Communist Worlds in Europe and Asia

[The books listed for the Soviet Union in Chapter XVII and for Eastern Europe in Chapter XIX should be consulted.] The most comprehensive treatment of Eastern Europe for the years after 1953 is F. Fejtö, *A history of the people's democracies: Eastern Europe since Stalin* (trans. 1971). H. Seton-Watson, *The East European revolution* (1950, 1956), may be supplemented by his insightful essay, *The "sick heart" of modern Europe: the problem of the Danubian lands* (1976). D. R. Shanon, *Soviet Europe* (1975), is a useful survey by a journalist, while Z. K. Brzezinski, *The Soviet bloc: unity and conflict* (1960; rev., 1967), a probing analysis by a political scientist, may be supplemented by the informative essays in S. Silvanian (ed.), *Eastern Europe in the 1970s* (1972). An outstanding study of Yugoslavia is D. Rusinow, *The Yugoslav experiment, 1948–1974* (1977).

The changes in the Soviet Union since 1953 are explored in A. Nove, *Stalinism and after*° (1975), and in R. McNeal, *The Bolshevik tradition: Lenin, Stalin, Khrushchev, Brezhnev*° (rev., 1974). L. R. Graham examines aspects of Soviet intellectual life in *Science and philosophy in the Soviet Union* (1972), and D. Joravsky a special episode in *The Lysenko affair* (1970). The background to present-day dissidence is explored in one of A. B. Ulam's many books, *Ideologies and illusions: revolutionary thought from Herzen to Solzhenitsyn* (1976). Two able journalistic surveys of the contemporary scene are H. Smith, *The Russians*° (1975), and R. G. Kaiser, *Russia: the people and the power*° (1975).

On the emergence of communism in China and on the regime since 1949, a number of books have already been cited in Chapter XVIII. Of the growing literature on the subject, only a few titles can be mentioned here. Two outstanding books by C. P. Fitzgerald are excellent introductions, *The birth of Communist China*° (rev., 1966) and *Mao Tse-tung and China* (1976). The Communist triumph and the nature of Chinese communism are explored in B. Schwartz, *Chinese communism and the rise of Mao*° (1951); D. Wilson, *The long march, 1935: the epic of Chinese communism's survival* (1972); the older and vivid E. Snow, *Red star over China* (reprinted 1968); the authoritative and balanced J. P. Harrison, *The long march to power: a history of the Chinese Communist party, 1921–1972* (1972); J. Guillermaz, *History of the Chinese Communist party, 1929–1949* (trans. 1972); and R. C. Thornton, *China: the struggle for power, 1917–1972* (1973). For documentation on the earlier years, C. Brandt, B. Schwartz, and J. Fairbank, *A documentary history of Chinese communism* (1952), is available. Three biographical accounts are S. Schram, *Mao Tse-tung*° (rev., 1967); S. Uhalley, *Mao Tse-tung: a critical biography*° (1975); and H. Suyin, *Wind in the tower: Mao Tse-tung and the Chinese Revolution,*

1949–1975 (1976). Chiang Kai-shek and the Nationalist defeat are studied in B. Crozier, *The man who lost China* (1976), a solid study despite the journalistic title. Books focusing on U.S. relations with China include H. Feis, *The China tangle: the American effort in China from Pearl Harbor to the Marshall mission*° (1953); W. I. Cohen, *America's response to China: an interpretive history of Sino-American relations*° (1971); F. R. Dulles, *American policy toward Communist China, 1949–1969* (1972); and J. K. Fairbank, *China perceived: images and policies in Chinese-American relations* (1977), by one of the most perceptive students of China. An interesting book on some Americans who early saw the vitality of Chinese communism is K. E. Shewmaker, *Americans and Chinese Communists, 1927–1945: a persuading encounter* (1971). The role of women is examined in M. Wolf and R. Witke (eds.), *Women in Chinese society* (1975), and D. Davin, *Woman-work: women and the party in revolutionary China* (1976).

The Emergent Nations: Asia and Africa

[The literature here is enormous, and no attempt can be made to cite the many studies of individual countries; the books mentioned in Chapters XV and XVIII also should be consulted.] Works of a general nature that serve as thoughtful introductions are R. Emerson, *From empire to nation: the rise to self-assertion of Asian and African peoples*° (1960), a book full of insights; H. Tinker, *Ballot box and bayonet: people and government in emergent Asian nations* (1964); M. Perham, *Colonial sequence, 1930–1949* (1967); R. von Albertini, *Decolonization: the administration and future of the colonies, 1919–1960* (1971); E. Kedourie, *Nationalism in Asia and Africa* (1971); and F. Brockway, *The colonial revolution* (1974). There are many informative volumes on the developing countries in the Modern Nations in Historical Perspective series.

The impact of modernization is examined historically and comparatively in C. E. Black, *The dynamics of modernization: a study in comparative history*° (1966); I. R. Sinai's two books, *The challenge of modernization*° (1964) and *In search of the modern world* (1968); and

D. A. Rustinow, *A world of nations: problems of political modernization*° (1967). An impressive, and discouraging, study is G. Myrdal, *Asian drama: an inquiry into the poverty of nations*° (3 vols., 1968), which may be supplemented by M. Lipton, *Why poor people stay poor* (1977), both emphasizing continuing mass poverty despite modernization and growing national wealth in the poorer countries. A valuable economic analysis is provided in P. Bairoch, *The economic development of the Third World since 1900*° (trans. 1975).

For the Middle East and its international implications, see, among many accounts providing a historical perspective, J. J. Malone, *The Arab lands of western Asia*° (1973); J. Berque, *Egypt: imperialism and revolution* (1972); A. Williams, *Britain and France in the Middle East and North Africa, 1914–1967* (1969); and H. M. Sachar, *Europe leaves the Middle East, 1936–1954* (1976). Studies by W. R. Polk, *The United States and the Arab world* (1965), and F. J. Khouri, *The Arab-Israeli dilemma* (1968), may be supplemented by a provocative book that covers events in the 1970s, E. R. F. Sheehan, *The Arabs, Israelis, and Kissinger: a secret history of American diplomacy in the Middle East* (1976).

For contemporary India and south Asia, the best introduction is W. Norman Brown, *India, Pakistan, and Bangladesh*, already cited. One finds a balanced assessment of achievements and shortcomings in K. Batia, *The ordeal of nationhood: a social study of India since independence, 1947–1970* (1971); and the same author also has written *Indira: a biography of Prime Minister Gandhi* (1974), which may be compared with Z. Masani, *Indira Gandhi: a biography* (1976), which illuminates contemporary India as well as its subject. R. Jahan, *Pakistan: failure in national integration* (1972), is a serious effort to assess the failure to integrate East Bengal which resulted in the emergence of Bangladesh. Developments in Indonesia may be approached through an excellent biographical account, J. D. Legge, *Sukarno: a political biography* (1972).

For Africa, to the general histories cited in Chapter XV, one may add J. Hatch, *A history of postwar Africa*° (1965); R. W. July, *The origins of modern African thought: its development in West Africa during the nineteenth and twentieth century* (1967); E. Mortimer, *France and the Africans, 1944–1960* (1969); R. I. Rotberg, *The rise of nationalism in central Africa: the making of Malawi and Zambia, 1873–1964* (1965); and A. G. Hopkins, *An economic history of West Africa* (1973), which examines economic developments from early times through independence. The stormy beginnings of the Congo, now Zaïre, as an independent nation, are studied in J. Gérard-Libois, *Katanga secession* (1966), and in C. Young, *Politics in the Congo: decolonization and independence* (1965). For southern Africa, a pressing problem is ably examined in G. Le May, *Black and white in South Africa*° (1971), and in a series of essays, L. Thompson and J. Butler (eds.), *Change in contemporary South Africa*° (1975).

The Western Countries [and Japan] since 1945

BRITAIN. [Many of the books cited for Chapter XIX also should be consulted.] W. Beveridge, *Full employment in a free society* (1944), is an expanded version of the wartime report on which subsequent welfare state developments were based. For these and other developments since 1945, one may turn to K. Hutcheson, *The decline and fall of British capitalism,* cited earlier; S. H. Beer, *British politics in the collectivist age* (1965); A. Sampson, *The new anatomy of Britain*° (1972); P. Gregg, *The welfare state: an economic and social history of Great Britain from 1945 to the present day* (1969); and M. Proudfoot, *British politics and government, 1951– 1970: a study of an affluent society* (1974).

FRANCE. The establishment and subsequent history of the Fourth Republic are best approached through G. Wright, *The reshaping of French democracy* (1948); E. M. Earle (ed.), *Modern France: problems of the Third and Fourth Republics* (1951); P. M. Williams, *Crisis and compromise: politics in the Fourth Republic*° (1964); A. Werth, *France, 1940–1955,* cited earlier; and D. MacRae, Jr., *Parliament, politics, and society in France, 1946–1958* (1967), an analytical study by a political scientist.

For the Fifth Republic, two informative volumes are P. M. Williams and M. Harrison, *Politics and society in de Gaulle's republic*° (1972), and H. W. Ehrmann, *Politics in France*° (rev., 1976). On the coming to power of de Gaulle, one may read D. Pickles, *Algeria and France* (1963), and C. S. Maier and D. S. White (eds.), *The thirteenth of May: the advent of de Gaulle's republic* (1968). Three important political studies are A. Kriegel, *The French Communists: profile of a people* (trans. 1972); R. Tiersky, *French Communism, 1920–1972* (1974); and R. E. M. Irving, *Christian democracy in France* (1973). For the social and economic changes in postwar France, many antedating the Fifth Republic, see E. R. Tannenbaum, *The new France* (1961); S. Hoffman and others, *In search of France,*° cited earlier; P. Bauchet, *Economic planning: the French experience* (trans. 1964); J. J. Carré and others, *French economic growth* (trans. 1975); J. Ardagh, *The new French revolution: a social and economic study of France, 1945–1968*° (1968); J. J. Servan-Schreiber, *The American challenge* (trans. 1968); and R. Gilpin, *France in the age of the democratic state* (1968). Recent developments are placed in historical perspective in J. C. Cairns, *France*° (1965), and D. Johnson, *France* (1969). Two studies emphasizing foreign affairs are A. Grosser, *French foreign policy under de Gaulle*° (1967), and W. W. Kulski, *De Gaulle and the world: the foreign policy of the Fifth French Republic* (1968). There are biographical accounts of de Gaulle by D. Schoenbrun° (1966), A. Werth° (1966), J. Lacouture (trans. 1966), and B. Crozier (1973), the latter the most detailed, but not entirely satisfactory. Despite the title, S. Hoffman, *Decline or renewal? France since the 1930s* (1974), focuses on the Fifth Republic and is informative on de Gaulle and his accomplishments. Aspects of French thought are explored in two difficult but rewarding books, H. S. Hughes, *The obstructed path: French social thought, 1930–1960*° (1968), and G. Lichtheim, *Marxism in modern France* (1966).

GERMANY, WEST AND EAST. The best study is A. Grosser, *Germany in our time*° (1971), while R. Dahrendorf, *Society and democracy in Germany* (1967), provides important insights. Two other useful introductions are M. Balfour, *West Germany*

(1968), and L. J. Edinger, *Politics in Germany*° (1968). On the occupation, the first postwar decade, and economic recovery, there are E. F. Ziemke, *The United States army in the occupation of Germany, 1944–1946* (1977), an outstanding study, and one of the final volumes in the 79-volume history of the American army in the Second World War; H. Zink, *The United States and Germany, 1945–1955* (1957); F. Golay, *The founding of the Federal Republic of Germany* (1958); and H. C. Wallich, *Mainsprings of the German revival* (1955). For the Adenauer years, see E. Alexander, *Adenauer and the new Germany* (1957), and R. Hiscocks, *The Adenauer era*° (1966). L. J. Edinger offers some psychoanalytical interpretations in a biography of the Social Democratic leader, *Kurt Schumacher: a study in personality and political behavior* (1965); and K. P. Tauber studies a special subject in great detail in *Beyond the eagle and swastika: German nationalism since 1945* (2 vols., 1967). G. A. Craig, *From Bismarck to Adenauer: aspects of German statecraft*, cited earlier, places recent German diplomacy in historical perspective. For the Eastern zone, J. P. Nettl, *The Eastern zone and Soviet policy in Germany, 1945–1950* (1951), may be supplemented by K. Sontheimer and W. Bleek, *The government and politics of East Germany* (1976). The conflict over Berlin is ably examined in J. M. Schick, *The Berlin crisis, 1958–1962* (1971).

ITALY. On the Italian republic, see M. Grindrod, *The new Italy: transition from war to peace* (1947) and *The rebuilding of Italy: politics and economics, 1945–1955* (1955); H. S. Hughes, *The United States and Italy,*° cited earlier; N. Kogan, *A political history of postwar Italy* (1966); G. Mammarella, *Italy after fascism: a political history, 1943–1965* (rev., 1966); and E. Wiskemann, *Italy since 1945* (1971). Economic developments are carefully studied in K. Allen and A. Stevenson, *An introduction to the Italian economy* (1975).

IBERIAN PENINSULA. S. G. Payne, *A history of Spain and Portugal*, already cited, is indispensable. On Spain: Payne, *Franco's Spain*° (1967) and the essays he has edited, *Politics and society in twentieth-*

century Spain,° also cited earlier, and G. Hills, *Spain* (1970), are informative for the postwar years, as is P. Preston (ed.), *Spain in crisis: the evolution and decline of the Franco regime* (1976). No significant study is available yet on the transition to a parliamentary democracy. On Portugal, there are available H. Kay, *Salazar and modern Portugal* (1976); A. De Figueiredo, *Portugal: fifty years of dictatorship* (1976); and A. H. De Oliveira Marques, *History of Portugal*° (rev., 1976), with an epilogue for the years since 1972.

JAPAN. E. O. Reischauer, *The United States and Japan*° (rev., 1965) and *Japan: the story of a nation*° (rev., 1974), are invaluable. The best study of the occupation is K. Kawai, *Japan's American interlude* (1960). Two important studies of economic developments are J. B. Cohen, *Japan's post-war economy* (1958), and G. C. Allen, *Japan's economic recovery* (1958). R. H. Minear, *Victor's justice: the Tokyo war crimes trial* (1971), is highly critical of the postwar judicial proceedings.

THE UNITED STATES. Although no listing on the contemporary United States is possible here, an introduction to the depression, war, and postwar years is provided in G. E. Mowry, *The urban nation, 1920–1960*° (1965); C. N. Degler, *Affluence and anxiety: the United States since 1945*° (1968); and W. E. Leuchtenburg, *A troubled feast: American society since 1945*° (1973). The black experience in America is told in J. H. Franklin, *From slavery to freedom*, cited earlier, and in A. Meier and E. M. Rudwick, *From plantation to ghetto*° (1966).

WESTERN EUROPE. A comprehensive introduction to Western Europe as a whole in the postwar era is provided with detail and insight by W. Laqueur, *Europe since Hitler*° (1972); less comprehensive but also useful is M. Crouzet, *The European renaissance since 1945*° (1971), which also treats Eastern Europe. For economic developments, M. M. Postan, *An economic history of Western Europe, 1945–1964*° (1967), and C. P. Kindleberger, *Europe's postwar growth* (1967), are important. The development of the postwar welfare state is carefully examined by the British study group, Political and Economic Planning, in *Economic planning and policies in Britain, France, and Germany* (1968), while A. Shonfield, *Modern capitalism: the changing balance of public and private power°* (1969), provides illuminating insights into a key aspect of contemporary economic life as a whole.

On postwar European economic cooperation and the movement toward unification, there are many studies, among which are G. Lichtheim, *The new Europe°* (1963); W. F. Knapp, *Unity and nationalism in Europe since 1945°* (1969); R. C. Mowat, *Creating the European Community* (1973); F. R. Willis, *France, Germany, and the new Europe, 1945–1967°* (1968); R. Morgan, *Western European politics since 1945°* (1973); and R. Pryce, *The politics of the European Community* (1974). Two useful collections of essays are S. R. Graubard (ed.), *A new Europe?°* (1964), and F. R. Willis (ed.), *European integration°* (1975). The historical background to unification may be explored in D. de Rougemont, *The idea of Europe* (trans. 1966); R. Albrecht-Carrié, *One Europe: the historical background of European unity* (1965); and J. Lukacs, *Decline and rise of Europe°* (1965). Special studies include H. E. Price, *The Marshall Plan and its meaning* (1966); J. Gimbel, *The origins of the Marshall Plan* (1976); W. Diebold, Jr., *The Schuman Plan* (1959); H. A. Schmitt, *The path to European union: from the Marshall Plan to the Common Market* (1962); W. O. Henderson, *The genesis of the Common Market* (1963); and U. W. Kitzinger, *The politics and economics of European integration* (1963).

International Relations since 1945

Several books on the wartime origins of the Soviet-Western rift, and "atomic bomb diplomacy" in 1945, have been described at the end of the previous chapter. Among attempts to reconstruct historically the major aspects of the Cold War with varying success are the following: P. Calvacoressi, *International politics since 1945°* (1968); L. Halle, *The Cold War as history* (1967); W. Knapp, *A history of war and peace, 1939–1965* (1967); J. Lukacs, *A new history of the Cold War°* (rev., 1966); D. Rees, *The age of containment: the Cold War°* (1967); D. Donnelly, *Struggle for the world: the Cold War, 1917–1965* (1965); A. Fontaine, *History of the Cold War* (2 vols., trans. 1968–1969), tracing its origins to 1917; and J. L. Clayton, *The economic impact of the Cold War* (1970). Valuable insights are provided in G. Kennan, *Russia and the West under Lenin and Stalin°* (1961) and *American diplomacy, 1900–1950°* (1951); E. H. Carr, *The Soviet impact on the Western world°* (1947); and L. F. Fischer, *Russia, America, and the world* (1961).

A large "revisionist" literature has appeared vehemently critical of the United States and generally blaming American foreign policy and American political or economic postwar ambitions for the Cold War. A sampling would include K. Ingram, *History of the Cold War* (1955); D. F. Fleming, *The Cold War and its origins, 1917–1960* (2 vols., 1961); W. A. Williams, *The tragedy of American diplomacy* (1959) and *American-Russian relations, 1781–1947* (1952); G. Kolko, *The politics of war . . . 1943 to 1945°* (1969) and, with J. Kolko, *The limits of power . . . 1945 to 1954°* (1972); D. Horowitz, *The free world colossus* (rev., 1971); and L. C. Gardner, *Architects of illusion* (1970). Other revisionist accounts, varying in their assessment of blame, would include T. G. Patterson, *Soviet-American confrontation: postwar reconstruction and the origins of the Cold War* (1973); B. Kuklick, *American policy and the division of Germany: the clash with Russia over reparations* (1972); L. A. Rose, *After Yalta* (1973) and *Dubious victory: the United States and the end of World War II* (1973); and G. C. Herring, *Aid to Russia, 1941–1946: strategy, diplomacy, and the origins of the Cold War* (1973).

Among other works that do not ignore American errors and miscalculations but reject conspiratorial interpretations are J. L. Gaddis, *The United States and the origins of the Cold War, 1941–1947°* (1972), a judicious study; L. E. Davis, *The Cold War begins: Soviet-American conflict over eastern Europe* (1974); and A. B. Ulam, *The rivals: America and Russia since World War II* (1971). Generally sympathetic to the American position are H. Feis, *From trust to terror: the onset of the Cold War, 1945–1950,°* cited earlier, and R. Aron, *The imperial republic: the*

United States and the world, 1945–1973 (trans. 1974). The revisionists receive harsh treatment in R. J. Maddox, *The new left and the origins of the Cold War* (1973); in J. Siracusa, *New left diplomatic histories and historians* (1973); and in R. W. Tucker, *The radical left and American foreign policy* (1971), a more balanced analysis. The quarrel persists over the interpretation of admittedly ambiguous documents, and many of the "new left" historians were undoubtedly motivated by opposition to the deep American involvement in the Vietnam war.

The founding of the United Nations is studied in R. B. Russell, *A history of the United Nations Charter: the role of the United States, 1940–1945* (1958), and among other subjects in F. P. King, *The new internationalism: Allied policy and the European peace, 1939–1945* (1973); some of the organization's subsequent history may be traced in C. M. Eichelberger, *The UN: the first twenty years* (1965). On nuclear weapons and international relations, the following interesting, and disturbing, books are recommended: P. M. S. Blackett, *Atomic weapons and East-West relations* (1956); H. A. Kissinger, *Nuclear weapons and foreign policy* (1957); G. Kennan, *Russia, the atom, and the West* (1958); H. Kahn, *On thermonuclear war°* (1960); D. E. Lilienthal, *Change, hope and the bomb°* (1963); and M. Lerner, *The age of overkill* (1964). H. D. Smyth, *Atomic energy for military purposes* (1945), and M. Gowing, *Britain and atomic energy, 1939–1945* (1964), are informative on the wartime development of the bomb.

The best general account of the Korean war is D. Rees, *Korea: the limited war* (1964), which may be supplemented by G. Henderson, *Korea: the politics of the vortex* (1968). On Vietnam, two successful efforts to explore Vietnamese history and to place recent events in historical perspective are A. B. Woodside, *Community and revolution in modern Vietnam* (1976), and W. J. Duiker, *The rise of nationalism in Vietnam, 1900–1941* (1976); also useful is J. F. Cady, *The history of postwar southeast Asia°* (1975). On guerrilla warfare in Vietnam and elsewhere, two outstanding books are W. Laqueur, *Guerrilla: a historical and critical study* (1977), and R. Asprey, *War in the shad-*

ows: the guerrilla in history* (1976); on related subjects, see J. B. Bell, *On revolt: strategies of national liberation* (1976), and A. Parry, *Terrorism* (1976). The American involvement in Vietnam may be studied in R. W. Van Alstyne, *The United States and east Asia* (1973); M. Kalb and E. Abel, *Roots of involvement: the United States in Asia, 1784–1971* (1971), by two skilled journalists; J. Schell, *The time of illusion°* (1976); A. M. Schlesinger, Jr., *The imperial presidency* (1973); and E. R. May, *"Lessons" of the past: the use and misuse of history in American foreign policy* (1973). Exceptionally useful for postwar American policy in general is S. Hoffman, *Gulliver's troubles, or the setting of American foreign policy* (1972).

Science and Thought

[The books described in Chapter XIV should be consulted as well as the histories of science listed in Chapter VII.] An intriguing survey of contemporary intellectual trends is R. N. Stromberg, *After everything: Western intellectual history since 1945°* (1975). A successful effort to reassess the idea of progress in the current era is W. Warren Wagar, *The belief in progress from Darwin to Marcuse*, already cited. H. Stuart Hughes, *An essay for our times* (1950), provides insights into modern cultural perplexities, and in *The sea change: the migration of social thought, 1930–1965* (1975), examines some key social thinkers who fled the Third Reich, a subject also explored in M. Jay, *The dialectical imagination . . . 1923–1950* (1973).

On the new physics, in addition to titles cited earlier, see B. Schonland, *The atomists, 1805–1933* (1968), and B. Cline, *The questioners: physicists and the quantum theory°* (1965). R. Clowes, *The structure of life* (1967), is informative on the biological revolution, and J. Watson, *The double helix* (1968), describes himself and other biologists at work. Various scientific developments and their implications are discussed in A. E. E. McKenzie, *The major achievements of science* (2 vols., 1960), C. D. Darlington, *The evolution of man and society* (1969); and K. Coutts-Smith, *The dream of Icarus* (1969). Useful introductions to the activities of the professional philosophers are provided in J. Passmore, *A hundred years of philosophy*

(1968); in A. J. Ayer and others, *The revolution in philosophy* (1956); and in M. White (ed.), *The age of analysis*° (1955), a convenient anthology. Aspects of modern religious thought are explored in S. P. Schilling, *Contemporary continental theologians* (1966), and an important subject is studied in G. Lewy, *Religion and revolution* (1974). An introduction to the complexities of contemporary art is provided in A. Neumeyer, *The search for meaning in modern art* (trans. 1964), H. Rosenberg, *The anxious object: art today and its audience* (1964), and G. Woods, *Art without boundaries, 1950–1970* (1972). On economic thought one may read M. Stewart, *Keynes and after* (1968), and C. Napoleoni, *Economic thought of the twentieth century* (1971). Many of the volumes listed in the final section of the Bibliography also are relevant to science, religion, thought, and society.

Contemporary Activist Movements

For the events of 1968, one may consult S. M. Lipset, *Rebellion in the university* (1972); R. Aron, *The elusive revolution* (1969); B. E. Brown, *Protest in Paris: anatomy of a revolt*° (1974); and A. Schnapp and P. Vidal-Nacquest (eds.), *French student uprising, 1967–1968* (1971), an annotated collection of documents. For insight into the emergence of youth as a social phenomenon, see the study by J. R. Gillis cited earlier, *Youth and history: tradition and change in European age relations, 1770 to the present,* and also L. S. Feuer, *The conflict of generations* (1969). For an introduction to the "new left" in the United States, one may turn to I. Unger, *The movement: a history of the American new left, 1959–1972* (1974). On the women's liberation movement, there is no historical account available for Europe or for the non-Western world comparable to M. P. Ryan, *Womanhood in America: from colonial times to the present* (1975), a concise and authoritative study. To the volumes cited in the introductory section, one may add W. O'Neill, *The woman's movement: feminism in the United States and England* (1969), and E. Boserup, *Women's role in economic development* (1970).

Past, Present, and Future

Although no attempt can be made to list the many assessments of contemporary problems, there may be some point in asking the reader to consider the titles and intents of these books: T. H. Von Laue, *The global city: freedom, power and necessity in the age of world revolutions* (1969); R. A. Nisbet, *Twilight of authority* (1975); B. Ward, *The West at bay*° (1948), *Faith and freedom*° (1954), *The rich nations and the poor nations*° (1962), *Five ideas that changed the world*° (1959) [which she identifies as nationalism, industrialism, colonialism, communism, and internationalism], and *The home of man*° (1976); E. Fischer, *The passing of the European age: a study of the transfer of Western civilization and its renewal in other continents* (1943, 1948); V. Bush, *Modern arms and free men: a discussion of the role of science in preserving democracy*° (1949); C. P. Snow, *The two cultures and the scientific revolution* (1959; rev., 1963); J. Barzun, *Science: the glorious entertainment* (1964); P. R. Ehrlich and A. H. Ehrlich, *Population, resources, environment: issues in human ecology* (1970); T. McKeown, *The modern rise of population* (1977); F. S. C. Northrop, *The meeting of East and West* (1946) and *The taming of the nations* (1952); R. Aron, *The century of total war* (1954); and A. J. Toynbee, *Civilization on trial* (1948) and *The world and the West* (1953).

To these may be added H. Arendt, *The human condition*° (1958); K. E. Boulding, *The meaning of the twentieth century* (1964); K. W. Deutsch, *Nationalism and its alternatives* (1969); J. Herz, *The nation-state and the crisis of world politics* (1976); M. Katz, *The things that are Caesar's* (1966) [on government and the governed]; J. K. Galbraith, *The new industrial state* (1967) and *Money: whence it came, where it went* (1975); E. F. Schumacher, *Small is beautiful: economics as if people mattered*° (1973, 1976); W. W. Rostow, *The world economy: history and prospect* (1977); L. S. Stavrianos, *The promise of the coming dark age*° (1976); R. A. Falk, *A study of future worlds* (1976); and R. G. Heilbroner, *An inquiry into the human prospect* (1974).

Problems and Readings*

Materials on science and intellectual developments are available in L. P. Williams (ed.), *Relativity theory: its origins and impact on modern thought* (1968), and in W. W. Wagar (ed.), *Science, faith, and man: European thought since 1914* (1968). Problem studies on international friction include N. A. Graebner (ed.), *The Cold War: a conflict of ideology and power* (rev., 1976); T. G. Patterson (ed.), *The origins of the Cold War* (1970); and L. C. Gardner (ed.), *Origins of the Cold War* (1970). Some other events are covered in T. W. Wallbank (ed.), *The partition of India: causes and responsibilities* (1966); P. P. Y. Loh, *The Kvomintang debacle of 1949: conquest or collapse?* (1965); and J. Baird (ed.), *The eve of the European empire: decolonialization after World War II* (1975).

Illustration
Sources

417 Kunsthistorisches Museum, Vienna; 462 Historiches Museum, Frankfurt am Main; 494, 495, 496 (above, below) The Mansell Collection; 497 New York Public Library; 498 (above) Staatsbibliothek Berlin; 498 (below) The Mansell Collection; 499 New York Public Library; 500 (above) Radio Times Hulton Picture Library; 500 (below) René-Jacques; 501 H. Roger-Viollet; 502 The American Numismatic Society; 542 Snark International, Art Gallery, Birmingham, England; 601 The American Numismatic Society; 644 The Mansell Collection; 645 New York Public Library; 646 (above, below), 647, 648 The Mansell Collection; 649 New York Public Library; 650, 651, 652 Radio Times Hulton Picture Library; 653 Photoworld, Inc.; 654 Popperfoto; 690 Sovfoto form USSR Magazine; 735 The American Numismatic Society; 791 Black Star, Fred Ward; 828 IBM; 829 Woodfin Camp & Associates/Marc & Evelyne Bernheim; 830 Rapho/Photo Researchers/Paolo Koch; 831 Woodfin Camp & Associates/Marc & Evelyne Bernheim; 832 Rapho/Photo Researchers/Sanford H. Roth; 834 United Nations/ILO; 835 Woodfin Camp & Associates/Marc & Evelyne Bernheim; 836 Rapho/Photo Researchers/Minoru Aoki; 837 Magnum/René Burri; 838 Rapho/Photo Researchers/Georg Gerster; 839 Rapho/Photo Researchers/Calogero Cascio; 840 NASA; 884 United Nations

Index

Dates given after names of rulers and popes are the years of reigns or pontificates; those given for all others are the years of birth and death.

Pronunciation is indicated where it is not obvious. With foreign words the purpose is not to show their exact pronunciation in their own language but to suggest how they may be acceptably pronounced in English. Fully Anglicized pronunciations are indicated by the abbreviation *Angl.* Pronunciation is shown by respelling, not by symbols, except that the following symbols are used for vowel sounds not found in English:

ø   Indicates the sound of ö as in Königsberg. To form this sound, purse the lips as if to say *o,* and then say *ay* as in *ate.*

U   indicates the sound of the French *u,* or of German ü. To form this sound, purse the lips as if to say *oo,* and then say *ee* as in eat.

aN, oN, uN, iN indicate the sounds of the French nasal vowels. Once learned, these are easily pronounced, roughly as follows: For aN, begin to pronounce the English word *on,* but avoid saying the consonant *n* and "nasalize" the *ah* sound instead. For oN do the same with the English *own;* for uN, with the English prefix *un-;* iN, with the English word *an.*

The sound of *s* as in the word *treasure* is indicated by *zh.* This sound is common in English, though never found at the beginning or end of a word. *igh* always indicates the so-called long *i* as in high. The vowel sound of *hoot* is indicated by *oo,* that of *hood* by ŏŏ.

Compared with English, the European languages are highly regular in their spelling, in that the same letters or combinations of letters are generally pronounced in the same way.

About
the Authors

ROBERT ROSWELL PALMER, Professor Emeritus of History at Yale University and now Adjunct Professor at the University of Michigan, was born in Chicago in 1909. After graduating from the University of Chicago, he received his doctorate from Cornell University in 1934. From 1936 to 1963 he taught at Princeton University, and was Dean of the Faculty of Arts and Sciences at Washington University in St. Louis from 1963 to 1966. He was President of the American Historical Association in 1970. Professor Palmer worked with the Historical Section of the Army Ground Forces from 1943 to 1945. He is the author of *Catholics and Unbelievers in Eighteenth Century France* (1939), *Twelve Who Ruled: The Year of the Terror in the French Revolution* (1941, 1958), and the two-volume *Age of the Democratic Revolution* (1959 and 1964), both volumes of which were History Book Club selections and the first of which won the Bancroft Prize in 1960. He has likewise written *The World of the French Revolution* (1970), which was also published in French in 1968, and *The School of the French Revolution* (1975). He edited the *Rand McNally Atlas of World History* (1957) and translated Georges Lefebvre's *Coming of the French Revolution* (1947). He has contributed to a variety of journals and collaborative volumes in this country and Europe.

JOEL COLTON was born in New York City in 1918. He received his A.B. from the City College of New York in 1937, his A.M. from Columbia University in 1940, and his Ph.D. from Columbia in 1950. In 1947 he joined the Department of History at Duke University and was chairman of the department from 1967 to 1974. He has served on the Board of Editors of the *Journal of Modern History* and as Consultant to the Advanced Placement Program of the College Entrance Examination Board. He was awarded a Guggenheim Fellowship, 1957–1958, a Rockefeller Foundation Fellowship, 1961–1962, and a National Humanities Endowment Senior Fellowship, 1970–1971. His articles and reviews have appeared in numerous professional publications such as the *American Historical Review* and the *Journal of Modern History*. He is the author of *Compulsory Labor Arbitration in France, 1936–1939* (1951), *Léon Blum: Humanist in Politics* (1966), and *Twentieth Century* (1968), a volume in the Great Ages of Man series. In 1969 his biography of Léon Blum appeared in a French translation. He has served as an officer and a member of several national committees of the American Historical Association, the Southern Historical Association, and the Society for French Historical Studies. Since 1974 he has been Director for Humanities at the Rockefeller Foundation in New York.

A Note
on the Type

The text of this book is set in CALEDONIA, *a Linotype face designed by W. A. Dwiggins. It belongs to the family of printing types called "modern face" by printers—a term used to mark the change in style of type-letters that occurred about 1800. Caledonia borders on the general design of Scotch Modern, but is more freely drawn than that letter.*

This book was composed, printed, and bound by American Book–Stratford Press, Inc., Saddle Brook, N.J.

The maps were executed by Jean Tremblay.

The text and cover were designed by Meryl Sussman Levavi

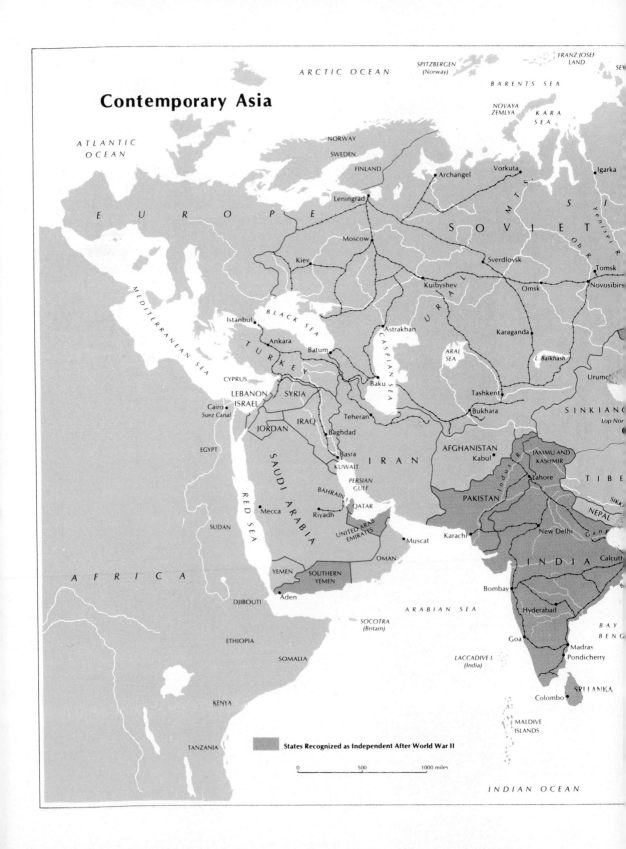

Contemporary Asia

ARCTIC OCEAN

SPITZBERGEN
(Norway)

FRANZ JOSEF
LAND

BARENTS SEA

NOVAYA
ZEMLYA

KARA
SEA

SEW

ATLANTIC
OCEAN

NORWAY

SWEDEN

FINLAND

Archangel

Vorkuta

Igarka

EUROPE

Leningrad

S O V I E T

URAL MTS.

Ob R.

Yenisei R.

Moscow

Sverdlovsk

Tomsk

Kiev

Kuibyshev

Omsk

Novosibirsk

Istanbul

BLACK SEA

Astrakhan

URAL R.

Karaganda

L. Balkhash

MEDITERRANEAN SEA

Ankara

Batum

CASPIAN SEA

ARAL
SEA

Urumch

T U R K E Y

Baku

Tashkent

SINKIANG

CYPRUS

LEBANON

SYRIA

Teheran

Bukhara

Lop Nor

ISRAEL

Cairo

Suez Canal

JORDAN

IRAQ

Baghdad

AFGHANISTAN

JAMMU AND
KASHMIR

TIBE

EGYPT

Basra

I R A N

Kabul

Lahore

SIKKI

KUWAIT

Indus R.

PAKISTAN

NEPAL

SAUDI ARABIA

PERSIAN
GULF

BAHRAIN

QATAR

New Delhi

Gange

RED SEA

Mecca

Riyadh

UNITED ARAB
EMIRATES

Muscat

Karachi

SUDAN

OMAN

I N D I A

Calcutt

YEMEN

SOUTHERN
YEMEN

Bombay

AFRICA

DJIBOUTI

Aden

ARABIAN SEA

Hyderabad

BAY
OF
BENG

ETHIOPIA

SOCOTRA
(Britain)

Goa

Madras

SOMALIA

LACCADIVE I.
(India)

Pondicherry

SRI LANKA

Colombo

KENYA

MALDIVE
ISLANDS

TANZANIA

States Recognized as Independent After World War II

0   500   1000 miles

INDIAN OCEAN

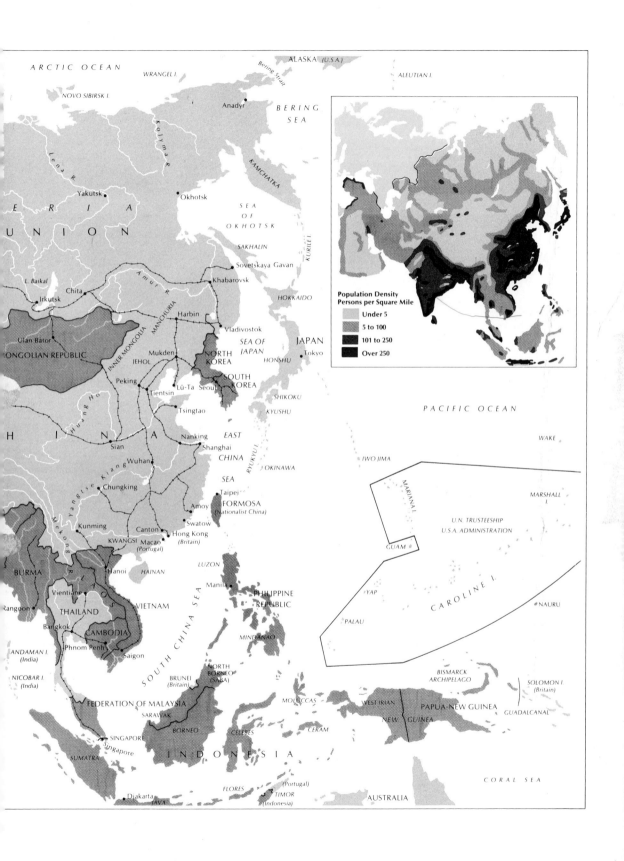

ARCTIC OCEAN

WRANGEL I.

NOVO SIBIRSK I.

Lena R.

Kolyma R.

ALASKA (U.S.A.)

Bering Strait

ALEUTIAN I.

Anadyr

BERING
SEA

KAMCHATKA

Yakutsk

Okhotsk

SEA
OF
OKHOTSK

E R I A

U N I O N

SAKHALIN

KURILE I.

Sovetskaya Gavan

Khabarovsk

HOKKAIDO

L. Baikal

Chita

Amur R.

Irkutsk

Harbin

MANCHURIA

Vladivostok

JAPAN

Ulan Bator

INNER MONGOLIA

Mukden

NORTH
KOREA

SEA OF
JAPAN

HONSHU

Tokyo

MONGOLIAN REPUBLIC

IEHOL

SOUTH
KOREA

Peking

Huang Ho

Lü-Ta Seoul

SHIKOKU

Tientsin

KYUSHU

H I N A

Sian

Tsingtao

Nanking

EAST
CHINA

Wuhan

Yangtse Kiang

Shanghai

RYUKYU I.

Chungking

SEA

OKINAWA

Mekong R.

Kunming

KWANGSI

Canton

Taipei

Amoy

FORMOSA
(Nationalist China)

Swatow

BURMA

Macao
(Portugal)

Hong Kong
(Britain)

HAINAN

LUZON

Hanoi

Rangoon

Vientiane

THAILAND

VIETNAM

Manila

PHILIPPINE
REPUBLIC

Bangkok

CAMBODIA

MINDANAO

ANDAMAN I.
(India)

Phnom Penh

Saigon

NICOBAR I.
(India)

NORTH
BORNEO
(SABA)

BRUNEI
(Britain)

FEDERATION OF MALAYSIA

MOLUCCAS

SARAWAK

CERAM

SINGAPORE

BORNEO

CELEBES

Singapore

I N D O N E S I A

SUMATRA

FLORES

(Portugal)

TIMOR
(Indonesia)

Djakarta

JAVA

**Population Density
Persons per Square Mile**

Under 5

5 to 100

101 to 250

Over 250

PACIFIC OCEAN

WAKE

IWO JIMA

MARIANA I.

MARSHALL
I.

U.N. TRUSTEESHIP
U.S.A. ADMINISTRATION

GUAM

YAP

CAROLINE I.

NAURU

PALAU

BISMARCK
ARCHIPELAGO

SOLOMON I.
(Britain)

WEST IRIAN

PAPUA-NEW GUINEA

GUADALCANAL

NEW GUINEA

SOUTH CHINA SEA

CORAL SEA

AUSTRALIA